A Reader in Christian Education

A Reader in Christian Education

Foundations and Basic Perspectives

Edited by

Eugene S. Gibbs

BAKER BOOK HOUSE
Grand Rapids, Michigan 49516

To my wife,

Judith,

for her support and encouragement.

Published by Baker Book House Company
P.O. Box 6287
Grand Rapids, Michigan 49516-6287

Printed in the United States of America

Library of Congress Cataloging-in-Publication Data

A Reader in Christian education foundations and basic perspectives / edited by Eugene S. Gibbs.
p. cm.
Includes bibliographical references and index.
ISBN 0-8010-3842-1
1. Christian education—Study and teaching. I. Gibbs, Eugene S.
BV1464.R42 1992
268—dc20 91-6910

Contents

Introduction 7

Part 1 Foundations

1. Erik H. Erikson: *Psychosocial Theorist*
   Eight Ages of Man *(1963)* 15
2. Carol Gilligan: *Sociodevelopmentalist*
   Psychological Theory and Women's Development *(1982)* 37
3. Lawrence Kohlberg: *Developmentalist*
   Moral Education in the Schools *(1966)* 57
4. Robert L. Selman: *Social-Cognitive Theorist*
   Social and Cognitive Understanding: **A Guide to Educational and Clinical Practice** *(1976)* 81
5. Jean Piaget: *Developmentalist*
   The Child and Reality *(1972)* 109
6. B. F. Skinner: *Psychologist*
   A Technology of Behavior *(1971)* 133
7. Jerome S. Bruner: *Psychologist*
   The Importance of Structure in Education *(1960)* 149
8. Paulo Freire: *Social Theorist*
   Pedagogy of the Oppressed: **Banking** *(1981)* 159
9. John Dewey: *Philosopher and Psychologist*
   Experience and Education *(1938)* 173
10. Malcolm S. Knowles: *Psychoeducationalist*
   Self-Directed Learning *(1975)* 181

Part 2 Basic Perspectives

11. Findley B. Edge
Experiential or Institutionalized Religion? *(1963)* 203

12. Gaines S. Dobbins
Translating New Testament Principles into Present-Day Practices *(1947)* 217

13. John H. Westerhoff III
The Shaking of the Foundations *(1976)* 231

14. George Albert Coe
What Is Christian Education? **The Starting Point of a Solution** *(1929)* 247

15. Randolph Crump Miller
The Clue to Christian Education *(1950)* 257

16. D. Campbell Wyckoff
The Gospel and Education *(1959)* 271

17. Lawrence O. Richards
Creative Bible Teaching *(1970)* 283

18. James Michael Lee
Religious Instruction as Social Science *(1971)* 295

19. Ted W. Ward
Facing Educational Issues *(1977)* 331

20. Donald M. Joy
A Proposal for Tomorrow *(1969)* 349

21. Lois E. LeBar
The Teaching-Learning Process *(1958)* 367

22. Thomas H. Groome
Shared Praxis in Praxis: **The Five Movements** *(1980)* 393

23. James W. Fowler
Stages of Faith *(1981)* 413

24. Sharon Parks
Imagination: **The Power of Adult Faith** *(1986)* 495

Bibliography 519

Index 523

Introduction

THE PURPOSE OF THIS BOOK IS TO PROVIDE PRIMARY SOURCE MATERIAL for students entering the field of Christian education. In order to think through and discuss with understanding the concepts and theoretical propositions of those on the cutting edge of the field, one must be familiar with basic positions. It may also help to engender something of a historical sensitivity to the discipline. It is nearly impossible to address questions of why one might do or refrain from doing something in the practice of ministry when one does not know basic ideas. One of the major weaknesses of Christian education is that much of its practice is "mindless," that is, not well thought out or developed according to any theoretical foundation. If an activity "works" in one church, it may well be tried in another church without regard as to how it might contribute to what the second church has set out to do. In more than thirty years of close contact with the church as observer, Christian-education and youth worker, Sunday-school teacher, researcher, and denominational board member, my feeling is that much Christian education at all levels is based on a poorly conceived, pragmatic philosophy bolstered by a few Bible verses. Many large Christian-education programs have little unity and no sense as to their direction. This is primarily because of the lack of any foundation in the areas of theological principles, learning theory, teacher development, or evaluation. As long as enrollments increase, it seems that any practice is justified. Christian educators must remember that some activity done in the name of learning may be "mis-educative."

Therefore, it is relevant that those beginning their formal schooling in the field of Christian education study foundational writings authored by persons concerned with social and behavioral science, biblical studies and theology, and educational planning. So, *A Reader in Christian Education* is designed to present such writings. Some have written about Christian education, whereas others have not thought about Christian education at all, but their work still has application and/or influence.

While writers from earlier centuries have made many important contributions to Christian education, the material in this volume is limited to twentieth-century authors. This is primarily because they are not found in other volumes, because they seem currently to make important contributions, and because their works are rarely found in any one place. Christian-education scholars will argue with the selection, no doubt. Space limitations have forced selection and choice of contents. The readings included are ones that I have found useful with my own students at colleges, seminaries, and graduate schools on both coasts, abroad, and now in the Midwest at Wheaton.

One of the distinctives of this book is that it contains *primary* source material. A careful attempt was made to present work that gets at the heart of the position of each author. The brief comments preceding and the reflection questions concluding each chapter are designed to give a little background and to introduce the reading, as well as to stimulate the reader's thinking. They are not intended to present a complete critique or summary of the position of each individual writer. Readers should be discriminating as they judge the strengths and weaknesses of each contribution. Scripture and one's personal theological position should be used to weigh the usefulness of the readings. Also, parts of any point of view may be rejected as unsatisfactory while other parts may be seen as valuable. Implications and applications need to be thought through.

This book is organized into two sections, Foundations and Basic Perspectives. The first part, Foundations, contains representative samples of the writings of psychologists, social-educational theorists, developmentalists, and one philosopher/psychologist. These readings are loosely grouped by topic. This material provides the base upon which some of the writings of the second part stand. The reader will probably recognize concepts from part 1 reappearing in part 2, applied to more specific Christian-education concerns. Part 2, Basic Perspectives, is also organized loosely by topic. The material covers some sixty years—that of George A. Coe first appeared in the 1920s, and the last three readings all were published during the 1980s.

Three authors in part 1, Erik Erikson, Paulo Freire, and Robert Selman, all show concern for social elements in human growth or education; three others, Jean Piaget, Lawrence Kohlberg, and Carol Gilligan, are considered developmentalists. Gilligan might also be grouped with those authors concerned with social elements in growth.

Jerome Bruner, B. F. Skinner, and Malcolm Knowles are psychologists whose work has been applied to education on a grand scale. Bruner looked at the main factors underlying learning to produce a theory of instruction. Skinner focused on the shaping of behavior in developing his learning theory. Knowles observed the differences among children, youth, and adults in regard to teaching and learning. In this book John Dewey stands alone. Sometimes he was a philosopher, sometimes a psychologist, but at all times an educator.

Erik Erikson presents a comprehensive theory of the psychosocial development of the individual. He seeks to demonstrate the building, stage upon stage, that characterizes the phenomenon. His presentation should help readers to see the "big picture" of human growth and change.

Although Carol Gilligan worked with Kohlberg, she investigated a specific kind of moral development, that of women. Citing Erikson's "eight stages," she concluded that men and women develop morally in different ways. *In a Different Voice* attempts to demonstrate this. Her concern for relationship and responsibility is refreshing and has generated much interest in professional circles.

Lawrence Kohlberg built a theory of moral decision-making on the general methodology and structure of Piaget. Kohlberg's work, with its emphasis on justice, has been influential in churches and schools, as well as with prison administrators and psychologists. In chapter 3, Kohlberg examines the cognitive theory of moral development and observes that the general education of children is intrinsically a moral education as well.

For the last thirty years Jean Piaget has been a dominant figure in developmentalism. His emphasis on active rather than passive learning, the qualitative stages of cognitive development, and the need for equilibrium have been major contributions. At the time Piaget was being widely read, the work of Kohlberg hit the American scene; Piaget gave the theoretical foundation for Kohlberg.

Role-taking, as presented by Robert Selman, is social because persons learn to see life or individual problems from the perspective of others. It seems to improve as social knowledge increases. Role-taking is related to the development of basic social categories; it seems to be a step between logical and moral thought. Chapter 4 focuses on social role-taking as a specific aspect of cognitive moral development.

The ideas of B. F. Skinner have been applied to education, social work, psychotherapy, and care of the retarded. He was able to ride the crest of the wave of behaviorism that broke fully on the American educational shore in the 1930s and 1940s and almost overwhelmed the educational establishment in the 1950s and 1960s. That it "works" has been a hard argument to overcome. Gradual change to produce major behavioral gains through reinforcement and timing became the Skinnerian "technology" of learning. Skinner radically breaks with the assumptions on which the preceding chapters are based; in contrast to the chapters that follow, Skinner's essay deals with general theory rather than specific issues and techniques of education.

Motivation, structure, sequence, and reinforcement form the outline for Bruner's position. Such innovative applications as "new math" came from his approach. His concern is for a theory of instruction rather than a theory of learning.

The work of Paulo Freire focuses on an interactive mode of education in contrast to a static, accumulative method. It looks at the social "usefulness" of a particular educational approach. Like Erikson and Selman, Freire shows concern for social elements of growth, but his view of human growth is narrower than theirs.

John Dewey was a philosopher who became professionally active at a time when psychology had separated from philosophy and became a discipline on its own. He kept one foot in each camp, philosophy and psychology, while trying to make applications of his ideas in education. His emphasis on students living life rather than preparing for life and his concept of the school representing the community were contributions that are now largely accepted.

If Malcolm Knowles did not coin the term *androgogy*, he at least popularized it. He has been able to show that children and adults learn, and so should be taught, in different ways. Adult experience, which was often thought to get in the way of learning, was made an asset in the work of Knowles. Adult education, especially that outside of schools, has made major changes due to his contributions.

These ten writers, thinkers, researchers, and activists lay a foundation for much of the current thinking about Christian education. This is evident in the Christian education statements in part 2.

In his 1975 book, Harold W. Burgess divides religious educators into four categories. These are the Traditional Theological, Social-Culture, Contemporary Theological, and Social-Science. The Traditional Theological approach is characterized by the use of normative, usually conservative, theological traditions as the basis for religious education. The effective presentation of the church's message is the goal of education. The Social-Culture approach is based on progressive education and liberal theology. It tends to focus on life and social activity. The Contemporary Theological approach emphasizes the relationship between religious education and the Christian community. Theology, generally of the neo-orthodox type, is normative. The Social-Science category is founded in the teaching-learning process. It seeks to maintain a value-free relationship to theology, using it as appropriate. As Burgess defines it, this category is basically behavioristic.

Of the authors whose work appears in this volume, Burgess identifies Lois LeBar with the Traditional Theological approach; George A. Coe with the Social-Culture approach; Randolph Crump Miller and D. Campbell Wyckoff with the Contemporary Theological; and James M. Lee with the Social-Science approach. Using the Burgess book as a guide, I would include Dobbins, Edge, and Richards in the first category and Groome in the third category. Joy, Ward, and Parks should be placed in a hybrid category, Social Science-Theological. This last designation differs from Burgess in that his definition limits social science to behaviorism, while it seems quite legitimate to include developmentalism within social science. It is at the point of developmentalism that Joy, Ward, and Parks are included.

Findley Edge has considered himself a progressive evangelical. He attacks the institutionalization of the church. Instead of the institution he wants to put experience with Christ as the base of the church. His challenge is for the church to regain its spiritual strength. This return to vitality is what he sees as the task of Christian education. This is primarily a theological task. In Christ, Edge believes, this can be accomplished.

Gaines Dobbins, a denominational worker, pastor, and professor, always sought to enhance the church; the local congregation was to be the recipient of his labors. His approach to Christian education was a biblical/theological one. Emphasis was on the Great Teacher, the Holy Spirit as interpreter, and the Bible. Most conservative church people will resonate with Dobbins's contribution.

An author who believes schooling-instruction has become a problem in Christian education is John Westerhoff. He thinks that the most important educative experiences for Christians develop out of the daily life of the congregation. He has been especially interested in the use of the same Scripture passages for education and for worship.

The work of Coe directly addresses what he sees as a critical issue, maybe *the* critical issue, of Christian education: whether to transmit the religion of the teacher to the students or encourage the students to create their own religious experience. Identifying this issue as important seems to come from a Deweyan approach to education and a commitment to liberal biblical scholarship.

Randolph Crump Miller, like Dobbins, has had a lengthy career in Christian education. Also like Dobbins, he takes a theological approach to the discipline. However, his perspective has been a somewhat right-of-center process theology. Bible, learner, and God form the source, interest, and chief end of Christian education.

Out of years of varied churchmanship comes the Christian education perspective of D. Campbell Wyckoff. He taught at Princeton Seminary for three decades. He also sees the need for a theological base for Christian education. Wyckoff believes that the contemporary church must deal with the problem of being bound to its culture as an institution and being bound to Christ as his servant.

Another writer with a long career as a minister and professor who also holds to theology as the foundation of Christian education is Lawrence Richards. He links the roles of home and church and cautions against too much reliance on a schooling approach to church education. Richards's influence among evangelicals has been strong, mainly due to his many books, lesson series, and teacher's materials. The material here focuses on Bible teaching.

The approach taken by James Michael Lee is unique. He believes that religion can and should be taught just like any other subject matter. This means using the best that is known about teaching-learning. Theology may provide the substance of content but should not drive method; that is a role for social science. While his books have provoked controversy, they have also provided much food for thought.

Ted Ward has been influential in the education of so many Christian educators that often 10 to 20 percent of the attendees at some professional meetings will be his former students. His blend of social science and evangelical theology has been helpful to many "non-students" as well. His overall goal is to move Christian education toward a sound Bible foundation while at the same time moving it toward the best social science.

Donald Joy is concerned with *how* people learn. He believes this ability to be God-given. By knowing something about how people learn, the educator becomes a partner with God in the process. He emphasizes the involvement of laypersons in the ministry of the church, primarily as models of the transforming power of Christ.

Another writer with a long career as a minister and professor who also holds to theology as the foundation of Christian education is Lois LeBar. She focuses on Christ and the connection of the Bible with the life of the learner. Her position is very life- and activity-oriented. It is strong on moving Christian teaching from the "felt" needs of the learner to the "substantive" needs of the learner. She also makes a strong place for the Holy Spirit in the teaching of Christians. The living out of the truths of the Bible in the life of the learner are the "proof of the pudding" for the Christian teacher.

When Thomas Groome's book, *Christian Religious Education,* appeared, it made an immediate impact on the field. He had brought together in a fine scholarly way parts that were emerging from varying sources. His "shared Christian praxis" is a practical approach that has been successfully used with children, youth, and adults. This dialectic process seems to many to be both good Bible teaching and good educational theory.

The faith development concept was introduced almost twenty years ago by James Fowler. During that time it has matured. It seems to have been misunderstood by many Christian educators who imposed their own definition of "faith" upon Fowler's theory. As the approach has gained better understanding, its usefulness has become apparent. The difficulty of the semiclinical research method was discouraging to some who might have provided empirical validity for the theory. Fowler's subsequent writing has fleshed out the Christian content for the structure. Faith-development theory bases its perspective on a view of faith that asks "Toward what or whom is your heart set?" The stage structure that is described provides valuable hooks upon which further thinking may be hung.

Sharon Parks focuses on the years of young adulthood as she develops her perspective on faith. She believes that one of the major tasks of this stage in the lifecycle is to make meaning through the use of the imagination. It is the imagination that enables young adults to "vision" their future, to consider what to "depend" on, and to contemplate God.

References

Burgess, Harold William. 1975. *An invitation to religious education.* Birmingham, Ala.: Religious Education Press.

Part 1

Foundations

1

Erik H. Erikson

Psychosocial Theorist

Eight Ages of Man

(1963)

ERIK ERIKSON WAS BORN IN GERMANY IN 1902. HIS EDUCATION WAS TYPICAL OF the middle class. Following secondary school he traveled in Europe developing his talent as a painter, primarily of portraits. While in Austria he painted the portrait of one of Sigmund Freud's children. This activity permitted him much time to converse with Freud, and he was subsequently invited to join the Psychoanalytic Institute of Vienna. There under the direction of Anna Freud, he focused his studies on children. After he completed his training in 1933, Erikson emigrated to the United States where he began a private practice in Boston and became associated with Massachusetts General Hospital and Harvard Medical School.

Erikson has held many important clinical and academic positions over the years. As a part of his theory development he studied Native Americans in South Dakota and California. Following this experience he published *Childhood and Society,* establishing himself as a theoretician and writer. He has won several awards as an author.

Three key concepts identified with Erikson are *epigenesis,* referring to growth and development; *the life cycle,* with eight ages of human life; and *the search for identity,* heightened during adolescence. Every stage in the life cycle presents the individual with potential hazards and potential for renewed growth, with a general focus for each. Erikson's insight has been that while persons are shaped by envi-

From *Childhood and Society*, 2d ed. (New York: Norton, 1963), 247–74.

ronmental and historical events, each one contributes to the environment and to the course of history. This psychosocial approach is probably quite limited to Western culture. However, it moves beyond Freud's focus on sexual forces and takes very seriously psychological development through the whole life cycle.

Erikson's work with life-culminating wisdom as well as his work with the linked concepts of hope, fidelity, and care, which he directly associates with the traditional values of hope, faith, and charity (something not found in many neo-Freudians) will be familiar to Christian educators. Figure 1.2, and the note following it, can be especially helpful. It allows for visualization of the life-cycle ages and allows one to note the cumulativeness of the cycle by taking into consideration the cells below the diagonal. The last column should be filled from bottom to top with hope, will, purpose, and so on, up to wisdom.

Basic Trust versus Basic Mistrust

The first demonstration of social trust in the baby is the ease of his feeding, the depth of his sleep, the relaxation of his bowels. The experience of a mutual regulation of his increasingly receptive capacities with the maternal techniques of provision gradually helps him to balance the discomfort caused by the immaturity of homeostasis with which he was born. In his gradually increasing waking hours he finds that more and more adventures of the senses arouse a feeling of familiarity, of having coincided with a feeling of inner goodness. Forms of comfort, and people associated with them, become as familiar as the gnawing discomfort of the bowels. The infant's first social achievement, then, is his willingness to let the mother out of sight without undue anxiety or rage, because she has become an inner certainty as well as an outer predictability. Such consistency, continuity, and sameness of experience provide a rudimentary sense of ego identity which depends, I think, on the recognition that there is an inner population of remembered and anticipated sensations and images which are firmly correlated with the outer population of familiar and predictable things and people.

What we here call trust coincides with what Therese Benedek has called confidence. If I prefer the word "trust," it is because there is more naïveté and more mutuality in it: an infant can be said to be trusting where it would go too far to say that he has confidence. The general state of trust, furthermore, implies not only that one has learned to rely on the sameness and continuity of the outer providers, but also that one may trust oneself and the capacity of one's own organs to cope with urges; and that one is able to consider oneself trustworthy enough so that the providers will not need to be on guard lest they be nipped.

The constant tasting and testing of the relationship between inside and outside meets its crucial test during the rages of the biting stage, when the teeth cause pain from within and when outer friends either prove of no avail or withdraw from the only action which promises relief: biting. Not that teething itself seems to cause all the dire consequences sometimes ascribed to it. As outlined earlier, the infant now is driven to "grasp" more, but he is apt to find desired presences elusive: nipple and breast, and the mother's focused attention and care. Teething seems to have a prototypal significance and may well be the model for the masochistic tendency to assure cruel comfort by enjoying one's hurt whenever one is unable to prevent a significant loss.

In psychopathology the absence of basic trust can best be studied in infantile schizophrenia, while lifelong underlying weakness of such trust is apparent in adult personalities in whom withdrawal into schizoid and depressive states is habitual. The reestablishment of a state of trust has been found to be the basic requirement for therapy in these cases. For no matter what conditions may have caused a psychotic break, the bizarreness and withdrawal in the behavior of many very sick individuals hides an attempt to recover social mutuality by a testing of the borderlines between senses and physical reality, between words and social meanings.

Psychoanalysis assumes the early process of differentiation between inside and outside to be the origin of projection and introjection which remain some of our deepest and most dangerous defense mechanisms. In introjection we feel and act as if an outer goodness had become an inner certainty. In projection, we experience an inner harm as an outer one: we endow significant people with the evil which actually is in us. These two mechanisms, then, projection and introjection, are assumed to be modeled after whatever goes on in infants when they would like to externalize pain and internalize pleasure, an intent which must yield to the testimony of the maturing senses and ultimately of reason. These mechanisms are, more or less normally, reinstated in acute crises of love, trust, and faith in adulthood and can characterize irrational attitudes toward adversaries and enemies in masses of "mature" individuals.

The firm establishment of enduring patterns for the solution of the nuclear conflict of basic trust versus basic mistrust in mere existence is the first task of the ego, and thus first of all a task for maternal care. But let it be said here that the amount of trust derived from earliest infantile experience does not seem to depend on absolute quantities of food or demonstrations of love, but rather on the quality of the maternal relationship. Mothers create a sense of trust in their children by that kind of administration which in its quality combines sensitive care of the baby's individual needs and a firm sense of personal trustworthiness within the trusted framework of their culture's life-style. This forms the basis in the child for a sense of identity which will later combine a sense of being "all right," of being oneself, and of becoming what other people trust one will become. There are, therefore (within certain limits previously defined as the "musts" of child care), few frustrations in either this or the following stages which the growing child cannot endure if the frustration leads to the ever-renewed experience of greater sameness and stronger continuity of development, toward a final integration of the individual life cycle with some meaningful wider belongingness. Parents must not only have certain ways of guiding by prohibition and permission; they must also be able to represent to the child a deep, an almost somatic conviction that there is a meaning to what they are doing. Ultimately, children become neurotic not from frustrations but from the lack or loss of societal meaning in these frustrations.

But even under the most favorable circumstances, this stage seems to introduce into psychic life (and become prototypical for) a sense of inner division and universal nostalgia for a paradise forfeited. It is against this powerful combination of a sense of having been deprived, of having been divided, and of having been abandoned that basic trust must maintain itself throughout life.

Each successive stage and crisis has a special relation to one of the basic elements of society, and this for the simple reason that the human life cycle and man's institutions have evolved together. In this chapter we can do little more than mention, after the description of each stage, what basic element of social organization is related to it. This relation is twofold: man brings to these institutions the remnants of his infantile mentality and his youthful fervor, and he receives from them—as long as they manage to maintain their actuality—a reinforcement of his infantile gains.

The parental faith which supports the trust emerging in the newborn, has throughout history sought its institutional safeguard (and, on occasion, found its greatest enemy) in organized religion. Trust born of care is, in fact, the touchstone of the *actuality* of a given religion. All religions have in common the periodical childlike surrender to a Provider or providers who dispense earthly fortune as well as spiritual health; some demonstration of man's smallness by way of reduced posture and humble gesture; the admission in prayer and song of misdeeds, of misthoughts, and of evil intentions; fervent appeal for inner unification by divine guidance; and finally, the insight that individual trust must become a common faith, individual mistrust a commonly formulated evil, while the individual's restoration must become part of the ritual practice of many, and must become a sign of trustworthiness in the community.[1] We have illustrated how tribes dealing with one segment of nature develop a collective magic which seems to treat the Supernatural Providers of food and fortune as if they were angry and must be appeased by prayer and self-torture. Primitive religions, the most primitive layer in all religions, and the religious layer in each individual, abound with efforts at atonement which try to make up for

1. This is the communal and psychosocial side of religion. Its often paradoxical relation to the spirituality of the individual is a matter not to be treated briefly and in passing (see *Young Man Luther*).

vague deeds against a maternal matrix and try to restore faith in the goodness of one's strivings and in the kindness of the powers of the universe.

Each society and each age must find the institutionalized form of reverence which derives vitality from its world-image—from predestination to indeterminacy. The clinician can only observe that many are proud to be without religion whose children cannot afford their being without it. On the other hand, there are many who seem to derive a vital faith from social action or scientific pursuit. And again, there are many who profess faith, yet in practice breathe mistrust both of life and man.

Autonomy versus Shame and Doubt

In describing the growth and the crises of the human person as a series of alternative basic attitudes such as trust versus mistrust, we take recourse to the term a "sense of," although, like a "sense of health," or a "sense of being unwell," such "senses" pervade surface and depth, consciousness and the unconscious. They are, then, at the same time, ways of *experiencing* accessible to introspection; ways of *behaving*, observable by others; and unconscious *inner states* determinable by test and analysis. It is important to keep these three dimensions in mind as we proceed.

Muscular maturation sets the stage for experimentation with two simultaneous sets of social modalities: holding on and letting go. As is the case with all of these modalities, their basic conflicts can lead in the end to either hostile or benign expectations and attitudes. Thus, to hold can become a destructive and cruel retaining or restraining, and it can become a pattern of care: to have and to hold. To let go, too, can turn into an inimical letting loose of destructive forces, or it can become a relaxed "to let pass" and "to let be."

Outer control at this stage, therefore, must be firmly reassuring. The infant must come to feel that the basic faith in existence, which is the lasting treasure saved from the rages of the oral stage, will not be jeopardized by this about-face of his, this sudden violent wish to have a choice, to appropriate demandingly, and to eliminate stubbornly. Firmness must protect him against the potential anarchy of his as yet untrained sense of discrimination, his inability to hold on and to let go with discretion. As his environment encourages him to "stand on his own feet," it must protect him against meaningless and arbitrary experiences of shame and of early doubt.

The latter danger is the one best known to us. For if denied the gradual and well-guided experience of the autonomy of free choice (or if, indeed, weakened by an initial loss of trust) the child will turn against himself all his urge to discriminate and to manipulate. He will overmanipulate himself, he will develop a precocious conscience. Instead of taking possession of things in order to test them by purposeful repetition, he will become obsessed by his own repetitiveness. By such obsessiveness, of course, he then learns to repossess the environment and to gain power by stubborn and minute control, where he could not find large-scale mutual regulation. Such hollow victory is the infantile model for a compulsion neurosis. It is also the infantile source of later attempts in adult life to govern by the letter, rather than by the spirit.

Shame is an emotion insufficiently studied, because in our civilization it is so early and easily absorbed by guilt. Shame supposes that one is completely exposed and conscious of being looked at: in one word, self-conscious. One is visible and not ready to be visible, which is why we dream of shame as a situation in which we are stared at in a condition of incomplete dress, in night attire, "with one's pants down." Shame is early expressed in an impulse to bury one's face, or to sink, right then and there, into the ground. But this, I think, is essentially rage turned against the self. He who is ashamed would like to force the world not to look at him, not to notice his exposure. He would like to destroy the eyes of the world. Instead he must wish for his own invisibility. This potentiality is abundantly used in the educational method of "shaming" used so exclusively by some primitive peoples. Visual shame precedes auditory guilt, which is a sense of badness to be had all by oneself when nobody watches and when everything is quiet—except the voice of the superego. Such shaming exploits an increasing sense of being small, which can develop only as the child stands up and as his awareness permits him to note the relative measures of size and power.

Too much shaming does not lead to genuine propriety but to a secret determination to try to get away with things, unseen—if, indeed, it does not result in defiant shamelessness. There is an impressive American ballad in which a murderer to be hanged on the gallows before the eyes of the community, instead of feeling duly chastened, begins to berate the onlookers, ending every salvo of defiance with the words, "God damn your eyes." Many a small child, shamed beyond endurance, may be in a chronic mood (although not in possession of either the courage or the words) to express defiance in similar terms. What I mean by this sinister reference is that there is a limit to a child's and an adult's endurance in the face of demands to consider himself, his body, and his wishes as evil and dirty, and to his belief in the infallibility of those who pass such judgment. He may be apt to turn things around, and to consider as evil only the fact that they exist: his chance will come when they are gone or when he will go from them.

Doubt is the brother of shame. Where shame is dependent on the consciousness of being upright and exposed, doubt, so clinical observation leads me to believe, has much to do with a consciousness of having a front and a back—and especially a "behind." For this reverse area of the body, with its aggressive and libidinal focus in the sphincters and in the buttocks, cannot be seen by the child, and yet it can be dominated by the will of others. The "behind" is the small being's dark continent, an area of the body which can be magically dominated and effectively invaded by those who would attack one's power of autonomy and who would designate as evil those products of the bowels which were felt to be all right when they were being passed. This basic sense of doubt in whatever one has left behind forms a substratum for later and more verbal forms of compulsive doubting; this finds its adult expression in paranoiac fears concerning hidden persecutors and secret persecutions threatening from behind (and from within the behind).

This stage, therefore, becomes decisive for the ratio of love and hate, cooperation and willfulness, freedom of self-expression and its suppression. From a sense of self-control without loss of self-esteem comes a lasting sense of good will and pride; from a sense of loss of self-control and of foreign overcontrol comes a lasting propensity for doubt and shame.

If, to some reader, the "negative" potentialities of our stages seem overstated throughout, we must remind him that this is not only the result of a preoccupation with clinical data. Adults, and seemingly mature and unneurotic ones, display a sensitivity concerning a possible shameful "loss of face" and fear of being attacked "from behind" which is not only highly irrational and in contrast to the knowledge available to them, but can be of fateful import if related sentiments influence, for example, interracial and international policies.

We have related basic trust to the institution of religion. The lasting need of the individual to have his will reaffirmed and delineated within an adult order of things which at the same time reaffirms and delineates the will of others has an institutional safeguard in the *principle of law and order*. In daily life as well as in the high courts of law—domestic and international—this principle apportions to each his privileges and his limitations, his obligations and his rights. A sense of rightful dignity and lawful independence on the part of adults around him gives to the child of good will the confident expectation that the kind of autonomy fostered in childhood will not lead to undue doubt or shame in later life. Thus the sense of autonomy fostered in the child and modified as life progresses, serves (and is served by) the preservation in economic and political life of a sense of justice.

Initiative versus Guilt

There is in every child at every stage a new miracle of vigorous unfolding, which constitutes a new hope and a new responsibility for all. Such is the sense and the pervading quality of initiative. The criteria for all these senses and qualities are the same: a crisis, more or less beset with fumbling and fear, is resolved, in that the child suddenly seems to "grow together" both in his person and in his body. He appears "more himself," more loving, relaxed, and brighter in his judgment, more activated and activating. He is in free possession of a surplus of energy which permits him to forget failures quickly and to approach what seems desirable (even if it also seems uncertain and even dangerous) with undiminished and more accurate direction. Initiative adds to autonomy the quality of undertaking, planning, and "attacking" a task for the sake of being active and on the move, where before self-will, more often than not, inspired acts of defiance or, at any rate, protested independence.

I know that the very word "initiative" to many, has an American, and industrial connotation. Yet, initiative is a necessary part of every act, and man needs a sense of initiative for whatever he learns and does, from fruit-gathering to a system of enterprise.

The ambulatory stage and that of infantile genitality add to the inventory of basic social modalities that of "making," first in the sense of "being on the make." There is no simpler, stronger word for it; it suggests pleasure in attack and conquest. In the boy, the emphasis remains on phallic-intrusive modes; in the girl it turns to modes of "catching" in more aggressive forms of snatching or in the milder form of making oneself attractive and endearing.

The danger of this stage is a sense of guilt over the goals contemplated and the acts initiated in one's exuberant enjoyment of new locomotor and mental power: acts of aggressive manipulation and coercion which soon go far beyond the executive capacity of organism and mind and therefore call for an energetic halt on one's contemplated initiative. While autonomy concentrates on keeping potential rivals out, and therefore can lead to jealous rage most often directed against encroachments by younger siblings, initiative brings with it anticipatory rivalry with those who have been there first and may, therefore, occupy with their superior equipment the field toward which one's initiative is directed. Infantile jealousy and rivalry, those often embittered and yet essentially futile attempts at demarcating a sphere of unquestioned privilege, now come to a climax in a final contest for a favored position with the mother; the usual failure leads to resignation, guilt, and anxiety. The child indulges in fantasies of being a giant and a tiger, but in his dreams he runs in terror for dear life. This, then, is the stage of the "castration complex," the intensified fear of finding the (now energetically erotized) genitals harmed as a punishment for the fantasies attached to their excitement.

Infantile sexuality and incest taboo, castration complex and superego all unite here to bring about that specifically human crisis during which the child must turn from an exclusive, pre-genital attachment to his parents to the slow process of becoming a parent, a carrier of tradition. Here the most fateful split and transformation in the emotional powerhouse occurs, a split between potential human glory and potential total destruction. For here the child becomes forever divided in himself. The instinct fragments which before had enhanced the growth of his infantile body and mind now become divided into an infantile set which perpetuates the exuberance of growth potentials, and a parental set which supports and increases self-observation, self-guidance, and self-punishment.

The problem, again, is one of mutual regulation. Where the child, now so ready to overmanipulate himself, can gradually develop a sense of moral responsibility, where he can gain some insight into the institutions, functions, and roles which will permit his responsible participation, he will find pleasurable accomplishment in wielding tools and weapons, in manipulating meaningful toys—and in caring for younger children.

Naturally, the parental set is at first infantile in nature: the fact that human conscience remains partially infantile throughout life is the core of human tragedy. For the superego of the child can be primitive, cruel, and uncompromising, as may be observed in instances where children overcontrol and overconstrict themselves to the point of self-obliteration; where they develop an over-obedience more literal than the one the parent has wished to exact; or where they develop deep regressions and lasting resentments because the parents themselves do not seem to live up to the new conscience. One of the deepest conflicts in life is the hate for a parent who served as the model and the executor of the superego, but who (in some form) was found trying to get away with the very transgressions which the child can no longer tolerate in himself. The suspiciousness and evasiveness which is thus mixed in with the all-or-nothing quality of the superego, this organ of moral tradition, makes moral (in the sense of moralistic) man a great potential danger to his own ego—and to that of his fellow men.

In adult pathology, the residual conflict over initiative is expressed either in hysterical denial, which causes the repression of the wish or the abrogation of its executive organ by paralysis, inhibition, or impotence; or in overcompensatory showing off, in which the scared individual, so eager to "duck," instead "sticks his neck out." Then also a plunge into psychosomatic disease is now common. It is as if the culture has made a man over-advertise himself and so identify with his own advertisement that only disease can offer him escape.

But here, again, we must not think only of individual psychopathology, but of the inner powerhouse of rage which must be submerged at this stage, as some of the fondest hopes and the wildest phantasies are repressed and inhibited. The resulting self-righteousness—often the principal reward for goodness—can later be most intolerantly turned against others in the form of persistent moralistic surveillance, so that the prohibition rather than the guidance of initiative becomes the dominant endeavor. On the other hand, even moral man's initiative is apt to burst the boundaries of self-restriction, permitting him to do to others, in his or in other lands, what he would neither do nor tolerate being done in his own home.

In view of the dangerous potentials of man's long childhood, it is well to look back at the blueprint of the life-stages and to the possibilities of guiding the young of the race while they are young. And here we note that according to the wisdom of the ground plan the child is at no time more ready to learn quickly and avidly, to become bigger in the sense of sharing obligation and performance than during this period of his development. He is eager and able to make things cooperatively, to combine with other children for the purpose of constructing and planning, and he is willing to profit from teachers and to emulate ideal prototypes. He remains, of course, identified with the parent of the same sex, but for the present looks for opportunities where work-identification seems to promise a field of initiative without too much infantile conflict or oedipal guilt and a more realistic identification based on a spirit of equality experienced in doing things together. At any rate, the "oedipal" stage results not only in the oppressive establishment of a moral sense restricting the horizon of the permissible; it also sets the direction toward the possible and the tangible which permits the dreams of early childhood to be attached to the goals of an active adult life. Social institutions, therefore, offer children of this age an *economic ethos,* in the form of ideal adults recognizable by their uniforms and their functions, and fascinating enough to replace the heroes of picture book and fairy tale.

Industry versus Inferiority

Thus the inner stage seems all set for "entrance into life," except that life must first be school life, whether school is field or jungle or classroom. The child must forget past hopes and wishes, while his exuberant imagination is tamed and harnessed to the laws of impersonal things—even the three R's. For before the child, psychologically already a rudimentary parent, can become a biological parent, he must begin to be a worker and potential provider. With the oncoming latency period, the normally advanced child forgets, or rather sublimates, the necessity to "make" people by direct attack or to become papa and mama in a hurry: he now learns to win recognition by producing things. He has mastered the ambulatory field and the organ modes. He has experienced a sense of finality regarding the fact that there is no workable future within the womb of his family, and thus becomes ready to apply himself to given skills and tasks, which go far beyond the mere playful expression of his organ modes or the pleasure in the function of his limbs. He develops a sense of industry—that is, he adjusts himself to the inorganic laws of the tool world. He can become an eager and absorbed unit of a productive situation. To bring a productive situation to completion is an aim which gradually supersedes the whims and wishes of play. His ego boundaries include his tools and skills: the work principle (Ives Hendrick) teaches him the pleasure of work completion by steady attention and persevering diligence. In all cultures, at this stage, children receive some *systematic instruction,* although . . . it is by no means always in the kind of school which literate people must organize around special teachers who have learned how to teach literacy. In preliterate people and in nonliterate pursuits much is learned from adults who become teachers by dint of gift and inclination rather than by appointment, and perhaps the greatest amount is learned from older children. Thus the *fundamentals of technol-*

ogy are developed, as the child becomes ready to handle the utensils, the tools, and the weapons used by the big people. Literate people, with more specialized careers, must prepare the child by teaching him things which first of all make him literate, the widest possible basic education for the greatest number of possible careers. The more confusing specialization becomes, however, the more indistinct are the eventual goals of initiative; and the more complicated social reality, the vaguer are the father's and mother's role in it. School seems to be a culture all by itself, with its own goals and limits, its achievements and disappointment.

The child's danger, at this stage, lies in a sense of inadequacy and inferiority. If he despairs of his tools and skills or of his status among his tool partners, he may be discouraged from identification with them and with a section of the tool world. To lose the hope of such "industrial" association may pull him back to the more isolated, less tool-conscious familial rivalry of the oedipal time. The child despairs of his equipment in the tool world and in anatomy, and considers himself doomed to mediocrity or inadequacy. It is at this point that wider society becomes significant in its ways of admitting the child to an understanding of meaningful roles in its technology and economy. Many a child's development is disrupted when family life has failed to prepare him for school life, or when school life fails to sustain the promises of earlier stages.

Regarding the period of a developing sense of industry, I have referred to *outer and inner hindrances* in the use of new capacities but not to aggravations of new human drives, nor to submerged rages resulting from their frustration. This stage differs from the earlier ones in that it is not a swing from an inner upheaval to a new mastery. Freud calls it the latency stage because violent drives are normally dormant. But it is only a lull before the storm of puberty, when all the earlier drives reemerge in a new combination, to be brought under the dominance of genitality.

On the other hand, this is socially a most decisive stage: since industry involves doing things beside and with others, a first sense of division of labor and of differential opportunity, that is, a sense of the *technological ethos* of a culture, develops at this time. We have pointed in the last section to the danger threatening individual and society where the schoolchild begins to feel that the color of his skin, the background of his parents, or the fashion of his clothes rather than his wish and his will to learn will decide his worth as an apprentice, and thus his sense of *identity*—to which we must now turn. But there is another more fundamental danger, namely man's restriction of himself and constriction of his horizons to include only his work to which, so the Book says, he has been sentenced after his expulsion from paradise. If he accepts work as his only obligation, and "what works" as his only criterion of worthwhileness, he may become the conformist and thoughtless slave of his technology and of those who are in position to exploit it.

Identity versus Role Confusion

With the establishment of a good initial relationship to the world of skills and tools, and with the advent of puberty, childhood proper comes to an end. Youth begins. But in puberty and adolescence all samenesses and continuities relied on earlier are more or less questioned again, because of a rapidity of body growth which equals that of early childhood and because of the new addition of genital maturity. The growing and developing youths, faced with this physiological revolution within them, and with tangible adult tasks ahead of them, are now primarily concerned with what they appear to be in the eyes of others as compared with what they feel they are, and with the question of how to connect the roles and skills cultivated earlier with the occupational prototypes of the day. In their search for a new sense of continuity and sameness, adolescents have to refight many of the battles of earlier years, even though to do so they must artificially appoint perfectly well-meaning people to play the roles of adversaries; and they are ever ready to install lasting idols and ideals as guardians of a final identity.

The integration now taking place in the form of ego identity is, as pointed out, more than the sum of the childhood identifications. It is the accrued experience of the ego's ability to integrate all identifications with the vicissitudes of the libido, with the aptitudes developed out of endowment, and with the opportunities offered in social roles. The sense of ego identity, then, is the accrued confidence that the inner sameness and continuity prepared in the past are matched by the sameness and continuity of one's meaning for others, as evidenced in the tangible promise of a "career."

The danger of this stage is role confusion (Erikson 1956). Where this is based on a strong previous doubt as to one's sexual identity, delinquent and outright psychotic episodes are not uncommon. If diagnosed and treated correctly, these incidents do not have the same fatal significance which they have at other ages. In most instances, however, it is the inability to settle on an occupational identity which disturbs individual young people. To keep themselves together they temporarily overidentify, to the point of apparent complete loss of identity, with the heroes of cliques and crowds. This initiates the stage of "falling in love," which is by no means entirely, or even primarily, a sexual matter—except where the mores demand it. To a considerable extent adolescent love is an attempt to arrive at a definition of one's identity by projecting one's diffused ego image on another and by seeing it thus reflected and gradually clarified. This is why so much of young love is conversation.

Young people can also be remarkably clannish, and cruel in their exclusion of all those who are "different," in skin color or cultural background, in tastes and gifts, and often in such petty aspects of dress and gesture as have been temporarily selected as *the* signs of an in-grouper or out-grouper. It is important to understand (which does not mean condone or participate in) such intolerance as a defense against a sense of identity confusion. For adolescents not only help one another temporarily through much discomfort by forming cliques and by stereotyping themselves, their ideals, and their enemies; they also perversely test each other's capacity to pledge fidelity. The readiness for such testing also explains the appeal which simple and cruel totalitarian doctrines have on the minds of the youth of such countries and classes as have lost or are losing their group identities (feudal, agrarian, tribal, national) and face world-wide industrialization, emancipation, and wider communication.

The adolescent mind is essentially a mind of the *moratorium*, a psychosocial stage between childhood and adulthood, and between the morality learned by the child, and the ethics to be developed by the adult. It is an ideological mind—and, indeed, it is the ideological outlook of a society that speaks most clearly to the adolescent who is eager to be affirmed by his peers, and is ready to be confirmed by rituals, creeds, and programs which at the same time define what is evil, uncanny, and inimical. In searching for the social values which guide identity, one therefore confronts the problems of *ideology* and *aristocracy*, both in their widest possible sense which connotes that within a defined world image and a predestined course of history, the best people will come to rule and rule develops the best in people. In order not to become cynically or apathetically lost, young people must somehow be able to convince themselves that those who succeed in their anticipated adult world thereby shoulder the obligation of being the best. We will discuss later the dangers which emanate from human ideals harnessed to the management of super-machines, be they guided by nationalistic or international, communist or capitalist ideologies. In the last part of this book we shall discuss the way in which the revolutions of our day attempt to solve and also to exploit the deep need of youth to redefine its identity in an industrialized world.

Intimacy versus Isolation

The strength acquired at any stage is tested by the necessity to transcend it in such a way that the individual can take chances in the next stage with what was most vulnerably precious in the previous one. Thus, the young adult, emerging from the search for and the insistence on identity, is eager and willing to fuse his identity with that of others. He is ready for intimacy, that is, the capacity to commit himself to concrete affiliations and partnerships and to develop the ethical strength to abide by such commitments, even though they may call for significant sacrifices and compromises. Body and ego must now be masters of the organ modes and of the nuclear conflicts, in order to be able to face the fear of ego loss in situations which call for self-abandon: in the solidarity of close affiliations, in orgasms and sexual unions, in close friendships and in physical combat, in experiences of inspiration by teachers and of intuition from the recesses of the self. The avoidance of such experiences because of a fear of ego loss may lead to a deep sense of isolation and consequent self-absorption.

The counterpart of intimacy is distantiation: the readiness to isolate and, if necessary, to destroy those forces and people whose essence seems dangerous to one's own, and whose "territory" seems to encroach on the extent of one's intimate relations. Prejudices thus developed (and utilized and exploited in politics and in war) are a more mature outgrowth of the blinder repudiations which during the struggle for identity differentiate sharply and cruelly between the familiar and the foreign. The danger of this stage is that intimate, competitive, and combative relations are experienced with and against the selfsame people. But as the areas of adult duty are delineated, and as the competitive encounter, and the sexual embrace, are differentiated, they eventually become subject to that *ethical sense* which is the mark of the adult.

Strictly speaking, it is only now that *true genitality* can fully develop; for much of the sex life preceding these commitments is of the identity-searching kind, or is dominated by phallic or vaginal strivings which make of sex-life a kind of genital combat. On the other hand, genitality is all too often described as a permanent state of reciprocal sexual bliss. This, then, may be the place to complete our discussion of genitality.

For a basic orientation in the matter I shall quote what has come to me as Freud's shortest saying. It has often been claimed, and bad habits of conversation seem to sustain the claim, that psychoanalysis as a treatment attempts to convince the patient that before God and man he has only one obligation: to have good orgasms, with a fitting "object," and that regularly. This, of course, is not true. Freud was once asked what he thought a normal person should be able to do well. The questioner probably expected a complicated answer. But Freud, in the curt way of his old days, is reported to have said: "Lieben und arbeiten" (to love and to work). It pays to ponder on this simple formula; it gets deeper as you think about it. For when Freud said "love" he meant *genital* love, and genital *love;* when he said love *and* work, he meant a general work-productiveness which would not preoccupy the individual to the extent that he loses his right or capacity to be a genital and a loving being. Thus we may ponder, but we cannot improve on "the professor's" formula.

Genitality, then, consists in the unobstructed capacity to develop an orgastic potency so free of pregenital interferences that genital libido (not just the sex products discharged in Kinsey's "outlets") is expressed in heterosexual mutuality, with full sensitivity of both penis and vagina, and with a convulsion-like discharge of tension from the whole body. This is a rather concrete way of saying something about a process which we really do not understand. To put it more situationally: the total fact of finding, via the climactic turmoil of the orgasm, a supreme experience of the mutual regulation of two beings in some way takes the edge off the hostilities and potential rages caused by the oppositeness of male and female, of fact and fancy, of love and hate. Satisfactory sex relations thus make sex less obsessive, overcompensation less necessary, sadistic controls superfluous.

Preoccupied as it was with curative aspects, psychoanalysis often failed to formulate the matter of genitality in a way significant for the processes of society in all classes, nations, and levels of culture. The kind of mutuality in orgasm which psychoanalysis has in mind is apparently easily obtained in classes and cultures which happen to make a leisurely institution of it. In more complex societies this mutuality is interfered with by so many factors of health, of tradition, of opportunity, and of temperament, that the proper formulation of sexual health would be rather this: A human being should be potentially able to accomplish mutuality of genital orgasm, but he should also be so constituted as to bear a certain amount of frustration in the matter without undue regression wherever emotional preference or considerations of duty and loyalty call for it.

While psychoanalysis has on occasion gone too far in its emphasis on genitality as a universal cure for society and has thus provided a new addiction and a new commodity for many who wished to so interpret its teachings, it has not always indicated all the goals that genitality actually should and must imply. In order to be of lasting social significance, the utopia of genitality should include:

1. mutuality of orgasm
2. with a loved partner
3. of the other sex
4. with whom one is able and willing to share a mutual trust
5. and with whom one is able and willing to regulate the cycles of
   a. work
   b. procreation
   c. recreation
6. so as to secure to the offspring, too, all the stages of a satisfactory development.

It is apparent that such utopian accomplishment on a large scale cannot be an individual or, indeed, a therapeutic task. Nor is it a purely sexual matter by any means. It is integral to a culture's style of sexual selection, cooperation, and competition.

The danger of this stage is isolation, that is, the avoidance of contacts which commit to intimacy. In psychopathology, this disturbance can lead to severe "character-problems." On the other hand, there are partnerships which amount to an isolation à deux, protecting both partners from the necessity to face the next critical development—that of generativity.

Generativity versus Stagnation

In this book the emphasis is on the childhood stages, otherwise the section on generativity would of necessity be the central one, for this term encompasses the evolutionary development which has made man the teaching and instituting as well as the learning animal. The fashionable insistence on dramatizing the dependence of children on adults often blinds us to the dependence of the older generation on the younger one. Mature man needs to be needed, and maturity needs guidance as well as encouragement from what has been produced and must be taken care of.

Generativity, then, is primarily the concern in establishing and guiding the next generation, although there are individuals who, through misfortune or because of special and genuine gifts in other directions, do not apply this drive to their own offspring. And indeed, the concept generativity is meant to include such more popular synonyms as *productivity* and *creativity,* which, however, cannot replace it.

It has taken psychoanalysis some time to realize that the ability to lose oneself in the meeting of bodies and minds leads to a gradual expansion of ego-interests and to a libidinal investment in that which is being generated. Generativity thus is an essential stage on the psychosexual as well as on the psychosocial schedule. Where such enrichment fails altogether, regression to an obsessive need for pseudo-intimacy takes place, often with a pervading sense of stagnation and personal impoverishment. Individuals, then, often begin to indulge themselves as if they were their own—or one another's—one and only child; and where conditions favor it, early invalidism, physical or psychological, becomes the vehicle of self-concern. The mere fact of having or even wanting children, however, does not "achieve" generativity. In fact, some young parents suffer, it seems, from the retardation of the ability to develop this stage. The reasons are often to be found in early childhood impressions; in excessive self-love based on a too strenuously self-made personality; and finally (and here we return to the beginnings) in the lack of some faith, some "belief in the species," which would make a child appear to be a welcome trust of the community.

As to the institutions which safeguard and reinforce generativity, one can only say that all institutions codify the ethics of generative succession. Even where philosophical and spiritual tradition suggests the renunciation of the right to procreate or to produce, such early turn to "ultimate concerns," wherever instituted in monastic movements, strives to settle at the same time the matter of its relationship to the Care for the creatures of this world and to the Charity which is felt to transcend it.

If this were a book on adulthood, it would be indispensable and profitable at this point to compare economic and psychological theories (beginning with the strange convergencies and divergencies of Marx and Freud) and to proceed to a discussion of man's relationship to his production as well as to his progeny.

Ego Integrity versus Despair

Only in him who in some way has taken care of things and people and has adapted himself to the triumphs and disappointments adherent to being, the originator of others or the generator of products and ideas—only in him may gradually ripen the fruit of these seven stages. I know no better word for it than ego integrity. Lacking a clear definition, I shall point to a few constituents of this state of mind. It is the ego's accrued assurance of its proclivity for order and meaning. It is a post-narcissistic love of the human ego—not of the self—as an experience which conveys some world order and spiritual sense, no matter how dearly paid for. It is the acceptance of one's one and only life cycle as something that had to be and that, by necessity, permitted of no substitutions: it thus means a new, a different love of one's parents. It is a comradeship with the ordering ways of distant times and different pursuits, as expressed in the simple products and sayings of such times and pursuits. Although aware of the relativity of all the various life-styles which have given meaning to human striving, the possessor of integrity is ready to defend the dignity of his own life-style against all physical and economic threats. For he knows that an individual life is the accidental coincidence of but one life cycle with but one segment of history; and that for him all human integrity stands or falls with the one style of integrity of which he partakes. The style of integrity developed by his culture or civilization thus becomes the "patrimony of his soul," the seal of his moral paternity of himself (". . . pero el honor / Es patrimonio del alma": Calderón). In such final consolidation, death loses its sting.

The lack or loss of this accrued ego integration is signified by fear of death: the one and only life cycle is not accepted as the ultimate of life. Despair expresses the feeling that the time is now short, too short for the attempt to start another life and to try out alternate roads to integrity. Disgust hides despair, if often only in the form of "a thousand little disgusts" which do not add up to one big remorse: *"mille petits dégôuts de soi, dont le total ne fait pas un remords, mais un gêne obscure"* (Rostand).

Each individual, to become a mature adult, must to a sufficient degree develop all the ego qualities mentioned, so that a wise Indian, a true gentleman, and a mature peasant share and recognize in one another the final stage of integrity. But each cultural entity, to develop the particular style of integrity suggested by its historical place, utilizes a particular combination of these conflicts, along with specific provocations and prohibitions of infantile sexuality. Infantile conflicts become creative only if sustained by the firm support of cultural institutions and of the special leader classes representing them. In order to approach or experience integrity, the individual must know how to be a follower of image bearers in religion and in politics, in the economic order and in technology, in aristocratic living and in the arts and sciences. Ego integrity, therefore, implies an emotional integration which permits participation by followership as well as acceptance of the responsibility of leadership.

Webster's dictionary is kind enough to help us complete this outline in a circular fashion. Trust (the first of our ego values) is here defined as "the assured reliance on another's integrity," the last of our values. I suspect that Webster had business in mind rather than babies, credit rather than faith. But the formulation stands. And it seems possible to further paraphrase the relation of adult integrity and infantile trust by saying that healthy children will not fear life if their elders have integrity enough not to fear death.

An Epigenetic Chart

. . . the emphasis is on the childhood stages. The foregoing conception of the life cycle, however, awaits systematic treatment. To prepare this, I shall conclude this chapter with a diagram. In this, as in the diagram of pregenital zones and modes, the diagonal represents the normative sequence of psychosocial gains made as at each stage one more nuclear conflict adds a new ego quality, a new criterion of accruing human strength. Below the diagonal there is space for the precursors of each of these solutions, all of which begin with the beginning; above the diagonal there is space for the designation of the derivatives of these gains and their transformations in the maturing and the mature personality.

The underlying assumptions for such charting are (1) that the human personality in principle develops according to steps predetermined in the growing person's readiness to be driven toward, to be aware of, and to interact with, a widening social radius; and (2) that society, in principle, tends to be so constituted as to meet and invite this succession of potentialities for interaction and attempts to safeguard and to encourage the proper rate and the proper sequence of their enfolding. This is the "maintenance of the human world."

But a chart is only a tool to think with, and cannot aspire to be a prescription to abide by, whether in the practice of child training, in psychotherapy, or in the methodology of child study. In the presentation of the psychosocial stages in the form of an *epigenetic chart* (fig. 1.1), . . . we have definite and delimited methodological steps in mind. It is one purpose of this work to facilitate the comparison of the stages first discerned by Freud as sexual to other schedules of development (physical, cognitive). But any one chart delimits one schedule only, and it must not be imputed that our outline of the psychosocial schedule is intended to imply obscure generalities concerning other aspects of development—or, indeed, of existence. If the chart, for example, lists a series of conflicts or crises, we do not consider all development a series of crises: we claim only that psychosocial development proceeds by critical steps—"critical" being a characteristic of turning points, of moments of decision between progress and regression, integration and retardation.

Figure 1.1
An Epigenetic Chart

III Locomotor-Genital			Initiative versus Guilt
II Muscular-Anal		Autonomy versus Shame, Doubt	
I. Oral-Sensory	Basic Trust versus Mistrust		
	1	2	3

It may be useful at this point to spell out the methodological implications of an epigenetic matrix. The more heavily-lined squares of the diagonal signify both a sequence of stages and a gradual development of component parts: in other words, the chart formalizes a progression through time of a differentiation of parts. This indicates (1) that each critical item of psychosocial strength discussed here is systematically related to all others, and that they all depend on the proper development in the proper sequence of each item; and (2) that each item exists in some form before its critical time normally arrives.

If I say, for example, that a favorable ratio of basic trust over basic mistrust is the first step in psychosocial adaptation, a favorable ratio of autonomous will over shame and doubt, the second, the corresponding diagrammatic statement expresses a number of fundamental relations that exist between the two steps, as well as some facts fundamental to each. Each comes to its ascendance, meets its crisis, and finds its lasting solution during the stage indicated. But they all must exist from the beginning in some form, for every act calls for an integration of all. Also, an infant may show something like "autonomy" from the beginning in the particular way in which he angrily tries to wriggle himself free when tightly held. However, under normal conditions, it is not until the second year that he begins to experience the whole *critical opposition of being an autonomous creature and being a dependent one;* and it is not until then that he is ready for a decisive encounter with his environment, an environment which, in turn, feels called upon to convey to him its particular ideas and concepts of autonomy and coercion in ways decisively contributing to the character and the health of his personality in his culture. It is this encounter, together with the resulting crisis, that we have tentatively described for each stage. As to the progression from one stage to the next, the diagonal

Figure 1.2
The Eight Stages of Man

VIII	Maturity							Ego Integrity versus Despair
VII	Adulthood						Generativity versus Stagnation	
VI	Young Adulthood					Intimacy versus Isolation		
V	Puberty and Adolescence				Identity versus Role Confusion			
IV	Latency			Industry versus Inferiority				
III	Locomotor-Genital		Initiative versus Guilt					
II	Muscular-Anal	Autonomy versus Shame, Doubt						
I	Oral-Sensory	Basic Trust versus Mistrust						
		1	2	3	4	5	6	7	8

indicates the sequence to be followed. However, it also makes room for variations in tempo and intensity. An individual, or a culture, may linger excessively over trust and proceed from I 1 over I 2 to II 2, or an accelerated progression may move from I 1 over II 1 to II 2. Each such acceleration or (relative) retardation, however, is assumed to have a modifying influence on all later stages.

An epigenetic diagram thus lists a system of stages dependent on each other; and while individual stages may have been explored more or less thoroughly or named more or less fittingly, the diagram suggests that their study be pursued always with the total configuration of stages in mind. The diagram invites, then, a thinking through of all its empty boxes: if we have entered Basic Trust in I 1 and Integrity in VIII 8, we leave the question open, as to what trust might have become in a stage dominated by the need for integrity even as we have left open what it may look like and, indeed, be called in the stage dominated by a striving for autonomy (II 1). All we mean to emphasize is that trust must have developed in its own right, before it becomes something more in the critical encounter in which autonomy develops—and so on, up the vertical. If, in the last stage (VIII 1), we would expect trust to have developed into the most mature *faith* that an aging person can muster in his cultural setting and historical period, the chart permits the consideration not only of what old age can be, but also what its preparatory stages must have been. All of this should make it clear that a chart of epigenesis suggests a global form of thinking and rethinking which leaves details of methodology and terminology to further study.[2]

2. To leave this matter truly open, certain misuses of the whole conception would have to be avoided. Among them is the assumption that the sense of trust (and all the other "positive" senses postulated) is an *achievement,* secured once and for all at a given state. In fact, some writers are so intent on making an *achievement scale* out of these stages that they blithely omit all the "negative" senses (basic mistrust, etc.) which are and remain the dynamic counterpart of the "positive" ones throughout life. The assumption that on each stage a goodness is achieved which is impervious to new inner conflicts and to changing conditions is, I believe, a projection on child development of that success ideology which can so dangerously pervade our private and public daydreams and can make us inept in a heightened struggle for a meaningful existence in a new, industrial era of history. The personality is engaged with the hazards of existence continuously, even as the body's metabolism copes with decay. As we come to diagnose a state of relative strength and the symptoms of an impaired one, we face only more clearly the paradoxes and tragic potentials of human life.

The stripping of the stages of everything but their "achievements" has its counterpart in attempts to describe or test them as "traits" or "aspirations" without first building a systematic bridge between the conception advanced throughout this book and the favorite concepts of other investigators. If the foregoing sounds somewhat plaintive, it is not intended to gloss over the fact that in giving to these strengths the very designations by which in the past they have acquired countless connotations of superficial goodness, affected niceness, and all too strenuous virtue, I invited misunderstandings and misuses. However, I believe, that there is an intrinsic relationship between ego and language and that despite passing vicissitudes certain basic words retain essential meanings.

I have since attempted to formulate for Julian Huxley's *Humanist Frame* (London: Allen and Unwin, 1961; New York: Harper and Brothers, 1962) a blueprint of essential strengths which evo-

For Reflection

1. What resources might be helpful for adults in the transition from developmental age to age?
2. What would the consequences be for the person who does not resolve the developmental crisis at a given age?
3. Why is identity formation in adolescence so important for life-cycle development?
4. In what way is adulthood a "linking" age?

References

Erikson, E. H. The problem of ego-identity. *Journal of American Psychiatric Association* 4, 1:56–121.

---

lution has built both into the ground plan of the life stages and into that of man's institutions. While I cannot discuss here the methodological problems involved (and aggravated by my use of the term "basic virtues"), I should append the list of these strengths because they are really the lasting outcome of the "favorable ratios" mentioned at every step of the chapter on psychosocial stages. Here they are:

Basic Trust versus Basic Mistrust: Drive and *Hope*
Autonomy versus Shame and Doubt: Self-Control and *Willpower*
Initiative versus Guilt: Direction and *Purpose*
Industry versus Inferiority: Method and *Competence*
Identity versus Role Confusion: Devotion and *Fidelity*
Intimacy versus Isolation: Affiliation and *Love*
Generativity versus Stagnation: Production and *Care*
Ego Integrity versus Despair: Renunciation and *Wisdom*

The italicized words are called *basic* virtues because without them, and their reemergence from generation to generation, all other and more changeable systems of human values lose their spirit and their relevance. Of this list, I have been able so far to give a more detailed account only for *Fidelity* (see *Youth, Change and Challenge*, E. H. Erikson, ed. [New York: Basic, 1963]). But here again, the list represents a total conception within which there is much room for a discussion of terminology and methodology.

2

Carol Gilligan

Sociodevelopmentalist

Psychological Theory and Women's Development

(1982)

At the time *In a Different Voice* was written Carol Gilligan was an associate professor of education at the Graduate School of Education, Harvard University. She studied under and worked with Lawrence Kohlberg of the Center of Moral Development at Harvard.

Professor Gilligan attempts to point out themes in human growth, especially moral development, that relate to males and females in different ways. She believes that existing schemes do not fit women well. This has resulted in the consideration of women's modes of growth being left out of theory construction. Much of the book's argument is based on three, primarily interview, studies; a college student study, an abortion decision study, and a rights and responsibilities study.

Gilligan proposes that the formation of female identity takes place within a relationship setting; that of men within the sphere of individuation. Femininity is defined in terms of attachment, masculinity in terms of separation. Male identity is threatened by intimacy, female identity by division. Boys play out-of-doors games more than girls do; they play more competitive games of many rules and with a range of age-mates. Girls play less competitive games that often end when disputes cannot be resolved. Differences such as these have led theorists—Piaget,

From *In a Different Voice: Psychological Theory and Women's Development* (Cambridge: Harvard University, 1982), 1–23.

Kohlberg, and Erikson are a few Gilligan names—to see female development at best lagging behind, at worst deficient.

Gilligan, on the other hand, suggests that women view morality in terms of concern for relationship and responsibilities rather than in the more male terms of rights and justice. Women value care; men devalue care. These observations often lead to the conclusion that women are less adult than men. A morality of rights is associated with separateness (male); a morality of responsibility is associated with connectedness (female). To men a "female" morality may appear inconclusive, while to women a "male" morality may seem indifferent. Perhaps both men and women would be enhanced if they could gain from the outlook of the other.

Introduction

Over the past ten years, I have been listening to people talking about morality and about themselves. Halfway through that time, I began to hear a distinction in these voices, two ways of speaking about moral problems, two modes of describing the relationship between other and self. Differences represented in the psychological literature as steps in a developmental progression suddenly appeared instead as a contrapuntal theme, woven into the cycle of life and recurring in varying forms in people's judgments, fantasies, and thoughts. The occasion for this observation was the selection of a sample of women for a study of the relation between judgment and action in a situation of moral conflict and choice. Against the background of the psychological descriptions of identity and moral development which I had read and taught for a number of years, the women's voices sounded distinct. It was then that I began to notice the recurrent problems in interpreting women's development and to connect these problems to the repeated exclusion of women from the critical theory-building studies of psychological research.

This book records different modes of thinking about relationships and the association of these modes with male and female voices in psychological and literary texts and in the data of my research. The disparity between women's experience and the representation of human development, noted throughout the psychological literature, has generally been seen to signify a problem in women's development. Instead, the failure of women to fit existing models of human growth may point to a problem in the representation, a limitation in the conception of human condition, an omission of certain truths about life.

The different voice I describe is characterized not by gender but theme. Its association with women is an empirical observation, and it is primarily through women's voices that I trace its development. But this association is not absolute, and the contrasts between male and female voices are presented here to highlight a distinction between two modes of thought and to focus a problem of interpretation rather than to represent a generalization about either sex. In tracing development, I point to the interplay of these voices within each sex and suggest that their convergence marks times of crisis and change. No claims are made about the origins of the differences described or their distribution in a wider population, across cultures, or through time. Clearly, these differences arise in a social context where factors of social status and power combine with reproductive biology to shape the experience of males and females and the relations between the sexes. My interest lies in the interaction of experience and thought, in different voices and the dialogues to which they give rise, in the way we listen to ourselves and to others, in the stories we tell about our lives.

Three studies are referred to throughout this [chapter] and reflect the central assumption of my research: that the way people talk about their lives is of significance, that the language they use and the connections they make reveal the world that they see and in which they act. All of the studies relied on interviews and included the same set of questions—about conceptions of self and morality, about experiences of conflict and choice. The method of interviewing was to follow the language and the logic of the person's thought, with the interviewer asking further questions in order to clarify the meaning of a particular response.

The *college student study* explored identity and moral development in the early adult years by relating the view of self and thinking about morality to experiences of moral conflict and the making of life choices. Twenty-five students, selected at random from a group who had chosen as sophomores to take a course on moral and political choice, were interviewed as seniors in college and then five years following graduation. In selecting this sample, I observed that of the twenty students who had dropped the course, sixteen were women. These women were also contacted and interviewed as seniors.

The *abortion decision study* considered the relation between experience and thought and the role of conflict in development. Twenty-nine women, ranging in age from fifteen to thirty-three, diverse in ethnic background and social class, some single, some married, a few the mother of a preschool child, were interviewed during the first trimester of a confirmed pregnancy at a time when they were considering abortion. These women were referred to the study through pregnancy counseling services and abortion clinics in a large metropolitan area; no effort was made to select a representative sample of the clinic or counseling service population. Of the twenty-nine women referred, complete interview data were available for twenty-four, and of these twenty-four, twenty-one were interviewed again at the end of the year following choice.

Both of these studies expanded the usual design of research on moral judgment by asking how people defined moral problems and what experiences they construed as moral conflicts in their lives, rather than by focusing on their thinking about problems presented to them for resolution. The hypotheses generated by these studies concerning different modes of thinking about morality and their relation to different views of self were further explored and refined through the *rights and responsibilities study.* This study involved a sample of males and females matched for age, intelligence, education, occupation, and social class at nine points across the life cycle: ages 6–9, 11, 15, 19, 22, 25–27, 35, 45, and 60. From a total sample of 144 (8 males and 8 females at each age), including a more intensively interviewed subsample of 36 (2 males and 2 females at each age), data were collected on conceptions of self and morality, experiences of moral conflict and choice, and judgments of hypothetical moral dilemmas.

In presenting excerpts from this work, I report research in progress whose aim is to provide, in the field of human development, a clearer representation of women's development which will enable psychologists and others to follow its course and understand some of the apparent puzzles it presents, especially those that pertain to women's identity formation and their moral development in adolescence and adulthood. For women, I hope this work will offer a representation of their thought that enables them to see better its integrity and validity, to recognize the experiences their thinking refracts, and to understand the line of its development. My goal is to expand the understanding of human development by using the group left out in the construction of theory to call attention to what is missing in its account. Seen in this light, the discrepant data on women's experience provide a basis upon which to generate new theory, potentially yielding a more encompassing view of the lives of both of the sexes.

Woman's Place in Man's Life Cycle

In the second act of *The Cherry Orchard,* Lopahin, a young merchant, describes his life of hard work and success. Failing to convince Madame Ranevskaya to cut down the cherry orchard to save her estate, he will go on in the next act to buy it himself. He is the self-made man who, in purchasing the estate where his father and grandfather were slaves, seeks to eradicate the "awkward, unhappy life" of the past, replacing the cherry orchard with summer cottages where coming generations "will see a new life." In elaborating this developmental vision, he reveals the image of man that underlies and supports his activity: "At times when I can't go to sleep, I think: Lord, thou gavest us immense forests, unbounded fields and the widest horizons, and living in the midst of them we should indeed be giants"—at which point, Madame Ranevskaya interrupts him, saying, "You feel the need for giants—They are good only in fairy tales, anywhere else they only frighten us."

Conceptions of the human life cycle represent attempts to order and make coherent the unfolding experiences and perceptions, the changing wishes and realities of everyday life. But the nature of such conceptions depends in part on the position of the observer. The brief excerpt from Chekhov's play suggests that when the observer is a woman, the perspective may be of a different sort. Different judgments of the image of man as giant imply different ideas about human development, different ways of imagining the human condition, different notions of what is of value in life.

At a time when efforts are being made to eradicate discrimination between the sexes in the search for social equality and justice, the differences between the sexes are being rediscovered in the social sciences. This discovery occurs when theories formerly considered to be sexually neutral in their scientific objectivity are found instead to reflect a consistent observational and evaluative bias. Then the presumed neutrality of science, like that of language itself, gives way to the recognition that the categories of knowledge are human constructions. The fascination with point of view that has informed the fiction of the twentieth century and the corresponding recognition of the relativity of judgment infuse our scientific understanding as well when we begin to notice how accustomed we have become to seeing life through men's eyes.

A recent discovery of this sort pertains to the apparently innocent classic *The Elements of Style* by William Strunk and E. B. White. A Supreme Court ruling on the subject of sex discrimination led one teacher of English to notice that the elementary rules of English usage were being taught through examples which counterposed the birth of Napoleon, the writings of Coleridge, and statements such as "He was an interesting talker. A man who had traveled all over the world and lived in half a dozen countries," with "Well, Susan, this is a fine mess you are in" or, less drastically, "He saw a woman, accompanied by two children, walking slowly down the road."

Psychological theorists have fallen as innocently as Strunk and White into the same observational bias. Implicitly adopting the male life as the norm, they have tried to fashion women out of a masculine cloth. It all goes back, of course, to Adam and Eve—a story which shows, among other things, that if you make a woman out of a man, you are bound to get into trouble. In the life cycle, as in the Garden of Eden, the woman has been the deviant.

The penchant of developmental theorists to project a masculine image, and one that appears frightening to women, goes back at least to Freud (1905), who built his theory of psychosexual development around the experiences of the male child that culminate in the Oedipus complex. In the 1920s, Freud struggled to resolve the contradictions posed for his theory by the differences in female anatomy and the different configuration of the young girl's early family relationships. After trying to fit women into his masculine conception, seeing them as envying that which they missed, he came instead to acknowledge, in the strength and persistence of women's pre-oedipal attachments to their mothers, a developmental difference. He considered this difference in women's development to be responsible for what he saw as women's developmental failure.

Having tied the formation of the superego or conscience to castration anxiety, Freud considered women to be deprived by nature of the impetus for a clear-cut oedipal resolution. Consequently, women's superego—the heir to the Oedipus complex—was compromised: it was never "so inexorable, so impersonal, so independent of its emotional origins as we require it to be in men." From this observation of difference, that "for women the level of what is ethically normal is different from what it is in men," Freud concluded that women "show less sense of justice than men, that they are more often influenced in their judgements by feelings of affection or hostility" (1925, 257–58).

Thus a problem in theory became cast as a problem in women's development, and the problem in women's development was located in their experience of relationships. Nancy Chodorow, attempting to account for "the reproduction within each generation of certain general and nearly universal differences that characterize masculine and feminine personality and roles," attributes these differences between the sexes not to anatomy but rather to "the fact that women, universally, are largely responsible for early child care." Because this early social environment differs for and is experienced differently by male and female children, basic sex differences recur in personality development. As a result, "in any given society, feminine personality comes to define itself in relation and connection to other people more than masculine personality does" (1974, 43–44).

In her analysis, Chodorow relies primarily on Robert Stoller's studies which indicate that gender identity, the unchanging core of personality formation, is "with rare exception firmly and irreversibly established for both sexes by the time a child is around three." Given that for both sexes the primary caretaker in the first three years of life is typically female, the interpersonal dynamics of gender identity formation are different for boys and girls. Female identity formation takes place in a context of ongoing relationship since "mothers tend to experience their daughters as more like, and continuous with, themselves." Correspondingly, girls, in identifying themselves as female, experience themselves as like their mothers, thus fusing the experience of attachment with the process of identity formation. In contrast, "mothers experience their sons as a male opposite," and boys, in defining themselves as masculine, separate their mothers from themselves, thus curtailing "their primary love and sense of empathic tie." Consequently, male development entails a "more emphatic individuation and a more defensive firming of experienced ego boundaries." For boys, but not girls, "issues of differentiation have become intertwined with sexual issues" (1978, 150, 166–67).

Writing against the masculine bias of psychoanalytic theory, Chodorow argues that the existence of sex differences in the early experiences of individuation and relationship "does not mean that women have 'weaker' ego boundaries than men or are more prone to psychosis." It means instead that "girls emerge from this period with a basis for 'empathy' built into their primary definition of self in a way that boys do not." Chodorow thus replaces Freud's negative and derivative description of female psychology with a positive and direct account of her own: "Girls emerge with a stronger basis for experiencing another's needs or feelings as one's own (or of thinking that one is so experiencing another's needs and feelings). Furthermore, girls do not define themselves in terms of the denial of pre-oedipal relational modes to the same extent as do boys. Therefore, regression to these modes tends not to feel as much a basic threat to their ego. From very early, then, because they are parented by a person of the same gender . . . girls come to experience themselves as less differentiated than boys, as more continuous with and related to the external object-world, and as differently oriented to their inner object-world as well" (1978, 167).

Consequently, relationships, and particularly issues of dependency, are experienced differently by women and men. For boys and men, separation and individuation are critically tied to gender identity since separation from the mother is essential for the development of masculinity. For girls and women, issues of femininity or feminine identity do not depend on the achievement of separation from the mother or on the progress of individuation. Since masculinity is defined through separation while femininity is defined through attachment, male gender identity is threatened by intimacy while female gender identity is threatened by separation. Thus males tend to have difficulty with relationships, while females tend to have problems with individuation. The quality of embeddedness in social interaction and personal relationships that characterizes women's lives in contrast to men's, however, becomes not only a descriptive difference but also a developmental liability when the milestones of childhood and adolescent development in the psychological literature are markers of increasing separation. Women's failure to separate then becomes by definition a failure to develop.

The sex differences in personality formation that Chodorow describes in early childhood appear during the middle childhood years in studies of children's games. Children's games are considered by George Herbert Mead (1934) and Jean Piaget (1932) as the crucible of social development during the school years. In games, children learn to take the role of the other and come to see themselves through another's eyes. In games, they learn respect for rules and come to understand the ways rules can be made and changed.

Janet Lever (1976), considering the peer group to be the agent of socialization during the elementary school years and play to be a major activity of socialization at that time, set out to discover whether there are sex differences in the games that children play. Studying 181 fifth-grade, white, middle-class children, ages ten and eleven, she observed the organization and structure of their playtime activities. She watched the children as they played at school during recess and in physical education class, and in addition kept diaries of their accounts as to how they spent their out-of-school time. From this study,

Lever reports sex differences: boys play out of doors more often than girls do; boys play more often in large and age-heterogeneous groups; they play competitive games more often, and their games last longer than girls' games. The last is in some ways the most interesting finding. Boys' games appeared to last longer not only because they required a higher level of skill and were thus less likely to become boring, but also because, when disputes arose in the course of a game, boys were able to resolve the disputes more effectively than girls: "During the course of this study, boys were seen quarrelling all the time, but not once was a game terminated because of a quarrel and no game was interrupted for more than seven minutes. In the gravest debates, the final word was always, to 'repeat the play,' generally followed by a chorus of 'cheater's proof'" (482). In fact, it seemed that the boys enjoyed the legal debates as much as they did the game itself, and even marginal players of lesser size or skill participated equally in these recurrent squabbles. In contrast, the eruption of disputes among girls tended to end the game.

Thus Lever extends and corroborates the observations of Piaget in his study of the rules of the game, where he finds boys becoming through childhood increasingly fascinated with the legal elaboration of rules and the development of fair procedures for adjudicating conflicts, a fascination that, he notes, does not hold for girls. Girls, Piaget observes, have a more "pragmatic" attitude toward rules, "regarding a rule as good as long as the game repaid it" (83). Girls are more tolerant in their attitudes toward rules, more willing to make exceptions, and more easily reconciled to innovations. As a result, the legal sense, which Piaget considers essential to moral development, "is far less developed in little girls than in boys" (77).

The bias that leads Piaget to equate male development with child development also colors Lever's work. The assumption that shapes her discussion of results is that the male model is the better one since it fits the requirements for modern corporate success. In contrast, the sensitivity and care for the feelings of others that girls develop through their play have little market value and can even impede professional success. Lever implies that, given the realities of adult life, if a girl does not want to be left dependent on men, she will have to learn to play like a boy.

To Piaget's argument that children learn the respect for rules necessary for moral development by playing rule-bound games, Lawrence Kohlberg (1969) adds that these lessons are most effectively learned through the opportunities for role-taking that arise in the course of resolving disputes. Consequently, the moral lessons inherent in girls' play appear to be fewer than in boys'. Traditional girls' games like jump rope and hopscotch are turn-taking games, where competition is indirect since one person's success does not necessarily signify another's failure. Consequently, disputes requiring adjudication are less likely to occur. In fact, most of the girls whom Lever interviewed claimed that when a quarrel broke out, they ended the game. Rather than elaborating a system of rules for resolving disputes, girls subordinated the continuation of the game to the continuation of relationships.

Lever concludes that from the games they play, boys learn both the independence and the organizational skills necessary for coordinating the activities of large and diverse groups of people. By participating in controlled and socially approved competitive situations, they learn to deal with competition in a relatively forthright manner—to play with their enemies and to compete with their friends—all in accordance with the rules of the game. In contrast, girls' play tends to occur in smaller, more intimate groups, often the best-friend dyad, and in private places. This play replicates the social pattern of primary human relationships in that its organization is more cooperative. Thus, it points less, in Mead's terms, toward learning to take the role of "the generalized other," less toward the abstraction of human relationships. But it fosters the development of the empathy and sensitivity necessary for taking the role of "the particular other" and points more toward knowing the other as different from the self.

The sex differences in personality formation in early childhood that Chodorow derives from her analysis of the mother-child relationship are thus extended by Lever's observations of sex differences in the play activities of middle childhood. Together these accounts suggest that boys and girls arrive at puberty with a different interpersonal orientation and a different range of social experiences. Yet, since adolescence is considered a crucial time for separation, the period of "the second individuation process" (Blos 1967), female development has appeared most divergent and thus most problematic at this time.

"Puberty," Freud says, "which brings about so great an accession of libido in boys, is marked in girls by a fresh wave of *repression*," necessary for the transformation of the young girl's "masculine sexuality" into the specifically feminine sexuality of her adulthood (1905, 220–21). Freud posits this transformation on the girl's acknowledgment and acceptance of "the fact of her castration" (1931, 229). To the girl, Freud explains, puberty brings a new awareness of "the wound to her narcissism" and leads her to develop, "like a scar, a sense of inferiority" (1925, 253). Since in Erik Erikson's expansion of Freud's psychoanalytic account, adolescence is the time when development hinges on identity, the girl arrives at this juncture either psychologically at risk or with a different agenda.

The problem that female adolescence presents for theorists of human development is apparent in Erikson's scheme. Erikson (1950) charts eight stages of psychosocial development, of which adolescence is the fifth. The task at this stage is to forge a coherent sense of self, to verify an identity that can span the discontinuity of puberty and make possible the adult capacity to love and work. The preparation for the successful resolution of the adolescent identity crisis is delineated in Erikson's description of the crises that characterize the preceding four stages. Although the initial crisis in infancy of "trust versus mistrust" anchors development in the experience of relationship, the task then clearly becomes one of individuation. Erikson's second stage centers on the crisis of "autonomy versus shame and doubt," which marks the walking child's emerging sense of separateness and agency. From there, development goes on through the crisis of "initiative versus guilt," successful resolution of which represents a further move in the direction of autonomy. Next, following the inevitable disappointment of the magical wishes of the oedipal period, children realize that to compete with their parents, they must first join them and learn to do what they do so well. Thus in the middle childhood years, development turns on the crisis of "industry versus inferiority," as the demonstration of competence becomes critical to the child's developing self-esteem. This is the time when children strive to learn and master the technology of their culture, in order to recognize themselves and to be recognized by others as capable of becoming adults. Next comes adolescence, the celebration of the autonomous, initiating, industrious self through the forging of an identity based on an ideology that can support and justify adult commitments. But about whom is Erikson talking?

Once again it turns out to be the male child. For the female, Erikson (1968) says, the sequence is a bit different. She holds her identity in abeyance as she prepares to attract the man by whose name she will be known, by whose status she will be defined, the man who will rescue her from emptiness and loneliness by filling "the inner space." While for men, identity precedes intimacy and generativity in the optimal cycle of human separation and attachment, for women these tasks seem instead to be fused. Intimacy goes along with identity, as the female comes to know herself as she is known, through her relationships with others.

Yet despite Erikson's observation of sex differences, his chart of life-cycle stages remains unchanged: identity continues to precede intimacy as male experience continues to define his life-cycle conception. But in this male life cycle there is little preparation for the intimacy of the first adult stage. Only the initial stage of trust versus mistrust suggests the type of mutuality that Erikson means by intimacy and generativity and Freud means by genitality. The rest is separateness, with the result that development itself comes to be identified with separation, and attachments appear to be developmental impediments, as is repeatedly the case in the assessment of women.

Erikson's description of male identity as forged in relation to the world and of female identity as awakened in a relationship of intimacy with another person is hardly new. In the fairy tales that Bruno Bettelheim (1976) describes an identical portrayal appears. The dynamics of male adolescence are illustrated archetypically by the conflict between father and son in "The Three Languages." Here a son, considered hopelessly stupid by his father, is given one last chance at education and sent for a year to study with a master. But when he returns, all he has learned is "what the dogs bark." After two further attempts of this sort, the father gives up in disgust and orders his servants to take the child into the forest and kill him. But the servants, those perpetual rescuers of disowned and abandoned children, take pity on the child and decide simply to leave him in the forest. From there, his wanderings take him to a land beset by furious dogs whose barking permits nobody to rest and who periodically devour one of the inhabitants. Now it turns out that our hero has learned just the right thing: he can talk with the dogs and is able to quiet them, thus restoring peace to the land. Since the other knowledge he acquires serves him equally well, he emerges triumphant from his adolescent confrontation with his father, a giant of the life-cycle conception.

In contrast, the dynamics of female adolescence are depicted through the telling of a very different story. In the world of the fairy tale, the girl's first bleeding is followed by a period of intense passivity in which nothing seems to be happening. Yet in the deep sleeps of Snow White and Sleeping Beauty, Bettelheim sees that inner concentration which he considers to be the necessary counterpart to the activity of adventure. Since the adolescent heroines awake from their sleep, not to conquer the world, but to marry the prince, their identity is inwardly and interpersonally defined. For women, in Bettelheim's as in Erikson's account, identity and intimacy are intricately conjoined. The sex differences depicted in the world of fairy tales, like the fantasy of the woman warrior in Maxine Hong Kingston's (1977) recent autobiographical novel which echoes the old stories of Troilus and Cressida and Tancred and Chlorinda, indicate repeatedly that active adventure is a male activity, and that if a woman is to embark on such endeavors, she must at least dress like a man.

These observations about sex difference support the conclusion reached by David McClelland (1975) that "sex role turns out to be one of the most important determinants of human behavior; psychologists have found sex differences in their studies from the moment they started doing empirical research." But since it is difficult to say "different" without saying "better" or "worse," since there is a tendency to construct a single scale of measurement, and since that scale has generally been derived from and standardized on the basis of men's interpretations of research data drawn predominantly or exclusively from studies of males, psychologists "have tended to regard male behavior as the 'norm' and female behavior as some kind of deviation from that norm" (81). Thus, when women do not conform to the standards of psychological expectation, the conclusion has generally been that something is wrong with the women.

What Matina Horner (1972) found to be wrong with women was the anxiety they showed about competitive achievement. From the beginning, research on human motivation using the Thematic Apperception Test (TAT) was plagued by evidence of sex differences which appeared to confuse and complicate data analysis. The TAT presents for interpretation an ambiguous cue—a picture about which a story is to be written or a segment of a story that is to be completed. Such stories, in reflecting projective imagination, are considered by psychologists to reveal the ways in which people construe what they perceive, that is, the concepts and interpretations they bring to their experience and thus presumably the kind of sense that they make of their lives. Prior to Horner's work it was clear that women made a different kind of sense than men of situations of competitive achievement, that in some way they saw the situations differently or the situations aroused in them some different response.

On the basis of his studies of men, McClelland divided the concept of achievement motivation into what appeared to be its two logical components, a motive to approach success ("hope success") and a motive to avoid failure ("fear failure"). From her studies of women, Horner identified as a third category the unlikely motivation to avoid success ("fear success"). Women appeared to have a problem with competitive achievement, and that problem seemed to emanate from a perceived conflict between femininity and success, the dilemma of the female adolescent who struggles to integrate her feminine aspirations and the identifications of her early childhood with the more masculine competence she has acquired at school. From her analysis of women's completions of a story that began, "after first term finals, Anne finds herself at the top of her medical school class," and from her observation of women's performance in competitive achievement situations, Horner reports that, "when success is likely or possible, threatened by the negative consequences they expect to follow success, young women become anxious and their positive achievement strivings become thwarted" (171). She concludes that this fear "exists because for most women, the anticipation of success in competitive achievement activity, especially against men, produces anticipation of certain negative consequences, for example, threat of social rejection and loss of femininity" (1968, 125).

Such conflicts about success, however, may be viewed in a different light. Georgia Sassen (1980) suggests that the conflicts expressed by the women might instead indicate "a heightened perception of the 'other side' of competitive success, that is, the great emotional costs at which success achieved through competition is often gained—an understanding which, though confused, indicates some underlying sense that something is rotten in the state in which success is defined as having better grades than everyone else" (15). Sassen points out that Horner found success anxiety to be present in women only when achievement was directly competitive, that is, when one person's success was at the expense of another's failure.

In his elaboration of the identity crisis, Erikson (1968) cites the life of George Bernard Shaw to illustrate the young person's sense of being co-opted prematurely by success in a career he cannot wholeheartedly endorse. Shaw at seventy, reflecting upon his life, described his crisis at the age of twenty as having been caused not by the lack of success or the absence of recognition, but by too much of both: "I made good in spite of myself, and found, to my dismay, that Business, instead of expelling me as the worthless imposter I was, was fastening upon me with no intention of letting me go. Behold me, therefore, in my twentieth year, with a business training, in an occupation which I detested as cordially as any sane person lets himself detest anything he cannot escape from. In March 1876 I broke loose" (143). At this point Shaw settled down to study and write as he pleased. Hardly interpreted as evidence of neurotic anxiety about achievement and competition, Shaw's refusal suggests to Erikson "the extraordinary workings of an extraordinary personality [coming] to the fore" (144).

We might on these grounds begin to ask, now why women have conflicts about competitive success, but why men show such readiness to adopt and celebrate a rather narrow vision of success. Remembering Piaget's observation, corroborated by Lever, that boys in their games are more concerned with rules while girls are more concerned with relationships, often at the expense of the game itself—and given Chodorow's conclusion that men's social orientation is positional while women's is personal—we begin to understand why, when "Anne" becomes "John" in Horner's tale of competitive success and the story is completed by men, fear of success tends to disappear. John is considered to have played by the rules and won. He has the *right* to feel good about his success. Confirmed in the sense of his own identity as separate from those who, compared to him, are less competent, his positional sense of self is affirmed. For Anne, it is possible that the position she could obtain by being at the top of her medical school class may not, in fact, be what she wants.

"It is obvious," Virginia Woolf says, "that the values of women differ very often from the values which have been made by the other sex" (1929, 76). Yet, she adds, "it is the masculine values that prevail." As a result, women come to question the normality of their feelings and to alter their judgments in deference to the opinion of others. In the nineteenth-century novels written by women, Woolf sees at work "a mind which was slightly pulled from the straight and made to alter its clear vision in deference to external authority." The same deference to the values and opinions of others can be seen in the judgments of twentieth-century women. The difficulty women experience in finding or speaking publicly in their own voices emerges repeatedly in the form of qualification and self-doubt, but also in intimations of a divided judgment, a public assessment and private assessment which are fundamentally at odds.

Yet the deference and confusion that Woolf criticizes in women derive from the values she sees as their strength. Women's deference is rooted not only in their social subordination but also in the substance of their moral concern. Sensitivity to the needs of others and the assumption of responsibility for taking care lead women to attend to voices other than their own and to include in their judgment other points of view. Women's moral weakness, manifest in an apparent diffusion and confusion of judgment, is thus inseparable from women's moral strength, an overriding concern with relationships and responsibilities. The reluctance to judge may itself be indicative of the care and concern for others that infuse the psychology of women's development and are responsible for what is generally seen as problematic in its nature.

Thus women not only define themselves in a context of human relationship but also judge themselves in terms of their ability to care. Women's place in man's life cycle has been that of nurturer, caretaker, and helpmate, the weaver of those networks of relationships on which she in turn relies. But while women have thus taken care of men, men have, in their theories of psychological development, as in their economic arrangements, tended to assume or devalue that care. When the focus on individuation and individual achievement extends into adulthood and maturity is equated with personal autonomy, concern with relationships appears as a weakness of women rather than as a human strength (Miller 1976).

The discrepancy between womanhood and adulthood is nowhere more evident than in the studies on sex-role stereotypes reported by Broverman, Vogel, Broverman, Clarkson, and Rosenkrantz (1972). The repeated finding of these studies is that the qualities deemed necessary for adulthood—the capacity for autonomous thinking, clear decision-making, and responsible action—are those associated with masculinity and considered undesirable as attributes of the feminine self. The stereotypes suggest a splitting of love and work that relegates expressive capacities to women while placing instrumental abilities in the masculine domain. Yet looked at from a different perspective, these stereotypes reflect a conception of adulthood that is itself out of balance, favoring the separateness of the individual self over connection to others, and leaning more toward an autonomous life of work than toward the interdependence of love and care.

The discovery now being celebrated by men in mid-life of the importance of intimacy, relationships, and care is something that women have known from the beginning. However, because that knowledge in women has been considered "intuitive" or "instinctive," a function of anatomy coupled with destiny, psychologists have neglected to describe its development. In my research, I have found that women's moral development centers on the elaboration of that knowledge and thus delineates a critical line of psychological development in the lives of both of the sexes. The subject of moral development not only provides the final illustration of the reiterative pattern in the observation and assessment of sex differences in the literature of human development, but also indicates more particularly why the nature and significance of women's development has been for so long obscured and shrouded in mystery.

The criticism that Freud makes of women's sense of justice, seeing it as compromised in its refusal of blind impartiality, reappears not only in the work of Piaget but also in that of Kohlberg. While in Piaget's account (1932) of the moral judgment of the child, girls are an aside, a curiosity to whom he devotes four brief entries in an index that omits "boys" altogether because "the child" is assumed to be male; in the research from which Kohlberg derives his theory, females simply do not exist. Kohlberg's (1958, 1981) six stages that describe the development of moral judgment from childhood to adulthood are based empirically on a study of eighty-four boys whose development Kohlberg has followed for a period of over twenty years. Although Kohlberg claims universality for his stage sequence, those groups not included in his original sample rarely reach his higher stages (Edwards 1975; Holstein 1976; Simpson 1974). Prominent among those who thus appear to be deficient in moral development when measured by Kohlberg's scale are women, whose judgments seem to exemplify the third stage of his six-stage sequence. At this stage morality is conceived in interpersonal terms and goodness is equated with helping and pleasing others. This conception of goodness is considered by Kohlberg and Kramer (1969) to be functional in the lives of mature women insofar as their lives take place in the home. Kohlberg and Kramer imply that only if women enter the traditional arena of male activity will they recognize the inadequacy of this moral perspective and progress like men toward higher stages where relationships are subordinated to rules (stage four) and rules to universal principles of justice (stages five and six).

Yet herein lies a paradox, for the very traits that traditionally have defined the "goodness" of women, their care for and sensitivity to the needs of others, are those that mark them as deficient in moral development. In this version of moral development, however, the conception of maturity is derived from the study of men's lives and reflects the importance of individuation in their development. Piaget (1970), challenging the common impression that a developmental theory is built like a pyramid from its base in infancy, points out that a conception of development instead hangs from its vertex of maturity, the point toward which progress is traced. Thus, a change in the definition of maturity does not simply alter the description of the highest stage but recasts the understanding of development, changing the entire account.

When one begins with the study of women and derives developmental constructs from their lives, the outline of a moral conception different from that described by Freud, Piaget, or Kohlberg begins to emerge and informs a different description of development. In this conception, the moral problem arises from conflicting responsibilities rather than from competing rights and requires for its resolution a mode of thinking that is contextual and narrative rather than formal and abstract. This conception of morality as concerned with the activity of care centers moral development around the understanding of responsibility and relationships, just as the conception of morality as fairness ties moral development to the understanding of rights and rules.

This different construction of the moral problem by women may be seen as the critical reason for their failure to develop within the constraints of Kohlberg's system. Regarding all constructions of responsibility as evidence of a conventional moral understanding, Kohlberg defines the highest stages of moral development as deriving from a reflective understanding of human rights. That the morality of rights differs from the morality of responsibility in its emphasis on separation rather than connection, in its consideration of the individual rather than the relationship as primary, is illustrated by two responses to interview questions about the nature of morality. The first comes from a twenty-five-year-old man, one of the participants in Kohlberg's study:

> [*What does the word morality mean to you?*] Nobody in the world knows the answer. I think it is recognizing the right of the individual, the rights of other individuals, not interfering with those rights. Act as fairly as you would have them treat you. I think it is basically to preserve the human being's right to existence. I think that is the most important. Secondly, the human being's right to do as he pleases, again without interfering with somebody else's rights.
>
> [*How have your views on morality changed since the last interview?*] I think I am more aware of an individual's rights now. I used to be looking at it strictly from my point of view, just for me. Now I think I am more aware of what the individual has a right to.

Kohlberg (1973) cites this man's response as illustrative of the principled conception of human rights that exemplifies his fifth and sixth stages. Commenting on the response, Kohlberg says: "Moving to a perspective outside of that of his society, he identifies morality with justice (fairness, rights, the Golden Rule), with recognition of the rights of others as these are defined naturally or intrinsically. The human's being right to do as he pleases without interfering with somebody else's rights is a formula defining rights prior to social legislation" (29–30).

The second response comes from a woman who participated in the rights and responsibilities study. She also was twenty-five and, at the time, a third-year law student:

> [*Is there really some correct solution to moral problems, or is everybody's opinion equally right?*] No, I don't think everybody's opinion is equally right. I think that in some situations there may be opinions that are equally valid, and one could conscientiously adopt one of several courses of action. But there are other situations in which I think there are right and wrong answers, that sort of inhere in the nature of existence, of all individuals here who need to live with each other to live. We need to depend on each other, and hopefully it is not only a physical need but a need of fulfillment in ourselves, that a person's life is enriched by cooperating with other people and striving to live in harmony with everybody else, and to that end, there are right and wrong, there are things which promote that end and that move away from it, and in that way it is possible to choose in certain cases among different courses of action that obviously promote or harm that goal.
>
> [*Is there a time in the past when you would have thought about these things differently?*] Oh, yeah, I think that I went through a time when I thought that

> things were pretty relative, that I can't tell you what to do and you can't tell me what to do, because you've got your conscience and I've got mine.
>
> [*When was that?*] When I was in high school. I guess that it just sort of dawned on me that my own ideas changed, and because my own judgment changed, I felt I couldn't judge another person's judgment. But now I think even when it is only the person himself who is going to be affected, I say it is wrong to the extent it doesn't cohere with what I know about human nature and what I know about you, and just from what I think is true about the operation of the universe, I could say I think you are making a mistake.
>
> [*What led you to change, do you think?*] Just seeing more of life, just recognizing that there are an awful lot of things that are common among people. There are certain things that you come to learn promote a better life and better relationships and more personal fulfillment than other things that in general tend to do the opposite, and the things that promote these things, you would call morally right.

This response also represents a personal reconstruction of morality following a period of questioning and doubt, but the reconstruction of moral understanding is based not on the primacy and universality of individual rights, but rather on what she describes as a "very strong sense of being responsible to the world." Within this construction, the moral dilemma changes from how to exercise one's rights without interfering with the rights of others to how "to lead a moral life which includes obligations to myself and my family and people in general." The problem then becomes one of limiting responsibilities without abandoning moral concern. When asked to describe herself, this woman says that she values "having other people that I am tied to, and also having people that I am responsible to. I have a very strong sense of being responsible to the world, that I can't just live for my enjoyment, but just the fact of being in the world gives me an obligation to do what I can to make the world a better place to live in, no matter how small a scale that may be on." Thus while Kohlberg's subject worries about people interfering with each other's rights, this woman worries about "the possibility of omission, of your not helping others when you could help them."

The issue that this woman raises is addressed by Jane Loevinger's fifth "autonomous" stage of ego development, where autonomy, placed in a context of relationships, is defined as modulating an excessive sense of responsibility through the recognition that other people have responsibility for their own destiny. The autonomous stage in Loevinger's account (1970) witnesses a relinquishing of moral dichotomies and their replacement with "a feeling for the complexity and multifaceted character of real people and real situations" (6). Whereas the rights conception of morality that informs Kohlberg's principled level (stages five and six) is geared to arriving at an objectively fair or just resolution to moral dilemmas upon which all rational persons could agree, the responsibility conception focuses instead on the limitations of any particular resolution and describes the conflicts that remain.

Thus it becomes clear why a morality of rights and noninterference may appear frightening to women in its potential justification of indifference and unconcern. At the same time, it becomes clear why, from a male perspective, a morality of responsibility appears inconclusive and diffuse, given its insistent contextual relativism. Women's moral judgments thus elucidate the pattern observed in the description of the developmental differences between the sexes, but they also provide an alternative conception of maturity by which these differences can be assessed and their implications traced. The psychology of women that has consistently been described as distinctive in its greater orientation toward relationships and interdependence implies a more contextual mode of judgment and a different moral understanding. Given the differences in women's conceptions of self and morality, women bring to the life cycle a different point of view and order human experience in terms of different priorities.

The myth of Demeter and Persephone, which McClelland (1975) cites as exemplifying the feminine attitude toward power, was associated with the Eleusinian Mysteries celebrated in ancient Greece for over two thousand years. As told in the Homeric *Hymn to Demeter*, the story of Persephone indicates the strengths of interdependence, building up resources and giving, that McClelland found in his research on power motivation to characterize the mature feminine style. Although, McClelland says, "it is fashionable to conclude that no one knows what went on in the Mysteries, it is known that they were probably the most important religious ceremonies, even partly on the historical record, which were organized by and for women, especially at the onset before men by means of the cult of Dionysos began to take them over." Thus McClelland regards the myth as "a special presentation of feminine psychology" (96). It is, as well, a life-cycle story par excellence.

Persephone, the daughter of Demeter, while playing in a meadow with her girlfriends, sees a beautiful narcissus which she runs to pick. As she does so, the earth opens and she is snatched away by Hades, who takes her to his underworld kingdom. Demeter, goddess of the earth, so mourns the loss of her daughter that she refuses to allow anything to grow. The crops that sustain life on earth shrivel up, killing men and animals alike, until Zeus takes pity on man's suffering and persuades his brother to return Persephone to her mother. But before she leaves, Persephone eats some pomegranate seeds, which ensures that she will spend part of every year with Hades in the underworld.

The elusive mystery of women's development lies in its recognition of the continuing importance of attachment in the human life cycle. Woman's place in man's life cycle is to protect this recognition while the developmental litany intones the celebration of separation, autonomy, individuation, and natural rights. The myth of Persephone speaks directly to the distortion in this view by reminding us that narcissism leads to death, that the fertility of the earth is in some mysterious way tied to the continuation of the mother-daughter relationship, and that the life cycle itself arises from an alternation between the world of women and that of men. Only when life-cycle theorists divide their attention and begin to live with women as they have lived with men will their vision encompass the experience of both sexes and their theories become correspondingly more fertile.

For Reflection

1. What do you see as strengths of a female morality? a male morality?
2. What do you see as weaknesses of a female morality? a male morality?
3. What would a "proper balance" look like?
4. How does Gilligan suggest conceptualizing the complexity of morality?

References

Bettelheim, B. 1976. *The uses of enchantment.* New York: Knopf.

Blos, P. 1967. The second individuation process of adolescence. In *The psychoanalytic study of the child*, vol. 22, ed. A. Freud. New York: International Universities Press.

Broverman, I., S. Vogel, D. Broverman, F. Clarkson, and P. Rosenkrantz. 1972. Sex-role stereotypes: A current appraisal. *Journal of Social Issues* 28: 59–78.

Chekhov, A. 1904. *The cherry orchard.* In *Best plays by Chekhov*, trans. S. Young. New York: Modern Library, 1956.

Chodorow, N. 1974. Family structure and feminine personality. In *Woman, culture, and society*, ed. M. Z. Rosaldo and L. Lamphere. Stanford: Stanford Univ. Press.

———. 1978. *The reproduction of mothering.* Berkeley: Univ. of California Press.

Edwards, C. P. 1975. Societal complexity and moral development: A Kenyan study. *Ethos* 3: 505–27.

Erikson, E. H. 1950. *Childhood and society.* New York: Norton.

———. 1968. *Identity: Youth and crisis.* New York: Norton.

Freud, S. 1905. *Three essays on the theory of sexuality.* Vol. 7.

———. 1925. *Some psychical consequences of the anatomical distinction between the sexes.* Vol. 19.

———. 1931. *Female sexuality.* Vol. 21.

Holstein, C. 1976. Development of moral judgment: A longitudinal study of males and females. *Child Development* 47: 51–61.

Horner, M. S. 1968. Sex differences in achievement motivation and performance in competitive and noncompetitive situations. Ph.D. diss., University of Michigan. University Microfilms # 6912135.

———. 1972. Toward an understanding of achievement-related conflicts in women. *Journal of Social Issues* 28: 157–75.

Kingston, M. H. 1977. *The woman warrior.* New York: Knopf.

Kohlberg, L. 1958. The development of modes of thinking and choices in years 10 to 16. Ph.D. diss., University of Chicago.

———. 1969. Stage and sequence: The cognitive-development approach to socialization. In *Handbook of socialization theory and research*, ed. D. A. Goslin. Chicago: Rand McNally.

———. 1973. Continuities and discontinuities in childhood and adult moral development revisited. In *Collected papers on moral development and moral education.* Moral Education Research Foundation, Harvard University.

———. 1981. *The philosophy of moral development.* San Francisco: Harper and Row.

Kohlberg, L., and R. Kramer. 1969. Continuities and discontinuities in child and adult moral development. *Human Development* 12: 93–120.

Lever, J. 1976. Sex differences in the games children play. *Social Problems* 23: 478–87.

Loevinger, J., and R. Wessler. 1970. *Measuring ego development.* San Francisco: Jossey-Bass.

McClelland, D. C. 1975. *Power: The inner experience.* New York: Irvington.

Mead, G. H. 1934. *Mind, self, and society.* Chicago: Univ. of Chicago Press.

Miller, J. B. 1976. *Toward a new psychology of women.* Boston: Beacon.

Piaget, J. 1932. *The moral judgment of the child.* New York: The Free Press.

———. 1970. *Structuralism.* New York: Basic.

Sassen, G. 1980. Success anxiety in women: A constructivist interpretation of its sources and its significance. *Harvard Educational Review* 50: 13–25.

Simpson, E. L. 1974. Moral development research: A case study of scientific cultural bias. *Human Development* 17: 81–106.

Stoller, R. J. 1964. A contribution to the study of gender identity. *International Journal of Psycho-analysis* 45: 220–26.

Strunk, W., Jr., and E. B. White. 1918. *The elements of style.* Reprint ed. New York: Macmillan, 1958.

Woolf, V. 1929. *A room of one's own.* New York: Harcourt, Brace and World.

3

Lawrence Kohlberg

Developmentalist

Moral Education in the Schools

(1966)

Professor Kohlberg trained in clinical psychology and child development at the University of Chicago, where he earned a Ph.D. Not satisfied with the traditional psychoanalytical explanation for the moral reasoning of children, Kohlberg began a creative line of research based on the cognitive developmental psychology of Jean Piaget and the educational philosophy of John Dewey (McKean 1985). Kohlberg accepted a position at Harvard in 1969 and founded a center for the study of moral development. Just prior to that his ideas gained widespread popularity. Two areas of the educational implications of his work are of special interest. They are "the level of justice in an educational community and the use of dilemma discussions for promoting moral development in students" (McKean 1985, 626). Kohlberg suggests that higher stages of cognitive moral judgment are promoted when people participate in a democratic setting. His theory supports the exposure of persons at lower moral stages to dilemma solutions one stage higher than their own. This seems to encourage them to restructure their own ways toward the higher stage.

In this reading Kohlberg tries to show that moral development (specifically cognitive moral decision-making) is not just relativistic, based on the immediate circumstances, chances of being caught, or opportunity for a reward, but that it is based

From *The School Review* 74 (Spring 1966): 1–30.

on an absolute structure, common to all. This structure is basically cognitive. It is divided into three levels, each with two stages.

The author seeks to make the case that teachers in public schools already engage in moralizing. They moralize about rules and values such as honesty. But most of the moral teaching, which he feels is mostly unplanned, is about trivial classroom management issues. His position is that it should be intentional and deal with broader, more important concerns. However, a public school in a democracy should not be formulating people's values for them. The schools should take the stimulation of development in the area of morality as their goal. This should result in helping children move up the stages of moral decision-making. When the specific approaches to moral development are novel, challenging, and life-related, Kohlberg contends, the learners will grow.

References

McKean, R. B. 1985. Lawrence Kohlberg. In *Baker encyclopedia of psychology,* ed. D. G. Benner. Grand Rapids: Baker.

For many contemporary educators and social scientists, the term "moral education" has an archaic ring, the ring of the last vestiges of the Puritan tradition in the modern school. This archaic ring, however, does not arise from any intrinsic opposition between the statement of educational aims and methods in moral terms and their statement in psychological terms. In fact, it was just this opposition which the great pioneers of the social psychology of education denied in such works as John Dewey's *Moral Principles in Education* (1911) and Emile Durkheim's *Moral Education* ([1925] 1961). Both of these works attempted to define moral education in terms of a broader consideration of social development and social functions than was implied by conventional opinion on the topic, but both recognized that an ultimate statement of the social aims and processes of education must be a statement couched in moral terms.

Unfortunately, the educational psychologists and philosophers who followed Dewey's trail retained his concern about a broad phrasing of the goals of education in terms of the child's social traits and values (e.g., cooperation, social adjustment, "democraticness," mental health) without retaining Dewey's awareness that intelligent thought about these traits and values required the concepts dealt with by moral philosophers and psychologists. More recently, however, thoughtful educators and psychologists have become acutely aware of the inadequacies of dealing with moral issues under cover of mental-health or group-adjustment labels. We have become aware, on the one hand, that these mental-health labels are not really scientific and value-neutral terms; they are ways of making value judgments about children in terms of social norms and acting accordingly. On the other hand, we have come to recognize that mental-health and social-adjustment terms do not really allow us to define the norms and values that are most basic as ideals for our children. The barbarities of the socially conforming members of the Nazi system and the other-directed hollow men growing up in our own affluent society have made us acutely aware of the fact that adjustment to the group is no substitute for moral maturity.

It is apparent, then, that the problems of moral education cannot be successfully considered in the "value-neutral" terms of personality development and adjustment. In this paper, I shall attempt to deal with some of the value issues involved in moral education but will approach these issues from the standpoint of research findings. I believe that a number of recent research facts offer some guide through the problems of moral education when these facts are considered from Dewey's general perspective as to the relationship between fact and value in education.

Research Findings on the Development of Moral Character Relevant to Moral Education in the Schools

One of the major reasons why the social functions of the school have not been phrased in moral-education terms has been the fact that conventional didactic ethical instruction in the school has little influence upon moral character as usually conceived. This conclusion seemed clearly indicated by Hartshorne and May's findings (1928–30) that character-education classes and religious-instruction programs had no influence on moral conduct, as the latter was objectively measured by experimental tests of "honesty" (cheating, lying, stealing) and "service" (giving up objects for others' welfare). The small amount of recent research on conventional didactic moral education provides us with no reason to question these earlier findings. Almost every year a professional religious educator or community-service educator takes a course with me and attempts to evaluate the effect of his program upon moral character. While each starts by thinking his program is different from those evaluated by Hartshorne and May, none comes away with any more positive evidence than did these earlier workers.

While recent research does not lead us to question Hartshorne and May's findings as to the ineffectiveness of conventional, formal moral education, it does lead us to a more positive view as to the possibility of effective school moral education of some new sort. In particular, recent research leads us to question the two most common interpretations of the Hartshorne and May findings: the interpretation that moral behavior is purely a matter of immediate situational forces and rewards and the interpretation that moral character is a matter of deep emotions fixed in earliest childhood in the home. Instead, recent research suggests that the major consistencies of moral character represent the slowly developing formation of more or less cognitive principles of moral judgment and decision and of related ego abilities.

The first interpretation of the Hartshorne and May findings mentioned was essentially that of these authors themselves. Their conclusions were much more nihilistic than the mere conclusion that conventional moral-education classes were ineffective and essentially implied that there was no such thing as "moral character" or "conscience" to be educated anyway. Hartshorne and May found that the most influential factors determining resistance to temptation to cheat or disobey were situational factors rather than a fixed, individual moral-character trait of honesty. The first finding leading to this conclusion was that of the low predictability of cheating in one situation for cheating in another. A second finding was that children were not divisible into two groups, "cheaters" and "honest children." Children's cheating scores were distributed in bell-curve fashion around an average score of moderate cheating. A third finding was the importance of the expediency aspect of the decision to cheat, that is, the tendency to cheat depends upon the degree of risk of detection and the effort required to cheat. Children who cheated in more risky situations also cheated in less risky situations. Thus, non-cheaters appeared to be primarily more cautious rather than more honest than cheaters. A fourth finding was that even when honest behavior was not dictated by concern about punishment or detection, it was largely determined by immediate situational factors of group approval and example (as opposed to being determined by internal moral values). Some classrooms showed a high tendency to cheat, while other seemingly identically composed classrooms in the same school showed little tendency to cheat. A fifth finding was that moral knowledge had little apparent influence on moral conduct, since the correlations between verbal tests of moral knowledge and experimental tests of moral conduct were low ($r = 34$). A sixth apparent finding was that where moral values did seem to be related to conduct, these values were somewhat specific to the child's social class or group. Rather than being a universal ideal, honesty was more characteristic of the middle class and seemed less relevant to the lower-class child.

Taken at their face value, these findings suggested that moral education inside or outside the school could have no lasting effect. The moral educator, whether in the home or in the school, could create a situation in which the child would not cheat, but this would not lead to the formation of a general tendency not to cheat when the child entered a new situation. Carried to its logical conclusion, this interpretation of the findings suggested that "honesty" was just an external value judgment of the child's act which leads to no understanding or prediction of his character. It suggested that concepts of good or bad conduct were psychologically irrelevant and that moral conduct must be understood, like other conduct, in terms of the child's needs, his group's values, and the demands of the situation. "While from the standpoint of society, behavior is either 'good' or 'bad,' from the standpoint of the individual it always has some positive value. It represents the best solution for his conflicting drives that he has been able to formulate" (Josselyn 1948). This line of thought was extended to the view that moral terms are sociologically as well as psychologically irrelevant. From the standpoint of society, behavior is not clearly good or bad either, since there are a multiplicity of standards that can be used in judging the morality of an action. As sociologists have pointed out, delinquent actions may be motivated by the need to "do right" or conform to standards, to both the standards of the delinquent gang and the great American standard of success.[1]

A second interpretation of the Hartshorne and May findings was somewhat less nihilistic. This interpretation was that suggested by psychoanalytic and neopsychoanalytic theories of personality (Freud [1930] 1955; Fromm 1949; Horney 1937). In this interpretation, moral instruction in the school was ineffective because moral character is formed in the home by early parental influences. Moral character, so conceived, is not a matter of fixed moral virtues, like honesty, but of deep emotional tendencies and defenses—of love as opposed to hate for others, of guilt as opposed to fear, of self-esteem and trust as opposed to feelings of inadequacy and distrust. Because these tendencies are basically affective, they are not consistently displayed in verbal or behavioral test situations, but they do define personality types. These types, and their characteristic affective responses, can be defined at the deeper levels tapped by personality projective tests, but they are also related to other people's judgments of the child's moral character. This point of view toward moral character was mostly clearly developed and empirically supported in the writing and research of Robert Havighurst (1949) and his colleagues (Peck and Havighurst 1960).

While both the "situational" and the "psychoanalytic" interpretations of moral-character research have some validity, recent research findings support a different and more developmental conception of moral character with more positive implications for moral education (Kohlberg 1963a, 1963b, 1964). While a specific act of "misconduct," such as cheating, is largely determined by situational factors, acts of misconduct are also clearly related to two general aspects of the child's personality development. The first general aspect of the

1. It is evident that the cheating behavior so extensively studied by Hartshorne and May does not represent a conflict between unsocialized base instinctual impulses and moral norms. The motive to cheat is the motive to succeed and do well. The motive to resist cheating is also the motive to achieve and be approved of, but defined in more long-range or "internal" terms. Moral character, then, is not a matter of "good" and "bad" motives or a "good" or "bad" personality as such. These facts, found by Hartshorne and May, have not yet been fully absorbed by some clinical approaches to children's moral character. If a child deviates a little he is normal; if he deviates conspicuously, he is believed to be "emotionally disturbed," i.e., to have mixed good and bad motives; if he deviates regularly or wildly, he is all bad (a "psychopathic" or "sadistic" personality).

child's development is often termed "ego strength" and represents a set of interrelated ego abilities, including the intelligent prediction of consequences, the tendency to choose the greater remote reward over the lesser immediate reward, the ability to maintain stable focused attention, and a number of other traits. All these abilities are found to predict (or correlate with) the child's behavior on experimental tests of honesty, teacher's ratings of moral character, and children's resistance to delinquent behavior (Kohlberg 1964).[2]

The second general aspect of personality that determines moral conduct is the level of development of the child's moral judgments or moral concepts. Level of moral judgment is quite a different matter from the knowledge of, and assent to, conventional moral clichés studied by Hartshorne and May. If one asks a child, "Is it very bad to cheat?" or "Would you ever cheat?" a child who cheats a lot in reality is somewhat more likely to give the conforming answer than is the child who does not cheat in reality (Kohlberg 1966a). This is because the same desire to "look good" on a spelling test by cheating impels him to "look good" on the moral-attitude test by lying. If, instead, one probes the reasons for the moral choices of the child, as Piaget and I have done (Piaget [1932] 1948; Kohlberg 1963a), one finds something quite different. As an example, we present the child with a series of moral dilemmas, such as whether a boy should tell his father a confidence about a brother's misdeed. In reply, Danny, age ten, said: "In one way, it would be right to tell on his brother or his father might get mad at him and spank him. In another way, it would be right to keep quiet or his brother might beat him up." Obviously, whether Danny decides it is right to maintain authority or right to maintain peer "loyalty" is of little interest compared to the fact that his decision will be based on his anticipation of who can hit harder. It seems likely that Danny will not cheat if he anticipates punishment but that he has no particular moral reasons for not cheating if he can get away with it. When asked, the only reason he gave for not cheating was that "you might get caught," and his teacher rated him high on a dishonesty rating form.

Danny's response, however, is not a unique aspect of a unique personality. It represents a major aspect of a consistent stage of development of moral judgment, a stage in which moral judgments are based on considerations of punishment and obedience. It is the first of the following six stages found in the development of moral judgment (Kohlberg 1963a):

Level I—Premoral

Stage 1—Obedience and punishment orientation. Egocentric deference to superior power or prestige, or a trouble-avoiding set. Objective responsibility.

2. These factors are also stressed in the work of Peck and Havighurst (1960), who found extremely high correlations between ratings of moral character and ratings of ego strength.

Stage 2—Naïvely egoistic orientation. Right action is that instrumentally satisfying the self's needs and occasionally other's. Awareness of relativism of value to each actor's needs and perspective. Naïve egalitarianism and orientation to exchange and reciprocity.

Level II—Conventional Role Conformity

Stage 3—Good-boy orientation. Orientation to approval and to pleasing and helping others. Conformity to stereotypical images of majority or natural role behavior, and judgment of intentions.

Stage 4—Authority and social-order-maintaining orientation. Orientation to "doing duty" and to showing respect for authority and maintaining the given social order for its own sake. Regard for earned expectations of others.

Level III—Self-Accepted Moral Principles

Stage 5—Contractual legalistic orientation. Recognition of an arbitrary element or starting point in rules or expectations for the sake of agreement. Duty defined in terms of contract, general avoidance of violation of the will or rights of others, and majority will and welfare.

Stage 6—Conscience or principle orientation. Orientation not only to actually ordained social rules but to principles of choice involving appeal to logical universality and consistency. Orientation to conscience as a directing agent and to mutual respect and trust.

Each of these stages is defined by twenty-five basic aspects of moral values. Danny's responses primarily illustrated the motivation aspect of stage 1, the fact that moral motives are defined in terms of punishment. The motivation for moral action at each stage, and examples illustrating them, are as follows:

Stage 1—Obey rules to avoid punishment. Danny, age ten: (Should Joe tell on his older brother to his father?) "In one way it would be right to tell on his brother or his father might get mad at him and spank him. In another way it would be right to keep quiet or his brother might beat him up."

Stage 2—Conform to obtain rewards, have favors returned, and so on. Jimmy, age thirteen: (Should Joe tell on his older brother to his father?) "I think he should keep quiet. He might want to go someplace like that, and if he squeals on Alex, Alex might squeal on him."

Stage 3—Conform to avoid disapproval, dislike by others. Andy, age sixteen: (Should Joe keep quiet about what his brother did?) "If my father finds out later, he won't trust me. My brother wouldn't either, but I wouldn't have a *conscience* that he (my brother) didn't." "I try to do things for my parents; they've always done things for me. I try to do everything my mother says; I try to please her. Like she wants me to be a doctor, and I want to, too, and she's helping me to get up there."

Stage 4—Conform to avoid censure by legitimate authorities and resultant guilt. Previous example also indicative of this.

Stage 5—Conform to maintain the respect of the impartial spectator judging in terms of community welfare or to maintain a relation of mutual respect. Bob, age sixteen: "His brother thought he could trust him. His brother wouldn't think much of him if he told like that."

Stage 6—Conform to avoid self-condemnation. Bill, age sixteen: (Should the husband steal the expensive black-market drug needed to save his wife's life?) "Lawfully no, but morally speaking I think I would have done it. It would be awfully hard to live with myself afterward, knowing that I could have done something which would have saved her life and yet didn't for fear of punishment to myself."

While motivation is one of the twenty-five aspects of morality defining the stages, many of the aspects are more cognitive. An example is the aspect of "The Basis of Moral Worth of Human Life," which is defined for each stage as follows:

Stage 1—The value of a human life is confused with the value of physical objects and is based on the social status or physical attributes of its possessor. Tommy, age ten: (Why should the druggist give the drug to the dying woman when her husband couldn't pay for it?) "If someone important is in a plane and is allergic to heights and the stewardess won't give him medicine because she's only got enough for one and she's got a sick one, a friend, in back, they'd probably put the stewardess in a lady's jail because she didn't help the important one."

(Is it better to save the life of one important person or a lot of unimportant people?) "All the people that aren't important because one man just has one house, maybe a lot of furniture, but a whole bunch of people have an awful lot of furniture and some of these poor people might have a lot of money and it doesn't look it."

Stage 2—The value of a human life is seen as instrumental to the satisfaction of the needs of its possessor or of other persons. Tommy, age thirteen: (Should the doctor "mercy kill" a fatally ill woman requesting death because of her pain?) "Maybe it would be good to put her out of her pain, she'd be better off that way. But the husband wouldn't want it, it's not like an animal. If a pet dies you can get along without it—it isn't something you really need. Well, you can get a new wife, but it's not really the same."

Stage 3—The value of a human life is based on the empathy and affection of family members and others toward its possessor. Andy, age sixteen: (Should the doctor "mercy kill" a fatally ill woman requesting death because of her pain?) "No, he shouldn't. The husband loves her and wants to see her. He wouldn't want her to die sooner; he loves her too much."

Stage 4—Life is conceived as sacred in terms of its place in a categorical moral or religious order of rights and duties. John, age sixteen: (Should the doctor "mercy kill" the woman?) "The doctor wouldn't have the right to take a life, no human has the right. He can't create life, he shouldn't destroy it."

Stage 5—Life is valued both in terms of its relation to community welfare and in terms of life being a universal human right.

Stage 6—Belief in the sacredness of human life as representing a universal human value of respect for the individual. Steve, age sixteen: (Should the husband steal the expensive drug to save his wife?) "By the law of society he was wrong but by the law of nature or of God the druggist was wrong and the husband was justified. Human life is above financial gain. Regardless of who was dying, if it was a total stranger, man has a duty to save him from dying."

We have spoken of our six types of moral judgment as stages. By this we mean more than the fact that they are age-related. First, a stage concept implies sequence; it implies that each child must go step by step through each of the kinds of moral judgment outlined. It is, of course, possible for a child to stop (become "fixated") at any level of development, but if he continues to move upward he must move in this stepwise fashion. While the findings are not completely analyzed on this issue, a longitudinal study of the same boys studied at ages ten, thirteen, sixteen, and nineteen suggests that this is the case. Second, a stage concept implies universality of sequence under varying cultural conditions. It implies that moral development is not merely a matter of learning the verbal values or rules of the child's culture but reflects something more universal in development which would occur in any culture. In order to examine this assumption, the same moral-judgment method was used with boys aged ten, thirteen, and sixteen in a Taiwanese city, in a Malaysian (Atayal) aboriginal tribal village, and in a Turkish village, as well as in America. The results for Taiwan and for America are presented in figure 3.1.

Figure 3.1 indicates much the same age trends in both the Taiwanese and the American boys. It is evident that in both groups the first two types decrease with age, the next two increase until age thirteen and then stabilize, and the last two continue to increase from age thirteen to age sixteen. In general, the cross-cultural studies suggest a similar sequence of development in all cul-

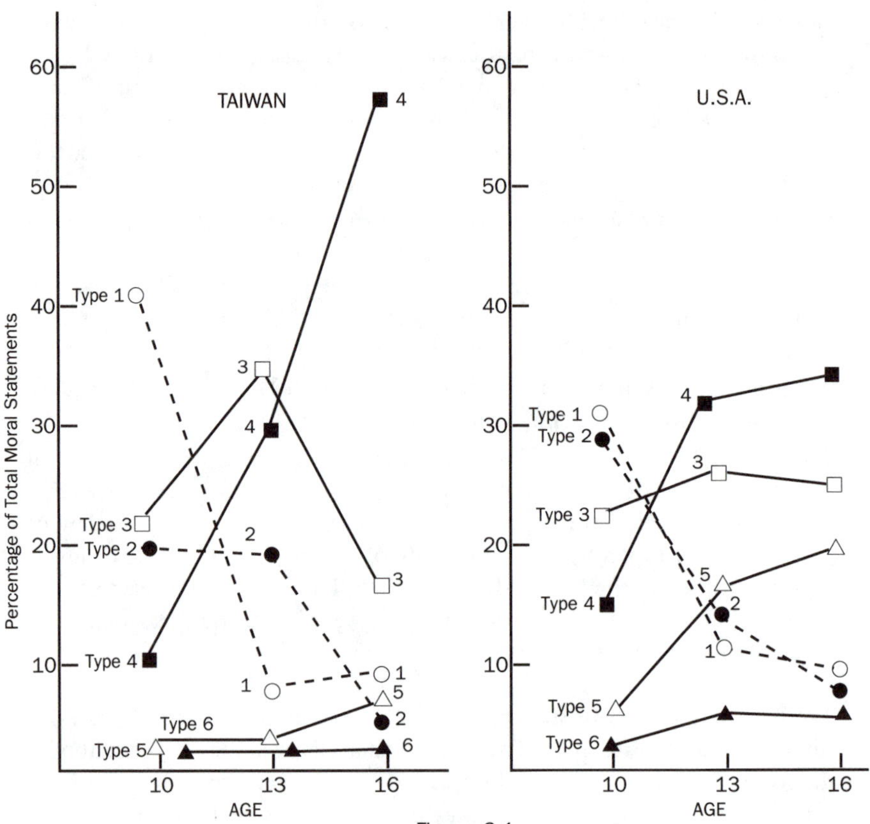

Figure 3.1
Mean percent of use of each of six stages of moral judgment at three ages in Taiwan and the United States.

tures, although they suggest that the last two stages of moral thought do not develop clearly in preliterate village or tribal communities.

In the third place, the stage concept implies personality consistency. We said that there was little consistency to honest behavior as such. There is, however, a high degree of consistency, a "g-factor" of moral stage, from one verbal moral situation to the next (Kohlberg 1966b).

In order to consider the relevance of these moral-judgment stages for our conceptions of moral character, we must consider a little further their relationship to moral conduct. We have already noted that verbal agreement to moral conventions does not generally predict to moral behavior. We noted that when Hartshorne and May measured the child's "knowledge" of the society's moral conventions (as opposed to his response to moral-attitude tests, assessing strength of verbal assent to these convictions), slightly better predictions were obtained; tests of moral knowledge correlated with experimental tests of cheating in the low 30s, about as well as a single cheating test correlates with another. These tests of moral knowledge require somewhat more cognitive understanding of cultural moral prescriptions than do verbal moral-attitude tests, and they are somewhat more age developmental. Our tests of moral judgment, which are more genuinely developmental and reflective of basic cognitive structuring of values than moral-knowledge tests, are still better predictors of moral conduct, however, if moral conduct is conceived in developmental terms.

In referring to a definition of moral conduct, in developmental terms, we refer to the implications of the fact found by Hartshorne and May and corroborated by more recent investigations (Kohlberg 1964)—the fact that such behaviors as honesty (resistance to cheating) do not increase with age during the elementary school years (Kohlberg 1964).[3] In contrast, we saw that moral judgment and values were developing in sequential fashion during these years. For the majority of these elementary school years, however, the child has not developed any clear or internal moral values or principles that condemn cheating, so it is not surprising that cheating behavior does not decline in these years. While most elementary school children are aware of, and concerned about, the harm done others by acts of aggression or theft (Krebs 1965), their only reason for not cheating is their fear of being caught and punished. Even at older ages, teachers give children few moral or mature reasons to think cheating is bad. Sixth-grade children tell us their teachers tell them not to cheat because they will get punished (stage 1) "or because the person you copied from might have it wrong and so it won't do you any good" (stage 2, expediency). In these years, then, resistance to cheating is not so much a matter of internal moral principles as of the situational and expediency factors stressed by Hartshorne and May. With regard to the type of cheating test situation used by Hartshorne and May, the critical issue for the subject's moral judgment is that of trust, what the experimenter or the teacher expects and what he has the right to expect. The experimenter explicitly leaves the subject unsupervised in a situation where he ordinarily expects supervision. This abandonment of control or authority is interpreted in varying ways. A very high degree of cheating in such a situation seems to primarily reflect a naïve abandon to the surface impression that the experimenter doesn't care. A lesser degree of cheating seems to reflect the child's belief that the experimenter doesn't care very much about his not cheating or he wouldn't leave him unsupervised and that a little cheating isn't too bad anyhow, so long as it is not too obvious and excessive or more than the others do.

3. This has sometimes been viewed as consistent with the psychoanalytic view that character is fixed at an early age in the home. In fact, this does not seem to be true, as there is little predictability from early moral conduct to later adolescent moral conduct.

In one study of sixth graders (Kohlberg 1966a) almost all (80 percent) of the children cheated somewhat. The majority of children at the premoral level of moral judgment (stages 1 and 2) cheated a great deal, and the majority of the children at the conventional level of moral judgment (stages 3 and 4) cheated a slight or moderate amount.[4] In contrast, adolescents at the level of moral principle (stages 5 and 6) do interpret the opportunity to cheat as involving issues of maintaining trust, contract, social agreement, and equality of reward for equal effort and ability. The one sixth grader in the Kohlberg study (1966a) at this level did not cheat at all. Among a group of college students also studied, only one of nine principled-level subjects cheated on an experimental test while about one-half of the twenty-six conventional-level subjects did so. (There were no premoral-level subjects in this group.)

Cheating, then, is not a good indicator of moral character until the child has developed in adolescence a set of inner moral principles that prohibit it. By that time, cheating behavior may reflect a lack of full development of moral values (i.e., a failure to reach the level of moral principles) or a discrepancy between action and moral values (a discrepancy due to a variety of possible deficits in ego strength or ego abilities).

More generally, then, there is some meaning to "moral character" as an aim of moral education if moral character is conceived in developmental terms rather than as a set of fixed conventional traits of honesty or responsibility.

Hartshorne and May's critique is justified insofar as it is a critique of a tendency of teachers to respond to isolated acts of deviance as indicating the child's bad or dishonest character. Specific acts of conformity or deviance in themselves reflect primarily situational wishes and fears rather than the presence or absence of conscience or moral character. Nevertheless, there is evidence that repeated misconduct tends to indicate general deficits or retardation of general moral-judgment capacities, or related guilt capacities, and the lack of internal ego control rather than simply situational values or emotional conflicts. While everyday judgments of moral character and worth are often psychologically erroneous, they do correlate with important consistencies in personality and development, which are positive from almost any viewpoint.

In addition to giving new meaning to notions of moral character, recent research also suggests that it may be possible to stimulate the development of moral character in the school. We said that there has been no recent research evidence to suggest revision of Hartshorne and May's finding that conventional moral- and religious-education classes had no direct influence on moral

4. The attitude of this latter group is probably well expressed by the following anonymous student article in a British school paper written after a siege of experimental studies of honesty: "The next test reminded me of the eleven plus exam. I had great fun doing these but they are sure to think I am barmy. But then they made a fatal mistake; they actually gave us our own papers to mark. We saw our mistakes in time and saved the day by changing the answers."

conduct as usually conceived. (More recently, ongoing research by Jacob Kounin also suggests that the teacher's use of various techniques of punishment and reward for misconduct has no relationship to the amount and type of misconduct that occurs in the classroom.) These negative results have usually been interpreted as indicating that only the home can have any real effect in moral teaching, because only the home teaching involves the intense and continuing emotional relationships necessary for moral teaching or for induction of potential guilt feelings for wrongdoing. In fact, the failure of conventional moral education in the school is probably not the result of the powerlessness of the school to influence the child's character but the result of the inadequacy of prevalent American conceptions of character education. These conceptions usually center on the training of good "habits" of honesty or responsibility, through preaching, example, punishment, and reward. This conception of character education appears to be just as ineffective in the home as it is in the school. Extensive research on parental practices has found no positive or consistent relationships between earliness and amount of parental demands or training in good habits (obedience, caring for property, performing chores, neatness, or avoidance of cheating) and their children's actual obedience, responsibility, and honesty. Amount of use of praise, of deprivation of physical rewards, or of physical punishment is also not found to relate consistently or positively to measures of moral character (Kohlberg 1963b, 1964).

There are, of course, a number of unique influences of the home on the development of character which the school cannot reproduce. These are not matters of specific moral training, however, but of the emotional climate in which the child develops. The only parent-attitude variables consistently found to relate to children's moral character are not "moral training" variables but variables of parental warmth (Kohlberg 1963b, 1964). These emotional-climate variables, however, only account for a very small percentage of the differences between children in moral development or moral character. Many of the environmental influences important in moral development are more cognitive in nature than either the "good habits" or the "early emotions" views have suggested. In part, this cognitive influence is meant in a relatively conventional mental-age or I.Q. sense. Intelligence quotient correlates well with maturity of moral judgment (31 to 53 at varying ages) and almost equally well with behavioral measures of honesty. At the kindergarten level, the capacity to make judgments of good or bad in terms of standards rather than in terms of punishment and egoistic interests is a capacity almost completely determined by cognitive development on Piaget tests of cognition (Krebs 1965).

We have discussed the influence of general intellectual advance upon the development of moral judgment. In addition, advances in a number of aspects of social concepts customarily thought of as part of the social-studies curriculum are correlated with advance in moral judgment. Children in the original Kohlberg study were asked to say how much and why various occupations (such as judge, policeman, soldier, artist, senator) were respected by most people, an apparent question of comprehension of social fact and function. Responses to this task could be scored in a fashion similar to the moral-judgment questions, and individual children's levels were similar on the two tasks.

This task pointed up the fact that some of the difficulties in moral development of lower-class children are largely cognitive in nature. Sociologists and social critics like Paul Goodman and Edgar Friedenberg have stressed the notion that the school not only transmits middle-class moral values at the expense of lower-class moral values but that there is a certain fundamental "immorality" or "inauthenticity" about these middle-class values to the lower-class child in comparison with lower-class values. While sociologists are correct in stressing class-linked value systems, they are not correct in postulating class-based differences in basic moral values. The lower-class parent and the middle-class parent show little difference in the rank order of moral values desired for their children; for example, both put honesty at the top of the list (Kohn 1959). In the Kohlberg studies of moral ideology middle-class and working-class children (matched for I.Q.) differed considerably. These differences, however, were developmental in nature. At one age, middle-class and working-class children differed in one way, at another in a different way. At all ages, however, the middle-class children tended to be somewhat in advance of the working-class children. The differences, then, were not due to the fact that the middle-class children heavily favored some one type of thought, which could be seen as corresponding to the prevailing middle-class pattern. Instead, middle-class and working-class children seemed to move faster and farther.

This finding becomes intelligible when it is recalled that the institutions with moral authority (law, government, family, the work order) and the basic moral rules are the same regardless of the individual's particular position in society. The child's position in society does to a large extent, however, determine his interpretation of these institutions and rules. Law and the government are perceived quite differently by the child if he feels a sense of understanding and potential participation in the social order than if he does not.[5]

5. The effect of such a sense of participation upon development of moral judgments related to the law is suggested by the following responses of sixteen-year-olds to the question, "Should someone obey a law if he doesn't think it is a good law?" A lower-class boy replies, "Yes, a law is a law and you can't do nothing about it. You have to obey it, you should. That's what it's there for." For him the law is simply a constraining thing that is there. The very fact that he has no hand in it, that "you can't do nothing about it," means that it should be obeyed (stage 1).

A lower-middle-class boy replies, "Laws are made for people to obey and if everyone would start breaking them. . . . Well, if you owned a store and there were no laws, everybody would just come in and not have to pay." Here laws are seen not as arbitrary commands but as a unitary system, as the basis of the social order. The role or perspective taken is that of a storekeeper, of someone with a stake in the order (stage 4).

An upper-middle-class boy replies, "The law's the law but I think people themselves can tell what's right or wrong. I suppose the laws are made by many different groups of people with dif-

The slower development of moral judgment of the working-class boys seemed largely accountable for by two factors, lesser understanding of the broader social order and lesser sense of participation in it. Both factors showed up especially in the social-concept task conceiving occupations but were apparent in their moral judgments as well. It seems likely that social-studies programs in the school could have considerably more positive effect upon these class-differentiating aspects of moral development than is true at present.

Our discussion of social class stressed opportunities for social participation and role-taking as factors stimulating moral development. Perhaps a clearer example of the importance of social participation in moral development is the finding that children with extensive peer-group participation advance considerably more quickly through the Kohlberg stages of moral judgment than children who are isolated from such participation (with both groups equated for social class and I.Q.). This clearly suggests the relevance and potential of the classroom peer group for moral education. In pointing to the effects of extrafamilial determinants upon moral development, we have focused primarily on their influence upon development of moral judgment. However, these same determinants lead to more mature moral behavior as well, as indicated by teachers' ratings and experimental measures of honesty and of moral autonomy (Kohlberg 1966a).

A Developmental Conception of the Aims and Nature of Moral Education

The facts, then, suggest the possibilities of useful planning of the moral-education component of schooling. Such planning raises more fundamental value issues, however—the issues as to the legitimate aims and methods of moral education in the American public schools. The writer would start by arguing that there are no basic value problems raised by the assertion that the school *should* be consciously concerned about moral education, since all schools necessarily are constantly involved in moral education. The teacher is constantly and unavoidably moralizing to children, about rules and values and about his students' behavior toward each other. Since such moralizing is unavoidable, it seems logical that it be done in terms of consciously formulated goals of moral development. As it stands, liberal teachers do not want to indoctrinate children with their own private moral values. Since the classroom social situation requires moralizing by the teacher, he ordinarily tends to limit and focus his moralizing toward the necessities of classroom management, that is, upon the

---

ferent ideas. But if you don't believe in a law, you should try to get it changed, you shouldn't disobey it." Here the laws are seen as the product of various legitimate ideological and interest groups varying in their beliefs as to the best decision in policy matters. The role of law-obeyer is seen from the perspective of the democratic policy-maker (stage 5).

immediate and relatively trivial behaviors that are disrupting to him or to the other children. Exposure to the diversity of moral views of teachers is undoubtedly one of the enlightening experiences of growing up, but the present system of thoughtlessness as to which of the teacher's moral attitudes or views he communicates to children and which he does not leaves much to be desired. Many teachers would be most mortified and surprised to know what their students perceive to be their moral values and concerns. My seven-year-old son told me one day that he was one of the good boys in school, but he didn't know whether he really wanted to be. I asked him what the differences between the good and bad boys were, and he said the bad boys talked in class and didn't put books away neatly, so they got yelled at. Not only is it highly dubious that his teacher's moralizing was stimulating his or any of the children's moral development, but it is almost inevitable that this be the case in an educational system in which teachers have no explicit or thought-out conception of the aims and methods of moral education and simply focus upon immediate classroom-management concerns in their moralizing.

The value problems of moral education, then, do not arise concerning the necessity of engaging in moral education in the school, since this is already being done every day. The value problems arise, however, concerning the formulation of the aims and content of such education. At its extreme, such a formulation of aims suggests a conception of moral education as the imposition of a state-determined set of values, first by the bureaucrats upon the teachers, and then by the teachers upon the children. This is the system of "character education" employed in Russia, as described by U. Bronfenbrenner (1962). In Russia, the entire classroom process is explicitly defined as "character education," that is, as making good socialist citizens, and the teacher appears to have an extremely strong influence upon children's moral standards. This influence rests in part upon the fact that the teacher is perceived as "the priest of society," as the agent of the all-powerful state, and can readily enlist the parents as agents of discipline to enforce school values and demands. In part, however, it rests upon the fact that the teacher systematically uses the peer group as an agent of moral indoctrination and moral sanction. The classroom is divided into cooperating groups in competition with one another. If a member of one of the groups is guilty of misconduct, the teacher downgrades or sanctions the whole group, and the group in turn punishes the individual miscreant. This is, of course, an extremely effective form of social control if not of moral development.

In our view, there is a third alternative to a state moral-indoctrination system and to the current American system of moralizing by individual teachers and principals when children deviate from minor administrative regulations or engage in behavior personally annoying to the teacher. This alternative is to take the stimulation of the development of the individual child's moral judgment and character as a goal of moral education, rather than taking as its goal either administrative convenience or state-defined values. The attractiveness of defining the goal of moral education as the stimulation of development rather than as teaching fixed virtues is that it means aiding the child to take the next step in a direction toward which he is already tending, rather than imposing an alien pattern upon him. An example of the difference may be given in terms of the use of the peer group. In Russia the peer-group structure is created by the teacher (i.e., he divides the classroom into groups), and the peer group is then manipulated by punishments and rewards so as to impose the teacher's or the school's values upon its deviant members. If one took the stimulation of the moral development of the individual child as a goal, one would consider the role of the peer group in quite a different way. In the previous section we discussed the fact that classroom isolates were slower in development of moral judgment than were integrates. This suggests that inclusion of the social isolates in the classroom peer group might have considerable influence on their moral development, though not necessarily an influence of immediate conformity to teacher or school demands.

The implementation of this goal would involve various methods to encourage inclusion of isolates such as are under investigation in a research project at the University of Michigan conducted by Ronald Lippett. Some of these methods involve creating a classroom atmosphere encouraging participation rather than attempting to directly influence sociometric integrates to include isolates. Some of these methods involve more direct appeal to integrated members of sociometric groups, but an appeal to the implementation of already existing social and moral values held by these children rather than an effort to impose the teacher's values upon them by reward or punishment. The process raises many valuable issues potentially stimulating the moral development of the integrates as well, since they must cope with the fact that, "Well, we were finally nice to him and look what he did." These issues involve the opportunity for the teacher to play a different and perhaps more stimulating and open role as a "moral guide" than that involved in supporting conformity to school rules and teacher demands.

A definition of the aims of moral education as the stimulation of natural development is most clear-cut in the area of moral judgment, where there appears to be considerable regularity of sequence and direction in development in various cultures. Because of this regularity, it is possible to define the maturity of a child's moral judgment without considering its content (the particular action judged) and without considering whether it agrees with our own particular moral judgments or values or those of the American middle-class culture as a whole. In fact, the sign of the child's moral maturity is his ability to make moral judgments and formulate moral principles of his own, rather than his ability to conform to moral judgments of the adults around him.[6]

6. A research indication of this comes from the Kohlberg study. After individual moral-judgment interviews, the children in the study were subjected to pressure from an adult and from

How in general, then, may moral maturity as an aim of education be defined? One general answer starts from the conception of maturity in moral judgment and then considers conduct in terms of its correspondence to such judgment. Maturity levels are most clearly apparent in moral judgment. Furthermore, the general direction of maturity of moral judgment is a direction of greater morality. Each of the Kohlberg stages of moral judgment represents a step toward a more genuinely or distinctly moral judgment. We do not mean by this that a more mature judgment is more moral in the sense of showing closer conformity to the conventional standards of a given community. We mean that a more mature judgment more closely corresponds to genuine moral judgments as these have been defined by philosophers. While philosophers have been unable to agree upon any ultimate principle of the good that would define "correct" moral judgments, most philosophers agree upon the characteristics that make a judgment a genuine moral judgment (Hare 1952; Kant 1949; Sidgwick 1901). Moral judgments are judgments about the good and the right of action. Not all judgments of "good" or "right" are moral judgments, however; many are judgments of esthetic, technological, or prudential goodness or rightness. Unlike judgments of prudence or esthetics, moral judgments tend to be universal, inclusive, consistent, and to be grounded on objective, impersonal, or ideal grounds (Kohlberg 1958). "She's really great, she's beautiful and a good dancer"; "the right way to make a martini is five to one"—these are statements about the good and right that are not moral judgments since they lack these characteristics. If we say, "Martinis should be made five to one," we are making an esthetic judgment, and we are not prepared to say that we want everyone to make them that way, that they are good in terms of some impersonal ideal standard shared by others, and that we and others should make five-to-one martinis whether they wish to or not. In a similar fashion, when Danny answered our "moral should" question, "Should Joe tell on his older brother?" in stage 1 terms of the probabilities of getting beaten up by his father and by his brother, he did not answer with a moral judgment that is universal (one that applies to all brothers in that situation and ought to be agreed upon by all people thinking about the situation) or that has any impersonal or ideal grounds. In contrast, the stage 6 statements quoted earlier not only specifically use moral words, such as "morally right" and "duty," but use them in a moral way; for example, "regardless of who it was" and "by the law of nature or of God" imply uni-

disagreeing peers to change their views on the questions. While maturity of moral judgment predicted to moral behaviors involving conformity to authority (e.g., cheating), it predicted better to behaviors involving maintaining one's own moral views in the face of pressure from authorities ($r = .44$). Among college students, not only were principled subjects much less likely to cheat, but they were much more likely to engage in an act of moral courage or resistance when an authoritative experimenter ordered them to inflict pain upon another subject (Kohlberg 1966a).

versality; "morally, I would do it in spite of fear of punishment" implies impersonality and ideality of obligation. Thus the value judgments of lower-level subjects about moral matters are not moral responses in the same sense in which the value judgments of high-level subjects about esthetic or morally neutral matters are not normal. The genuinely moral judgment just discussed is what we mean by "judgments of principle" and "to become morally adult is to learn to make decisions of principle; it is to learn to use 'ought' sentences verified by reference to a standard or set of principles which we have by our own decision accepted and made our own" (Hare 1952).

How can the teacher go about stimulating the development of moral judgment? We have already rejected the notion of a set curriculum of instruction and exhortation in the conventional moral virtues, a conception killed by Hartshorne and May's demonstration of ineffectiveness. Dewey (1911) pointed to the inadequacy of such a conception long ago and traced it to the fact that it assumed a divorce between moral education and intellectual education on the one side, and a divorce between education and real life on the other. To put Dewey's critique more bluntly, both conventional character-education classes or preaching and conventional moralizing by teachers about petty school routines are essentially "Mickey Mouse" stuff in relationship to the real need for moral stimulation of the child. To be more than "Mickey Mouse," a teacher's moralizings must be cognitively novel and challenging to the child, and they must be related to matters of obvious, real importance and seriousness.

It is not always necessary that these matters be one of the immediate and real-life issues of the classroom. I have found that my hypothetical and remote but obviously morally real and challenging conflict situations are of intense interest to almost all adolescents and lead to lengthy debate among them. They are involving because the adult right answer is not obviously at hand to discourage the child's own moral thought, as so often is the case. The child will listen to what the teacher says about moral matters only if the child first feels a genuine sense of uncertainty as to the right answer to the situation in question. The pat little stories in school readers in which virtue always triumphs or in which everyone is really nice are unlikely to have any value in the stimulation of moral development. Only the presentation of genuine and difficult moral conflicts can have this effect.

It is obvious, however, that discussion of such more remote but important moral conflicts as are involved in the situations we have used are only a supplement to the discussion of the more immediate "real-life" issues of classroom life. The most serious and vital value issues represented by school life are not moral values per se but are intellectual in nature. As Dewey points out in discussing moral education, the serious business of the school is, and should be, intellectual. The principal values and virtues the teacher attends to are intellectual. However, the teacher may attend to these values and virtues either with awareness of their broader place in moral development or without such awareness. If such awareness is not present, the teacher will simply transmit the competitive-achievement values that dominate our society. He will train the child to think that getting a good mark is an absolute good and then suddenly shift gears and denounce cheating without wondering why the child should think cheating is bad when getting a good mark is the most important value. If the teacher has a greater awareness of the moral dimensions of education, his teaching of the intellectual aspects of the curriculum will illustrate the values of truth, integrity, and trust in intellectual affairs and intellectual learning in such a way as to carry over to behaviors like cheating.

We have mentioned that to stimulate development of moral communication by the teacher should involve issues of genuine moral conflict to the child and represent new cognitive elements. There is also an important problem of match between the teacher's level and the child's involved in effective moral communication. Conventional moral education never has had much influence on children's moral judgment because it has disregarded this problem of developmental match. It has usually involved a set of adult moral clichés that are meaningless to the child because they are too abstract, mixed up with a patronizing "talking down" to the child in concrete terms beneath his level. In fact, the developmental level of moral-education verbalizations must be matched to the developmental level of the child if they are to have an effect. Ideally, such education should aim at communicating primarily at a level one stage above the child's own and secondarily at the child's own level. Experimental demonstration of this principle is provided in a study by E. Turiel (1966). Turiel ascertained the moral level of sixth graders on the Kohlberg stages, matched them for I.Q., and divided them into three experimental groups (and a fourth control group). All the groups (except the controls) were then exposed to short role-playing and discussion sessions with the experimenter centered on hypothetical conflict situations similar to those used in the Kohlberg tests. For one experimental group, the experimenter presented a discussion using moral judgments and reasons *one level above* the child's own. For a second group, the experimenter used moral judgments *two levels above* the child's own. For the third group, the experimenter used moral judgments *one level below* the child's own. All the children were then retested on the original test situations as well as on the situations discussed with the experimenter. Only the children who were exposed to moral judgments one level above their own showed any appreciable absorption of the experimenter's moral judgments. The children exposed to judgments one level below their own showed some absorption (more than those exposed to judgments two levels above) but not nearly as much as those exposed to one level above. Thus, while children are able to understand moralizing that is talking down beneath their level, they do not seem to accept it nearly as much as if it is comprehensible but somewhat above their level. It is obvious that the teacher's implementation of this principle must start by his careful listening to the moral judgments and ideas actually expressed by individual children.

So far, we have talked about the development of moral judgment as an aim of moral education. The sheer ability to make genuinely moral judgments is only one portion of moral character, however. The remainder is the ability to apply these judgmental capacities to the actual guidance and criticism of action. Thus, in addition to stimulating the development of general moral judgment capacities, a developmental moral education would stimulate the child's application of his own moral judgments (not the teacher's) to his actions. The effort to force a child to agree that an act of cheating was very bad when he does not really believe it (as in the case of the author of the school-newspaper article) will be effective only in encouraging morally immature tendencies toward expedient outward compliance. In contrast, a more difficult but more valid approach involves getting the child to examine the pros and cons of his conduct in his own terms (as well as introducing more developmentally advanced considerations).[7]

In general, however, the problem of insuring correspondence between developing moral judgments and the child's action is not primarily a problem of eliciting moral self-criticism from the child. One aspect of the problem is the development of the ego abilities involved in the non-moral or cognitive tasks upon which the classroom centers. As an example, an experimental measure of high stability of attention (low reaction-time variability) in a simple, monotonous task has been found to clearly predict resistance to cheating in Hartshorne and May's tests ($r = .68$) (Grim, Kohlberg, and White 1968). The encouragement of these attentional ego capacities is not a task of moral education as such but of general programming of classroom learning activities.

Another aspect of the encouragement of correspondence between the child's moral values and his behavior is more difficult and fundamental. In order to encourage the application of his values to his behavior, we need to make sure that the kinds of behavior demands we make have some match to his already existing moral values. Two major types of mismatch occur. One type, which we have already mentioned, occurs when teachers concentrate on trivial classroom routines, thus moralizing issues that have no moral meaning outside the classroom. If the teacher insists on behavioral conformity to these demands and shows no moral concerns for matters of greater relevance to the child's (and the society's) basic moral values, the child will simply assume that his moral values have no relevance to his conduct in the classroom. It is obvi-

7. This is actually more valuable for acts of good conduct than for acts of bad conduct. We expect children to justify defensively acts of misconduct. If we take the trouble to find out, however, we will often be surprised that the acts of good conduct we praise are valued by the child himself for immature reasons and that we are really rewarding "selfish" rather than moral values. In such cases it is relatively easy to foster the application of developmentally more advanced values in the child's repertoire to his own behavior.

ous that the teacher must exert some influence toward conformity to trivial classroom rules, but there are two things he can do to minimize this sort of mismatch. The first is to insure that he does communicate some of his values with regard to broader and more genuinely moral issues. The second is to treat administrative demands as such and to distinguish them from basic moral demands involving moral judgment of the child's worth and moral sanctions. This does not imply that no demands should be treated as moral demands but that the teacher should clearly distinguish his own attitudes and reactions toward moral demands from his more general conformity demands. The second form of mismatch between the teacher's moral demands and the child's moral values arises from the fact that the teacher feels that certain behavioral demands are genuine moral demands, but the child has not yet developed any moral values that require these behaviors. We gave as an example the fact that resistance to cheating on tests does not derive from anything like moral values in young children aged five to seven, whereas resistance to theft and aggression do correspond to more spontaneous and internal moral values at this age. Given this fact, it does not seem wise to treat cheating as a genuine moral issue among young children, while it may be with older children. In general, the teacher should encourage the child to develop moral values relevant to such behavior as cheating but should not treat the behavior as a moral demand in the absence of such values.

It is clear, then, that a developmental conception of moral education does not imply the imposition of a curriculum upon the teacher. It does demand that the individual teacher achieve some clarity in his general conceptions of the aims and nature of moral development. In addition, it implies that he achieve clarity as to the aspects of moral development he should encourage in children of a given developmental level and as to appropriate methods of moral communication with these children. Most important, it implies that the teacher starts to listen carefully to the child in moral communications. It implies that he becomes concerned about the child's moral judgments (and the relation of the child's behavior to these judgments) rather than about the conformity of the child's behavior or judgments to the teacher's own.

For Reflection

1. What role does the peer group play in Kohlberg's scheme?
2. Give a brief definition for a "stage system."
3. Can Christian values fit Kohlberg's stages? In what ways?
4. What qualifies as a "moral" judgment compared to other judgments?

References

Bronfenbrenner, U. 1962. Soviet methods of character education: Some implications for research. *American Psychologist* 17: 550–65.

Dewey, J. 1911. *Moral principles in education.* Boston: Houghton Mifflin.

Durkheim, E. [1925.] 1961. *Moral education.* Reprint ed. Glencoe, Ill.: Free Press.

Freud, S. [1930.] 1955. *Civilization and its discontents.* Reprint ed. London: Hogarth.

Fromm, E. 1949. *Man for himself.* New York: Rinehart.

Grim, P., L. Kohlberg, and S. White. 1968. Some relationships between conscience and attentional processes. *Journal of Personality and Social Psychology* 8:239–52.

Hare, R. M. 1952. *The language of morals.* New York: Oxford Univ. Press.

Hartshorne, H., and M. A. May. 1928–30. 3 Vols. New York: Macmillan.

Havighurst, R. J., and H. Taba. 1949. *Adolescent character and personality.* New York: Wiley.

Horney, K. 1937. *The neurotic personality of our time.* New York: Norton.

Josselyn, I. M. 1948. *Psychosocial development of children.* New York: Family Service Association.

Kant, I. 1949. *Fundamental principles of the metaphysic of morals.* Trans. T. K. Abbott. Reprint ed. New York: Liberal Arts.

Kohlberg, L. 1958. The development of modes of moral thinking and choice in the years ten to sixteen. Ph.D. diss., University of Chicago.

———. 1963a. The development of children's orientations toward a moral order: I. Sequence in the development of moral thought. *Vita Humana* 6: 11–33.

———. 1963b. Moral development and identification. In *Child psychology,* ed. H. Stevenson. Chicago: Univ. of Chicago Press.

———. 1964. The development of moral character and ideology. In *Review of child development research,* ed. M. Hoffman and L. Hoffman. New York: Russell Sage Foundation.

———. 1966a. Cognitive stages and preschool education. *Human Development* 9:5–17.

———. 1966b. Stage and sequence: The developmental approach to moralization. In *Moral processes,* ed. M. Hoffman. Chicago: Aldine.

Kohn, M. 1959. Social class and parental values. *American Journal of Sociology* 64: 337–51.

Krebs, R. 1965. The development of moral judgment in young children. Master's thesis, Committee on Human Development, University of Chicago.

Peck, R. F., and R. J. Havighurst. 1960. *The psychology of character development.* New York: Wiley.

Piaget, J. [1932.] 1948. *The moral judgment of the child.* Reprint ed. Glencoe, Ill.: Free Press.

Sidgwick, H. 1901. *Methods of ethics.* London: Macmillan.

Turiel, E. 1966. An experimental analysis of developmental stages in the child's moral judgment. *Journal of Personality and Social Psychology* 3, 6: 611–18.

4

Robert L. Selman
Social-Cognitive Theorist

Social and Cognitive Understanding: A Guide to Educational and Clinical Practice

(1976)

Within the context of cognitive-developmental moral judgment, Selman focuses on social role-taking, or the ability to take the perspective of other persons. Other research indicates that the role-taking ability improves with age, continues into adolescence, and is correlated both with measures of intelligence and with emotional balance. The previous studies seem to imply, at least to Selman, that role-taking improves as a result of the accumulation of social knowledge. He has used structural analysis to describe stages in the development of role-taking ability. These indicate qualitative changes in the person's understanding of the perspectives of self and of others.

Selman defines the structure of each role-taking stage with the answers to the following questions:

> How does the child differentiate the perspectives of self and other? How does the child coordinate or relate his perspective to that of another? In what way are the new differentiations and coordinations of

From *Moral Development and Behavior: Theory, Research, and Social Issues,* ed. Thomas Lickona (New York: Holt, Rinehart, and Winston, 1976), 299–316.

> a given state based upon, but more advanced than, those of the previous stage? (301)

He also defines the content of role-taking with which the child develops concepts about basic categories of social experience. He uses the answers to the following questions:

> What is the child's conception of the subjective aspects of self and other? What is his understanding of another's capabilities, personality attributes, expectations and desires, feelings and emotions, motives, potential reactions, and social judgments? (301)

Role-taking development plays a part in four areas of the child's life: general problem-solving, communication and persuasion, understanding feelings, and understanding concepts of fairness and justice.

The excerpt from Selman's writing that follows contains descriptions of the stages of role-taking, as well as the dilemma and probe questions used in the semiclinical interview format to determine the stage of development in the child.

Other research by Selman and by others seems to indicate that role-taking may be a form of social cognition intermediate between logical and moral thought. Moral judgment is a consideration of how people *should* act and social role-taking is a consideration of how they do *in fact* act and think. So role-taking may be necessary, but is insufficient by itself, for moral decision-making.

A table depicts parallels between social role-taking and moral judgment stages; the last half of the article deals with applications of theory to practice for the educator, the clinician, and the developmentalist. Special attention is given to social-cognitive structures as a link between social perception-taking and behavior.

The notion that the human capacity for judgment about morals proceeds according to a predictable series of universal stages is not new. As long ago as 1909 John Dewey pointed to the significance of such a concept. Yet even today few professionals directly concerned with social development, social adjustment, or social intervention in the lives of children view such cognitive-moral stages as applicable to the day-to-day business of the psychological handling of children's social and emotional behavior.

One example of this attitude can be found in the recent movement within schools toward affective education, aimed at children's development of humanistic values, altruism, sympathy, and increased social awareness. Many adherents of this movement feel that a moral judgment stage approach, concerned with rational issues such as justice and fairness, is too cold and calculating for use within a humanistic or affectively oriented context. Likewise, for the professionals wedded to the psychodynamic approach traditionally used in clinics for children with emotional or behavioral difficulties, the cognitive-developmental stage approach seems to disregard nonjudgmental or irrational factors such as fantasy, interpersonal dynamics, and unconscious drives in the explanation of interpersonal behavior.

My research has indicated, however, that descriptions of social-cognitive stages, within the context of a theory of ego development, can be usefully applied to both educational and clinical intervention. The base of these stages is sufficiently broad to be valuable in diagnosing children's behavior and in planning and evaluating efforts to improve children's social functioning.

Consider a short clinical vignette. An 8-year-old boy is referred to a guidance clinic or a school psychologist because he is continually getting into fights with his classmates. His teacher is particularly upset because she observes that when classmates accidentally bump him in the hall or during recess, he reacts by getting angry, fighting, and accusing his peers of starting the trouble. The teacher's concern extends beyond the child's development to the well-being of the entire class.

In such a case, different theoretical approaches to the understanding of development, particularly of human development, particularly to social behavior, would stress different steps in trying to understand this child. For example, a dynamically oriented viewpoint might first focus on the child's anger and aggression and try to analyze their source. Such an approach might assume that the child was projecting his own aggressive feelings and hostility onto his peers and then reacting in kind, or that he was displacing feelings really directed toward his father or some other important oedipal figure.

A cognitive-developmentalist, however, would take a different approach to understanding this child's behavior. He would try first to see things through the child's eyes. He might ask whether this troubled 8-year-old has differentiated cognitively between purposive and unintentional behavior. Most children understand by the age of 6 or 7 that other people usually have reasons underlying their actions, and that their actions can be partially explained or justified in terms of these reasons. At this stage, children can distinguish between willed, purposive activity (psychological causality) and strictly mechanical, overt behavior (physical causality). Before this stage of understanding, children often decide the rightness or wrongness of an act on the basis of its observable consequences rather than on the intentions of the actor. They are unable to differentiate one viewpoint from another, or even the reasons behind the actions of others from the actions themselves.

Determining the stage of cognitive or social development of a particular child leads the professional to understand how the child looks at the world, and to avoid expectations of conceptual and emotional abilities that the child has not yet developed. Far from disdaining the value of understanding the child's interpersonal dynamics, this approach enhances that understanding by exploring the stage underlying his behavior and by identifying the next stage toward which his development can be directed.

For the past several years I have used the Piagetian structuralist-developmental approach in focusing my research on the description of successive stages in the development of the ability to take the perspective of another (social role-taking), and on the relation of this ability to theoretically parallel stages in the development of moral thought. This chapter begins by devoting considerable space to defining a developmental sequence of role-taking ability (using reasoning about moral dilemmas as the context), in the hope of clarifying the logical structures that underlie important aspects of this large sphere of social development. It then speculates about how role-taking and moral judgment stages may fit within the context of a cognitive-developmental theory of ego development, and then goes on to discuss various implications of the cognitive-developmental approach for social intervention.

Social Role-Taking Stages and Their Relation to the Development of Moral Judgment

Some Theoretical Comments

Over the years role-taking has been studied from a variety of theoretical orientations. Research findings have indicated that role-taking ability and accuracy of social perception improve with age (Ausubel 1952; Feffer and Gourevitch 1960; Flavell 1968) and that development in this area continues into adolescence (Flavell 1968; Moore 1958; Taft 1955). Other research has correlated role-taking ability with psychometric measures of intelligence (DeVries 1970; Neale 1966; Selman 1971a, 1971b) and with emotional balance (Chandler 1971; Soloman 1963; Taft 1955).

These findings have shown that role-taking is clearly a developed capacity, but none of them has illustrated the qualitative nature of this development. In my research, I have used structural analysis to define developmental transformations (or stages) in order to describe the development of role-taking ability. Therefore, instead of viewing progression in role-taking simply as the result of a quantitative accumulation of social knowledge, I have viewed it in terms of qualitative changes in the child's structuring of his understanding of the relation between the perspectives of self and others.

In defining the *structural aspect* of a particular stage of role-taking the following questions are asked: How does the child differentiate the perspectives of self and other? How does the child coordinate or relate his perspective to that of another? In what way are the new differentiations and coordinations of a given stage based upon, but more advanced than, those of the previous stage? The answers to these questions define the structure of each successive role-taking stage.

My analysis of role taking also considers *content*, which is defined by the following: What is the child's conception of the subjective aspects of self and other? What is his understanding of another's capabilities, personality attributes, expectations and desires, feelings and emotions, motives, potential reactions, and social judgments? These categories of role-taking content are seen as developing concepts about basic categories of social experience. They are closely related to role-taking structure because their own form is partially defined for the child by his structural role-taking stage.

In other words, a child's development from a structural stage in which he can take only one point of view at a time to a stage in which he can see another's view as related to his own, is paralleled by a change in his conceptions of personality development, motivation, and other elements of social relations.

Role-taking development plays an important part in a wide range of human social behaviors. In our research we have studied the part it plays in four general areas of application: (1) children's general social problem-solving ability (e.g., ability to play cooperative or competitive games, such as hide-and-seek); (2) children's communicative and persuasive abilities; (3) children's understanding of the feelings of others (sympathy, empathy); and (4) children's understanding of fairness and justice, and the development of moral reasoning. This last aspect is the focus of this paper.

A Brief Description of Role-Taking Stages in the Context of Moral Reasoning

A structural analysis of stages attempts to look for the organization and order underlying thought or behavior, and to formalize the organization according to mathematical or logical models (Gardner 1973). The utility of such an analysis rests upon the ability of others to see the logic of the stage sequences, and thereby to recognize the order as described. Stages of social and moral judgment must justify their application to social intervention and education by being readily understandable to teachers, therapists, and educators. (If only stage theorists can see the stages in everyday life, useful application is a long way off.) Therefore, it seems appropriate to describe in detail each of the successive stages of role-taking as they play a part in reasoning about moral issues.

In studying the development of role-taking and in devising this analysis, I have followed the open-ended clinical method first used by Piaget (1929) in his study of children's understanding of physical concepts and later applied by Kohlberg (1969) to the study of moral thought. This method entails the use of dilemmas to engage the child in social or moral thought. Although the dilemmas are standardized, the ensuing discussion is open-ended (hence clinical). The following are some examples of sociomoral dilemmas and types of role-taking probe questions used in determining stage definition. The first two are taken from Kohlberg's original method (1969).

Heinz's dying wife needs a special drug. He has offered the druggist who discovered the drug half-payment now (all the money he has) and the rest at a later date. The druggist-inventor has refused. Heinz must decide whether or not to steal the drug.

Role-Taking Questions:

1. Would a good husband steal the drug for his wife?
2. What do you think the husband would do if he didn't love his wife?
3. What would his wife think if he did not steal it? What would she want him to do?
4. Would you steal the drug to save your own life?
5. What would you do if you were the husband?

The second dilemma is also from Kohlberg (1969):

Two young brothers are in serious trouble, and need money to leave town in a hurry. Karl, the older one, breaks into a store and steals 500 dollars. Bob, the younger one, goes to an old retired man who had been known to help others. Bob tells the man that he is very sick and needs $500 to pay for an operation. He wasn't really sick at all, and he has no intention of paying the man back. Although the man doesn't know Bob very well, he loans him the money. So Bob and Karl skip town, each with $500.

Role-Taking Questions:

1. Who would feel worse, the man who lent his money but didn't get it back, or the man whose store was robbed?
2. How would you feel in this situation if you lent some money and didn't get it back?
3. Why is trust so important to people?
4. What will the lender do when he finds out that he won't get his money back?

The next example of an open-ended sociomoral dilemma is for younger children (aged 4 to 10) and taps the lower stages of role taking:

Holly is an 8-year-old girl who likes to climb trees. She is the best tree climber in the neighborhood. One day while climbing down from a tall tree, she falls off the bottom branch but does not hurt herself. Her father sees her fall. He is upset and asks her to promise not to climb trees any more. Holly promises.

Later that day, Holly and her friends meet Shawn. Shawn's kitten is caught up in a tree and can't get down. Something has to be done right away, or the kitten may fall. Holly is the only one who climbs trees well enough to reach the kitten and get it down, but she remembers her promise to her father.

Role-Taking Questions:

1. Does Holly know how Shawn feels about the kitten?
2. How will Holly's father feel if he finds out she climbed the tree?
3. What does Holly think her father will do if he finds out that she climbed the tree?
4. What would you do in this situation?

Role-taking stages within moral reasoning are scored on the basis of the subject's responses to both standardized and open-ended probe questions which focus on three structural aspects of role taking: (1) the subject's own point of view, (2) the different viewpoints of each character in the dilemma, and (3) the relationships among these various perspectives. In addition, an analysis is made of the subject's conception of persons and of the social nature of human behavior, particularly his conception of the motives and feelings of others as this applies to his ethical judgments.

Stage 0: Egocentric Role-Taking (About Ages 4 to 6)[1]

Structural Aspects

Distinguishing perspectives. Stage 0 is characterized by the child's inability to make a distinction between a personal interpretation of social action (either by self or other) and what he considers the true or correct perspective. Therefore, although the child can differentiate self and other as entities, he does not differentiate their points of view.

Relating perspectives. Just as the child does not differentiate points of view, he does not relate perspectives. He is very likely to give his mother a bag of jelly beans for her birthday, not necessarily because he likes jelly beans or because he thinks that she will like jelly beans, but because "jelly beans are liked." At this egocentric level the child does not reflect upon thoughts of self or other. For example:

Q *What do you think Holly will do, save the kitten or keep her promise?*
A She will save the kitten because she doesn't want the kitten to die.

1. Age ranges for all stages represent only an average approximation based on our studies to date.

Q *How will her father feel when he finds out?*
A Happy, he likes kittens.
Q *What would you do if you were Holly?*
A Save the kitten so it won't get hurt.
Q *What if Holly doesn't like kittens? What will she do?*
A She won't get it.
Q *What if her father punishes her if she gets the kitten down?*
A Then she will leave it up there.
Q *Why?*
A Because she doesn't want to get in trouble.
Q *How will she feel?*
A Good, she listened to her father.

Analysis. A child at Stage 0 is unable to conceptualize differences between one character's perspective (Holly's) of the situation and that of another (Holly's father). The child focuses on the act of rescuing the kitten, and thinks all the participants do likewise. If the interviewer refocuses the child's attention on the punitive consequences of breaking the promise to the father, the child orients to the father's viewpoint, still maintaining a consensus among characters and showing no awareness of inconsistency.

Conception of Persons

At Stage 0 the child is able to "predict" or read off another's emotions (such as sad, mad, happy) in those situations where the child knows his own response. He bases his judgments of others on observable action, not covert psychological data. He lacks the social-cognitive ability to get under the skin of another person and to see the cause-effect relation between someone's reasons and their actions. For example:

Q *Would you climb the tree to get the kitten down?*
A Yes, it might get hurt.
Q *How will Holly feel if her father punishes her for climbing the tree?*
A Sad.
Q *Why?*
A Because her father hit her.
Q *How do you know she will feel sad?*
A She'll cry.
Q *Why did her father hit her?*
A Because she climbed the tree.
Q *Did Holly have a good reason for climbing the tree?*
A I don't know.
Q *Would you climb the tree?*
A No, I don't want to get hit.

Analysis. At no point does the child at Stage 0 refer to a possible explanation of action on a covert psychological level, for example, at the level of intentions (which emerges at the next stage). The psychological state of sadness is simply "read off" from the overt behavior of crying.

Stage 1: Social-Informational Role-Taking (About Ages 6 to 8)

Structural Aspects

Distinguishing perspectives. At Stage 1 the child sees himself and the other as actors with potentially different interpretations of the same social situation, largely determined by the data each has at hand. He realizes that people feel differently or think differently because they are in different situations or have different information.

Relating perspectives. The child is still unable to maintain his own perspective and simultaneously put himself in the place of others in attempting to judge their actions. Nor can he judge his own actions from their viewpoint. He has yet to see reciprocity between perspectives, to consider that his view of the other is influenced by his understanding of the other's view of him (Stage 2). He understands the subjectivity of persons, but does not understand that persons consider each other as subjects. As he makes moral applications at Stage 1, the child still assumes that only one perspective is "right" or "true"—the authority's or his own—even though he recognizes the existence of different viewpoints. For example:

Q *Who would feel worse, someone who lent money and was not going to get it back, or a storeowner who was robbed of the same amount?*

A The storeowner who was robbed. Because the storeowner knows somebody stole it, but the man who loaned the $500 doesn't know for sure that he won't get it back.

Analysis. The child reasons from the social fact that the storeowner knows immediately that he has been robbed to the "objective" conclusion that the storeowner will "subjectively" feel bad, but that the lender will not feel as bad because he does not realize that he will lose his money. At stages of role taking higher than Stage 1, the focus will be less on who knows what and more on the relative points of view of the storeowner viewing an impersonal robbery as compared to the old man viewing a broken trust.

Conception of Persons

Whereas at Stage 0 the child considers other persons as information collectors, that is, perceivers of social data, at Stage 1 the child sees other persons as information processors, that is, interpreters of social situations. The child now understands that to be a person means to have evaluative abilities. He consequently realizes that both himself and another, as persons, can make distinctions between intentional and unintentional actions. This understanding of intentionality is a marked change from Stage 0, and it leads to the understanding of the concept of personal reasons as cause for choices or actions. For example:

Q *Do you think Holly's father would get angry if he found out she climbed the tree?*
A If he didn't know why she climbed the tree, he would be angry. But if Holly tells him why she did it, he would realize she has a good reason.[2]

Stage 2: Self-Reflective Role-Taking (About Ages 8 to 10)

Structural Aspects

Distinguishing perspectives. At Stage 2 the child is aware that people think or feel differently, because each person has his own uniquely ordered set of values or purposes. In moral terms this role-taking development leads to a relativistic belief that no person's perspective is absolutely right or valid.

Relating perspectives. A major development at Stage 2 is the ability to reflect on the self's behavior and motivation as seen from outside the self, from the other's point of view. The child recognizes that the other can also put himself in the child's shoes, so the child is able to anticipate the other's reactions to his own motives or purposes. However, these reflections do not occur simultaneously or mutually. They occur only sequentially. Thus the child cannot "get outside" the two-person situation and view it from a third-person perspective. For example:

Q *What punishment does Holly think is fair if she climbs the tree?*
A None.
Q *Why not?*
A She knows that her father will understand why she climbed the tree, so she knows that he won't want to punish her at all.

2. Excerpting sentences from the open-ended interviews in order to provide examples of role-taking stages is always dangerous. It is, in a way, antithetical to the nature of a structural analysis, which searches for the organization of thought underlying a wide range of the child's ideas, not an isolated instance. Because higher stages incorporate lower ones, it is more likely that scoring errors will be made in the direction of scoring a child's thinking too low rather than too high. Therefore in this particular example, the statement is indicative of thinking that is at least Stage 1. Only through the examination of the entire protocol can one be sure that higher-stage role-taking is not present.

Analysis. The subject takes the perspective of the daughter who realizes that the father will in turn understand the daughter's reasoning (motives). At Stage 2 therefore the subject realizes that his taking of another's point of view is directly influenced by his own assumption of how another will take his perspective.

Conception of Persons

At Stage 2 the child understands that the motives of one individual can be in conflict or can be ordered by the individual in a relativistic hierarchy. Because the child begins to think of others as multimotivated rather than unmotivated, he begins to see that altruistic (other-oriented) and instrumental (self-interested) motives may conflict in his mind and another's. The child can now conceive of persons doing things they may not want to do, and vice versa. For example:

Q *Do you think Holly would climb the tree?*
A Yes. She knows her father will understand why she did it.
Q *What do you think Holly's father would want Holly to do? In this situation would he want her to go up and get the kitten or not?*
A No.
Q *Why not?*
A Because he would be changing his order, and he wouldn't be a good father if he changed his mind. The father may think breaking a promise is worse, but he'd understand that Holly thinks saving the kitten's life is more important.
Q *Would all fathers think this way?*
A No, it depends on what they think is more important.

Stage 3: Mutual Role-Taking (About Ages 10 to 12)

Structural Aspects

Distinguishing perspectives. At Stage 3 the child can differentiate the self's perspective from the generalized perspective, that is, the point of view taken by an average member of a group. In a dyadic situation the child distinguishes each party's point of view from that of a third person. He can be an impartial spectator and maintain a disinterested point of view.

Relating perspectives. The child at Stage 3 discovers that both self and other can consider each party's point of view simultaneously and mutually. Each can put himself in the other's place and view himself from that vantage before deciding how to react (the Golden Rule). In addition, each can consider a situation from the perspective of a third party who can also assume each individual's points of view and consider the relationships involved. Such an endless chain of role-taking leads in the moral domain to the development of conventional rules for deciding between the claims of individuals. For example:

Q *Would the judge think Heinz was right to steal the drug?*
A I think the judge would have thought that it wasn't right for Heinz to steal, but now that he had done it and the judge had heard his side of the story, the judge would feel that Heinz was doing what he thought was right. Heinz realizes that the judge will consider how he felt.

Analysis. Two aspects of this example indicate Stage 3 reasoning. First, the subject attributes to each party the ability to consider each other's point of view. Second, he understands that the judge is aware of Heinz's self-reflection ("the judge would feel that Heinz was doing what he thought was right"). This awareness that each of the participants in a dyad is mindful of the self-reflective process in the other characterizes Stage 3 role taking.

Conception of Persons

A child at Stage 3 knows that all persons have a conception of the shared nature of social facts and interpersonal relationships. Trust, friendship, and mutual respect and expectations are viewed as dyadic or mutual. At Stage 2, the concept of friend is defined from only one perspective: A friend is someone who does the self a favor and acts kindly from the self's perspective. At Stage 3, the concept of friend is defined in interpersonal or mutual terms, which go beyond simple reciprocity. A temporal component also emerges as the child begins to perceive consistency of actions by each member of the relationship over time as necessary to the definition of mutual relations. For example:

Q *Suppose it wasn't Heinz's wife who was dying of cancer, but it was Heinz's best friend; his friend didn't have any money and there was no one in his family who wanted to steal the drug; do you think Heinz would steal the drug for his friend in that case?*
A He'd really have to be the top friend to do it. Because I mean, you put yourself in your friend's place and you think, "Would he do it for me?" I guess it would depend on what kind of friends they have been. If they each have proven their friendship to each other, then maybe he would do it. It all depends on how strong a relationship it is, how long they've been friends.

Analysis. At Stage 3 the child is aware that social relations have a certain depth, consistency, and temporal dimension. Friendship is not viewed as an immediate process of reciprocal back scratching, but as the product of a series of interchanges over time that validate mutuality. The child also realizes that certain actions may have different meanings for different persons, based on each one's previous social experiences. Understanding of a person's subjectivity is much more complex than, for example, the Stage 1 realization of different perspectives based simply on different social information. Thus mutuality at Stage 3 is evidenced in both structure (a simultaneous coordination of perspectives) and concept of the person (the understanding that both self and other hold mutual expectations).

Stage 4: Social and Conventional System Role-Taking (About Ages 12 to 15+)

Structural Aspects

Perspective taking. At Stage 4 perspective taking is raised from the level of the dyad to the level of a general social system involving a group or social perspective. The adolescent at Stage 4 views the social system within which he operates as a construction of conventional perspectives which all members share in mutual relationship with his own. At Stage 3 the subject considers the activity of the impartial observer as taking the perspective of both the self and the other; at Stage 4 the subject realizes that each self considers the shared point of view of the *generalized other* (the social system) in order to facilitate accurate communication with and understanding of others. For example:

Q *What do you think the judge would do in Heinz's case?*
A I'm afraid he'd have to convict him. When Heinz stole the drug, he knew it was wrong from society's point of view. He also knew that if he were caught, he'd be convicted because he'd realize the judge would have to uphold the law.
Q *Why?*
A The judge has to think about the way it would look to everybody else. If they see Heinz getting no punishment, they might think they can get away with stealing. Heinz should realize this and take some form of punishment.
Q *Would the judge think Heinz was right or wrong to do what he did?*
A The judge is not supposed to be a philosopher. Even if the judge thought Heinz was morally right, from the legal point of view, the judge has to consider the law of the people.

Analysis. Conceptions such as law and morality are based upon the idea of a consensual group perspective. The mutuality which first developed at Stage 3 is expanded at Stage 4 to subordinate the dyadic relation to the group perspective.

Conception of Persons

At Stage 4 the relationship between judgment and action within each individual's social decision-making process is now viewed as a complex intrapersonal system analogous in nature to an interpersonal social system. The developing conception of personality (or character) reflects the subject's understanding that the other's thoughts and actions are a function of an intrapsychic organization of developing beliefs, values, and attitudes, and that this allows the prediction of the other's future actions and the understanding of his past actions. People may have different perspectives on internal values as well as on external social actions. For example:

Q *Who would feel worse, the storeowner who was robbed or the man who was cheated out of a loan?*

A Well that's really hard to say. You would have to know what each guy is really like. Like maybe the guy who lent the money was the kind of guy who realized that he might not get it back. He might not expect thanks or stuff like that. Then he might not be upset at all, or just a little sad because he realizes that people may not be honest. On the other hand, if he is the kind of guy who expects a lot from people, he may really be hurt, or it may break his faith in human nature. In general I'd say the guy who lent the money would feel a broken personal trust. You'd have to know the guys to be sure.

Recent studies [see Kuhn et al. 1977] indicate a general correspondence between moral stages and Piagetian stages of cognitive development. The Piaget cognitive stages appear to be necessary but not sufficient conditions for the parallel moral stages. The same necessary-but-not-sufficient relation seems to exist between role-taking stages and moral stages (Selman 1971a, 1972). Conceptually, role-taking can be described as a form of social cognition intermediate between logical and moral thought.

According to this outlook the child's cognitive stage indicates his level of understanding of physical and logical problems, while his role-taking stage indicates his level of understanding of the nature of social relations, and his moral judgment stage indicates the manner in which he decides how to resolve social conflicts between people with different points of view. Moral judgment considers how people *should* think and act with regard to each other, while social role taking considers how and why people do *in fact* think about and act toward each other. The stage at which the moral claims of self and others are considered builds on the structurally parallel role-taking stage of understanding the relationship between the perspectives of self and others. If the subject has not reached a given stage of role taking, he cannot apply this stage of social cognition to the moral domain. Table 4.1 presents the parallel stage sequences for role taking and moral judgment.

My own empirical evidence, as well as that of others (Giraldo 1972; Hickey 1972; Kuhn 1972; Moir 1971; Thrower 1972), supports this analysis of the relationship between role-taking and moral judgment. For example, these stud-

Table 4.1 Parallel Structured Relations between Social Role-Taking and Moral Judgment Stages

Social Role-Taking Stage	***Moral Judgment Stage***
Stage 0—Egocentric Viewpoint (Age Range 3–6)[a]	Stage 0—Premoral Stage
Child has a sense of differentiation of self and other but fails to distinguish between the social perspective (thoughts, feelings) of other and self. Child can label other's overt feelings but does not see the cause and effect relation of reasons to social actions.	Judgments of right and wrong are based on good or bad consequences and not on intentions. Moral choices derive from the subject's wishes that good things happen to self. Child's reasons for his choices simply assert the choices, rather than attempting to justify them.
Stage 1—Social-Informational Role Taking (Age Range 6–8)	Stage 1—Punishment and Obedience Orientation
Child is aware that other has a social perspective based on other's own reasoning, which may or may not be similar to child's. However, child tends to focus on one perspective rather than coordinating viewpoints.	Child focuses on one perspective, that of the authority or the powerful. However, child understands that good actions are based on good intentions. Beginning sense of fairness as equality of acts.
Stage 2—Self-Reflective Role Taking (Age Range 8–10)	Stage 2—Instrumental Orientation
Child is conscious that each individual is aware of the other's perspective and that this awareness influences self and other's view of each other. Putting self in other's place is a way of judging his intentions, purposes, and actions. Child can form a coordinated chain of perspectives, but cannot yet abstract from this process to the level of simultaneous mutuality.	Moral reciprocity is conceived as the equal exchange of the intent of two persons in relation to one another. If someone has a mear intention toward self, it is right for self to act in kind. Right defined as what is valued by self.
Stage 3—Mutual Role Taking (Age Range 10–12)	Stage 3—Orientation to Maintaining Mutual Expectations
Child realizes that both self and other can view each other mutually and simultaneously as subjects. Child can step outside the two-person dyad and view the interaction from a third-person perspective.	Right is defined as the Golden Rule: Do unto others as you would have others do unto you. Child considers all points of view and reflects on each person's motives in an effort to reach agreement among all participants.
Stage 4—Social and Conventional System Role-Taking[b] (Age Range 12–15+)	Stage 4—Orientation to Society's Perspective
Person realizes mutual perspective taking does not always lead to complete understanding. Social conventions are seen as necessary because they are understood by all members of the group (the generalized other) regardless of their position, role, or experience.	Right is defined in terms of the perspective of the generalized other or the majority. Person considers consequences of actions for the group or society. Orientation to maintenance of social morality and social order.

[a] Age ranges for all stages represent only an average approximation based on our studies to date.

[b] Higher stages of role taking and their relation to Kohlberg's Stages 5 and 6 have been defined by Byrne (1975).

ies, using a variety of role-taking measures, found subjects whose role-taking reasoning exceeded their structurally parallel moral judgments. The reverse, significantly, was not true. These measures have shown that in normal populations, role-taking stage generally paralleled moral stage or exceeded it by only one stage. In a study of young adult delinquents, however, the role-taking of many subjects was far superior (by two or more stages) to their moral thinking. These subjects had a relatively mature conception of the way the social world operated, but a retarded sense of what it should be like (Hickey 1972).

In a study (Thrower 1972) of institutionalized orphanage children ranging in age from 10 to 18, both moral and role-taking stages were depressed well below levels achieved by normal control groups. Just as in the study of delinquents, each role-taking stage was found to be a necessary but not sufficient condition for the corresponding moral stage.

Theory to Practice: Applications of Social-Cognitive Analyses to Intervention

Because Piagetian developmental theory has been thought by many to apply only to cognitive development, its potential application to clinical and social education areas has not been realized. The chapter turns now to this question: How can universal stages of social development (role-taking and moral judgment) serve professionals such as educators and clinical psychologists directly concerned with enhancing social and cognitive development in children?

From a cognitive-developmental perspective, both education and psychotherapy seek the optimal rate of development of children through social-cognitive and cognitive stages. This developmental stage perspective becomes an invaluable and unique tool, a common concept that can coordinate the different outlooks and terminologies of the clinician, educator, and developmentalist.

Implications for Social and Affective Education

The most common criticism of the cognitive-developmental approach is that the individual's social or moral judgments do not necessarily determine his actual behavior. Critics frequently charge cognitive-developmental psychology with a failure to consider the role of a person's affective or "gut" reactions in shaping his social conduct. Would he really do what he says he ought to do or will do? Might he not be too frightened, too self-interested, too concerned about his family? Where do feelings fit in?

While the adequacy of the cognitive-developmental approach to deal with these questions could be debated on theoretical grounds, the answer to the criticism is in part empirical. A number of recent studies of a variety of different populations at various ages has shown that the cognitive-developmental approach in moral discussion groups stimulates movement to higher moral stages (Blatt and Kohlberg 1975; Colby, Fritz, and Kohlberg 1974; Hickey

1972). How this movement relates to behavior and to feelings about the self has also been explored (see Kohlberg and Selman 1972; Scharf, Hickey, and Kohlberg 1973). A summary of these studies indicates that although the correspondence of judgment and action is never simple, better judgment *may* lead to more consistent social behavior and more realistic feelings about the self.

My own experience with intervention (Selman and Lieberman 1975) has been with children going through what is often called latency (roughly ages 6 to 12). Whereas late adolescence can be seen as a critical period for the development of principled moral thought (Kohlberg's Stages 5 and 6), the ages of 8 or 9 to 12 can be seen as an important period for the development of general social thought and interpersonal experience. Therefore my goals have been different from those of previous efforts with adolescents (Blatt and Kohlberg 1975), although upward movement through social-cognitive stages remains a common criterion for all intervention.

Both adolescents and adults may frequently choose not to take another's perspective, but the younger child often lacks the ability to do so. Because of the conviction that moral thought rests on the ability to take another's perspective, our intervention programs for preadolescents have focused on helping children to understand the social reasoning of others and to relate others' social points of view to their own. To this end, we have developed a filmstrip series of moral value dilemmas—dealing with issues such as rules, trust, property rights, and fairness—to help children aged 6 to 12 move through the lower stages of social-cognitive development (to Stage 3).[3] The dilemmas are used by the teacher to stimulate discussion of values in a variety of formats ranging from small "buzz groups" to structured classroom debate.

The emphasis of this filmstrip series is primarily on social cognition—getting children to understand more and reason better about the mutual aspects of social relationships. Educating children to understand and evaluate the reasoning of others in relation to their own depends on a great deal of role-taking; in this sense, our program is very cognitively oriented. Nevertheless, children's feelings become inescapable issues when they begin to think about their own reactions and relationships to others. What would they do, for example, if they had to decide whether to rescue a kitten or keep a promise not to climb trees? The actual social and moral conflicts of the classroom, as the second- and third-grade teachers who have worked with the filmstrip program came to realize, prove to be most natural material for stimulating both affective and cognitive involvement in moral issues. In fact, our valuation of this approach (Selman and Lieberman 1975) indicates that social educational gains were greatest in classrooms where teachers maintained the cognitive-developmental methods defined in our program, even after the actual program had ended.

Recognizing the social-cognitive stages of each child helps the teacher in

3. The filmstrips, entitled *First Things: Social Reasoning* (1974) and *First Things: Values* (1971), are published by Guidance Associates, New York.

several ways. First, she can better understand the behavior of her class by understanding how her children view social relationships, rights, and obligations. This kind of diagnosis also helps the teacher to determine her own expectations for her students' developmental goals. Most of all, it helps the teacher not to overestimate the affective as well as cognitive capacity of children. For example, before attaining Stage 3 role-taking and moral judgment, children do not have adequate understanding of such central interpersonal concepts as trust, love, friendship, and their concomitant affective attitudes. They achieve this affective awareness only as they achieve the parallel social-cognitive stage awareness. This does not mean that children cannot act in a trusting or loving way before they reach certain social-cognitive stages. It does imply, however, that children must reach these stages before they can reflect upon and truly understand the meaning and reason for their actions in a mature sense.

The basic integration of cognition and affect is perhaps best summarized by Hirst and Peters (1970):

> In most of the standard works on child development, studies are classified under the heading of physical, intellectual, social, and emotional development; but what distinguishes, say, emotional development from social development? And how is intellectual development to be distinguished from either of them? . . . Emotions such as jealousy, guilt, pity, and envy cannot be characterized without reference to moral and social concepts such as rules, ownership, and rights. . . . The tendency to disregard the importance of cognition in this area has led to the neglect of the specific features of interpersonal understanding as a mode of experience which is of manifest importance in the recognition of emotions and motives in oneself and others. . . . The result is that the development of stages in interpersonal understanding remains uncharted in any precise way; so also does the development of emotions and motives (49–50).

It is my belief that the integrated conception of role-taking and moral judgment stages constitutes a first step in the development of what Hirst and Peters call "stages of interpersonal understanding," and that role-taking links cognitive to both emotional and moral functioning. To take the perspective of others is to begin to understand their feelings and emotions as well as their motives and reasons.

This approach can be just as useful for understanding the social development of inadequately functioning children in the clinic as for educating normal children in the classroom.

Cognitive-Developmental Applications to Clinical Diagnosis

Child clinicians do not usually conceptualize children's social-emotional deficits in terms of retarded moral thinking, or define role-taking gains as the aim of therapeutic intervention. Most clinicians would, however, accept "ego development" as a valid therapeutic goal. Indeed, clinical, educational, and developmental psychologists generally agree that ego development as a concept provides a fundamental definition of the person, his core beliefs about himself, and his relation to the social and physical world.

From the cognitive-developmental point of view, ego-development research looks for structural levels in the growth of the child's understanding of the following basic categories of knowledge:

1. *The physical domain:* Conceptions of physical objects and of the relation of the self to these objects (for example, the relation of the self to time, space, and movement of objects).
2. *The logical domain:* Conceptions of classes and subclasses, relations, and the ordering of relations between classes.
3. *The social domain:* Conceptions of the self, the relation of self to others (role-taking), and the means for resolving conflicts of different selves (moral reasoning).

Picture a rectangular ego-development grid. Across the horizontal axis of the grid is an array of content categories (1, 2, 3) to be understood and acted upon by the child. On the vertical axis is a developmental sequence of stages for each of the content areas. Theoretically, at each stage a common structural unity runs across the different content areas.

A clinical analysis of horizontal aspects of development can be of value at two levels. At the superordinate level, a child's stage of functioning can be compared *across* the basic horizontal dimensions of ego development, for example, the logical, the social (role-taking), and the moral. In my own research, investigation is under way to see whether a wide discrepancy between a child's moral judgment and role-taking stage (instances where the role-taking stage exceeds the moral judgment stage by two or more levels) indicates behavioral problems (e.g., boredom in school, fighting, and other antisocial behavior) as well as structural signs of disequilibrium. Similar analyses are possible comparing cognitive and social-cognitive stage development.

At the subordinate level, a scatter analysis can be made of subissues within a given category. At this level the interplay of content and structure is most visible. In my research on role taking (Selman 1976), for example, I have divided role-taking content into various concepts and defined stage development for each of them. My concepts revolve around the two basic categories of social experience defined and elaborated by George Herbert Mead in his book *Mind, Self, and Society* (1934): (1) conceptions of the nature of the *self* (conceptions of personality, motives, and self-reflection) and (2) conceptions of the nature of *society* (conceptions of roles and relations, the nature of "social reality"). A stage-developmental analysis across concepts can yield a specific clinical profile that shows the areas in which the child is lagging and those in which he is functioning at an age-typical stage. Even more important, such an analysis can indicate areas of difficulty in the child's social and emotional functioning; these findings will complement the information gained from other clinical tools which do not focus on children's social and physical concepts.

Two Case Studies: A Window on the World of the Child

For the past several years I have been attempting to prove to my own satisfaction the actual substance of cognitive-developmental stages. Do they really exist in the minds of children as well as in the minds of cognitive-developmentalists? Can the same consistent patterns of thought be identified in children's day-to-day activities as well as in their verbal responses to the standardized questionnaires of research?

Because my interest has been the application of developmental approaches by teachers and clinicians who must deal directly with children, I decided on the case-study approach of using dialogue with children as a medium for "real-life" stage analysis. Working with children with a variety of social and emotional problems at the Judge Baker Child Guidance Center in Boston, I sought to understand the functioning of the child from a cognitive-developmental as well as from a psychodynamic viewpoint.

Undertaking to substantiate a pet theory by the clinical approach proves a humbling experience. A child, in all his complexity, has a way of overwhelming the clinician with data—so much so that theory appears to have less and less to do with the total "variance of behavior" of the child. A child's developmental stage of reasoning often seems of little use in explaining all the causes of deviant behavior (and probably "normal" behavior as well). Nevertheless, my clinical experience leads me to believe that describing the child's developmental stage does provide one kind of understanding of the child. Developmental stages also provide criteria for the evaluation of a therapeutic or interventive effort by observing whether or not there has been movement to a higher stage (Kohlberg and Mayer 1972).

As an illustration of clinical stage analysis, let us consider the case histories of two children whose behavior can in part be better understood by the application of social-cognitive stages. These are children whom I saw over several weeks in diagnostic work at the Judge Baker clinic.

Case 1: Tommy B. Tommy B. was an extremely hyperactive and aggressive 8-year-old boy with a chaotic family background. He was unable to function in a traditional public school. Since he seemed able to learn in one-to-one tutoring and treatment, he was placed in a special class with four or five other children his age. Although he was able to do well academically in this special class, he exhibited patterns of social behavior with his teacher and with his therapists that were indicative of social-cognitive arrest.

During our diagnostic sessions, Tommy would come into my office and insist that I buy him a present or give him one of the toys in the office. When I refused or was unable to meet his request, he became furious. First, he would attempt to gain his objective by saying that he wouldn't be my friend. When I asked him in various ways to define what he meant by "friend," or how else I could be his friend, he was unable to consider anything but the immediate situation.

If I complied with Tommy's wishes, his anger would quickly dissipate, and for some time he would play with his toy. But as soon as another request was refused, he would insist once again that I hated him, and that he wouldn't be my friend. No continuity of relationship seemed possible; Tommy's social relations seemed, rather, a series of individual encounters, each with its own social meaning. When I asked him questions or tried in other ways to ascertain his conception of what our or any relationship meant, he would always refer to some concrete desired object and say that he would not be my friend if I didn't give it to him. When I asked him if he ever thought about what I might want him to do for me in order to be his friend (reciprocal role-taking), he showed no comprehension of the question. When I tried to help him understand his own reasons for his actions, I could elicit no signs of improved understanding.

Similarly, if the teacher in Tommy's special class did not pay extra attention to him, he would sulk and claim she hated him. When he discovered her home phone number, he began to call her up at 6:00 A.M. on weekdays and Sundays in a pathetic effort to gain more individual attention. When the teacher could no longer meet or comply with this aspect of Tommy's behavior and tried to explain to him that such calls were annoying to her, Tommy, furious and unable to see her side, claimed she hated him.

Clearly, the boy felt strong affective deprivation and, from a dynamic view, was behaving much like a narcissistic infant. However, in addition to suffering powerful affective needs and tragic desperation, Tommy lagged at Stage 0 social logic from a cognitive-developmental point of view at an age when most children are in transition between Stages 1 and 2 in both role-taking and moral judgments. In the moral domain, Tommy's justification for the judgment, "I should get X." was "Because I want it." In other words, Tommy showed no conception of reasons as justifications or causes of actions or desires. Good was what he wanted; bad was what he did not want (moral Stage 0).

In the role-taking domain Tommy had one perspective: not his or another's perspective, but *the* perspective. His accusation that teacher and therapist hated him could be understood in terms of his inability to see our social perspectives, to view the situation as we might view it, for example, to consider the teacher's perspective on receiving early morning phone calls. Not to meet his needs was, according to his precausal logic, to hate him. In this sense, Tommy's social-cognitive development was at least temporarily arrested at Stage 0. Interestingly, his cognitive (conceptions of physical and logical) development, as assessed by Piagetian cognitive measures, had progressed to a transitional, operational stage beyond the precausal level. This cognitive assessment also contained evidence of slight developmental retardation, but was taken diagnostically as evidence that Tommy had the capacity for social-cognitive development.

As Tommy's social world became more chaotic, meaningful interaction with others was becoming more difficult—a difficulty that might be expected to affect all spheres of his ego development, including the cognitive. As he isolated himself, he began to maintain his own primitive system of logic, unchecked or unchallenged by the thoughts of others (peer or parental).

Even though Tommy wanted to relate to the other children in the class, he literally did not know how (basically, because for him friendship meant simply that other children would do things for him or be nice to him). When the other children asked for some basic evidence of interpersonal reciprocity—for example, that he share class material equally with others (Stage 1 moral judgment)—he did not comprehend, so he could not comply. Reciprocity to him meant action for the self (Stage 0 role-taking); it had no meaning in terms of understanding others' subjective needs as separate and different from his own.

Tommy was functioning at a level most children pass through at ages 4 and five. Through close contact with this child—watching him play, watching him interact with others, listening to his requests, and focusing on how he justified his actions—it was possible to see the nature of his stage of social and logical thought, and to understand something of the logic behind his behavior. Therapeutic treatment with Tommy could in turn be evaluated in terms of his progress to higher moral and role-taking stages.

Given that his cognitive level exceeded his social level, it seemed as though Tommy could make social-cognitive gains in a milieu in which he could be helped to comprehend social situations, their implicit rules, and the expectations of others. He was enrolled over the summer in a therapeutic camp at which the counselors' strategy with Tommy was to continually emphasize the reasons behind their social actions and to make as clear as possible for him the structure of the social interaction at the camp. The reasons behind the nature and rules of social games were carefully explained to him, as were the motives of counselors and other campers.

Apparently the strategy was successful. At the beginning of camp, sociometric peer ratings showed Tommy to be one of the least liked children. By the end of the eighth week, he not only had improved his conception of friendship but also had managed to win the friendship of many of the children in his cabin. A reanalysis of his social thinking indicated that he had developed a functioning conception of social and moral intentionality from Stage 0 to Stage 1.

Our structural-developmental analysis does not "explain" Tommy's behavior, but it helps to define his behavior so that a therapeutic plan of action can be chosen. It also provides a guideline for eventual evaluation of the treatment program.

Case 2: Marty S. Marty S. was an adolescent of 14 years who was brought to the clinic by his mother because she felt he was isolated and friendless. The previous year he had developed a school phobia, which caused him to miss half the year, to repeat a grade, and to have almost no peer relations. Marty's phobia seemed to be related to a very low sense of self-esteem and a related fear of the natural social environment, including peers and teachers. We asked Marty to respond to the standard Kohlberg dilemma about Heinz, the man whose wife was dying of cancer. His answers follow:

Q *Should Heinz steal the drug to save his wife's life?*
A If he loves her, he should. If he doesn't love her, he won't. He doesn't want to get in trouble and end up in jail.
Q *Why is loving her important?*
A Because, if he needs her he should steal it. If he doesn't, why take the chance?
Q *Should Heinz steal the drug if he were dying? Should he steal it to save his own life?*
A No.
Q *Why not?*
A I wouldn't . . . I wouldn't steal it to save myself.
Q *Why not?*
A I'm not worth that much. I'd be all sick and wouldn't want to be alive.
Q *What do you mean, you're not worth that much?*
A Well, I'm not important, I don't have a lot of money, for example.
Q *Would you steal it to save a pet?*
A Sure, a pet wants to live as much as the wife. A pet is a friend so I would steal it for the pet.
Q *What about for a friend?*
A I don't have any friends.

At a later point in treatment, Marty expounded his ideas on the death penalty for convicted murderers.

A I don't see why they have life imprisonment. They should just kill them. If I were sent up for life, I wouldn't want to live. Besides the government would save lots of money. Life imprisonment is a dumb law.

Q *What about from the prisoner's point of view? How would they like that law?*
A They don't want to spend their whole life in jail. They probably would want to die.

Although most 14-year-olds have developed to Stage 3 or 4 in their role-taking ability and to Stage 3 in moral judgment, Marty appeared to be functioning at Stages 1 and 2 in both areas. Although he was aware that others may have a different viewpoint, his attempt to take the inmate's perspective regarding life imprisonment was not clearly separated from and then related to his own; hence it was characteristic of Stage 1. Marty gave no evidence that he could consider the reciprocity of perspective involved in understanding that some prisoners might prefer life imprisonment even if he didn't, nor did he seem able to weigh the perspectives of self and other (Stage 2).

His moral judgment appeared to be a mixture of Stages 1 and 2. He had a very instrumental orientation (Stage 2) concerning what Heinz's attitude toward his wife should be. More significant from a clinical point of view, however, his conception of the value of his own life appeared to be at Stage 1: an equation of moral with material worth ("I'm not important, I don't have a lot of money"). This Stage 1 materialistic conception of the value of his own life corresponds to and helps us understand the cognitive basis for Marty's extremely low level of self-esteem and self-worth. The implication here is not that cognition is cause and feelings are effect, but that cognition and feelings about the self and about others are inseparable.

Differences between the level of Marty's view of the social world and the level of his conceptions of the physical world proved particularly interesting. He had good scientific ability. On physics tests similar to those used by Piaget and Inhelder (1958) to test for cognitive operations, Marty showed the ability to think at least at a low level of formal operations (Piaget's highest stage). However, his social isolation was so complete that he apparently had little opportunity to test his own social-cognitive theories against those of his peers and thus performed at a concrete operational level in the social area.

Marty's inadequate social development was clear in the content as well as the structure of his thought. He believed that the Army was watched over by the President, and that if he, Marty, were to enlist and the Army did not uphold its contracts with him, the President would sue the Army for him. Such a simplistic conception of the social system is not uncommon in children half Marty's age, and is another indication of his social-cognitive retardation.

Marty's judgmental stage scores across all moral issues were not uniformly low. He held some Stage 3 conceptions on issues of family relations. However, his Stage 1 conception of the value of (his own) life was an accurate structural reflection of the content area of his personality, which was quite fragile and immature.

Our point in presenting these cases is not to claim that cognitive and social-cognitive developmental measures should replace other clinical tools or conceptions, but that the cognitive-developmental approach has a place in the diagnosis and treatment of children.

Conclusion

One way cognitive-developmental theory may be of use in enriching the clinical understanding of social and emotional development of individuals or in providing guidelines for social or moral intervention, is to take the direction of what Loevinger (1973) has called a *strand theory of ego development.* This theoretical approach construes ego development as consisting of various conceptual domains, each with its own set of interrelated stages, together defining an ego-development grid as discussed earlier. The notion of different concept domains does not imply that ego development occurs without some unifying, binding force. A host of studies has shown that various stage measures of ego, moral, and social development are highly correlative in both a conceptual and empirical sense.

The application of cognitive-developmental theory to social issues also requires the clarification of the relation of judgment to action. A structural-developmental approach does not predict specific actions, but describes the general form of thinking most likely to underlie a wide range of an individual's judgments in a particular issue domain or across several domains. It may be true that both adults and children can say one thing (reflecting perhaps their highest level of judgment) and do another, but this does not mean that they do not have a reason for what they do, or that there is not a structure underlying their reasons. Although there is no simple one-to-one correspondence between action and structure, the cognitive-developmental approach makes it clear that an analysis of reasoning is one necessary condition for the complete understanding of social behavior.

In essence, cognitive-developmental and social-cognitive analyses do not "explain" the causes of behavior; rather, they present a way of organizing and "describing" behavior, and this description then becomes useful for intervention because of the invariant and hierarchical nature of the stages. The stages provide the criteria that allow us to make claims about the adequacy of any structural change in reasoning.

It is also clear that applying social-cognitive stages to educational and clinical practice requires a shift in emphasis from the study of the development of concepts across persons to the study of the particular quality of an individual's thinking. This is not an easy task, but it is an essential one. Stages of cognitive and social-cognitive development will become as sterile (and probably as abused) as IQ points if the structural level of an individual's judgment is taken as a product, rather than understood as a process of social reasoning within the broader context of a given *individual child's* social experience. Stage analysis will best serve teachers and clinicians interested in child development if it deemphasizes reliance on standardized assessment and emphasizes the professional's need to understand the child's view of his life experience and to maintain with him an open-ended and mutual dialogue.

For Reflection

1. What is the relationship between social-cognitive awareness and affective awareness?
2. How is role-taking a part of understanding *self* motives and reasons as well as those of others?
3. Why would role-taking be an important concept for church teachers of third-and fourth-graders? Give an example.

References

Ausubel, D. P. 1958. *Theory and problems of child development.* New York: Grune and Stratton.

Blatt, M., and L. Kohlberg. 1975. The effects of classroom moral discussion upon children's level of moral development. *Journal of Maoral Education* 4: 129–61.

Byrne, D. 1975. Role-taking in adolescence and adulthood. Ph.D. dissertation, Harvard University.

Chandler, M. J. 1971. Egocentrism and childhood psychopathology. Paper presented at the meeting of the Society for Research in Child Development, April, Minneapolis.

Colby, A., B. Fritz, and L. Kohlberg. 1974. The relation of logical and moral judgment stages. Unpublished manuscript, Harvard University.

DeVries, R. 1970. The development of role-taking as reflected by behavior of bright, average, and retarded children in a social guessing game. *Child Development* 41: 759–70.

Feffer, M. H., and V. Gourevitch. 1960. Cognitive aspects of role-taking in children. *Journal of Personality* 28: 383–96.

Flavell, J. H. 1971. The development of inferences about others. Paper presented at the Interdisciplinary Conference on Our Knowledge of Persons: Personal Perception and Inter-Personal Behavior, December, State University of New York at Binghampton.

Gardner, H. 1973. *The quest for mind.* New York: Knopf.

Giraldo, M. 1972. Egocentrism and moral development. Ph.D. dissertation, Catholic University, Washington, D.C.

Hickey, J. 1972. Stimulation of moral reasoning in delinquents. Ph.D. dissertation, Boston University.

Hirst, P., and R. Peters. 1970. *The logic of education*. London: Routledge.

Kohlberg, L. 1969. Stage and sequence: The cognitive-developmental approach to socialization. In *Handbook of socialization theory and research,* ed. D. A. Goslin, 347–480. Chicago: Rand McNally.

Kohlberg, L., and R. Mayer. 1972. Development as the aim of education. *Harvard Educational Review* 42, 4.

Kohlberg, L., and R. Selman. 1972. *Preparing school personnel relative to values: A look at moral education in the schools*. Washington, D.C.: ERIC Clearinghouse on Teacher Education.

Kuhn, D. 1972. The development of role-taking ability. Unpublished manuscript, Columbia University.

Kuhn, D., Langer, J., Kohlberg, L., and Haan, N. 1977. The development of formal operations in logical and moral judgment.*Genetic Psychology Monographs* 95: 97–188.

Loevinger, J. 1973. Recent research on ego development. Invited address at the annual meeting of the Society for Research in Child Development, March 31.

Mead, G. H. 1934. *Mind, self and society*. Chicago: University of Chicago Press.

Moir, D. J. 1971. Egocentrism and the emergence of conventional morality in preadolescent girls. Master of arts in education thesis, University of Canterbury, Christchurch, New Zealand.

Moore, O. K. 1958. Problem-solving and the perception of persons. In *Person perception and interpersonal behavior,* ed. R. Tagiuri and L. Petrullo, 131–50. Stanford: Stanford University Press.

Neale, J. M. 1966. Egocentrism in institutionalized and noninstitutionalized children. *Child Development* 37: 97–101.

Piaget, J. 1929. *The child's conception of the world*. London: Routledge.

Piaget, J., and B. Inhelder. 1958. *The growth of logical thinking from childhood to adolescence*. New York: Basic.

Scharf, P., J. Hickey, and L. Kohlberg. 1973. Moral stages and their application to work in prisons. Unpublished manuscript, Harvard University.

Selman, R. L. 1971a. The relation of role-taking to the development of moral judgment in children. *Child Development* 42: 79–91.

———. 1971b. Taking another's perspective: Role-taking development in early childhood. *Child Development* 42: 1721–34.

———. 1972. The relation of role-taking and moral judgment stages: A theoretical and empirical analysis. Unpublished manuscript, Harvard University.

———. 1976. Toward a structured analysis of developing interpersonal relations concepts: Research with normal and disturbed preadolescent boys. In *Tenth Annual Minnesota Symposium on Child Development,* ed. A. Pick, 156–200. University of Minnesota Press.

Selman, R. L., and M. Lieberman. 1975. Moral education in the primary grades: An evaluation of a developmental curriculum. *Journal of Educational Psychology* 67: 712–16.

Soloman, L. 1963. Experimental studies of tacit coordination: A comparison of schizophrenic and normal samples. Paper presented at the Brocton Veteran's Administration Hospital Colloquium Series.

Taft, R. 1955. The ability to judge people. *Psychological Bulletin* 52: 1–23.

Thrower, J. S. 1972. The effects of group home and foster care on development of moral judgment. Ph.D. dissertation, Harvard University.

5

Jean Piaget

Developmentalist

The Child and Reality (1972)

A citizen of Switzerland, Jean Piaget began to impress the academic world as a child. He wrote scientific papers from age 10 through his teen years. He completed his undergraduate studies at age 18 and received a Ph.D. degree in natural sciences from the University of Neuchatel at age 21.

Piaget was very interested in psychology and philosophy. To expand his knowledge he studied at several European clinics and laboratories, including Alfred Binet's lab school in Paris. In 1929 he went to the University of Geneva and was associated with the J. J. Rousseau Institute. In 1949 he became director of Geneva's Psychology Laboratory. Piaget was fascinated with the wrong answers children gave to test questions. He also carefully studied his own three children. These studies and his background in zoology led Piaget to believe that nature made a major contribution to how the children went about obtaining knowledge. He produced hundreds of articles and dozens of books on various aspects of cognitive development. Some psychologists identify Piaget with the study of cognitive growth in the same way they identify Freud with the study of emotional growth (Sprinthall and Sprinthall 1987).

Ironically, one of Piaget's greatest contributions was also a hindrance to the acceptance of his theories, especially in the United States, where behaviorism prevailed in the psychological communities. Piaget believed that the human mind

From *The Child and Reality: Problems of Genetic Psychology*, trans. Arnold Rosin (New York: Grossman, 1972), 49–91.

is not a passive, blank slate waiting to be marked upon, nor is it merely potential responses waiting for the appropriate stimuli. Piaget held that the mind is very active during the process of learning, interacting with new material, which causes the mental scheme to be initially "out of balance." The organism does not like this condition and thus seeks "equilibrium" or a balanced condition. This theory, called genetic epistemology by Piaget, did not fit the predominantly behavioristic outlook of the 1930s in American psychology—neither did his research methodology. Furthermore, his books had to be translated from French in order to gain a widespread audience here. However, by the mid-1960s educators began to read Piaget's work and found it a helpful alternative to behaviorism. Within a few years his approach to cognitive development had made a major impact on educational psychologists and on classroom teachers.

The two chapters that follow present the stage theory and, especially in "Child Praxis," the two major ideas that are at the heart of the "active mind" concept: assimilation and accommodation.

References

Sprinthall, N. A., and R. C. Sprinthall, eds. 1987. *Educational psychology: A developmental approach*. New York: Random House.

The Stages of Intellectual Development in the Child and Adolescent

The stages of intellectual development form a privileged case and we cannot generalize to other fields. If for example we take the development of a child's perception or the development of language, we observe a completely different and much greater continuity than in the field of logico-mathematical operations. In the field of perception, in particular, I would be unable to give you a chart of stages similar to the one I offered you from the point of view of intellectual operations, for we rediscover this continuity from the organic point of view, a continuity which can be broken up in a conventional manner but which does not offer very distinct natural breaks.

To the contrary, in the field of intellectual operations we witness this dual phenomenon: On the one hand, we see structures form which we can follow step-by-step from the earliest main features and, on the other, we witness their completion, that is, the formation of levels of equilibrium. Take for example the organization of whole numbers: We can follow this structuration based on numbers 1, 2, 3, and so forth, until the moment when the child discovers the series of numbers and at the same time the first arithmetic operations. At a given moment, this kind of structure is thus formed and leads to its level of equilibrium. This equilibrium is so stable that the whole numbers will no longer be modified during an entire lifetime while integrating themselves into more complex systems (fractional numbers, etc.). We are therefore in the presence of a privileged field in the heart of which we witness the formation of structures and their completion, where different structures can succeed one another or integrate themselves according to multiple combinations.

In this particular field and, I repeat, without my posing the problem of generalization, I shall call *stages* the breaks which fit the following characteristics.

1. If stages are to exist, first of all the *order of succession of acquisitions must be constant.* I speak not of the chronology but of the order of succession. The stages in a given population can be characterized by a chronology, but this chronology is extremely variable. It depends on the individual's previous experience, and not only on his maturation; and it depends above all on the social milieu which can hasten or delay the appearance of a stage, or even prevent the manifestation. We find ourselves here in the presence of considerable complexity, and I would be unable to make a statement on the value of the average ages of our stages so far as any population is concerned. I consider only the ages relative to the populations which we have studied; they are therefore essentially relative. If it is a question of stages, the order of succession of conduct is to be considered constant; that is, one characteristic will not appear before another in a certain number of subjects and after another in another group of subjects. Here, where we witness such alternations, the characteristics at stake are not utilizable from the point of view of stages.

2. Then there is *the integrative characteristic,* that is, that the structures constructed at a given age become an integral part of the structures of the following age. For example, the notion of the permanent object which is constructed at a sensorimotor level will be an integral element of the notions of future conservation (when there will be conservation of a unit, or of a collection, or even of an object whose spatial appearance is distorted). Similarly, the operations which we will call concrete will constitute an integral part of the formal operations, in the sense that the latter will constitute a new structure but based on the former. (The second thus constitute operations carried out on other operations.)

3. Together with Mlle. Inhelder, we have always tried to characterize a stage not by the juxtaposition of foreign characteristics but by a *whole structure.* This notion acquires a precise meaning in the field of intelligence, more precise than elsewhere. On the level of concrete operations, for example, a structure will be a grouping with the logical grouping characteristics found in the classification or in the successions. Later, on the level of the formal operation, the structure will be the group of the four transformations which I shall soon mention, or the network. Thus we mean structures which can be characterized by their laws of totality in such a manner that once such a structure

is achieved, one can determine every operation it covers. Considering that the child achieves this or that structure, it is thus known that he is capable of a multiplicity of distinct operations, and at first often without any visible relation among them. Here is the advantage of the notion of structures: When structures are complex, a series of operational schemes with no apparent connection among them can be reduced to greater unity; this is the whole structure as such which characterizes a stage.

4. A stage thus includes both a level of *preparation* on the one hand and of *completion* on the other. For formal operations, for example, the stage of preparation will be the whole period from eleven to thirteen or fourteen years, and the completion will be the level of equilibrium which appears at that time.

5. However, since the preparation of later acquisitions can involve more than a stage (with various overlapping among certain preparations, some shorter and others longer), and since there are various degrees of stability in the completions, in any series of stages there must be a distinction between the *process of formation,* or of birth, and the *final forms of equilibrium* (in the relative sense). Only the latter constitute the whole structures mentioned in paragraph 3: whereas the formative operations are presented in aspects of successive differentiations of such structures (differentiation of the earlier structure and preparation of the following one).

Finally, I would like to insist on the notion of *lag* (of operations), to which we will return, for it can create an obstacle to the generalization of stages and introduce considerations of caution and limitation. Lags characterize the repetition or the reproduction of the same formative operation at various levels. We distinguish *horizontal lags* and *vertical lags.*

We will speak of horizontal lags when the same operation applies to different content. In the field of concrete operations, for example, a child aged seven or eight will know how to seriate quantities of material or lengths. He will know how to classify, count, and measure them, and will likewise acquire notions of conservation relative to these contents. But he will be incapable of all these operations in the field of weights, whereas on an average of two years later, he will be able to generalize them by applying them to this new content. From the formal point of view, the operations are the same in both cases but applied to different fields. In this case, we will speak of horizontal lag within the same period.

A vertical lag, on the contrary, is the reconstruction of a structure by means of other operations. At the close of the sensorimotor period, an infant achieves what with H. Poincaré we call a *group of displacements:* The infant will know how to orient himself in his apartment with detours and return. But this *group* is only practical and by no means representative. Several years later when it is a matter of representing the same displacements, that is, imagining or interiorizing them in operation, we rediscover similar stages of formation but this time on another level, that of the representation. It is a matter of other operations, and in this case we will call it vertical lag.

We will divide intellectual development into three important periods.[1]

The Period of Sensorimotor Intelligence

This first period extends from birth to the appearance of language, that is, approximately the first two years of existence. We subdivide it into six stages:

1. *Reflex exercises:* From zero to one month.

2. *First habits:* Beginning of primary stable conditionings and circular reactions (that is, relative to the body proper: for example sucking his thumb). From one to four-and-a-half months.

3. *Coordination of vision and prehension* and beginning of secondary circular reactions (that is, relative to the manipulated limbs). Beginning of coordination of qualitative spaces, until then undifferentiated, but without searching for lost objects; and beginning of differentiation between aims and means, but without referring to previous aims while acquiring new conduct. From about four-and-a-half to eight or nine months.

4. *Coordination of the secondary schemes* with, in certain cases, utilization of known means to achieve a new objective (several new means possible for one and the same goal and several goals possible for one and the same means). Beginning of search for the lost object but without coordination of successive displacements (and localizations). From about eight or nine to eleven or twelve months.

5. *Differentiation of schemes of action by tertiary circular reaction* (variation of conditions by exploration and directed groping) and *discovery of new means.* Examples: supporting devices (drawing a blanket to bring to the floor the object placed on it; negative reaction if the object is alongside or beyond the support), use of string or stick (by groping). Search for the disappeared object with localization in function of perceptible successive displacements and beginning of organization of the practical group of displacements (detours and returns in actions). From about eleven or twelve to eighteen months.

6. *Beginning of the interiorization of the schemes and solution of a few problems with action stopping and sudden understanding.* Example: direction of the stick when it has not been acquired by groping during stage 5. Generalization of the group practice with, incorporated into the system, a few nonperceptible displacements. From about eighteen to twenty-four months.

These six stages present a rather striking character if we compare them to the stages of future representative thought, in the sense that they form a kind of prefiguration according to the term cherished by our president Michotte (analogous in a sense to the prefiguration of the notional, which he often

1. We will speak of *periods* to designate the important unities and speak of *stages,* then of *substages,* to describe their subdivisions.

mentions in regard to perception). Actually, on this practical level, we are witnessing an organization of movements and displacements which, first centered on the body itself, gradually decentralize and lead to a space in which the child situates himself like an element among others (hence a system of permanent objects including his body on the same ground as the others). On a small scale and on the practical level, we see here exactly the same operation of progressive decentration which we will then rediscover on the representative level in terms of mental operations and not simply of actions.

The Period of Preparation and of Organization of Concrete Operations of Categories, Relations, and Numbers

We will call concrete operations those we bear on manipulable objects (effective or immediately imaginable manipulations), in contrast to operations bearing on propositions or simple verbal statements (logic of propositions).

This period extending from about two to eleven or twelve years can be divided into a subperiod *A* of functional preparations of the operations[2] but of preoperatory structure, and a subperiod *B* of operatory structuration itself.

The Subperiod of Preoperatory Representations. This subperiod can itself be subdivided into three stages:

1. From two to three-and-a-half or four years: *appearance of the symbolical function and beginning of the interiorization of the schemes of action in representations.* This stage is the one on which we have the least information on the operations of thought, for it is not possible to question the child before the age of four in a continuous conversation; but this negative fact alone is a characteristic indication. The positive facts are the following. (1) The appearance of the symbolical function in its various forms: language, symbolic play (or imagination) in contrast to the simple play of exercise, postponed imitation, and probably beginnings of the mental image conceived as internal imitation. (2) Plan of the nascent representation: difficulties of application to nonproximate space and to nonpresent time of the schemes of object, space, time, and causality already used in the effective action.

2. From four to five-and-a-half years: *representative organizations founded either on static configurations or on an assimilation to the action itself.* Duality of states and transformation is the characteristic of the first representative structures revealed on this level by questions about objects to be manipulated. The first are thoughts as configurations (compare the role of perceptive configurations or figural collections to this level of nonconservation of totalities or quantities), and the second are thoughts assimilated to actions.

2. If we call *operations* the interiorized, reversible, and solidary actions of whole structures such as the *groupings, groups,* and *networks.*

3. From five-and-a-half to seven or eight years: *articulated representative regulations.* Intermediary phase between nonconservation and conservation. Beginnings of connection between states and transformations, thanks to representative regulations enabling these to be thought in semireversible forms. (Examples: increasing articulations of classifications, relations of order.)

The subperiod of concrete operations. This stage extending from seven or eight to eleven or twelve years is characterized by a series of structures on the point of completion which can be carefully studied and their form analyzed. On the logical level, they all amount to what I call *groupments,* that is, they are not yet *groups* nor are they *networks* (with lack of boundaries for some and greater boundaries for others, these are half-networks): such are the classifications, the successions, the correspondences point-by-point, the simple or successive correspondences, the multiplicative operations (matrices). On the arithmetic level, I will add the additive and multiplicative groups of whole and fractional numbers.

This period of concrete operations can be divided into two stages: one of simple operations and the other of completion of certain whole systems especially in the fields of space and of time. In the field of space, it is the period when the child of only about nine or ten reaches the systems of coordinates or of references (representation of verticals and horizontals in relation to these references). This is also the level of the coordination of whole systems of perspectives, the level which marks the greatest system on the concrete plane.

The Period of Formal Operations

Finally there is the third and last period, that of *formal operations.* Here, as early as eleven or twelve (first stage) with an equilibrium level about thirteen or fourteen (second stage), we witness a great many transformations which are relatively rapid at the time of their appearance and extremely varied. We were able to reach these conclusions chiefly through the fine studies made by Mlle. Inhelder on inductive reasoning and on the experimental method among children and adolescents. At that age operations appear as different from one another as the following. First combinative operations: Until then there was only simple interlocking of sets and elementary operations, but not what mathematicians call *sets of parts,* which are the starting point for these combinations. On the contrary, the combination begins at about eleven or twelve and creates the network structure. On this same level, proportions appear, as well as the capacity for reasoning and self-representation according to two reference systems at the same time, the structures of mechanical equilibrium, et cetera. Let us study, for example, the relative movements of a snail on a small plank which will be moved in a direction opposite the snail, and the calculation of the result of these movements, one in relation to the other and in relation to a system of external reference. In this case we see (and they are found again in the mechanical equilibriums, etc.) the intervention of four coordinated operations: a direct operation *(I)* and its opposite *(N),* but also the direct operation and the opposite of the other system which formed the reciprocal of the first *(R)* and the negative of this reciprocal or correlative (*NR* = *C*). This group of four transformations *INRC* appears in a series of different fields in these logico-mathematical problems but also in problems of proportions even independently of school knowledge.

Above all, what appears in this last level is the logic of propositions, the capacity to study statements and propositions and no longer only objects placed on the table or immediately represented. The logic of statements also supposes the combinative network and the group of four transformations *(INRC),* that is, the two complementary aspects of a new whole structure taking in every operatory mechanism which we see formed at this level.

I will end by saying that these three important periods with their particular stages form operations of successive equilibrium, steps toward equilibrium. The moment the equilibrium is reached on a point, the structure is integrated into a new system being formed, until there is a new equilibrium ever more stable and of an ever more extending field.

It is worth recalling that equilibrium is defined by reversibility. To say that there is a step toward equilibrium means that the intellectual development is characterized by a growing reversibility. The reversibility is the most apparent characteristic of the act of intelligence which is capable of detours and returns. Thus this reversibility increases at a regular rate, level-by-level, during the course of the stages which I have just briefly described. It is presented in two forms: one which can be called inversion or negation which appears in schoolroom logic or arithmetic; the other, which we could call reciprocity, appears in the operations of relations. In every level of concrete operations, inversion and reciprocity are two processes traveling side-by-side and at the same time, but without meeting in a unique system. With the group of four *INRC* transformations, on the contrary, we have inversion, reciprocity, negation of the reciprocal, and the same transformation, that is, the synthesis in a single system of these two forms of reversibility until then parallel but with no connection between them.

In this privileged field of intellectual operations, we thus arrive at a simple and regular system of stages, but it is perhaps characteristic of such a field of perception that I am unable to furnish its stages.

Child Praxis

Praxis or action is not some sort of movement but rather a system of coordinated movements functioning for a result or an intention. To take but one example, the displacement of an arm which interferes in the act of putting on or of removing a hat is not praxis; a praxis consists of an action in its totality and not of a partial movement within this action. Praxis is an *acquired* as opposed to a reflex coordination; this acquisition can derive not only from the child's experience or education in the large sense (instruction, example), but also eventually from the internal operations of equilibrium which expresses a regulation or a stabilization acquired from coordination.

Thus characterized, praxis consists of two possible forms of coordination, the first constantly at work and the second capable of superimposing itself upon or of deriving from the first. We will call the first *internal coordination*, that which gathers several partial movements into a whole act, whether some of these partial movements previously existed in an isolated state (which is not the rule but can be observed), whether coordinated for the first time, or even whether the result of a progressive differentiation during gradual coordinations. We will call *external coordinations* the coordinations of two or several acts of praxis into a wholly new praxis of superior order, the earlier ones remaining capable of functioning in separate states.

The psychological problems which are now posed and which become directly or indirectly part of the clinical problems of apraxia, can be grouped into three major headings: (1) those of the mode of coordination (internal or external) peculiar to praxis; this will lead among others to choosing among the explicative models such as the associationist ones, the gestalts, or the assimilative schemes; (2) those of the relations between the coordinations proper of praxis and intelligence; and (3) those of relations between these coordinations and the symbolical function, particularly the mental picture. The problems in (2) are themselves subdivided into two groups. On the sensorimotor levels of development, that is, before language, the question arises if, specifically, the coordinations of praxis are gradually directed by an outer practical intelligence (in this case, the contents of this intelligence should be discovered) or if, on the contrary, the sensorimotor intelligence is nothing more than the very coordination of the actions. The problems in (2) are therefore the same as those in (1) on these initial levels of the development. After the construction of the symbolical function, the problems in (2) make one wonder what are the relations between praxis and the fundamental mechanism of representative intelligence, that is, the mechanism of the *operations;* these to be conceived precisely as actions of a certain kind, interiorized actions coordinated in well-defined structures (logico-mathematical structures, chiefly geometrical). As for the problems in (3), they are partially independent of those in (2), if we admit that knowledge or gnosis includes two distinct aspects: the operative aspect to which I just alluded, and the figurative aspect (perception, mental picture) intervening among others in the symbolical function in regard to the elaboration of the significants or symbolizers (for example, the picture).

To deal with the three kinds of problems, we are first going to study the sensorimotor levels, then the relations between praxis and the operations of representative intelligence, and finally, the relations between praxis and mental pictures.

Between the newborn child's almost entirely reflex behavior (but with the diffused cortical control emphasized by Minkovski) and the appearance of language or of the symbolical function, there exists a series of levels whose very succession is already instructive in the modes of coordination which characterize praxis and its relation to intelligence.

In the first of these stages, certain complex reflexes, like those of sucking, give rise to a kind of exercise and of internal consolidation due to their functioning, which announce the formation of schemes in behavior.

We call *schemes* of an action the general structure of this action, conserving itself during these repetitions, consolidating itself by exercise, and applying itself to situations which vary because of modifications of milieu. In this respect, sucking reflexes create a scheme (which is not the case of all the other reflexes but only of some of them) which manifests itself among others by the functional consolidation I just mentioned, but also by a certain number of generalizations (empty sucking, sucking any object in the presence of the lips) and of recognitions (finding the nipple again when moving slightly aside and distinguishing it from the surrounding teguments).

As early as the second stage, the presence of such schemes permits certain new acquisitions (new in relation to the original hereditary structures), thanks to the incorporation of new elements into the initial circuit: After sucking his thumb during fortuitous contact, the baby will be able, first, to hold it between his lips, then to direct it systematically to his mouth for sucking between feeding. Already we are in the presence of a praxis.

With the third stage, marked by the coordination of vision and prehension (coordination, according to Tournay, due to a myelinization of the pyramidal fasciculus, but which in addition requires an undeniable part of exercise),[3] the possibility of thus intentionally seizing the objects appearing in the close visual field creates the formation of a series of new schemes.[4] To mention only one, a child seizes among others a cord hanging from the top of its cradle; this shakes the top with all the objects which we had hung there (celluloid

3. With our three children, this coordination was formed at six months, four-and-a-half months, and three months and three days, hence with considerable age difference but in similar order to the whole context of their activities.

4. Beginning with the scheme of intentional prehension itself, quite distinct from the earlier reflex prehension due to the fact that the intentional prehension includes the possibility of "releasing," that is, choosing not to take. (This is not to be confused with the scheme, appearing much later, of purposely dropping an object from his hands.) The difference between this intentional prehension with the possibility of not taking is, as Ajuriaguerra pointed out to us, comparable to the active visual exploration (fixations and displacements of the intentional glance) as opposed to the roaming and gripping glance.

dolls filled with granules to produce sound). Soon afterward, when the objects had been removed from the top, we attached another object and the child, having watched this, at once sought the cord and pulled it while again watching the object hanging there. Subsequently, the balancing of a presented object from three to six feet from the cradle and even the interruption of repeated whistling gave rise to looking for and pulling the cord.

During a fourth stage, the child no longer limits himself to reproducing the sequences discovered by chance (circular reactions), but he uses the schemes thus discovered by coordinating them, one of these schemes assigning a goal to the action and one of the others serving as a means of achieving the goal. Or again, by presenting a new object, the child applies to it in turn (as exploration) each of the known schemes, in order to determine the practical significance or the use of this object, and he will grasp it to look at it, to suck it; he will shake it, rub it against the side of the cradle, hit it with one hand while holding it with the other. In short, the stage is characterized both by a growing mobility of the schemes of action and by the appearance of what we called earlier the external coordination between acts of praxis.

During the fifth stage (beginning of the second year), the external coordinations are accompanied by a differentiation of the schemes as a function of experience; for example, reaching an object too far away by pulling the support (carpet) on which it had been placed, with variations in accordance with the situations. Here, therefore, there is simultaneous external coordination of schemes capable of functioning separately and there is discovery of new means by accommodating the schemes to the unexpected facts of experience.

Finally, during the sixth stage, which coincides with the first manifestations of the symbolic function, a beginning of interiorization of the external coordination between the schemes is manifested in the form of insight or of invention of new means. One of my children, for example, in order to reach an object placed in a slightly opened box of matches, began by feeling the box in various ways (fifth-stage behavior). Then after a pause during which he had observed quite carefully the much-too-small opening, he slipped his finger into this opening and thus solved the problem. This beginning of interiorization of the coordinations is often accompanied by symbolical gestures favoring the formation of the nascent representation. Thus while glancing at the opening which he wishes to enlarge, this child opened and closed his mouth several times, not because the coveted object in the box was to be eaten (he saw that this was a thimble), but more probably to symbolize the desired solution (to increase the opening).

Such being the stages of formation of elementary praxis peculiar to the sensorimotor period of development, let us now ask ourselves of what do the coordinations which characterize them consist.

First, it is worth noting that such development could not be reduced to an associationist model by learning or by conditioning interpreted in the sense of associations. Indeed, a scheme is more than a mere "hierarchical family of habits" (in the Hull sense) due to cumulative associations, for a new acquisition consists not only of associating a new stimulus or a new response-movement to stimuli or to previous movements *a, b,* and *c.* Any new acquisition consists of *assimilating* an object or a situation to a previous scheme by thus enlarging it. It is insufficient, for example, to explain the habit of thumb sucking by saying that the infant has *associated* his thumb to a sucking movement, for the real conditioning problem is to know why it stabilizes itself, when, like any association, it is merely of a temporary nature. Indeed, the thumb stimulus releases the sucking response only if it assumes a significance as a function of the scheme of this response, that is, if it is assimilated as a sucking object. Psychoanalysts would simply say that it is a breast symbol, but this apparent simplicity consists of attributing to the subject somewhat too precociously the very complex symbolical function.[5] Let us therefore satisfy ourselves by saying that it is assimilated to a sucking scheme and let us try to specify the meaning of these terms.

Assimilation thus understood is a very general function presenting itself in three nondissociable forms: (1) functional or reproductive assimilation, consisting of repeating an action and of consolidating it by this repetition; (2) recognitive assimilation, consisting of discriminating the assimilable objects in a given scheme; and (3) generalizing assimilation, consisting of extending the field of this scheme. Hence assimilation, on the behavior level, is merely the continuation of the biological assimilation in the large sense—any reaction of the organism to the milieu consisting of assimilating the milieu to the structures of the organism. Just as, when a rabbit eats cabbage, he is not changed into cabbage but, on the contrary, the cabbage is changed into rabbit, so in all action or praxis, the subject is not absorbed in the object, but the object is used and "included" as relative to the subject's actions.

It is therefore assimilation which is the source of schemes, with the exception of the original reflex and hereditary schemes which orient the first assimilations: Assimilation is the operation of integration of which the scheme is the result. Moreover it is worth stating that in any action the driving force or energy is naturally of an affective nature (need and satisfaction) whereas the structure is of a cognitive nature (the scheme as sensorimotor organization). To assimilate an object to a scheme is therefore simultaneously to tend to satisfy a need and to confer on the action a cognitive structure.

Thus, what we have called internal coordination of schemes is therefore

5. One could, it is true, limit oneself to saying that the thumb=pleasure=breast. But this amounts exactly to what we call the assimilation of the thumb to the sucking theme, any assimilation being both cognitive (utilization or comprehension) and affective (satisfaction). In this respect, see the following paragraph.

nothing more than the product of cumulative assimilations. As for the external coordination between schemes, it is a question then of reciprocal assimilation. For any object, for example, capable of being seen (compare oculo-cephalogyric reflexes) and seized, the coordination of the vision and the prehension includes a reciprocal assimilation of the corresponding schemes, the object becoming *both* something to see and to seize.

Thus conceived, the schemes of assimilation are not confused with the gestalts, although in certain cases, a scheme can present gestalt characteristics. A gestalt is an organization obeying laws of compensation or of intrinsic and independent equilibrium of the acquired experience: symmetry, regularity, simplicity, etc. Thus a scheme can obey the gestalt laws (symmetrical arm movements). The organization of a scheme, however, is much greater and results both in the subject's activities (which are a function of the utilization as well as of the laws of "good form") and of his acquired experience (accommodations to objects). The laws of compensation and of equilibrium of schemes stem therefore from the activities like those of the subject (to compensate an outer disturbance in order to satisfy a need) and not the so-called preformed geometrical laws.

It thus becomes relatively easy to solve the problem of the relation between sensorimotor praxis and intelligence (problems on which the interpretation of the ideomotor apraxia partially depend). If the mode of coordination of actions is truly of an assimilating nature and not simply associative, it becomes futile to subordinate the actions or praxis to a so-called intelligence which would be external to them and would consist then of a kind of faculty difficult to understand, unless of the first fact. There certainly exists a sensorimotor intelligence, and as early as the fourth stage, the mobility and external coordination of the schemes lead to a subordination of the means to the goals; the characterizing of this as intelligent action could not be denied (and this *a fortiori* with the discovery of the new means of the fifth stage and the insights of the sixth). But this intelligence is nothing more than the very coordination of the actions, and as early as the most elementary actions, we again find in the assimilation a kind of sketch or prefiguration of judgment: The infant who discovers that an object is to be sucked, to be balanced, or to be pulled orients himself in an uninterrupted line of assimilations leading directly to the superior behavior which the physicist uses when he assimilates (he also!) heat to movement or a scale to a system of work.

That is why as early as the sensorimotor praxis, the substructures of subsequent knowledge are outlined. The search for disappearing objects (long impossible, then developing gradually) leads to the scheme of the permanence of objects, which is a point of departure for the subsequent notions of conservation. The displacements in space are gradually organized into a scheme which takes form from what geometers call a group of displacements, and this scheme, already almost reversible[6] at the fifth and sixth stages, will play an important role in the organization of representative space, once reconstructed on the level of thought by interiorization of the actions in operation. The causality, the temporal series (order of succession) are not imposed on praxis from without by intelligence but develop under the effect of their coordination and constitute the substructures of the subsequent notions of cause, order, time, etc.

Let us now study child praxis as developed after the construction of the symbolical function, noting especially those whose disturbances correspond to what is known as constructive apraxia.

The symbolical function results from a differentiation between the significants and the signified (until now undifferentiated, as in the case of the perceptive signs or signals of conditioning). The symbols and signs, once differentiated from their significations, make it then possible to evoke objects and situations actually nonperceived, forming the beginning of representation. The significants, which differentiate between one or one-and-a-half and two years, so far as symbols proper are concerned, are: (1) symbolical play (representation of objects and actions by gestures) dissociating itself from the mere play of functional exercise; (2) postponed imitation (with its multiple varieties leading to graphic imitation or drawing); (3) mental pictures doubtless resulting from interiorized imitations. At the time when these various categories of symbols are formed, there is also acquisition (by imitation) of the systems of social signs, the principal one being speech.

Thus the symbolical function makes this interiorization of actions possible or at least strengthens it considerably. We noted the beginnings at the sixth sensorimotor stage: In addition to their material and effective development, the actions become more and more capable of being carried out in thought or symbolically. This interiorization, however, supposes a reconstruction on the level of thought, which is long and laborious: It is one thing for the child, for example, to coordinate his displacements in a group, enabling him to find himself again in his garden or between his house and school, and another to be able to represent these displacements in thoughts, respecting the group rules (returns and detours), and to outline these paths by drawing, language, or simply by arranging the paths and the house on a model prepared for this purpose. It is only after the age of seven or eight that representation rediscovers this group structure which was already active in the sensorimotor organization at the fifth and sixth stages.

Thus interpreted, representation or representative thought consists of two different aspects which should be clearly distinguished if we wish to state with

6. In the mathematical sense of the word and not neurological. Indeed, a group consists of the direct, reverse compositions (returns) and identical and associative ones (detours).

some rigor the nature of the psychological trouble intervening in a constructive apraxia: the figurative aspect and the operative aspect.

The figurative aspect of thought is everything related to the configurations as such, in opposition to the transformations. Guided by perception and supported by the mental picture, the figurative aspect of representation plays an important role (abusively important and precisely at the expense of transformations) in the preoperatory thought of the child aged two to seven, before the operations are constructed in the sense I have just defined. Thus, when we pour a liquid from container *A* into a narrower and taller container *B*, the child aged four to six generally still believes that the quantity of the liquid increases because the level is higher. He reasons thus only on the configurations *A* and *B* by comparing them directly without the intermediary of the system of transformations (which would offer him the relation: higher but narrower; therefore equal quantity). After the age of seven or eight, on the contrary, he believes in the conservation of the quantity of liquid because he reasons on the transformation and subordinates the configuration to it.

The operative aspect of thought relates to transformations and is thus related to everything that modifies the object, from the moment of the action until the operations. We will call operations the interiorized (or interiorizable), reversible actions (in the sense of being capable of developing in both directions and, consequently, of including the possibility of a reverse action which cancels the result of the first), and coordinated in structures, known as operatory, which present laws of composition characterizing the structure in its totality as a system. Addition, for example, is an operation because it stems from collecting actions, because it includes a reversal (subtraction), and finally because the system of addition and subtraction includes laws of totality.[7] The operatory structures, for example, are the classifications, seriations, correspondences, matrices, series of numbers, spatial metrics, or projective transformations. A large number of logical, mathematical, and physical operations develop for the most part spontaneously in the child aged six or seven and are completed as of the eleventh or twelfth year by propositional or formal operations, making the adolescent's hypothetico-deductive deduction possible.

If we admit this distinction between the figurative and operative aspects of thought, it is then immediately evident that operations stem from the sensorimotor schematization, even if the symbolical function and the figurative representation are required for their interiorization and expression. Indeed, it should be well understood that an operation is not the representation of a transformation; it is, in itself, an object transformation, but one that can be done symbolically, which is by no means the same thing. Thus an operation remains an action and is reduced neither to a figure nor to a symbol.

7. Group laws, etc.

Thus the essential problem of praxis interpretation is to dissociate what is due to the figurative aspect and to the operations as such, in such a manner that in a constructive act of praxis, for example, we can diagnose what stems from intelligence or what stems only from the symbolical figuration.

Particularly in regard to space and the spatial disorders so important in apraxia, it should be understood above all that the spatial relations simply "given" in appearance between the external objects are in no way reduced in point of fact to pure systems of perceptions or of imagined representations but include operatory constructions far more complex than they appear. Although there exist vertical and horizontal positions locatable by postural and proprioceptive means and although directions can be estimated visually in relation to that of the glance (Donders' law), the prevision of the horizontal level of water in a slanted jar, for example, is not accessible to a normal child until about the age of nine, because it supposes a whole system of references bound up with Euclidian metric operations—the axes of coordinates capable of being constructed on the representative level only at the end of the long formation of measure operations. Even the conservation of lengths and distances, in a case of change in the arrangement of objects, is only acquired as a function of reversible operations, and is by no means acquired by the merely perceptive method or by the play of mental pictures only.

We must therefore turn to a precise investigation of the eventual operations in play if we wish to understand the details of troubles in a constructive act of praxis. Thus in the drawings of small bicycles so suggestive (and so similar to those of children aged five to six) furnished by Hécaen, Ajuriaguerra, and Massonnet in the case of right lesions (1960: 270), we can ask ourselves to what extent the lacunae are due to the relations of causality, temporal series, spatial representations as figurative, topological relations (the chain "enclosing" the indented wheel), the absence of coordinates in the plan. When we are told that "the copy of the Rey complex figure proves very defective," is this due to perception, to the graphic quality as such, or to many spatial operations which intervene implicitly in the success of this excellent overall proof but which cannot serve to dissociate the operative from the figurative aspect of the operation in play?

To specify the eventual relation between operations and praxis, it is now worth adding that, during the development of thought, operations go through three successive stages. During the first, between the ages of two and seven or eight, thought remains preoperatory, in the sense that the operations gradually form themselves but without achieving logical reversibility or adequate total structure, and they remain dominated by the figurative aspect of the representations.

In the second stage (from seven or eight to eleven or twelve), certain operations are completed and organized in logically reversible structures. But (and this is important to the praxis problem) the operations remain concrete in the sense that they are limited to the field of manipulation of the objects and do not yet include simply verbal manipulation on the hypothetico-deductive level. In regard to seriation, for example, a child aged seven to eight succeeds in arranging, according to their increasing size, a series of small rulers (between ten and sixteen and a half centimeters) one above the other and in arranging them without hesitation according to a method (first, the smallest of all, then the smallest of those which remain). This is a fine example of praxis of an operatory character. Similarly, at the age of nine to ten, he will be able to arrange distinct weights (with objects of equal volume), which constitutes another operatory praxis. However these concrete operations alone will not enable him to solve the Burt test which is based on the same operations of seriation but on a hypothetico-deductive level: Edith is more blonde than Suzanne. Edith is darker than Lili. Which of the three is the darkest? Finally, at about the age of eleven or twelve, the propositional or hypothetico-deductive operations are constituted which can function beyond any object manipulation and no longer concern praxis.

Moreover, it is essential to note that, in addition to the acts of intelligence proceeding by concrete operations and tending to solve a problem of truth (with a true or false solution), there exists a considerable set of acts of intelligence tending to solve purely practical problems (which solutions are expressed in success or failure). Such in particular are the behaviors studied by A. Rey in his work on *L'intelligence pratique chez l'enfant* and by Bussmann in his volume on *Le transfert dans l'intelligence pratique de l'enfant.* For example, the withdrawal of an object from a container by using various stems as intermediaries (an early study of this kind having been furnished by two German psychologists, Lippmann and Bogen, *Naive Physik).* It is a question, in this case, of praxis in the strictest sense of the term, since the aim of these actions is principally of a utilitarian nature (to achieve a material result) and no longer cognitive, as in the acts of classification, seriation, or correspondence. But the interest of the research by Rey, Bussmann, and others was precisely to show the close analogy between the child's failures or successes and the operations of his thought itself at the levels considered. One of Rey's goals was to control this kind of prelogic which we pointed out in the child in the verbal area, if it could be found again in the area of practical intelligence. In the preface to Rey's first work, we insisted on the parallelism obtained. We could insist even more so today since we no longer limit ourselves to using verbal methods and have revealed the late character of concrete operations, that is, of the logic of object manipulation. In the context of practical intelligence, our pupil Bussmann revealed the transitions which exist between the sensorimotor assimilation and the particularly logical generalization. From the viewpoint of the interpretation of the varieties of apraxia, this continuity between the practical intelligence and the particularly cognitive intelligence, if we can so state (hence the system of the logico-mathematical or logico-physical operations), seems instructive to us by emphasizing the relation of praxis and gnosis, in other words, of the basic unity of action and of intelligence in its operative aspect.

There now remains to be examined the figurative aspect of knowledge and of actions, especially the problems of image and of symbolical behavior.

The classic theories of apraxia would consider acts based on pictures. A. A. Grünbaum, on the contrary, interprets pictures as deriving from acts. From the psychological viewpoint, he is unquestionably right, and psychologists (Lotze, Dilthey, and others) have long shown that the picture does not consist of a mere continuation of perception but that it includes a propulsive element (compare Morel's, Schifferli's, and Rey's work). From the electroencephalographic viewpoint, Gastaut observes the same beta waves during the mental representation of the bending of the hand as during effective bending; Adrian has made similar observations. Using electrographics, Jacobsen, Allers, and Schminsky observed light peripheral activities (movement outlines) during the representation of arm movements simultaneous with the activities registered during the act itself thus represented. In short, the picture and the figurative aspect of thought as well as the operative aspect of thought and the operations themselves derive from the sensorimotor activities. How then should one conceive of this dual relation while maintaining the distinction of these two figurative and operative aspects of all knowledge?

We have just seen that the essential mechanism of the sensorimotor intelligence consists of a schematizing assimilation, and it is from this that the subsequent operations of representative thought proceed.

A scheme of assimilation, however, is constantly submitted to the pressure of the circumstances and can differentiate in accordance with the objects to which it is applied. We will call *accommodation*[8] this differentiation of response to the action of the objects on the schemes, synchronized with assimilation of the objects to the schemes. Equilibrium can then occur between assimilation and accommodation: Such is the result of an act of intelligence. But a primacy of accommodation can also occur and, in this case, the action is modeled on the object itself—for example, when the object becomes more interesting than the assimilating use the subject can make of it. Such more or less purely accommodating behavior indeed forms what is known as *imitation* and we can follow stage-by-stage the progress of this imitation on the sensorimotor levels in close correlation with the progress of intelligence (or equilibrium between assimilation and accommodation).

8. In analogy to what biologists call *accommodates*, that is, the distinct phenotypical variations of the genotypical characteristics.

Thus our hypothesis is that the figurative aspects of thought derive from imitation and that it is imitation which assures the transition of sensorimotor to representative thought by preparing its necessary symbolism. On the one hand, at the sensorimotor levels, there is only imitation to constitute a kind of representation by gesture (naturally quite distinct from representation in thought which will eventually derive from it). On the other hand, the advent of the symbolical function, that is, as we have seen the differentiation of the significants and the signified, is due precisely to the progress of imitation which first becomes capable of functioning in its deferred form[9] (deferred imitation already constituting a true representation). This furnishes to symbolical games (beginning about the age of one and a half) their entire gestural symbolism which, as we are going to see now, forms the point of departure of the mental picture as interiorized imitation.

As early as 1935 (334–55ff.) we insisted on this role of transition between the sensorimotor and the representative played by imitation. H. Wallon brilliantly returned to this idea in *De l'acte a la pensée,* by emphasizing the importance of the postural system and attitudes in the birth of representation. Thus we agree with Wallon on this point, but we do not believe that this relation is valid only for the figurative aspect of thought, whereas the operative aspect (which constitutes the chief characteristic of acts of intelligence in opposition to their symbolical expression) continues the energy as such.

To return to the image, we therefore suggest conceiving it as an interiorized imitation,[10] and all research that we were able to do and are still doing on the development of the child's mental pictures reveals to what extent imagery (pictures) remains static and short before completion of operations, and above all to what extent imagery remains subordinated to operations instead of preparing and directing them. It is surprising, for example, to note the child's difficulties at the preoperatory levels in imagining the stages of a curve's transformation (in the form of wire thread) into a rectilinear shaft, or the rotation of a shaft around a pivoting center, or of the gradual growth in height of a stem placed on another, then shifted, or of a cube slipping on another, before

9. That is, basically as early as its beginning in the absence of the model (in opposition to the early imitations in the presence of the model and continuing during its absence).

10. The first reason is of a genetic order: The behaviors of the first eighteen months appear to reveal the absence of pictures until what can be called the played picture (compare the infant who opens and closes his mouth before increasing the opening of a half-opened box) and the interiorized picture. The other reasons are the following: A sonorous picture (evoking the sound of a word, a melody, etc.) is accompanied by a production sketch, like the representation of a gesture. A visual picture continues not the perception as receiver but the sensorimotor activity of exploration which imitates the object's silhouette. (Compare Morel's and Schifferli's experiments on the ocular movements accompanying the picture and parallel to those which intervene in the perceptive activities during the very presentation of the object).

the spatial operations are constructed, with the conservation of the sizes during displacements.

This duality of image and operation seems important to us for the study of apraxia. One of the classic tests of apraxia, which consists of imitating a transitive act without an object present, is based on imitative representation of the act and not on its execution in an operative situation. It is only starting at a certain level that the imagined representation of the act can play a role in the improvement of its execution, and when it is a question of somewhat complex acts for their anticipation to be necessary to the success; but it is easy to furnish a series of examples of acts correctly carried out by the child, where their representation is defective. The most remarkable example of imagined (pictured) representation capable of offering a precise anticipation of the acts and even of substituting for them, is the spatial intuition of the geometer who succeeds with surprising mobility in imagining every possible transformation of a figure, whereas a nongeometer, whom Plato[11] in his *Republic* proscribed, "sees" only a few. This geometrical intuition, though developed to a certain degree in any normal subject beginning at the level of concrete operations, remains, as we have just seen, oddly static and unfinished prior to this level. There is nothing easier for a five-year-old child, for example, than to pivot a rod at 90° until at a horizontal position (one end being fixed). This child's drawing, however, will disclose only the extreme positions; he is incapable of representing the intermediary slanted positions. Similarly, a child aged four to five, taking the same way from home to school and back, will find a systematic difficulty in reproducing it (even in outline) on a model and will be satisfied with motor memories ("I go like that, then I turn, etc."), indicating by gestures rectilinear movements, or sudden turnings, but without evocations of reference points or of the way as such.

Generally, spatial pictures are thus dependent on actions and operations and not the contrary, and the mathematician's geometrical intuition is only an internal imitation of the operations which he is capable of doing according to an increasingly refined logic. Certain acts probably suppose at almost every level an imagined anticipation, for example, of drawing (oriented by Luquet's "internal model"). But these are figurative acts, so to speak (the drawing is a graphic imitation as part of imitation in general), and the rule does not seem valid to us for operative acts (=transformation and not reproduction of an object).

As for the corporal scheme, unfortunately we were unable to do research on this subject and therefore cannot make a statement on the picture's role in the actions exercised on the body itself. But whether this role proves necessary or not, we would have to ask ourselves to what point the construction of this

11. Plato is said to have inscribed, "Let no man ignorant of geometry enter here," above the entrance to his Academy.—Trans.

scheme is precisely not bound up with imitation itself which we studied in regard to the first eighteen months (Piaget 1959) (following P. Guillaume's fine work on the learned and not innate character of this imitation). The child, for example, long knows his face only tactually and does not place it in relation to the faces perceived visually on others: Until the age of one year a yawning by others is not at all contagious (if the experimenter yawns noiselessly!). The errors committed are far more instructive than the successes: To a model opening and closing its eyes, the child will reply among other actions by opening and closing his mouth. If the corporal scheme were partly constructed as a result of imitation, the relation between the picture (or interiorized imitation) and the act would create a particular problem in this delimited field which would thus be midway between operative situations (as the intuition of space of objects) and figurative situations (as drawing).

Frankly, there is still nothing more ambiguous than the notion of the corporal scheme, despite the fine work by Head, Bartlett, Pick, Schilder, Conrad, and many others. In concluding their excellent work on *Méconnaissances et hallucinations corporelles* (Mason 1952), Hécaen and Ajuriaguerra summarized well the present state of the act, but what is quite clear is the absence of a somewhat systematic genetic study, despite work by Wallon, Zazzo, Lezine, and others. Thus for the present, we can only conclude with Schilder: If somatognosis includes a set of perceptive facts, especially proprioceptive, it supposes above all a spatial setting integrating into a functional whole our perceptions, our postures, and our gestures. Thus it is extremely probable that in this setting are integrated not only the contributions of the body itself, but also the almost constantly indispensable reference which is visual, auditive, and partly tactilo-kinesthetic knowledge (as during imitation learning) of others' bodies and of what is common to every human body (and perhaps even animals). This is why, in the present fragmentary state of knowledge, we would be inclined to believe that somatognosis is established between the elementary sensorimotor schemes (which include the knowledge of hands, but not that of the whole body) and the truly figurative symbolical behavior (pictures) and, requires as still-to-be representative or symbolical figurative instrument only imitation itself, whose role precisely is to assure the connection between the body proper and that of others.

Moreover, there remains to be specified how far we should extend the notion of corporal knowledge. But if we go so far as to include the notions of left and right and their application to the bodies of others as well as to ones' own body (see Head's proof and our results on the difficulty, before about the age of seven, to designate the experimenter's left and right hand when seated facing the subject), it will be important to recall that even relations of this kind, while including an operatory and logical aspect, become part of the reciprocity setting whose point of departure is again furnished by imitation (in a one-way or mutual direction).

If a conclusion is expected of us, we might end this report by seeking points of contact between such a study of praxis and the analysis of apraxia. Ajuriaguerra and Hécaen suggest a new classification of apraxia based on the following trilogy:

1. *Sensorikinetic apraxia* is characterized by an alteration of the sensorimotor synthesis with automatization of the gesture, but with no trouble in representing the act.

2. *Somato-spatial apractognosis* is characterized by spatial disorganization of the relations between the body and the external objects with no sensorimotor troubles. It is a question therefore of the somatognostic troubles causing gesture disadaptations, including disturbances of left-right relations or certain dressing apraxia. In addition, there are often visual perceptivo-motory alterations but without this necessarily signifying primary perceptive troubles.

3. *Apraxia of symbolical formation* is characterized by disorganization of symbolical and categorical activity (ranging from the agnosia of utilization to frequent trouble with verbal formation).

To compare this list with what we have seen of normal praxis, we at once note certain correspondence but also note that a question, rather a central one, remains.

These three categories of apraxia correspond closely to three genetic levels: sensorikinetic apraxia to the sensorimotor level; somato-spatial apraxia to an intermediary level between the elementary sensorimotor behaviors and the behaviors made possible by the symbolical function, the intermedial level whose point of departure we suggested is found in the behavior of imitation; apraxia of symbolical formation, finally, to the level characterized by representations in their dual figurative and operative aspect.

But the remaining question precisely relates to this dual aspect of representative thought: Does apraxia of symbolical formation result from alterations of the operations as such or only from the gestural symbolism, imagined or even verbal, serving to represent them? We dislike the term *categorical* used by Gelb and Goldstein, Wallon, and others to designate the notional or conceptual settings which correspond to the verbal settings, for in this language "the symbolical and categorical activity," as one says too easily, seems to constitute only a one and the same "activity" of which, in point of fact, the only "active" characteristic would be to allow abstraction! Certainly it is conceivable that this is so, but our effort consists in doubting such unity. Believe me, thinking cannot be reduced to speaking, to classifying into categories, nor even to abstracting. To think is to act on the object and to transform it. When an automobile breaks down, an understanding of the situation does not consist in describing the engine's observable failure but in knowing how to take it apart and reassemble it. In the presence of a physical phenomenon, comprehension begins only by transforming the facts in order to dissociate the factors and to make them vary separately—an action not of categorizing but of acting to produce and to reproduce.[12] Even in pure geometry, knowledge does not consist of describing the figures but of transforming them to the point of being able to reduce them to basic groups of transformations. In short, "In the beginning was the Act," as Goethe said,[13] and the operation followed! Thus it seems to us, there remains to be established with some care to what extent contructive apraxia, ideatory apraxia, and in general apraxia of symbolical formation concern only symbolizing, that is, representation of the gesture, the design, the picture, or even the language, or if they are related to the symbolized itself, that is, to actions and operations.

For Reflection

1. What approaches to instruction might facilitate assimilation?
2. What implications do you see for Christian education of Piaget's stage theory?
3. How does accommodation differ from assimilation?
4. Explain disequilibration.

References

Ajuriaguerra, J., and H. Hécaen. 1960. *Le cortex cerebral.* 2d ed. Paris: Masson.

Hécaen, H., and Ajuriaguerra, J. 1952. *Méconnaissances et hallucinations corporelles.* Paris: Masson.

Piaget, J. 1935. *La Naissance de l'intelligence chez l'enfant.* Neuchatel, Switzerland: Delachaux and Niestle.

———. 1959. *La formation du symbole chez l' enfant.* 2d ed. Neuchatel, Switzerland: Delachaux and Niestle.

12. To achieve the "mode of production of the phenomena," despite the ban pronounced by Auguste Comte.

13. *Faust*, Part One, Scene III—Trans.

6

B. F. Skinner
Psychologist

A Technology of Behavior
(1971)

If John Watson can be called the "father of behaviorism," surely Burrhus Frederic Skinner has earned the title "eldest son of behaviorism." He received the Ph.D. at Harvard in 1931 and returned to join the faculty in 1948. Skinner's work in behavioral psychology has had a powerful effect on education, especially since the late 1950s. "Precision teaching" and the general use of behavior objectives are two of the results of his influence. In his numerous writings Skinner has applied his theories of operant behavior to mental illness, politics, and counseling. He vigorously advocates materialistic humanism.

What follows is the first chapter of B. F. Skinner's well-known book, *Beyond Freedom and Dignity,* attacking the concept of "the autonomous man" and showing how a science of behavior could lead to the evolution of cultures. Included, too, are the final two pages of chapter 8, "The Design of a Culture." Professor Skinner argues that the concepts of freedom and dignity have played important roles in the maintenance of the autonomous-man ideal. If the woes of the world are to be overcome, according to the author, these concepts must be discarded. Instead, we should focus on the physical and social environments, based on the results of experimental analysis of behavior, that is, advanced approaches to behavioristic psychology. Explanations of human behavior need to be given in terms of genetic endowment and personal history rather than in the mentalistic terms of state of

From *Beyond Freedom and Dignity* (New York: Alfred A. Knopf, 1971), 3–25.

mind or feelings. Of course, no place or need remains for the traditional concept of God. The only way to change humans is to change their environment.

Pulling these ideas together, Skinner calls for a technology of behavior. It will be able to bring the interaction between environment and organism to our understanding. Freedom, dignity, and the autonomous man call for the individual to bear personal responsibility for conduct and take credit for achievement. The technology of behavior will shift responsibility and credit to the environment. Questions of who will use and control the technology are misplaced. Instead, they should address the quality of the environment.

Of all the writings of B. F. Skinner this book seems to take behaviorism, the analysis of behavior, and the technology of behavior to its logical conclusion.

In trying to solve the terrifying problems that face us in the world today, we naturally turn to the things we do best. We play from strength, and our strength is science and technology. To contain a population explosion we look for better methods of birth control. Threatened by a nuclear holocaust, we build bigger deterrent forces and anti-ballistic-missile systems. We try to stave off world famine with new foods and better ways of growing them. Improved sanitation and medicine will, we hope, control disease; better housing and transportation will solve the problems of the ghettos; and new ways of reducing or disposing of waste will stop the pollution of the environment. We can point to remarkable achievements in all these fields, and it is not surprising that we should try to extend them. But things grow steadily worse, and it is disheartening to find that technology itself is increasingly at fault. Sanitation and medicine have made the problems of population more acute, war has acquired a new horror with the invention of nuclear weapons, and the affluent pursuit of happiness is largely responsible for pollution. As Darlington has said, "Every new source from which man has increased his power on the earth has been used to diminish the prospects of his successors. All his progress has been made at the expense of damage to his environment which he cannot repair and could not foresee" (1970, 1332).

Whether or not he could have foreseen the damage, man must repair it or all is lost. And he can do so if he will recognize the nature of the difficulty. The application of the physical and biological sciences alone will not solve our problems because the solutions lie in another field. Better contraceptives will control population only if people use them. New weapons may offset new defenses and vice versa, but a nuclear holocaust can be prevented only if the conditions under which nations make war can be changed. New methods of agriculture and medicine will not help if they are not practiced, and housing is a matter not only of buildings and cities but of how people live. Overcrowding can be corrected only by inducing people not to crowd, and the environment will continue to deteriorate until polluting practices are abandoned.

In short, we need to make vast changes in human behavior, and we cannot make them with the help of nothing more than physics or biology, no matter how hard we try. (And there are other problems, such as the breakdown of our educational system and the disaffection and revolt of the young, to which physical and biological technologies are so obviously irrelevant that they have never been applied.) It is not enough to "use technology with a deeper understanding of human issues," or to "dedicate technology to man's spiritual needs," or to "encourage technologists to look at human problems." Such expressions imply that where human behavior begins, technology stops, and that we must carry on, as we have in the past, with what we have learned from personal experience or from those collections of personal experiences called history, or with the distillations of experience to be found in folk wisdom and practical rules of thumb. These have been available for centuries, and all we have to show for them is the state of the world today.

What we need is a technology of behavior. We could solve our problems quickly enough if we could adjust the growth of the world's population as precisely as we adjust the course of a spaceship, or improve agriculture and industry with with some of the confidence with which we accelerate high-energy particles, or move toward a peaceful world with something like the steady progress with which physics has approached absolute zero (even though both remain presumably out of reach). But a behavioral technology comparable in power and precision to physical and biological technology is lacking, and those who do not find the very possibility ridiculous are more likely to be frightened by it than reassured. That is how far we are from "understanding human issues" in the sense in which physics and biology understand their fields, and how far we are from preventing the catastrophe toward which the world seems to be inexorably moving.

Twenty-five hundred years ago it might have been said that man understood himself as well as any other part of his world. Today he is the thing he understands least. Physics and biology have come a long way, but there has been no comparable development of anything like a science of human behavior. Greek physics and biology are now of historical interest only (no modern physicist or biologist would turn to Aristotle for help), but the dialogues of Plato are still assigned to students and cited as if they threw light on human behavior. Aristotle could not have understood a page of modern physics or biology, but Socrates and his friends would have little trouble in following most current discussions of human affairs. And as to technology, we have made immense strides in controlling the physical and biological worlds, but our practices in government, education, and much of economics, though adapted to very different conditions, have not greatly improved.

We can scarcely explain this by saying that the Greeks knew all there was to know about human behavior. Certainly they knew more than they knew about the physical world, but it was still not much. Moreover, their way of thinking about human behavior must have had some fatal flaw. Whereas Greek physics and biology, no matter how crude, led eventually to modern science, Greek theories of human behavior led nowhere. If they are with us today, it is not because they possessed some kind of eternal verity, but because they did not contain the seeds of anything better.

It can always be argued that human behavior is a particularly difficult field. It is, and we are especially likely to think so just because we are so inept in dealing with it. But modern physics and biology successfully treat subjects that are certainly no simpler than many aspects of human behavior. The difference is that the instruments and methods they use are of commensurate complexity. The fact that equally powerful instruments and methods are not available in the field of human behavior is not an explanation; it is only part of the puzzle. Was putting a man on the moon actually easier than improving education in our public schools? Or than constructing better kinds of living space for everyone? Or than making it possible for everyone to be gainfully employed and, as a result, to enjoy a higher standard of living? The choice was not a matter of priorities, for no one could have said that it was more important to get to the moon. The exciting thing about getting to the moon was its feasibility. Science and technology had reached the point at which, with one great push, the thing could be done. There is no comparable excitement about the problems posed by human behavior. We are not close to solutions.

It is easy to conclude that there must be something about human behavior which makes a scientific analysis, and hence an effective technology, impossible, but we have not by any means exhausted the possibilities. There is a sense in which it can be said that the methods of science have scarcely yet been applied to human behavior. We have used the instruments of science, we have counted and measured and compared, but something essential to scientific practice is missing in almost all current discussions of human behavior. (The term *cause* is no longer common in sophisticated scientific writing, but it will serve well enough here.)[1]

Man's first experience with causes probably came from his own behavior: things moved because he moved them. If other things moved, it was because someone else was moving them, and if the mover could not be seen, it was because he was invisible. The Greek gods served in this way as the causes of physical phenomena. They were usually outside the things they moved, but they might enter into and "possess" them.[2] Physics and biology soon aban-

1. What is no longer common in sophisticated scientific writing is the push-pull causality of nineteenth-century science. The causes referred to here are, technically speaking, the independent variables of which behavior as a dependent variable is a function. See Skinner (1953), chap. 3.

2. On "possession," see Skinner (1969), chap. 9.

doned explanations of this sort and turned to more useful kinds of causes, but the step has not been decisively taken in the field of human behavior. Intelligent people no longer believe that men are possessed by demons (although the exorcism of devils is occasionally practiced, and the daimonic has reappeared in the writings of psychotherapists), but human behavior is still commonly attributed to indwelling agents. A juvenile delinquent is said, for example, to be suffering from a disturbed personality. There would be no point in saying it if the personality were not somehow distinct from the body which has got itself into trouble. The distinction is clear when one body is said to contain several personalities which control it in different ways at different times. Psychoanalysts have identified three of these personalities—the ego, superego, and id—and interactions among them are said to be responsible for the behavior of the man in whom they dwell.

Although physics soon stopped personifying things in this way, it continued for a long time to speak as if they had wills, impulses, feelings, purposes, and other fragmentary attributes of an indwelling agent. According to Butterfield (1957), Aristotle argued that a falling body accelerated because it grew more jubilant as it found itself nearer home, and later authorities supposed that a projectile was carried forward by an impetus, sometimes called an "impetuosity." All this was eventually abandoned, and to good effect, but the behavioral sciences still appeal to comparable internal states. No one is surprised to hear it said that a person carrying good news walks more rapidly because he feels jubilant, or acts carelessly because of his impetuosity, or holds stubbornly to a course of action through sheer force of will. Careless references to purpose are still to be found in both physics and biology, but good practice has no place for them; yet almost everyone attributes human behavior to intentions, purposes, aims, and goals. If it is still possible to ask whether a machine can show purpose, the question implies, significantly, that if it can it will more closely resemble a man.

Physics and biology moved farther away from personified causes when they began to attribute the behavior of things to essences, qualities, or natures. To the medieval alchemist, for example, some of the properties of a substance might be due to the mercurial essence, and substances were compared in what might have been called a "chemistry of individual differences." Newton complained of the practice in his contemporaries: "To tell us that every species of thing is endowed with an occult specific quality by which it acts and produces manifest effects is to tell us nothing." (Occult qualities were examples of the hypotheses Newton rejected when he said "Hypotheses non fingo," though he was not quite as good as his word.) Biology continued for a long time to appeal to the *nature* of living things, and it did not wholly abandon vital forces until the twentieth century. Behavior, however, is still attributed to human nature, and there is an extensive "psychology of individual differences" in which people are compared and described in terms of traits of character, capacities, and abilities.

Almost everyone who is concerned with human affairs—as political scientist, philosopher, man of letters, economist, psychologist, linguist, sociologist, theologian, anthropologist, educator, or psychotherapist—continues to talk about human behavior in this prescientific way. Every issue of a daily paper, every magazine, every professional journal, every book with any bearing whatsoever on human behavior will supply examples. We are told that to control the number of people in the world we need to change *attitudes* toward children, overcome *pride* in size of family or in sexual potency, build some *sense of responsibility* toward offspring, and reduce the role played by a large family in allaying *concern* for old age. To work for peace we must deal with the *will to power* or the *paranoid delusions* of leaders; we must remember that wars begin in the *minds* of men, that there is something suicidal in man—a *death instinct* perhaps—which leads to war, and that man is aggressive by *nature*. To solve the problems of the poor we must inspire *self-respect*, encourage *initiative*, and reduce *frustration*. To allay the disaffection of the young we must provide a *sense of purpose* and reduce feelings of *alienation* or *hopelessness*. Realizing that we have no effective means of doing any of this, we ourselves may experience a *crisis of belief* or a *loss of confidence*, which can be corrected only by returning to a *faith in man's inner capacities*. This is staple fare. Almost no one questions it. Yet there is nothing like it in modern physics or most of biology, and that fact may well explain why a science and a technology of behavior have been so long delayed.

It is usually supposed that the "behavioristic" objection to ideas, feelings, traits of character, will, and so on concerns the stuff of which they are said to be made. Certain stubborn questions about the nature of mind have, of course, been debated for more than twenty-five hundred years and still go unanswered. How, for example, can the mind move the body? As late as 1965 Karl Popper could put the question this way: "What we want is to understand how such nonphysical things as *purposes, deliberations, plans, decisions, theories, tensions*, and *values* can play a part in bringing about physical changes in the physical world" (1966, 15). And, of course, we also want to know where these nonphysical things come from. To that question the Greeks had a simple answer: from the gods. As Dodds (1951) has pointed out, the Greeks believed that if a man behaved foolishly, it was because a hostile god had planted ἄτη (infatuation) in his breast. A friendly god might give a warrior an extra amount of μένος [might or force], with the help of which he would fight brilliantly. Aristotle thought there was something divine in thought, and Zeno held that the intellect *was* God.

We cannot take that line today, and the commonest alternative is to appeal to antecedent physical events. A person's genetic endowment, a product of the evolution of the species, is said to explain part of the workings of his mind and his personal history the rest. For example, because of (physical) competition during the course of evolution people now have (nonphysical) feelings of aggression which lead to (physical) acts of hostility. Or, the (physical) punishment a small child receives when he engages in sex play produces (nonphysical) feelings of anxiety which interfere with his (physical) sexual behavior as an adult. The nonphysical stage obviously bridges long periods of time: aggression reaches back into millions of years of evolutionary history, and anxiety acquired when one is a child survives into old age.

The problem of getting from one kind of stuff to another could be avoided if everything were either mental or physical, and both these possibilities have been considered. Some philosophers have tried to stay within the world of the mind, arguing that only immediate experience is real, and experimental psychology began as an attempt to discover the mental laws which governed interactions among mental elements. Contemporary "intrapsychic" theories of psychotherapy tell us how one feeling leads to another (how frustration breeds aggression, for example), how feelings interact, and how feelings which have been put out of mind fight their way back in. The complementary line that the mental stage is really physical was taken, curiously enough, by Freud, who believed that physiology would eventually explain the workings of the mental apparatus. In a similar vein, many physiological psychologists continue to talk freely about states of mind, feelings, and so on, in the belief that it is only a matter of time before we shall understand their physical nature.

The dimensions of the world of mind and the transition from one world to another do raise embarrassing problems, but it is usually possible to ignore them, and this may be good strategy, for the important objection to mentalism is of a very different sort.[3] The world of the mind steals the show. Behavior is not recognized as a subject in its own right. In psychotherapy, for example, the disturbing things a person does or says are almost always regarded merely as symptoms, and compared with the fascinating dramas which are staged in the depths of the mind, behavior itself seems superficial indeed. In linguistics and literary criticism what a man says is almost always treated as the expression of ideas or feelings. In political science, theology, and economics, behavior is usually regarded as the material from which one infers attitudes, intentions, needs, and so on. For more than twenty-five hundred years close attention has been paid to mental life, but only recently has any effort been made to study human behavior as something more than a mere by-product.

The conditions of which behavior is a function are also neglected. The mental explanation brings curiosity to an end. We see the effect in casual discourse. If we ask someone, "Why did you go to the theater?" and he says,

3. Ibid., chap. 8.

"Because I felt like going," we are apt to take his reply as a kind of explanation. It would be much more to the point to know what has happened when he has gone to the theater in the past, what he heard or read about the play he went to see, and what other things in his past or present environments might have induced him to go (as opposed to doing something else), but we accept "I felt like going" as a sort of summary of all this and are not likely to ask for details.

The professional psychologist often stops at the same point. A long time ago William James (1884) corrected a prevailing view of the relation between feelings and action by asserting, for example, that we do not run away because we are afraid but are afraid because we run away. In other words, what we feel when we feel afraid is our behavior—the very behavior which in the traditional view expresses the feeling and is explained by it. But how many of those who have considered James's argument have noted that no antecedent event has in fact been pointed out? Neither "because" should be taken seriously. No explanation has been given as to why we run away *and* feel afraid.

Whether we regard ourselves as explaining feelings or the behavior said to be caused by feelings, we give very little attention to antecedent circumstances. The psychotherapist learns about the early life of his patient almost exclusively from the patient's memories, which are known to be unreliable, and he may even argue that what is important is not what actually happened but what the patient remembers. In the psychoanalytic literature there must be at least a hundred references to felt anxiety for every reference to a punishing episode to which anxiety might be traced. We even seem to prefer antecedent histories which are clearly out of reach. There is a good deal of current interest, for example, in what must have happened during the evolution of the species to explain human behavior, and we seem to speak with special confidence just because what actually happened can only be inferred.

Unable to understand how or why the person we see behaves as he does, we attribute his behavior to a person we cannot see, whose behavior we cannot explain either but about whom we are not inclined to ask questions. We probably adopt this strategy not so much because of any lack of interest or power but because of a longstanding conviction that for much of human behavior there *are* no relevant antecedents. The function of the inner man is to provide an explanation which will not be explained in turn. Explanation stops with him. He is not a mediator between past history and current behavior, he is a *center* from which behavior emanates. He initiates, originates, and creates, and in doing so he remains, as he was for the Greeks, divine. We say that he is autonomous—and, so far as a science of behavior is concerned, that means miraculous.

The position is, of course, vulnerable. Autonomous man serves to explain only the tings we are not yet able to explain in other ways. His existence depends upon our ignorance, and he naturally loses status as we come to know more about behavior. The task of a scientific analysis is to explain how the behavior of a person as a physical system is related to the conditions under which the human species evolved and the conditions under which the individual lives. Unless there is indeed some capricious or creative intervention, these events must be related, and no intervention is in fact needed. The contingencies of survival responsible for man's genetic endowment would produce tendencies to *act* aggressively, not feelings of aggression. The punishment of sexual behavior changes sexual *behavior*, and any feelings which may arise are at best by-products. Our age is not suffering from anxiety but from the accidents, crimes, wars, and other dangerous and painful things to which people are so often exposed. Young people drop out of school, refuse to get jobs, and associate only with others of their own age not because they feel alienated but because of defective social environments in homes, schools, factories, and elsewhere.

We can follow the path taken by physics and biology by turning directly to the relation between behavior and the environment and neglecting supposed mediating states of mind. Physics did not advance by looking more closely at the jubilance of a falling body, or biology by looking at the nature of vital spirits, and we do not need to try to discover what personalities, states of mind, feelings, traits of character, plans, purposes, intentions, or the other perquisites of autonomous man really are in order to get on with a scientific analysis of behavior.

There are reasons why it has taken us so long to reach this point. The things studied by physics and biology do not behave very much like people, and it eventually seems rather ridiculous to speak of the jubilance of a falling body or the impetuosity of a projectile; but people do behave like people, and the outer man whose behavior is to be explained could be very much like the inner man whose behavior is said to explain it. The inner man has been created in the image of the outer.

A more important reason is that the inner man seems at times to be directly observed. We must infer the jubilance of a falling body, but can we not *feel* our own jubilance? We do, indeed, feel things inside our own skin, but we do not feel the things which have been invented to explain behavior. The possessed man does not feel the possessing *demon* and may even deny that one exists. The juvenile delinquent does not feel his *disturbed personality*. The intelligent man does not feel his *intelligence* or the introvert his *introversion*. (In fact, these dimensions of mind or character are said to be observable only through complex statistical procedures.) The speaker does not feel the *grammatical rules* he is said to apply in composing sentences, and men spoke grammatically for thousands of years before anyone knew there were rules. The respondent to a questionnaire does not feel the *attitudes* or *opinions* which lead him to check items in particular ways. We do feel certain states of our bodies associated with behavior, but as Freud pointed out, we behave in the same way when we do not feel them; they are by-products and not to be mistaken for causes.

There is a much more important reason why we have been so slow in discarding mentalistic explanations: it has been hard to find alternatives. Presumably we must look for them in the external environment, but the role of the environment is by no means clear. The history of the theory of evolution illustrates the problem. Before the nineteenth century, the environment was thought of simply as a passive setting in which many different kinds of organisms were born, reproduced themselves, and died. No one saw that the environment was responsible for the fact that there *were* many different kinds (and that fact, significantly enough, was attributed to a creative Mind). The trouble was that the environment acts in an inconspicuous way: it does not push or pull, it *selects.* For thousands of years in the history of human thought the process of natural selection went unseen in spite of its extraordinary importance. When it was eventually discovered, it became, of course, the key to evolutionary theory.

The effect of the environment on behavior remained obscure for an even longer time.[4] We can see what organisms do to the world around them, as they take from it what they need and ward off its dangers, but it is much harder to see what the world does to them. It was Descartes (1662) who first suggested that the environment might play an active role in the determination of behavior, and he was apparently able to do so only because he was given a strong hint. He knew about certain automata in the Royal Gardens of France which were operated hydraulically by concealed valves. As Descartes described it, people entering the gardens "necessarily tread on certain tiles or plates, which are so disposed that if they approach a bathing Diana, they cause her to hide in the rosebushes, and if they try to follow her, they cause Neptune to come forward to meet them, threatening them with his trident." The figures were entertaining just because they behaved like people, and it appeared, therefore, that something very much like human behavior could be explained mechanically. Descartes took the hint: living organisms might move for similar reasons. (He excluded the human organism, presumably to avoid religious controversy.)

The triggering action of the environment came to be called a "stimulus"—the Latin for *goad*—and the effect on an organism a "response," and together they were said to compose a "reflex." Reflexes were first demonstrated in small decapitated animals, such as salamanders, and it is significant that the principle was challenged throughout the nineteenth century because it seemed to deny the existence of an autonomous agent—the "soul of the spinal cord"—to which movement of a decapitated body had been attributed. When Pavlov showed how new reflexes could be built up through conditioning, a full-

4. Ibid., chap. 1.

fledged stimulus-response psychology was born, in which all behavior was regarded as reactions to stimuli. One writer put it this way: "We are prodded or lashed through life" (Holt 1931). The stimulus-response model was never very convincing, however, and it did not solve the basic problem, because something like an inner man had to be invented to convert a stimulus into a response. Information theory ran into the same problem when an inner "processor" had to be invented to convert input into output.

The effect of an eliciting stimulus is relatively easy to see, and it is not surprising that Descartes' hypothesis held a dominant position in behavior theory for a long time, but it was a false scent from which a scientific analysis is only now recovering. The environment not only prods or lashes, it *selects*. Its role is similar to that in natural selection, though on a very different time scale, and was overlooked for the same reason. It is now clear that we must take into account what the environment does to an organism not only before but after it responds. Behavior is shaped and maintained by its consequences. Once this fact is recognized, we can formulate the interaction between organism and environment in a much more comprehensive way.

There are two important results. One concerns the basic analysis. Behavior which operates upon the environment to produce consequences ("operant" behavior) can be studied by arranging environments in which specific consequences are contingent upon it.[5] The contingencies under investigation have become steadily more complex, and one by one they are taking over the explanatory functions previously assigned to personalities, states of mind, feelings, traits of character, purposes, and intentions. The second result is practical: the environment can be manipulated. It is true that man's genetic endowment can be changed only very slowly, but changes in the environment of the individual have quick and dramatic effects. A technology of operant behavior is, as we shall see, already well advanced, and it may prove to be commensurate with our problems (Ulrich, Stachnik, and Mabry, 1966, 1970).

That possibility raises another problem, however, which must be solved if we are to take advantage of our gains. We have moved forward by dispossessing autonomous man, but he has not departed gracefully. He is conducting a sort of rearguard action in which, unfortunately, he can marshal formidable support. He is still an important figure in political science, law, religion, economics, anthropology, sociology, psychotherapy, philosophy, ethics, history, education, child care, linguistics, architecture, city planning, and family life. These fields have their specialists, and every specialist has a theory, and in almost every theory the autonomy of the individual is unquestioned. The inner man is not seriously threatened by data obtained through casual observation or from studies of the structure of behavior, and many of these fields deal only with groups of people, where statistical or actuarial data impose few restraints

5. On "operant" behavior, see Skinner (1953), chap. 5.

upon the individual. The result is a tremendous weight of traditional "knowledge," which must be corrected or displaced by a scientific analysis.

Two features of autonomous man are particularly troublesome. In the traditional view, a person is free. He is autonomous in the sense that his behavior is uncaused. He can therefore be held responsible for what he does and justly punished if he offends. That view, together with its associated practices, must be reexamined when a scientific analysis reveals unsuspected controlling relations between behavior and environment. A certain amount of external control can be tolerated. Theologians have accepted the fact that man must be predestined to do what an omniscient God knows he will do, and the Greek dramatist took inexorable fate as his favorite theme. Soothsayers and astrologers often claim to predict what men will do, and they have always been in demand. Biographers and historians have searched for "influences" in the lives of individuals and peoples. Folk wisdom and the insights of essayists like Montaigne and Bacon imply some kind of predictability in human conduct, and the statistical and actuarial evidences of the social sciences point in the same direction.

Autonomous man survives in the face of all this because he is the happy exception. Theologians have reconciled predestination with free will, and the Greek audience, moved by the portrayal of an inescapable destiny, walked out of the theater free men. The course of history has been turned by the death of a leader or a storm at sea, as a life has been changed by a teacher or a love affair, but these things do not happen to everyone, and they do not affect everyone in the same way. Some historians have made a virtue of the unpredictability of history. Actuarial evidence is easily ignored; we read that hundreds of people will be killed in traffic accidents on a holiday weekend and take to the road as if personally exempt. Very little behavioral science raises "the specter of predictable man." On the contrary, many anthropologists, sociologists, and psychologists have used their expert knowledge to prove that man is free, purposeful, and responsible. Freud was a determinist—on faith, if not on the evidence—but many Freudians have no hesitation in assuring their patients that they are free to choose among different courses of action and are in the long run the architects of their own destinies.

This escape route is slowly closed as new evidences of the predictability of human behavior are discovered. Personal exemption from a complete determinism is revoked as a scientific analysis progresses, particularly in accounting for the behavior of the individual. Joseph Wood Krutch (1967) has acknowledged the actuarial facts while insisting on personal freedom: "We can predict with a considerable degree of accuracy how many people will go to the seashore on a day when the temperature reaches a certain point, even how many will jump off a bridge . . . although I am not, nor are you, compelled to do either." But he can scarcely mean that those who go to the seashore do not go for good reason, or that circumstances in the life of a suicide no not have some bearing on the fact that he jumps off a bridge. The distinction is tenable only so long as a word like "compel" suggests a particularly conspicuous and forcible mode of control. A scientific analysis naturally moves in the direction of clarifying all kinds of controlling relations.

By questioning the control exercised by autonomous man and demonstrating the control exercised by the environment, a science of behavior also seems to question dignity or worth. A person is responsible for his behavior, not only in the sense that he may be justly blamed or punished when he behaves badly, but also in the sense that he is to be given credit and admired for his achievements. A scientific analysis shifts the credit as well as the blame to the environment, and traditional practices can then no longer be justified. These are sweeping changes, and those who are committed to traditional theories and practices naturally resist them.

There is a third source of trouble. As the emphasis shifts to the environment, the individual seems to be exposed to a new kind of danger. Who is to construct the controlling environment and to what end? Autonomous man presumably controls himself in accordance with a built-in set of values; he works for what he finds good. But what will the putative controller find good, and will it be good for those he controls? Answers to questions of this sort are said, of course, to call for value judgments.

Freedom, dignity, and value are major issues, and unfortunately they become more crucial as the power of a technology of behavior becomes more nearly commensurate with the problems to be solved. The very change which has brought some hope of a solution is responsible for a growing opposition to the kind of solution proposed. This conflict is itself a problem in human behavior and may be approached as such. A science of behavior is by no means as far advanced as physics or biology, but it has an advantage in that it may throw some light on its own difficulties. Science *is* human behavior, and so is the opposition to science. What has happened in man's struggle for freedom and dignity, and what problems arise when scientific knowledge begins to be relevant in that struggle? Answers to these questions may help to clear the way for the technology we so badly need.

In what follows, these issues are discussed "from a scientific point of view," but this does not mean that the reader will need to know the details of a scientific analysis of behavior. A mere interpretation will suffice. The nature of such an interpretation is, however, easily misunderstood. We often talk about things we cannot observe or measure with the precision demanded by a scientific analysis, and in doing so there is much to be gained from using terms and principles which have been worked out under more precise conditions. The sea at dusk glows with a strange light, frost forms on the windowpane in an unusual pattern, and the soup fails to thicken on the stove, and specialists tell us why. We can, of course, challenge them: they do not have "the facts," and what they say cannot be "proved," but they are nevertheless more likely to be right than those who lack an experimental background, and they alone can tell us how to move on to a more precise study if it seems worthwhile.

An experimental analysis of behavior offers similar advantages. When we have observed behavioral processes under controlled conditions, we can more easily spot them in the world at large. We can identify significant features of behavior and of the environment and are therefore able to neglect insignificant ones, no matter how fascinating they may be. We can reject traditional explanations if they have been tried and found wanting in an experimental analysis and then press forward in our inquiry with unallayed curiosity. The instances of behavior cited in what follows are not offered as "proof" of the interpretation. The proof is to be found in the basic analysis. The principles used in interpreting the instances have a plausibility which would be lacking in principles drawn entirely from casual observation.

The text will often seem inconsistent. English, like all languages, if full of prescientific terms which usually suffice for purposes of casual discourse. No one looks askance at the astronomer when he says that the sun rises or that the stars come out at night, for it would be ridiculous to insist that he should always say that the sun appears over the horizon as the earth turns or that the stars become visible as the atmosphere ceases to refract sunlight. All we ask is that he can give a more precise translation if one is needed. The English language contains many more expressions referring to human behavior than to other aspects of the world, and technical alternatives are much less familiar. The use of casual expressions is therefore much more likely to be challenged. It may seem inconsistent to ask the reader to "keep a point in mind" when he has been told that mind is an explanatory fiction, or to "consider the idea of freedom" if an idea is simply an imagined precursor of behavior, or to speak of "reassuring those who fear a science of behavior" when all that is meant is changing their behavior with respect to such a science. The book could have been written for a technical reader without expressions of that sort, but the issues are important to the nonspecialist and need to be discussed in a nontechnical fashion. No doubt many of the mentalistic expressions imbedded in the English language cannot be as rigorously translated as "sunrise," but acceptable translations are not out of reach.

Almost all our major problems involve human behavior, and they cannot be solved by physical and biological technology alone. What is needed is a technology of behavior, but we have been slow to develop the science from which such a technology might be drawn. One difficulty is that almost all of what is called behavioral science continues to trace behavior to states of mind, feelings, traits of character, human nature, and so on. Physics and biology once followed similar practices and advanced only when they discarded them. The behavioral sciences have been slow to change partly because the explanatory entities often seem to be directly observed and partly because other kinds of explanations have been hard to find. The environment is obviously important, but its role has remained obscure. It does not push or pull, it *selects,* and this function is difficult to discover and analyze. The role of natural selection in evolution was formulated only a little more than a hundred years ago, and the selective role of the environment in shaping and maintaining the behavior of the individual is only beginning to be recognized and studied. As the interaction between organism and environment has come to be understood, however, effects once assigned to states of mind, feelings, and traits are beginning to be traced to accessible conditions, and a technology of behavior may therefore become available. It will not solve our problems, however, until it replaces traditional prescientific views, and these are strongly entrenched. Freedom and dignity illustrate the difficulty. They are the possessions of the autonomous man of traditional theory, and they are essential to practices in which a person is held responsible for his conduct and given credit for his achievements. A scientific analysis shifts both the responsibility and the achievement to the environment. It also raises questions concerning "values." Who will use a technology and to what ends? Until these issues are resolved, a technology of behavior will continue to be rejected, and with it possibly the only way to solve our problems.

For Reflection

1. How might it be possible to reject Skinner's worldview, but still use the essential elements of behaviorism productively in Christian education? Is this possible?
2. How is the idea of "designing a culture" the same as or different from the idea of "Christ transforming culture"?
3. Is the concept of "the autonomous person" essential for Christian education? Explain why or why not.
4. Explain the sense in which the environment *selects* rather than pushes or pulls at people.

References

Butterfield, H. 1957. *The origins of modern science.* London.

Darlington, C. D. 1970. *The evolution of man and society.* Quoted in *Science* 168: 1332.

Descartes, R. 1662. *Traité de l'homme.*

Dodds, E. R. 1951. *The Greeks and the irrational.* Berkeley: University of California Press.

Holt, E. B. 1931. *Animal drive and the learning process.* New York: Henry Holt.

James, W. 1884. What is an emotion? *Mind* 9: 188–205.

Krutch, J. W. 1967. *New York Times Magazine,* July 30.

Popper, K. R. 1966. *Of clouds and clocks.* St. Louis: Washington University Press.

Skinner, B. F. 1953. *Science and human behavior.* New York: Macmillan.

———. 1969. *Contingencies of reinforcement: A theoretical analysis.* New York: Appleton-Century-Crofts.

Ulrich, R., T. Stachnik, and J. Mabry, eds. 1966, 1970. *Control of human behavior.* Vols. 1 and 2. Glenview, Ill.: Scott, Foresman.

7

Jerome S. Bruner

Psychologist

The Importance of Structure in Education (1960)

Professor Bruner studied physiological psychology at Harvard during the 1930s, but with the rise of national socialism in Germany he shifted his interest to social psychology. In 1941 he completed a dissertation on Nazi propaganda techniques. After the war he returned to Harvard to do research in human perception, especially in children. He came to believe that people formulated their perceptions to remain consistent with their experiences from the past. Bruner's research developed into an interest in cognitive psychology, the study of how people obtain knowledge and grow intellectually. Not long after he founded the Harvard Center for Cognitive Studies in 1960, his work began to have an impact on education. This excerpt, a chapter from one of the earlier writings of Bruner, *The Process of Education,* describes the heart of his approach: "structure."

Bruner suggests from his empirical studies that most learning is based on four principles. The first is "motivation." All children have an inborn will to learn. However, they need some rewards to initiate certain actions. These should be primarily intrinsic if the actions are to be sustained. Children should be encouraged to explore alternatives through the phenomena of activation, maintenance, and direction.

From *The Process of Education* (New York: Vintage, 1960), 17–31.

The second principle is "structure." The well-known short version of this principle is that knowledge from any subject area can be organized according to its essential structure so that it can be understood by almost anyone. The structure can be characterized by means of mode of presentation, economy, and power. Bruner poses the structure question to education thusly, ". . . how to construct curricula that can be taught by ordinary teachers to ordinary students and at the same time reflect clearly the basic or underlying principles of the various fields of inquiry" (1960, 18).

The third principle is "sequence." This refers to the order in which key aspects of a subject are presented. Bruner believes this is important because intellectual growth follows its own sequence. He also sees sequence linked to motivation.

Learning requires "reinforcement," the fourth principle, by means of feedback. Feedback must come at the time self-evaluation is taking place—not too early, not too late. Explorations may be confused or extinguished if the timing is not just right.

All of these principles aim at equipping the learner to become a self-sufficient problem-solver.

The first object of any act of learning, over and beyond the pleasure it may give, is that it should serve us in the future. Learning should not only take us somewhere; it should allow us later to go further more easily. There are two ways in which learning serves the future. One is through its specific applicability to tasks that are highly similar to those we originally learned to perform. Psychologists refer to this phenomenon as specific transfer of training; perhaps it should be called the extension of habits or associations. Its utility appears to be limited in the main to what we usually speak of as skills. Having learned how to hammer nails, we are better able later to learn how to hammer tacks or chip wood. Learning in school undoubtedly creates skills of a kind that transfers to activities encountered later, either in school or after. A second way in which earlier learning renders later performance more efficient is through what is conveniently called nonspecific transfer or, more accurately, the transfer of principles and attitudes. In essence, it consists of learning initially not a skill but a general idea, which can then be used as a basis for recognizing subsequent problems as special cases of the idea originally mastered. This type of transfer is at the heart of the educational process—the continual broadening and deepening of knowledge in terms of basic and general ideas.

The continuity of learning that is produced by the second type of transfer, transfer of principles, is dependent upon mastery of the structure of the subject matter. . . . That is to say, in order for a person to be able to recognize the applicability or inapplicability of an idea to a new situation and to broaden his learning thereby, he must have clearly in mind the general nature of the phenomenon with which he is dealing. The more fundamental or basic is the idea he has learned, almost by definition, the greater will be its breadth of applicability to new problems. Indeed, this is almost a tautology, for what is meant by "fundamental" in this sense is precisely that an idea has wide as well as powerful applicability. It is simple enough to proclaim, of course, that school curricula and methods of teaching should be geared to the teaching of fundamental ideas in whatever subject is being taught. But as soon as one makes such a statement a host of problems arise, many of which can be solved only with the aid of considerably more research. We turn to some of these now.

The first and most obvious problem is how to construct curricula that can be taught by ordinary teachers to ordinary students and that at the same time reflect clearly the basic or underlying principles of various fields of inquiry. The problem is twofold: first, how to have the basic subjects rewritten and their teaching materials revamped in such a way that the pervading and powerful ideas and attitudes relating to them are given a central role; second, how to match the levels of these materials to the capacities of students of different abilities at different grades in school.

The experience of the past several years has taught at least one important lesson about the design of a curriculum that is true to the underlying structure of its subject matter. It is that the best minds in any particular discipline must be put to work on the task. The decision as to what should be taught in American history to elementary school children or what should be taught in arithmetic is a decision that can best be reached with the aid of those with a high degree of vision and competence in each of these fields. To decide that the elementary ideas of algebra depend upon the fundamentals of the commutative, distributive, and associative laws, one must be a mathematician in a position to appreciate and understand the fundamentals of mathematics. Whether schoolchildren require an understanding of Frederick Jackson Turner's ideas about the role of the frontier in American history before they can sort out the facts and trends of American history . . . is a decision that requires the help of the scholar who has a deep understanding of the American past. Only by the use of our best minds in devising curricula will we bring the fruits of scholarship and wisdom to the student just beginning his studies.

The question will be raised, "How can we enlist the aid of our most able scholars and scientists in designing curricula for primary and secondary schools?" The answer has already been given, at least in part. The School Mathematics Study Group, the University of Illinois mathematics projects, the Physical Science Study Committee, and the Biological Sciences Curriculum Study have indeed been enlisting the aid of eminent men in their various fields, doing so by means of summer projects, supplemented in part by yearlong leaves of absence for certain key people involved. They have been aided in these projects by outstanding elementary and secondary school teachers and, for special purposes, by professional writers, film makers, designers, and others required in such a complex enterprise.

There is at least one major matter that is left unsettled even by a large-scale revision of curricula in the direction indicated. Mastery of the fundamental ideas of a field involves not only the grasping of general principles, but also the development of an attitude toward learning and inquiry, toward guessing and hunches, toward the possibility of solving problems on one's own. Just as a physicist has certain attitudes about the ultimate orderliness of nature and a conviction that order can be discovered, so a young physics student needs some working version of these attitudes if he is to organize his learning in such a way as to make what he learns usable and meaningful in his thinking. To instill such attitudes by teaching requires something more than the mere presentation of fundamental ideas. Just what it takes to bring off such teaching is something on which a great deal of research is needed, but it would seem that an important ingredient is a sense of excitement about discovery—discovery of regularities of previously unrecognized relations and similarities between ideas, with a resulting sense of self-confidence in one's abilities. Various people who have worked on curricula in science and mathematics have urged that it is possible to present the fundamental structure of a discipline in such a way as to preserve some of the exiting sequences that lead a student to discover for himself.

It is particularly the Committee on School Mathematics and the Arithmetic Project of the University of Illinois that have emphasized the importance of discovery as an aid to teaching. They have been active in devising methods that permit a student to discover for himself the generalization that lies behind a particular mathematical operation, and they contrast this approach with the "method of assertion and proof" in which the generalization is first stated by the teacher and the class [is then] asked to proceed through the proof. It has also been pointed out by the Illinois group that the method of discovery would be too time-consuming for presenting all of what a student must cover in mathematics. The proper balance between the two is anything but plain, and research is in progress to elucidate the matter, though more is needed. Is the inductive approach a better technique for teaching principles? Does it have a desirable effect on attitudes?

That the method of discovery need not be limited to such highly formalized subjects as mathematics and physics is illustrated by some experimentation on social studies carried out by the Harvard Cognition Project. A sixth-grade class, having been through a conventional unit on the social and economic geography of the southeastern states, was introduced to the north-central region by being asked to locate the major cities of the area on a map containing physical features and natural resources, but no place names. The resulting class discussion very rapidly produced a variety of plausible theories concerning the requirements of a city—a water transportation theory that placed

Chicago at the junction of the three lakes, a mineral resources theory that placed it near the Mesabi range, a food-supply theory that put a great city on the rich soil of Iowa, and so on. The level of interest as well as the level of conceptual sophistication was far above that of control classes. Most striking, however, was the attitude of children to whom, for the first time, the location of a city appeared as a problem, and one to which an answer could be discovered by taking thought. Not only was there pleasure and excitement in the pursuit of a question, but in the end the discovery was worth making, at least for urban children for whom the phenomenon of the city was something that had before been taken for granted.

How do we tailor fundamental knowledge to the interests and capacities of children? This is a theme we shall return to later, and only a word need be said about it here. It requires a combination of deep understanding and patient honesty to present physical or any other phenomena in a way that is simultaneously exciting, correct, and rewardingly comprehensible. In examining certain teaching materials in physics, for example, we have found much patient honesty in presentation that has come to naught because the authors did not have a deep enough understanding of the subject they were presenting.

A good case in point is to be found in the usual attempt to explain the nature of tides. Ask the majority of high school students to explain tides and they will speak of the gravitational pull of the moon on the surface of the earth and how it pulls the water on the moon's side into a bulge. Ask them now why there is also a bulge of less magnitude on the side of the earth opposite to the moon, and they will almost always be without a satisfactory answer. Or ask them where the maximum bulge of the incoming tide is with respect to the relative position of the earth and moon, and the answer will usually be that it is at the point on the earth's surface nearest to the moon. If the student knows there is a lag in the tidal crest, he will usually not know why. The failure in both cases comes from an inadequate picture of how gravity acts upon a free-moving elastic body, and a failure to connect the idea of inertia with the idea of gravitational action. In short, the tides are explained without a share of the excitement that can come from understanding Newton's great discovery of universal gravitation and its mode of action. Correct and illuminating explanations are no more difficult and often easier to grasp than ones that are partly correct and therefore too complicated and too restricted. It is the consensus of virtually all the men and women who have been working on curriculum projects that making material interesting is in no way incompatible with presenting it soundly; indeed, a correct general explanation is often the most interesting of all. Inherent in the preceding discussions are at least four general claims that can be made for teaching the fundamental structure of a subject, claims in need of detailed study.

The first is that understanding fundamentals makes a subject more comprehensible. This is true not only in physics and mathematics, where we have principally illustrated the point, but equally in the social studies and literature. Once one has grasped the fundamental idea that a nation must trade in order to live, then such a presumably special phenomenon as the Triangular Trade of the American colonies becomes altogether simpler to understand as something more than commerce in molasses, sugar cane, rum, and slaves in an atmosphere of violation of British trade regulations. The high school student reading *Moby Dick* can only understand more deeply if he can be led to understand that Melville's novel is, among other things, a study of the theme of evil and the plight of those pursuing this "killing whale." And if the student is led further to understand that there are a relatively limited number of human plights about which novels are written, he understands literature the better for it.

The second point relates to human memory. Perhaps the most basic thing that can be said about human memory, after a century of intensive research, is that unless detail is placed into a structured pattern, it is rapidly forgotten. Detailed material is conserved in memory by the use of simplified ways of representing it. These simplified representations have what may be called a "regenerative" character. A good example of this regenerative property of long-term memory can be found in science. A scientist does not try to remember the distances traversed by falling bodies in different gravitational fields over different periods of time. What he carries in memory instead is a formula that permits him with varying degrees of accuracy to regenerate the details on which the more easily remembered formula is based. So he commits to memory the formula $s = 1/2\ gt^2$ and not a handbook of distances, times, and gravitational constants. Similarly, one does not remember exactly what Marlow, the commentator in *Lord Jim,* said about the chief protagonist's plight, but, rather, simply that he was the dispassionate onlooker, the man who tried to understand without judging what had led Lord Jim into the straits in which he found himself. We remember a formula, a vivid detail that carries the meaning of an event, an average that stands for a range of events, a caricature or picture that preserves an essence—all of them techniques of condensation and representation. What learning general or fundamental principles does is to ensure that memory loss will not mean total loss, that what remains will permit us to reconstruct the details when needed. A good theory is the vehicle not only for understanding a phenomenon now but also for remembering it tomorrow.

Third, an understanding of fundamental principles and ideas, as noted earlier, appears to be the main road to adequate "transfer of training." To understand something as a specific instance of a more general case—which is what understanding a more fundamental principle or structure means—is to have learned not only a specific thing but also a model for understanding other things like it that one may encounter. If a student could grasp in its most human sense the weariness of Europe at the close of the Hundred Years' War and how it created the conditions for a workable but not ideologically absolute Treaty of Westphalia, he might be better able to think about the ideological struggle of East and West—though the parallel is anything but exact. A carefully wrought understanding should also permit him to recognize the limits of the generalization as well. The idea of "principles" and "concepts" as a basis for transfer is hardly new. It is much in need of more research of a specific kind that would provide detailed knowledge of how best to proceed in the teaching of different subjects in different grades.

The fourth claim for emphasis on structure and principles in teaching is that by constantly reexamining material taught in elementary and secondary schools for its fundamental character, one is able to narrow the gap between "advanced" knowledge and "elementary" knowledge. Part of the difficulty now found in the progression from primary school through high school to college is that material learned earlier is either out of date or misleading by virtue of its lagging too far behind developments in a field. This gap can be reduced by the kind of emphasis set forth in the preceding discussion.

Consider now some specific problems that received considerable discussion at Woods Hole. One of them has to do with the troubled topic of "general science." There are certain recurrent ideas that appear in virtually all branches of science. If in one subject one has learned them well and generally, that achievement should make the task of learning them again in different form elsewhere in science much easier. Various teachers and scientists have raised the question whether these basic ideas should not be "isolated," so to speak, and taught more explicitly in a manner that frees them from specific areas of science. The type of idea can be easily illustrated: categorization and its uses, the unit of measure and its development, the indirectness of information in science and the need for operational definition of ideas, and so forth. With respect to the last, for example, we do not *see* pressure or the chemical bond directly but infer it indirectly from a set of measures. So too body temperature. So too sadness in another person. Can these and similar ideas be presented effectively and with a variety of concrete illustrations in the early grades in order to give the child a better basis for understanding their specific representation in various special disciplines later? Is it wise to teach such "general science" as an introduction to disciplinary sciences in the later grades? How should they be taught and what could we reasonably expect by way of easier learning later? Much research is needed on this promising topic—research not only on the usefulness of such an approach, but also on the kinds of general scientific ideas that might be taught.

Indeed, it may well be that there are certain general attitudes or approaches toward science or literature that can be taught in the earlier grades that would have considerable relevance for later learning. The attitude that things are connected and not isolated is a case in point. One can indeed imagine kindergarten games designed to make children more actively alert to how things affect or are connected with each other—a kind of introduction to the idea of multiple determination of events in the physical and the social world. Any working scientist is usually able to say something about the ways of thinking or attitudes that are a part of his craft. Historians have written rather extensively on this subject as far as their field is concerned. Literary men have even evolved a genre of writing about the forms of sensibility that make for literary taste and vigor. In mathematics, this subject has a formal name, "heuristic," to describe the approach one takes to solving problems. One may well argue, as it was argued at Woods Hole by men in widely differing disciplines, that it might be wise to assess what attitudes or heuristic devices are most pervasive and useful, and that an effort should be made to teach children a rudimentary version of them that might be further refined as they progress through school. Again, the reader will sense that the argument for such an approach is premised on the assumption that there is a continuity between what a scholar does on the forefront of his discipline and what a child does in approaching it for the first time. This is not to say that the task is a simple one, only that it is worthy of careful consideration and research.

Perhaps the chief arguments put forward in opposition to the idea of such efforts at teaching general principles and general attitudes are, first, that it is better to approach the general through the specific and, second, that working attitudes should be kept implicit rather than being made explicit. For example, one of the principal organizing concepts in biology is the persistent question, "What function does this thing serve?"—a question premised on the assumption that everything one finds in an organism serves some function or it probably would not have survived. Other general ideas are related to this question. The student who makes progress in biology learns to ask the question more and more subtly, to relate more and more things to it. At the next step he asks what function a particular structure or process serves in the light of what is required in the total functioning of an organism. Measuring and categorizing are carried out in the service of the general idea of function. Then beyond that he may organize his knowledge in terms of a still more comprehensive notion of function, turning to cellular structure or to phylogenetic comparison. It may well be that the style of thought of a particular discipline is necessary as a background for learning the working meaning of general concepts, in which case a general introduction to the meaning of "function" might be less effective than teaching it in the context of biology.

As for "attitude" teaching or even the teaching of heuristic in mathematics, the argument runs that if the learner becomes too aware of his own attitudes or approach, he may become mechanical or trick-oriented in his work. No evidence exists on the point, and research is needed before any effort is made to teach in this way. Work is now going on at Illinois on training children to be more effective in asking questions about physical phenomena, but much more information is needed before the issue is clear.

One hears often the distinction between "doing" and "understanding." It is a distinction applied to the case, for example, of a student who presumably understands a mathematical idea but does not know how to use it in computation. While the distinction is probably a false one—since how can one know what a student understands save by seeing what he does—it points to an interesting difference in emphasis in teaching and in learning. Thus one finds in some of the classic books on the psychology of problem solving (such as Max Wertheimer's *Productive Thinking*) a sharp line drawn between "rote drill" and "understanding." In point of fact, drill need not be rote and, alas, emphasis on understanding may lead the student to a certain verbal glibness. It has been the experience of members of the School Mathematics Study Group that computational practice may be a necessary step toward understanding conceptual ideas in mathematics. Similarly one may try to give the high school student a sense of styles by having him read contrasting authors, yet final insight into style may come only when the student himself tries his hand at writing in different styles. Indeed, it is the underlying premise of laboratory exercises that doing something helps one understand it. There is a certain wisdom in the quip made by a psychologist at Woods Hole: "How do I know what I think until I feel what I do?" In any case, the distinction is not a very helpful one. What is more to the point is to ask what methods of exercise in any given field are most likely to give the student a sense of intelligent mastery over the material. What are the most fruitful computational exercises that one can use in various branches of mathematics? Does the effort to write in the style of Henry James give one an especially good insight into that author's style? Perhaps a good start toward understanding such matters would be to study the methods used by successful teachers. It would be surprising if the information compiled failed to suggest a host of worthwhile laboratory studies on techniques of teaching—or, indeed, on techniques of imparting complex information generally.

A word is needed, finally, on examinations. It is obvious that an examination can be bad in the sense of emphasizing trivial aspects of a subject. Such examinations can encourage teaching in a disconnected fashion and learning by rote. What is often overlooked, however, is that examinations can also be allies in the battle to improve curricula and teaching. Whether an examination is of the "objective" type involving multiple choices or of the essay type, it can be devised so as to emphasize an understanding of the broad principles of a subject. Indeed, even when one examines on detailed knowledge, it can be done in such a way as to require an understanding by the student of the connectedness between specific facts. There is a concerted effort now under way among national testing organizations like the Educational Testing Service to construct examinations that will emphasize an understanding of fundamental principles. Such efforts can be of great help. Additional help might be given to local school systems by making available to them manuals that describe the variety of ways in which examinations can be constructed. The searching examination is not easy to make, and a thoughtful manual on the subject would be welcome.

For Reflection

1. What might the curriculum be for a Sunday school lesson for fifth-graders, over one of Saint Paul's missionary journeys, if the structure of the subject were a prime concern?
2. How might theologians and educationists be directly involved in developing Christian-education curriculum that reflects Bruner's concerns?
3. How is discovery learning related to considerations of structure?
4. In what ways would an emphasis on "concepts" and "principles" be superior to an emphasis on "facts" and "details"?

8

Paulo Freire

Social Theorist

Pedagogy of the Oppressed: Banking

(1981)

Paulo Freire, former professor of history and philosophy of education at the University of Recife, Brazil, and formerly of the staff of the World Council of Churches, developed a perspective on literacy education that has tended to transcend the simple skills of reading and writing. In his work with rural peasants he has suggested that literacy changes attitudes, knowledge, and behavior and challenges unjust social structures and oppressive educational models. His approach to adult literacy education became national policy for Brazil in the 1960s. However, following a military coup d`etat, the administration of the country recognized the subversive character of Freire's approach and had him jailed and then exiled.

Freire's model centers on freedom through critical thinking, which leads to changed perceptions and action. When the Brazilian peasants changed from passivity to activity, the government and the power elite of the country viewed the change as nonsupportive of the status quo. This process of education may lead the oppressed to analyze their own social situation and seek, in their action, release from oppression. This means change (Ewert 1977, 9–10).

From *Pedagogy of the Oppressed,* trans. Myra Bergman Ramos (New York: Continuum, 1981), 57–74.

This model results in a *praxis* approach to education, regardless of the specific content. Reflection drives action, which leads to further reflection, which leads to more informed action. This depends more on dialogue than monologue, transformation rather than adaptation, problem-posing rather than problem-solving. The "opposite" approach–in which the teacher is all-knowing and dispenses information to the passive learner–is what Freire calls the *banking* concept of education.

According to Freire the teacher's thinking is authenticated only by the authenticity of the students' thinking. And true thought has meaning only when generated by action. Banking transforms learners into receiving objects, prohibiting their creative power. This also prevents responsible action, causing people to suffer.

This problem-posing, dialogic, *praxis* approach to education may have broad application. It could lead to self-learning, to encouragement of adult students in everyday settings, and to heightened motivation.

References

Ewert, D. M. 1977. Freire's concept of critical consciousness and social structure in rural Zaire. Unpublished doctoral dissertation, University of Wisconsin.

A careful analysis of the teacher-student relationship at any level, inside or outside the school, reveals its fundamentally *narrative* character. This relationship involves a narrating subject (the teacher) and patient, listening objects (the students). The contents, whether values or empirical dimensions of reality, tend in the process of being narrated to become lifeless and petrified. Education is suffering from narration sickness.

The teacher talks about reality as if it were motionless, static, compartmentalized, and predictable. Or else he expounds on a topic completely alien to the existential experience of the students. His task is to "fill" the students with the contents of his narration—contents which are detached from reality, disconnected from the totality that engendered them and could give them significance. Words are emptied of their concreteness and become a hollow, alienated, and alienating verbosity.

The outstanding characteristic of this narrative education, then, is the sonority of words, not their transforming power. "Four times four is sixteen; the capital of Pará is Belém." The student records, memorizes, and repeats these phrases without perceiving what four times four really means, or realizing the true significance of "capital" in the affirmation "the capital of Pará is Belém," that is, what Belém means for Pará and what Pará means for Brazil.

Narration (with the teacher as narrator) leads the students to memorize mechanically the narrated content. Worse yet, it turns them into "containers," into "receptacles" to be "filled" by the teacher. The more completely he fills the receptacles, the better a teacher he is. The more meekly the receptacles permit themselves to be filled, the better students they are.

Education thus becomes an act of depositing, in which the students are the depositories and the teacher is the depositor. Instead of communicating, the teacher issues communiqués and makes deposits which the students patiently receive, memorize, and repeat. This is the "banking" concept of education, in which the scope of action allowed to the students extends only as far as receiving, filing, and storing the deposits. They do, it is true, have the opportunity to become collectors or cataloguers of the things they store. But in the last analysis, it is men themselves who are filed away through the lack of creativity, transformation, and knowledge in this (at best) misguided system. For apart from inquiry, apart from the praxis, men cannot be truly human. Knowledge emerges only through invention and reinvention, through the restless, impatient, continuing, hopeful inquiry men pursue in the world, with the world, and with each other.

In the banking concept of education, knowledge is a gift bestowed by those who consider themselves knowledgeable upon those whom they consider to know nothing. Projecting an absolute ignorance onto others, a characteristic of the ideology of oppression, negates education and knowledge as processes of inquiry. The teacher presents himself to his students as their necessary opposite; by considering their ignorance absolute, he justifies his own existence. The students, alienated like the slave in the Hegelian dialectic, accept their ignorance as justifying the teacher's existence—but, unlike the slave, they never discover that they educate the teacher.

The *raison d'être* of libertarian education, on the other hand, lies in its drive towards reconciliation. Education must begin with the solution of the teacher-student contradiction, by reconciling the poles of the contradiction so that both are simultaneously teachers *and* students.

This solution is not (nor can it be) found in the banking concept. On the contrary, banking education maintains and even stimulates the contradiction through the following attitudes and practices, which mirror oppressive society as a whole:

(a) the teacher teaches and the students are taught;
(b) the teacher knows everything and the students know nothing;
(c) the teacher thinks and the students are thought about;
(d) the teacher talks and the students listen—meekly;
(e) the teacher disciplines and the students are disciplined;
(f) the teacher chooses and enforces his choice, and the students comply;
(g) the teacher acts and the students have the illusion of acting through the action of the teacher;
(h) the teacher chooses the program content, and the students (who were not consulted) adapt to it;

(i) the teacher confuses the authority of knowledge with his own professional authority, which he sets in opposition to the freedom of the students;
(j) the teacher is the subject of the learning process, while the pupils are mere objects.

It is not surprising that the banking concept of education regards men as adaptable, manageable beings. The more students work at storing the deposits entrusted to them, the less they develop the critical consciousness which would result from their intervention in the world as transformers of that world. The more completely they accept the passive role imposed on them, the more they tend simply to adapt to the world as it is and to the fragmented view of reality deposited in them.

The capability of banking education to minimize or annul the students' creative power and to stimulate their credulity serves the interests of the oppressors, who care neither to have the world revealed nor to see it transformed. The oppressors use their "humanitarianism" to preserve a profitable situation. Thus they react almost instinctively against any experiment in education which stimulates the critical faculties and is not content with a partial view of reality but always seeks out the ties which link one point to another and one problem to another.

Indeed, the interests of the oppressors lie in "changing the consciousness of the oppressed, not the situation which oppresses them" (de Beauvoir 1963, 34); for the more the oppressed can be led to adapt to that situation, the more easily they can be dominated. To achieve this end, the oppressors use the banking concept of education in conjunction with a paternalistic social action apparatus, within which the oppressed receive the euphemistic title of "welfare recipients." They are treated as individual cases, as marginal men who deviate from the general configuration of a "good, organized, and just" society. The oppressed are regarded as the pathology of the healthy society, which must therefore adjust these "incompetent and lazy" folk to its own patterns by changing their mentality. These marginals need to be "integrated," "incorporated" into the healthy society that they have "forsaken."

The truth is, however, that the oppressed are not "marginals," are not men living "outside" society. They have always been "inside"—inside the structure which made them "beings for others." The solution is not to "integrate" them into the structure of oppression, but to transform that structure so that they can become "beings for themselves." Such transformation, of course, would undermine the oppressors' purposes; hence their utilization of the banking concept of education to avoid the threat of student *conscientização*.

The banking approach to adult education, for example, will never propose to students that they critically consider reality. It will deal instead with such vital questions as whether Roger gave green grass to the goat, and insist upon the importance of learning that, on the contrary, Roger gave green grass to the rabbit. The "humanism" of the banking approach masks the effort to turn men into automatons—the very negation of their ontological vocation to be more fully human.

Those who use the banking approach, knowingly or unknowingly (for there are innumerable well-intentioned bank-clerk teachers who do not realize that they are serving only to dehumanize), fail to perceive that the deposits themselves contain contradictions about reality. But, sooner or later, these contradictions may lead formerly passive students to turn against their domestication and the attempt to domesticate reality. They may discover through existential experience that their present way of life is irreconcilable with their vocation to become fully human. They may perceive through their relations with reality that reality is really a *process*, undergoing constant transformation. If men are searchers and their ontological vocation is humanization, sooner or later they may perceive the contradiction in which banking education seeks to maintain them, and then engage themselves in the struggle for their liberation.

But the humanist, revolutionary educator cannot wait for this possibility to materialize. From the outset, his efforts must coincide with those of the students to engage in critical thinking and the quest for mutual humanization. His efforts must be imbued with a profound trust in men and their creative power. To achieve this, he must be a partner of the students in his relations with them.

The banking concept does not admit to such partnership—and necessarily so. To resolve the teacher-student contradiction, to exchange the role of depositor, prescriber, domesticator, for the role of student among students would be to undermine the power of oppression and serve the cause of liberation.

Implicit in the banking concept is the assumption of a dichotomy between man and the world: man is merely *in* the world, not *with* the world or with others; man is spectator, not re-creator. In this view, man is not a conscious being *(corpo consciente);* he is rather the possessor of *a* consciousness: an empty "mind" passively open to the reception of deposits of reality from the world outside. For example, my desk, my books, my coffee cup, all the objects before me—as bits of the world which surrounds me—would be "inside" me, exactly as I am inside my study right now. This view makes no distinction between being accessible to consciousness and entering consciousness. The distinction, however, is essential: the objects which surround me are simply accessible to my consciousness, not located within it. I am aware of them, but they are not inside me.

It follows logically from the banking notion of consciousness that the educator's role is to regulate the way the world "enters into" the students. His task is to organize a process which already occurs spontaneously, to "fill" the students by making deposits of information which he considers to constitute true knowledge.[1] And since men "receive" the world as passive entities, education should make them more passive still, and adapt them to the world. The educated man is the adapted man, because he is better "fit" for the world. Translated into practice, this concept is well suited to the purposes of the oppressors, whose tranquility rests on how well men fit the world the oppressors have created, and how little they question it.

The more completely the majority adapt to the purposes which the dominant minority prescribe for them (thereby depriving them of the right to their own purposes), the more easily the minority can continue to prescribe. The theory and practice of banking education serve this end quite efficiently. Verbalistic lessons, reading requirements,[2] the methods for evaluating "knowledge," the distance between the teacher and the taught, the criteria for promotion: everything in this ready-to-wear approach serves to obviate thinking.

The bank-clerk educator does not realize that there is no true security in his hypertrophied role, that one must seek to live *with* others in solidarity. One cannot impose oneself, nor even merely coexist with one's students. Solidarity requires true communication, and the concept by which such an educator is guided fears and proscribes communication.

Yet only through communication can human life hold meaning. The teacher's thinking is authenticated only by the authenticity of the students' thinking. The teacher cannot think for his students, nor can he impose his thought on them. Authentic thinking, thinking that is concerned about *reality,* does not take place in ivory tower isolation, but only in communication. If it is true that thought has meaning only when generated by action upon the world, the subordination of students to teachers becomes impossible.

Because banking education begins with a false understanding of men as objects, it cannot promote the development of what Fromm calls "biophily," but instead produces its opposite: "necrophily."

> While life is characterized by growth in a structured, functional manner, the necrophilous person loves all that does not grow, all that is mechanical. The necrophilous person is driven by the desire to transform the organic into the inorganic, to approach life mechanically, as if all living persons were things. . . . Memory, rather than experience; having, rather than being, is what counts. The necrophilous person can relate to an object—a flower or a person—only if he possesses it; hence a threat to his possession is a threat to himself; if he loses

1. This concept corresponds to what Sartre calls the "digestive" or "nutritive" concept of education, in which knowledge is "fed" by the teacher to the students to "fill them out." See Jean-Paul Sartre, "Une idée fundamentale de la phénomenologie de Husserl: L'intentionalité," *Situations I* (Paris, 1947).

2. For example, some professors specify in their reading lists that a book should be read from pages 10 to 15—and do this to "help" their students!

> possession he loses contact with the world. . . . He loves control, and in the act of controlling he kills life. (Fromm 1964, 41)

Oppression—overwhelming control—is necrophilic; it is nourished by love of death, not life. The banking concept of education, which serves the interests of oppression, is also necrophilic. Based on a mechanistic, static, naturalistic, spatialized view of consciousness, it transforms students into receiving objects. It attempts to control thinking and action, leads men to adjust to the world, and inhibits their creative power.

When their efforts to act responsibly are frustrated, when they find themselves unable to use their faculties, men suffer. "This suffering due to impotence is rooted in the very fact that the human equilibrium has been disturbed." But the inability to act which causes men's anguish also causes them to reject their impotence, by attempting ". . . to restore [their] capacity to act. But can [they], and how? One way is to submit to and identify with a person or group having power. By this symbolic participation in another person's life, [men have] the illusion of acting, when in reality [they] only submit to and become a part of those who act" (Fromm 1964, 31).

Populist manifestations perhaps best exemplify this type of behavior by the oppressed, who, by identifying with charismatic leaders, come to feel that they themselves are active and effective. The rebellion they express as they emerge in the historical process is motivated by that desire to act effectively. The dominant elites consider the remedy to be more domination and repression, carried out in the name of freedom, order, and social peace (that is, the peace of the elites). Thus they can condemn—logically, from their point of view—"the violence of a strike by workers and [can] call upon the state in the same breath to use violence in putting down the strike" (Niebuhr 1960, 130).

Education as the exercise of domination stimulates the credulity of students, with the ideological intent (often not perceived by educators) of indoctrinating them to adapt to the world of oppression. This accusation is not made in the naïve hope that the dominant elites will thereby simply abandon the practice. Its objective is to call the attention of true humanists to the fact that they cannot use banking educational methods in the pursuit of liberation, for they would only negate that very pursuit. Nor may a revolutionary society inherit these methods from an oppressor society. The revolutionary society which practices banking education is either misguided or mistrusting of men. In either event, it is threatened by the specter of reaction.

Unfortunately, those who espouse the cause of liberation are themselves surrounded and influenced by the climate which generates the banking concept, and often do not perceive its true significance or its dehumanizing power. Paradoxically, then, they utilize this same instrument of alienation in what they consider an effort to liberate. Indeed, some "revolutionaries" brand as "innocents," "dreamers," or even "reactionaries" those who would challenge this educational practice. But one does not liberate men by alienating them. Authentic liberation—the process of humanization—is not another deposit to be made in men. Liberation is a praxis: the action and reflection of men upon their world in order to transform it. Those truly committed to the cause of liberation can accept neither the mechanistic concept of consciousness as an empty vessel to be filled, nor the use of banking methods of domination (propaganda, slogans—deposits) in the name of liberation.

Those truly committed to liberation must reject the banking concept in its entirety, adopting instead a concept of men as conscious beings, and consciousness as consciousness intent upon the world. They must abandon the educational goal of deposit-making and replace it with the posing of the problems of men in their relations with the world. "Problem-posing" education, responding to the essence of consciousness—*intentionality*—rejects communiqués and embodies communication. It epitomizes the special characteristic of consciousness: being *conscious of*, not only as intent on objects but as turned in upon itself in a Jasperian "split"—consciousness as consciousness *of* consciousness.

Liberating education consists in acts of cognition, not transferrals of information. It is a learning situation in which the cognizable object (far from being the end of the cognitive act) intermediates the cognitive actors—teacher on the one hand and students on the other. Accordingly, the practice of problem-posing education entails at the outset that the teacher-student contradiction be resolved. Dialogical relations—indispensable to the capacity of cognitive actors to cooperate in perceiving the same cognizable object—are otherwise impossible.

Indeed, problem-posing education, which breaks with the vertical patterns characteristic of banking education, can fulfill its function as the practice of freedom only if it can overcome the . . . contradiction. Through dialogue, the teacher-of-the-students and the students-of-the-teacher cease to exist and a new term emerges: teacher-student with students-teachers. The teacher is no longer merely the-one-who-teaches, but one who is himself taught in dialogue with the students, who in turn while being taught also teach. They become jointly responsible for a process in which all grow. In this process, arguments based on "authority" are no longer valid; in order to function, authority must be *on the side of* freedom, not *against* it. Here, no one teaches another, nor is anyone self-taught. Men teach each other, mediated by the world, by the cognizable objects which in banking education are "owned" by the teacher.

The banking concept (with its tendency to dichotomize everything) distinguishes two stages in the action of the educator. During the first, he cognizes a cognizable object while he prepares his lessons in his study or his laboratory; during the second, he expounds to his students about that object. The students are not called upon to know, but to memorize the contents narrated by the teacher. Nor do the students practice any act of cognition, since the object towards which that act should be directed is the property of the teacher rather than a medium evoking the critical reflection of both teacher and students. Hence in the name of the "preservation of culture and knowledge" we have a system which achieves neither true knowledge nor true culture.

The problem-posing method does not dichotomize the activity of the teacher-student: he is not "cognitive" at one point and "narrative" at another. He is always "cognitive," whether preparing a project or engaging in dialogue with the students. He does not regard cognizable objects as his private property, but as the object of reflection by himself and the students. In this way, the problem-posing educator constantly re-forms his reflections in the reflection of the students. The students—no longer docile listeners—are now critical co-investigators in dialogue with the teacher. The teacher presents the material to the students for their consideration, and reconsiders his earlier considerations as the students express their own. The role of the problem-posing educator is to create, together with the students, the conditions under which knowledge at the level of the *doxa* is superseded by true knowledge, at the level of the *logos.*

Whereas banking education anesthetizes and inhibits creative power, problem-posing education involves a constant unveiling of reality. The former attempts to maintain the *submersion* of consciousness; the latter strives for the *emergence* of consciousness and *critical intervention* in reality.

Students, as they are increasingly posed with problems relating to themselves in the world and with the world, will feel increasingly challenged and obliged to respond to that challenge. Because they apprehend the challenge as interrelated to other problems within a total context, not as a theoretical question, the resulting comprehension tends to be increasingly critical and thus constantly less alienated. Their response to the challenge evokes new challenges, followed by new understandings; and gradually the students come to regard themselves as committed.

Education as the practice of freedom—as opposed to education as the practice of domination—denies that man is abstract, isolated, independent, and unattached to the world; it also denies that the world exists as a reality apart from men. Authentic reflection considers neither abstract man nor the world without men, but men in their relations with the world. In these relations consciousness and world are simultaneous: consciousness neither precedes the world nor follows it.

> La conscience et le monde sont dormés d'un même coup: extérieur par essence `a la conscience, le monde est, par essence relatif à elle. (Sartre 1947, 32)

In one of our culture circles in Chile, the group was discussing (based on a codification) the anthropological concept of culture. In the midst of the discussion, a peasant who by banking standards was completely ignorant said: "Now I see that without man there is no world." When the educator responded: "Let's say, for the sake of argument, that all the men on earth were to die, but that the earth itself remained, together with trees, birds, animals, rivers, seas, the stars . . . wouldn't all this be a world?" "Oh no," the peasant replied emphatically. "There would be no one to say: 'This is a world.'"

The peasant wished to express the idea that there would be lacking the consciousness of the world which necessarily implies the world of consciousness. *I* cannot exist without a *not-I.* In turn, the *not-I* depends on that existence. The world which brings consciousness into existence becomes the world *of* that consciousness. Hence, the previously cited affirmation of Sartre: *"La conscience et le monde sont dormés d'un même coup."*

As men, simultaneously reflecting on themselves and on the world, increase the scope of their perception, they begin to direct their observations towards previously inconspicuous phenomena:

> In perception properly so-called, as an explicit awareness [*Gewahren*], I am turned towards the object, to the paper, for instance. I apprehend it as being this here and now. The apprehension is a singling out, every object having a background in experience. Around and about the paper lie books, pencils, inkwell, and so forth, and these in a certain sense are also "perceived," perceptually there, in the "field of intuition"; but whilst I was turned towards the paper there was no turning in their direction, nor any apprehending of them, not even in a secondary sense. They appeared and yet were not singled out, were not posited on their own account. Every perception of a thing has such a zone of background intuitions or background awareness, if "intuiting" already includes the state of being turned towards, and this also is a "conscious experience," or more briefly a "consciousness of" all indeed that in point of fact lies in the co-perceived objective background. (Husserl 1969, 105–6)

That which had existed objectively but had not been perceived in its deeper implications (if indeed it was perceived at all) begins to "stand out," assuming the character of a problem and therefore of challenge. Thus, men begin to single out elements from their "background awarenesses" and to reflect upon them. These elements are now objects of men's consideration, and, as such, objects of their action and cognition.

In problem-posing education, men develop their power to perceive critically *the way they exist* in the world *with which* and *in which* they find themselves; they come to see the world not as a static reality, but as a reality in process, in transformation. Although the dialectical relations of men with the world exist independently of how these relations are perceived (or whether or not they are perceived at all), it is also true that the form of action men adopt is to a large extent a function of how they perceive themselves in the world. Hence, the teacher-student and the students-teachers reflect simultaneously on themselves and the world without dichotomizing this reflection from action, and thus establish an authentic form of thought and action.

Once again, the two educational concepts and practices under analysis come into conflict. Banking education (for obvious reasons) attempts, by mythicizing reality, to conceal certain facts which explain the way men exist in the world; problem-posing education sets itself the task of demythologizing. Banking education resists dialogue; problem-posing education regards dialogue as indispensable to the act of cognition which unveils reality. Banking education treats students as objects of assistance; problem-posing education makes them critical thinkers. Banking education inhibits creativity and domesticates (although it cannot completely destroy) the *intentionality* of consciousness by isolating consciousness from the world, thereby denying men their ontological and historical vocation of becoming more fully human. Problem-posing education bases itself on creativity and stimulates true reflection and action upon reality, thereby responding to the vocation of men as beings who are authentic only when engaged in inquiry and creative transformation. In sum: banking theory and practice, as immobilizing and fixating forces, fail to acknowledge men as historical beings; problem-posing theory and practice take man's historicity as their starting point.

Problem-posing education affirms men as beings in the process of *becoming*—as unfinished, uncompleted beings in and with a likewise unfinished reality. Indeed, in contrast to other animals who are unfinished, but not historical, men know themselves to be unfinished; they are aware of their incompletion. In this incompletion and this awareness lie the very roots of education as an exclusively human manifestation. The unfinished character of men and the transformational character of reality necessitate that education be an ongoing activity.

Education is thus constantly remade in the praxis. In order to *be*, it must *become*. Its "duration" (in the Bergsonian meaning of the word) is found in the interplay of the opposites *permanence* and *change*. The banking method emphasizes permanence and becomes reactionary; problem-posing education—which accepts neither a "well-behaved" present nor a predetermined future—roots itself in the dynamic present and becomes revolutionary.

Problem-posing education is revolutionary futurity. Hence it is prophetic (and, as such, hopeful). Hence, it corresponds to the historical nature of man. Hence, it affirms men as beings who transcend themselves, who move forward and look ahead, for whom immobility represents a fatal threat, for whom looking at the past must only be a means of understanding more clearly what and who they are so that they can more wisely build the future. Hence, it identifies with the movement which engages men as beings aware of their incompletion—an historical movement which has its point of departure, its subjects and its objective.

The point of departure of the movement lies in men themselves. But since men do not exist apart from the world, apart from reality, the movement must begin with the men-world relationship. Accordingly, the point of departure must always be with men in the "here and now," which constitutes the situation within which they are submerged, from which they emerge, and in which they intervene. Only by starting from this situation—which determines their perception of it—can they begin to move. To do this authentically they must perceive their state not as fated and unalterable, but merely as limiting—and therefore challenging.

Whereas the banking method directly or indirectly reinforces men's fatalistic perception of their situation, the problem-posing method presents this very situation to them as a problem. As the situation becomes the object of their cognition, the naïve or magical perception which produced their fatalism gives way to perception which is able to perceive itself even as it perceives reality, and can thus be critically objective about that reality.

A deepened consciousness of their situation leads men to apprehend that situation as an historical reality susceptible of transformation. Resignation gives way to the drive for transformation and inquiry, over which men feel themselves to be in control. If men, as historical beings necessarily engaged with other men in a movement of inquiry, did not control that movement, it would be (and is) a violation of men's humanity. Any situation in which some men prevent others from engaging in the process of inquiry is one of violence. The means used are not important; to alienate men from their own decision-making is to change them into objects.

This movement of inquiry must be directed towards humanization—man's historical vocation. The pursuit of full humanity, however, cannot be carried out in isolation or individualism, but only in fellowship and solidarity; therefore it cannot unfold in the antagonistic relations between oppressors and oppressed. No one can be authentically human while he prevents others from being so. Attempting *to be more* human, individualistically, leads to *having more*, egotistically: a form of dehumanization. Not that it is not fundamental *to have* in order *to be* human. Precisely because it *is* necessary, some men's *having* must not be allowed to constitute an obstacle to others' *having*, must not consolidate the power of the former to crush the latter.

Problem-posing education, as a humanist and liberating praxis, posits as fundamental that men subjected to domination must fight for their emancipation. To that end, it enables teachers and students to become subjects of the educational process by overcoming authoritarianism and an alienating intellectualism; it also enables men to overcome their false perception of reality. The world—no longer something to be described with deceptive words—becomes the object of that transforming action by men which results in their humanization.

Problem-posing education does not and cannot serve the interests of the oppressor. No oppressive order could permit the oppressed to begin to question: Why? While only a revolutionary society can carry out this education in systematic terms, the revolutionary leaders need not take full power before they can employ the method. In the revolutionary process, the leaders cannot utilize the banking method as an interim measure, justified on grounds of expediency, with the intention of *later* behaving in a genuinely revolutionary fashion. They must be revolutionary—that is to say, dialogical—from the outset.

For Reflection

1. What is the key concept in this reading in regard to teacher-learner relationship?
2. Identify a banking education experience of your own. How might it have been improved?
3. Give a positive example of problem-posing education in contrast to problem-solving. In instruction, how can -solving become -posing?
4. What are the dangers of Freire's approach to adult education?

References

de Beauvoir, S. 1963. *El pensamiento de la derecha*. Buenos Aires: Ediciones Siglo Viente. Originally published as *La pensée de droite, aujord'hui*. Paris: Schenhof.

Fromm, E. 1964. *The heart of man*. New York: Harper and Row.

Husserl, E. 1969. *Ideas—general introduction to pure phenomenology*. London: G. Allen and Unwin, Ltd.

Niebuhr, R. 1932/1960. C. Scribner's Sons. *Moral man and immoral society*. New York: C. Scribner's Sons.

Sartre, J.-P. 1974. *Situations I*. Paris: Gallimard.

9

John Dewey

Philosopher and Psychologist

Experience and Education

(1938)

John Dewey was the consummate representative of progressive education. He did not see education as preparation, but life in action. School was society in miniature, not a retreat from reality for a time. His view of the mind as an active tool of adjustment led him to highly value the "scientific method" as a strategy to facilitate thinking.

Dewey was born into a God-fearing family in Vermont in 1859. As a child he attended church and Sunday school with faithfulness, but he seems to have generally rejected supernaturalism. This may have been in part because he saw institutional religion as restricting creative thinking. He received a degree from the University of Vermont and taught school before entering graduate school at Johns Hopkins University. He earned the Ph.D. in philosophy by writing a dissertation on Kant. In 1884 he became an instructor in psychology and philosophy at the University of Michigan. In the mid-1890s Dewey moved to the University of Chicago to assume the chair of philosophy, psychology, and pedagogy. He began to develop his pragmatic instrumentalism philosophy while working, along with his wife, at the university's laboratory school. From this experience came the strong views on educational psychology that reflected his philosophy of education. In 1904 Dewey moved to Columbia University and continued to teach there for almost five decades. He had great influence on the many graduate stu-

From *Experience and Education* (New York: Macmillan, 1950), 12–22, 113–16.

dents in education and through them on American education in general. His many books and articles were also influential.

Dewey believed that while humans may have many faults, they also have great potential. He rejected both the mechanistic and the romantic views of persons. He felt that facing the challenges of life was the best way to stimulate human growth, and so he emphasized the social environment as an educational agent. He saw good education as being learner-centered rather than teacher-centered; *learn by doing* was his byword. Careful, reflective thinking that leads to problem-solving was part of doing.

The passages that follow express what, for Dewey, was the nature of education. Experience can be a good teacher, but also can be miseducative if it does not lead to growth. Experiences need to be connected to each other. When this happens, learning becomes exciting and stretching. Such learning requires planning and planning requires a philosophy. Dewey calls for a philosophy of education based on a philosophy of experience; experience subordinated to intelligence and direction.

The Need of a Theory of Experience

In short, the point I am making is that rejection of the philosophy and practice of traditional education sets a new type of difficult educational problem for those who believe in the new type of education. We shall operate blindly and in confusion until we recognize this fact; until we thoroughly appreciate that departure from the old solves no problems. What is said in the following pages is, accordingly, intended to indicate some of the main problems with which the newer education is confronted and to suggest the main lines along which their solution is to be sought. I assume that amid all uncertainties there is one permanent frame of reference: namely, the organic connection between education and personal experience; or, that the new philosophy of education is committed to some kind of empirical and experimental philosophy. But experience and experiment are not self-explanatory ideas. Rather, their meaning is part of the problem to be explored. To know the meaning of empiricism we need to understand what experience is.

The belief that all genuine education comes about through experience does not mean that all experiences are genuinely or equally educative. Experience and education cannot be directly equated to each other. For some experiences are miseducative. Any experience is miseducative that has the effect of arresting or distorting the growth of further experience. An experience may be such as to engender callousness; it may produce lack of sensitivity and of responsiveness. Then the possibilities of having richer experience in the future are restricted. Again, a given experience may increase a person's automatic skill in a particular direction and yet tend to land him in a groove or rut; the effect again is to narrow the field of further experience. An experience may be immediately enjoyable and yet promote the formation of a slack and careless attitude; this attitude then operates to modify the quality of subsequent experiences so as to prevent a person from getting out of them what they have to give. Again, experiences may be so disconnected from one another that, while each is agreeable or even exciting in itself, they are not linked cumulatively to one another. Energy is then dissipated and a person becomes scatterbrained. Each experience may be lively, vivid, and "interesting," and yet their disconnectedness may artificially generate dispersive, disintegrated, centrifugal habits. The consequence of formation of such habits is an inability to control future experiences. They are then taken, either by way of enjoyment or of discontent and revolt, just as they come. Under such circumstances, it is idle to talk of self-control.

Traditional education offers a plethora of examples of experiences of the kinds just mentioned. It is a great mistake to suppose, even tacitly, that the traditional schoolroom was not a place in which pupils had experiences. Yet this is tacitly assumed when progressive education as a plan of learning by experience is placed in sharp opposition to the old. The proper line of attack is that the experiences which were had, by pupils and teachers alike, were largely of a wrong kind. How many students, for example, were rendered callous to ideas, and how many lost the impetus to learn because of the way in which learning was experienced by them? How many acquired special skills by means of automatic drill so that their power of judgment and capacity to act intelligently in new situations was limited? How many came to associate the learning process with ennui and boredom? How many found what they did learn so foreign to the situations of life outside the school as to give them no power of control over the latter? How many came to associate books with dull drudgery, so that they were "conditioned" to all but flashy reading matter?

If I ask these questions, it is not for the sake of wholesale condemnation of the old education. It is for quite another purpose. It is to emphasize the fact, first, that young people in traditional schools do have experiences; and, secondly, that the trouble is not the absence of experiences, but their defective and wrong character—wrong and defective from the standpoint of connection with further experience. The positive side of this point is even more important in connection with progressive education. It is not enough to insist upon the necessity of experience, nor even of activity in experience. Everything depends upon the *quality* of the experience which is had. The quality of any experience has two aspects. There is an immediate aspect of agreeableness or disagreeableness, and there is its influence upon later experiences. The first is obvious and easy to judge. The *effect* of an experience is not borne on its face. It [presents] a problem to the educator. It is his business to arrange for the kind of experiences which, while they do not repel the student, but rather engage his activities are, nevertheless, more than immediately enjoyable since they promote having desirable future experiences. Just as no man lives or dies to himself, so no experience lives and dies to itself. Wholly independent of desire or intent, every experience lives on in further experiences. Hence the central problem of an education based upon experience is to select the kind of present experiences that live fruitfully and creatively in subsequent experiences.

Later, I shall discuss in more detail the principle of the continuity of experience or what may be called the experiential continuum. Here I wish simply to emphasize the importance of this principle for the philosophy of educative experience. A philosophy of education, like any theory, has to be stated in words, in symbols. But so far as it is more than verbal it is a plan for conducting education. Like any plan, it must be framed with reference to what is to be done and how it is to be done. The more definitely and sincerely it is held that education is a development within, by, and for experience, the more important it is that there shall be clear conceptions of what experience is. Unless experience is so conceived that the result is a plan for deciding upon subject-matter, upon methods of instruction and discipline, and upon material equipment and social organization of the school, it is wholly in the air. It is reduced to a form of words which may be emotionally stirring but for which any other set of words might equally well be substituted unless they indicate operations to be initiated and executed. Just because traditional education was a matter of routine in which the plans and programs were handed down from the past, it does not follow that progressive education is a matter of planless improvisation.

The traditional school could get along without any consistently developed philosophy of education. About all it required in that line was a set of abstract words like culture, discipline, our great cultural heritage, . . . actual guidance being derived not from them but from custom and established routines. Just because progressive schools cannot rely upon established traditions and institutional habits, they must either proceed more or less haphazardly or be directed by ideas which, when they are made articulate and coherent, form a philosophy of education. Revolt against the kind of organization characteristic of the traditional school constitutes a demand for a kind of organization based upon ideas. I think that only slight acquaintance with the history of education is needed to prove that educational reformers and innovators alone have felt the need for a philosophy of education. Those who adhered to the established system needed merely a few fine-sounding words to justify existing practices. The real work was done by habits which were so fixed as to be institutional. The lesson for progressive education is that it requires in an urgent degree, a degree more pressing than was incumbent upon former innovators, a philosophy of education based upon a philosophy of experience.

I remarked incidentally that the philosophy in question is, to paraphrase the saying of Lincoln about democracy, one of education of, by, and for experience. No one of these words, *of, by,* or *for*, names anything which is self-evident. Each of them is a challenge to discover and put into operation a principle of order and organization which follows from understanding what educative experience signifies.

It is, accordingly, a much more difficult task to work out the kinds of materials, of methods, and of social relationships that are appropriate to the new education than is the case with traditional education. I think many of the difficulties experienced in the conduct of progressive schools and many of the criticisms leveled against them arise from this source. The difficulties are aggravated and the criticisms are increased when it is supposed that the new education is somehow easier than the old. This belief is, I imagine, more or less current. Perhaps it illustrates again the *Either-Or* philosophy, springing from the idea that about all which is required is *not* to do what is done in traditional schools.

I admit gladly that the new education is *simpler* in principle than the old. It is in harmony with principles of growth, while there is very much which is artificial in the old selection and arrangement of subjects and methods, and artificiality always leads to unnecessary complexity. But the easy and the simple are not identical. To discover what is really simple and to act upon the discovery is an exceedingly difficult task. After the artificial and complex is once institutionally established and ingrained in custom and routine, it is easier to walk in the paths that have been beaten than it is, after taking a new point of view, to work out what is practically involved in the new point of view. The old Ptolemaic astronomical system was more complicated with its cycles and epicycles than the Copernican system. But until organization of actual astronomical phenomena on the ground of the latter principle had been effected, the easiest course was to follow the line of least resistance provided by the old intellectual habit. So we come back to the idea that a coherent *theory* of experience, affording positive direction to selection and organization of appropriate educational methods and materials, is required by the attempt to give new direction to the work of the schools. The process is a slow and arduous one. It is a matter of growth, and there are many obstacles which tend to obstruct growth and to deflect it into wrong lines.

I shall have something to say later about organization. All that is needed, perhaps, at this point is to say that we must escape from the tendency to think of organization in terms of the *kind* of organization, whether of content (or subject-matter), or of methods and social relations, that mark traditional education. I think that a good deal of the current opposition to the idea of organization is due to the fact that it is so hard to get away from the picture of the studies of the old school. The moment "organization" is mentioned imagination goes almost automatically to the kind of organization that is familiar, and in revolting against that we are led to shrink from the very idea of any organization. On the other hand, educational reactionaries, who are now gathering force, use the absence of adequate intellectual and moral organization in the newer type of school as proof not only of the need of organization, but to identify any and every kind of organization with that instituted before the rise of experimental science. Failure to develop a conception of organization upon the empirical and experimental basis gives reactionaries a too easy victory. But the fact that the empirical sciences now offer the best type of intellectual organization which can be found in any field shows that there is no reason why we, who call ourselves empiricists, should be "push-overs" in the matter of order and organization.

Experience—The Means and Goal of Education

In what I have said I have taken for granted the soundness of the principle that education in order to accomplish its ends both for the individual learner and for society must be based upon experience—which is always the actual life-experience of some individual. I have not argued for the acceptance of this principle nor attempted to justify it. Conservatives as well as radicals in education are profoundly discontented with the present educational situation taken as a whole. There is at least this much agreement among intelligent persons of both schools of educational thought. The educational system must move one way or another, either backward to the intellectual and moral standards of a pre-scientific age or forward to ever greater utilization of scientific method in the development of the possibilities of growing, expanding experience. I have but endeavored to point out some of the conditions which must be satisfactorily fulfilled if education takes the latter course.

For I am so confident of the potentialities of education when it is treated as intelligently directed development of the possibilities inherent in ordinary experience that I do not feel it necessary to criticize here the other route nor to advance arguments in favor of taking the route of experience. The only ground for anticipating failure in taking this path resides to my mind in the danger that experience and the experimental method will not be adequately conceived. There is no discipline in the world so severe as the discipline of experience subjected to the tests of intelligent development and direction. Hence the only ground I can see for even a temporary reaction against the standards, aims, and methods of the newer education is the failure of educators who professedly adopt them to be faithful to them in practice. As I have emphasized more than once, the road of the new education is not an easier one to follow than the old road but a more strenuous and difficult one. It will remain so until it has attained its majority and that attainment will require many years of serious co-operative work on the part of its adherents. The greatest danger that attends its future is, I believe, the idea that it is an easy way to follow, so easy that its course may be improvised, if not in an impromptu fashion, at least almost from day to day or from week to week. It is for this reason that instead of extolling its principles, I have confined myself to showing certain conditions which must be fulfilled if it is to have the successful career which by right belongs to it.

I have used frequently in what precedes the words *progressive* and *new* education. I do not wish to close, however, without recording my firm belief that the fundamental issue is not of new versus old education nor of progressive against traditional education but a question of what anything whatever must be to be worthy of the name *education*. I am not, I hope and believe, in favor of any ends or any methods simply because the name progressive may be applied to them. The basic question concerns the nature of education with no qualifying adjectives prefixed. What we want and need is education pure and simple, and we shall make surer and faster progress when we devote ourselves to finding out just what education is and what conditions have to be satisfied in order that education may be a reality and not a name or a slogan. It is for this reason alone that I have emphasized the need for a sound philosophy of experience.

For Reflection

1. How can thinking be doing? How can reflection be living life?
2. Do "problem-solving" and church ministry fit together? How or why not?
3. What might a focus on "experience" look like in Christian education?

10

Malcolm S. Knowles

Psychoeducationalist

Self-Directed Learning

(1975)

Malcolm Knowles could rightly be called, if not the "father," then the "wise uncle" of adult education. He has been a human relations development consultant to business, industry, and government, a high school instructor, the executive director of the Adult Education Association of the U.S.A., and a professor, principally at Boston University and North Carolina State University. He has written numerous books and articles. His approach to adult education is based on an *organismic model* which represents the adult as an interactive, developing organism, rather than as an empty machine (Knowles 1973). This leads to an *andragogical theory of adult learning.* (Knowles learned the term *andragogy* from colleagues in Yugoslavia and popularized it in this country.) It establishes a different way of educating adults from that used with children *(pedagogy)* (Knowles 1973). Andragogical theory assumes that as persons mature their self-concept moves from dependence toward self-directedness. As persons mature they accumulate experience that provides great reservoirs for learning. As people grow older their readiness to learn is based less on biological factors or external stress and more on the developmental tasks required to perform social roles. Adults are more problem-centered in regard to learning while children have been conditioned to have a more content-centered orientation (Knowles 1973).

From *Self-Directed Learning: A Guide for Learners and Teachers* (Chicago: Association/Follett, 1975), 14–21, 23–28, 60–63, 99–104, 110–15.

Knowles's book, *Self-Directed Learning: A Guide for Learners and Teachers,* is practical. It briefly presents the teacher's role as that of a facilitator of learning rather than that of a content transmitter. Instead of being concerned with what content needs to be covered, how it can be organized into manageable pieces and a logical sequence, and what are the most efficient means of transmission, the teacher is concerned with setting the learning climate, planning for optional procedures and decision-making, diagnosing needs, helping to set goals, suggesting learning plans, engaging in activities, and evaluation. Beyond these, the reading that follows gives almost step-by-step plans for adult educators, including charts, check lists, and other resources.

References

Knowles, Malcolm. 1973. *The adult learner: A neglected species.* Houston: Gulf Publishing Company

Inquiry Project 1: Why Self-Directed Learning?

It is a tragic fact that most of us only know how to be taught; we haven't learned how to learn. Why is this a tragic fact? There are both immediate and long [-term] reasons.

One immediate reason is that there is convincing evidence that people who take the initiative in learning (pro-active learners) learn more things, and learn better, than do people who sit at the feet of teachers passively waiting to be taught (reactive learners). . . . They enter into learning more purposefully and with greater motivation. They also tend to retain and make use of what they learn better and longer than do the reactive learners.

A second immediate reason is that self-directed learning is more in tune with our natural processes of psychological development. When we are born we are totally dependent personalities. We need parents to protect us, feed us, carry us, and make decisions for us. But as we grow and mature we develop an increasingly deep psychological need to be independent, first, of parental control, and then, later, of control by teachers and other adults. An essential aspect of maturing is developing the ability to take increasing responsibility for our own lives—to become increasingly self-directing.

A third immediate reason is that many of the new developments in education—the new curriculums, open classrooms, nongraded schools, learning resource centers, independent study, nontraditional study programs, external degree programs, universities-without-walls, and the like—put a heavy responsibility on the learners to take a good deal of initiative in their own learning.

Students entering into these programs without having learned the skills of self-directed inquiry will experience anxiety, frustration, and often failure, and so will their teachers. The rapid spread of this problem in high schools, technical institutes, community colleges, colleges and universities, and adult education is precisely what has caused this book to be written.

But there is also a long [-term] reason why it is tragic that we have not learned how to learn without being taught, and it is probably more important than all of the immediate reasons put together. Alvin Toffler calls this reason "future shock." The simple truth is that we are entering into a strange new world in which rapid change will be the only stable characteristic. And this simple truth has several radical implications for education and learning.

For one thing, this implies that it is no longer realistic to define the purpose of education as transmitting what is known. In a world in which the half-life of many facts (and skills) may be ten years or less, half of what a person has acquired at the age of twenty may be obsolete by the time that person is thirty. Thus, the main purpose of education must now be to develop the skills of inquiry. When a person leaves schooling he or she must not only have a foundation of knowledge acquired in the course of learning to inquire but, more importantly, also have the ability to go on acquiring new knowledge easily and skillfully the rest of his or her life.

A second implication is that there must be a somewhat different way of thinking about learning. Typically, we think of learning as what takes place in school—it is "being taught." To be adequate for our strange new world we must come to think of learning as being the same as living. We must learn from everything we do; we must exploit every experience as a "learning experience." Every institution in our community—government agency, store, recreational organization, church—becomes a resource for learning, as does every person we have access to—parent, child, friend, service provider, doctor, teacher, fellow worker, supervisor, minister, store clerk, and so on and on. Learning means making use of every resource—in or out of educational institutions—for our personal growth and development.

A third implication is that it is no longer appropriate to equate education with youth. In the civilization of our forefathers it may have been possible for people to learn in their youthful years most of what they would need to know for the rest of their life, but this is no longer true. Education—or, even better, learning—must now be defined as a lifelong process. The primary learning during youth will be the skills of inquiry and the learning after schooling is done will focus on acquiring the knowledge, skills, understanding, attitude, and values required for living adequately in a rapidly changing world.

To sum up: the "why" of self-directed learning is survival—your own survival as an individual, and also the survival of the human race. Clearly, we are not talking here about something that would be nice or desirable; neither are we talking about some new educational fad. We are talking about a basic human competence—the ability to learn on one's own—that has suddenly become a prerequisite for living in this new world.

Inquiry Project 2: What Is Self-Directed Learning?

In its broadest meaning, "self-directed learning" describes a process in which individuals take the initiative, with or without the help of others, in diagnosing their learning needs, formulating learning goals, identifying human and material resources for learning, choosing and implementing appropriate learning strategies, and evaluating learning outcomes. Other labels found in the literature to describe this process are "self-planned learning," "inquiry method," "independent learning," "self-education," "self-instruction," "self-teaching," "self-study," and "autonomous learning." The trouble with most of these labels is that they seem to imply learning in isolation, whereas self-directed learning usually takes place in association with various kinds of helpers, such as teachers, tutors, mentors, resource people, and peers. There is a lot of mutuality among a group of self-directed learners.

Two Approaches to Education

Perhaps the full meaning of self-directed learning can be made clearer by comparing it with its opposite, which was referred to in Inquiry Project 1 as being "taught." To make the labels parallel, let's call it "teacher-directed learning."

It might be worthwhile to mention in passing that the body of theory and practice on which teacher-directed learning is based is often given the label *pedagogy*, from the Greek words *paid* (meaning "child") and *agogus* (meaning "leader"). Pedagogy has come to be defined as the art and science of teaching, but its tradition is in the teaching of children. The body of theory and practice on which self-directed learning is based has come to be labeled "andragogy," from the combining form *andr* of the Greek word *aner* (meaning "man"). Andragogy is defined, therefore, as the art and science of helping adults (or, even better, maturing human beings) learn. These definitions do not imply that children should be taught pedagogically and adults should be taught andragogically. Rather, the two terms simply differentiate between two sets of assumptions about learners, and the teacher who makes one set of assumptions will teach pedagogically whether he or she is teaching children or adults, whereas the teacher who makes the other set of assumptions will teach andragogically whether the learners are children or adults. In fact, many of the current innovations in schooling, such as open classrooms, nongraded schools, learning laboratories, community schools, and nontraditional study programs, are premised on andragogical assumptions about children and youth as learners.

The assumptions about learners on which these two approaches are based are summarized in Learning Resource A. You might find it helpful to scan it quickly now, and then turn back here and read the paragraphs below for any further explanation you may want.

Teacher-directed learning assumes the learner is essentially a dependent personality and that the teacher has the responsibility of deciding what and how the learner should be taught; whereas self-directed learning assumes that the human being grows in capacity (and need) to be self-directing as an essential component of maturing, and that this capacity should be nurtured to develop as rapidly as possible.

Teacher-directed learning assumes that the learner's experience is of less value than that of the teacher [and] the textbook writers and materials producers as a resource for learning, and that therefore the teacher has the responsibility to see to it that the resources of these experts are transmitted to the learner; whereas self-directed learning assumes that the learner's experiences become an increasingly rich resource for learning which should be exploited along with the resources of experts.

Teacher-directed learning assumes that students become ready to learn different things at different levels of maturation, and that a given set of learners will therefore be ready to learn the same things at a given level of maturation; whereas self-directed learning assumes that individuals become ready to learn what is required to perform their evolving life tasks or to cope more adequately with their problems, and that each individual therefore has a somewhat different pattern of readiness from other individuals.

Teacher-directed learning assumes that students enter into education with a subject-centered orientation to learning (they see learning as accumulating subject matter) and that therefore learning experiences should be organized according to units of content; whereas self-directed learning assumes that this orientation is a result of their previous conditioning in school and that their natural orientation is task- or problem-centered, and that therefore learning experiences should be organized as task-accomplishing or problem-solving learning projects (or inquiry units).

Teacher-directed learning assumes that students are motivated to learn in response to external rewards and punishments, such as grades, diplomas, awards, degrees, and fear of failure; whereas self-directed learning assumes that learners are motivated by internal incentives, such as the need for esteem (especially self-esteem), the desire to achieve, the urge to grow, the satisfaction of accomplishment, the need to know something specific, and curiosity.

As you reflect on these differing assumptions, does it occur to you that both sets of assumptions may be true—that all teacher-directed learning is not necessarily bad and that all self-directed learning is not necessarily good? No doubt there are learning situations in which we are indeed dependent (as when approaching an entirely new and strange area of inquiry), in which our experience is in fact of little worth (as when we have had no previous experience within the area of inquiry), in which our readiness to learn is really determined by our level of maturation regarding the area of inquiry, in which we are rightly focusing on accumulating subject matter, and in which we are actually motivated by external pressures. Perhaps what makes the difference between pedagogical and andragogical education is not so much the difference in the assumptions underlying their theory and practice as it is the attitude of the learners. If self-directed learners recognize that there are occasions on which they will need to be taught, they will enter into those taught-learning situations in a searching, probing frame of mind and will exploit them as resources for learning without losing their self-directedness.

Inquiry Project 3: What Competencies Are Required for Self-Directed Learning?

The competencies required to excel in teacher-directed learning, every *A*-student will tell you, include the ability to listen attentively, the ability to take careful notes, the ability to read speedily and with good comprehension, and the ability to predict exam questions and cram for them. This may seem to be a caricature of teacher-directed learning competencies, but aren't these in reality the ones we have come to rely upon in school?

Self-directed learning, however, requires a very different set of competencies. A list of the more general and important competencies are contained in Learning Resource B.

You might find it useful to turn to Learning Resource B now and rate the degree to which you already possess each of these competencies. Then check out your ratings with a group of two or three peers and a teacher to get their help in testing how realistic your ratings are.

Inquiry Project 4: Designing a Learning Plan

There are a variety of ways one can go about designing a plan for learning. Perhaps the simplest is to follow the steps of scientific inquiry:

1. What is the question I want an answer to?
2. What are the data I need to answer this question?
3. What are the most appropriate and feasible sources of these data?
4. What are the most efficient and effective means I can use to collect these data from these sources?
5. How shall I organize and analyze these data to get an answer to my question?
6. How will I report my answer and test its validity?

But I want to suggest a somewhat more elaborate and rigorous format: a *learning contract*. My students report that it helps them organize their learning more efficiently, induces them to be more creative in identifying learning resources and developing learning strategies, and forces them to get better evidence of their accomplishments. It is capable of being used in any content area.

The Learning Contract

A contract is usually defined as "a binding agreement between two or more persons or parties," and it is in fact becoming more and more common for teachers to make contracts with students for course work and grades, and for nontraditional study institutions to enter into contracts with students specifying what must be accomplished to earn a particular degree. For the purpose of this learning project in self-directed learning, however, I suggest that you contract with yourself. You are contracting with yourself to become a self-directed learner, and your contract will specify how you will go about it and how you will know when you are there.

Here are some suggestions for building your learning contract:

1. Turn to Learning Resource C and reproduce on three or four sheets of typing paper the four-column form of the contract (1. Learning Objectives; 2. Learning Resources and Strategies; 3. Evidence of Accomplishment; and 4. Criteria and Means of Validating).

2. Scan down Column 1 of the sample contract in Learning Resource C and, on the basis of the assessment you made in Inquiry Project 3, write into Column 1 of your contract form any objectives that you feel it would be useful for you to work toward. Add any other objectives not in this list that you can think of on your own.

3. Go now to Column 2 of your contract form and for each learning objective identify one or more learning resources and strategies that you think will help you accomplish that objective. Learning Resources J [see the section Questioning Strategies and Techniques] and K describe some learning strategies that are relevant to various kinds of objectives; you may well think of others.

4. Now you are ready for Column 3, in which for each objective you specify what evidence you will collect to help you measure the degree to which you have accomplished that objective. Learning Resource C and Learning Resource N [see Types of Evidence for Different Objectives] will give you some ideas about what kinds of evidence are appropriate for different objectives. You, in turn, may think of other kinds of evidence that will have meaning for you.

5. Column 4 provides space for you to indicate what criteria you will use for judging the evidence, and what means you will use to convince yourself of the validity of the evidence. Learning Resource O [see Some Examples of Rating Scales] may suggest ideas for this step. This is probably the most difficult part of the whole process, so don't try to be too ambitious about being scientific. The important thing is that you have some experience in weighing the evidence about what you have learned and judging how convincing it is to you.

6. At this point, you will find it helpful to check out your learning contract with a teacher or a group of peers. You can ask them such questions as:

a. Are the learning objectives clear, understandable, and realistic?
b. Can they think of other objectives you might consider?
c. Do the learning strategies seem reasonable?
d. Can they think of other resources and strategies you might consider?
e. Does the evidence seem relevant to the various objectives?
f. Can they suggest other evidence you might consider?
g. Are the criteria and means for validating the evidence clear, relevant, and convincing?
h. Can they think of other ways to validate the evidence you might consider?

7. From the responses you get from the . . . consultants, you may wish to modify your contract.

Now you are ready to engage in the learning strategies specified in your contract.

Have a rewarding experience.

Learning Resource A

A Comparison of Assumptions and Processes of Teacher-Directed (Pedagogical) Learning and Self-Directed (Andragogical) Learning

(Please read as poles on a spectrum, not as black-and-white differences)

Assumptions

About	Teacher-directed learning	Self-directed learning
Concept of the learner	Dependent personality	Increasingly self-directed organism
Role of learner's experience	To be built on more than used	A rich resource for learning
Readiness to learn	Varies with levels of maturation	Develops from life tasks and problems
Orientation to learning	Subject-centered	Task- or problem-centered
Motivation	External rewards and adjustments	Internal incentives, curiosity

The body of theory and practice on which teacher-directed learning is based is often given the label *pedagogy*, from the Greek words *paid* (meaning "child") and *agogus* (meaning "leader")—thus being defined as the art and science of teaching children.

The body of theory and practice on which self-directed learning is based is coming to be labeled *andragogy*, from the Greek word *aner* (meaning "man")—thus being defined as the art and science of helping adults (or even better, maturing human beings) learn.

Process Elements

Elements	Teacher-directed learning	Self-directed learning
Climate	Formal Authority-oriented Competitive Judgmental	Informal Mutually respectful Consensual Collaborative Supportive
Planning	Primarily by teacher	By participative decision-making
Diagnosis of needs	Primarily by teacher	By mutual assessment
Setting goals	Primarily by teacher	By mutual negotiation
Designing a learning plan	Content units Course syllabus Logical sequence	Learning projects Learning contracts Sequenced in terms of readiness
Learning activities	Transmittal techniques Assigned readings	Inquiry projects Independent study Experiential techniques
Evaluation	Primarily by teacher	By mutual assessment of self-collected evidence

Learning Resource B

Competencies of Self-Directed Learning: A Self-Rating Instrument	I possess these competencies to the following degree:			
	None	**Weak**	**Fair**	**Strong**
1. An understanding of the differences in assumptions about learners and the skills required for learning under teacher-directed learning and self-directed learning, and the ability to explain these differences to others.				
2. A concept of myself as being a non-dependent and a self-directing person.				
3. The ability to relate to peers collaboratively, to see them as resources for diagnosing needs, planning my learning, and learning; and to give help to them and receive help from them.				
4. The ability to diagnose my own learning needs realistically, with help from teachers and peers.				
5. The ability to translate learning needs into learning objectives in a form that makes it possible for their accomplishment to be assessed.				
6. The ability to relate to teachers as facilitators, helpers, or consultants, and to take the initiative in making use of their resources.				
7. The ability to identify human and material resources appropriate to different kinds of learning objectives.				
8. The ability to select effective strategies for making use of learning resources and to perform these strategies skillfully and with initiative.				
9. The ability to collect and validate evidence of the accomplishment of various kinds of learning objectives.				
10. ____________				
11. ____________				

Learning Resource C

Learning Contract

Name: John Doe | **Learning Project: Self-Directed Learning**

	1 **Learning Objectives**	2 **Learning Resources and Strategies**	3 **Evidence of Accomplishment**	4 **Criteria and Means of Validating Evidence**
1.	To develop an understanding of the theory and practical implications of teacher-directed learning and self-directed learning.	Inquiry Projects 1, 2 & 3. Read Brown, Eble, Houle, and Tough. Learning Resource A.	A written or oral presentation of the definitions, rationales, assumptions, and required skills of each.	Make presentation to a high school student, college student, teacher, and adult friend and have them rate it on a 5-point scale as to: (1) clarity, (2) comprehensiveness, and usefulness to them.
2.	To enhance my self-concept as a self-directing person.	Learning Resource D. Inquiry Project 4.	Creating of a satisfying learning contract.	Rating of the contract by two peers and a teacher as to degree of self-directedness it demonstrates.
3.	To gain skill in relating to peers collaboratively.	Learning Resource E. Learning Resource F.	Performance as a helper and helpee in a learning project with two or more peers.	Rating by the peers on my effectiveness as a helper and my openness to feedback as a helpee.
4.	To increase my skill in diagnosing my own learning needs.	Inquiry Projects 3 & 4. Learning Resource B. Learning Resource G.	Self-assessment as per Learning Resource G.	Rating by an expert on adequacy of model and accuracy of assessment.
5.	To increase my ability to translate learning needs into learning objectives.	Inquiry Projects 3 & 4. Learning Resource I.	Inquiry Project 4.	Rating by two peers and a teacher of objectives in contract as to measurability.
6.	To gain skill in making use of teachers as helpers and resources.	Inquiry Project 4. Learning Resource J.	Utilization of a teacher as a consultant and information source.	Rating by teacher used in Inquiry Project 4 of my skill in getting help and information.
7.	To increase my ability to identify human and material resources appropriate to different kinds of learning objectives.	Inquiry Project 4.	Resources identified in Inquiry Project 4.	Rating of resources by two peers and a teacher as to (1) variety, (2) appropriateness, (3) authoritativeness, and (4) feasibility.
8.	To increase my ability to select effective learning strategies.	Inquiry Project 4. Learning Resource K.	Strategies identified in Inquiry Project 4.	Same as above.
9.	To increase my ability to collect and validate evidence of accomplishment of objectives.	Inquiry Project 4. Learning Resource N. Learning Resource O.	Identification of evidence and criteria and means of validation in Inquiry Project 4.	Rating of adequacy of evidence and criteria and means of validation by two peers and a teacher according to criteria of (1) appropriateness of objectives, (2) sufficiency, and (3) convincingness.
10.				
11.				

Questioning Strategies and Techniques

Self-directed learning means learners engaging in inquiry. Inquiry means getting answers to questions through the collection and analysis of data. The prerequisite skill of inquiry, therefore, is the ability to formulate questions that can be answered by data.

Unfortunately, this is a skill that few of us have learned through our schooling. Rather, we have been taught to ask questions that can be answered by authority (a teacher, a textbook) or by faith. For example, "What grade will the teacher give me?" is a question that can be answered only by authority; "Will the teacher grade fairly?" is a question that usually can be answered only by faith; "What will be the effect on my grade of two different ways of studying?" however, is a question that can be answered through inquiry (using an experimental design).

A plan of inquiry involves asking six specific process questions and testing their adequacy against certain criteria, as follows:

1. What is the question you want to get an answer to?
   With the criteria of adequacy being:
   a. Is it a question worth asking?
   b. Is it a question you really care about?
   c. Is it a question that is answerable by data?
   d. Is the question clear and understandable to others?
2. What data are required to answer this question?
   With the criteria of adequacy being:
   a. Have subquestions requiring different kinds of data been identified?
   b. Are you clear about the data required to answer this particular question and no other?
   c. Are these data available to you within your limitations of time, money, etc.?
3. What are the sources of the required data?
   With the criteria of adequacy being:
   a. Are the sources feasible for you, i.e., within your reach and competence?
   b. Are the sources reliable and authentic repositories of the particular data you require?
   c. Are the requirements for data from primary versus secondary sources clearly delineated?
4. What means will be used to collect the data?
   With the criteria of adequacy being:
   a. Are these the most efficient and effective means for collecting these particular data from these sources?

   b. Are the means within your competence to use, or do you need further training for them?
   c. Will these means produce reliable and valid data?
   d. Will they produce data that will answer the question you are asking?

5. How will the data be analyzed so as to answer the question you are asking?
   With the criteria of adequacy being:
   a. Are the methods of analysis within your competence to use, or do you require further training for them?
   b. Will these methods of analysis produce a clear and significant answer to the specific question raised?
   c. Are these the most efficient and relevant methods of analysis for the data provided and the question posed?
6. How will the answer to the question be presented?
   a. Will the answer be clearly supported by the data?
   b. Is this form of presentation the most efficient and understandable possible?*

Students can learn a great deal about questions and their effective use from just being allowed opportunities to formulate some and carry out investigations of them. However, informal learning about questions should not exclude formal instruction. Students can have periods of time designated for focusing on their process of inquiry or problem-solving. Such focus would naturally deal with questions. Here students can analyze the types of questions they have been asking. Are they satisfied with their questions? Have they considered their questions productive in directing them to designated goals? What is the type of question they most commonly formulate?

Students who are presented opportunities to inquire within the discovery curriculum will most likely develop felt needs for formal discussion of questions. Students who are active in learning need to have time scheduled for analyzing just how they proceed. We can discuss with students the several types of questions according to some guide such as Bloom.[1] We should be sure that it is a guided discussion rather than just an exposition. We can present for discussion the idea that various types of questions will provide certain types of data. We might direct consideration as to what students do in questioning when they wish to formulate a generalization.

*Reprinted, with permission, from Francis P. Hunkins, *Questioning Strategies and Techniques* (Boston: Allyn and Bacon, 1972), 73–75.

1. The reference is to Benjamin S. Bloom, ed., *Taxonomy of Educational Objectives, Handbook I: The Cognitive Domain* (New York: McKay, 1956).

Before commencing formal discussion of questions, the teacher assigns students the task of listing some of the major questions they used in dealing with particular research topics. This list can then be considered in class group discussion. Students can analyze and criticize the different questions listed. Just what are the characteristics of the many questions asked? Why do you suppose this question was asked? If a student wished to develop a generalization, should he have asked primarily comprehension questions?

Such focus on questions also can lead to a consideration of the numerous questioning strategies the students used. Students engaged in oral investigation with a team partner might record their questions as they consider data. The tapes could then be studied to check if certain types of questions were used at the beginning of the inquiry and other types at the end. Where did the student put his most significant questions in relation to his search? Did he comprise a list of significant questions to search for, or did he just react to specific types of data and then draw questions from this experience?

Students also should have time for practicing at writing various types of questions and for judging the questions of others. Students can be grouped in teams of two and use each other as sounding boards regarding their questions. Perhaps the class can develop certain guides in formulating the several types of questions. The development of criteria for effective questions can be a class task. Here students could do some reading of the question and its importance. Students could read about inquiry in articles published in school magazines.

Related to writing diverse questions is being able to identify questions in written materials. Students, perhaps in teams, can analyze questions in textbooks and various supplementary books. Such analysis could focus on the intent of the questions. Also, if students wished to gain information other than that asked for in the material, what types of questions would they have to state?

Types of Evidence for Different Objectives

Different types of evidence are required for assessing the accomplishment of different objectives. The examples below may provide guidance in thinking of ways you might go about getting evidence that is appropriate for your objectives.

Objective	*Types of Evidence*
Knowledge	Reports of knowledge acquired, as in essays, examinations, oral presentations, audiovisual presentations.

Learning Resource K

Relating Methods to Objectives*

Type of Objectives	*Most Appropriate Methods*
Knowledge (Generalizations about experience; internalization of information)	Lecture, television, debate, dialogue, interview, symposium, panel, group interview, colloquy, motion picture, slide film, recording, book-based discussion, reading, programmed instruction
Understanding (Application of information and generalizations)	Audience participation, demonstration, dramatization, Socratic discussion, problem-solving project, case method, critical incident process, simulation games
Skills (Incorporating new ways of performing through practice)	Skill practice exercises, role-playing, in-basket exercises, participative cases, simulation games, human relations training groups, nonverbal exercises, drill, coaching
Attitudes (Adoption of new feelings through experiencing greater success with them than with old feelings)	Experience-sharing discussion, sensitivity training, role-playing, critical incident process, case method, simulation games, participative cases, group therapy, counseling
Values (The adoption and priority arrangement of beliefs)	Value-clarification exercises, biographical reading, lecture, debate, symposium, colloquy, dramatization, role-playing, critical incident process, simulation games, sensitivity training

*Adapted from Malcolm S. Knowles, *The Modern Practice of Adult Education* (New York: Association Press, 1970), 294.

Understanding	Examples of utilization of knowledge in solving problems, as in critical incident cases, simulation games, proposals of action projects, research projects with conclusions and recommendations.
Skills	Performance exercises, with ratings by observers.
Attitudes	Attitudinal rating scales; performance in role playing, critical incident cases, simulation games, sensitivity groups, etc., with feedback from observers.
Values	Value rating scales; performance in value clarification groups, critical incident cases, simulation games, etc., with feedback from observers.

Some Examples of Rating Scales

The instruments reproduced on the next few pages are examples of rating scales that were constructed by students in one of my courses (ED 559E: Adult Learning) to collect or validate evidence of accomplishment of various objectives.

They are presented here in the hope that they may stimulate ideas for constructing your own instruments.

Evaluation

Course: ______________________________

Learner: ______________________________

Evaluator: cc

Objective 1: To develop a better understanding of current learning concepts and theories.

Learning Strategy: To attend class regularly and to participate in class activities and discussions.

	Low				High
1. Was my participation adequate?	1	2	3	4	5
2. Were my questions relevant to the discussion?	1	2	3	4	5
3. Did I take up too much class time for my own observations and remarks?	1	2	3	4	5
4. Did I help other class members by evaluating them when asked to do so?	1	2	3	4	5
5. Was my attendance at class meetings regular?	1	2	3	4	5

Evaluation

Course: ______________________________

Learner: ______________________________

Evaluator: Inquiry Group

Objective 2: To develop knowledge of the changes adults, particularly those over sixty years of age, experience as they develop.

Learning Strategy: To read in various sources about people over sixty; to conduct and tape interviews with three people in this age group and with the director of a program of volunteer community service for retired senior citizens.

	Low				High
1. Is my reading list appropriate for a study of people over sixty?	1	2	3	4	5
2. Was the reading material useful in the preparation of the group presentation?	1	2	3	4	5
3. Was my participation in the preparation of the interviewer's guide helpful to the group?	1	2	3	4	5
4. Were the interviews appropriate methods of study for learning about people over sixty?	1	2	3	4	5
5. Were the interviews useful in the preparation of the class presentation?	1	2	3	4	5

Evaluation

Course: ______________________________

Learner: ______________________________

Evaluator: Consultation Group

Objective 3: To develop technical skill in using new methods and techniques for the class presentation.

Learning Strategy: To take photographs of people interviewed; to help select other visual material for slides; to help prepare the tape for the narrator; to help coordinate the slides and sound.

	Low				High
1. Were the photographs appropriate for the program?	1	2	3	4	5
2. Were the photographs useful to the program?	1	2	3	4	5
3. Was the recording of the "rough" tape for the narrator a contribution to the group project?	1	2	3	4	5
4. Was the help I gave in coordinating the sound and visuals valuable to the group?	1	2	3	4	5
5. Do you think I developed new skills in this learning experience?	1	2	3	4	5

For Reflection

1. How might a “learning contract” be helpful in a Christian education setting?
2. Do you think a teacher of adults who thinks mainly in pedagogical terms could make the adjustment to andragogy? Explain.
3. What is a “plan of inquiry”? How does it work?
4. Why is evaluation important in the adult education process?

Part 2

Basic Perspectives

11

Findley B. Edge

Experiential or Institutionalized Religion? (1963)

Findley B. Edge, who considers himself a "progressive" evangelical, was for many years professor of religious education at the Southern Baptist Theological Seminary. He influenced several generations of Christian educators, especially Southern Baptists. Professor Edge identifies several major personal influences on his thinking: Gaines Dobbins, his teacher at Southern Seminary; Ernst Ligon, of Union College, New York, and the head of the Character Research Project; and Randolph C. Miller of Yale (Mayr 1983).

The call, a sort of open letter, made by Edge in this, the opening chapter of his book, is as valid today as it was twenty-five years ago. It is a call away from a church that is based primarily upon institutional loyalty toward a church that is based upon experience in Christ. It sets, for Edge, the agenda for Christian education for at least the remainder of the century. Much of his concern comes from his observation that American churches were increasing in membership and buildings, but diminishing in spiritual strength. Following the call, Edge describes how the contemporary church has mired itself in institutionalism. He begins with the experience of Judaism, advances to the early church, then considers the church from the reformation to the present. He challenges today's church to

From *A Quest for Vitality in Religion: A Theological Approach to Religious Education* (Nashville: Broadman, 1963), 15–31.

return to the vitality of the New Testament. This is presented throughout as a task of Christian education: ". . . the educational program of the church . . . is a primary means by which and through which the ministry of the church is realized." (30) Since at its essence this task is theological, it emphasizes Edge's perspective that Christian (religious) education is basically a theological endeavor.

In the remaining chapters of his book, under the following headings, Edge explores several proposals that he believes essential to the task of Christian education: The Nature and Meaning of the Christian Life, How One Enters the Christian Life, Seeking a Regenerate Church Membership. At the end of this selection, Edge invites all concerned Christians to ponder his proposals and enter into a dialogue with each other. His optimism that solutions can be found stem, not from his great confidence in Christians, but from his great confidence in Christ.

References

Mayr, M., ed. 1983. *Modern Masters of Religious Education.* Birmingham: Religious Education Press.

Two paradoxical phenomena may be seen in the religious life of the United States today. On the one hand are numerous evidences that religion is in the midst of a period of unparalleled success. On the other, a crescendo of voices, raised both in question and warning, point up the fact that something is seriously wrong with modern Christianity.

Which of these conflicting views is correct? Is it possible that there is a real measure of accuracy in both views? If so, which view is more critical and, therefore, demands our primary concern?

Evidences of Revival

It is obvious that there has been a revival of religion in this generation. Church membership has reached an all-time high. In 1850 only 16 percent of the population were members of any church. During the next fifty years, by 1900, this had risen to 36 percent. In 1940 church membership was 49 percent, while in 1960 it had risen to 63.4 percent. In the two decades between 1920 and 1940 church membership increased only 6 percent; while in the two decades between 1940 and 1960 it increased 14.4 percent. In 1943 (more adequate statistics are given for this year than in 1940) there were approximately 213,000 Sunday schools with an enrollment of just over 25,000,000. In 1960 there were over 286,000 Sunday schools with an enrollment of over 44,000,000 (National Council of the Churches of Christ 1960). This is an increase of a million per year in enrollment for nearly twenty years—a remarkable growth.

Attendance at the services in the churches has likewise increased. "Opinion polls of attendance at church by adults indicated that 41 percent of the respondents attended in the week preceding the interview in 1939 as compared to 51 percent in 1957" (Winter 1961, 30). One of the most remarkable areas of growth has been that of finances. Between 1940 and 1960 contributions to churches more than doubled. In 1940 total gifts of more than $1,100,000,000, were reported. In 1960 total gifts were a little over $2,300,000,000. In 1950 the per-capita giving was $30.51. In 1960 it was $62.25. Despite inflation this is a significant gain.

Church construction has soared to new heights. New churches are being built; old churches are being remodeled, or new space is being added. It is true that building is directly related to the economy, and we have had prosperous years recently. Yet in comparing the present building surge with another prosperous year, 1928, we find there is approximately a 400 percent increase at the present time. Church building has become "the fourth largest private building category" as religious bodies have "erected tangible symbols of their devotion" (Marty 1959, 15).

Statistics alone cannot measure the depth of religious concern, nor are these the only evidences of success that might be cited. However, they do give an indication of the progress being made and the interest and attention currently given to religion by a majority of our population.

What Kind of Religion Is It?

Many evidences thus point to the fact that for the past two decades in particular there has been a rather remarkable renaissance in religion. Some call it a "revival of religion"; some, an "interest in religion"; others refer to it as a "surge of piety." However it may be characterized, it cannot be denied that there has been a definite "upswing" in religion. Although the forward progress has slowed to some extent recently, the optimism of many concerning the future of religion in the United States is undiminished.

The question being raised with increasing frequency and with growing concern, however, is: What kind of religious revival are we experiencing in our generation? Is it in reality a revival of the Christian faith, the faith of the New Testament, or is it something other than the Christian faith? Have we developed a religion that holds to the external forms of the New Testament faith but places something else at the center?

In answer to this question Claire Cox (1961, 1–2) says,

> There is a new-time religion in the land. It has made the church more popular and prosperous than ever before. It also has made the church less pious. . . .

> What this religious phenomenon is no one is exactly sure. Many a churchman has spent painful hours pondering the question. There is no doubt about the heightened religious interest. . . . But the religious upsurge appears against a dismal backdrop of payola, television quiz show "fixes," police scandals, increasing rape, murder, robbery and embezzlement, and rising rates of juvenile delinquency, alcoholism, and divorce.

Roy Eckardt (1958, 43) calls the religion which is having such a resurgence in America today "folk religion."

> The real justification of the phrase "folk religion" is the fact that the "turn to religion" is very much a popular movement. . . . Folk religion is religion for the "folks." It is characterized by the fact that it holds both the people and religion in high esteem. . . . Piety can resolve basic human problems of both a personal and social nature, and this without very great difficulty. Religion is marked by its utility.

Others suggest that instead of the religion of the New Testament, in reality we have developed a "new American religion" which tends to be identified with the highest ethical standards of modern society. The interest in and commitment to this "new American religion" is very deep and very real. The only difficulty is that this is not the New Testament faith. Will Herberg (1955, 89–90), in his penetrating analysis of modern religion, says that today we have a sort of "religion in general" that affirms the "American way of life." Church members are more deeply committed to the American way than they are to "the way" of the first century. In fact they seem to have identified the American way and "the way" as being synonymous. When probed deeply, the average American is more concerned about and opposed to one who threatens the American way of life than to one who might threaten his religion.

The warning being raised is that this "new American religion" has lost much of the essence and vitality that was characteristic of New Testament Christianity. Marty (1959, 108) describes the change that has taken place in this fashion:

> From the days when reformed Christians came to America . . . to the present, Protestantism has carried on an exciting dialogue with its environment. The characteristic result we have described as *erosion*. Constant friction rubbed rough edges away. Protestant particularity and the offense of its witness tended to be worn smooth; uncongenial aspects in the American environment were absorbed. Church (or churches) and world made their peace. Religion was Americanized and America was religionized, and both were accepted complacently.

It should not be inferred from what has been said or will be said that there are not those people in our churches who have a genuine personal faith and a deep commitment to Jesus Christ. Unfortunately, these are the exception and not the rule. The average member of our churches neither reflects an intelligent awareness of the deeper demands of the Christian faith as a radical way of life, nor does he demonstrate a serious commitment of himself to that way of life.

Certainly the typical church member believes in God. In fact polls indicate that over 90 percent of our total population attest to their belief in God. But what kind of God is it in which the typical member believes? Is he the God of Abraham, Isaac, and Jacob? Is he the one so holy and majestic that mortal man bows in his presence in reverence and awe? No, this is not the temper of our times. Americans have not only come to "know" God, they have become "chummy" with him. To one he is a "living doll"; to another he is the "man upstairs." We are on his side and he is on our side. This God "smiles on society, and his message is a relaxing one. He does not scold you; he does not demand of you. He is a gregarious God and he can be found in the smiling, happy people of the society about you. As the advertisement puts it, religion can be fun" (Whyte 1956, 254).

Certain leading psychiatrists are writing today that belief in God is essential for a sound, integrated personality. Politicians are proclaiming that only a return to God can preserve our way of life. Scientists are saying that a spiritual transformation is essential if our civilization is to survive. So, in our generation, there has been a "turning to God," a return to religion.

This modern infatuation with religion was typified in a recent cartoon. A man was pictured in clerical garb. On his lapel was a large (campaign-size) button with the words: "I Like God." God would get his vote. In fact God would get the vote of the majority of Americans. They "like God." Yet this "belief in God" does not seriously affect the minor or major relationships of most people. Although the overwhelming majority professes to a belief in God, "three out of four admit they never think of God in relation to their own lives or associate Him with their behavior" (Whitman 1962, 81–2). When there is a conflict between the ways of God and current social mores, the latter is almost always the course that is followed.

What we have failed to understand is that our return has been to "religion" and not to Christianity; our revival has been a "religious" revival and not, primarily, a revival of Christianity. What the typical church member does not understand is that God does not exist to give us peace of mind, to save our way of life, nor even to save our civilization. As Perry says, "the God of Christian faith is no bell-hop catering to our needs as we define them and to our vanities and aspirations. We are God's servants, citizen-subjects of his kingdom, performing his service when he beckons" (Perry 1958, 16). When God demands of his people a radical break with the evils and injustices of modern society, when he demands a radical break with the "cult of conformity" that has engulfed modern religion, the one who would be Christian rather than merely religious has no choice but to obey. We must serve God. God does not exist to serve us.

Although it is true that a majority of present-day Americans are members of some church, this does not mean that they have given themselves to God to do his will "on earth even as it is done in heaven." The fact is that the labor union, the manufacturers' association, or the professional society of which they are members exerts far more influence on their attitudes, values, and courses of action. These relationships demand and get more real loyalty from the average man than does the church to which he belongs.

Modern society expects the church to make a comfortable adjustment to current social norms, and the church usually has been ready to comply. The distinction between church and world, between the people of God and the people of the world, has largely been lost. The masses join the churches with a minimum of commitment and with a minimum being expected of them.

> Success-minded congregations make it all too clear in their solicitation that admission to the church is by handshake with the smiling pastor. The church that opens its door so easily loses its potency. . . . Few are asked to take the form of a servant, but all are frequently asked to take a packet of envelopes for financial contributions. No one is religious because everyone is "religious" (Marty 1959, 117).

How is it that such a situation exists in the life of churches today? Undoubtedly there are numerous reasons. For example, many people have united with a church for other than Christian reasons. Some have joined for purely business reasons rather than on the basis of a personal commitment to Jesus Christ. The public schoolteacher knows that she will be more readily accepted by the community if she joins the church. The insurance man knows it is good business if he is active in the life of a church. In *Sincerely, Willis Wayde,* a novel by John P. Marquand, the hero, an up-and-coming young executive, moves to a new community, joins the church, and becomes a solicitor for the every-member canvass.

> Willis Wayde is a complete secularist without the vaguest glimmering of what the Christian religion is all about. But he knows that the up-and-coming young executive, moving into a suburban community of other up-and-coming young executives, is expected to be identified with a Protestant church (Hutchinson 1957, 113).

Also, in belonging to a church an individual may be fulfilling no more than a basic desire of modern man, the desire to belong, to be identified with and accepted by his fellow man. It is true that he may have a vague admiration for an Isaiah, an Elijah, or an Amos, but he has no real identification with these "zealots for the Lord." To exhibit such nonconformity, to hold such an uncompromising position before his fellow man would be impossible for him. His need for belonging, his need to be accepted is too great. The religion of the modern man

> is thus frequently a religiousness without serious commitment, without real inner conviction, without genuine existential decision. What should reach down to the core of existence, shattering and renewing, merely skims the surface of life, and yet succeeds in generating the sincere feeling of being religious. Religion thus becomes a kind of protection the self throws up against the radical demand of faith (Herberg 1955, 276).

Is Christianity Becoming Institutionalized?

The thoughtful observer views contemporary religion with mixed emotions. He may be raised to the heights of rejoicing as he views the many evidences of success, of genuine concern for the unreached and unsaved, of unselfish dedication and service on the part of many. On the other hand, he may be plunged almost to the depths of despair, for the thoughtful observer cannot help but be aware that there are also disturbing evidences of tendencies toward externalism, superficiality, and institutionalism in modern religious life.

There is always good and bad, strength and weakness, in the expression of religion at any given time. Weakness may show up even when the church is at its best, and some strength is there when the church is at its worst. This analysis of the current religious situation does not mean to imply that our understanding, appropriation, and expression of religion today has been a complete failure. The question is whether, through the passing years, we have unconsciously wandered from and thus tended to lose the essential spirit and vitality of the faith of the New Testament, so that today we merely are holding on to some of the external forms of that faith.

In assessing the modern religious situation, some people emphasize the other side of the picture. "What is wrong," they ask, "with religion becoming a vogue in American life? . . . Let's be glad for the faithful fifties. If this generation will move with the winds of God as we now see them stirring in our American life, we may see one of the most memorable acts of God in the history of mankind" (Eckhardt 1958, 158). If one feels that the religion of today is the religion of the New Testament, or a reasonable facsimile thereof, then one will agree with the previous statement. Those holding this view will feel that a book such as this is out of place and does more damage than good. They feel we need to stop criticizing, stop "rocking the boat." They feel we need to get together to promote and expand the religion of today with every ounce of energy that is within us.

On the other hand, if religion as it is being expressed today, in the main, is not the religion of the New Testament and only in certain external forms is it even a partial facsimile thereof, then to perpetuate the current religious expression is to bring upon us the judgment of God. Thus, one's reaction to the current religious situation is determined by one's answer to the question: What is the nature and essence of New Testament religion? To explore this question and to suggest a possible answer is one purpose of this study.

First we must consider what is meant by "institutionalism" in religion. It is no broadside condemnation of institutions and organizations *per se*. They are both necessary and desirable instruments for the orderly and adequate propagation of the faith. They provide an effective means by which converts to the movement are made. They provide the structure in which and through which guidance is given to the adherents through teaching and study. They provide an effective means of cooperation by which the adherents as a group can accomplish tasks which are too large and complicated for individuals to do alone. Thus, it would be utterly impossible for any movement to survive without institutions and organizational structure. Certainly it would be impossible for any adequate propagation of the values of the movement to be made without such institutions. Institutions are not inherently evil. Rather they are a valid and valuable part of any significant movement.

What, then, is meant by "institutionalism"? Religion becomes institutionalized when its adherents are related primarily to the church as an institution or to the organizations of the church rather than to the living God. The religious life manifested is not the free and open outworking of a deep, spiritual relationship with God. Rather, in institutionalized religion the primary expression of a person's religion is that he supports the organizations by his attendance; he supports the institution by his gifts; and in general he merely lives a "good" life.

Acknowledging this as a real trend today would depend, in part, upon the religious group or groups with which one has had contact and also, in part, upon the criteria used in making one's evaluation. To be precise in such a subjective matter is virtually impossible. It is the conclusion of one writer, however, that

> approximately one half of the official membership of the churches, possibly as much as two thirds, are religiously tied to an organization rather than personally bound to God or his teachings—a surprising fact in view of the Protestant understanding of faith. It is ironical that Protestantism, after rebelling against the institutional character of Roman Catholicism, should emerge in the 1960s with a membership predominantly oriented to organizational activities (Winter 1961, 100).

Religion becomes institutionalized when the church turns its concern inward upon itself, when it is more concerned with its own existence and progress than it is with the mission for which it was founded. Hendrik Kraemer (1958, 127) says this is exactly what is happening in the modern church.

> . . . The Church as such is introvert, and considered as such by public opinion. It has been bred for centuries into the Church and therefore it is felt as natural by Church people themselves and by public opinion . . . the mind of the Churches is bent, above all, on its own increase and well-being. It is Church-centred. It is self-centred.

It is true that Protestants have demonstrated an interest in and concern for the unreached masses. We have taken a definite pride in the fact that our Sunday school enrollment has increased twenty million in less than twenty years. The increase in church membership likewise has been a source of pride. But this very outreach, which indeed is a fundamental part of the Christian mission in the world, too often seems only to have contributed to the growth of the church as an *institution*. The churches have not seriously attempted to transform the world, nor have we led the people whom we have reached and enlisted to be active instruments in remaking the world.

One primary motive that underlies the multitudinous activities carried on by the minister and the people is to build up and enlarge the institution. In their minds this has come to be identified with "doing the will of God." The truth of this statement is demonstrated by noting the question which ministers and other staff members generally ask each other: What's your Sunday school enrollment now? How many baptisms did you have last year? What's your church budget? "The church-as-an-institution is more concerned to enhance the institution than it is to minister to the real needs of people or to transform the world. In such a situation, the office of the minister becomes the job of a promoter" (Meister 1961, 254–55).

Religion becomes institutionalized when means become ends and ends become means. Institutions and organizations which were designed and intended to be used as a means of serving people may become ends, and the loyalty of people is determined by their service to the institution.

> We have reached a time when conventional American Protestant churches are inordinately concerned with upholding the existence, the authority, and the sanctity of their own organizational structures. Forms of organization which originated as *means* to enable the church to function "decently and in order" in performing its redemptive mission, have become ends to be served. . . . Instead of using organizations to serve people, we use people to serve organizations. . . . This is fatal. The church which seeks to save its own life will lose it, just as surely as the person who seeks to save his life will lose it (Meister 1961, 253–54).

The announcements made in church about certain meetings are indicative of the emphasis on organizational ends. For example, we often hear the Sunday school superintendent announcing: "The regular Sunday school associational meeting will be held this afternoon at Red Fork Church. Brother Smith is our new associational superintendent and he is trying real hard to have a good attendance. Let's all try to be present and support him in his work." Or: "We're having the associational Training Union meeting in our church this afternoon. It would be embarrassing if some other church should have more in attendance than we do. Let's all try to come."

Support the organization. This is the emphasis! Attend the meeting. This is how to demonstrate your loyalty! Little or nothing is said about the real purpose of the meeting or about what the meeting is to do for those who attend. Of course there is a vague idea that those who attend "might be helped." But if the attendance of the organizations goes down, it is the task of the leadership of the church to increase this attendance. The loyalty and devotion of the church members are largely determined by their faithful attendance at the meetings of the church. What they do or do not do for Christ *in the world* is not the central concern. The organizations must be served!

Religion becomes institutionalized when it is more concerned with the correctness of one's belief than it is with the quality of one's life. Institutions are founded to propagate values that are held in highest esteem by a group. In the beginning of a movement the life of the group is directed by and lived under the demand of these values. However, as these values are passed on to succeeding generations, increasing emphasis is placed on belief in and acceptance of these values, but less and less is there adherence to and expression of these values in life. Emphasis is placed on belief rather than life.

Religion becomes institutionalized when the "spirit" of religion is lost and only the form remains. Worship may be taken as an example. The true spirit of worship may be found both in a highly liturgical service of worship or in an informal service of worship. Likewise, both the liturgical or the informal service may become institutionalized; that is, the spirit may be lost and only the form remain. This principle applies also to religion in its expression in life. Expressions of religion in life, such as prayer and giving, may be outward expressions of a deep inner experience or they may be routine forms.

> Religion not infrequently exhibits a tendency to become departmentalized, to move from the centre of experience to its margins. . . . Convictions become dogmas. Religious activities degenerate into meaningless and worthless forms. The institutions of religion which were the organs through which it found much of its expression and got much of its work done, become extraneous overhead organizations that lay a deadening hand upon the spirit. Finally, religion loses its moral and spiritual sensitiveness. The soul of religion is dead. In the name of God it fastens its dead weight upon progress, opposing the discovery of truth, stoning the prophets, and standing as the arch-champion of things as they are. And so it turns out that institutionalized, dogmatic, anti-social, and unethical "religion" becomes an obstacle in the way of God, crucifying His Son and defeating His purpose, so that God has had to set aside repeatedly in the course of history institutionalized forms of religion and their over-zealous custodians in

> order to make way for the prophets of reality and the religion of the spirit (Bower 1925, 138–39).

The question may be raised legitimately: If it is true that we have wandered so far from the essence of New Testament religion, why is this not apparent to more people? Indeed, why is it not apparent to all? Two answers may be given. First, this change comes about so slowly and imperceptibly one is not aware that it is happening. Evil slips in, becomes respectable, and finally is accepted as normal. The spirit and vitality which give life to religion slip away until only the external forms remain. Second, if such is the case in our day, this would not be the first time such a thing has happened in the religious life of a people and was not apparent to all—not even to the religious leaders.

In the middle of the eighth century before Christ, according to all outward appearances, religion was flourishing in Israel. It was presumed that the Israelites were pleasing to God. The people were meticulous in their observance of the sacrifices and other religious ceremonies. The sanctuaries throughout the land were filled with worshipers. They were living in prosperous times, a certain evidence of God's favor upon them they felt; and, in return, they were generous in their support of religion. Yet to the consternation and bewilderment of the people, the prophet Amos declared that Israel was hovering on the brink of destruction. All the outward evidences of religious success and all the outward religious displays were merely deceptive coverings for the decay that was at the heart of the nation's life. Into the midst of their smug complacency this herdsman hurled his words of doom. No wonder he aroused the hostility of the official clergy (Amos 7:10–17)! The people must have felt that here was another "fanatic" trying to disturb their situation (Smart 1960, 172). But from the vantage point of history, we are able to understand that Amos saw what God saw, and what the religious people of that day were too blind to see; namely, that their religion was merely a beautiful shell and that the inner vitality, the inner life, was dead.

A Radical Reformation Needed

If there is any measure of accuracy in the analysis given thus far, then the situation facing modern religion is not merely serious, it is critical. "The situation, rightly seen, shakes us as a church to the very roots of our being and challenges the validity of what passes as Christianity among us" (Smart 1960, 162). There may be those who will think that this problem is only academic in nature, pursued by a seminary professor as a sort of intellectual exercise. Not so! There is no problem more serious facing religion today. It touches the very center of the life and ministry of all Christians. We seek to serve the living God, but we serve him primarily through the life and work of the church. If in any way and for any reason the church follows some other way than *the way*, then our life and ministry as Christians correspondingly "misses the mark," and we are deceived at the very center of our being.

If it is true that there is a decided tendency toward institutionalism in the life of the modern church, is there any indication that the church is willing to change the pattern of its life and seek to recapture vital, experiential religion? This is not an easy question to answer. It is certainly possible for the church to do so. On the other hand, the road back to experiential religion is so difficult that the church may not be willing to pay the price. Elton Trueblood (1952, 32–33) is hopeful:

> There have been different great steps at different times in Christian history, because one of the most remarkable features of the Christian faith is its ability to reform itself *from the inside*. However vigorous the outside critics of the Church may be, the inside critics, who love the movement which they criticize, are far more vigorous and searching. Reformation is not accidental or exceptional, but characteristic and intrinsic. The crust forms repeatedly, but there is always volcanic power to break through it.

There is also hope in the increasing awareness and concern being evidenced by pastors and laymen alike. All the apparent success has not eliminated the disturbing fear that something is seriously wrong with the religious life of today. More and more these questions of deep concern are being raised, not by those who are hostile to the denomination or religious group, but by those who are most deeply committed to it. More and more these questions are being discussed openly in church and denominational meetings. Even now some of the churches are beginning serious and searching self-analysis. This self-appraisal will undoubtedly prove to be an agonizing experience. Where it will lead the church, no one knows.

> The whole gamut of new, stirring awareness and inner disturbance, manifested in a revival of apostolic sensitivity; of experiments in new Christian living and evangelism; of new stimulating theological thinking; . . . is the sure indication of a rising feeling that a radical Reformation of the Church is due. Probably more radical than the Reformation of the 16th century, because the pressure both of the Spirit and of the world are upon us to rethink and reshape the response to the divine calling of the Church (1958, 99).

If the blight of institutionalism is to be eliminated, if we are to recapture the vitality of the New Testament faith, the church must come to have a deeper and clearer understanding of herself, her life, and work. For this reason the educational program of the church, which is a primary means by which and through which the ministry of the church is realized, must rest upon a solid theological foundation. To state certain aspects of this theology, to enunciate a philosophy of education that grows out of this theology, and to suggest some practical implications of this philosophy that will serve as a guide for the life and work of the church is the purpose of this book.

This is an attempt to understand the experiential nature of New Testament Christianity and to take a serious look at ourselves in light of these findings. Certain of the proposals that will be suggested may seem to some to be drastic. Their practice did not seem so in New Testament times. They seem thus to us only because we have unconsciously wandered so far from the New Testament pattern and let ours become such a soft and easy religion. Without knowing it, we have traveled rather far down the road of institutionalism. Whether we like it or not, only drastic action will even begin to meet the seriousness of our situation. Trueblood is right in saying:

> If, in this situation, one truth is more obvious than any other, it is that *we cannot win except by a radical change.* If all we have to offer is the tame routine of the conventional church, with slight improvements in technique, we might as well give up. The modern church will not make a sufficient difference by a slight improvement in the anthems or by a little better preaching or by a little better organization of the Sunday Schools. Many of these are fairly good already, but not much seems to happen, so far as the pagan order is concerned (Trueblood 1952, 28).

The churches today face a difficult question. Shall they continue the relatively easy type of religion which can be popular and thus appeal to the masses; or shall they submit themselves to the difficult and radical element of discipline and self-denial which was characteristic of the New Testament faith? Since the masses tend to avoid suffering, this way cannot be popular. The present generation has grown up in this popular, easy religion. Because this is all the religion they know, they tend to feel that this is what religion ought to be. But in more thoughtful moments there comes the haunting and disturbing thought that perhaps—just perhaps—the difficult way, the way of radical change, may be the only way to power, the only way to vital, experiential religion.

Thus, the church today is called upon to go through the painful process of reevaluating herself—her essential nature, her ministry and mission in the modern world. Because of the difficulties involved these changes will come about only when, and if, the leadership of the church comes to have a deeper and clearer understanding of what the church is and what the church should be about in today's world.

For Reflection

1. How does "folk religion" fit into Edge's presentation? Can you give some personal examples?
2. Why is institutionalism so bad?
3. What is the "radical reformation" the author proposes?

References

Bower, W. C. 1925. *The curriculum of religious education.* New York: Charles Scribner's Sons.

Cox, C. 1961. *The new-time religion.* Englewood Cliffs, N.J.: Prentice-Hall.

Eckardt, R. 1958. *The surge of piety in America.* New York: Association Press.

Herberg, W. 1955. *Protestant, Catholic, Jew.* Garden City, N.Y.: Doubleday.

Hutchinson, P. 1957. *The new ordeal of Christianity.* New York: Association Press.

Kraemer, H. 1958. *A theology of the laity.* London: Lutterworth Press.

Marty, M. E. 1959. *The new shape of American religion.* New York: Harper and Bros.

Meister, J. 1961. "Requirements of renewal." *Union Quarterly Review* (March 1961) 16.

National Council of the Churches of Christ in the U.S.A. 1960. *Yearbook of American churches.* New York: National Council of the Churches of Christ in the U.S.A.

Perry, E. 1958. *The gospel in dispute.* Garden City, N.Y.: Doubleday.

Smart, J. D. 1960. *The rebirth of ministry.* Philadelphia: Westminster.

Trueblood. E. 1952. *Your other vocation.* New York: Harper and Bros.

Whitman, A. 1962. "What not to tell a child about God." *Reader's Digest* (February).

Whyte, Jr., W. H. 1956. *The organization man.* New York: Simon and Schuster.

Winter, G. 1961. *The suburban captivity of the churches.* Garden City, N.Y.: Doubleday.

12

Gaines S. Dobbins

Translating New Testament Principles into Present-Day Practices

(1947)

Although I have personally met and worked with several of the authors whose work appears in this book and have served on professional task forces with some, Gaines Dobbins is the only one who was my teacher for a whole semester toward the end of his very long and productive career. A teacher/administrator at Southern Baptist seminaries for almost fifty years, Dobbins also helped pioneer journalism, church administration, and Christian education as seminary subjects for his denomination and for evangelicals in general. Professor Dobbins taught more than twelve thousand students internationally, as well as in the United States. In addition, he was a denominational executive well recognized for his efficient and innovative work. His writing ministry began in 1915 and included at least five thousand articles, more than thirty books, and innumerable pamphlets and curriculum materials (Dobbins 1978).

Professor Dobbins was known to many as "Mr. Southern Baptist" because of his wide-ranging work and his many contacts, personally and through his writings, with thousands of Baptist church members. Initially, Dobbins saw himself as a pastor and theologian. Later, as a seminary faculty member, he created his own version of two practical theology disciplines, Sunday school pedagogy (religious education) and church efficiency (church administration). His approach to *Building Better Churches* reflects this focus, in that it is essentially pastoral (Dobbins 1978).

From *Building Better Churches: A Guide to the Pastoral Ministry* (Nashville: Broadman, 1947), 83–98.

The book is organized into three parts: Restoring New Testament Principles; Achieving Ends through Efficient Organization; and Meeting Needs through Pastoral Ministries. The chapter reprinted here briefly recapitulates the first part and then applies the author's New Testament principles in practical language. The chapter is based on two questions plainly stated: "Is there a clear-cut New Testament pattern that can be followed?" and "If . . . followed, will this pattern produce most richly the fruit of a true Christianity?" Dobbins's answer is affirmative, but he considers it revolutionary. His approach to this revolutionary answer might seem routine in the church world of the 1990s, but it is still to be accomplished on any wide basis. To the theologically conservative reader, Dobbins's material will not seem unusual, but well stated with its emphases on Christ the Great Teacher, Holy Spirit as interpreter, the Bible as chief textbook, and every Christian a server and witness bearer; it is "dead center" in the thinking of most evangelicals.

References

Dobbins, A. C. 1978. Gaines S. Dobbins. *Review and Expositor* 75. 3.

The minister, having faced the facts of a changing world, having confronted his complex task, having surveyed his field and his forces, having sought to rediscover the New Testament church pattern, and having undertaken to evaluate changed and changing conceptions of the church, will doubtless experience mingled emotions of depression and enthusiasm as he sets himself to the task of translating New Testament principles into present-day practice in the light of history and contemporary conditions. The molds into which the life of his church and denomination were poured have given it shape, which he feels helpless to change. Tradition and sentiment are powerful forces which change the minister more effectually than he can ordinarily change them. Much rationalizing has been indulged in by sincere men in the effort to bring the Scriptures to the support of sectarian views and practices. The completely unbiased mind is a fiction. Yet there have been few periods in Christian history when life was so fluid as at the present. Change is the order of the day. The minister may well be thrilled by the possibilities of progress in his field, as in education, medicine, transportation, communication, social sciences, political science, and other major fields of human interest.

What sort of church would it be that undertook intelligently and fearlessly to fashion itself according to the basic principles of the New Testament? On what vital functions would it major? What would be revealed as to its strength and weakness? What would it give up as encumbrances inherited from a traditional past but clearly of doubtful value in the living present? The two fundamental criteria would be (1) New Testament confirmation, and (2) functional value. The assumption is made that if the first test is met, the second will likewise be met, and vice versa. Such a church would set up for itself the following minimum ideals.

The Church, a Regenerate Body

Christian Church Members Should Be Different

This difference should result from an inward change growing out of a personal experience in which the shift of life's center has been from self to Christ. Individuals who have undergone this experience are "twice-born"; they are "new creatures in Christ Jesus." That this change cannot be brought about by any form of baptism or any other ceremony or sacrament is the testimony of the New Testament, of common sense, of experience, and of psychology. That it cannot be induced in an infant or in any other subject incapable of the personal experience of repentance and faith is equally clear. This prerequisite experience is not to be confused with knowledge of the Bible or ability to pass tests concerning doctrines and church practices. It may not safely be assumed because of a public avowal of religion and request for church membership. It flows no more from the dry-eyed acceptance of a creedal statement than from the tearful outburst of religious emotion.

Christian Church Members Should Manifest This Difference

Jesus himself set up the test: "By their fruits ye shall know them." Fruit bearing, however, is an end result, not an instantaneous achievement. "First the blade, then the ear, then the full grain in the ear" (Mark 4:28). The significant quality of the mustard seed is not its minuteness of size but its life germ which enables it to push upward through the earth toward the sun until it becomes full-grown and fruitful. The quality of life that emerges from stage to stage of the individual's development is the observable proof of the unseen change which took place when he became rightly related to God through his experience with Jesus Christ.

A Church Should Engender and Develop This Difference

A church cannot bring about the new birth any more than the maternity ward can create the life of the babe born under its care. A church can bring together the sinner and the Saviour, and a church can furnish the conditions in which the experience of salvation occurs. The question is, How may a church best meet the requirements of bringing the needy soul to the saving Christ and then nurture the newborn life to strength and usefulness? Obviously a church, to do this, must believe in its necessity. It may seek to meet the need by a ceremony that brings the sacramentally saved child into the church fold; or it may lead through nurture to a saving experience after baptism; or it may posit the regenerating experience as the condition of entrance into church membership, with nurture of the implanted life to follow. The question, then, simply becomes: Which of these procedures will more surely guarantee the same ultimate objective? It is readily admitted that those who come into the church according to the former views may come later to a saving experience; likewise it is readily admitted that those who come into the church according to the latter view may be mistaken and will either fall away or undergo a saving experience subsequently. But when we ask, (1) Which is confirmed by the New Testament? and (2) Which has greater functional value? the answer seems obvious.

The Church, a Beloved Community

In the Christian Community There Is Equality

Love cannot flourish in an atmosphere where some assume an attitude of superiority over others as their inferiors. The infinite worth of every individual is basic in the teachings of Jesus. Selfish ambition is truly the sin "whereby angels fell." "Clergy" and "laity" are convenient distinctions which have little basis in New Testament teaching. Of course, there are distinctions of ability and devotion among church members, and some may be leaders while others are followers, but the "priesthood of all believers" forbids the exercise of lordship over the humblest member and opens the door of opportunity for the least to become the greatest. Democracy as conceived by the New Testament is more than a mode of government; it is a way of life. It makes reverence for personality normative in human relationships. It lights the candle of hope for the underprivileged and lays upon the privileged the burden of greater service. It repudiates all dictatorship, all totalitarianism, all coercion in the realm of things spiritual. It guarantees the "four freedoms." It is the star that guides humanity on its slow and tortuous way to the goal of the good life for all. In the nature of the case, the "beloved community" must be in the form of a spiritual democracy.

The Christian Community Manages Its Own Affairs

The highest development of individuals and of groups cannot be reached when they are under the control of others. The ideal of intelligent parents is the transfer of authority from themselves to the children as quickly as they are able to receive it. Love fails when authoritarianism replaces voluntarism. Sacrifice for the common good is of the essence of true community. The New Testament exhortation, "Let us work that which is good toward all men, and especially toward them that are of the household of the faith" (Gal. 6:10), does not appeal to the self-regarding motive but to the highest altruism. The demonstration of Christianity must begin at home. But there is no warrant for the interference with the affairs of a "household of faith" on the part of any individual or group. There may be mutual concern, to be sure, but every church should manage its own affairs. True, this proves often to be the hard way, and outside authority may sometimes appear to be wise and necessary; but if the end in view is an intelligent self-determining, self-criticizing, Spirit-led, religiously mature body of Christians, then the danger is worth all that it may cost in granting to them complete autonomy.

A Church Should Provide the Conditions of Vital Fellowship

If a Christian church is a beloved community, a confraternity, a fellowship of likeminded believers, its polity should be conducive to the realization of this ideal. What sort of church will best produce and maintain true Christian community? A church ruled by priests? a church governed by bishops? a church under the control of synods and conferences? a church whose affairs are in the hands of a "board of deacons" or a "presbytery"? a church with the pastor as its dictator? or a church in which all responsibility for the management of all its affairs is in the hands of all its members? Applying our criteria, we ask (1) Which of these conceptions is closest to the New Testament pattern? and (2) Which promises greatest functional values? The answer would not seem difficult to discover.

The Church, a Company of Worshipers

Worship Is Essential to the Christian Life

Worship is at the heart of all religion—pagan, Jewish, Christian. Worship is characteristic of all men everywhere through all time. In a scale of values there will be good, better, best, and then the best that is or ever can be. Men worship whatever they look upon as the Other and the Highest; that is, whatever they regard as supremely worthful. The quality of their life is more clearly determined by what men worship than by any other single thing. A religion without worship would be inconceivable. Christianity's immeasurable superiority over other religions is nowhere more evident than in its object, practice, and purposes of worship. Its object of worship is the God of the Lord Jesus Christ made real through the presence of the Holy Spirit. Its practice of worship is within the sphere of spirit and of truth. Its purpose of worship is to maintain vital union between the worshiper and God through the mediator, Jesus Christ, and the illuminator, the Holy Spirit. From this fellowship with each other in the presence of God flow life's most precious values. A church may do much else besides worship, but it will do little else of consequence without worship. A church may well be described as a company of worshipers.

In Worship Believers Find Free Access to God

God is a Spirit, and his worship, to be acceptable, must be spiritual. But men are material, and they find it difficult to hold God in the center of attention without some visible or audible means of worship. Purely mystical or unmediated experiences of God are rare. A controversy that rent the medieval Catholic Church into Eastern and Western divisions was occasioned by the introduction of images in worship. Rejecting images, some churches make much of symbols. Other churches propose to stimulate and guide the experience of worship through beautiful and elaborate rituals. Still others make preaching central in worship. The Quakers feel that silence is most conducive to their experience of worship. The highly emotional groups think that their worship is most satisfying when it verges on the hysterical. However wisely or mistakenly, all of these bodies seek through worship to find access to God. The measure of a church's worth may well be in terms of the enriching and ennobling or sterilizing and impoverishing experiences of its people in worship.

A Church Should Provide the Conditions of Fruitful Worship

On the one hand, a church may seek to induce the mood of worship through an awe-inspiring cathedral; on the other hand, it may seek the same mood through plain bare walls and backless pews. An elaborate ritual may provide the medium of worship in one type of church; in another, the medium may be a wholly unplanned extemporaneous service. Some churches put the ceremonies of worship at the center with preaching incidental; others put preaching at the center with the ceremonies of worship incidental. Some Christian bodies insist on a prescribed order; others insist that worship should be free. One large group of churches consider baptism and the Supper to be *sacraments,* the outward signs of invisible grace; another large group consider baptism and the Supper to be *ordinances,* symbols and reminders of truth but possessing no saving power. What shall we conclude? What kind of worship is most satisfying? Under what conditions will worship prove most fruitful? We apply our criteria: (1) What form of worship is closest to the New Testament in teaching and practice? and (2) What form of worship produces greatest values? Under this searchlight the extremes of both formal and formless worship fade out, and in the center stands free worship gathered about vital preaching, enriched through spiritual aids to worship and in an architectural setting of beauty and simplicity.

The Church, a Winner of Believers

Believers Are Won to Saving Faith through Persuasion

To the first two inquirers Jesus said, "Come and see!" They came away from their long interview fully persuaded that they had found the Messiah. They then used their influence to persuade each his brother to become a believer. This process of intelligent persuasion continued throughout the ministry of our Lord, so that on the day of Pentecost there were already one hundred and twenty convinced believers. The witness of these men and women, climaxed by the persuasive preaching of Peter, led three thousand new believers into the church on one memorable day. There is no hint of the use of any other means of bringing new members into the church apart from persuasion. We read in Acts that Paul "persuaded the people," that he "persuaded the Jews and the Greeks," that he was charged with having "persuaded and turned away much people," and that at Rome when the people came to see him, "he expounded the matter, testifying the kingdom of God, and persuading them concerning Jesus." He summed up his mission and his method, saying, "Knowing therefore the fear of the Lord, we persuade men . . . We are ambassadors therefore on behalf of Christ, as though God were entreating by us: we beseech you on behalf of Christ, be ye reconciled to God" (2 Cor. 5:11, 20). There is no mistaking the proposal of the New Testament that believers be won to saving faith through persuasion.

Every Christian Should Bear a Winning Witness

The most satisfying of all life's experiences is that of becoming a Christian. A new world of peace, happiness, and security is entered. The first impulse following this spiritual awakening and remaking of life is to share the experience with another. If there is no such impulse, the reality of the experience may well be suspected. If the impulse is allowed to die without expression, the vitality of the church may well be called in question. Misunderstandings at this point have caused fatal damage. Mistakenly it has been assumed that there need be no such experience, sacramentalism and intellectualism being substituted. Equally mistakenly, it has been assumed that disciple winning is the business of professional religionists, the result being the neglect of witness bearing by the great majority. The contrasting dangers must be recognized—dependence on sacramental regeneration without the necessity of personal experience, or overemphasis on emotional experience. The middle course lies in the competency of the witness of every Christian who has had a transforming experience and who knows how to share this experience intelligently with others.

Disciplemaking Should Be a Church's Perennial Business

Evangelism, properly conceived, is not the occasional concern of a church but its continuous concern. Sin and death take no holiday. If the church has the one remedy for sin and the only antidote for death, its guilt would be immeasurably great if it neglected for a single day to make known the salvation for the want of which a soul perished. Churches should make the decision for themselves and not have it thrust upon them: Will they depend upon sacraments, creedal statements, ceremonial observances, intellectual assent, made effectual and available through infant baptism followed by indoctrination; or will they place their dependence upon persuasion leading to a personal experience through repentance and faith to be shared with others at all times and in all walks of life? We submit the answer to our twofold test: (1) Which conforms more nearly to the New Testament proposal?; and (2) Which will produce the richer fruitage of believers?

The Church, a Teacher of Disciples

Salvation and Education Are Inseparably Related

Salvation is not by education, but salvation is not apart from education. The gospel proposes only two conditions for salvation—repentance of sin and faith in the Lord Jesus Christ. Repentance and faith will be followed by confession and obedience, but these are proofs and not conditions of salvation. Eternal life is the gift of God and cannot be earned through any merit of the recipient. But what is repentance? Could one repent who does not *know* the demands of the moral law, God's requirement of righteousness, Christ's standard of conduct? What is faith? Could one exercise saving faith in a Saviour whom one does not *know*, about whose life and teachings one is ignorant, concerning whose love and power one has not heard? How could confession be made of that which one does not understand? How could obedience be given to that about which one has no knowledge? Paul's logic is inescapable: "Whosoever shall call upon the name of the Lord shall be saved. How then shall they call upon him whom they have not believed? and how shall they believe in him of whom they have not heard? and how shall they hear without a preacher? and how shall they preach, except they be sent?" (Rom. 10:13–15). Preaching and teaching, the two main methods of Christian education, are indispensable means of leading toward Christ, to Christ, and into the service and likeness of Christ.

The Art of Christian Living Must Be Learned

It has been said that religion is "caught, not taught." There is a sense in which this is true, in that religious experience is induced far more by contact with contagious Christian personalities than by knowledge of facts and truths. Here again we face a wide cleavage. Some would say that the Christian life is the outcome of a process of Christian nurture. Some would hold that the new life is imparted through baptism and then sustained through the nurture of the church. Others would say that the new life is imparted as an inheritance from one or more believing parents, and is nurtured through Christian home life and associations and teaching within the church. Still others, rejecting both sacramental and hereditary salvation, would make the generation of the Christian life dependent upon a process of nurture according to which the child is gradually led from ignorance to knowledge, from unbelief to faith, nurture thus replacing evangelism in the older sense.

In contrast, many believe that Christian education cultivates the soil and plants the seed, but that the new life appears only when a definite personal commitment to Christ is made on the basis of a definite change of heart toward self and sin, salvation to be followed by a lifetime of nurture of the new life from germination to maturity. Human elements are recognized, but in this view God takes the initiative and regeneration is wrought by the Holy Spirit through the grace of Jesus Christ.

A Church Should Serve as a Christian School

A church, thus conceived, is not a religious institution with a school attached; it is essentially a school. Christ is the Great Teacher, the Holy Spirit is his interpreter, the Bible is the chief textbook; the minister is the chief officer of the school, about him are gathered teachers and staff; every church member is an enrolled student, all others who can be reached are sought as learners to be led toward Christ and then to him and into church membership through conversion. In this conception there is no antagonism between evangelism and Christian nurture, between faith and knowledge. Each reinforces the other in the achievement of common ultimate ends. Preaching, teaching, and training constitute a triumvirate of means in human hands under divine direction for the purposes of Father, Son, and Holy Spirit. A church may ignore evangelism and place all its emphasis on nurture; or it may ignore nurture and put all its emphasis on evangelism. Or a church may wisely combine evangelism and nurture, nurture and evangelism, in balanced proportions. What course it shall follow may well be determined by our familiar questions: (1) Which is nearer to the New Testament model? (2) Which will bring richer returns?

The Church, a Server of Humanity

Christianity Is a Religion of Service

When Peter, in the maturity of his Christian experience, sought a single phrase that would describe Jesus Christ, he spoke of him as one "who went about doing good." A rapid glance through the New Testament confirms this description. Matthew records that "Jesus went about all the cities and villages, . . . healing all manner of disease and all manner of sickness" (Matt. 9:35). The great majority of his miracles were miracles of healing. To the twelve he "gave authority over unclean spirits, to cast them out, and to heal all manner of disease and all manner of sickness" (Matt. 10:1). His commissions to his apostles included healing of body and of mind. He spoke of himself as a servant and made service the mark of true greatness among his followers. John, the forerunner of Christ, put heavy stress upon the social implications of the Messiah's coming and reign, replying to the question, "What must we do?" in terms of generous sharing, honest dealing, upright living, peace, and contentment (Luke 3:10–15).

The early Christians caught the spirit of Christ and, like him, "went about doing good." They healed the sick, cared for the poor, helped the needy, shared their goods with one another, comforted the sorrowing, preached salvation from sin unto righteousness. A church, to be true to its Founder and to the New Testament example, must deal with contemporary problems of sin and suffering; it must educate the social sympathies of its people; it must deal fearlessly with injustice and exploitation; it must throw its weight against war as a means of settling national disputes; it must present a Christian view of race and race relations; it must courageously confront corruption in high places as well as in low; it must be concerned with the welfare of the family, and stand as the unafraid champion of womanhood, childhood, and manhood. It must send regenerate men and women out into an immoral society to transform evil into good, wrong into right, injustice into justice, not so much by political measures as by the leavening process of Christian influence. It must produce members of society who take seriously the basic principle of Christ that "whosoever will save his life shall lose it: and whosoever will lose his life for my sake shall find it" (Matt. 16:25).

Service Tests the Genuineness of Faith

Scarcely would any group of any name contest the proposition that Christianity is a religion of service. The point of dispute arises as to the place of service in the redemptive plan. Some would say that "good works" are stored to the credit of the Christian and will so shorten his stay in purgatory. In the event of a superabundance of good works, the superfluity may be passed to the account of one who is short. Others would hold that good deeds are balanced against bad deeds, and whichever outweighs will determine final fate. Still others would say that we are to be rewarded or punished in accordance with the deeds done in the flesh, and that faith must have its complement of good works in order to be recognized as possessing saving power.

In contrast with those who hold these views, in which faith and works are both somehow necessary to salvation, stand those who would make faith the sole ground of salvation. To them grace would not be grace if it were conditioned on man's merit. If man could earn his salvation in part, they insist, he could conceivably earn it altogether, and this would void the necessity of Christ's atoning death. Carrying this to its logical extreme in the doctrine of election, some would say that the election of certain individuals to eternal life means the election of others to eternal death, hence the number of the saved is absolutely fixed from eternity. Human choice and instrumentality would therefore be of no avail.

A Church Should Translate Its Doctrines into Deeds

Whatever its doctrinal position, a church is under necessity of putting profession into practice. Catholics, Protestants, evangelicals, whatever their name, must either carry on or sponsor a program of practical activities if they expect to be taken seriously by the community. Human needs cry aloud for fulfillment, and a church interested in ideas only and insensitive to human welfare would have little right to be called a church. What sort of church will render maximum service? Will it be a church organized under professional leadership, with priests and nuns giving full time to a service program? Will it be a church that preaches and teaches what it conceives to be fundamental Christianity, and then depends upon these principles to work themselves out in the lives of its people? Will it be a church with a social gospel, implemented by a social service program under the leadership of a trained staff of social workers? Or will it be a church that preaches and teaches full-rounded Christian truth with the definite purpose of applying the gospel to actual human conditions through the inspired and directed service of every member? The answer will best appear when two familiar criteria are applied: (1) Which ideal approaches most nearly the New Testament pattern? and (2) Which in practice would yield most fruitful results?

The Church, an Agency of the Kingdom

"The Kingdom" Is the Ultimate End of the Redemptive Purpose

The phrases *kingdom of God* and *kingdom of heaven* were constantly on the lips of Jesus. His first recorded proclamation was, "Repent ye; for the kingdom of heaven is at hand" (Matt. 4:17). Matthew further records that Jesus "went about all the cities and the villages . . . preaching the gospel of the kingdom" (Matt. 9:35). Almost he exhausted language in his explanation and illustration of the meaning of the kingdom. He likened the kingdom to seed, to leaven, to a pearl, to a householder, to a marriage feast, to ten virgins, to a man traveling into a far country; he spoke of his disciples as children of the kingdom; he declared that his kingdom was not of this world; he offered to give to his disciples the keys of the kingdom; on many occasions he opened up the mysteries of the kingdom; he taught his disciples to pray for the coming of the kingdom.

Jesus' concept of the kingdom of God was grasped by Paul and other New Testament writers and played a powerful part in the life of the early churches. The final consummation will be when Christ "shall deliver up the kingdom to God, even the Father; when he shall have abolished all rule and all authority and power" (1 Cor. 15:24). John heard great voices in heaven, and they said, "The kingdoms of this world are become the kingdoms of our Lord, and of his

Christ: and he shall reign for ever and ever" (Rev. 11:15). The kingdom had its beginning when Jesus came; it will have its completion when he reigns in the hearts of all men everywhere.

"The Kingdom" Is a Present and a Future Reality

Perhaps no other term in the New Testament has been the subject of so much controversy as the "kingdom of God," or the "kingdom of heaven." Scholarship is practically agreed that the two terms are synonymous. Some would identify "the kingdom" with "the church." If the idea of the "universal church" is accepted, its identification with "the kingdom" naturally follows. An "invisible church," consisting of the redeemed of all time, has likewise been made identical with "the kingdom." It has been popular in recent years to identify the kingdom with social aims and endeavors, looking to the progressive establishment of the "the good society," in which will be at length realized some kind of social Utopia. Dispensationalists hold that the *kingdom of heaven* signifies the messianic rule on earth of Jesus Christ, after the return of the king in glory; that is, after his second coming, Jesus will sit on the throne at Jerusalem and rule in a material way over the earth.

In contrast to these views of the kingdom as church universal, church invisible, church militant, church millennial, is the view that the church is not to be identified with the kingdom nor the kingdom with the church, but that the kingdom of God is a spiritual order, a realm of relationships between God and the saved, the reign of God through Christ mediated by the Holy Spirit over obedient believers everywhere. A church is an instrumentality for bringing persons into this relationship and thus into this realm in which the reign of God through Christ is operative. That is, the kingdom is not an organization to be promoted, nor a movement to be advanced, nor a social ideal to be realized, but a relationship to be entered and a spiritual order into which others are to be brought through persuasive witnessing.

A Church Should Seek to Bring the Kingdom to All Men and All Men into the Kingdom

Whether we speak of building the kingdom, or advancing the kingdom, or promoting the kingdom, or waiting for the kingdom, or entering into the kingdom, we imply that the business of a church is to bring more and more people into saving relationship with Christ that the prayer which he taught may be ultimately realized: "Thy kingdom come. Thy will be done, as in heaven, so on earth." This calls imperatively for evangelism and missions, the bringing of more and more persons into saving relationship with Jesus Christ and under his lordship until the consummation of the ages. What sort of church will best bring this about? What view of ultimate ends will best vitalize immediate means? What forms of organization and activity will give a church its strongest home base and its farthest outward reach? What animating spirit will best sustain its kingdom passion? What practical program will best produce regenerate persons in a Christian society around the world? Unhesitatingly we apply our questions: (1) What approaches most closely the New Testament ideal? and (2) Experimentally, what has produced and is producing the most satisfying results?

Ends and means are sometimes strangely confused. Tradition exerts powerful influence which increases with time. When each successive board is cut according to the measure of the one preceding, the final result is surprisingly different from the original. The gradualness of departure from the original pattern of the church as given in the New Testament prevented or mitigated the sense of shock; each successive departure had its apparent justification; in course of time the departure was accepted as having the values of the original. Rationalization remains an effective method by which good reasons are given for questionable actions.

The twofold question which the intellectually honest thinker must face regarding the church and its polity emerges: Is there a clear-cut New Testament pattern which can be followed? If intelligently followed, will this pattern produce most richly the fruits of a true Christianity? If the answer is affirmative, then the minister is challenged to dare to reject the accretions of tradition, the barnacles of expediency, the inheritances of denominational practice, and humbly but boldly put New Testament principles into practical operation in the conduct of the church's affairs. A denominational label is not the chief essential. The supremely important matter is clear understanding of and wholehearted committal to the principles which lie clearly revealed in the teachings of Jesus as interpreted and practiced by his immediate followers and recorded in the Book we call the New Testament. "By their fruits ye shall know them" will be the sufficient test of the methods which are used and the kind of church and denominational life which follows.

Ours is an age of revolution. Inevitably the churches are undergoing change. Why not seize on this opportunity to make changes back to the New Testament rather than farther away from it?

For Reflection

1. What seems to you to be the critical component of community as the author presents it?
2. How are community and "company of worshipers" related?
3. In what ways are salvation and education related?
4. Give an example of nurture and evangelism in proper balance.

13

John H. Westerhoff III

The Shaking of the Foundations

(1976)

John Westerhoff grew up in a reverent but nonreligious home. After several less than satisfactory church experiences through childhood and youth he entered Harvard Divinity School. At several points in his abortive church journeys different people identified John as a man of God or as a person destined for the ministry. When John entered Harvard to continue his search for meaning, his search was at its intellectual height. The stimulation and variety of this enriching university environment allowed him to find some direction for his life. At age 22 he acknowledged a call to the ministry and was taken under the care of the United Church of Christ, where he was eventually ordained. Following this he spent eight years in the parish ministry. In all the churches he served it became evident to him that educative approaches, other than schooling, that were born out of the daily and weekly life of the congregation were effective for people of all ages, but especially for adults.

Following these years in the parish ministry, Professor Westerhoff worked for the United Church Board of Homeland Ministry. Increasingly he was involved in speaking about and writing about education. He became convinced that worship, evangelism, education, social action, and all the church's other ministries could not be separated. From these experiences he decided that his own ministry

From *Will Our Children Have Faith?* (New York: Seabury, 1976), 1–25, 78.

needed to be more focused on helping prepare people for the ministry as he now conceived it. With encouragement he began a doctoral program through Teachers College Columbia University and Union Theological Seminary. Shortly after finishing the program, he was in a severe auto accident and spent extended time in the hospital, which provided needed time for contemplation. An invitation came to join the faculty at Duke Divinity School. Westerhoff accepted and soon after embraced the Episcopal Church. During this time he also wrote *Will Our Children Have Faith?* (Mayr 1983).

Professor Westerhoff believes that the schooling-instruction paradigm is the basic problem with contemporary Christian education. It is also the environment within which questions about the discipline must be addressed. "We have accepted the assumptions of the schooling-instructional paradigm and missed the anomalies which make it no longer viable for our educational mission and ministry" (Mayr 1983, 10). He illustrates the problem with brief discussions of the small church and ethnic churches. He then points to what he calls the broken ecology, consisting of community, family, Protestant-related public schools, church, popular religious periodicals, and Sunday school. Most of these have changed substantially over the last forty years. The ecology is much more heterogeneous. This condition leaves the previous pattern of Christian education without its former support network. Westerhoff then briefly describes his concerns about religious socialization and the difference between religion and faith. Herein lies the heart of his concern for Christian education.

References

Mayr, M., ed. 1983. *Modern masters of religious education.* Birmingham, Ala.: Religious Education Press.

> The immediate future of liberal Protestant education is uncertain. Despite its appearance of modernity and relentless relevance, mainstream Protestantism is rooted in the ethos of the last century. [The issue that faces us is] do we have the courage to acknowledge the shaking of the foundations?
>
> Robert W. Lynn

It is a truism that Christian faith and education are inevitable companions. Wherever living faith exists, there is a community endeavoring to know, understand, live, and witness to that faith. Still, an accurate description of education in the church today is difficult. Here and there exemplary educational ministries flourish, but in many more places anxiety, confusion, frustration, despair, and even failure exist. While generalizations may be difficult, few would defend the contemporary health and vitality of Christian education within mainline Protestant Churches. Since 1957 when *Life* magazine dubbed the Sunday school the most wasted hour of the week, increasing numbers of church persons have admitted that their educational ministries are less than adequate for the day. The church school, despite numerous bold innovations and even a few modern success stories, is plagued with disease. There may be disagreement over the severity of the illness and the prognosis of recovery, but there is no debate as to whether or not all is well. Differing diagnoses, however, do exist. For example, it appears that many church educators are sure that we are dealing with a surface infection, while I am convinced that we face a very serious disease.

This conviction is not entirely new. *Colloquy* was born in 1968 and for eight years as founder and editor, I advocated the need for radical change in church education. In 1970, just before the walls of mainline Protestant church education began to show its cracks, I published a series of works which boldly suggested that an alternative for church education was needed. I have now concluded that it is not enough simply to conceive of alternative programs for church education; fundamental issues once clearly resolved need to be explored afresh. No longer can we assume that the educational understandings that have informed us, or the theological foundations that have undergirded our efforts, are adequate for the future. A continuing myopic concern for nurture, understood primarily as schooling and instruction and undergirded by increasingly vague pluralistic theologies, will not be adequate for framing the future of religious education. Today we face an extremely radical problem which only revolution can address. We must now squarely face the fundamental question: Will our children have faith?

Beginnings

The roots of our problem go back to the turn of the century and a joke: "When is a school not a school?" The answer: "When it is a Sunday school!" Coming when it did, this characteristic comment triggered a reaction throughout mainline Protestantism. A new generation of leaders, in what was commonly referred to as religious education, emerged. They were embarrassed by the Sunday school and impressed by the emerging public school system with its new understandings of child development and pedagogy. The Sunday school, they believed, was outmoded and needed to be replaced. The times, they concluded, called for both the birth of a new church school (modeled after the public schools) and the introduction of religious instruction into the nation's common schools. Thus, in 1903 the Religious Education Association was founded with the dual purposes of inspiring the religious forces of our country with an educational ideal and the educational forces with a religious one.

The church school envisioned by these women and men of the progressive era conformed to an image of the best in public education. A new profession was born to create and sustain the church school. Seminaries developed departments of religious education and conferred degrees, directors and ministers of religious education were employed by the churches, and denominations responded with a new educational bureaucracy. The old-time people's Sunday school had begun to be transformed into the professional's church school. Soon religious education, influenced by liberal theology, was identified with church schooling and the instruction of children, youth, and adults according to the methods of modern pedagogy.

Gradually the theological foundations of the religious education movement began to crumble, and by the late 40s and 50s most mainline denominations had adopted, in varying degrees, the theology of neo-orthodoxy. Religious education changed its name to Christian education, but the image of the church school and religious instruction remained intact. Large educational plants modeled after modern public school architecture and equipped with the latest in educational technology were built wherever economically feasible. More professionals were hired by local churches to direct these burgeoning educational institutions attached to local churches, and denominational curriculum resources erupted as big business.

During the 60s a few significant voices spoke out for a broader understanding of Christian education—Randolph Crump Miller, D. Campbell Wyckoff, C. Ellis Nelson, Robert Havighurst, Roger Shinn, Ross Snyder, Rachael Hendrilite, and Sara Little, to name a few. They boldly attempted to make the case that effective programs of Christian education needed to be planned in the light of the total mission and ministry of the church. They acknowledged that the church teaches most significantly through nurture in a worshipping, witnessing community of faith, and they clearly explained that explicit instruction in the church schools was only a small part of Christian education. Nevertheless, even they placed special emphasis on the church school and on instruction; few heard their call for a broader perspective.

We now find ourselves in the 70s with the foundations of neo-orthodoxy eroded, and seemingly unable to envision any significant alternative to the church school. Rachael Hendrilite reminds us that we can't go home again, C. Ellis Nelson emphasizes religious socialization, and Randolph Crump Miller shifts his attention to theological foundations. A few voices, like Edward A. Powers in his book, *Signs of Shalom*, repeat the earlier call for a broader understanding of Christian education and an attempt to provide a new theological foundation. Nevertheless, local church folk still ask for help in revitalizing their church schools without any particular theological foundation. A host of panaceas in the form of methodologies or new variations on the church school, such as family clusters, flourish for a time and denominations still strive to produce better curriculum resources.

Vast amounts of money continue to be spent on teacher training, educational technology, and buildings. Numerous colleges have developed degree programs in Christian education to supply churches with economical semiprofessionals to save and revitalize their church schools. Denominations develop public relations campaigns to save the church school, and salvation by a new curriculum is still promised. A few reversals in past trends, or even a leveling off in the attendance decline, give people new hope, but still our educational ministries flounder. A broader perspective from which to evaluate, plan, and engage in Christian education is still not understood or accepted. Some continue to offer a prophetic word and preach about alternatives, but little appears to change. Why?

The Problem

I am convinced that the very foundations upon which we engage in Christian education are shaking. And while a host of builders attempt with varying degrees of success to shore them up, there is a dearth of architects engaged in designing new structures. The church's educational problem rests not in its educational program, but in the paradigm or model which undergirds its educational ministry—the agreed-upon frame of reference which guides its educational efforts.

Every field of endeavor operates out of some common frame of reference or identity. Most often we take this orientation for granted; it guides our work, helps us shape our questions, and provides us with insights for solutions to our problems. The paradigm within which we labor tells us what to do and provides us with a language to share our efforts with others.

Religious educators hold in common certain assumptions about their endeavor. The language of religious education—subject matter, what we want someone else to know—is an expression of those understandings. The set of assumptions, orientation, and frame of reference which informs us is expressed in the paradigm by which we engage in educational ministry. Since the turn of the century, in spite of nods to other possibilities, Christian educators and local churches have functioned according to a *schooling-instructional paradigm*. That is, our image of education has been founded upon some sort of a "school" as the context *and* some form of instruction as the means. Seminaries, denominational bureaucracies, educational professionals, and local church lay persons have all shared this common perspective.

Within the confines of this model, a great number of imaginative, important, and relevant contributions to Christian education have been made; and a significant influence on the lives of adults, youth, and children can be observed. It is only natural, therefore, that we have assured ourselves that improving the techniques and resources of schooling and instruction will continue to solve our educational problem and meet our educational needs. But, limited by a once helpful model, we have blindly and unconsciously proceeded as if there were no other possible way. Attempts to broaden that perspective, while intellectually acknowledged, are functionally resisted, and so we continue to let the schooling-instruction paradigm define our problem and establish the criteria for choosing questions to be addressed. As a result, only particular issues are acknowledged and only certain questions answered. The schooling-instructional paradigm isolates us from new possibilities while continuing to occupy most of our attention in teaching, research, practice, and resource development. To compound our difficulties, we find it functionally difficult to imagine or create any significant educational program outside it.

Of course, this is not uniquely a problem of the church. The church mirrors society in that education in the United States operates according to a similar paradigm. Any attempt to de-school society or question the adequacy of instruction is either ignored or met with hostility. The schooling-instructional paradigm has dominated our thinking for some time, but not always. Recall that Plato, in all his discussions of education, gives little attention to schools. As far as Plato was concerned, it is the community that educates, by which he meant the multiplicity of formal and informal forces which influence persons.

In this century, John Dewey began his important career by assuring us that all of life educates, and that instruction in schools represents only one small part of our total education. Futhermore, he insisted that there were many forms of deliberate education. At that point Dewey was a Platonist, but late in his life, confronted by urbanization and the technological revolution, he reflected on education in American society and contended that education in the home, church, and community was no longer adequate for the day. Supported by this conclusion, he made the great twentieth-century theory jump: the school must do it. From that moment on education in the United States has been functionally coexistent with schooling and instruction. If persons are killed on the highways, we add driver education; if girls have children out of wedlock, we add sex education. No matter what the problem or need, we organize a course. Schooling and instruction have become the panaceas for all our needs. Of course our schooling and instructional methods are continually reformed, but our faith in them is never questioned.

The church, mirroring the culture, operates according to a similar paradigm, and for about the same reasons. Professional religious educators at the turn of the century didn't feel that the old Sunday school, with its dependence upon other related institutions—home, country, church, and public school—could do the job. Thus, they focused their attention on a reformed church school that could do the job by itself. Consequently, no matter what the church's needs, our typical solution has been to develop courses of instruction for the church's school.

I contend that we have become victimized by this schooling-instructional understanding of religious education and imprisoned by its implications. As long as it informs our labors, significant alternatives will have difficulty being born or sustained.

While admitting that learning takes place in many ways, church education has functionally equated the context of education with schooling and the means of education with formal instruction. The public schools have provided us with our model of education, and insights from secular pedagogy and psychology have been our guides. A church school with teachers, subject matter, curriculum resources, supplies, equipment, age-graded classes, classrooms, and, where possible, a professional church educator as administrator, has been the norm. All this must change.

Anomalies

While some paradigm is necessary if we are to engage in any significant endeavor, any particular frame of reference may limit our awareness of new possibilities and act as a barrier to alternative understandings. Unaware of the character and limitations of the paradigm which informs our efforts, we are in danger of missing the anomalies—irregularities or deviations—that question our frame of reference. Even as we operate according to some agreed-upon understandings, it is important to be aware of the anomalies that question its viability. Of course, anomalies are not easily spotted or acknowledged.

Jerome Bruner once carried out an experiment in which he took a deck of cards and flashed them on a screen at differing rates of speed. In that deck he had placed a red ace of spades and a black four of hearts and at first no one saw the unusual cards. Rather, they corrected them and reported a black four of spades and red ace of hearts. Some sensed that something was not right—that an anomaly was present—but even when Bruner flashed the cards slowly, one at a time, some persons couldn't spot any anomalies. In a similar way, assumptions can limit our awareness, and while assumptions help us to achieve a stable consensus, they are typically conservative and so make it difficult to alter our understandings and ways, even in the face of compelling evidence that we should do so.

This, I contend, is the problem we face in Christian education today. We have accepted the assumptions of the schooling-instructional paradigm and missed the anomalies which make it no longer viable for our educational mission and ministry.

The Small Church

Following the lead of the public school movement, religious educators focused their attention on church schools—new educational institutions. Soon these institutions were divorced from the people and from church life, and rarely were they able to meet the needs of any but our larger, sophisticated, suburban churches.

Recently, I discovered the large, important world of the small church. As a professional church educator, I had often ignored these thousands of small churches and, like other church educators, I had gotten used to talking about educational plants, supplies, equipment, curriculum, teacher training, age-graded classes, and learning centers with individualized instruction. Lately, I've been confronted by churches which share a pastor and will probably never be able to afford the services of a professional church educator. At best they have a couple of small inadequate rooms attached to their church building, no audiovisual equipment, few supplies, an inadequate number of prospective teachers, and not enough students for age-graded classes. The Sunday church schools in these small mainline Protestant churches are sick—in part because they have tried to become modern church schools and failed. The Sunday school "statistics board" in front of their churches dramatizes their situation and denominational programs, most of which they are unable to use, and creates feelings of inadequacy and failure.

Depression results from the realization that the great majority of Protestant churches have fewer than two hundred members. Many of these churches have nevertheless faithfully striven to turn their Sunday schools into church schools and have failed. The severity of the problem is great. One anomaly, the schooling-instruction paradigm, can be seen in the realization that most small churches will never be able to mount up or support the sort of schooling and instruction upon which religious education has been founded since the turn of the century.

Ethnic Churches

Also consider the numerous ethnic churches in our country. At one time I was the liaison person for the United Church Board for Homeland Ministries with our churches in Hawaii, and on one of my visits I met with the members of a number of small native Hawaiian churches. They still called their church schools Sunday schools, although through the years they had obediently and faithfully striven to develop a Christian education program like that recommended by the church's educational professionals. They struggled to raise money to build classrooms, they bought the denomination's curriculum resources, and they sent their people to teacher-training workshops and lab schools. And yet attendance continued to drop, teachers were difficult to secure and, more seriously, the faith was not being adequately transmitted or sustained.

They asked me why they were failing, and I was stumped. They were doing everything we had suggested and still they were unsuccessful. In desperation, I asked them to tell me about the days when they were succeeding. They explained that a number of churches gathered each Sunday evening for a luau. Young and old came together to sing hymns, tell the gospel story, witness to their faith, discuss their lives as Christians, minister to each other's needs, eat, and have fellowship. They did almost everything natural to their culture except dance, which we had taught them was "immoral." When they finished describing their old educational programs, I could think of nothing but to suggest they return to having luaus, knowing that those committed to schooling and instruction would think me mad.

A Broken Ecology

While most of our Protestant churches are small, some seventy percent of all church members reside in churches of three hundred or more people, and one might conjecture that the schooling-instruction paradigm is viable in these churches. During the last few years I have visited a number of large dynamic church schools directed by qualified, creative, professional staffs. And I have found that there are quite a few churches where the dream of "the perfect" church school has been actualized. In these churches, most of the teachers are well-trained and many have developed their own exemplary curriculum resources. The educational plants, equipment, supplies, and organization would make many a public school envious. Attendance at church school has not significantly diminished, and there is still enthusiasm for their many innovative programs. And yet, in almost every case they have evaluated their achievements and found them lacking. The modern church school at its very best is less than adequate for our day. The reason is another anomaly in the schooling-instructional paradigm.

During the first third of this century an "ecology"—a pattern of relations between organisms and their environment—of institutions was consciously engaged in religious education. First, there was the community. Life in any typical American town nurtured persons in a Protestant ethos and atmosphere. Others—Roman Catholics, Jews, and others—lived and were nurtured in their own homogeneous communities.

Second, the family was basically secure, extended, and stable. There was little mobility; both parents were frequently home and shared family life together. And if not living under the same roof, relatives lived nearby and were in continuous interaction with the family. Divorce was less frequent, few women worked outside the home, and families were larger. There were few one-parent families and almost no interfaith marriages. Most persons were nurtured, married, and died within a hundred miles of their birth. In this environment, the family provided a natural setting and made a significant contribution to a person's religious education.

Third, most public schools were Protestant parochial schools. From the daily morning ritual of Bible reading (King James Version) and the Lord's prayer (with a Protestant benediction) to the textbooks complete with moral and religious lessons (The McGuffey Readers), children acquired general foundational Protestant religious education. Roman Catholics, in turn, supported their own parochial school system to educate their children.

Fourth, there was the church. The typical church was a community neighborhood congregation where all ages knew each other and regularly interacted. Many hours were spent at the church, not only in worship but in a variety of social activities. Here persons were socialized in the shared understandings and ways on their particular denomination.

Fifth, a great number of popular religious periodicals provided the major source of "entertainment" and religious education in the home.

Sixth and last, the Sunday school completed this ecology of institutions deliberately engaged in religious education. (Roman Catholics depended on courses in religion taught by nuns in the parochial schools.) The Sunday school was especially important in that it was a lay-directed organization where women could play a significant leadership role. It provided an intergenerational setting where persons could celebrate Easter, Christmas, Thanksgiving, Missionary Day, and Dedication Day. Always concerned about community, celebration, the religious affections, and the biblical story, these Sunday schools included plays and musicals, games, hikes and hunts, homecomings and family gatherings, parties and picnics, social service projects and community activities.

These six institutions intentionally worked together to produce an effective educational ecology.

But now an anomaly is found in our changing situation, for today most communities (especially those in which we find our larger churches) are heterogeneous. A pluralism of religious and secular persuasions interact and compete, and no longer can the community be counted upon to transmit a particular set of understandings and ways.

The family has changed also. Families are smaller and children often lack any significant direct interaction with the grandparents and relatives. Increasingly, both parents work outside the home, actual or functional one-parent families are on the increase, interfaith marriages are common, and the average family moves frequently and is typically without roots. Many functions of the family once carried out in the home have been assumed by the society. Day-care centers for children, retirement homes for the aging, recreation organizations for youth, and hospitals for the care of the sick are but a few examples of these now transferred functions.

The public school is now the religiously neutral institution intended by the Constitution, where at best religion can be taught *about* and studied objectively. Fewer Roman Catholics now send their children to parochial schools.

Today the church is rarely the center of people's social and community life; it is not uncommon for families to go away on weekends and find their numerous needs met in a diversity of secular groups. Television and an array of mass secular media have replaced religious publications.

So we are left with a church school (or parish Confraternity of Christian Doctrine [C.C.D.] program) struggling to do alone what it took an ecology of six institutions to do in the past. It cannot be done, but the schooling-instructional paradigm ignores this changing situation.

The Hidden Curriculum

For a variety of reasons, the schooling-instructional paradigm inadequately addresses the educational needs of both the small and large church. More important, however, is an anomaly in the schooling-instructional paradigm that affects them both, namely, the manner in which this paradigm eliminates the processes of religious socialization from the concern and attention of church educators and parishioners.

By socialization I mean all those formal and informal influences through which persons acquire their understandings and ways of living. For example, I have friends who have one child. The mother is a professional journalist who travels a great deal, and the father has willingly performed most of the parenting functions for their young daughter. On one occasion I observed the little girl playing house. Noticing that she was holding a doll, I inquired, "Who are you?" "I'm the father," she explained. "Oh, where is the mother?" I asked. "Well, she's away writing a story." That is socialization. No one intentionally sat down and taught this young girl that fathers take care of children and mothers work; she learned it without a school or instruction.

Education correctly understood is not identical with schooling. It is an aspect of socialization involving all deliberate, systematic, and sustained efforts to transmit or evolve knowledge, attitudes, values, behaviors, or sensibilities. The history of religious education, therefore, needs to include the family, public schools, community ethos, religious literature, and church life. Schooling, on the other hand, is only one specific and very limited form of education. The schooling-instructional paradigm has made this small part into the whole and, by accepting this understanding, we have typically forgotten that even in the school the "hidden curriculum" of socialization is at work influencing what is learned.

Recently, I have been engaged in the study of schools and sex-role stereotyping. While visiting an elementary school, the principal thought I should visit a class using a new unit on human sexuality. What amazed him was my greater interest in walking through the halls. He asked to join me in my walk, and we observed the following: female teachers go into both the boys' and girls' rooms while male teachers go only into the boys' room; girls and boys are encouraged to play very different sorts of games; teachers correct or punish boys and girls in significantly different ways; there are no male teachers in the kindergarten and no female administrators; photographs in classrooms consistently have men and women in sex-defined roles. Later we talked and I tried to explain that no intentional course of study could adequately counter the hidden curriculum of that school. Indeed, it was daily life in that school which primarily affected persons' understandings and ways.

The same can be said about the church and the church school, but the schooling-instructional paradigm tends to isolate the process of socialization from our consideration. Because the informal hidden curriculum in our churches is often more influential than the formal curriculum of our church schools, the schooling-instructional paradigm will always be less than adequate for the evaluation and planning of Christian education. For example: Once I taught a senior high class in worship, in which we learned that the offering was a symbolic, communal act in response to the gospel of the people's intentions and commitments for life in the world. The class decided that the church's offering of money once a year for racial justice did not meet the criteria of an offering, and they suggested asking the congregation to place on the altar an offering of signed fair housing pledge cards. After a few minutes of discussion at a board meeting, the church's adult leaders turned down the suggestion on political and economic grounds. Where was the more significant learning, in the church school class or at the board meeting? We can teach about equality in our church schools, but if our language in worship excludes women, if positions of influence and importance are held only by men or those from upper socioeconomic classes, or if particular races are either implicitly or explicitly excluded from membership, a different lesson is learned. Naming rooms in churches after wealthy donors may only teach children that the Christian life is one of gaining affluence. If we organize the church so that whenever time or talents are requested it is for serving the institutional needs, people are not apt to learn that the Christian life is one of mission in the world. And so it goes. As long as we operate by a schooling-instructional paradigm numerous significant influences will be ignored.

The Wrong Questions

We continue to accept the established as real; we assume that if we know more about teaching and learning, we can solve our educational problems. Faced by curricular needs we turn to technology and neglect new ways of being together. Faced with nonresponsive students, we turn to psychology to understand and control behavior instead of reflecting on the meaning of two persons in relationship. Confronted by difficulties in classroom discussion, cooperation, or morale, we consider the latest group-dynamics technique instead of rethinking the nature of community. When facing new problems we typically respond by focusing even more sharply on formal teaching and learning, believing that it is possible, with new knowledge and techniques, to build a workable school for the church, train an adequate number of capable teachers, and provide more useful curriculum resources for quality church education. In bondage to this inadequate understanding, we interpret any small success or reversal of existing negative trends in church schooling as a confirmation of the old paradigm's validity. This anomaly in the schooling-instructional paradigm, therefore, relates to the sources of influence which inform its life.

We have permitted the behavioral sciences to give us a source of false optimism. We have assumed that the more we know about people and learning, the more effective will be our educational efforts. We have believed that if stages of thinking can be identified, then both resources and teaching techniques to answer all our educational needs can be designed. However, our deepest problems may be of a different nature. Perhaps we need to rethink and reshape the institutions within which people dwell, and begin struggling with what it means to be Christian together.

Another example results from the unfortunate fact that the schooling-instructional paradigm encourages adults to be with children in ways that assert their power over them. The language of teaching, learning, behavioral objectives, and subject matter tend to produce a mind-set that results in the tendency to inflict on children adult ways of being in the world. It is difficult for us simply to be with the neophyte in song, worship, prayer, storytelling, service, reflection, and fellowship. We always seem to want to do something to or for them so they will be like us or like what we would like to be.

But education grounded in Christian faith cannot be a vehicle for control; it must encourage an equal sharing of life in community, a cooperative opportunity for reflection on the meaning and significance of life. Surely we must share our understandings and ways with children, but we also must remember that they have something to bring to us and what we bring to children is always under God's judgment. Of course, it is easier to impose than reflect, easier to instruct than share, easier to act than to interact. It is important, however, to remember that to be with a child in Christian ways means self-control more than child-control.

To be Christian is to ask: What can I bring to another? Not: What do I want that person to know or be? It means being open to learn from another person (even a child) as well as to share one's understandings and ways. To speak of schooling and instruction leads us in other directions and to other conclusions. Should we not ask: Is schooling and instruction in a Christian community necessary for education? Or is living as a Christian with others inherently educational? If we attend to being Christian with others, need we attend to schooling and instruction? By focusing on schooling and instruction, we have ignored these issues and questions that are so important for Christian faith.

Religion or Faith

We have too easily linked the ways of secular education with religion. Dependence upon the practice, rhetoric, and norms of secular psychology and pedagogy is risky business. Perhaps there is something unique about education in religious communities. That uniqueness is made clear in the last anomaly I wish to mention.

This anomaly surfaces in the awareness of what purposes schooling and instruction best serve. Recall the question asked in the Gospel according to Saint Luke: "When the Son of Man comes will he find faith on earth?" (Luke 18:8). Surely he will find religion (institutions, creeds, documents, artifacts, and the like), but he may not find faith. Faith is deeply personal, dynamic, ultimate. Religion, however, is faith's expression. For example, religion is concerned about institutions (churches), documents, statements of belief (Bible and theology), and our convictions and moral codes. Religion is important, but not ultimately important. Educationally, religion is a means not an end; faith is the only end. Faith, therefore, and not religion, must become the concern of Christian education.

The anomaly of the schooling-instructional paradigm is found in its natural and primary concern with religion. You can teach about religion, but you cannot teach people faith. Thus, this paradigm places Christian education in the strange position of making secondary matters primary. Teaching people *about* Christianity is not very important. Religion at best is an expression of someone's faith which, under proper conditions, can lead others to faith. Bach wrote the "B Minor Mass" as an expression of his faith, and I have faith in part because I am moved to faith whenever I hear it. However, knowing all about the "B Minor Mass" is not to be confused with having faith; indeed, one can know all about it and not be Christian at all.

It appears that as Christian faith has diminished, the schooling-instructional paradigm has encouraged us to busy ourselves with teaching *about* Christian religion. As our personal commitment to Christ has lapsed, many church persons have turned for solace to teaching children what the Bible says, what happened in the history of the church, what we believe, and what is right and wrong. Sometimes, even when the school has succeeded, it has only produced educated atheists. For many today, Christian religion as taught in our church schools stands between them and God. The schooling-instructional paradigm easily leads us into thinking that we have done our jobs if we teach children all *about* Christianity.

There is a great difference between learning about the Bible and living as a disciple of Jesus Christ. We are not saved by our knowledge, our beliefs, or our worship in the church; just as we are not saved by our actions or our religion. We are saved by the anguish and love of God, and to live according to that truth is to have faith.

Faith cannot be taught by any method of instruction; we can only teach religion. We can know about religion, but we can only expand in faith, act in faith, live in faith. Faith can be inspired within a community of faith, but it cannot be given to one person by another. Faith is expressed, transformed, and made meaningful by persons sharing their faith in an historical, tradition-bearing community of faith. An emphasis on schooling and instruction makes it too easy to forget this truth. Indeed, the schooling-instructional paradigm works against our necessary primary concern for the faith of persons. It encourages us to teach about Christian religion by turning our attention to Christianity as expressed in documents, doctrines, history, and moral codes. No matter what the rhetoric of our purposes, the schooling-instructional paradigm, modeled after modern psychology and pedagogy, leads us to focus on religion rather than faith. If for no other reason than this, the schooling-instructional paradigm needs to be questioned.

A Bankruptcy

I have concluded, therefore, that the schooling-instructional paradigm is bankrupt. An alternative paradigm, not merely an alternative educational program, is needed. But that is easier said than done. Our dilemma is exemplified in a Sufi story about a person who, having looted a city, was trying to sell an exquisite rug. "Who will give me a hundred pieces of silver for this rug?" he cried. After the sale was completed, a comrade approached the seller and asked, "Why did you not ask more for that priceless rug?" "Is there a number larger than one hundred?" asked the seller.

Until we can imagine an alternative to our present schooling-instructional paradigm, our efforts at Christian education will be inadequate and increasingly ineffective. However, a new paradigm cannot be created in a vacuum. Christian education is dependent upon theological underpinnings, a fact that we have forgotten on occasion; relying, rather, upon insights from philosophy, the social sciences, or general education. Before we can explore an alternative paradigm, we must reflect on our theological convictions, so to that task we turn. But first a word of hope.

Unless hope is aroused and alive there is little reason to struggle with an alternative paradigm. Remember, therefore, that hope has its foundations in dissatisfactions with the present. Hope is founded upon the death of the old and the birth of the new. There are those who are troubled by death, the unknown, the new, but the Christian faith finds hope for tomorrow in the destruction of old ways and understandings.

Questioning our schooling-instructional paradigm provides us with significant opportunity to rethink what we are about in religious education. It is not wise to depend on our own short, unreflective pasts or on our current endeavors to provide insight for the future, for when we do, we too easily accept the established as real. The future is in our imaginations and with God. In that conviction is our hope. As we celebrate the death of past understandings, we go forth, as pilgrims in faith, in search of new ones to support our educational ministry. We affirm the need to grapple with the radical question: Will our children have faith?

Conclusion

Using the radical nature and character of a faith community as the context or place for Christian education means using every aspect of our church's life for education—our rituals and preparation for participation, the experiences we have and provide within the community of faith, and the individual and corporate actions we inspire and equip persons to engage in. It means examining and judging our total life as a community of faith to see how well we live and transmit our Christian story or tradition, how well we minister to the total needs of whole persons in community, and how well we prepare and motivate individuals and communities to act on behalf of God's coming community in the world. This means understanding religious education in terms of a continuing struggle to reform the church.

If we make our life in a community of faith the context of Christian education, it will mean living each day under the judgment and inspiration of the gospel to the end that God's community comes and God's will is done. The willingness to affirm and accept this understanding is the challenge of Christian education today; it is also the basis for an answer to the question: Will our children have faith?

For Reflection

1. What does the author think is so bad about schooling as a model?
2. In what ways is socialization important to Christian education thinking?
3. Think of an example from your experience of a hidden curriculum in Christian education.

14

George Albert Coe

What Is Christian Education? The Starting Point of a Solution

(1929)

George Albert Coe held positions in theology and philosophy at the University of Southern California and at Northwestern University. From 1909 until 1922 he was professor of religious education at Union Theological Seminary, New York. He concluded his active teaching career with five years at Teachers College, Columbia University. He continued to write, and it is from this time, early in retirement, that the current selection comes.

Coe was greatly influenced by John Dewey. In turn he influenced what is often called the "liberal" period in religious education (Cully 1960)—a time during the last two decades of the nineteenth century and the first two of the twentieth, when European biblical criticism and liberal theology was having great success in American universities and seminaries. In the middle of this period, 1903, the Religious Education Association (REA) was formed. Coe was active in the association from the start. As a result of his positions at Union Seminary and Columbia University, his several books and numerous articles were widely read. Along with the REA, Coe contributed to the perception that the liberal approach to religious education with its "scientific" applications was the only legitimate and substantive way for the discipline to proceed. His considerable intellect and energy were

From *What Is Christian Education?* (New York: Charles Scribner's Sons, 1929), 327–38.

dedicated to this end. His work, along with that of a very few others, helped to bring religious education out of its infancy and into the accepted range of practical theology.

In the following excerpt from Coe's writing, he introduces "the Christian teacher's dilemma." By this he means whether teachers should transmit through their personalities and values their own religion to the student or whether they should help the student to create what Coe calls "a new world." He suggests that the student, instead of trying to imitate Jesus, should adopt his spirit, goals, and principles. These are then to be applied in contemporary situations, giving birth to new, individual modes of conduct. He then gives some brief examples taken from his own time (1900–1929). From this he concludes that the focus of Christian education should be not on the past but on the future. "Reconstruction, continuous reconstruction" is seen by Coe as the essence of the work of God in all humans.

References

Cully, D. B. 1960. *Basic writings in Christian education.* Philadelphia: Westminster.

Religion Changes in the Act of Teaching It

At what point shall we begin the attempt to rethink the nature of Christian education? Perhaps the simplest procedure that moves within the concrete, and does not wander off into abstract definitions, is this: Imagining a teacher and a pupil together, each responding to the other, to ask what this relationship between the two is. What is it to be a teacher, and what is it to be a pupil, where Christian education is going on?

A distinction between the two individuals comes at once to the surface. I do not refer to the fact that usually one is considerably older than the other, for sometimes this age relation is reversed. The important difference is that, whereas the teacher acts in a representative capacity, speaking for the church, or for God, or for a cause or a curriculum, the pupil represents nobody but himself. Let us examine this contrast and some consequences of it.

The teacher certainly is an agent or an instrument, but is he nothing more than this? Is he a lamp that grows incandescent and warm only when and because someone else presses a button? Is he merely an animated tool? Everybody, Catholic and Protestant alike, will answer that what the teacher himself is, his individual personality, what he is by virtue of his own choices, efforts, and habits, is a vital factor in the teacher-pupil relationship.

For Catholics this answer might conceivably call attention to a rather odd difference in standpoint within their church. According to the Roman doctrine, in the sacrifice of the mass, which is regarded as the central channel through which the saving grace of God flows into the church, the character of the officiating priest is nonessential. He may be a bad Catholic and a bad man, he may be drunk or trifling at the time, but if he has been properly ordained, and if he says mass according to the prescribed formula, the full value of the sacrifice is realized. On the other hand, a bad Catholic or bad man, or one drunk or trifling at the time, even if he had been ordained, and even if he spoke Catholic doctrine and ideals without a flaw, could not be a good teacher of the Catholic religion. Why this discrepancy between the minimal requirement for mediating God to a congregation and the minimal qualifications of a teacher who is to stand in the presence of a child? I shall leave the answer to any Catholic who may be interested in the question.

Probably Catholics and Protestants would give the same reason for their insistence upon truly Christian character and earnestness in the teacher, namely, that what the teacher is mingles itself inextricably with what he says, so that response of the pupil is a response to the teacher as well as to the curriculum that he uses, the church that commissions him, and the God on whose behalf the church speaks through him.

In fact, that which we can be most certain of whenever we undertake to teach is some interplay between the teacher and the pupil, with some resulting modification of the pupil's personality. This, indeed, is psychologically inevitable, and it has far-reaching implications.

The first of these implications will now be stated, but others will be postponed for a time. The personality principle implies that Christian education, as well as the Christian teacher, is not a mere tool or instrument of our religion, but the actual fulfillment, or attempt at fulfillment, of the ends of our religion in the teacher-and-learner relationship.

Something like this has been said many times, but whether the full meaning and consequence of it have been perceived may be doubted. For it signifies that what is most personal and free in each of the persons concerned can be educational in the most Christian sense. The pupil, as we have remarked, speaks for nobody but himself. The teacher, in turn, though he is a messenger and transmitter, is such by his own conviction and voluntary loyalty. This loyalty of his adds impressiveness to the message and to the authority back of it, making concrete, near, and warm what otherwise would not seem so close. Moreover, the teacher adjusts himself to the pupil, varying the form of words, the emphasis and angle of thought, and the type of attitude, to suit the age, the experience, and the individuality of the other. Thus, into the relationship there is injected a meaning to which the teacher's own individuality clings and must cling, and likewise a meaning to which the pupil's individuality clings.

Consider, now, that personality is a sensitive, changing thing, and that no two personalities are exactly alike. Any two Christians are Christians in at least slightly different ways, probably in ways that are not slight. Pupils, likewise, are individual and different from one another; their spiritual responses, though couched in identical words, are not exactly the same. Here, then, are two necessarily variable elements. Though we reduce the variation to the lowest possible point, we do not quite extinguish it.

These variations or shadings in religion, taking place in the acts of teaching and learning it, have received entirely inadequate consideration. One probable reason is that, like biological variations, they are usually slight and therefore apparently not important.

In fact, they are not always slight, but even when they are they have a way of accumulating that is not unimportant. Religions can change their complexion almost insensibly along with the other changes in their adherents and pupils. A church population, Protestant or Catholic, that makes the transition from weakness to power, from poverty to wealth, or from crudity to culture, drifts into changed religious attitudes. It does so by accumulating such slight individual variations as have been described.

Christian education participates in these variations not only because the teacher's convictions reflect them, but also because he is, and is known by the pupil to be, a representative of his church. Through the teacher the church as a whole says, "Follow us"; or, if it says, "Follow Jesus," the pupil assumes, in the absence of specific information to the contrary, that following Jesus consists in what his professed disciples do. Thus the prevailing habits of Christians, which are changing habits, supply an interpretative background to anything that teacher or textbook or sermon or the Bible says, and to any worship or other activity that is included in the church program.

This background meaning shifts because ideas and conduct shift. General formulas of approval and disapproval may remain the same while particular acts, attitudes, and notions exchange places to any extent in the scale that reaches from what is praised, through what is permitted, to what is condemned. Practices in which the religious society acquiesces become standards, at least standards of the religiously permissible. One can see this from the short history of the motorcar, or from the history of race relations during the last hundred years. The atrophy of a custom—family prayers, for example—is reflected in a changed sense of duty, though there be no change in the formulas of piety. Even sudden and profound spiritual displacements can occur, as in the Great War, without formal acknowledgment. It is then the emotional situation that does the effective teaching. The same curriculum material may have been taught in 1913, 1918, and 1928, but how different the kinds of Christianity that it represented to the pupil! All this "not-in-the-curriculum" meaning is mediated to the pupil by the personal presence of the teacher.

What shall the Christian teacher do about this kind of inescapable fact? He will, of course, endeavor to hand on to his pupil the best thing in the religious inheritance, and over and above what he intentionally hands on he will almost automatically transmit much more. Education always is transmission; no one need fear that it ever will cease to be this. But the other factor, likewise inevitable, is minimized by Catholics and fumbled by Protestants. It is true that Protestants sentimentalize over the importance of "the teacher's personality"; they sometimes even substitute winsomeness for sound work within the curriculum. But never, I think, has it been recognized that precisely in the personal relations between teacher and pupil the religion of the churches undergoes modification either slowly or rapidly, and never has this process of modification been taken purposefully in hand and given deliberate direction.

The concept that now emerges is that of the possibility of a church that, through its educational system, exercises voluntary selection among possible changes in its religion, some of which are bound to occur. Changes unforeseen and not fully voluntary will continue to take place—the complexity of the details, and the unpredictable factors in personality assure this—but mere drift can be reduced; it can be recognized as such and therefore modified far earlier than is now the case, and there can be conscious and controlled development, growth, in the qualities of our religion.

The Christian Teacher's Dilemma

Almost invariably the assumption has prevailed that the work of the Christian teacher is to transmit a religion, and that the contribution of the teacher's personality is simply and solely that of a reinforcement of the transmission process. We now see that this "simply and solely" is a psychological impossibility. When teachers of religion become psychologically awake and thoroughly realistic, they will perceive that they must take a voluntary attitude toward a flow in religion that cannot in any case be wholly prevented. They will be face to face with a practical dilemma: Shall the personality factor in teaching be so used as to secure the maximum of conformity and the minimum of change, or so as to produce attitudes of freedom in the presence of conditions that might lead to change? There will dawn upon the mind the possibility of religious creativeness through Christian education, whereupon the relation of transmission to creation within the educative process will have to be worked out. Practically everything that remains to be said in this volume concerns this practical dilemma and its relation on the one hand to existing defects in religious education, and on the other hand to the achievement of something new and better but still Christian. Therefore some pages will now be devoted to a preliminary illumination of the alternatives between which we shall have to choose.

It is not within our power to determine whether education shall be both transmission from the past and response to the present—it is bound to be in some measure each of these—but we can select one or the other of them as the primary function, and we can make either of them contributory to the other. Accordingly, the Christian teacher's practical dilemma takes this form: Shall the primary purpose of Christian education be to hand on a religion, or to create a new world?

A dim inkling that education is not mere transmission pervades the schooling of both the state and the church. For no school endeavors to perpetuate, whole and unchanged, any culture whatever. When we teach literature, we select the specimens according to our own taste, not according to the taste of our ancestors. When we teach history or biography, we ourselves determine what shall be foreground and what background. And when we come to morals, again we select. We do it rather drastically, too, for we never tell the young the whole truth about the conduct of the present adult generation, nor about the standards that it in practice accepts. By maintaining discreet silence concerning parts of our civilization, we hope to save the coming generation from civilization as we ourselves practice it.

Wherever the schools do not avow this policy they come perilously near the edge of duplicity. The schools of the state scarcely ever tell the whole truth about how the government is run and what it has done; instead, they cover up or slur over the blunders and the wrongs committed by our nation, causing pupils to believe that our better national qualities are more commanding than they ever have been. Thus, professing to transmit a political culture, the schools idealize it by a process of selection that really implies condemnation as well as praise, the need of reconstruction as well as of transmission.

An almost identical educational policy prevails in the schools of the church. No Sunday school, church college, or theological seminary paints an impartially realistic picture of the state of our religion, or with some exceptions in theological schools—of any past state of it. No church, however holy it thinks itself, goes the whole length of complete self-revelation. When God, incarnated in children, peers about our ecclesiastical garden, every denomination resorts to fig leaves.

This selective function of education, normal and proper though it be, is seldom fully avowed by school administrators; it is seldom thorough, and the implication that education should squarely accept the duty of social criticism and reconstruction is scarcely ever accepted. No, the dominant concern is that the rising generation should not get too far away from precedents, should not become too unlike us.

As it is not within our power to determine whether education shall be both transmission from the past and response to the present, so it is beyond our scope to permit or forbid selection among the possible responses to the present. Selection takes place anyhow, whether consciously or unconsciously, whether by successive yieldings to circumstances or by a continuous plan. The one thing that we can do is to make deliberate choices, and consolidate them into a policy, instead of drifting, or being only partly steered by others, dead or alive, while we vainly imagine that we are wholly guided by them. If we should conclude that our job as teachers is not, first and foremost, to hand on something that already exists, but to enter creatively into the flow of present experience, a part of our problem would then take this form: Is there anything creative in the religion that has been handed down to us, any principle that provides for a self-transcending and self-transforming process within the historic faith itself? If so, this principle might conceivably approve itself as a guide to original, unprescribed, and unprecedented responses to our present world, which is itself unprecedented, and we should then have a creative education that is nevertheless Christian. Let us look at this concept a little more closely.

The Concept of a Creative Education That Is Christian

That God is now, as through all history, creating a spiritual or moral order of righteousness and goodwill is a very old item in Christian thinking. At least, words like these are old. But the concept of continuous creation, it appears, has been hard to grasp; the nearest that most minds come to it is the notion of a quantitative increase of something that is qualitatively finished and complete. The growth of the kingdom of God has been conceived as "more of the same"—more geographic areas covered, more members in the church, more resources at command, more faithfulness in doing duties that the saints long ago performed to the full. Growth, in the sense of qualitative change, the coming into being of something unprecedented and unpredictable from the past, involving possibly the superseding of some ancient good—this notion of the inexhaustible vitality of the divine has not been common.

Oddly enough, however, it has been many times declared that imitation, even of the Master, does not suffice. He was unmarried, and at the crucial period of his life he lived outside of the family; apparently he had so settled place of abode, and it is not clear that he made any economic contribution to his own support. In short, he did not have our particular problems to meet, and to imitate his conduct is no solution of them. Therefore, instead of imitating him, we are to adopt his spirit, his ends and principles of action, and by applying them in our situations develop modes of conduct of our very own.

The growth of social consciousness and conscience within the Christian churches during the last thirty and more years has brought to the surface a most interesting phase of this idea. The Gospels give us no direct guidance concerning capital and labor, property, the profit system, corporations, government ownership, social insurance, international law, and so on, though these are the sphere of severest moral strains of our time. Nevertheless, no one doubts that in Jesus' approach to life there is something that does bear upon this whole area of modern social struggle, and that if we take this approach we shall produce unprecedented modes of social life and unprecedented good. How our modern mass life can become Christian we simply do not know and cannot know except by experimentation; we must create the good life or we shall miss it. Already we see that the old sorts of goodness, the Christian life of other generations, are inadequate and sometimes obstructive, and it dawns upon us that *we* cannot be Christian unless we take upon ourselves the burdens and the risks of re-creating in some measure our Christianity itself.

This re-creation, these phases of religious living that Jesus never thought of, can yet be Christian in the sense of carrying forward something that Jesus started or something to which he gave impetus; and his mode of approach to life (as distinct from the particular things he did, and the particular connections in his thought) is universally valid because it is the way of perpetual discovery and perpetual creation. It may be—I shall show that this is the fact—that we cannot maintain vital continuity with Jesus unless we do take his road of discovery and creation. It is quite possible . . . to attempt a kind of continuity that is self-defeating. The churches have broken away from Jesus time and again at the very points where they thought they were exalting him. I do not see how we can ever really outgrow him; the issue for us is whether we will be creators with him, evoking the unprecedented by our own thinking, experimenting, daring, and suffering. Reconstruction, continuous reconstruction, is of the essence of the divine work in and through the human.

Of course we cannot reconstruct anything unless we are acquainted with it; we cannot take a creative part in the moral order without intelligence as to its present and its past. But the focal point of true education is not acquaintance with the past, it is the building forth of a future different from the present and from the past. Moreover, creative education implies that the nature and the degree of this difference are to be determined within and by means of the educative processes; they cannot be dictated or imposed; they cannot be discovered by exegesis of any historical document.

This, in a preliminary and schematic way, is what is meant by creative education that is likewise Christian. Looked at from the standpoint of the learner's experience, what has been said means that learning to be a Christian should be, essentially and primarily, an experience of free creativity. Looked at from the standpoint of the teacher, it means fellowship of teacher and pupil in forming and executing purposes that are unprecedented as well as those that follow precedent. From the standpoint of the church, it means ecclesiastical self-reconstruction in and through fresh approaches to the surrounding world. . . .

What, Then, Is Christian Education?

It is the systematic, critical examination and reconstruction of relations between persons, guided by Jesus' assumption that persons are of infinite worth, and by the hypothesis of the existence of God, the Great Valuer of Persons.

For Reflection

1. What does Coe have to say about Christian character?
2. How does Coe's liberal theology shape his approach to Christian education (as far as can be told by the excerpt)?
3. What does Coe mean by a "creative education"?
4. How can reconstruction be continuous?

15

Randolph Crump Miller

The Clue to Christian Education (1950)

The milieu from which *The Clue to Christian Education* arose was one of personal loss, family adjustment of the most basic kind, and professional change for its author. Soon after writing the first chapter as a lecture manuscript, Professor Miller's wife died at age thirty-five of polio. He and his four daughters, all under age nine, sought solace in this tragedy in relationship with God and the fellowship of the church where he was pastor. The meaning of relationship, of theology, and of the living of life came to the forefront in his thinking. After six months he could again take up the writing of the book (Mayr 1983).

Randolph Miller began his teaching career at Pacific School of Religion in Berkeley, California, with courses in philosophy of religion, the department where he prepared for the Ph.D. at Yale. Since it was a small seminary he also had to teach apologetics and some Christian education. As he gained more and more confidence he taught more and more Christian education and less theology.

In 1952 Miller moved from Pacific School of Religion to Yale Divinity School to accept a position in Christian education. It was through his work at Yale and as the editor of *Religious Education* for the Religious Education Association that Professor Miller came most to influence the field of Christian education. He continued to write curriculum and serve on committees for its preparation, and wrote

From *The Clue to Christian Education* (New York: Charles Scribner's Sons, 1950), 1–17.

other books as well. However, *The Clue* represents some of his best ideas. He did not deviate too far over the years from the conviction that theology must be the foundation upon which any theory of Christian education should be built. Nevertheless, his thinking was influenced in later years by process theology.

Miller considers *The Clue* to be a conservative expression of his solution to the debate, popular at the time of its writing, about whether Christian education should be content-centered, as in "traditional" education, or life- or pupil-centered, as in "progressive" education. Miller's answer was *neither.* Theology, he said, should be the foundation of Christian education, not its primary focus. "The chief source of all our teaching is the Bible, the chief interest of our teaching is the learner, and the chief end of our teaching is the God and Father of Jesus Christ" (p. 16). Theology could bridge the gap between content and method; it could aid in establishing the proper relationship between truth and life. Faith and grace should be in the foreground, and theology should be in the background of Christian education.

The chapter reprinted here gives an overview of Miller's position on Christian education theory. Such expressions as "accepting Jesus as Lord and Savior" and the place given to evangelism in his theory, as well as the quotation from Ephesians, will all ring familiar to evangelical readers. Much of Miller's writing is encompassing, with a broad outlook. He seems proud, too, that the ideas written in *The Clue to Christian Education* were first tried and proven to his satisfaction in the give and take of Saint Alban's Church, where he pastored and which for its first seven years was a store-front church.

References

Mayr, M., ed. 1983. *Modern masters of religious education.* Birmingham, Ala.: Religious Education Press.

There is something new in the theory and practice of Christian education. It is coming out of parents' and teachers' meetings in terms which they do not often understand; it is being expressed by pastors in their dissatisfaction with both the older methods of teaching and the newer and progressive methods; it is being illustrated by the demand for new lesson materials, by the experiments being made among the educational leaders of the various denominations, and by the increasing cooperation between home and church.

It is hard to put one's finger on the exact problem, because the difficulty now confronting us in being expressed primarily in negative terms. There is increasing dissatisfaction with the content-centered teaching which is still prevalent, and there is also widespread distrust of the so-called life-centered teaching. This vagueness of analysis is further illustrated by the enthusiasm with which new tricks have been tried. There are no answers to the basic problem in novel teaching methods, in the use of motion pictures and other visual aids, or in expanded time for the education of both children and adults, important as these things are.

Some of the difficulties of the older materials were overcome by turning to the experience of the learner as a basic element in educational procedure. The earlier methods had been catechetical, or ungraded, or Bible-centered, with no thought for the religious needs and experiences of the pupils. To get away from this emphasis on content, it was decided to begin at the "growing edge" of the learner and lead him through his increased interests and insights toward a fuller and richer Christian life. Too often, the procedure was reversed, so that "a little child shall lead them" not to the deepest truths of Christian living, but to the vagaries of childhood or the mutual interchange of ignorance of high school students in a bull session or the prejudices of ill-informed adults. As a matter of fact, the main goal of education was lost sight of just as much in life-centered as in content-centered teaching, for the goal of all education is quite clearly to learn "truth," and there is no easy way to acquire or impart "truth."

This points to the fundamental weakness in practically all educational theory: *a failure to grasp the purpose of Christian education and to impart Christian truth.* "Ye shall know the truth, and the truth shall make you free," we are told; but when the emphasis has been on truth, there has been no method adequate to impart it; and when there have been effective methods, there has been no fundamental truth to guide them. Our philosophy of educational method has been sound at the expense of theology, while both true and false theologies have been presented without the methods to bring them to life in the experiences of the learners.

Let us illustrate this thesis: It is true that a little child learns primarily through activity, and that what he sees or touches or smells is of greater significance than what he hears. He can learn great lessons about God because he can see, touch, or smell a flower or a doll or a baby. But too often he achieves romantic and unrealistic views of natural processes because the interpretation is not fundamentally either scientific or Christian, and as a result he will have to unlearn this meaning of nature as he grows older.

A child in the fifth grade may spend a great deal of time making a relief map of Palestine. This is an enjoyable occupation, and he will be able to show the routes which Jesus followed from Nazareth to Jerusalem, and he will understand the deadness of the Dead Sea and the sudden storms on the Lake of Galilee. Too often such knowledge will bring him no closer to seeing what it means to accept Jesus as the Christ, and while his geographical insights may have improved greatly and he may have become a quite adequate mapmaker, he will be no farther along the road to becoming a Christian. This type of worthwhile and exciting activity will keep him occupied, and the methodology is fundamentally sound, but unless "something new has been added," it will result in an actual stoppage of Christian growth.

The examples on the other side are equally frustrating. There was a time when the same Bible story was taught to each age-group and all learners were treated alike, because, if the story were in the Bible it had to be taught some day. While it is generally admitted that this is impossible today even in the smallest ungraded church school, there are still many hangovers in educational circles. First-grade children are expected to recite and understand the Apostles' Creed. Uniform lessons are still among the best sellers of church-school materials. The catechism is still taught in terms of set questions and answers. Some parents and church-school leaders are disturbed when their children do not learn by rote Bible verses which are so many meaningless jumbles to the youngsters, although it is recognized that the right use of memorization is valuable.

The dissatisfaction with the dilemmas has led the writers of church-school courses to seek a new solution. They have not worked out a theory, but there is in their efforts a hint to the proper theory. The newest Bible courses have not been placed simply on a problem-solving level. It has been discovered that the Bible is not only the source of potential solution to many problems, but that it has within it the power to suggest new questions to which it has the answer. So it has been that courses have been worked out which make full use of the specific problems of a particular age-group, but which lead them also into the mystery of the Bible as something worth knowing in itself. The same thing has been done with church history, so that whereas historical processes and events are understood in terms of modern problems, they are also comprehended within the framework of the situations actually facing the historical actors and writers. Clues to a solution of the problem have also been provided by the writers of courses on worship, for it has been discovered that worship is the experience-centered method *par excellence* for educational purposes, that worship is an activity of one who knows himself to be in the presence of God, to whom the worshiper brings his own difficulties and in the presence of whom he finds solace and power and blessing. Courses on Christian ethics have also stumbled on this same truth, that the central beliefs of the Christian tradition are relevant to present-day living.

I

But the insights of such discoveries, important as they are, do not quite get at the heart of the problem. *The major task of Christian education today is to discover and impart the relevance of Christian truth.* The one missing topic in most educational schemes today is *theology,* and in theology properly interpreted lies the answer to most of the pressing educational problems of the day. The new element in educational theory is the discovery of the organic relation between doctrine and experience, between content and method, between truth and life.

Now before this is misunderstood, two things must be said. This is not a plea to return to a content-centered curriculum, for it is perfectly clear that an emphasis on content as an end in itself leads to verbalism, whereby the learner repeats the words but is not concerned with the meaning. That is like trying to Christianize a parrot, and success cannot be achieved by that method. In the second place, it is not a desire to return to indoctrination, for indoctrination implies a kind of authority which is consistent with controlled propaganda rather than with the growth of individuals in the Christian way of life.

But if neither content nor indoctrination provides the clue, how can theology be at the center of the curriculum? The answer is that theology is *not* at the center. *The center of the curriculum is a twofold relationship between God and the learner. The curriculum is both God-centered and experience-centered. Theology must be prior to the curriculum!* Theology is "truth-about-God-in-relation-to-man." In order to place God and man at the center of the Christian educational method, we must have adequate knowledge of the nature and working of both God and man, and of God's relationships to particular pupils.

For example, it would be possible to work out a sound curriculum based on the Apostles' Creed (assuming that the creed is true in so far as it may be proved by Scripture and made meaningful in experience). But the creed would be placed *back of* the curriculum rather than in it. It would be introduced into the curriculum in terms of the relevance of Christian truth to the experiences and capacities of the learners, until at the proper level it could be studied as a summary of truths which are relevant to Christian living today. Most of us would not think of this as an adequate curriculum, unless it were enriched by the many implications of the creed . . . , but there would be a depth of meaning and a richness of experience provided by even so inadequate a curriculum which are lacking in most modern approaches to Christian education.

The task of Christian education is not to teach theology, but to use theology as the basic tool for bringing learners into the right relationship with God in the fellowship of the church. We have tried the Bible as a tool, and have ended up with some knowledge of the Bible but with no basic principles for using it properly. It is true that Holy Scripture is the basic authority for theology, but it is also evident that theology is a guide to the meaning of the Bible. Theology provides the perspective for all subjects, and yet all subjects are to be taught in terms of the interests and capacities of the learners in their relationship to God and to their fellow men.

When we say that truth is the underlying principle of the curriculum, this does not mean that we can be dogmatic about it. We need to recognize the great varieties of concepts held to be true by various individuals and denominations calling themselves Christian, and then to grant that our teachers will be bound to a theological system in terms of their own loyalty and freedom. The degrees of authority and freedom will vary from communion to communion, and from congregation to congregation within a communion, so that the writer of lesson materials and the teacher of a class will still have to use their own intelligence in making selections of theological tools for religious instruction.

There is great danger in this approach, as we have said, for it opens the door to the emphasis on content at the expense of Christian growth, and it could bring us back to the old idea of indoctrination, but the safeguard against this error is the insistence that there is a proper *relationship* between content and method. It is this relationship which needs further investigation. If we are right in our assumption that theology lies back of the curriculum and is to be introduced into it in the light of the "growing edge" of the learner, we need to understand the relation of theology to Christian living at the various age-levels, and this involves what is even more fundamental: the relevance of theology for all of life.

A person's behavior is guided by his deepest convictions, for what he believes in his inmost self determines his actions. His motivations are organically related to this theology. He may hold these concepts consciously or unconsciously. He may behave in a way foreign to a creed which he deceives himself into thinking he accepts, and thus may indicate that his basic drives are other than what he professes (and the hypocrite is one who professes one set of beliefs and acts according to another set). The complexity of his personality and the confusion of his motives may blur the picture of the relation between his beliefs and his behavior. But when the principle of this relationship is applied consistently and with due regard for all the factors, it will be discovered that the beliefs which are *habitually* held (and thus taken seriously even when one is not conscious of them) are the normal bases for action.

If this be true, it is of the greatest significance for Christian education. It explodes both the traditional view and the progressive one, for the traditional view insists that beliefs be accepted within the framework of a certain vocabulary regardless of their relevance, while the progressive view ultimately is reduced to the solving of a problem within the frame of reference of that problem and without regard to the wider cosmic or metaphysical point of view. If theology comes into the foreground of Christian teaching, there is great danger that beliefs will be held which are not part of one's basic personality pattern, whereas if theology is disregarded there is no sense of ultimate purpose.

Theology in the background; faith and grace in the foreground might well be the slogan for this new point of view. The center of the educational process is neither theology nor the individual learner. *The purpose of Christian education is to place God at the center and to bring the individual into the right relationship with God and his fellows within the perspective of the fundamental Christian truths about all of life*—a Christian view of the universe, a Christian view of God who is know in experience and in the historical process, a knowledge of Jesus Christ who is to be accepted as Lord and Savior, a view of man which actually accounts for the experiences of damnation and salvation, an acceptance of the church as a people-church in a covenant relationship with God, and the experience of the learner in terms of the *realities* underlying these concepts. When such a relationship between content and method is achieved, theology becomes relevant to Christian living, and education is almost synonymous with evangelism. Evangelism has often been ignored or misunderstood in modern educational circles, but its essential purpose can never be ignored if Christian education is to remain a vital force in the life of the church. To evangelize is to confront men with Jesus Christ, so that they will put their trust in God through him, and by the power of the Holy Spirit live as Christ's disciples in the fellowship of the church.

The person who by faith comes to this position is said to be integrated. The integration of the personality which is the goal of religious instruction can never be achieved in terms of ideals alone (as in character education), or of beliefs alone (as in indoctrination), or of social adjustment alone (as in much modern psychiatry). Just at the point where Christianity is unique, its educational philosophy and its methods have fallen down. The weakness of the good man who lacks religion is that his personality is centered on ideals, and he becomes like the Pharisee in Jesus' parables. The charge against religious fanatics is that they know Bible verses and creeds, but have little insight into the meaning of Christlikeness. The trouble with many who have made good social adjustments is that they lack the divine discontent which is the only motivation for making a better world.

There must be a deeper integration. Theology, in so far as it represents truth, points in the direction of a Christian answer: . . . Christian integration lies in the relationship between God and man. It is the integration which results from a deep and abiding personal relationship between God and man. It flows from a right religious adjustment which is a basic process of living. It is more than intellectual or emotional or volitional activity, for it involves the total personality in relation to the ultimate reality, who is God. The human integration of a child does not evolve from his *idea* of his parents. It comes from his *relationship* with his parents. So also, his religious integration does not come primarily from his *idea* of God. It comes from his *personal relationship* with God.

It is central to the educational theory of these chapters to recognize the radical nature of Christian integration. Modern studies in psychology point toward the same emphasis: a man's integration is in terms of the organic relation between himself and his environment, not in terms of ideas or values but in terms of the situation in which he find himself. It is Christian theology which adds a further element, that central in the Christian's environment is the living God and that the frame of reference for Christian living is he in whom we live and move and have our being. The Epistle to the Ephesians describes it as "reaching maturity, reaching the full measure of development which belongs to the fulness of Christ—instead of remaining immature, blown from our course and swayed by every passing wind of doctrine, by the adroitness of men who are dexterous in devising error; we are to hold by the truth, and by our love to grow up wholly unto Him" (Eph. 4:13–15, Moffat).

No current educational theory adequately accounts for this end product of a sound program of Christian education. That children have grown up in the church and come to a religion of maturity is an acknowledged fact, but it has never been the conscious aim of the educational system within the churches as far as statements of purpose and method are concerned. Horace Bushnell's *Christian Nurture,* with its concern for the relationship between home and church as the matrix of Christian nurture, came the closest to seeing this point of view, but those who used Bushnell's insights never adequately comprehended the organic connection between content and method, and they blurred the necessary relation between home and church. Out of the tremendous concern for the present situation in Christian educational circles, Paul Vieth's *The Church and Christian Education* deals with all the factors involved, and Ernest Ligon's *A Greater Generation* is an important contribution to understanding the role of parents in the church's program, but it has not been made clear how we can use the most effective of modern educational methods to teach a profoundly Christian theology in terms of the relationship between deeply held convictions and Christian behavior.

Those who are aware of the theological deficiencies in modern education have failed to see clearly the answer to the problem. The solution is not to inject theology into an otherwise non-theological approach to Christian education, for that is to get caught in the vicious circle of repeating the cycle of old mistakes. Theology, which is truth from a Christian perspective, must be the presupposition of any curriculum. There is a proper theological perspective for using the Bible, for examining the life of Christ, for approaching Christian history, for studying the meaning of worship and of the sacraments, for finding the Christian answer to individual behavior problems, for looking on the social situation, and for building Christian fellowship between the churches.

For the churches corporately to find an answer to such problems as these, means that the educators must become theologians, and the theologians must become educators, and the writers of lesson materials must be grounded thoroughly in both educational theory and theological method. Every aid must be sought from the findings of child and adult psychology, secular educational experience, and the sociology of learning, and in so far as the underlying theological presuppositions are sound, the church's educational system may make use of the findings of all the sciences related to secular educational theory.

II

Other elements enter the picture as we examine the clue to Christian education. There are the practical problems of insufficient funds, inadequate time during the week for Christian education, untrained teachers in the church schools, untrained and sometimes indifferent clergy, and improper equipment. These are difficult barriers to overcome even when the theory is sound, although it is not our purpose to deal with them in these chapters.

There are other elements in the theory of education which must be brought to bear on the present situation. The first of these is an understanding of the place of the home in the educational development of little Christians. It is a generally acknowledged fact that the little child gets his fundamental training in religious and character development before he is exposed to any kind of formal education in school or church. The patterns of his reactions to all kinds of stimuli are built into habits during the early years. There is little chance that the church in one hour or so per week (and against the background of a secular home and school) can do more than build on the habit patterns already established. Therefore, it is important that the significance of the relation between home and church be realized within the elementary educational theory of the church. The Christian home may be the greatest aid to the church, and through their mutual interdependence there is the opportunity for a more sound and permanent Christian education.

Experiments along these lines are being carried out in many areas of the church's life. There are experiments in the preschool age-group, where parents are assisted by the church in providing the conditions under which Christian growth may be furthered. So far, the church has not been prepared to provide adequate guidance to parents, but the realizing of the need for this type of cooperation merits our hope that something significant may develop in terms of a new educational philosophy.

Cooperation between parents and the church is really just beginning at the point where the child enters church school, but often that is where they are cut off. Yet if there is to be any significant relationship between what is done at church school and the child's daily life, the cooperation of parents is equally necessary at this point, and throughout the adolescent period as well. Some new lesson materials make a place for the parents in their methods, and in more advanced plans parents must actually take part in the Sunday schedule and then be ready to make reports on the progress of their children. While parents at the beginning of such an experiment are unprepared to give much help, by proper education they may become more effective than the average teacher. At this point, the educational theory is sound but it needs to be implemented as it is put into more widespread practice.

Because religion deals so much with intangibles, with subtly changing attitudes, and with the development and growth of the spirit, it is often hard to measure progress. Parents have been enlisted to assist in measuring the improved spiritual characteristics of their children, and teachers have been instructed in recognizing the changes which indicate successful teaching. In the past, too often the only measure of a child's religious growth has been in his ability to memorize or recite various selections of words, which as an end in itself might be a worthwhile exercise in memory but which has practically no effect on the child's relation to God. In reaction against content-centered teaching, we have quite rightly discarded the emphasis on memory work as a token in itself of Christian development, but we still have not discovered how to make the truths of the Christian gospel relevant to everyday living in terms which can be observed. The intangibles have remained too intangible to be seen, and yet only as Christians learn to practice and bear witness to the gospel can there be any significant growth in wisdom and in favor with God and man. Our clue to Christian education does not point to an easy answer to this question, but it poses the problem in different terms, in that is insists that *Christian growth is a process of increased integration centered on the living God who is in our midst.*

In modern society, the home usually finds that the basic implications of daily living are based upon a secular philosophy. The family exists in a society which is governed by the mechanics of industrialism and by the economics of the profit system, and it is against this cultural infiltration that the Christian home must work. It is not a problem of building a Christian home in a Christian society (and indeed the problem has never been that simple); it is rather the discovery of the relevance of the Christian home within a society which permits, condones, and approves many unchristian motives and actions.

Our fundamental educational procedures in the public schools are based primarily upon the principles of a secular society. While it is true that Christianity provides the religious nucleus of American culture, it is also evident that the predominant educational philosophy of the United States is a pragmatic and instrumentalist approach which has little or no place for religion. The public schools, important and significant as they are in American culture, are hardly allies of the Christian church and Christian home in the field of basic theological motives and assumptions. The school may well be an ally in terms of cooperative activities, and it may supplement the work of the church and home without distorting what the Christian is trying to achieve, but there is an underlying difference of philosophy which must be recognized.

The child is exposed first of all to the influence of his parents, and this is where the crucial influence on character development takes place. At a certain point, the schools begin to have as much as or more influence than the parents, although the parents never cease to have an obligation in this regard. The church is always on the sidelines, making use of whatever experiences the home and school and community provide for a Christian interpretation of life. This means that the church should often sit in judgment on the child's experiences which run in opposition to the basic assumptions of a Christian society. At other times, the church will find in these experiences rich and abiding meanings which are ways of opening the child's awareness of God.

The church also provides a new set of experiences, which are the product of the church's life of worship, study, fellowship, and service. These are small elements in the time span of the child, totaling at most only a little over an hour or two per week, but their significance far outweighs the brevity of the experiences. If conditions in the home and school are sufficiently related to what happens in church, the church becomes relevant as a basis for providing the deeper and richer meanings of life. But in many instances, the church provides an isolated kind of experience, where the child fails to see the relevance of what is happening, and thus he sees religion as divorced from life. This is due not only to a false concept of the church's relation to society or to the inadequacy of educational method. The real failure is due to the inability to relate theology to life, and thus we are back to our original analysis that the weak link in modern Christian education is the failure to realize the proper place of the relevant truths of Christianity *behind* the child-centered and God-centered experiences of the learners. When theology is meaningful and related to life, it is possible to make use of the experiences of all of life to build a Christian perspective in the light of the learner's situation and age-group, illuminating those experiences with the peculiarly Christian experiences of worship, sacrament, preaching, study, fellowship, and work as found within the life of the church.

III

The clue to Christian education is the rediscovery of a relevant theology which will bridge the gap between content and method, providing the background and perspective of Christian truth by which the best methods and content will be used as tools to bring the learners into the right relationship with the living God, who is revealed to us in Jesus Christ, using the guidance of parents and the fellowship of life in the church as the environment in which Christian nurture will take place.

I believe this clue rests in the picture of Jesus as a teacher or rabbi in the Gospels. He always assumed the basic truth of belief in God. He taught that God was our Father. He referred constantly to the fundamental truths revealed in the Old Testament. His theology was relevant to every situation in which he found himself. But he always taught in terms of a particular problem or of a specific individual or group. He related his theology to life. He spoke to the "growing edge" of his hearers, and he always led them beyond himself to a deeper loyalty to the Father. His parables were always "life situations" to his hearers, and they saw the application of his teaching to their problems. He never watered down his theology, but he always made it speak to the situation. He did not speak or teach in abstractions.

So also, we are dealing with real children and real adults, and theology is simply "truth-about-God-in-relation-to-man." As adults, we should have mature beliefs, but we should teach these beliefs in terms of the experiences and capacities of the children and older learners, leading them always from their "growing edge" to the deeper meanings and appreciations of life. The chief source of all our teaching is the Bible, the chief interest of our teaching is the learner, and the chief end of our teaching is the God and Father of Jesus Christ.

Because Christianity is primarily an historical rather than a metaphysical religion, the center of the approach to God will be through Jesus Christ, and Jesus will always be seen against the historical background of the Incarnation. While one would not tell a kindergarten child that the Christmas story tells of the birth of the "incarnate Lord" and expect him to understand the phraseology, it would be necessary for the teacher and the writer of the lesson material to know this and to teach so that the child would not learn something foreign to this belief. Some educators might even decide that it would be better not to emphasize the "baby Jesus" at the expense of later Christian faith, for sometimes a child fails to get beyond thinking of Jesus as a baby. In other words, method and content would be judged both by mature theological considerations and by sound knowledge of how the child's personality reacts.

We have acquired a great deal of information concerning the behavior and thoughts of the little child, we have experimented widely and wisely with the learning process at all age-levels, and we have made great use of these new insights, but we have never brought theology to bear upon them. Theology has been taught in opposition to child psychology, and this has been done at the expense of both theology and the child. The new task is to make theology relevant, realizing that the goal of Christian education is Christian truth, that truth may be acquired only through the interpretation of experience, and that we become Christians only as we use truth to place ourselves in commitment to the living God revealed to us in Jesus Christ and through the fellowship of the church.

For Reflection

1. Is the argument between content and method still current? If so, how is it formulated now?
2. Why does Miller think a thorough understanding of the learner is important for Christian education?
3. Do you agree with Miller about theology not being the focus of Christian education? Why? What role should it play?
4. What definition of "relationship with God" seems consistent with this chapter?

16

D. Campbell Wyckoff

The Gospel and Education
(1959)

From the mid-1950s D. Campbell Wyckoff has made an impact on the field of Christian education through his writings and his teaching, principally at Princeton Theological Seminary. He served at that institution more than thirty years. The experiences out of which his contributions have come have been varied. From rural missions to high school teaching to youth director of the New York Federation of Churches, Professor Wyckoff hammered out the beginnings of his Christian education perspectives through church service. He became more and more convinced that a theological base was needed for effective Christian education. This growing conviction led him, with the encouragement of his graduate-school mentors, to write a doctoral dissertation at New York University on the theories of knowledge and responsibility in the theology of Jonathan Edwards.

The first book Wyckoff wrote after taking the chair of Christian education at Princeton was based on his inaugural address "Toward an Informed and Valid Practice of Christian Education." That book was *The Gospel and Christian Education,* a chapter of which is reprinted here.

Wyckoff is identified with what Harold W. Burgess has called the contemporary theological approach to Christian education (Burgess 1975). Although this suggests a neo-orthodox influence, it is more accurate to place Wyckoff at the conservative end of that perspective.

From *The Gospel and Christian Education: A Theory of Christian Education for Our Times* (Philadelphia: Westminster, 1959), 97–112.

Wyckoff believed that the church has historically faced a dilemma, made acute by the mid-twentieth century: How can the church, though bound by its culture, at the same time fulfill its role as servant of its Lord? A half-cultural, half-Christian solution would by no means satisfactorily resolve the dilemma; a fully Christian perspective is required. He says, "Our theological commitments in Christian education . . . are to a position that is supernaturalistic, biblical, Christocentric, and ethical" (69). While the development of a theory of Christian education may need to draw from the fields of philosophy, history, psychology, sociology, communications, it has to start with theology and the life and work of the church.

"The Gospel and Education" lays a basic biblical/theological foundation for a theory of Christian education. The intention is that the theory would be in dynamic tension with and informative to practice.

References

Burgess, H. W. 1975. *An introduction to religious education.* Birmingham: Religious Education Press.

Mayr, M., ed. 1983. *Modern masters of religious education.* Birmingham: Religious Education Press.

At the same time that it is the responsibility of Christian education to be the church's effective servant, it is also up to it to be in a position to know and to contest the inroads of the cultural situation at the necessary points. To do this, it needs a theory that is adequate, both theologically and educationally. That theory, in order to be useful, has to be expressed in terms that can be readily understood and grasped by everyone involved in Christian education, including the layman and the learner.

In order to be readily communicable, the whole theory may well be informed by a guiding principle that is at once adequate, simple, and clear. This guiding principle can give Christian education sure direction by infusing its objectives, its curriculum principles, and its principles of administration. It will also focus the various elements that make up Christian education (all the concerns of the Christian faith and the Christian life), so that their meaning and use will be unmistakably clear.

It has been variously suggested that elements like the Bible, Christian doctrine, problem-solving, "life," experience, the child, the person, the church, and the person of Christ might serve as the basis for such a guiding principle.

The element that seems, however, to hold most promise of being able to focus the other elements, to give unmistakable guidance to Christian education, and at the same time to be adequate both from a theological and an educational point of view, is the gospel.

It appears, then, that the most promising clue to orienting Christian education theory so that it will be both worthy and communicable is to be found in recognizing and using the gospel of God's redeeming activity in Jesus Christ as its guiding principle.

The Basic Guide for Christian Education Theory

The suggestion that the gospel be used as the basic guide for Christian education theory is supported by five arguments:

1. Revelation—the Word of God—is central in Christian education theory.
2. The gospel—God's redeeming activity in Jesus Christ—is the very heart and point of the Word he has spoken to men in their self-centered helplessness throughout the ages, and the very heart and point of the Word he speaks to men today.
3. The gospel is the clue to the meaning of history.
4. The gospel is the clue to the meaning of existence.
5. The gospel is the reason for the church's existence; it brings the church into existence; it sustains the church; it informs, directs, and corrects the church.

After discussing each of these points, we will be in a position to see whether the gospel can be properly used as the basis for a guiding principle.

The Word of God

. . . In ordinary speech a word is a way of getting something across so that it will be understood. . . . The Word of God is God's way of getting himself, in the most complete sense, across to men:

> The Word of God is God's attempt to get the nature of his being and his will across to us so that we shall understand it. Of course, it is more than the spoken word. As a rule, we regard the Word of God as not so much spoken as written, written in a book. But this again is not by any means the whole concept of the Word. Look again at ordinary words and you see what is involved. To help people to understand something, you can show them what it is; you can tell them what it is; and you can make it possible for them constantly to be reminded of it. God uses all these methods: demonstrating, telling, and reminding us of his nature, existence, and truth. He shows us what he is like; here is the Word made flesh, Jesus Christ, pre-existent, existent in history, and eternally existent as the living Christ, the living Lord. He leaves us a written record of what he is like; here is the Bible, the Word in written form. Furthermore, he continually illu-

mines our understanding of what he is like; here is the testimony of the Spirit to the Word within our hearts.

The Word of God is revelation. It is God's disclosure of himself, his revelation of himself.

In a deep sense the Word of God is spoken to us; God discloses himself to us. We have the opportunity and the responsibility to listen, to understand, to answer, and to become and do what is clearly implied. This is a dynamic encounter, by the very nature of the Word not so much an encounter with an idea or proposition as an encounter of a person-to-person kind.

Because we are rational beings, and always try to think out the meaning of our experience by translating it into ideas, we respond to the Word of God by trying to explain to ourselves and to other people what the encounter means to us. This gives rise to theology and doctrine, the formulation of the Christian faith. Let us come directly to the point—What is the Christian faith? What is our interpretation of our encounter with the Word of God?

The Christian faith has a source; its doctrine of God speaks to this matter. It deals with a problem; its doctrines of man and sin explain what this problem is. It believes that the problem has been solved; the doctrines of the covenant, the incarnation, the atonement, and the living Word attempt to explain how God has dealt with and solved the human problem. It believes that God has entrusted his work in the world to his people, and that he guides them by his Spirit; here it develops its doctrine of the church, including the church's ministry of the Word and sacraments and the church's mission. Christian faith has a goal; its belief about its goal is the subject of its doctrine of the fulfillment of personal destiny and human history. God's revelation of the meaning of life and history is thus the source and subject of the Christian faith.

It has been amply demonstrated that such an understanding of the Christian faith is absolutely indispensable to a theory of Christian education that is theologically worthy. Any Christian education theory that did not make this central would be distorted and would lack permanent value. Revelation, and the Christian faith as the witness to revelation, are thus central to Christian education theory.

The purpose of Christian education has often been glibly and superficially described as "to teach people about God." In a deep sense, this *is* the purpose of Christian education. And if it is, then the Word of God—his telling us who he really is—is the very heart of it. And the theological witness to the Word is of major importance in enabling men to listen to the Word, understand, answer, and become and do what is demanded.

The Gospel—the Heart of the Word

To a person or to a world so wrapped up in itself that it has never considered such a possibility, the fact of God's having revealed himself, the fact that in so doing he has revealed the meaning of life and history, the fact that he has made the human problem clear and has solved it, comes—if it does not seem like utter foolishness—as news, *good* news, *the* good news.

The New Testament writers saw in Jesus Christ the climax and fulfillment of the whole drama of history and revelation. The fact of who he was and what he did was the best news that man had ever received, or could ever receive. Such phrases as "the Word made flesh" and "the living Word" are a sort of symbolic shorthand by which the tremendous significance of the gospel is indicated.

The definition of the term *gospel* in the concordance of *The Westminster Study Edition of The Holy Bible* (1948) is this: "The word means 'good news,' 'glad tidings.' Hence it is used of the message proclaimed by Jesus himself concerning the coming Kingdom of God, and then of the story of God's redeeming activity through the life, death, and resurrection of Jesus Christ, proclaimed by the apostles and recorded by the Evangelists."

The gospel is the Bible's essential unity, since it is the gospel that the Old Testament anticipates, and since it is the gospel that constitutes the message of the New Testament. At its climax, according to Millar Burrows (1946), the Old Testament proclaims the expectation of the gospel:

> Failure to do God's will as he has revealed it incurs judgment; but God does not leave the guilty without hope: he offers the undeserving sinner redemption and reveals the way to obtain it. The promise of the new covenant includes forgiveness. This note sounds strongly in the later prophets, . . . who again and again proclaims the good news of deliverance. This is the origin of the Christian word "gospel." The law shows what God requires and the penalties of disobedience; the gospel shows the way of deliverance when man has failed to meet the requirements. This is what Paul means by justification, God's free gift to the sinner.

The gospel constitutes the message of the New Testament. In his analysis of the word *gospel* (100), Alan Richardson says:

> After the death and resurrection of Jesus the content of the gospel, as it is understood by the apostolic church, is Christ himself. It is no longer simply "the gospel of the Kingdom of God" (though, of course, that is involved), but is "the gospel of Jesus Christ, the Son of God"—a phrase in which every word must be given its full significance. It is "the gospel of God," the saving message which God has addressed to the world, first by way of anticipation in the Scriptures, and now finally in the living Word, Jesus Christ. It is therefore supremely the message of the cross and the resurrection, and it is "the power of God unto salvation to every one that believeth." The church itself is built upon this one gospel and is indeed a fellowship in the gospel. The gospel must always be received personally by faith. For those who thus receive it the gospel is always "news," breaking in freshly upon them and convincing them afresh, though they may first have heard it and accepted it long ago."

It was in the mid-1930s that, browsing in a bookstore on upper Amsterdam Avenue in New York, I came across Principal Alex. Martin's *The Finality of Jesus for Faith* (1933). It was a period when the churches were given to "religiousness," or to a combination of literalistic pedantry and sentimental emotionalism. Into such an atmosphere Principal Martin's direct witness to the gospel came with intense clarity. It has been my polestar ever since. . . .

Thus, the gospel—God's redeeming activity in Jesus Christ—is the very heart and point of the Word he has spoken to men in their helplessness throughout the ages, and the very heart and point of the Word he speaks to men today.

The Meaning of History

The gospel is the clue to the meaning of history. God deals with man through the medium of history. The perception of history and historical relationships is man's God-given way of finding himself and the meaning of his life in the continuum of time.

Meaningful history is, looked at from a thoroughly realistic perspective, the account of God's relationships with man. History *past* is the story of what he has done with, for, and through man. History *present* is his current activities with, for, and through man. History *future* is what he intends to do with, for, and through man.

Suddenly, then, the Bible, with the gospel as its major motif, comes into perspective as "holy history." In this context it is clear that through his relations with the Hebrew people God *indicated* his redemptive purpose in history. Through the birth, life, death, resurrection, and ascension of his Son in history, he has *established* his redemptive purpose in history beyond the shadow of a doubt. In the same events he has *guaranteed* the victorious conclusion of his historical activity.

When the redemptive activity of God makes itself known to a man or a people it comes as *the* good news. Thus the gospel of Jesus Christ is God's revelation of the meaning of man's historical life.

Cultures rise, flourish, and decline in history. Their achievements and their conflicts are historical. In each culture, whatever its achievements or conflicts may be, the church is God's historical instrument, with a message to deliver. It is the gospel that constitutes the message that the church has to deliver to each historical culture, else how can the culture know the meaning of the history of which it is a part?

The Meaning of Existence

But look at the matter, not from the perspective of the long sweep of God's purpose in history, which may seem very remote and impersonal, but from the perspective of the individual life, one's personal existence.

God's redemptive purpose seems to *me* to be very far removed unless *I* am involved in it. My immediate existence consists so largely of the world of my private thoughts and feelings that I tend to perceive my surroundings in terms of the patterns into which I have channeled my subjective needs. I do see what is around, but unwittingly I see it the way I want to see it, the way I am habituated to see it.

Yet I want to live, and to live fully. As I try to do so, I seem to be prevented from it. The great desire of my heart, the thing that will make my life complete, is within my grasp. But even as I reach out for it, it eludes me. Or, if I do succeed in grasping it, it turns out to be not what I thought it would be, and is hardly worth the having.

I realize that what prevents me from living fully is that I see everything essentially from only one vantage point, and that from within. The world turns out to be not what it seems because my apprehension of it is completely distorted by my own desires, my preconceptions, my habits—in a word, by my whole point of view.

Someone tells me that what prevents me from living fully is my sin. Not so much the wrong things I do—they are more results than causes—but a whole warped attitude toward life. The universe as I see it revolves around me. I need to get outside myself, to gain perspective, to see things in *true* proportions and relationships.

Then the enormity of the situation dawns on me. It is arrogantly presumptuous of me to look at life as I do from my human, personal, egocentric point of view. I have simply been ignoring God. I have dethroned him from my life. My sin is thus radical sin, and deserving of death. This deserved penalty I would have to pay for having ignored and dethroned my God.

At the depth of my predicament I hear of the incarnation and the atonement (or I hear of the manger, the teacher, the healer, the cross, and the empty tomb). Then the overwhelming point of a sentence that perhaps had become obscure because of my having used it too much or too early speaks to me—"God so loved the world that he gave his only Son, that whoever believes in him should . . . have eternal life."

And as I respond, the old *I* does die, and he gives me a new birth of life in him.

This is *the* good news. Thus the gospel of Jesus Christ is God's revelation and living achievement of the meaning of existence, even of individual, personal existence.

The Gospel and the Church

In discussing the church and its educational work, I said that the church is the human instrumentality brought into being by God in Christ to continue his ministry of redemption to the world. Plainly, the gospel was and is the soul of that ministry.

The gospel is the reason for the church's existence. The reality of the gospel, its power, and the imperative for its communication brought the church into being. The gospel sustains the church in performing its functions . . . in every generation and in every culture. The gospel, as the church's essential message, informs, directs, and corrects the church.

Thus, in a situation where the church and the culture are in tension (as they always are to some degree), it is the church's business to communicate the gospel. The gospel is what the church says to the culture. The church knows something that the culture does not know but needs to know. It is the work of the church to employ every means to deliver that urgently needed message.

The church's own members live in the tension between the church and the world. If they are, in this situation, to perceive, accept, and fulfill the gospel, every means must be employed to help them to grasp it in all its implications.

To those outside the church's fellowship the gospel must also be communicated by every available means, that they too may perceive, accept, and fulfill it, if that be God's will.

Connections between the Gospel and Christian Education

One of the ministries by which the church communicates the gospel to its members and to those outside is the ministry of teaching. The teaching function of the church is:

1. To deliver the message that in man's extreme need God has forgiven and redeemed him in Jesus Christ. This is urgent.
2. To help those inside and those outside the church to prepare themselves for response to that message.
3. To show them how to respond.
4. To help them to see and work out the fullness of the implications of the message of the gospel for themselves and their world.

If one way by which the church communicates the gospel is by teaching, then the gospel is of central concern to Christian education. Because it sustains such a vital relationship to the church's teaching ministry, there are certain specific connections between the gospel and Christian education that can be pointed out, bringing the whole matter into focus at this point.

Christian education (defined in the fullest sense to include the church and the Christian home) has a task of preparation for response, demonstration of how to respond, and guidance in mature response as it seeks to make persons aware of their living encounter with the gospel. In *In One Spirit* (1958, 17) I put it this way:

> The individual has his choice. He may remain in tragic bondage to self, society, and culture. This is what is meant by "the human predicament." On the other hand he may become a free person, by God's Spirit, through his response in complete devotion to Jesus Christ. Christian education seeks to prepare the individual to respond in faith by the power of the Holy Spirit, to show him how he may respond to the living Word as it is spoken to him, and to guide him into increasingly mature and effective ways of responding to the Holy Spirit and doing the Father's will. This is why Christian education is called the nurture of the Christian life.

The emphasis is clearly on how one becomes a free person through response to the gospel.

This, in turn, makes it even more evident than before that Christian education in the church (again, using the term in the fullest sense) is responsible for assisting persons to perceive the gospel, to accept it, and to see its demands and fulfill them. There is never a time in a person's life or in the life of the church when any one of these aspects may be separated from the other two, but it is helpful in seeing the church's educational task with persons of different levels of experience to point out that in childhood the emphasis is likely to be more on perceiving the gospel, in youth on accepting it, and in maturity on discovering and meeting its ever-changing requirements.

Thus Christian education definitely implies the closest attention to the gospel and to its work at every point. When we examine the objectives of Christian education we will see them in the light of the gospel. When we look at educational procedures, it will be chiefly in the context of the gospel. And when we describe the educational programs and institutions involved (including church and home), the major concern will be with communicating the gospel and nurturing faithful discipleship in the light of it.

Christian education is inextricably bound up with the gospel, but what of education in general? Here, again, some things that have been said before come into focus. Education has to be concerned with helping persons to see things as they are and to come to grips with life. Its indispensable emphasis is on human becoming—the development of free and mature persons. We have seen how the various aspects of so-called secular education—technical education, liberal education, and moral and religious education—can be carried on in the light of the gospel if the learner approaches them from a fully Christian perspective. Something of the results of that approach in increased insights, higher achievement of competence, and a greater sense of having come to terms with life, have been hinted at.

The teacher in so-called secular education, as well as the learner, can do his work within a Christian perspective. If the gospel is what it claims to be, it involves living relationships and a quality of life even more than it does the use of any particular words or the expression of any particular sectarian ideas.

The teacher who, in a secular school, lives and teaches in the assurance of God's redeeming love for him in Jesus Christ, provides a living witness that needs no special words in the classroom. Such a teacher need not, indeed cannot, hide who he is, how he became what he is, what he does as a result, and what it means to him. His whole life, from personal devotions to responsible social action, girds him for his witness.

But the words themselves need not be missing. They cannot be the subject of exhortation in the public classroom. Yet it is the responsibility of every teacher, and especially teachers of subjects dealing with the expression of human needs and values, to point out, among the various approaches to the problems of life, the fact that there is a Christian gospel, and that it provides a distinctive approach to understanding and dealing with human problems.

These are some of the relationships of the gospel to education—both church education and education in general. Consideration of these relationships has brought us to the place where we can summarize the possibility of the gospel as the criterion for education. Is it adequate? Is it simple? Is it clear?

The gospel provides an adequate basis for guiding Christian education because it is integral to the Word of God, because it is the clue to the meaning of history, because it is the clue to the meaning of existence, because it brings the church into existence and gives it its imperative, and because (in educational terms) it is the clue to human becoming.

The gospel provides a simple basis for the guidance of Christian education because, for all its profundity, it may be put in a simple proposition (God's redeeming work on man's behalf in Jesus Christ) and in concrete terms (as concrete as the manger, the teacher, the healer, the cross, and the empty tomb) without losing anything really essential.

The gospel provides a clear basis for the guidance of Christian education because it is easily and readily understandable at many different educational and experience levels.

Conceived as a principle that may be used to assist and guide in the development of objectives, curriculum principles, and principles of administration, this center and focus on the gospel in Christian education may be stated thus: If Christian education will focus its attention on the gospel, it will be properly oriented and conceived. Around the gospel the other elements of Christian education may be grouped, but it is the one element that can stand alone and give the others meaning. The gospel is the essential element in establishing the institutions of Christian education and devising their curriculums.

Here then, in the form of a guiding principle, is summarized the conviction that the central concern of, and norm for, the educational life and work of the church is the gospel—in all its implications for the revelation of God, for the nature and condition of man, for the meaning of history, for individual and social salvation and responsibility, for the significance and mission of the church, and for the fulfillment of human destiny.

For Reflection

1. Why is the gospel so important to Christian education?
2. What might a Christian-education theory be like without the gospel?
3. What is the relationship of the gospel to the church?
4. What is the teaching function of the church and what does it have to do with free personal response?
5. What are the similarities and differences between "secular" and Christian education?

References

Burrows, M. 1946. *An outline of biblical theology.* Philadelphia: Westminster.

Martin, P. A. 1933. *The finality of Jesus for faith.* Edinburgh: T. & T. Clark.

Richardson, A. 1950. *A Theological wordbook of the Bible.* New York: Macmillan.

Wyckoff, D. C. 1958. *In one spirit.* New York: Friendship.

17

Lawrence O. Richards

Creative Bible Teaching
(1970)

The author is widely known in evangelical Christian education circles. He is a graduate of the University of Michigan, Dallas Theological Seminary, and the joint doctoral program at Garrett Seminary and Northwestern University (focus on Christian education and social psychology). Richards has taught at Wheaton College, developed his own line of Sunday school curriculum, lectured extensively, and worked directly with churches. His work comes out of all these experiences and an intensive sense of personal stress and renewal. His books, curriculum materials, and other written contributions number into the dozens. Overall they have been very well received.

Richards presents his theological position on Christian education in *A Theology of Christian Education*. He emphasizes "whole-personness," and his general approach to Christian education is a "socialization" perspective. That is, he considers the best way to nurture faith is through the social contacts an individual has in the family, church, and community. Richards encourages the church to facilitate the growth at home as well as in its own educational processes. He sees the critical issues in Christian education as the roles of Scripture and teacher and personal relationships. He encourages informal and nonformal educational activities rather than limiting education to a schooling point of view. In fact, he feels the church has seriously restricted itself by making too strong an investment in a formal schooling model.

The following excerpt from *Creative Bible Teaching* demonstrates Richards's view of using the Bible. In his discussion he shows his concern for Scripture, teacher, and curriculum. These, as well as a strong concern for interpersonal life-sharing, are themes repeated in much of his writing.

From *Creative Bible Teaching* (Chicago: Moody, 1970), 11–19, 122–27, 139–42.

This Bible

"It's a great book, this Bible we teach!"

That's what Chuck thought as he taught the Bible to his high school class. A great book. God's book! A book that God would use to lead his lively, noisy bunch of guys into a vital, exciting walk with Christ.

That's what Chuck thought.

And he couldn't understand why his faithful, week-by-week Bible teaching didn't seem to touch his teens. Chuck taught. He taught the Bible. But the Bible just didn't seem to work.

There are many teachers like Chuck in our churches. Teaching the Bible—but without effect.

And we'd better begin . . . by asking why.

I once visited a church that helps to bring Chuck's problem, and perhaps yours, into clearer focus. I remember it as a very disturbing church. Oh, it was fundamental—and conservative—and evangelical. What disturbed me wasn't what was said in the pulpit or taught in the classes. What disturbed me was the people.

For one thing, they repulsed "outsiders." One of the farmers went into a feedstore and overheard the tail end of a questionable joke. With a grim and condemning glare at the laughing pair, he turned on his heel and stomped out. Another church family turned down invitation after invitation from neighbors, until the neighbors stopped asking them over. To the folk of the area, the people in this church were a peculiar, forbidding clan with unknown beliefs, but with many known don'ts.

And if you had seen them, you too might have wondered why. Why, when the Bible was believed and known, weren't these people more like those in the early church? Why weren't they men and women marked by their *love,* not their lists; men and women who were far more concerned with communicating Christ to their neighbors than with condemning them for their sins?

Now, I'm not creating a mythical "fundamentalist" and criticizing all believers by clubbing him. I'm describing an actual church. It may or may not be like your church. But it does exist. And the fact that it exists forces us to ask an important question: *How can people who believe the Bible, and who know the Bible, become spiritually warped?*

If we're honest, we can all think of individuals who are warped. Like the youth from a Christian home, brought up through the Sunday school, taught the Bible from toddlerhood, who goes off to college and immediately "loses" his faith. Or the businessman I know who, after training in a famous Bible institute, took a mistress while his wife was carrying their second child. Or the cantankerous old saint who can correct the pastor on any biblical topic, but who can't get along with anyone, and actively feuds with church leaders. Every church has people like these: people who know the Bible, but whose lives are warped out of its pattern. And we wonder, *Why should this be?*

One easy answer is this: "Of course! We're all sinners." No Christian is freed from the warping presence of sin, even though the Bible says we can be free from sin's power. While this is true, it's no solution. When we turn to sin for the explanation, we're really saying that we don't *expect* Christians to be Christlike! That, after all, if we're all sinners, it's only natural that we behave like sinners.

But conservatives do expect Christians to be different. We don't expect *natural* behavior of those whom Christ has touched; we expect *supernatural* behavior. We expect those who know Christ and his Word to be transformed.

That's why people like Chuck and you and me teach the Bible. We believe that men who are by nature sinners and lost can discover themselves in the mirror of the Scriptures. We believe that there they can hear the gospel. We believe that they can learn the good news that God loves us sinners and forgives all who put their trust in his Son Jesus Christ, who became Man and died to bear our sins. A person who receives this message from God and trusts himself to Christ is changed inside. And we believe that through the Word of God, applied by the Spirit of God, this new life within a person can become progressively more dominant, until experience is transformed and the very life of Christ overflows and controls the believer.

We believe this. And this is our problem.

The people in the church I described believed the Bible. They claimed Christ. The youth at one time professed to believe, as did the adulterer and the old critic. And each had gone on to learn more and more Bible. *But the Bible they learned did not transform.* And again we're forced to ask, Why?

How is it that a book, given by God to transform, seems so unproductive when taught in the very churches where it is most honored and best known? And unproductive it seems to have been. Our Christian education has often produced warped personalities; our teaching has often failed to straighten twisted lives. Warping is so common that we've become used to it! Used to shaking our heads about "lost faith" in college and dropouts in high school. Used to congregations and individuals without vitality or dedication or reality in their walk with Christ. Used to an exploding population and a sputtering evangelism. Used to living day after day with men and women who need the Savior, and used to saying nothing to them about him. Used to reading and studying and teaching the Bible without seeing God use it to transform. Are we successful in reproducing the biblical faith in our twentieth-century world? Have we "turned the world upside down" as did the early church? Are our churches filled with spiritual giants?

Hardly! Teaching the Bible as we teach it has not transformed men as our theology says the Word of God should. But why not? Is it possible that we haven't really understood the nature of the Bible we teach? Is it possible that we haven't been teaching the Bible in a way that harmonizes with God's purposes in giving it? . . .

The theology of neo-orthodoxy has now passed from favor in the denominational seminaries. As yet no theology has replaced it as dominant, although the views of Tillich, Bultmann, and Altizer have all had their adherents.

But the neo-orthodox years did serve to focus the attention of Christian educators on the nature of the Bible. And they led to the development of a new theory of the nature and purpose of Scripture that does dominate Christian education today. This theory rests on a distinctive concept of what revelation is, what the place of the Bible is in revelation, and how the Bible should be taught.

And in this respect we have been done a service. For development of this theory has forced us to examine the new view—and our own. We have been forced to look honestly at our own Bible teaching and to ponder why the teaching of the Bible in our churches has been so unproductive in terms of transformed, dedicated, Christ-centered lives if, as we believe, the Bible *is* the written Word of God. We have been forced to ask *theological* questions about our *teaching* of the Bible.

How we need this. How we need not merely to assert the fact of propositional revelation, but to understand the nature of that revelation and to see its implications for our Bible teaching.

Not long ago one of my students at Wheaton College introduced me to teacher Chuck by describing his experience as a high schooler in Sunday school. Here's what my student wrote:

> In our Sunday school class, Chuck followed the book to the letter and usually read the material. The class was all boys and we were from "good" homes, so we behaved fairly well at first; but when we found how far we could push Chuck and how to get a rise out of him, we really cut loose. Even though we used good material and he was prepared, we had little if any net gain from the class. We began to mock Chuck outside of class, and it wasn't long before the attitude spread to the material he was teaching.
>
> As I look back I see that Chuck was sincere and dedicated, but not prepared to teach six or eight teenage boys. As I grew older and less critical I thought of those class sessions at times, especially when the young people would get together and we would laugh about them. But it was hard to remember a class when there was any attempt to relate current events or link up the lesson to daily life. We had nothing to challenge us when we were beginning to challenge what we had been taught, and to test these "adult" ideas that had been thrown at us. We had no occasion to express our imaginative thoughts or sense of humor in the class situation at all, for Chuck believed in a highly structured, formal teaching sit-

> uation, and God's Word was serious business. We were told this, but never really given any sound basis for believing it.

We can't dismiss Chuck as simply another bad teacher—though he certainly was that. We can't charge Chuck with liberalism or with being a "neo." Chuck held firmly to a conservative view of Scripture. To him teaching the Bible and learning it was "serious business."

But Chuck could and did teach the Bible without challenge, without relationship to life, without relevance. Taught the way Chuck taught it, the Bible did not promote spiritual growth; it stunted it!

That's what I meant earlier. Perhaps the Bible hasn't proven effective because we haven't understood how to teach it. Spiritual warping may be the fault of the teacher. The Book of God, given to transform, may be ineffective in the churches where it is most honored because it has been taught wrongly.

You see, God never intended the Bible to be taught as the Chucks among us teach it. And, *if they truly understood the nature of Scripture, they could never teach the Bible as they do!*

As conservative, evangelical Christians, we believe firmly that God uses his Word to transform. Let's make sure we know *how* he uses it before we dare to teach.

Person to Person

"Yes sir, I would like to join the church. I think I'd make a good member. I got the highest grade in church membership class."

"But do you know God?"

"I took a test on Bible, and knew 93 percent of the answers. The national average for that test is only 38 percent."

"But do you know God?"

"When I was growing up I memorized Scripture daily. I review the verses even now. I can quote over two thousand verses."

"But do you know God?"

"Right now I'm working on memorizing whole books of the Bible. I'm just finishing Romans, and the next book I plan to start on is Ephesians."

"But do you know God?"

This is a fair question. Those who know the Bible do not necessarily know God. To the contemporary Christian educator this is an extremely significant fact.

This should be one of the major goals of the Bible teacher: not to keep the learners dependent on him, but to equip them to study the Word independently, and to study it in such a way that they grow. When your teaching conforms to the pattern given in Colossians and you involve your class in the process, your students will develop the ability they need to grow.

Figure 17.1
The Pattern of Self-Guided Application

Principle	Varied Application	Examination of Sensitive Area	Personal Decision
Joy in sacrificing self for others	by listening by visiting sick by helping sick by shopping for sick by baby-sitting by cleaning by having people over by giving up best place or best job ← by putting another first	How do we compete for first place, rather than give? Why? → in church ← at home on job etc.	I will try this week to . . . →

The Process of Guided Self-Application

The pattern described. Stated simply, the pattern (fig. 17.1) is this:

In practice, decisions and responses will normally be made outside of class. During the week when situations arise, each individual will be faced anew with the opportunity to respond. But through the creative process in class you will have equipped your students with eyes opened to new meanings for God's truth, with new sensitivity to its relevance in their lives.

The process illustrated. [Take a] John the Baptist lesson. How might you teach it, using the guided self-application process? Let's see.

You've covered the content and begun generalizing. After some discussion, your teens suggest two qualities John had that they agree other Christians should share:

He pleased God, unconcerned about personal popularity.
He didn't place great importance on material things.

Now in various ways you lead your [students] to see how these qualities would show up in life today. What pressures of popularity exist in the high school world? You think together of times when the desires of the crowd and of God pull different ways. And you get their ideas down on the chalkboard (see fig. 17.2). Moving on, you talk together of ways their friends put a premium on things. These too you record. This is varied application.

Figure 17.2
Guided Self-Application Process:
Record of John the Baptist Class

Generalization	Varied Application	Examination of Sensitive Area	Personal Decision
Please God, not popularity	Cliques Questionable dress fads How about unfriendly witnessing? When hear dirty joke Dates before school work? Do things just to fit in? How "buy" popularity? Friends with unpopular kid? What to do when others cheat Dancing? Invite to Bible club?	Stand up for Christ in locker room How about outsiders? What needs in our group? Why not popular attitude? How to choose friends, get to know for self, meet need?	Invite outsider in Lunch
Not place stress on things	Money habits? Giving? Up-to-date fashions? After-school job vs. study What life goals? Ashamed of poor home? Ashamed of parents' education, manners? Car to get date? How important good looks? Envy others' looks, strength? Know people for themselves	(etc.)	Date carless teen (etc.)

As your class suggests various applications, you notice that the idea of "outsiders" comes up several times. These are the kids who don't fit in, those who aren't in the "in" crowd. Often they are the kids without sharp clothes, a year behind the fashions; the ones without cars, without the looks or wealth that labels others "acceptable." So you now guide your class to think together about this group (closer examination of sensitive area). How would a person like John relate to these kids? What would his attitude be? His actions? What *does* count about a person, if not his money or clothes or appearance? Which is really important: meeting another's needs or making sure of our standing with the gang?

You close the class by pointing out John's greatest quality, the one you haven't discussed. John put Jesus Christ first. And you ask, "If you really want to put Christ first in your life, how might you do it this week? How might you follow him, rather than the crowd, or see people and things from his viewpoint?"

The results? Sally expresses her decision to try to bring a new girl into her group of special friends. Tom the football player, blushing, tells of his determination to speak up for Christ when the talk gets rough in the locker room. Gwen decides to ask an "outsider" to lunch with her in the school cafeteria the very next day. And popular Jan says she'll even accept a date from one of her carless hopefuls!

Well, you think as you leave class, *serious or funny, they do respond. Tom in his quiet, serious way; Gwen, as usual, fluttery and enthusiastic; even superficial Jan.*

And you thank God. Because you realize that while you were the "teacher," it was God who taught.

Choosing Curriculum

In the view of most conservatives, the Bible speaks for itself. We resent (rightly) the idea that some church authority must speak before we can know the true meaning of a passage, or before we can respond to God, who communicates himself to us in his Word. In some churches, and to some individuals, this resentment carries over to Sunday school and other curricula. Writers and editors are viewed suspiciously as claimants of an authority not really theirs.

Certainly no writer or editor can stand as an authority. Even Paul, who actually had apostolic authority, commended the Berean believers for *not* taking his word for truth without checking. Each of us is personally responsible to search the Scriptures to see if the things taught are true. But users of curriculum materials normally aren't seeking an extrabiblical authority. They're users because they need help! They need the help of men trained in theology, just as a pastor needs the help of his commentaries and study resources. And laymen definitely need the help of those educationally expert.

It's help—not authority—that a good curriculum is designed to give.

Values of a curriculum. We see the values when we look at a few of the problems facing us in Christian education. Take, for example, the problem of progressive change. As children mature, they pass through stages marked by changing needs, interests and patterns of thinking and response. This is important, as the Hebrew text of Proverbs 22:6 points up. Children when old will not depart from the "way" they have been taught—*when taught the truths needed in the manner suitable at each stage of development.*

Most of us know that children pass through characteristic periods of change and development. But how many know the implications of these patterns well enough to be sure that a particular approach is geared to the way of thinking and feeling of their class? Few know the Word well enough to choose concepts and passages and stories that fit their students' changing pattern of needs. This is one advantage of using a curriculum. Curriculum writers can be (and usually are) experts on the characteristics of the age groups for which they write. Most laymen, possibly excepting public school teachers, need the expert help and guidance such people can give.

Another problem curricula help solve is sourced in the rapidly changing educational programming of the public schools. Each year new teaching techniques are developed. A lay Sunday school teacher isn't able to keep up. But an editor or writer can. Take, for instance, the primary department editor of one evangelical publisher. Go into her office, and you'll find master lists of vocabulary levels expected in various stages of first, second, and third grades. You'll find current school texts and *My Weekly Reader*. From these resources teaching methods are constantly checked, and new ways of learning introduced into Sunday school lessons. Such lessons are kept challenging and interesting, as new learning skills just mastered in the public schools are called for weekly.

Another closely related problem is found in the variety of resources now used in the public schools. A Christian publisher can match them and provide a variety of learning materials, including visuals, workbooks, take-home papers. When these are used, interest is increased, truths better grasped, and practical applications encouraged. No layman can produce the quantity and quality of supplementary teaching aids that publishing houses make available today.

Finally, there's the need for overall planning. Children develop in loose stages, usually of two or three years' duration. Most Sunday schools are graded to fit these stages, with nursery, beginner, primary, junior departments. When lessons are planned at a publishing house, the editor thinks in terms of the whole stage—the whole two or three years or more. The needs of the age group can be covered in a planned pattern of teaching that, left to themselves, few laymen would devise. For these and other reasons, good curriculum materials are an aid to creative Bible teaching. The creative teacher can draw on and adapt resources that few, if any, laymen can bring to their teaching without curriculum. The problem, then, isn't whether or not to use a curriculum; it's how to choose a good curriculum to use.

Marks of a good curriculum. It's a complicated task, evaluating curriculum. First the overall grading plan is studied. The theology of the materials is determined. The pedagogy and relevance of the lessons at each age level are tested. Anyone interested in learning specifically how to test the Sunday school materials of various publishers and rank them can find out.[1] Our purpose at this point is simply to point out that, in the first and second sections of this book, a teacher or pastor can see crucial areas that must be right if a curriculum is to help laymen teach the Bible. What are they?

A correct view of Scripture and its function. Few conservatives choose curriculum materials that reflect the contemporary view of revelation. Conservatives hold to a propositional concept of revelation: that God reveals true information in his Word. Materials which teach and reflect the view of the new orthodox simply are not acceptable, although some use them because of denominational pressures.

Many evangelical publishers, independent and denominational alike, provide materials that are based securely on the orthodox belief. But too few of these are as clear in their focus on the *function* of propositional revelation. They lose sight of the fact that revelation takes us beyond information to contact with God, and that it calls for appropriate response. . . .

Another error, often found in children and youth materials, is to call for a conduct response, but *not the response demanded by the passage studied.* At times the lessons of most conservative publishers fall into this error. The writer wants the children to be kind and to share. So a passage, such as the feeding of the five thousand, is selected. The focus is on the little boy who shared his lunch. And from this passage, the commandment "You ought to share" is taught. But is this the meaning of the passage? Is "you ought to share" the teaching? Is sharing the appropriate response? Actually, little is said of the boy. He's not focal; Christ is. His act of sharing isn't held up for others to imitate. Jesus Christ's power to meet every need is demonstrated for us to trust.

It's easy to set up our rules of conduct and then to find passages that seem to indicate some biblical support. But this isn't teaching the Bible. It's teaching a legalism that can become crushing. Such teaching obscures for teacher and learner alike the God who reveals himself, and who demands not conformity to a code but response to a Person; a life lived not in cold conformity, but in spontaneous response to God the Spirit.

When a publisher's lessons characteristically fall into either pattern—information without response, or warped response—the lessons should be rejected.

A creative concept of Bible teaching. A good curriculum seeks to raise students' levels of Bible learning. Good curriculum follows (either in individual lessons or units of lessons) the pattern suggested in Colossians 1. Good cur-

1. For a guide to evaluating curriculum, including a carefully developed rating scale, see Lawrence O. Richards, *The Key to Sunday School Achievement* (Chicago: Moody, 1965), chap. 4.

riculum reflects an awareness of the gaps that block response to God. Its lessons aim at response; they exhibit a structure which leads into the Word, explores the Word, and guides students to explore relevance and plan response. In a good curriculum, application is planned for flexibility, maximum student participation, and student self-discovery of the life implications of Bible truths. And good lessons reflect the writer's awareness of structural factors that help create the desire to learn.

What it really boils down to is this: good curriculum has a distinctive philosophy of Bible teaching, and this philosophy is carefully applied in developing each lesson series.

In point of view, few publishers spell out their position on the theological and educational issues raised in this book. Even if they did, users would still have to check their practice against their claimed philosophy! And so the responsibility returns to the users, who expect and pay publishers for Bible teaching *help*. It's up to the men and women in our local churches to select lessons that are theologically and educationally sound.

Using Curriculum Effectively

Published curricula are an aid, but not the answer. All lesson materials are limited in value. When used as a crutch even the best can stifle the freedom and spontaneity, so essential to creative Bible teaching, which the writer hopes to encourage.

A teacher then needs a healthy attitude toward his lesson materials. He'll look to them with appreciation for guidance in the choice of truths relevant to the age group he teaches. He'll expect ideas on the meaning of the passages taught, and a teaching plan that will lead to student response. He'll be glad for new methods and approaches lessons may suggest, and for visuals and other teaching materials. But he will not view his materials as setting a pattern he must follow in class.

A slavish reliance on printed plans, while helpful perhaps for an inexperienced teacher, cuts deply into the potential for creativity. It's not hard to see why. Creative teaching is a process in which students are vitally involved. Often in this process, ideas are developed and needs revealed which no writer can plan for, nor teacher predict. The teacher has to feel free in such cases to respond to the lead of his class and spontaneously follow the guidance of the Holy Spirit. This may mean shortening some learning activities, adding unplanned ones, eliminating some that were planned. This kind of freedom just isn't possible to the teacher who relies slavishly on printed materials.

What then does the teacher need as he enters class? Not a detailed series of steps which he plans to take. He needs instead an overview of the process he hopes to stimulate. He needs a flexible view of the end toward which that process must move. And he needs a view so clear that he can feel free to adapt or change his plans in response to classroom developments, so clear that even with changes he still can lead his students to the climax of learning—response to the God who has spoken to them in his Word.

This need for spontaneity helps us see more clearly what a layman needs to become a creative Bible teacher. He needs first of all an understanding of the nature of the Bible he teaches. Next he needs a clear understanding of how that Bible must be taught, a philosophy of teaching. Finally he needs to develop skill in planning and using learning activities (methods) that will enable him to implement his philosophy!

For Reflection

1. What does Richards seek as the purpose of the Bible in Christian education?
2. What is the role of the teacher?
3. How does Richards suggest making the Bible live?
4. What does he believe will happen to the church when the approach to Bible teaching presented in the excerpt is accomplished?

18

James Michael Lee

Religious Instruction as Social Science

(1971)

James Michael Lee grew up in New York City, where he attended Catholic schools. Early on he was drawn to a life of service to Christ and struggled with whether he should consider the priesthood. He decided that a career as scholar/teacher would offer the most service opportunity for a person with his talents, abilities, and interests. After receiving a master's degree in history from Columbia University, he completed the Ph.D. in education from Teachers College. While at Teachers College, an experience not altogether satisfying, Lee acquired the following basic principles and foci that have become fundamental to his approach to religious education:

> education must start with the learner . . . developmentally; learning takes place primarily according to the psychophysiological functioning of the learner and not primarily with the logical content of the subject matter; content is everything the learner acquires from the teacher, and not just the logical dimensions of the subject matter; the effectiveness of teaching and learning are ascertained by careful empirical research, and not by well-intentioned guesses or speculative opinions; the purpose of education is to foster personal growth in one way or another. (Mayr, 275–76)

From *The Shape of Religious Instruction: A Social Science Approach* (Mishawaka, Ind.: Religious Education Press, 1971), 182–224.

Lee became a college professor and a few years later joined the faculty of Notre Dame University. Within a few years, as the chair of the education department, he initiated a doctoral program in religious education. His time at Notre Dame was not free from controversy, especially in relation to the Catholic hierarchy, and after eight years he left for a faculty position at the University of Alabama, Birmingham.

One of Lee's unique contributions to the field of religious education was the founding of Religious Education Press (REP). The publishing company was begun while he was at Notre Dame and continues to be the only publisher that exclusively markets scholarly books in religious education.

One of the reasons that Lee has been controversial as a scholar is his insistence that religious instruction is a branch of social science rather than of theology. *The Shape of Religious Instruction* lays the foundation for the social-science approach. He believes that instruction in religion is basically the same as instruction in any other school subject: It must follow the principles of learning. Teaching that misses such principles will be ineffective.

Lee is the author of two other books, *The Flow of Religious Instruction* and *The Content of Religious Instruction.* This trilogy establishes his comprehensive and systematic theory of religious instruction. It is intended to be helpful for both Catholic and Protestant educators.

References

Mayr, M., ed. 1983. *Modern masters of religious education.* Birmingham, Ala.: Religious Education Press.

> "You're the illogical one, Meyer.
> You want omelettes for breakfast,
> but you don't want to crack the eggs."
>
> —Morris L. West[1]

I . . . treat[ed] the nature and methodology of both theological science and social science in order to lay the groundwork for an exploration of the question: "Is religious instruction a branch of theological science or a branch of social science?" The answer to this question is of paramount practical importance because on it depend the entire axis and thrust of every aspect of the work of religious instruction. Thus, for example, if we state that religious instruction is a branch of theological science, the preparation of religion teachers will take the form of a primary, if not at times an exclusive, emphasis on deepening the trainees' theological insights and understanding. If, on the

1. Morris L. West, *The Devil's Advocate* (New York: Morrow, 1959), 274.

other hand, we take the position that religious instruction is a branch of social science, the preparation of religion teachers will revolve around the improvement of those understandings and skills which will enable the trainees to most effectively facilitate desired religious behaviors in learners. . . . I intend to reintroduce some of those properties of social science . . . in order to ascertain whether or not religious instruction can be properly said to be a branch of social science. Naturally, I will not now go over each property at length, nor for that matter will I include all the properties of social science. I will present only as much material as is required to illumine the basic point. It is my hope that . . . the reader [can] extract enough information to enable him to make for himself a more lengthy examination of the implications and consequences which result from the placing of religious instruction within the confines of either theological science or social science.

In seeking to ascertain whether religious instruction is a theological science or a social science, it might well be that the very phrase *religious instruction* offers a clue. It will be noted that "religious" is the adjective and "instruction" is the noun. In other words, the term *religious* specifies the kind of instruction that is done. Religious instruction, then, is situated within the total context of instruction, whether instruction is viewed vertically (early childhood instruction, elementary school instruction, secondary school instruction, university instruction, instruction for the professions, instruction for adults; Wyckoff 1967, 393) or horizontally (science instruction, reading instruction, social studies instruction, language instruction).

The substantive noun *instruction* bears witness that religious instruction is characterized by the same objectives, processes, and operational principles as other kinds of instruction, while at the same time being particularized as a certain kind or form of instruction. Perhaps an analogy drawn from philosophy might be helpful here. In the Aristotelian tradition, any substance is conceived as having both being (*esse*) and specificity (*talis*). Thus, a particular substance shares with all other substances similarities which are most fundamental and most ordaining, while also stamped with features which particularize it as this kind of thing rather than that kind. *Esse* provides the existential and ordaining framework for *talis,* much as instruction provides the existential and ordaining framework for the way in which religion operates in this context.

What I am suggesting is that there is a vast difference between religious instruction and instructional religion. Religious instruction is the process of facilitating behavioral modification in learners along religious lines. Instructional religion is the process by which the exercise of religion has educational outcomes as by-products. In a certain theological sense, of course, all instruction is religious and all religion is instructional, and so the ontological distinction between religious instruction and instructional religion is not watertight. In an organically interrelated world, there is considerable overlapping with everything. Yet there is a difference between a church service which is an act of religion and the classroom situation which is an act of instruction. The activities carried out in a church service are shaped primarily by the fact that worship participation constitutes an act of religion whereas the activities of a classroom setting are shaped primarily by the fact that class participation constitutes an act of instruction. Religious instruction and instructional religion alike aim at facilitating a change in behavior; however, the way in which each of these enterprises goes about its facilitation process varies considerably depending on whether the activity is substantively religion or substantively instruction. Any way one wishes to slice it, a church is a church and not a classroom, and a classroom is a classroom and not a church. Indeed, the lack of awareness of this fundamental distinction on the part of both clergy and teachers has resulted in church services sometimes being operated as classes, and classes being turned into prayer meetings.

At this time I do not wish to treat at any length the interrelationship of theology and instruction since these two are joined in the ongoing work of religious instruction. . . . I wish simply to indicate that in religious instruction, religion is done within the general context and ground of the instructional process. In other words, I am suggesting that the very phrase *religious instruction eo ipso* cannotes that religious instruction belongs to social science rather than to theological science.

The Empirical Character of Religious Instruction

One of the chief characteristics of social science, it will be recalled, is its empirical base. Social science, then, is oriented toward working with observable phenomena in such a way that conclusions about the present and future operations of these phenomena are empirically tested and verified. Theological science, on the other hand, tends to operate primarily within a speculative rather than an empirical framework. Of course, theological science is in as close a contact with *a posteriori* data as possible; nonetheless it does not utilize any empirical or objective controls to ascertain the validity and reliability of these *a posteriori* data. Thus Philip Phenix (1966) can remark that whereas social-science theorists like Gordon Allport and Rollo May have a disciplined and empirically verified knowledge of human nature and its integrative drives, theologians such as Johann Metz merely have *a priori* dogmatic premises about human nature.[2]

Put another way, theological science makes statements about human behavior which speculatively follow from certain basic principles but which, from the standpoint of empirical testing and verification, are untested assumptions. An example will perhaps serve to illustrate this point. Ecclesiastical leaders of most Christian churches, from the Roman Church to the Anglican Church to

2. Philip Phenix, it might be noted, is a philosopher of education and sometime theologian.

the Lutheran Church and so on, have down through the centuries asserted that the clerical and religious role of itself bears witness to Jesus and his lifeway, and brings about a closer relationship of the clergyman or religious with his or her spiritual children. A social-science orientation suggests that this is a statement about human behavior, which until empirically tested remains at the level of an assumption. As a matter of fact, there is some empirical evidence which indicated that the theological statement about the behavioral effect of a clerical or religious role is not true. Peter Grande's experimental investigation is relevant in this connection. Grande (1964) studied the behavioral rapport of adolescents in Catholic secondary schools who were counseled by two different groups of counselors who had the same professional training. One group of counselors were laymen; the other group was composed exclusively of clergymen and religious. The investigator found that the rapport achieved by the youths with the lay counselors was superior to that with the clerical or religious counselors. One conclusion of the study was that the youth's awareness that the counselor is a clergyman or religious *eo ipso* lessens the degree of rapport achieved with the counselor. In other words, the religious role seems to act as a barrier inhibiting rapport and indeed inhibiting the client's communication of some personality characteristics.[3] As I have mentioned elsewhere (Lee 1963a), the personality of the counselor after a period of time becomes more functionally important to the client than does his status role; in this way clergymen and religious can indeed achieve effective rapport with their clients. However, this does not at all nullify the fact that theological statements about the positive behavioral effect of the religious role remain at the level of assumptions. The reason is that theological science is intrinsically inadequate to probe the behavioral cause-effect relationship existing between two or more observable human transactional patterns. Speculation can provide a possible clue into why a person behaves in a particular manner; however, it remains for empirical methodology to test and verify this clue. Theological speculation is particularly helpful when some or all of the phenomena under investigation are supernatural in character, and therefore not amenable to empirical methodology.

Religious instruction has as a major concern the discernment of the kind of curriculum and pedagogical methodologies which cause effective learning to take place. Perhaps a contrast between the theological approach and the social-science approach to this problem might be useful in our discussion. Throughout the second half of the nineteenth century, the catechism of the theologian Joseph Deharbe was the most important single vehicle for religious instruction in the Catholic Church in Germany. The pedagogical principle from which Deharbe was operating was that "the most sublime, comprehensive and significant truths are the most abstract truths and can only be taught

3. The instrument which Grande used to measure the degree of rapport experienced by the clients was the Anderson and Anderson Rapport Rating Scale.

as such" (Deharbe, cited in Goldbrunner 1965, 41). One of the most influential religious educators in Germany and Austria in the twentieth century has been the theologian Josef Jungmann who writes: "As a result of the careful ordering of these associated parts (in the catechism) the good news character of the dogmatic structure will be made apparent. Through unswerving concentration on what is taught the chances are that the children will remember basic facts of the Christian faith, even under the most unfavorable circumstances" (1959, 143). Argus Communications, theologically-oriented publishers of *Choose Life,* a popular series of so-called religion non-textbooks in the 1960s and 1970s, declare that this series ". . . begins where revelation happens in the student's experience . . . The materials meet the young person where he is. They draw upon everyday experiences of ordinary life: the spoken word, the newspaper headline, the Madison Avenue gimmick, the sophisticated catchphrase, the tongue-in-cheek editorial, the serious scholar's report, the sights and sounds that are all around us—the world of the 'now' generation" (Kennedy 1968, 5).

A social-science perspective of these statements by Deharbe, Jungmann, and Argus is that they are interesting assumptions which remain assumptions until some hard empirical data can be adduced for their support. The statements of all three sources are declarations about concrete human behaviors. What is the empirical evidence to corroborate Deharbe's claim that abstract truths are the most sublime of all truths, and indeed can be taught only in an abstract form? Did Deharbe or anyone else test the truth or falsity of this assumption by finding out how, in reality, children do in fact learn? What is the empirical support for Jungmann's assertion that a careful ordering of the curriculum around a logical axis will indeed make the kerygmatic thrust of dogmatic truths apparent to the learners? Also, what evidence does Jungmann advance to bolster his affirmation that "unswerving concentration on what is taught" will help insure that the child will learn what the curriculum makers intend for him to learn? What empirical investigations have been made to ascertain if real-life children actually do acquire from a curriculum structure what Jungmann states flatly they will acquire? Where are the hard data to confirm Argus's *a priori* assumption that its instructional materials begin where revelation happens in the student's experience? How does Argus know when revelation happens in a young person's experience? Argus also claims that its materials meet the young person where he is. Are there any empirical data to support the contention that the "sophisticated catchphrase," or the "tongue-in-cheek editorial," the "Madison Avenue gimmick," or indeed the "serious scholar's report" are where the youth in a rural backwoods community is existentially at? How culture-fair is the Argus series? What empirical research has Argus employed even in such a methodologically primitive category as insuring that the vocabulary and concepts used are consonant with the empirically verified norms of the adolescent population at which the series is aimed?

It may well be that the *a priori* assumptions made by theologians and theologically-oriented religious educators are true. The point I am attempting to make is that the task of religious instruction is to enhance the probability of the individual's acquiring the desired learning outcome. In order to maximize this probability, we must have data which indicate how learning takes place, and what pedagogical conditions optimally promote this learning. This is fundamentally the work of social science. Effective religious instruction cannot operate on untested assumptions.

To be sure, untested assumptions abound in the literature. It would not be surprising if religion teachers, dependent as they are on leadership from the specialists, operate their own pedagogy on the basis of these untested assumptions rather than on the basis of what has been empirically validated. Despite the mass of hard data on child and adolescent development, it is astonishing to discover how many religious instruction writers employ untested assumptions about child and adolescent development instead of seeking to test their assumptions either experimentally or by a comparison with the extant empirical data. A few examples will suffice to concretize the point. Anna Barbara, an American religion teacher at the secondary level, declares that "psychologically, the adolescent is ripe for eschatology" (1963, 466). Barbara's statement represents a generalization about adolescent behavior—but where are her empirical data to indicate whether her generalization is valid or not? Perhaps she gleaned her generalization from the high school youth whom she taught. If this is so, her statement remains at the hypothetical level only, since she has not tested it within the context of methodological controls. Pierre Ranwez, a European theologian with an interest in religious instruction, states that obedience is the child's first virtue, and that obedience practiced in love constitutes the basic Christian attitude (1963, 90). The second part of his statement is a theological affirmation, while the first part is a declaration of child development. Where are the empirical data to confirm Ranwez's generalization that obedience is the child's first virtue? Certainly most child psychologists would disagree on the basis of the relevant empirical research findings.[4] While Ranwez's assumption is rejected by the hard data, there is evidence to indicate that as late as the early 1960s, Catholic clergy tended to base their parochial school programs on this assumption. Thus, for example, Gerhard Lenski's empirical study revealed that 81 percent of the Catholic clergy investigated ranked obedience as far more important than intellectual autonomy

4. See Elizabeth B. Hurlock, *Child Development*, 4th ed. (New York: McGraw-Hill, 1964); Arthur T. Jersild, *Child Psychology*, 6th ed. (Englewood Cliffs, N.J.: Prentice-Hall, 1968); Lawrence J. Stone and Joseph Church, *Childhood and Adolescence*, 2d ed. (New York: Random House, 1968); Justin Aronfreed, *Conduct and Conscience* (New York: Academic Press, 1968); Leonard Berkowitz, *The Development of Motives and Values in the Child* (New York: Basic, 1964); John Bowlby, *Child Care and Growth of Love*, ed. and abr. Margery Fry (London: Penguin, 1953); Hugh Hartshorne, *Childhood and Character* (Boston: Pilgrim, 1919).

as a key learning outcome in the school (1961, 240). Randolph Crump Miller, one of America's leading theologically-oriented Protestant religious educators, writes that the primary school child "wants to be a member of the church and know that he is recognized as such. At seven he will like the church's worship as an aid to his inner life. He will be sufficiently aware of death to ask questions about it" (1950, 112). What data exist to confirm that the primary school child wants to be a member of the church? Why does not Miller adduce hard data to support his contention that at seven, the child likes the church's worship as an aid to his inner life? What does the research say on the primary school child's concept of death?

In highlighting the importance of empirically verified data for the work of religious instruction, I am not suggesting that social science provides the entire framework for religious instruction. To be sure, the work of the supernatural constitutes a central variable in the enterprise of religious instruction. However, the supernatural cannot be measured by empirical procedures. Indeed, theological science itself seems hard pressed to make any sort of accurate assessment of the supernatural effects of religious instruction. But the evaluation and improvement of a particular religion class or religion curriculum are dependent upon the degree to which the learner's behavior is being modified along desired religious lines. Consequently some sort of judgment must be made about the relative effectiveness of teaching method *x* compared with teaching method *y*, or of curriculum *a* compared with curriculum *b*. It is proper to assume, I think, that an increase in faith and charity and other supernatural virtues will cause a related change in the religious behavior of the learner to the extent that he has acquired one or more of these supernatural qualities. If supernatural enhancement has no visible effect on one's daily living, perhaps the Christian religion is in vain. Empirical methodology, then, is useful in assessing the religious effects on the learner's life of one or other teaching method or curriculum structure or instructional materials. From the data, we may make a legitimate inference as to the augmentation of this or that supernatural quality in the learner. For example, if we study two groups of matched youths, being taught by different instructional methods, and observe over a protracted period of time that Group A practices love of neighbor more than Group B does, then we may infer that the instructional method used with Group A is more effective than the method used with Group B in producing those behaviors identified with the virtue of charity.

Verification in Religious Instruction

In theology, verification for propositions comes from faith or from the Bible or from tradition, or from natural reasoning, or from the magisterium (or the church). In other words, verification comes from a speculative, authoritative source which in an important way lies external to the phenomena.

In M. D. Chenu's words, ". . . theology, being the child of faith, can only exist in submission to the Word of God, in loyalty to its mysteries, in obedience to its dogmas and consequently in the absence of any evidence for its basic principles" (1964, 89). In social science, on the other hand, verification for propositions comes from controlled observation and empirical testing of the phenomena and their relation, according to the method of difference or one of the other general methods. Let us look at a typical religious instruction activity in order to ascertain which method of verification is most appropriate. A teacher in a certain religion class wishes to have his students learn to relate the Christian teaching of love of neighbor to their everyday life. How does this teacher verify that he has succeeded in his attempt? Will the magisterium provide him with an accurate answer? Of what help are Scripture and tradition in assessing the effectiveness of the lesson? Does faith somehow provide the answer to the lesson's level of success? Or perhaps is it necessary to use empirical methods to ascertain the degree to which these students are in fact relating their class learnings to their out-of-class life?

An empirical study conducted by Milton Rokeach (1970), a social scientist, will possibly illustrate this point. This investigator explored the relation between an individual's religious values and the degree of his compassionate social outlook. From the viewpoint of theological science, there would obviously be a high correlation, since the person having more expressly religious values would presumably be living a richer life of faith; further, such a person is in closer contact with the Bible, and his elevated level of church attendance and fidelity to the magisterium (or church) would serve in addition to produce a high correlation. Rokeach's carefully conducted attitudinal survey of over one thousand adult Americans in a national sample revealed that religious values are more or less irrelevant as guides in ascertaining the degree of compassionate social outlook. Indeed, Rokeach noted that the findings suggest a pervasive social outlook among those with high religious values which seems incompatible and often opposite to the compassion taught in the Sermon on the Mount. For example, the respondents were asked whether they had felt anger on learning the news of Martin Luther King's murder, or whether the assassination had made them "think about the many tragic things that have happened to Negroes and that this was just another one of them." Those persons who scored highest on religious values, notably in their emphasis on salvation as a prime Christian value, were insensitive to such feelings—"it never occurred to me." On the other hand, those not so salvation-minded were most likely to have experienced such reactions of compassion. Rokeach's investigation confirms and extends earlier social-science findings that an individual's belief in Christian teachings often bears no relation to his concern with Christian moral practice.

Jesus frequently made use of empirical verifiers to confirm the truth and validity of his teachings for those to whom he was giving religious instruction. Again and again we read in the Gospels something akin to what he told the nobleman whose son lay sick at Capernaum: "You must see signs and miracles happen, or you will not believe" (John 4:48). Jesus, then, employed empirically observable and testable experiences to act as verifiers for the supernatural cause-effect relation which he stated as true. The use of such verifiers, obviously, accomplished a pedagogical purpose. An illustration of Jesus' use of empirical verifiers in his work of religious instruction is as follows:

> When he returned to Capernaum some time later, word went round that he was back; and so many people collected that there was no room left, even in front of the door. He was preaching the word to them when some people came bringing him a paralytic carried by four men, but as the crowd made it impossible to get the man to him, they stripped the roof over the place where Jesus was; and when they had made an opening, they lowered the stretcher on which the paralytic lay. Seeing their faith, Jesus said to the paralytic, "My child, your sins are forgiven." Now some scribes were sitting there, and they thought to themselves, "How can this man talk like that? He is blaspheming. Who can forgive sins but God?" Jesus, inwardly aware that this was what they were thinking, said to them, "Why do you have these thoughts in your hearts? Which of these is easier: to say to the paralytic, 'Your sins are forgiven,' or to say, 'Get up, pick up your stretcher and walk?' But to prove to you that the Son of Man has authority on earth to forgive sins"—he said to the paralytic—"I order you: get up, pick up your stretcher, and go off home." And the man got up, picked up his stretcher at once and walked out in front of everyone, so that they were all astounded and praised God saying, "We have never seen anything like this." (Mark 2:1–12).

What I am suggesting in this section, and indeed in this entire chapter, is that social science is far more helpful than is theological science in verifying both the level and effectiveness of religious instruction. In fact, theological science by its very nature is not equipped to verify the level of effectiveness of the teaching-learning process.

T. W. Dean writes that confronted with the mysteries of the world, man feels a positive need to acknowledge the transcendence of God (1963, 246). How would theological science verify this to be the fact that Dean says it is? Some theologians might hold that such a need represents a wishful projection on the part of man. Others might note that confrontation with the mysteries of the world leads man to seek the God within rather the God "up there." And so forth. Dean is making a statement about human behavior—psychological behavior, to be precise. Attempts to verify this behavior by theological science result in all sorts of conflicting speculative theories.

The German theologians who gave birth to the Munich Method for religious instruction based much of their approach on the notion that understandings give rise to convictions and to improved religious attitudes (Goldbrunner 1965a, 43). Once again, theologians are making statements which by their very nature cannot be verified by the methodology proper to theological science. To be sure, social-science research investigations have concluded that understandings do not necessarily give rise to convictions, and when they do so, it is within the framework of selected conditions. There are other more powerful ways of effecting convictions than by improving understanding. Perhaps an example will reinforce my point. One social-science researcher found in his study that penitentiary inmates and college students, when asked to rank the Ten Commandments in the order of importance to themselves, came to a high degree of similarity in their responses (Simpson, 1933). The college students had a deeper understanding of the Ten Commandments than did the penitentiary inmates. However, this higher level of understanding of the Ten Commandments on the part of the college students did not result in their having convictions about the relative personal worth of these commandments which were substantially different from those of the penitentiary inmates.

Catholic theologians for centuries have strongly believed in the efficacy of retreats to significantly alter the attitudes and convictions of those individuals making the retreat. These theologians have further asserted that a closed retreat is more effective in altering attitudes and convictions than is an open retreat.[5] The special retreat masters as well as parish clergymen have repeatedly testified that significant changes were wrought in the attitudes, values, and lives of those making the retreats. But in recent decades, other retreat masters and clergymen have reported that retreats had relatively little effect on the retreatants. Is theological methodology capable of assessing this contradictory evidence and establishing the truth or falsity of one of these statements? Thomas Hennessey (1962) decided to employ the tools of social science to learn the answer and so make a verification. Hennessey's study dealt with the changes and with the permanence of changes in the religious ideals of Catholic high school students following a closed retreat and a control group in an open three-day retreat. He investigated an experimental group of these youths in a closed three-day retreat. Hennessey's data indicated a pronounced improvement in the former group as compared with the latter in expressed religious ideals at the conclusion of the respective retreats. Five months later, however, there were no statistical differences between the groups in the area of religious ideas; in fact, the religious attitudes of students were just about as they had been before the retreat. Whereas the attitudes had not been altered, religious practices such as church attendance had improved in the experimental group.

5. A closed retreat is that period of prayer and spiritual reflection conducted in an environment devoid of any contact with the outside, temporal, everyday world. Such retreats are typically held in monasteries or so-called retreat houses situated in some isolated milieu which promotes withdrawal from the world. An open retreat is that period of prayer and spiritual reflection conducted in an environment in which there is contact with the outside world. Retreatants in such milieux typically return home in the evenings, listen to the radio or watch television, read secular magazines—all in addition to the regular horarium of prayer and spiritual reflection.

The Place of Prediction in Religious Instruction

One of the primary aims of social science is to predict future behavior or occurrences on the basis of laws derived from empirically observed and verified phenomena. Prediction of the learner's behavior is of paramount importance in religious instruction; indeed, it might be said that a cardinal objective of all pedagogical activity is to modify the learner's behavior along desired lines. The religion teacher operates on the probability that a certain product content and a certain instructional process will cause a desired learning outcome in the student. For example, in his attempt to teach students to appreciate the Christian value of suffering, the teacher will utilize teaching method *x* in preference to method *y* because he predicts method *x* will be more effective in this case.

This kind of prediction is uniquely the work of social science and not of theological science. It is social science that is methodologically equipped to empirically ascertain which set of pedagogical variables interacts in such a way that the learning outcome of this interaction can be accurately forecast by the teacher or by the appropriate educational authorities. To predict that desired learning outcomes will take place in students, the social scientist tests which conditions must exist and how these conditions must be shaped in order to forecast that an individual will effectively learn one particular thing rather than either another thing or nothing at all. It is the work of social science, not of theological science, to evolve both laws of teaching and laws of learning from empirically verified facts. And it is by the judicious use of these empirically derived laws that the religion teacher goes about his work of facilitating learning as optimally as possible. One important function of a law of learning is to enable the teacher to choose that pedagogical approach and strategy which will most effectively bring about the desired learning outcome. Thus the law essentially has a predictive function. For example, it is a law of learning that positive reinforcement results in significantly higher retention of learned material than no reinforcement. Hence if an adolescent learns that compassion is a deeply Christian virtue, the teacher will attempt to reinforce this learning by some positive reward. In doing so, the teacher is guided by yet another law of learning, namely, that the more immediate is the reinforcement of the learned behavior, the higher is the retention. In selecting the suitable kind of immediate reinforcement, the teacher acts on still another law of learning, namely that peer-group reinforcement is more effective for adolescents than is reinforcement from the teacher.

Let us say that a teacher is working with a group of parents in evolving a preschool religious education program for their toddlers. What should he suggest concerning the punishment of their little ones for various kinds of offenses? A conservative theologian might urge fair but rigorous punishment, in keeping with the biblical maxim, "Do not withhold correction from a child, for if you strike him he shall not die. You shall beat him with the rod and deliver his soul from hell" (Prov. 23:13–14). A liberal theologian might counsel a more moderate approach. A social scientist, on the other hand, would find out what the empirical research has to report on the effects of punishment and nonpunishment on the present and future conduct of children. He would discover among other things that the more severely children are punished for aggression by their mothers, the more aggressive they become during their preschool years (Sears et al. 1953, 214). By using the tools of this science, the social scientist occupies a more favored position in predicting future behavior than does the theologian employing the tools of his science.

Perhaps another example will illustrate the point I am making. Beginning with the Council of Trent, Catholic theologians and indeed the magisterium itself forcefully have stated that an environment totally isolated from the world provides the most effective training milieu for its future priests. The theologians at the Second Vatican Council reversed this centuries-old position, predicting that an environment providing contact with the world and with so-called secular persons would produce a more effective priest. Using their own research tools, social scientists have made independent research investigations into the comparative results of isolated versus nonisolated seminary environments in predicting the effectiveness of future priests trained in each of these milieux. John Murray attempted to assess the influence which traditional seminary training exerted on personality. Murray found an increase in psychological deviancy during the seminary years, and a sharp regression toward the normal after ordination when the young men perforce left the confines of the isolated seminary setting (1957).[6] Richard Vaughan investigated the personality change in students who lived in traditional isolated Roman Catholic seminaries versus those who lived in university-based Roman Catholic seminaries. Vaughan's study examined four groups of seminarians, two of which lived either on a university campus in separate boarding facilities or in a residential seminary while attending all their classes on a university campus. The other two groups were domiciled in the traditional isolated seminary milieu. Each group was tested twice by the investigator: once before entering the seminary and again after completing from one to nine years as seminarians. All four groups received the first two years of their training in an isolated seminary setting. Groups B and C attended classes for one year at a university. Group A spent the entire time in a traditional isolated seminary as did Group D also; however, Group D began teaching after six or seven years of training. Vaughan's study concluded that "those students who received all their training in the traditional seminary environment showed the greatest shift in the direction of abnormality." He further found that whereas changing the loca-

6. Murray used 400 Catholic college students, major and minor seminarians, and priests in his sample population. His instruments were the Minnesota Multiphasic Personality Inventory and the Guilford-Zimmerman Temperament Survey.

tion of training from the traditional isolated seminary setting to a university campus failed to offset the effects of previous self-centered training in the case of junior college seminarians, it did so to a degree in the case of the more mature university seminarians (1970).[7] Surely the social science research conducted by such men as Murray and Vaughan serves as more reliable predictors than do the pronouncements of theologians vis-à-vis the effect on student personality of traditional isolated seminary environments versus university-based seminary milieux.

To be an effective teacher is to so shape the learning environment that its conditions will be optimally conducive to the attainment of a desired learning outcome. Unless the teacher consciously and deliberatively shapes the instructional environment, he will not be able to predict the learning outcome. Lacking this, teaching is reduced to chance, to some sort of vague get-together. It is the purpose of social science to furnish the teacher with those hard data, those facts, and those laws which enhance the probability that the students will learn what is meant to be learned. The attitude of a theologian toward the work of prediction in religious instruction is quite the opposite, as the following quotation from Gabriel Moran demonstrates: "The Spirit works where he wills and how he wills, and it is not for man to control him. The catechist, like the apostle, invites man to respond to God, but when, where, and under what conditions is not for the catechist to decide. What the catechist can do is show what a Christian life is by living one" (1966, 67). In terms of religious instruction, I believe Moran's view misses the mark. The pedagogical problem is not controlling the actions of the Spirit, but rather shaping the learning conditions in such a way that the Spirit will be enabled to most fruitfully operate. Indeed, I suspect it is bad theology to imply that no intimate connection exists between the supernatural world and the natural world. If the Scriptures show anything, they show that God's holy men were constantly engaged in a struggle to shape political, social, cultural, environmental, and pedagagical conditions so that the Spirit could act in an effective manner. The notion of willy-nilly chance promoting the effective operation of the Spirit seems quite foreign to the activities recounted in the Bible.

Hard empirical data, then, together with empirically-derived laws enable the teacher and curriculum builder to predict which variables will most effectively achieve the learning of desired outcomes under given conditions. This procedure is of its nature proper to social science rather than to theological science, as is illustrated by the following quotation from a European theologian interested in religious instruction: "The catechist himself should not begin with God and then treat of Christ, the church, the sacraments and the moral law. He should begin rather with the sacramental life, discuss our attitudes

7. For additional data on seminary preparation, see James Michael Lee and Louis J. Pulz, eds., *Seminary Education in a Time of Change* (Notre Dame, Ind.: Fides, 1965).

toward it and the frustrations we experience, and only then delve into those matters which cast light and clarity on Christian living" (Jungmann 1959, 362). What this theologian is doing is attempting to predict the order in which topics should be introduced in the curriculum to optimally promote learning. His decision on the ordering was made on theological grounds. But on what basis does theological science predict that such-and-such a curricular ordering does indeed result in facilitating learning? Does the whole matter of determining what does or does not facilitate learning properly fall within the competence of theological science? Or is such a determination more in line with the work of social science which has as its axis the critical testing and verifying of past causative factors in the teaching-learning process so that, as a consequence, we can predict what will happen when similar kinds of teaching-learning activities take place?

The Conditionality of Religious Instruction

The teaching-learning process always takes place within some kind of existential context. Interactive relations among phenomena never occur in isolation. A person learns a particular product or process because all the conditions necessary to cause this learning are present and interacting in such a way as to produce a particular learning outcome. If any of the conditions change, then it is possible that the learning might not be produced. For example, a young person might be able to readily learn the meaning of a particular scriptural passage in a class taught early in the day, but experience considerable difficulty in grasping the meaning when the class is taught after his lunch period. In this case, time is a significant condition which, when altered, affects the rate and quality of learning.

It would seem that social scientists tend to be more deeply aware of the results of altering contextual conditions than do theological scientists. The reasons for this do not seem to have been explored to any degree of depth. Perhaps it is because conditionality forms such an intimate part of the investigative method of social science. In any event, the greater sensitivity to conditionality on the part of social scientists enables them to explain and predict more accurately than the theologian those conditions which promote or hinder religious learning. An example might illustrate this point. Angela Dolores Goldbeck, a religion teacher who bases her pedagogy on theological science, writes as follows: "Talking with God, discussing the joys and sorrows, the painful process of growing up, and other problems with this Friend, has to be done in the quiet of one's own heart. Therefore, a time should be provided after the religion lesson, with 'heads down' on folded arms, to think of something heard or enjoyed during that lesson. . . . Needless to say, a real personal love for Christ, and through him of the Father and the Holy Spirit, is one of the major consequences of this growth in informal meditation for God can never be outdone in generosity" (1966, 20–21). Goldbeck's position on the effectiveness of a "heads down" meditative period might hold true with the children in her particular class. However, suppose the conditions were changed so that Goldbeck's pupils came from a different social class, or that they belonged to a totally different culture, or that they were brain-damaged, and so forth. Under such altered conditions, the effectiveness of her teaching method may or may not hold true. In other words, the effectiveness of her method, strictly speaking, cannot be generalized to other than her own group of children; broadly speaking, statements about the effectiveness of her method can be generalized to situations in which the population and the other conditions are similar to the original situation. (Parenthetically, a social scientist would pose several serious questions to Goldbeck on the basis of her statements. What substantiating data does Goldbeck have for her statement that talking with God has to be done in the quiet of one's own heart? What data does Goldbeck adduce to show that her lesson was indeed effective in terms of promoting real personal love for Christ? In this connection, Goldbeck supports her position that the "heads down" method is effective because God can never be outdone in generosity. Is this adequate verification of the effectiveness of the "heads down" method? Operationally defined, what are Goldbeck's criteria for real personal love for Christ?)

Social scientists have learned from the data that there is a host of conditions which, when altered, significantly change the interactive relations in any given context. It has been found, for example, that crime is more prevalent among men, persons from low socioeconomic groups, certain minority groups, urban dwellers, and the less religious, than among women, persons from high socioeconomic groups, majority group members, rural dwellers, and the more religious (Berelson and Steiner 1964). In other words, a person's sex, socioeconomic group, membership in minority or majority group, place of residence, and religiosity are all conditions which significantly influence the rate of his criminality or probable criminality. Similarly, it has been found that school life and school performance are also greatly influenced by a host of conditions, including the learner's sex, socioeconomic environment, familial setting, and so forth (Lee 1963b). Indeed, it has been found that the school environment itself represents an important condition serving to stimulate or stifle learning (Coleman 1961). A review of the pertinent empirical research concludes that even such a relatively "minor" condition as group size can affect the performance and learning of members of the group (Thomas and Fink 1963).

What I am suggesting is that it is the work of social science rather than the work of theological science to supply the facts and the laws indicating the causal relationship of a collection of conditions upon learning. The teacher acts as a social scientist, not as a theologian, when he makes the decision that the deployment of one reaching strategy (condition) in preference to another teaching strategy (condition) will bring about the desired learning outcome.

And it is this act of structuring the conditions in such a way as to bring about desired learning which is the very essence of religious instruction.

Replication in Religious Instruction

The religion teacher is continuously seeking to increase the effectiveness of his pedagogical activity. In the process of doing this, he continuously seeks empirical tests to ascertain whether some pedagogical approach or strategy which seemed effective in the past is still effective. Or again, he seeks to test whether the conditions in his present instructional setting are sufficiently similar to those prior instructional milieux in which teaching method *x* has consistently been found by social scientists to be more effective than teaching method *y*. In other words, to maintain and improve his instructional effectiveness, the religion teacher in his own way is seeking to replicate the conditions which either he himself or social scientists have found will insure that the students attain desired learning outcomes.

Research conducted by social scientists on teaching effectiveness or on learning outcomes tends to have more objective validity and reliability than do "homemade" empirical tests constructed by the religion teacher in his particular setting. Therefore, the religion teacher will naturally be in close contact with the relevant research data so that he might replicate in his own classroom those conditions which social-science investigations have demonstrated bring about effective learning. Let me give two examples of how a religion teacher might go about this. In the 1930s and 1940s, there was much experimentation in public schools on the effectiveness of the so-called core curriculum. The core curriculum is one which centers around interdisciplinary problems of both eternal and personal concern. Subject matter is brought into the learning situation as it is needed to solve the problem being studied, without respect to precise subject-matter boundaries. Thus, for example, a study of the problem of social injustice might bring in such diverse subject areas as the history of the American Negro, music of the slaves, literature on man's inhumanity to man, religious writings on the topic, surveys of black attitudes, and so forth. The conclusions of carefully conducted research investigations into the learning outcomes derived from core as compared with those derived from subject-centered classes have almost consistently revealed the superiority of core. The results of the eight-year study, for example, showed that students from schools with core curriculum scored higher in college than did matched students from schools utilizing the traditional design (Aiken 1942). Wayne Wrightstone's report of a study comparing students in experimental core classes with matched pupils from the traditional curriculum in New York City high schools discovered that core pupils received significantly higher scores in all subjects except Latin grammar (1936). Results of other studies on core came to much the same conclusions (Lee 1963b). Reviewing all this research on the core curriculum, the religion teacher in a particular church-related high school decides that he would like to enhance student learning by embarking on a core curriculum. Working with the teachers, students, parents association, and school officials he secures enough students to form an experimental group of youth who will opt for the core curriculum. Then he sets about to create conditions which are sufficiently similar to the instructional and curricular conditions of the original experiments. Next, he replicates the core program, with the assurance that there is a strong probability that he will achieve results similar to those obtained in earlier experiments. In other words, this religion teacher is using the replicability of social science to improve the instructional program.

Whereas my first example centers around the replication of an experiment, my second example will be based on replication of a survey to improve the instructional program. In 1961 Gerhard Lenski reported the results of a carefully-conducted piece of survey research which concluded that the Catholic schools investigated appeared not to be developing those attitudes, beliefs, values, and intellectual orientations which make it possible for individuals to enjoy working (1961, 248). A religion teacher in a Protestant school setting might wonder if Lenski's findings could also point to one outcome of his own school program. Or a Catholic religion teacher might be eager to learn whether Lenski's 1961 data are applicable to his school during the current year. Both of these teachers can administer Lenski's instrument, either in its original form or in a revised version, to ascertain the impact of the school program on work attitudes. By replicating Lenski's survey, utilizing a social-science approach, these religion teachers can separate what is fact from what is fiction or what is wishful thinking on the part of teachers, school officials, and parents.

The Function of Objectivity in Religious Instruction

All along the line, the religion teacher must make sure that each individual is really learning what the teacher, the individual himself, and the rest of the group perceive he is learning. Just because a teacher or a parent believes that an individual has acquired a specified learning outcome is no proof that the individual has indeed acquired that outcome. In other words, the teacher must objectively verify the extent to which the individual has acquired the desired learning outcome. The process of objective verification of learning outcomes is more suited to the work of empirically-oriented social science than to that of theological science. In the process of objectively verifying the acquisition of learning outcomes, the religion teacher utilizes an many controls as possible to insure a filtering out of subjective bias or expectancy on his part. Thus, for example, he administers a standardized test to an individual, or he uses objectively derived measuring instruments to assess the degree to which the individual has operationalized the hypothesized learning outcome in his life. To illustrate: the religion teacher believes that method *x* is superior to method *y* in causing a particular learning outcome. How does the teacher really know that his students are achieving a higher rate of learning as a result of method *x*? Perhaps the teacher has a conscious or unconscious emotional preference for method *x*. Possibly the students prefer method *x* because it is more enjoyable and they express greater satisfaction with this method (learner satisfaction may or may not be related to the degree of learning which has taken place). Objective criteria are needed to establish the reality of the situation.

Some illustrations might serve to throw additional light on this point. Billy Graham believes he has accomplished a great deal of permanent behavior modification along religious lines for the crowds who have attended his prayer gatherings. Yet an objective empirical follow-up study discovered little if any such change among a significant percentage of those who attended Graham's services (Vernon 1967, 45).

Daniel Brown, a theologically-oriented university professor, has proposed a method which he personally perceives as effective for teaching the Old Testament to college students. His method is to concentrate on one area of the Israel phenomenon, "thus reducing the material to what can be properly handled in a semester and doing so as a privileged example of a living tradition, a tradition continuing today, which the student can enter into and make his own, thus bringing out the true relevance of the Old Testament to his personal life." While he does not spell out his specific pedagogical methodology, it seems safe to infer that Brown relies pretty much on lectures, assigned readings, written assignments, and an examination (1968–69). From a social-science viewpoint, Brown's perception of the effectiveness of his teaching methodology poses several serious problems relating to objective criteria. Are Brown's students learning as effectively as Brown perceives they are? After all, *to be* is not the same as *to be perceived*. What are the criteria Brown uses for assessing whether or not his evaluation of their written assignments and final examination is truly objective? In other words, what objective controls are built into the evaluation procedure to insure that Brown does or does not consciously or unconsciously compose and/or evaluate the assignments and the test in such a way as to be perceived by him as justifying his judgment about the effectiveness of his class? What objective evidence does Brown bring forward to verify that his method is more effective than other teaching methods in causing learning? Assuming for a moment that Brown's method is instructionally effective in his own case, what objective criteria does he employ to generalize that this pedagogical method is effective for all other teachers as well?

Randolph Crump Miller, a theologically-oriented Protestant specialist in religious education, writes: "In most cases, it is my opinion that eighth- and ninth-graders will attack content that is external to themselves. This is why a course on Old Testament is sound procedure. It is history, which many of them enjoy" (1956, 69). The personal opinion of so experienced a religious education specialist as Miller surely carries weight; however, there is considerably more validity to empirically-derived objective verification. There is indeed empirical research to support Miller's belief that external content is not too meaningful to eighth- and ninth-graders; these data constitute a more sound and objective verifier than does Miller's subjective opinion. A course in Old Testament itself is sound procedure if it is appropriate to the maturational level of the eighth- and ninth-graders in question. Objective evidence on the psychological stages of these children, rather than one's personal opinion, should serve as the basis for assessing the effectiveness of a course on Old Testament.

Throughout the world in recent years, there has been a great deal of anxiety on the part of older people in particular that sexual practices, notably among young adults, are deteriorating considerably from the "good old days." Theologians and religious educators have voiced concern in this area. But the social scientist asks the question: What is the objective verification that sexual practice today is considerably more permissive than in the "good old days"? In France in the 1960s, some social scientists sought an objective answer to this question. It is an empirically verified fact that the period of human gestation is normally nine months. By the use of statistical methods, it is possible to infer with reasonable accuracy the degree of deviation from this mean point. The French social scientists then examined parish records for a three-hundred-year period, from the mid-seventeenth century up until the year of their study. They compared the day-month-year of a couple's marriage with the day-month-year of the birth of their first child. If the interval was significantly less than nine months (with statistical allowances for the probability of a nonnormal gestation period), the social scientists inferred there was sexual permissiveness. The conclusion was that no matter what major variable was taken into account—war or peace, famine or plenty, eighteenth or twentieth century, and so forth—the rate[8] of inferred premarital pregnancy tended to be approximately the same. Such a study provides objective rather than impressionistic data.

All sciences are characterized by a certain degree of objectivity. Yet it seems safe to assert that social science of its very nature represents a greater attempt than that made by theological science to insure a total objectivity. Theologians declare that theology inevitably bears the mark of its time. Theology is influenced by the period in which it is done, and in turn seeks to influence that period as well. This does not mean that theological science is shaped totally by an era, but rather that the way in which it is done reflects to a significant extent the Zeitgeist (Rahner and Vorgrimler 1965). One need only think of the biblical and theological interpretations of slavery and the black man formulated in different epochs or in different parts of the world to see the influence of the Zeitgeist on theologizing. Further, as Theodor Filthaut observes, the Zeitgeist has exerted considerable impact on the content and

8. One-third of all the marriages recorded in the parish registers.

shape of any kind of religious instruction which is primarily theological in derivation (1965, 1). Indeed, as M. D. Chenu has reminded us, theology takes on very different colors when viewed by different minds (1959, 63). We have the Augustinian school and the Thomist school, the Protestant school and the Catholic school, the fundamentalist school and the liberal school, and so on. To be sure, when after painstaking care, a theologian assembles his data he really is not objectively free to draw any conclusions which the data themselves suggest. In the final analysis, it is not the objective analysis of the data which is the decisive factor (as in the case of social science) but rather some force outside that data themselves. For Catholics, it is fundamentally the magisterium which determines the parameters within which the data may be analyzed and interpreted (Chenu 1959, 48–49). Paul Tillich nicely sums up the forces external to the data which are decisive in any Protestant analysis and interpretation of the data:

> In every assumedly scientific theology there is a point where individual experience, traditional valuation, and personal commitment must decide the issue. This point, often hidden to the authors of such theologies, is obvious to those who look at them with other experiences and other commitments. If an inductive approach is employed, one must ask in what direction the writer looked for his material. And if the answer is that he looks in every experience, one must ask what characteristic of reality or experience is the empirical basis of his theology. Whatever the answer may be, an a priori of experience and valuation is implied. The same is true of a deductive approach, as developed in classical idealism. The ultimate principles in idealist theology are rational expressions of an ultimate concern; like all metaphysical ultimates, they are religious ultimates at the same time. A theology derived from them is determined by the hidden theology implied in them. In both the empirical and the metaphysical approaches [to theology], as well as in the much more numerous cases of their mixture, it can be observed that the a priori which directs the induction and the deduction is a type of mystical experience (1951, 8–9).

Social science utilizes empirical controls all along the way to insure objectivity. In so doing, it is very helpful to the work of religious instruction. To facilitate learning in a black child, for example, it is crucial that we know in an objective manner how this black child does in fact learn. Our theology of the black child is not of itself a vital factor in facilitating desired learning outcomes in him; such a theology becomes a significant process variable only when it somehow interacts with other variables which affect learning. Thus, for example, if one holds a theology that blackness is an external manifestation of divine displeasure, then this theology becomes a significant process variable only to the extent that such a theology results in the teacher's behaving in a hostile or derogatory fashion toward the child (behaviors proved to correlate negatively with the facilitation of learning).

The Quantitative Aspect of Religious Instruction

Religious instruction aims at facilitating Christian living in the learner's total behavioral pattern. Consequently, it is important that the teacher and the student have some clear idea of the extent to which a particular Christian behavior is being facilitated. It is the purpose of quantification to provide both teacher and learner with some measure of precision as to the degree and extent to which the desired learning outcomes are being achieved. Indeed, the very concept of effective learning connotes some sort of quantified measure, crude or refined, by which an individual can assess whether or not he is actually attaining the desired behavioral outcomes. A religion teacher might say to himself that pedagogical method *x* is more effective than method *y*. However, unless there is some sort of quantitative measure to differentiate the effectiveness of the two methods, it is not possible to objectively assert that method *x* is more effective than *y*. Further, this religion teacher will wish to ascertain how much more effective method *x* is, so that he can make wise instructional decisions. Suppose, for example, that the implementation of method *x* demands a great deal more time, effort, and financial expense than does method *y*. An analysis of the results of each method reveals method *x* is indeed the more effective, but only by a few percentage points. Such quantitative data can help the teacher judge whether all the extra time, effort, and financial expense involved in method *x* pay the proportionate learning dividends.

Social-science survey research done on American students has concluded that men consistently score higher on tests of theoretical, political, and economic values, whereas women score higher on tests of religious, social, and aesthetic values (Berelson and Steiner 1964, 574). This kind of quantified data is of significant assistance to the religion teacher in helping him differentiate his instructional activities. Further, by delving deeper into the data, the religion teacher can learn the degree to which women score higher than men on religious values. The amount of instructional differentiation which the teacher must provide in order to insure effective learning of religious values by his male and female students will vary according to the level of difference in the scores on the religious values scale.

One of the claims made by teachers and educational officials of Sunday school programs and church-related schools is that the students in these learning experiences acquire personal religious models who can serve as concrete ideals with whom to identify in fashioning their own Christian living. This is a claim; but what are the factual data? Here again quantitative measures can indicate the extent to which such personal religious models do act as concrete ideals for the learners. In this way, the teachers and educational officials can assess with some degree of accuracy the effectiveness of their religion programs in the area of providing personal religious models for the students. A 1957 study by Robert Morocco revealed that 62 percent of the students in

Catholic secondary schools chose a religious personage as their primary personal ideal. The most frequently mentioned names were Fulton Sheen (a prominent bishop and popular television personality of the time) and the blessed mother Mary—Jesus was named by only nine students (1957).

Quantification is proper to social science rather than to theological science. Indeed, when theological science incorporated quantification into its work, various unfortunate results came about. For example, in the Catholic Church, God's mercy was placed in quantified form by a theological system called indulgences. Thus an individual could gain an indulgence of seven years and seven quarantines for performing this act, or an indulgence of six years for doing another act. Again, some moral theologians appeared to be employing quantitative or quasi-quantitative procedures in ascertaining how far an individual could go before he passed from the state of venial sin to that of mortal sin.

While theologically-oriented specialists in religious instruction would doubtless deny its social-science character, nonetheless their writings often reflect an implicit quantification of which they might be unaware. Thus, for example, Johannes Hofinger writes: "From the standpoint of religious pedagogy . . . a dialogue Mass is preferable even to a sung or solemn high Mass. This is not a question of the highest form of celebration, objectively speaking, but of the form of the Mass most fitted to give our children and young people a proper understanding of the teaching and the meaning of the Mass, and one which will help them to participate as intensively and meaningfully as possible" (1962, 41–42). Hofinger is here implying that children and young people learn more (quantitative) from a dialogue Mass than from a sung or solemn high Mass. All comparisons in the degree or level of pedagogical effectiveness perforce are in expressed or implied quantitative terms. (Parenthetically, I might note that Hofinger does not offer any hard data to support his contention that a dialogue Mass is a more effective pedagogical vehicle for children and young people than is a sung or solemn high Mass. Theological presuppositions are no substitute for empirically verified data in this regard.)

I should add that I do not mean to suggest in this section that religious instruction is at bottom quantitative, or that all religious instruction can be quantitatively measured. What I am saying is that the assessment and improvement of religious instruction must as far as possible utilize quantitative procedures if it is to provide valid and reliable indications and measures of the degree of its effectiveness.

Value-Freedom in Religious Instruction

It will by recalled from the last chapter that one of the characteristics of social science is that it is value-free. In other words, it does not assign value judgments to the results of its activity. A theological scientist, for example, might categorize a particular act as sinful or heretical, while a social scientist would categorize the same act as a personality malfunction or a socially disruptive activity.

For religious instruction, value-freedom means that the teaching process itself can facilitate behavioral modification toward one system of values more or less as readily as toward a different system of values. In other words, the process of producing learning outcomes can take place regardless of the values the teacher wishes the individual to attain. For example, a teacher in a Methodist Sunday school will use many of the same general pedagogical techniques to facilitate Methodist-type behaviors in his students as a Catholic CCD teacher will employ in facilitating Catholic-type behaviors in his students.

For religious instruction, value-freedom means that the process or effectiveness of behavioral modification is not normally subjected to theological judgments. For example, the magisterium or church or faith is not competent to judge whether teaching method *x* is more effective than teaching method *y* in facilitating a particular charitable behavior in the learner. Nor is theological science competent to judge the manner in which a person learns. For example, basing his evidence on the opinion of theologians, Josef Goldbrunner asserts that a "child acts only from an ethics of obedience and not out of personal decision" (1965a, 35). Such psychological judgments clearly fall outside the scope of theological methodology and theological science in general.

When I say that religious instruction is value-free, I am not suggesting that religious instruction is unconcerned with values. Quite the contrary: both the process and product outcomes of religious instruction are themselves values. Christian living, the goal of religious instruction, is a supreme value. Moreover, religious instruction accepts the benchmark values of Christianity as the framework within which it operates. Hence religious instruction cannot violate any Christian principles in its work of behavioral modification. It is in this domain of values that a synapse is effected between the process of religious instruction and theological science. One of the crucial roles which theological science plays in the work of religious instruction is to provide the parameters and the overall direction within which and toward which the process of religious instruction works. I will discuss this point in greater length in the next chapter.

It is precisely in this matter of accepting and facilitating theological value structures that religious instruction differs sharply from religious counseling. The religion teacher's function is to facilitate certain desired values in the learner, while the work of the religious counselor is to accept unconditionally the client's values no matter how erroneous they may be.[9] The counselor's personal religious convictions, or the tenets of the religious denomination sponsoring the relationship he is having with his client, must not

9. For a discussion of this point, see James Michael Lee and Nathaniel J. Pallone, *Guidance and Counseling in Schools: Foundations and Processes* (New York: McGraw-Hill, 1966), 302–4, and passim.

interfere with the client's self-actualizing (Segal 1959). For example, if an adolescent explains that he is having guilt feelings about masturbation, attributing such feelings to felt conflicts between his physiopsychological needs and his Roman Catholic religion, the counselor does not seize the opportunity to discuss the morality of masturbation (Curran 1960). He simply listens and reacts in a neutral way, without making any value judgment one way or the other, but merely expressing unconditional positive regard for the client's beliefs qua beliefs. Religious counseling is concerned with value but primarily the value of the person self-actualizing and the incorporation by the client into his own self-system of those values he perceives will promote his own self-actualization.[10] Religious instruction, on the other hand, aims at the conscious and deliberative modification of desired values on the part of the learner.

The Facilitation Process in Religious Instruction

The facilitation process in religious instruction is a uniquely social-science activity. Facilitation is the enabling function; it is the process by which the learner is helped to modify his behavior in desired directions. Facilitation is the arrangement of instructional conditions so as to optimally promote learning. Properly and essentially considered, facilitation is a content-free process; however, the way in which learning is facilitated in a particular religious class does, of course, take on some of the coloring of the specified outcome to be facilitated. Theological science does not afford significant assistance in the ways to facilitate behavioral modification; rather it lends assistance to the work of religious instruction by suggesting fruitful directions toward which the behavior might be modified.

A failure on the part of theologians to recognize the social-science character of the facilitation process in religious instruction has led to some silly and pietistic statements. The following might be considered representative: "The human teacher is always subordinate to the Holy Spirit in the catechizing of the child . . . Catechesis is not an event between the catechist and the child, but between God and the child."[11] Indeed such statements smack of ontologism and angelism. Religious instruction is not a mystical experience; it is first and foremost an interaction between the learner and the conditions which have been consciously and deliberatively shaped in such a way that he will acquire the desired learning outcomes. Of course, God resides in all things, including the religion lesson. But history has shown that God works through human and other natural agents in causing the behaviors he wishes. Until

10. For a full-length treatment of the relationship of counseling to values, see Charles A. Curran, Counseling and Psychotherapy: The Pursuit of Values (New York: Sheed & Ward, 1968).

11. The first of these two sentences is from Gabriel Moran, *Catechesis of Revelation*, p. 116; the second is from Franz Arnold as quoted in ibid., pp. 116–17.

religious instruction is demythologized of the prevalent attitude reflected in such statements as I have just cited, I believe it will remain quagmired in the same overpresumptuous reliance on God and overneglect of human and natural resources which have caused such nonprofessionalism in the field for centuries. God cannot—and I suspect will not—be dragged in by the heels to make every religion class a paragon of behavioral facilitation. I rather believe that God works in and through the natural order. In religious instruction this means that educational experiences must be planned carefully and implemented skilfully if they are to have the intended effects on the learner (Bloom 1963, 387).

The cumulative effect of all sorts of variables operating within the learning situation is what causes the individual to learn one thing rather than another. It is within the competency of social science to isolate those variables which are most productive of learning, and so structure them that the desired learning outcome is achieved. This conscious control and deliberative structuring of the learning situation is at the heart of the facilitation process. Because both the scientific discernment of the significant instructional variables which affect learning, and also the arrangement of these variables to produce effective learning fall outside the competency of theological science, theologically-oriented religious educators have had to stumble around and guess how a lesson could be structured to facilitate the desired learning outcomes. The results of this theological speculation sometimes have been mistaken and other times irrelevant. For example, Johannes Hofinger states flatly that the most effective way of facilitating young children in the primary school grades to enter more completely into a living union with Jesus is through a biblical-historical approach, which leads to Jesus through the telling of the story of salvation. To buttress his contention, Hofinger cites this method as the way in which Paul attempted to facilitate religious learning in his speech in the synagogue of the Pisidian Antioch, and the way in which Augustine urged religious instruction to be facilitated. To further support his position, Hofinger adduces theological arguments including that of the history of salvation's being at the center of the joyous Christian message (1962).

There are obvious minor flaws in Hofinger's arguments. For example, Paul's audience at Antioch were all adults, as were most of those whom Augustine had in mind—and adults learn quite differently from children, as common sense, to say nothing of social-science data, indicates. But the major weakness in any attempt to make theology do the work of facilitation is that theological science *eo ipso* is not geared to the facilitation of behavioral modification. It is clearly outside the province of theological science to discover and predict the psychological and instructional conditions under which children learn. For example, how is theology equipped to predict the effects of television versus classroom discussion in shaping the attitudes of learners? Indeed, in the case of Hofinger's contention there are some hard data which suggest that the biblical-historical method is inappropriate and ineffective in facilitation in young children the very learning outcomes which Hofinger says will result.[12]

By virtue of the kind of science it is, social science occupies a uniquely favored position to discover, explain, and predict the effect of a host of instructional variables which facilitate or impede the attainment of desirable learning outcomes. For example, social science has discovered that the very words used by a teacher or other person in communicating with another individual do significantly facilitate or impede the acquisition of the content and coloration of the message. The research investigation conducted by William Verplanck illustrates this. Verplanck's experiment was carried out in a series of ordinary conversations between two people: the subject who was not informed in any way that he was taking part in an experiment and the experimenter. Twenty-four subjects participated. Each experimenter engaged the subject in conversation on a variety of topics for at least one-half hour. The half-hour was divided into three discrete periods of ten minutes each. During the first ten-minute period, the experimenter engaged in normal conversation and recorded the rate of the subject's opinion output. A comparative baseline of the subject's rate of opinion utterance was thereby established. During the second ten-minute period, the experimenter positively reinforced every opinion-statement made by the subject. This positive reinforcement was effected by the experimenter's verbally agreeing with every opinion stated by the subject, or by making a nodding or smiling affirmation if he could not verbally interrupt. In the last of the three ten-minute periods the experimenter tried to extinguish all the subject's opinion-statements. He did this by withdrawing all reinforcement, that is, by failing to respond at all in the case of some subjects or by negative reinforcement, that is, by disagreeing with every opinion-statement in the case of other subjects. The results of the study are as informative as they are dramatic. The subjects' rate of speaking during the entire half-hour period did not change. However, what did change markedly was the amount of opinion-statements made by the subjects. All twenty-four subjects showed an increase in the relative frequency of opinion-statements during the second time period, that is, when the experimenter was positively reinforcing their opinion-statements. On the other hand, twenty-one of the twenty-four subjects showed a decrease in the relative frequency of opinion-statements during the third time period, namely, when the experimenter was extinguishing their opinion-statements by withholding all reinforcements or by disagreeing with them (Verplanck 1955). The significance of the Verplanck study for religious

12. Ronald Goldman, *Religious Thinking from Childhood to Adolescence* (New York: Seabury, 1968); also David Elkind, "The Child's Conception of His Religious Identity," *Lumen Vitae* 19 (December 1964): 635–46; also Christian Van Bunnen, "The Burning Bush: The Symbolic Implications of the Bible Story among Children from 5–12 Years," *Lumen Vitae* 19 (June 1964): 327–38.

instruction is that it again illustrates that student behavior is in fact shaped by significant variables within the teacher's repertoire of instructional behaviors. In the work of religious instruction, surely it is God who gives the increase, but it must be the learning situation which plants, and the teacher who waters. To facilitate is both to plant and to water.

Behavior Modification and Religious Instruction

Religious instruction works toward effecting in the learner a behavioral modification along religious lines. Such behavioral modifications might be in the area of cognition affectivity or more globally, the learner's lifestyle. Basically, learning is a change in behavior; therefore, the modification of an individual's behavior is an operational way of expressing learning. The Scriptures abound with incidents in which Jesus modified an individual's behavior. He taught Peter to have faith and John to have humility. He effected the conversion of the Samaritan woman at the well and enabled his companions on the road to Emmaus to gain insight. In short, Jesus went around doing good, that is, in one way or another modifying the behavior of all who would learn from him.

In order to effectively modify behavior, the religion teacher or curriculum builder must first, know the conditions which bring about behavior change and second, arrange for the concrete structuring of these conditions in such a way that the learner's behavior is in fact modified in the desired direction. Consequently, the religion teacher and the curriculum builder must be conversant with the empirical data on how a learner actually learns, and how to facilitate that kind of behavioral modification which is really possible, given the existential conditions of the learner. In other words, in the work of causing behavior modification in the learner, the teacher is a practicing social scientist.

While theological science is useful in suggesting directions toward which the learner's behavior can be fruitfully modified, it is the work of social science which actually secures and effects the behavior modification itself. For example, there has been dispute among theologians throughout the centuries as to the most propitious moment for first communion, and whether a child should make first communion in the company of his peer-group or of his parents. The duration of this theological dispute and the variegation of opinions serve as an indication that a real solution to this question is not within the scope of theological science. Social-science investigation can reveal the actual facts of the psychological maturation, readiness, and development of children of different age levels, together with the kinds of interactions they have with parents and peer-group members. On this basis, a decision can be intelligently made as to the moment and the accompanying group most propitious for the reception of first communion.

Both theologians and theologically-oriented religious educators tend to develop curricula for religious instruction programs from the standpoint of the logical development of theological science. A social scientist, on the other hand, tends to develop his curricula from the existential situation of the learner—how he does in fact learn, the conditions conducive to facilitating learning, and so forth. A theologian like Marcel van Caster suggests that in the teaching of the eschatological dimension of Christianity, the religion teacher should "take as his starting-point the fact of Christ's resurrection; put the Christian's death explicitly in relation to the death of Christ and the meaning of his death" (1963, 455). A social scientist would take as his starting point the way in which the particular group of individuals he is teaching do in fact learn. Their age level, psychophysiological needs, socioeconomic background, cultural milieu—all these have been shown by the hard data to bear a very significant relationship to the way in which learning actually occurs. It may well be that the empirical data suggest that the resurrection is an inappropriate starting point, or again, the data might reveal that the resurrection does represent an effective starting point in terms of where the learners are existentially at. What I am saying is that *a priori* assumptions about religious instruction, no matter how sound they might be from the standpoint of theological science, do not of themselves suggest the most effective mode of facilitation behavioral modificating for this or that group of learners.

Shaping the Learning Environment to Promote Religious Instruction

It is the total environment in which the teaching-learning process takes place, and not simply any one variable within that environment such as the teacher or the curriculum, which works toward producing the desired learning outcomes. The task of the religion teacher is to skilfully shape the learning environment so that all the conditions will work together to cause the intended behavioral modification. The religion teacher as a practicing social scientist controls and shapes all the variables which are known to exert a significant influence on the acquisition of learning outcomes—pedagogical strategy, materials, curriculum, socioemotional climate, institutional setting, physical and human environmental variables within that shaped situation interact to cause learning. Because of the difference in their respective natures, it is within the scope of social science—not theological science—first to identify those variables which cause learning, second to structure those variables in a situational fashion so as to bring about the desired learning, and finally to assess whether or not the desired behavioral modification actually occurred.

In that theological science by its nature is not equipped to structure environmental variables to bring about the desired modifications in behavior, its efforts in this direction have been on a hit-or-miss basis. This is in sharp contrast to a social-science approach to the problem; social science is geared to reduce chance to a minimum in the cause and prediction of behavior. Perhaps an example will illustrate the results which follow from hit-or-miss efforts when theologians rather than social scientists are put in charge of shaping the learning environment. Novitiates and convents for the training of women religious represent learning environments shaped by theologically-oriented persons in such a way as to bring about desired behavioral modifications in the young women living within their confines. Social-science data have revealed that this kind of environment has scored a direct "hit" rather than a "miss" in terms of producing the desired behavioral modification. Thus, for example, Marie Francis Kenoyer (1961) conducted a careful empirical study of two groups of matched Catholic girls, one of which had entered the religious life and the other which remained in the lay life. Both groups were matched prior to group A's entering the convent or novitiate. After a number of years had elapsed, Kenoyer employed psychological assessment devices to compare the two groups of girls. The study found that the girls in religious life perceived themselves as more submissive, more self-abasement-oriented, more in need of being dominated, and more shy than the matched group of lay women. Kenoyer concluded that this difference in personality traits was due to the effect of the convent environment on group A.

Other instances can be related to indicate that environments shaped by theologically-oriented individuals failed to produce the anticipated learning outcomes. Let me give one illustrative case. Catholic theologians and theologically-oriented individuals failed to produce the anticipated learning outcomes. Let me give one illustrative case. Catholic theologians and theologically-oriented religious authorities have for centuries decried coeducation of youth. Pius XI stated flatly that coeducation frequently was based on naturalism and a denial of original sin. Surveying creation from the vantage point of theological science, Pius noted that divine and natural law indicate that coeducation of youth is highly deleterious to the natural and supernatural development of young men and women (1936). The Pian prohibition on coeducation of youth was reinforced in a 1958 *instructio* of the Sacred Congregation of Religious which states from a theological position that coeducation in Catholic high schools is permissible only in localities where the bishop deems this evil gravely necessary. In such situations, the Sacred Congregation has listed specific precautions which must be taken; for example, boys and girls must be housed in different classrooms or at least on opposite sides of the same classroom where separate classrooms are not possible, and they must enter and leave the school at different times. Religious are not permitted to conduct coeducational secondary schools. Further, religious who teach in these schools must be men or women whose virtue has been proved by experience—a provision which probably excludes young religious from teaching in such schools (1958). Despite these weighty theological viewpoints, social-science data have not indicated harmful effects of coeducational environments on the development or religious behavior of youth.[13] Indeed, there are some data which suggest that segregation of the sexes at the secondary and university levels has unfortunate behavioral results. For example, the study by Alice Wessell and Mary Rita Flaherty (1964) revealed that after one year in a Catholic women's college, the girls tested were significantly less feminine than when they entered the college.

Theologically-oriented Protestant and Catholic officials have erected church-related colleges in the belief that the environments at such institutions are conducive to producing heightened religious growth and development in the students. These officials use theological verifiers to buttress their frequent statements that they can "really feel the religious atmosphere in the air at St. Z College." Yet there are some social-science data to suggest that while these theological verifiers might endow the church official with a personal sense of satisfaction and well-being, nevertheless these verifiers are not providing a valid picture of what is really going on. Thus, for example, a longitudinal investigation by Marie Edmund Harvey concluded that in the eastern Catholic women's college studied, there was no significant change in the religious attitude of students from freshman to senior year (1964). Harvey's findings are similar to those of Robert Hassenger who investigated the impact of a midwest Catholic women's college environment on the religious attitudes of its students. Seniors at this college were only minimally different from the freshmen in terms of religious attitudes and values (1967b). In one of the most complete reviews of the empirical research on the impact of the Catholic college environment on the student, Hassenger concludes that these environments do not seem to be too significant in altering the religious attitudes and values of the students along the lines intended by the college officials. Rather, the religious attitudes and values of the seniors seem to be quite consistent with those they held as freshmen—although beginning in the late 1960s, there appears to be a trend for the religious attitudes and values of seniors to be moving in a direction away from that desired by the religious officials of the college (1967a).

Both the shaping and the assessing of the educational impact of a learning environment upon individuals are tasks for social science rather than for theological science. To be sure, theological science has a key role to play in religious education; however, this role is something other than the structuring of the learning situation.

The Christian Learning Laboratory and Religious Instruction

The religion class at its most fulsome is a laboratory for Christian living. Such a laboratory represents a learning environment so shaped that the product and process outcomes of the lesson are achieved through the direct expe-

13. For various studies on this point, see James Michael Lee and Nathaniel J. Pallone, *Guidance and Counseling in Schools: Foundations and Processes.*

riencing of them. As John Dewey has suggested, the rise of modern science has shown that there is no such thing as genuine knowledge or fruitful understanding—and I might add, mature attitude and value development—except as the offspring of doing, in the broad sense of this term. Individuals have to do something with knowledge or understanding or values; they cannot merely attain these outcomes in their heads (Dewey 1916, 321). Man is an integer, that is, a being who is called on by his nature to effect an integration in his own lifestyle of being and doing. Commenting on the celebrated Hawthorne experiment conducted by social scientists, Marshall McLuhan observes that this investigation demonstrates behaviorally that when individuals are permitted to join their energies to the process of learning and discovery in a laboratory setting, the resultant increased efficiency is "phenomenal" (1964, ix.).

Because of their respective natures and thrusts, social science, not theological science, is equipped to shape the learning conditions necessary for the development, implementation, and assessment of a learning laboratory for Christian living. André Godin notes that theologians and theologically-oriented religion teachers are *eo ipso* unacquainted with the effects of socioemotional climate on the teaching-learning process, or in knowing what pedagogical strategy is most appropriate for producing a specific kind of learning (1962).[14] It is only through the understanding of and skill in social science that the religion teacher can so environ the pedagogical conditions that desired learning outcomes are caused in the individual.

Conclusion

Religious instruction falls within the domain of social science rather than theological science. This is not to imply that religious instruction has little or no relation to theology; rather, it is to point out that religious instruction borrows its fundamental structure and thrust from social science. Each science has its own structure and operational procedures which shape the orientation and direction of those areas or disciplines which it incorporates.

I am further suggesting in this chapter that the traditional view of religious instruction as a branch of practical theology has been responsible for a substantial diminution of the potential effectiveness of religious instruction over the centuries. André Godin has observed in this connection that the theological base for religious instruction has caused religion teachers and curriculum builders to let everything slide along as if experimental techniques, shaping the learning environment, statistical discrimination, and facilitation do not exist

14. This article represents a highly sensitive and penetrating analysis of the relationship of social science and theology in the work of religious instruction. Godin's contribution is especially commendable and courageous in light of the continual misunderstanding and opposition he has encountered from the social press of the theologically-oriented milieu in which this social scientist operates.

or are of very minor concern (1962). Religious instruction, then, has its own ontology distinct from theology, but certainly not removed from theology.

At bottom, what the social-science approach to religious instruction does is to radicate it in the teaching-learning process. By this I mean that the central task of religious instruction becomes the conscious and deliberative facilitation of specified behavioral goals. Incorporating as fully as possible the process and product content of theological science, whether old or new, the prime function of religious instruction is the study into and the implementation of a planned structuring of the learning situation. Quite obviously, then, theology plays a vital and indispensable role in this kind of religious instruction; however, it is theology which is being integrated and plugged into the social science of the teaching-learning situation, not vice versa, as has formerly been the case.

Second, the social-science approach views the environment in which the learning of religion takes place not as constituting a supportive milieu for "getting across" the subject matter of theology, but rather a key factor—and indeed in some ways the controlling force—in the here-and-now dynamic of the learning process. The elements of social time and social space, with all their ramifications, are crucial to the type of teaching-learning which occurs. To be sure, the classroom group is of and in itself a unique psychosocial system, with its own unique psychosocial structure. Again, theology is indispensable here; but the shift in emphasis that I am suggesting is that theology is utilized as only one directional force in the classroom group. This, of course, substantially differs from the typical religion teacher's emphasis in which the classroom milieu is perceived simply as a motivational tool to interest the students in religion, or to "get them going" in carrying out the theological themes of the lesson.

Third, the social-science approach regards religious instruction as a conscious and deliberative joint effort of teacher and students to effect selected behavioral modifications in the learners. The classroom becomes a laboratory for Christian living, a planned and operationalized milieu for facilitating in the students desired changes in behavior. Theology remains as a mode of prime importance; however, theology is used as one, and only one, of the factors involved in the educational structuring of the learning environment to produce these behavioral goals, instead of the *terminus ad quem* of classroom activity (Lee 1970, 1–2).

Placing religious instruction within the domain of social science helps to insure that its future will be brighter than its past. In this connection I believe that Gabriel Moran provides the fundamental structural blueprint for the future of religious instruction when he remarks that the future development of religious instruction cannot consist of either content *or* method, that old dichotomy of what hopefully is a bygone era in religious instruction. To be fruitful, the future development of religious instruction must grow along the lines of the inner relationship of content and method, both in human life and in Christian faith. What religious instruction most needs is to take as its axis sophisticated methodological issues. By methodology here is meant a style of behaving and communicating.[15] This chapter has attempted to show that it is social science, rather than any other kind of science, which is uniquely equipped to most fruitfully address itself to that style of behaving and communicating which Moran terms "sophisticated methodology." Certainly it is the social-science approach which can enable religious instruction to effectively predict, facilitate, and shape religious behaviors in the learner.

For Reflection

1. How does Lee distinguish between theological "science" and social "science"?
2. What does he mean by "verification of religious instruction"?
3. How would the Christian education you have experienced be different if it had been based on the foundation of Lee's social science approach?

References

Aiken, W. 1942. *The story of the eight-year study.* New York: Harper.

Barbara, A. 1963. Straining toward the future: Eschatological perspectives in teaching the Eucharist to adolescents. *Lumen Vitae* 18 (Sept.).

Berelson, B., and G. A. Steiner. 1964. *Human behavior: An inventory of scientific findings.* New York: Harcourt, Brace, and World.

Bloom, B. S. 1963. Testing cognitive ability and achievement. *Handbook of research on teaching,* ed. N. L. Gage. Chicago: Rand McNally.

Brown, D. 1968–69. Teaching the Old Testament to American students. *Living Light* 5 (Winter): 65–74.

Caster, M. van. 1963. The subject of eschatology in catechesis. *Lumen Vitae* 18 (Sept.).

Chenu, M. D. 1964. *Is theology a science?* New York: Hawthorn.

Coleman, J. S. 1961. *The adolescent society.* New York: The Free Press.

Curran, C. A. 1960. The concept of sin and guilt in psychotherapy. *Journal of Counseling Psychology* 7 (Fall): 192–97.

15. Moran uses the word *thinking* instead of *behaving.* I trust he will excuse my substitution. This insight into a new structure of religious instruction represents, in my perception at least, one of Gabriel Moran's most profound comments on the nature and structure of religious instruction. It is not altogether clear, however, whether Gabriel Moran (himself a theologian) would agree that it is social science rather than theology which is the vehicle for the sophisticated methodological axis he advocates. See Gabriel Moran, "The Future of Catechetics," in *Living Light* 5 (Spring 1968): 8.

Dean, T. W. 1963. The training of adolescents to prayer. *Lumen Vitae* 58 (June).

Dewey, J. 1916. *Democracy and education*. New York: Macmillan.

Filthaut, T. 1965. The concept of man and catechetical method. *New catechetical methods,* ed. J. Goldbrunner, trans. M. V. Reid. Notre Dame: Univ. of Notre Dame Press.

Godin, A. 1962. The importance and difficulty of scientific research in religious education: The problem of criterion. *Religious Education* 57 (July–Aug.): S–169.

Goldbeck, A. D. 1966. Another necessity—Helping children to pray. *Living Light* 3 (Fall): 20–21.

Goldbrunner, J. 1965a. Catechesis and encounter. *New catechetical methods,* ed. J. Goldbrunner, trans. M. V. Reid. Notre Dame: Univ. of Notre Dame Press.

Goldbrunner, J. 1965b. Catechetical method. *New catechetical methods,* ed. J. Goldbrunner, trans. M. V. Reid. Notre Dame: Univ. of Notre Dame Press.

Grande, P. P. 1964. Rapport in the school counseling interview in relation to selected personality characteristics of religious and laymen (nonreligious) counselors. Unpubl. Ph.D. diss., Univ. of Notre Dame.

Harvey, M. E. 1964. A study of religious attitudes of a group of Catholic college women. Unpubl. master's thesis, Fordham Univ.

Hassenger, R. 1967a. Impact of Catholic colleges. In *The shape of Catholic higher education*. Chicago: Univ. of Chicago Press.

Hassenger, R. 1967b. Portrait of a Catholic women's college. In *The shape of Catholic higher education*. Chicago: Univ. of Chicago Press.

Hennessey, T. C. 1962. A study of the changes and the permanence of changes in the religious ideals of Catholic high school students after a closed retreat. Unpubl. Ph.D. diss., Fordham Univ.

Hofinger, J. 1962. *The art of teaching Christian doctrine: The good news and its proclamation*. 2d. ed. Notre Dame: Univ. of Notre Dame Press.

Jungmann, J. A. 1959. *Handing on the faith*. Trans. and rev. A. N. Fuest. New York: Herder and Herder.

Kennedy [Arlin], P. 1968. Introduction: Religious education for young adults. *Ultimate concern: Teacher's manual*. Chicago: Argus.

Kenoyer, M. F. 1961. The influence of religious life on three levels of perceptual processes. Unpubl. Ph.D. diss., Fordham Univ.

Lee, J. M. 1963a. Counseling versus discipline: Another view. *Catholic Counselor* 7 (Spring): 114–19.

———. 1963b. *Principles and methods of secondary education*. New York: McGraw-Hill.

———. 1970. Foreword. *Toward a future for religious education,* eds. J. M. Lee and P. Rooney. Dayton, Ohio: Pflaum.

Lenski, G. 1961. *The religious factor*. Garden City, N.Y.: Doubleday.

McLuhan, M. 1964. *Understanding media: The extensions of man*. New York: McGraw-Hill.

Miller, R. C. 1950. *The clue to Christian education*. New York: Scribner's.

———. 1956. *Biblical theology and Christian education.* New York: Scribner's.

Moran, G. 1966. *Catechesis of revelation.* New York: Herder and Herder.

Morocco, R. R. 1957. A study of the ideals expressed by a selected group of parochial and public school students. Unpubl. master's thesis, The Catholic Univ. of America.

Murray, J. B. 1957. Training for the priesthood and interest test manifestations. Unpubl. Ph.D. diss., Fordham Univ.

Phenix, P. H. 1966. Religious education in the secular city: Myth and mystery in the secular city. *Religious Education* 61 (March–April).

Pius XI. 1936. *Christian education of youth.* Trans. National Catholic Welfare Conference. Washington, D.C.: NCWC.

Rahner, K., and H. Vorgrimler. 1965. *Theological dictionary,* ed. C. Ernst, trans. R. Strachan. New York: Herder and Herder.

Ranwez, P. 1963. The awakening of a child's sense of son. *Lumen Vitae* 18 (March).

Rokeach, M. 1970. Faith, hope, and bigotry. *Psychology Today* (April): 33–37, 58.

Sacra Congregatio de Religiosis. 1958. Instructio de juvenum utriusque sexus promiscua institutione. *Acta Apostolicae Sedis* 50 (Feb. 24).

Sears, R., et al. 1953. Some child-rearing antecedents of aggression and dependency in young children. *Genetic Psychology Monographs* 57 (May).

Segal, S. J. 1959. Religious factors and values in counseling: The role of the counselor's religious values in counseling. *Journal of Counseling Psychology* 6 (Winter): 270–79.

Simpson, R. M. 1933. Attitudes toward the Ten Commandments. *Journal of Social Psychology* 4: 223–30.

Thomas, E. J., and C. F. Fink. 1963. Effects of group size. *Psychological Bulletin* 60 (July): 371–84.

Tillich, P. 1951. *Systematic theology.* Vol. 1:8–9. Chicago: Univ. of Chicago Press.

Vaughn, R. P. Seminary training and personality change. *Religious Education* 55 (Jan.): 56–59.

Vernon, G. M. 1967. Measuring religion: Two methods compared. In *The sociology of religion,* ed. R. D. Knudten. New York: Appleton-Century Crofts.

Verplanck, W. S. 1955. The control of the content of conversation: Reinforcement of statements of opinion. *Journal of Abnormal and Social Psychology* 56 (Nov.): 668–76.

Wessell, A., and S. M. R. Flaherty. 1964. Changes in CPI scores after one year in college. *Journal of Psychology* 57 (Jan.): 235–38.

Wrightstone, J. W. 1936. *Appraisal of experimental high school practices.* New York: Teachers College, Columbia Univ.

Wyckoff, D. C. 1967. Religious education as a discipline: Toward a definition of religious education as a discipline. *Religious Education* 62 (Sept.–Oct.).

19

Ted W. Ward

Facing Educational Issues (1977)

For many years Ted Ward was professor of education at Michigan State University. His work there in values development in education, Theological Education by Extension (TEE), and nonformal education became widely known. Over a period of more than two decades he supervised the doctoral education of dozens of evangelical Christians who have become leaders in various areas of ministry in North America and overseas. Many of these men and women are involved in a variety of Christian education endeavors.

Dr. Ward, especially through his speaking and teaching, has probably been the most influential constructive critic of Christian education from the evangelical perspective during the past thirty years. Now a professor of Christian education and world missions at Trinity Evangelical Divinity School, he continues to direct doctoral students and to express his interest in worldwide ministry.

At the time *Church Leadership Development* was produced, Ward was at Michigan State and was fully engaged as the friendly critic of Christian education. He spoke to groups of church teachers, college leaders, and camp directors. Often his message revolved around the quip that much of "Christian education is neither." As the reader will see from the excerpt that follows, this was not idle banter.

Professor Ward sees much of Christian education as fragmented rather than holistic, too propositional and not developmental enough, too abstract rather than experiential, and generally undisciplined or lacking in structure. While the issue of

From the National Christian Education Study Seminar, *Church Leadership Development* (Glen Ellyn, Ill.: Scripture Press, 1977), 31–46. Mimeographed.

leadership is addressed directly in this excerpt, it is an overall perspective on Christian education that Ward is presenting.

The call is for a return to biblical and theological scholarship on the one hand, and the approach of social science on the other, so that Christian education can be as Christian and as educational as possible. Understanding human development and using its insights in leadership, or any other aspect of ministry, is often an emphasis for Ward. Bringing the Bible and developmentalism together, as in the section dealing with Matthew 23:1–7, is a challenge that has been met by many Christian educators as they respond to the thinking of Ward.

One word of caution: this paper contains strong medicine. It is compounded of a mixture of love and indignation that unfortunately includes traces of foreign particles. These particles, which may be seen as anger or nastiness, have floated through even the smallest pores of one man's filter of compassion.

This paper is not intended for widespread publication; it is a discussion piece intended for serious professional dialog. The motive is to heal; the procedure is to cauterize, to expose and burn away, so that the process of healing will not be interrupted by the bursting forth of the running sores of secularism that infect the church in North America.

But that is too grand. The paper is not that ambitious, certainly not that adequate. Instead, it is the sharing of a conviction based upon a thesis with which not everyone will agree. May it at least be given attention and prayerful consideration. The conviction is that the church of Jesus Christ is being inadequately served by its educational components; the thesis is that much or most of the blame lies in the failure of us all to challenge the educational validity and the theological relevancy of the patchwork of programs called "Christian education."

The author has been heard before on this subject, and since he tends to deal with the theoretical issues first and treat practical matters as being secondary, the activists are often disappointed. With reference to this current paper, a happy condition prevails: it is the middle paper of three; at last the author is located where he feels most confident: bridging between theological perspectives and practical planning. So the challenge to be completely candid and as thorough as possible, given the space and time restrictions, is warmly accepted. The author may never have a better chance to be blunt. Let the reader beware!

Problem I: Christian Education

I regretfully confess to being the originator of a little dab of graffiti that has, by now, found its way to the walls of some of the leading theological education establishments of the land: "Christian education is neither." I do not regret having started this little prank, but I do regret the need for having to raise the challenge. Though there are notable exceptions (some of my best friends are in Christian education), in far too many cases Christian education is neither thoroughly Christian nor soundly educational.

Too many of its programs lack foundation and substance in matters of human development and instructional facilitation; the social-science research upon which the formal study of education must be grounded is often neglected. Christian *education*? "Christian programs" might come closer—and one watered-down course in child development plus one confusing excerpt from behaviorism called "educational psychology" doesn't begin to solve the problem.

As for being "Christian," the claim is even more farfetched—a handful of proof-texts about the Pentateuchal origins of Christian education (God knows they didn't have Sunday schools) and, ironically, the mandatory recitals about the central role of home and family. Then the courses push wildly into the mass of programmed activities that tend to divide and isolate families and that reduce the whole marvelous matter of redemption and growing in grace to a series of informational chunks which are to be dumped on people at just the right moments of life. Christian education? At its best, maybe it is; but as I've seen it and experienced it in dozens of shapes and forms in various institutions and local churches, "Christian education is neither."

The educational aspects of the church need to be reexamined and revised. The following complaints cry out for healing; until they are dealt with, nothing much is going to change for the better.

Christian education has become a conglomeration of events and programs dealing with bits and pieces of supposedly needed learning. It is *fragmented* when what it needs is to be more comprehensive, thorough, and related to body, soul, and spirit; in short, *holistic*.

Christian education is too often *propositional*, concerned with getting the right information into people and conditioning them to make the right responses, when what we really need is an educational environment that is nourishing and *developmental*.

Christian education is so often *abstract*, concerned with the disputations of the clergy when people are asking for help with practical matters; the complex life of today demands *experiential* learning.

Christian education is *undisciplined* in the sense that it lacks clearly defined disciplinary structure. What exactly is it based on? Is it based on theology? Not even the "Christian colleges" really make good on that, with their devotion to pre-Christian Greek liberal arts maxims. What we need is a new rigor of responsible scholarship, bringing into education for the church a clearer sense of disciplinary linkage with both theology and social science.

Problem II: Leadership

Studying the brochures for leadership training programs, seminars, and conferences leads me to conclude that we have entered the "management era." Not that this trend is a good thing, but it's important to know what's happening to us. Either side of the argument *sounds* good. The church needs efficient management in order to do its work effectively, *or*, the church is not a factory. Since its major reason for being is hard to quantify, management techniques from business and industry are irrelevant. Indeed, truth may lie in between or in some third position; but meanwhile, we have to decide how to respond to the mounting enthusiasm for management by objective (MBO), linear models of planning for goal achievement, reductionism of calling and mission to individualistic concepts of time management, and all the rest of the spillovers from systems logic as applied to profit-motive competition management.

Government is also being affected by this spillover—and the results are not very good, even in pragmatic terms. In any enterprise where the output cannot be reduced to fairly simple and easily-agreed-upon coinage—such as "the bottom line" of dollar gains over dollar costs or some specific counting of product output. These borrowings from business enterprise are deceptively inappropriate. Insidiously, they focus attention on some one or two criteria of "success" and overlook most anything not closely linked to those particular, narrowly defined criteria. This observation, now widely noted and hotly debated among educational planners, goes a long way to explain the ambivalence of many people about so-called church growth. Surely quantitative growth is a worthy outcome, but does it make a good goal? Except for such planners as those of General Motors, for whom more cars mean more money, simplistic goals can work against the more vital values. One must be concerned about the desirable beauties of life that can be destroyed by making them objectives: having many friends, having a good reputation, enjoying leisure time, to name a few. These are never really achieved if they are primary goals.

The craze to apply management techniques to the church is made more destructive because of the pseudo-scientism from which it gets its own righteousness. One looks hard and far to find more simplistic notions of what science is for! The bringing of scientific understandings to bear on all sorts of issues and problems of human nature and social transactions in and for the church is too important to be prostituted as a gimmick.

For example, consider the key problem: confusion between leadership and management. (Even *Time* magazine [Nov. 8, 1976] calls headline attention to this issue.) Granted, it is easier to apply scientific findings to the tasks of management than to the processes of leadership. In the compulsive interest of being scientific, some people simply do a sleight of hand and, hocus-pocus, *leadership* is now management! And thus all the "scientific" resources are relevant. But sadly, those who advocate science aren't very scientific about it! They preach science but they don't practice science.

Science unfolds in the defining of terms, the describing of phenomena, and the searching for similarities, dissimilarities, and relationships.

Defining

In the interests of science rightly applied and in the best interests of Christian education, the term *leadership* should be defined with care and attention to the biblical commitments and historical presuppositions of Christianity. *Leadership* is not a precise word. Anything from General Patton's swagger stick to Mahatma Gandhi's shrunken, bony body can be included. Endless-loop debates over what a leader is, what makes a leader, how to train a leader, and so forth, should be adequate warning that the semantic game doesn't pay. For the Christian community, the issue isn't leadership, anyway, it is *servanthood.* "Let those who would be great among you become your servants." "He who is least among you, this is the one who is great" (Matt. 20:28; Luke 22:26; Mark 9:35). "The kings of the Gentiles lord it over them, and those who have authority over them are called benefactors . . . *Not so with you . . . !*" (Luke 22:25, emphasis added). The church must define leadership differently. To do less, especially to borrow the secular frame of reference and concepts, is to secularize the church.

Leadership as it should be in the church demands a dynamic definition of the sort that social scientists call a *model.* Leadership is not what one *does* so much as what one *is* within the given contexts of the development of the body of believers. Leadership is not so much bringing people out of a wilderness as it is sharing a journey. This sharing is as a peer ("You have but one teacher, you are all brothers . . . and do not be called leaders, for one is your leader, Christ" [Matt. 23:8, 10]), and sharing is to be done as would a servant. In the church, those who lead (better to say *minister*?) are to serve as agents of the Holy Spirit's gifts to the church. Perhaps there are points of similarity between the Christian and the secular definition of leadership, but they are much less important than the points of dissimilarity.

Describing

Judging by the current fads, the following terms constitute a description of the church leader at work. *Inducing*, *motivating*, and *congratulating.* With all the emphasis on leading as something to be done *to* people, it is not surprising that the heart of the behavioristic view of human learning finds its way into the church. Indeed, when the role of the leader centers on getting people involved, inducing them to do something that the leader (or "the program") has decided they need to do, and rewarding them selectively for "appropriate" behavior (good works), we see the whole vicious menace not only of philosophical determinism but also of sociological elitism, smack dab in the middle of the sanctuary of God.[1] We need to get serious about describing what passes as "leadership" and evaluate it against firm criteria.

As for the criteria, we need a theological framework for understanding leadership in the church. Any human enterprise is entitled to define its presuppositions and to describe its philosophical biases: why should the church be slow to put forth its presuppositions and biases on the basis of biblical theology? Slowness in this key matter is likely due to one or another of these problems: delegation of "Christian education" to the less theoretical tacticians of the church; isolation of the preaching-studying minister from the developmental flow of the lives of the congregation; the unchallenged assumption that the Bible offers little to the theological foundation of the educator beyond the handful of recited proof-texts; or simple neglect (after all, theological scholarship sometimes values Hebrew verb points higher than the understanding of human behavior). Help!

We must change the *induce*, *motivate*, and *congratulate* model of leadership into *accept*, *share*, and *grow together* or we have no business at all putting the word *Christian* ahead of the word *leadership*.

Searching for Relationships

The scientist seeks to understand in order to explain and predict. In complex human settings it is all the scientist can do to explain; prediction is a very iffy matter. The social scientist is usually satisfied just to be able to understand the relationships. Thus, from a scientific point of view, the questions change: no longer is it "What leadership style gets best results?" but "How does this or that leadership process relate to particular persons, situations, and needs?" In other words, generalizations such as "best" and "most effective" are expanded to "best *for whom*?", "*for what*?", "*when*?", and the spotlight pattern is enlarged to look at whole situations and complex sets of relationships. What a leader *knows*, what he or she *does*, and what he or she *is*, all become part of the whole picture. In this broader view, the particular distinctives of leadership for the church become more visible: to lead the church is to be engaged in *process*—the ongoing work of God in lives—hardly a repetition of a sequence of mechanical operations. The process is highly *developmental*, not tightly structured and programmed, and the most significant output is, itself, a *continuing fulfillment* (washing, renewal, and perfection) rather than the arrival at some end state or nirvana.

1. Determinism is the assumption that life is completely "programmed" and thus beyond one's own will or control. "What will be will be." "We are what our environment makes us." Ultimately, determinism runs afoul of biblical teaching on the crucial issue of whether or not a person can be responsible for what he or she does in life.

Problem III: Separation—Distinctives or Distance?

The practical outcomes of separation are one convincing evidence that the effects of the fall hang over the redeemed as well as the unredeemed. They are stultifying and sometimes ugly. While there is good wisdom in keeping one's distance from snares, the biblical teachings on separation of the Christian give us no basis for ignoring or being unresponsive to the needs of mankind, nor can they gives us a basis for ignoring scientific and scholarly inquiry in the secular pursuits of science.

The development of leadership for the church has much to learn from research done on human behavior, human learning, and social development. Should it be necessary for Christians to rerun every experiment or to ignore any findings that haven't been baptized? (I find it ironic that Christians have been fascinated by natural science research, raising the challenge—the issue of evolution—but have stubbornly ignored or refused to accept the value of social science until rather recently.) A Christian in science sooner or later learns how to make two judgments about the worth of a given research study: (1) the scientific core and "replicability" of the inquiry, and (2) the presuppositions of the research or the way these affect the conclusions that the researcher has drawn. There are plenty of research studies that scientists (whether Christian or secular) must discard on the basis of the first question. They lack scientific worth. And there are many that the Christian must reanalyze on the basis of biblical presuppositions. Many times the *findings* are respectable enough, and a simple reanalysis of the findings on the basis of biblical presuppositions, particularly about the nature of man, brings out *conclusions* that are very valuable for the Christian.

Indeed, there are ways to bring Christian education into a closer and more responsible relationship with the world of social science research. Properly handled, this poses no threat to the integrity of the church.

But there is another separation that may not be so easy to handle. Sad to say, the church in North America has largely accepted the nonbiblical distinctions between clergy and laity and between educational ministry and pastoral ministry. It is the latter which will be addressed, though it is, in large part, a natural extension of the delegational concepts that come from separating the clergy from the rest of the flock.

Education in the church needs to be redefined. In common practice, "Christian education" is whatever the "senior pastor" wants to delegate. Not only does this demean the central importance of the development of the Christian, but it also gets the pastor too far off the mark of what should be his greatest responsibility: nurture. The reference here to education as *the development of the Christian* reflects my nonschooling view of education. As I see it, something is not education merely because it can be carried out in a school; it is educational because it facilitates human development! Sad to say, preaching to the saints is rarely thought of as being educational. And while we're at it, consider: if liturgy isn't educational, it is simply ritual.

The separation between pastoral and educational roles is the great mother of the proliferation of disjointed programs. Say what you will, the basic criterion of "success" for the director of Christian education too often is how much program action he/she has underway. How many classes? How many groups? How many programs? parties? And, of course, how many young people are involved? I despair: How can the qualitative questions get any attention in the face of the current fad of counting things and making church-growth charts?

When separation of the church or particularly of the educational mission of the church is a matter of distance—either of distance from the needs of mankind or of distance from much-needed sources of basic insight into human nature—separateness does not fulfill its biblical intention. Leadership people in Christian education should turn things around until separation is a matter of *distinctiveness.* Education for the church should be everything good from whatever sources of ideas and procedures, but it should be *distinct.* It is most important that we know the theological and philosophical premises on which we are educating, and it is important not to bring in practices, procedures, and materials simply because they have "caught on" in the secular educational setting. We need to do well what we do, but do nothing that does not pass the tests of contributing to the development of the Christian as God intended and to the development of the church as a unified body.

A Growing Split in Social Science

Social science is a divergent field. There are all sorts of positions on all sorts of issues. You can easily get a debate going on almost any subject, including some that would seem to be long foreclosed—for example, do we really gain practical insights from experimental research? Do the animal lab studies mislead us into making wrong generalizations about humans? Is political science really a science?

Modern science has emerged from the need to describe and understand. Even so, social science's several specialties, sociology, psychology, anthropology, political science, and perhaps geography and history, have come into being not as fields of applied engineering but as explanatory and descriptive scholarship. In the twentieth century, the desire to "do something practical" has become a prominent feature of certain of the social sciences, particularly psychology. Beginning with those who were committed to helping people with disorders (i.e. the psychoanalysts), the activism has broadened.

Two categories of application of the social sciences have emerged. (This oversimplification is flawed in several particulars; for example, it doesn't even suggest a third category which the psychoanalysts themselves [make up].) The two, the behaviorists and the developmentalists, are increasingly in conflict and are becoming more evenly matched despite an earlier serious setback handed the developmentalists. That near extinction of developmentalism was a result of their own excessive tendency to label people and to be too firm in their predictions.

Crucial differences in the views of man held, respectively, in the two "camps" account for the liveliness of the conflict. The Christian may see certain features of the respective views of which the secular scholar is perhaps unaware. For example, the alert Christian will reject the behaviorist's assumption that man is merely a high-form animal and can be described in propositions drawn from pigeon, rat, and primate research. The alert Christian will also have trouble with the behaviorist's determinism, and with the presupposition that the more educated should decide what the less educated should learn. Equally unacceptable, of course, is the social-learning view that the child is a "blank slate" to be written on by parents, preachers, teachers, friends, and others. A Christian should not be content with any view of leadership that sees structuring the environment and controlling the contingency systems of rewards and punishments as the ultimate basis of determining what will be learned and what will be believed.

Somewhat more compatible with the biblical view of man are the key presuppositions of the developmental view: Development is a process of unfolding, following patterns that are genetically programmed and, within broad limits, in common with all mankind; environment affects but does not control development; the intellective processes are deeply interlocked with physical and emotional aspects of the person; the person has broad responsibility for affecting his or her own destiny.

Both social learning and behaviorism in education are marked by a high degree of planning *for* people; developmentalism in education is more inclined toward planning *with* people. Tightly programmed instructional strategies are usually based on the assumptions that the designer knows what the learner needs and can anticipate or predict the particular experiential sequence which will result in the needed learning; a behaviorist is more comfortable with programmed instruction of this sort.

In one respect the behaviorist of today is nothing more than a "highly armed" version of the ancient social-learning strategist dating back to the pre-Christian Greek era or before. They share many traits in common, including their view of knowledge as a sort of "out there" stuff that must be acquired by bringing it into one's knowledge storehouse, a task most easily accomplished with the help of a teacher whose job it is to organize it into appropriate bundles.

It seems ironic that the Christian education field contains so much behaviorism! Behaviorism's basic tenets are antithetical to Christianity! But Christians are apparently more comfortable with knowledge as perceptual information rather than as developed experience. Surely this is justified to some extent, since the Bible is our authoritative basis. But wait! The Bible itself is a developmental document—developmentally unfolding God's processes of dealing redemptively with man.

Many developmentalists are humanists (whose "man is the measure of all things" fails the biblical test of truth). Perhaps then, Christians, and especially Christian educators, tend to reject them, consequently failing to recognize the crucial validity of a developmental posture on teaching and learning.

The growing split in social science between developmentalism and behaviorism affects all educators. We each need to know where we stand and why. A small handful of us are describing our own position as "creational developmentalism" to identify both our belief in God as source and origin, and our views of the nature of man, though fallen, as capable of unfolding and developing in ways that reflect the grandeur and beauty of the Creator's great goodness.[2]

The Case for Developmental Leadership

The Bible makes frequent reference to vines, grain, and trees in order to make abstract points more concrete. The long-standing explanation is that since the people among whom the biblical incidents occurred were mostly agrarian folk, this heavy use of analogies from farming made the messages more understandable. Reasonable enough; but the developmentalist sees more. The analogies are not just agrarian, most are botanical. Aside from the heavy use of the shepherd-sheep relationship and an occasional donkey or ox, the heavy emphasis is on things that grow as plants. The features that are given attention create a sort of master analogy: human development and the process of maturity are like those of the plant: Its nature and pattern of unfolding is within it. Its environment (water, light, and air) significantly affects or alters its rate of growth and sometimes determines its physical survival, but it is not the determinant of the nature or growth pattern of the plant. Purposing (goal-setting) within the plant is not the crucial issue. God provides for the growth ("lilies . . . take no thought for tomorrow"); blooming is a fulfilling phase, not a constant condition; fruit is a seasonal matter; and dormancy is normal. What a boost to mental health is provided by this non-compulsive biblical analogy. One even gets the impressions that it's O.K. to shrivel a bit on dry days, get brittle from overexposure to the wind, and have periods when barrenness isn't even embarrassing! Could such a view be part of Paul's awareness of this freedom in Christ (1 Cor. 10:29; Gal. 5:1)?

2. The concept does not imply innate goodness of man, though it does accept that the Creator has graciously provided man a moral conscience, capable of enlightening him to the ways of the created moral universe, though inadequate in itself to establish righteousness before God, q.v., Romans 1:18–2:16.

Going one step beyond these particulars of the botanical model, we can suggest some propositions about leadership. Consider the leader as a gardener (not the farm *owner*—be careful). In the current fad of houseplant care, it is expected that the gardener will talk to the plants; even singing to them is alleged to help. Be that as it may, one thing that gardeners *don't* do now or in Bible times is to exhort the plants to be plants. No amount of lecturing, argument, or even shouting will change a tomato plant into a cucumber or make a rose bloom. The gardener cares for the environmental needs so that the plant can be what it is, in itself; so that it can develop into its own fulfillment. The gardener doesn't bring on the bloom, the plant does—because it is in its nature. The gardener facilitates; that is, he or she helps to assure the conditions that the plant needs.

The botanical analogies also remind us that there are all sorts of plants in the world—all sorts of *good* plants. What a pity if we didn't have watermelon vines! And what a pity if *all* we had were watermelon vines—everywhere, as far as you could see, watermelons, watermelons, watermelons. *The church needs leadership that values differences!*

The competent gardener knows the plants and provides for them according to their particular needs. Isn't the "new nature in Christ" deserving of such a gentle, loving treatment? Do leaders in the church need a big stick or a watering pot? Surely a little hoeing of weeds is important, but here, too, the Bible speaks: When the hoeing of weeds would likely also disturb the roots of the good grain, put the hoe away until the Lord of the Harvest comes to do his own sorting out! *The church needs nonjudgmental leadership.* "Do not judge lest you be judged yourselves" (Matt. 7:1).

Things that come in for heavy judgment of the Lord of the Harvest are those that violate their nature, particularly trees that don't bear fruit. But a good gardener knows you have to give a tree many years to demonstrate its nature—some much more than others. How damaging to count success in terms of short-range goals! *The church needs patient leadership—faithful leadership,* not suspicious leadership. "Love is patient . . . love is not jealous" (1 Cor. 13:4).

Pruning is part of the picture, but it is attuned to the nature of the plant. Pruning helps grape vines and roses; but it would be absurd to prune a carrot. The good gardener doesn't come down on everything with the same tactics. The church needs leadership that accommodates individual development characteristics.

I've seen many beautiful gardens, ranging from my daughter's greenhouse bedroom to the magnificent sprawling gardens of Europe. I've learned to expect one thing to always be true. In every beautiful garden not only are there many varieties and species of growing things, each encouraged and supported to be the very best of what it is within itself, but somewhere in the shadows is a gardener. Rarely out front, but usually just out of sight—watching, caring, enjoying—is a very happy, loving gardener. Gardeners are a funny bunch: They like people to enjoy and praise the gardens, but they don't need much praise themselves. I'll never forget the gardener in Geneva who had spent about an hour happily showing the little group of Americans one after another of the specimens in a magnificent but small public park. The conversation shifted from the beauty of the garden to his competency as a great gardener. We turned from the flowers to pursue our questions about how he brought it all about. But to our surprise, he had disappeared. *The church needs leadership that plays down its own importance.*

These may sound more like the remarks of a poet than of a scientist. I was asked to bring a paper on "what the new research in education suggests about developing effective leadership for the church." What I have said here may not fulfill expectations behind the original request, but I believe I am doing what I was asked to do. The truth is that there are vast shelves of research reports that have one or another bits to add to our understanding of effective leadership in the church. They can be divided into two categories: those bits that give more about the techniques and technologies for changing people, and those bits that help us better understand what human development is all about and how it can be facilitated. As time goes on, I'm less and less interested in the first—with advancing age comes ever lower confidence in my ability to decide how other people should age change. And I am more and more convinced that in the second category of research there is little that is fundamentally new. Perhaps it would be better to say that the second category reiterates, amplifies, and finds new application of the developmental concepts we find in the Bible. And so it should be. The Author of the Bible is the Creator of the magnificent sixth-day creature. As we study this creature—personal attributes and social transactions—we recognize more of the detail lying within human development, that most complex process which sprang from those seven words: "Let us make man in our image."

The research on human development, learning, and social transaction is saying this to me: Leadership is a serving relationship that has the effect of facilitating development of human beings. With this sort of definition in hand, we can draw from the most significant research of the past thirty years: Jean Piaget on cognitive development, Erik Erikson on stages of life, Carl Rogers on personhood and human transactions, Cartwright and Zander on human groups, Ron Lippitt on leader behaviors and change, Claude Levi-Strauss on social structure, Lawrence Kohlberg on moral development, Biddle and Thomas on role-taking, Jerome Kagan on bio-social development, Flavell on self-actualization, Bernice Neugarten on adult socialization, Jane Loevinger on ego strength, Urie Bronfenbrenner on family development, and many others whose studies interlock and complement.

But is it practical? Can we say anything further than generalizations about what leadership ought to be? Always we come back to these questions, and the theorist is not turned off. It was once said, "There is nothing more practical than good theory." The following section is illustrative of the practical advice that can come from the developmental research. The content of this example, motivation, is the key to effective leadership.

Understanding Motivation Developmentally

A major issue, perhaps *the* major issue of leadership is the matter of motivation. High on any list of leadership skills is the leader's capacity to motivate. How much do we really know about this process?

Motivation is still largely a mystery. Among the findings of social science are all sorts of information about moral judgment, for example, but very little about moral action. It is now fairly clear how people determine what they *should do,* but we lack understanding of the basis on which a person decides actually *to do* something. Thus we still must speculate about the important matter of what causes a person to act on his or her motivations. All we can say now is that moral behavior has at least three facets: *knowing* to do, *willing* to do, and *strength* to do.

We need to know more, but that should be no excuse for failing to use wisely what we do know. We should be aware of the basic facts about motivation; and we should know what they suggest about ways to help people. There are several important things that we can know from the research on human development.

For example, we know these things about motivation as a process:

1. The roots of motivation are deep within a person. Motivation comes from inside!
2. Motivations are complex, and in no two persons is the pattern of motivation exactly alike.
3. In certain ways, we are all very much alike as human beings. The ways we are basically alike underlie our motivations.
   a) We all have essentially the *same basic human needs*, though we may find different ways to meet these needs.
   b) We all develop through the *same stages of intellectual (cognitive) function*, though we develop at different rates.
   c) We all develop through the *same stages of moral judgment*, though we each may get "stuck" at different stages.

The research suggests these things about our own motivation:

1. We are rarely aware of all our own motivations.
2. We can become more aware of our own motivations.

3. As we better understand where our own motivations come from, we become more able to accept another person's motivations.
4. Our opinions and prejudices about an experience or object will affect to some extent whether or not we are motivated by the experience or object.
5. We cannot always be sure in advance whether or not we will find an experience or object to be motivating.
6. A wider range of motivations can be awakened through a wider variety of experiences.

We have ways to see the motivations of others:

1. If one knows enough about how people develop, particularly about the stages of development people move through, it is possible to predict the particular factors that might make an experience or object motivating to a person.
2. We can often see a distinction between *intrinsic motivations* (motivations imbedded in the person's own experience), and *extrinsic motivations* (motivations that are attached to the experience by another person's arbitrary action). The distinction is like the difference between enjoyment of raising flowers because of the (intrinsic) satisfaction of it, versus the reward of getting (extrinsic) blue ribbons at the flower show.
3. Two persons might be motivated by a given experience or object for two very different reasons.

The research even enlightens us about the matter of motivating other people.

1. Whatever is done to "motivate" a person must somehow connect with the roots of motivation—drives, urges, needs—within that person.
2. Relating a motivational emphasis to the person's own development will increase the likelihood of engaging the person's motivations.
3. We cannot *give* motivation to a person, though we can expose the person to an experience or object that might relate to the person's basic motivation.
4. The basic legitimate motivational activities are the following:
   a) *Sharing* (involving another person in one's own experience) is the most effective means of motivation through exposure to new exp riences; setting examples plays a part.
   b) *Encouragement* (selectively encouraging the worthy things a person is experiencing) has a positive motivational effect.

c) *Stimulation*, sometimes called prodding, works well only if the person being prodded is quite accepting and has respect for the one who provides the stimulus.
d) *Association*, helping a person see the similarities between a new experience or object and one for which he or she already has a motivation, can help the motivation to "transfer."
e) *Facilitation*, helping a person accomplish and be successful in an experience, will help him or her gain satisfaction and thus gain motivation.

But through it all we recognize that there are hazards in motivating others.

1. Only a fine line separates motivating from manipulating. The key issue is whether or not what one does to "motivate" overpowers the other person's own judgment and needs. Manipulation involves serious moral and ethical issues.
2. When we engage in manipulation, it shows our own lack of respect for the soundness and reasonableness of our purposes.
3. A person motivated (manipulated) against his or her better judgments will likely turn against the manipulator sooner or later.
4. Plotting and manipulating, even if they catch the "target" person's attention, may turn him or her off cold!

Back to the Scripture, with Developmental Perspective

What would happen to "Christian education" if the teachings of Jesus were taken seriously? For one thing, there would be less emphasis on talk and more on action. But changes in leadership style would be even more noticeable.

Much of "Christian education" is patterned on secular instructional and cultural approaches to teaching and learning. From Sunday school to seminary the approaches are adaptations of the ancient Greek academic traditions—traditions that were well established by the time of Christ.

The Greek concepts of knowledge and learning were sharply in contrast with those of the Hebrew Scriptures; Jesus deliberately chose not to adopt them. He built no school, put himself in no high-status lectureships, and raised no funds to perpetuate his teachings through an endowed institution. He could have done so; among the elite of that day, such practices were more acceptable than what he chose to do. He selected a handful of candidates and lived among them, an itinerant community of friends.

Toward the end of his earthly ministry with this close circle of disciples, he stated very clearly what he had been demonstrating for three years. The most influential leader the world has ever known went on record squarely against the prevailing secular approach to leadership. What he said has been largely ignored down through the years because the secular concept of leadership seems more reasonable than Christ's propositions.

"Leaders must lead. To lead one must have authority. And to lead with authority one must be prestigiously and conspicuously above those who are to be led. Preferably the leader must deserve and merit his position and lead with honor and competence. Leaders have command and 'presence,' and great leaders exercise authority." Thus it is among the Greeks and Romans.

"It shall not be so among you," Jesus said (Matt. 20:25–60). Since Jesus rejected the time-honored secular concept of leadership, what did he suggest instead? "Whoever is to be great among you, let him serve you. Whoever wants to be the chief leader shall be your servant" (Matt. 20:26–27).

Is servanthood—the text suggests the lowest servanthood, that of a slave—perhaps a punishment for wanting to be a leader? Or maybe the point here is that one should prove his humility through a probationary servanthood. (Americans are especially fond of the idea that true greatness is a dramatic rising from a lowly beginning.) No, the true message of this Scripture is clarified in a hard-to-accept jolt: Jesus refers to *himself* as the example of the servant-leader—"Just as I did not come to be served, but to *serve,* and *to give my life* . . ." How powerful this contrast becomes in Paul's review of it: "Have this attitude in you which was also in Christ Jesus, who, although he existed in the form of God, did not regard equality with God a thing to be held onto, but emptied himself, taking the form of a bondservant, and being made in the likeness of men. And being found in appearance as a man, he humbled himself by becoming obedient to the point of death, even death on a cross" (Phil. 2:5–8). So *this* is what Jesus had in mind as a contrast with the elegant, secular view of prestigious leadership! It is hardly an appealing alternative. What would the church look like if leadership were defined in these terms?

As if his straightforward rejection of the secular ("Gentile" or Greek) concept of leadership weren't enough, Jesus brings it up again (Matt. 23:1–12), this time in reference to what had gone wrong in the synagogues and temple: those who sit in Moses' seat, taking responsibility for the religious leadership of God's people, (1) have made a faulty division between word and deed. They talk a good line but they don't put it into action. (2) They take it upon themselves to tie up neat bundles of tasks for their followers. They see leadership as a matter of deciding what others should do, but they don't actually get down to the hard part themselves. (3) They make their good works highly visible and take their satisfactions from the praises of men. (4) They perpetuate and expand on the traditions of "pomp and circumstance" so as to make themselves more distinct from the common people. (5) They bask in the honors of their rank and accept favors and privileges as if they were entitled to them. (6) The like to be called by a distinctive title that represents their authority and prestige: Rabbi!

"Do not be called Rabbi," said Jesus, as if to summarize his rejection of this whole secular leadership style that had infected the worship of Jehovah. Why not be called Rabbi? "Because you have but one teacher—you are all brothers!"

He was talking to his disciples, to the apostles upon whose shoulders rested the vital responsibility of continuing after his departure to carry out the most dynamic leadership task ever assigned to a group of human beings. And not one of these men was to let himself be called "Rabbi"—honored religious teacher and leader. And if this weren't clear enough (perhaps to close all the loopholes), he goes on to point out that he is talking broadly about *leadership*: "Don't call anyone 'Father.'" You can't create relationships with labels; make relationship-building your approach, not labeling. "And don't let anyone call you 'Leader,' because you have only one leader, Christ!" He follows this with a deliberate review of what he had said earlier about leadership: "You know your leaders by their servanthood."

What changes in our concept of the church would result from taking Jesus seriously? The mind boggles. And what about changes in the education of leadership persons for the church? Leadership for the church is what theological education is all about, lest we forget! The issue that demands more careful attention is *what concept of leadership is being practiced and taught.* What is its source? Christ or culture?

The six faults pointed out by Jesus in Matthew 23:1–7 might serve well as evaluative criteria for "Christian education." If we assume the logical contrast with the faulty conditions to be the appropriate criteria, here is an example of how the list would look:

1. Emphasis on *knowing* is to be accompanied by emphasis on *doing*. Human development is a holistic matter—you can't split off one aspect of the person to deal with. Further, enhancement of mental processes (such as recall of information) is an insufficient goal of education.
2. People are to help in identifying their own needs and should participate in goal-setting. Leading is a matter of working encouragingly as a sharer of experiences. It is not the place of the leader to determine what the learner needs and to prepackage and prescribe a load of tasks.
3. Those who teach are to show, by precept *and by example*, the value of avoiding the praises of men, doing nothing for self-glorification or for the gratification of self-serving rewards. Instead, the beauty and deeper satisfaction of glorifying God and bringing encouragement and honor to others should be sought.
4. Traditions and symbols are to be evaluated against the criterion of servanthood. Whatever would attract attention to the glorification

of the merits and efforts of any person other that Christ should be brought under specific scrutiny. "Let each of you regard one another as more important than himself" (Phil. 2:3).

5. Access to resources, matters of convenience, and other privileges are to be shared as peers. If special treatment is in order, such as circumstances that can be alleviated by temporary granting of preferential treatment, the criterion should be *need*, not rank, status, age, seniority, or gender.
6. The whole environment is to reflect the unity of a true community. The lordship of Christ and the mutual indebtedness of all—teachers and learners alike—to the reality of his presence as sole Teacher should not be compromised by titles of distinction and honorific symbols of rank or prestige. The main issue is less the use or non-use of titles but more the seeking after true functional relationships within the family of Christ.

Some of these criteria may need to be compromised or softened to some extent for effective nurturing of children whose motivations and values are still in the self-oriented early stages. But for normal adolescents and adults, "Christian education" would be more truly *Christian* if these criteria were observed. Why don't we see more of it? The ease with which certain of Jesus' teachings are overlooked by those who claim to be engaged in his work is amazing indeed.

What can scientific research and sound educational theory offer to the development of more appropriate leadership in the church? A more thorough grounding in what is known about human development, for one thing, and a new impetus to get our theology into action, for another!

For Reflection

1. What is the "management era" in leadership training? How does Professor Ward respond to this?
2. How are *leadership* and *servanthood* related? Different?
3. Describe *developmental leadership*. Give a good example of leadership and/or a bad example of leadership. Can you judge these by the developmental description?
4. How would your own experience as a leader need to change if it were to conform to Ward's suggestions?

20

Donald M. Joy

A Proposal for Tomorrow
(1969)

Donald Joy has been associated for many years with Asbury Theological Seminary as professor of human development and Christian education. He took this position shortly after writing this book, which stems from his varied experiences in church curriculum projects in the United States and from work abroad with the Protestant Religious Education team, a group who worked with chapels of the United States Air Force European Command. The book also reflects the concerns growing out of his graduate work at the University of Indiana.

Professor Joy believes that insights about about *how* people learn are crucial for Christian educators. He is concerned with whether Christian education is *Christian* in goals, techniques, and content, and concerned with the larger question of whether it is *education*. These issues are appropriate for Christian educators to consider if they believe the human capacity for learning and the means of acquiring knowledge are God-given. Effective teaching in Christian education, for Joy, is "working with the grain" put into human beings at creation by the Creator and accumulated history.

Three of the author's personal convictions give rise to his book, *Meaningful Learning in the Church.*

1. Man is a specially endowed creature with a capacity to know and to learn. If he is to be well served by the church, we must be attentive to the ways of

From *Meaningful Learning in the Church* (Winona Lake, Ind.: Light and Life, 1969), 126–52.

> knowing and to the emerging strategies of learning so as to help human beings grasp the vision of themselves and their world which is the distinctive property of the Christian faith (10).

Related to this is his belief that the great malady of contemporary American culture is the loss of a clear sense of destiny which invests self and all others with immeasurable worth.

> 2. The grand ideas of the Christian faith as expressed in Holy Scripture and in the person of Jesus Christ concerning the nature of man, the world, God, sin, and salvation constitute the most ennobling and driving vision ever entertained in the mind of beings on this planet; it remains for men who are possessed by this faith and who are its custodians to communicate it meaningfully to all persons who can be brought under its influence (11).
>
> 3. The most convincing specimen of the power of Jesus Christ in the world is the typical lay-volunteer teacher who may need abundant help in making his teaching effective, but who brings to his task—by virtue of his own commitment to Christ—a complex set of skills for communicating Christian concepts, values, and attitudes (13).

Joy is impressed with the potential of lay leadership in Christian education to be a living "incarnation" of God in the world. That person is proof that Jesus Christ makes a difference in people's lives. A congregational program staffed wholly by professionals could not alone be demonstration of Christ's-transforming power.

There are great hazards facing anyone who would attempt to make predictions in these times. Some people still claim that "history repeats itself" and that, therefore, it is easy to predict the future by knowing one's history. But the old assertion—which may have had an element of validity during the long centuries of man's primitive existence—is hardly adequate for today. It collapses chiefly on the fact that history cannot repeat itself; we are not feeding the same elements into it. These are new times. We know ourselves better than did any generation before. We know our environment better. We know the real nature of our problems or are much nearer finding out. This is not to say that a golden tomorrow is guaranteed; indeed, tomorrow may be ushered out by a wave of atomic mushrooms. Or it may be left in shambles in the wake of some insane race revolution. But it will be different from any previous time—and hence not easily predictable.

Although we imagine that nuclear and space developments are our greatest signs of change, it may well be that history will record of us that equally significant changes were brought on by less flamboyant discoveries. The process of education, for example, is being radically changed as we come to better know human nature and human potential. Not everyone is interested in going to the moon. Some thoughtful scientists are trying to break through into an understanding of the seat of man's real problems: motivation, thinking, learning, and the formation of values (conscience).

After making the observations of the previous nine chapters, I am probably obligated to say something about their implications for the immediate future of learning in the church. I choose not to predict what shape church education will take in twenty-five years. Instead, I wish only to set down what it seems to me are desirable and possible developments for tomorrow—now.

The "Concept Curriculum"

It becomes evident that the most urgent educational ministry for persons in the church is instruction which leads to the development of significant concepts. Traditional Sunday school lessons tend to be taught either as Bible events cast in interesting stories or as Bible content set forth as "ground to cover." The use of rich Bible material in either of these ways creates the impression that if one knows the story or has covered the ground he has no further need to consider the Bible material. It also suggests that the Bible is merely a book to be known, when, in fact, it is a book which must be brought to life as its grand ideas catch the vision of men.

It is true that certain of the key concepts require a grasp of the flow of events over a sustained period of time, so at some point a person must acquire the big picture of God's work through history. God's acts of redemption form a general parallel concept which has the appearance of "ground covering." But the learner need not plow through the vast stretches of the centuries at a snail's pace in once-a-week intervals; indeed, if he did, he would almost certainly lose the big picture and be lost in a field of largely disconnected facts and events. Perhaps such "high altitude" concepts should be explored in a more concentrated curriculum than the once-a-week Sunday school.

Most concepts have an individuality and a complexity that make them worthy of intensive and recurring exploration. Noah, for example, might be met by students looking at the acts of God in history, but there is a great deal more to discover about him than his place in time. Suppose that in our master list of concepts worthy of exploration the concept of "grace" is included. Noah is a person of whom Scripture records that he "found grace in the eyes of the Lord" (Gen. 6:8). In developing a working definition of "grace," we should carefully examine Noah's relationship to God. In fact, many young adults who have come up through Sunday school seem never to have formed the concept of "grace" in anything like an adequate way. Suppose, again, that our master list of concepts worth knowing as an adult contains the concept of "perfection." We may find ourselves going back to Noah again to discover what Scripture means when it says that Noah was "perfect" in his generation (Gen. 6:9). We will, of course, make a depth exploration of Jesus' words in

Matthew 5:48. But an adequate concept of "perfect" when applied to believers in God requires patient and repeated weaving together of a wide range of perceptions. Both of these examples illustrate how a concept curriculum, whether designed by denominational curriculum planners or developed by parents for use with their own children, differs significantly from a curriculum that is planned to "cover the ground." Indeed, a concept curriculum might seem sometimes to cover very little ground and to cover it very slowly, for great ideas take time to grow. They tend to stimulate spontaneous adventures in learning which are costly of time.

An immediate need is for the development of a master list of Christian education concepts. It would identify those issues, principles, and values which are of abiding concern to mankind. Age-level perceptions should be defined for each of these, and a hierarchy and structure given to the entire list.[1]

The next step would require that for each concept a complete set of procedures be developed, tested, and refined for use in teaching the concept. Procedures would be needed for dealing with the required perceptions at each level.

The master list of concepts for Christian education must be developed by drawing on resource persons with the best competences available in theology, psychology, and anthropology. A continuing study should be maintained as concepts are identified, defined, revised, and enlarged.

After the master list is available, the procedures should be developed by bringing to the task the best energies of learning experts and curriculum development specialists. The procedures for each concept should be carefully validated through actual teaching in pilot and research settings.

These two kinds of working commissions require calling together a task force of persons having scarce resources. Not many publishers could afford a panel of such men on their staffs. Besides, if the resource persons are to maintain their skills, they are more likely to do so in research and educational settings than in actual materials' preparation employment. The implications then become clear. Denominational curriculum developers and publishers must turn to research and high-skill talents most often found in colleges, seminaries, and universities. These experts should be engaged for specialized services as needed.

At this moment theological and psychological resources might be readily available in college and seminary faculty persons. The traditional liberal arts colleges and seminaries, however, are rarely engaged in front-line research. It seems reasonable to predict that a call for help from the curriculum develop-

1. Three useful taxonomies cataloging learners' basic needs, learners' engagement in the learning tasks, and possible results of learning are incorporated in *Tools of Curriculum Development for the Church's Educational Ministry* (Anderson, Ind.: Warner, 1967), 23–70. A taxonomy of "concepts" would differ somewhat from even the third of these and especially would need the additional classification indicating both the logical and the urgency order of the many concepts.

ers might provide an impetus to educational research and Christian education specialization in the denominational colleges and graduate schools. In addition, the curriculum developers might act to reach research scholars, graduate students, and research specialists whose energies might be harnessed. They could contribute to the task of identifying concepts and developing the educational procedures for building them in the minds of children, young people, and adults in the church.

The "Spiral Curriculum"

Jerome Bruner of Harvard offers us a theory to the effect that any concept which is worth knowing as an adult can be taught in some intellectually honest form to any person of any age. That is, there are "percepts" that may be explored within any age or ability level which contribute to building the larger "concept."

Suppose, in our research, that we discover there are a dozen (or a hundred) concept families which have abiding significance in the life of a person. Then, these concepts need to be scheduled for exploration by every growing person periodically during his lifetime. Bruner suggests that even the elementary child's curriculum should be tested in every point to determine whether his learning has abiding and expanding value to him (Bruner 1960, 52). He thinks that those things should be discarded which do not contribute in some way to the large concepts which will be useful to him as an adult.

This is not to say that a preschool or an early elementary child should be expected to deal precisely and definitively with a concept such as "Christian perfection." But there are numerous perceptions he might grasp which are useful to him now and which also begin to build a foundation for a well-formed concept to sustain him as an adult. His earliest insights into the concept may be represented to him by action or by images. Most surely he will open up his early understandings along intuitive lines more than along analytical ones. But foundational percepts of his concepts of "Christian perfection" include (1) his perception of constant love as an attribute of parents, (2) his earliest impressions of the God who has loved him constantly and perfectly, (3) his own inward yearning for harmonious and satisfying relationships, and (4) his inclination to work for closure—completed tasks and full-blown ideas, for example. These begin to lay a base for an increasingly well focused idea of God's image restored through the grace of Jesus Christ in men who are re-created and made whole persons in the image of God's Son.

By calling for a "spiral curriculum," I am only urging that the concepts our students need should be arranged mechanically for recurring exploration and development. At the minimum, a spiral curriculum for the Sunday school would schedule these concepts, not only for an orderly progression along a horizontal time plane, but also for an orderly repetition of concept exploration at the higher levels. Timing and spacing should be determined by the span of the age-level cycles, presumably bringing each concept up for additional exploration during the span of each cycle. I have suggested earlier that the traditional grouping of preschool, early elementary, upper elementary, junior high, and senior high age-group cycles would seem both to serve developmental purposes and to offer sufficient breadth for a comprehensive coverage of essential concepts.

Closing the Generation Gap

If it is true, as the Cornell research seems to suggest, that the American society is pulling apart at the peer culture seams,[2] church education ministries might find ways of helping to mend the tear in our culture. A distinctive feature of the Judeo-Christian strain in history has been its vision that the home is the fountainhead of moral and spiritual values and instruction in a particular life style. The Cornell research found that Russian peer groups serve the national interest in shaping children's values by social pressure. This socialistic model of conscience development is particularly well suited in a culture where a rapid change in mass viewpoint and values is wanted. Both the Judeo-Christian and the democratic view of man have been that we are obligated to our own history. We have held that long-treasured values are not quickly erased from the minds of any people without jeopardizing the future of humanity. Hence, these viewpoints have tended to hold the family in high regard as the custodian of values, in contrast to the more laboratory-like situation in which a government or a particular leader imposes a new set of values by applying peer and political pressure according to personal, economic, or insane whims.

It may be of profound importance, therefore, that we find ways of restoring the initiative for moral instruction to the American home. In the proposal I am making, there are two specific kinds of action that seem to be open to us in closing the generation gap.

One potential solution is in creating a home curriculum which will provide parents with a conversation agenda. Perhaps only parents who have a high interest in the Christian nurture of their children will respond to such a program, but then parents who make commitments to Christ and the church tend to be those who want to be the best parents. With a "spiral curriculum" which gives recurring attention to the great issues, principles, and values of the Christian faith, a home curriculum becomes an immediate possibility. By careful timing in the church study schedule, all age levels could be exploring within the same concept at the same time. At home there could then be rein-

2. See discussion in chap. 9 [of *Meaningful Learning in the Church*], 111, 112. See also Urie Bronfenbrenner, "The Split-Level American Family," *Saturday Review*, vol. 50, no. 40:60–66, October 7, 1967.

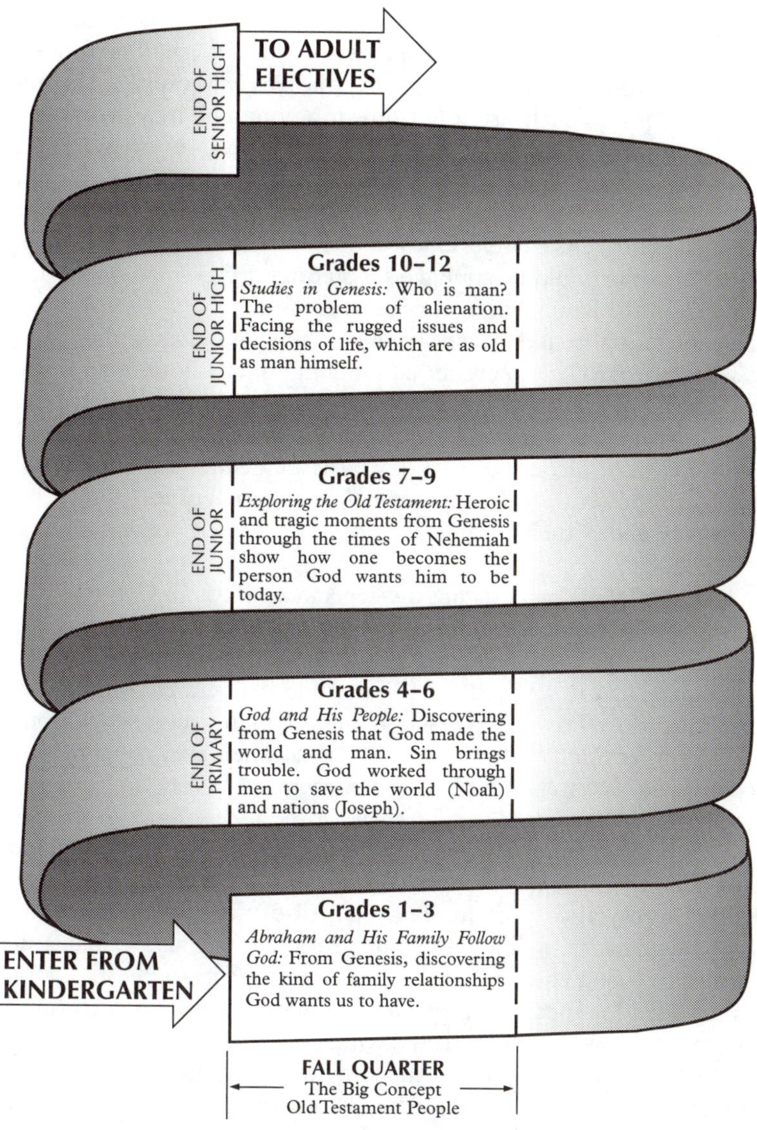
TO ADULT ELECTIVES
END OF SENIOR HIGH
Grades 10–12
Studies in Genesis: Who is man? The problem of alienation. Facing the rugged issues and decisions of life, which are as old as man himself.
END OF JUNIOR HIGH
Grades 7–9
Exploring the Old Testament: Heroic and tragic moments from Genesis through the times of Nehemiah show how one becomes the person God wants him to be today.
END OF JUNIOR
Grades 4–6
God and His People: Discovering from Genesis that God made the world and man. Sin brings trouble. God worked through men to save the world (Noah) and nations (Joseph).
END OF PRIMARY
Grades 1–3
Abraham and His Family Follow God: From Genesis, discovering the kind of family relationships God wants us to have.
ENTER FROM KINDERGARTEN
FALL QUARTER
The Big Concept
Old Testament People

forcing conversations on the common concept. Two immediate benefits emerge: (1) Parents, the most significant persons in the lives of children, have an opportunity to speak on the most important issues of life in the presence of their children. Many parents would welcome that opportunity, but few have the initiative to create their own religious education program. Consequently, in the harried and stratified family life of our culture, many children never hear their parents speak on the issues of faith and life. (2) Children join the education team as they contribute to conversations in which other children are forming ideas. It is no secret that a twelve-year-old can often make clear to a six-year-old things which a parent gropes helplessly to explain. The modes of representation evidently are more similar among children themselves than between children and adults. What is more, the values of an idolized big brother or sister go a long way in influencing a younger child in the family. A home curriculum would bring all these influences to bear on the formation of values. The curriculum could follow a daily dinner-table devotional and discussion format or could be arranged for an extended evening or Sunday afternoon session the family might choose to set aside.

Parents must also understand that a formal religious curriculum at home is not all-sufficient. The "phantom curriculum" of any household is spun out in the day-by-day attitudes and opinions which are expressed by parents. Perhaps the home curriculum could keep this phantom dimension in the minds of parents. Without dictating its content, the guidelines might help them see the potential power of their own viewpoints on moral issues, of their behavior under stress, and of their attitudes toward other persons both within the home and outside it.

A second way of consolidating the generations through Christian education ministries in the church would involve temporary but periodic breaking down of the airtight age-level groupings in the church. Again, with a concept curriculum arranged in a timed spiral, we could deliberately shuffle people to spread their ideas. For example, selected junior high young people could help for two or three Sundays in the primary classes. There they could participate in discovery and in conversations having a bearing on the concept being explored. Or we could bring selected families together for three sessions to share insights and do further exploration together on the concept being considered. It is conceivable that in a given church, traditional groups might be suspended for three weeks above the junior level. All of the constituency might be engaged systematically either in seminars for the whole family, in instructional assistance in young children's classes, or in cross-generation exploration seminars grouped for specialized or intensive work. Such a restructuring of the classes would provide a potentially exciting culmination to a period of exploration with one's own peers. At the same time it would tend to cement the entire church community as the flow of common concepts spread across the generations. The pastor's pulpit role in all of this might be open to equally creative innovation.

Programmed Instruction in the Church

Programmed instruction refers to the use of teaching techniques or devices which provide the learner with a series of learning steps, each of which is rewarded if properly completed. The so-called teaching machine is one form of programmed instruction. The typical machine presents a small piece of information which must be learned before you can proceed to the next "frame." The "reward" may consist of candy, money, or simply the satisfaction of having a right answer.

Two factors combine which tend to reduce the usefulness of programmed instruction for the church. First, the church possesses a large body of ideas or concepts which it wishes to convey to the young and to the newly recruited; programmed instruction is more easily adapted for use with highly factual bodies of information than with concepts. Second, the church tends to rely upon interpersonal dialogue as the most effective means of developing those ideas or concepts in the minds of its adherents; programmed instruction tends to be most useful for individual, often "solo," study.

This is not to say, however, that concepts cannot be programmed or arranged for "reinforcement learning." Indeed, United States servicemen subjected to Communist "education" in Korea gave us a vivid demonstration that ideas can be shaped by indoctrination which is accompanied by a system of rewards and punishment. But Russian psychology, which first gave us the conditioned response theory and the assumption that higher order learning was essentially the same as that of Pavlov's dogs, is reported to be turning to more active symbolical approaches to problem solving among children. At the same time American psychologists tend to be hanging on to the Pavlovian notions (Bruner 1965, 92).

Since we will want to keep alive the highest respect for the individual in all church education, we will not be likely to use the relatively "closed system" of mental manipulation in developing the grand concepts of the Christian faith. At the same time we are obligated to examine our instructional tasks to see whether there are not some which could better be handled by programmed learning. What are the heavy factual informational parts of our teaching ministry? What are the factual understandings which underlie our concept formation adventures?

Consider, for example, that large numbers of persons come into the fellowship of the church with virtually no religious training in their childhood background. They enter their respective classes on a Sunday morning without basic information or frames of reference badly needed to participate meaningfully in the class. Perhaps the church should develop several study laboratories to fill in the gaps:

Names and categories of Bible books
Condensed history of Bible events
Compact "tree" of Bible people
Denominational history
Basic beliefs: catechism

Such laboratories could be programmed into small sections for fitting into bits of time available before public services. A system of appropriate rewards could be developed. The programs could be "branched," so that when one was mastered adequately it would lead to another.

There might be other uses for such laboratories. Children and young people enrolled in the regular ministries of the church might use them at intervals to find whether their mastery of certain understandings was progressing satisfactorily. Then, too, the performance one showed in the laboratories might have a bearing upon his placement in classes in other phases of the ministry of the church.

We might adopt a guiding principle that any highly compact and precise kind of information which the church wishes to teach should be considered for programmed instruction. We would program it out of respect for the energies of the student and also to conserve limited class time for the kinds of learning which require interaction, discussion, and the formation of complicated attitudes, values, and understandings.

"Live Curriculum" for an Adult Elective

Among the most restless persons in the church are those young adults neither caught yet by the concerns of parenthood, nor trapped by their own childhood. These are creative and energetic persons whose commitment to Christ thrusts them forward to create a better world. Indeed, there are many adults who fully sense their parental responsibilities and are at the same time searching urgently for some means of dealing realistically and meaningfully with the problems of their times.

A large number of young adults want to bring their own times and situations into focus in the light of the Bible and of the revelation of God in Christ. But it is not easy for a publisher to bring out curriculum materials that get at the issues of demonstrations, assassinations, riots, and campus sit-ins *as they are occurring*. The curriculum can speak to the perennial needs of mankind, of course, but cannot deal with the volatile, earthshaking issues and events. By the time the discussion guides get into print the event will have long been passed and the issue will have probably become vastly more complicated.

The typical Sunday school lesson is outlined and sent on its way to final production about four years ahead of its use in a class. Publishers who operate with "short deadlines" still require that lesson manuscripts be in hand one year ahead of use. And when one thinks of all of the complicated supporting media needed for the vast array of curriculum one publisher puts together, it is easy to understand the need for long-range planning and scheduling.

It must be asked, however, whether a single discussion guide could not be released "live" to the thoughtful and energetic adult classes which demand to know how they can relate Christ's concern in the complicated social and moral climate of their times. Consider the fact that live television can now take us into a hut in the remotest village in the world and that this morning's news, complete with pictures, will be printed and in the hands of millions of people tonight. One could easily ask what motivations have pushed the secular society to act with such vigor in mass circulation of information and viewpoint. But if he did, he would also have to ask why Christian motivation to share information and interpretation of events remains content with virtually no instant means of communication. Even some denominational news magazines work with about a one-hundred-day blackout time between the editors and the readers.

Let me propose that a creative team of Christian education specialists could prepare, on a week-by-week basis, a discussion guide. It might be only four pages geared to current issues and concerns to which Christian adults might address themselves. The format could incorporate reprinted news excerpts, leading questions which Christians must ask of their own history and their own consciences. There could be citations to potential biblical resources and insights leading to action. This "Living Issues" adult curriculum could be compiled for a given week within a forty-eight-hour period and multilithed from typescript and stripped news excerpts. The whole thing could be ready for mailing within four days from conception. Lightweight multiple copies could be airmailed to distant points. A special subscription rate could be devised for single copies which would be specially prepared for photocopying at the point of use. This proposal has many potential variations. I offer it here chiefly to illustrate that in the church we have not yet taken advantage of our communications technology to spur the church to action or to shape its conscience rapidly. Yet we live in an era in which powerful forces are at work to change our values and commitments.

A Formula for Meaningful Teaching

I have . . . offered [no] simple solutions to [the] complex and unusual opportunities which confront us. I have tried to illustrate the need for creative and discovery-oriented teaching in the church and to give illustrations that inspire both excitement and hope that learning in the church can become more meaningful for all of us.

Let me close by suggesting what may seem to be an overly simple formula that you may apply to any learning session. I have reduced it to four key words. You may find better ones, but these form a chain which, it seems to me, is a particularly strong one with which to pull for meaningful learning. The four key words are "intersect," "investigate," "infer," and "implement." Here is how they interlock in a teaching-learning session:

Learning requires that the path of the student's interest is brought to *intersect* with a given idea, concept, or body of information. We sometimes speak glibly about "attention-getting devices." As a last resort, such devices are instru-

ments of intersecting student interest. More powerful intersection occurs when the needs of the person are met directly by the learning experience. We always ask: What are the living concerns of these students? What are their deepest needs? What do they *think* their deepest needs are? Can I lead them from the supposed need to the real one? What events in their immediate environment can I capitalize on to gain entrance to lead them to significant learning? Who are their heroes? How can I bring their devotion to those heroes to intersect with a higher call to commitment? Can this concept or this body of information be organized in such a way that it is relevant to the needs and experiences of this particular learning audience? So, for the curriculum developer, the writer, and the teacher, there is always this first claim: What we teach must first be set on a collision course such that it intersects with the awareness and interest of the person who needs to learn. If we take seriously our hypothesis that any concept worth possessing can be taught in some intellectually honest way to any child at any age, then we must find the "intellectually honest" way to represent the concept to the student so as to have obvious meaning to him.

Once the learner has intersected with the gold mine route leading to the rewarding concept, he needs help to *investigate* and work the rich conceptual field. If we follow discovery as a principal mode of inquiry, we will lead the learner to the resources, ask him to form tentative rules or hypotheses, test them, and arrive at working principles. He will probe, explore, unmask, and synthesize his findings in the act of discovery. We will moderate the learning experience, but rarely dictate. We will question the learner, helping him to test the integrity of his hypotheses, to determine whether he has asked appropriate questions and whether he has asked those questions of the best resources. If he is satisfied with a weak or erroneous hypothesis, we will cite him to further resources. It becomes evident that investigation thus becomes the principal phase of the learning formula for the acquisition of new information and for processing it into working principles. Notice, however, that what I am proposing differs radically from either an authoritarian or a "covering the ground" strategy of teaching. At the same time biblical resources come in for maximum use, not so much as anecdotal material, but as the source of ultimate authority for life and experience. Thus, Bible material is not encountered repeatedly in story form, but it becomes the mining field in which concepts take shape and working principles are formed. It is reasonable to believe every issue under exploration will lead ultimately and significantly to a serious examination of Bible material. Finally, the investigation will lead to formation of a new insight—a working hypothesis or rule growing out of the collision of God's truth with the student's real life. Insight is not an activity; it is a product of intersection and investigation.

When the learner has intersected with learning and has proceeded to investigate the resources available to him, his third obligation in meaningful learning is to *infer*—to draw inferences from his findings, which he can apply to real life. Here the teacher helps him to ask the critical questions: What are the implications of this finding for my day-to-day life? What generalizations can I derive from this particular concept as I have defined it? Whereas the investigative operation may often follow a convergent kind of thinking, the inferential operation requires abundant use of divergent thinking. Christian values can be applied to changing cultures only if imagination, insight, and creativity are brought to bear upon interpreting fixed principles and translating them for unpredictable situations.

Once inferences have been made and implications defined, it then remains for the learner to *implement* those understandings in actual practice. We indulge in a dangerous practice if we stop short of implementation in any learning experience in the church. If we stop with investigation, we have merely tasted of knowledge for the sake of knowledge. If we stop with inference, we have contented ourselves with being diagnosticians. Each of us who is related in any way to the educational ministry of the church must finally ask himself, for every learning event, "To what extent does this session, or this exploratory activity, bring the learner into a position such that he can actively put his understanding to work?" It is a dangerous error for us to suppose that since we are concerned with teaching "moral truth" we cannot be expected to develop performance skills. Indeed, it could be successfully argued that one does not, in fact, possess moral truth unless its impact is demonstrated in the quality of life and behavior which follows.

Now, having set forth this simple formula for effective teaching, I will close by relating it to . . . this model of "Life-Changing Learning."

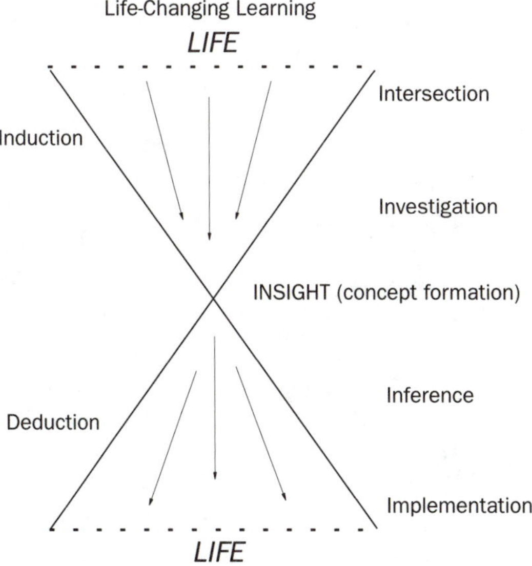

Notice that the learning experience of a person begins when real life is intersected by new ideas. They may come from some source outside of himself or even from his stumbling upon some "message" right in his environment. As he processes his observations, investigates the evidence, and forms tentative rules (hypotheses) which will help him make sense of new observations in relation to his old ones, he arrives finally at "insight." Insight comes only after he has sorted, discarded, and refined his rules until he has found the best hypothesis for dealing with his new information and all of his old understandings. From this moment on, he must draw inferences from his new insight. This leads, inevitably, to changes in his behavior—in his life. The quality of his living is changed. When he behaves differently we may say that he has implemented his learning.

Take an example: Suppose that I am the product of an essentially Caucasian, American culture. I grow up near an Indian reservation. From my earliest infancy I have heard people say that Indians are lazy, that they drink heavily, and that, in short, they are no good. My feeling for Indians is well fixed before I even start to school; my attitudes are well developed before I think about Christ's claim on my life. I may even be converted and still hold the same opinions about Indians; nothing in the religious life of my church directly reminds me of Indians—except references by missionaries to the residents of India, which they carefully avoid calling "Indians." Those in India are remote from me, are in desperate poverty, and need my compassion. But it is just here that I am confronted with a problem. Intersecting my peaceful life is a teaching: "God . . . hath made of one blood all nations of men . . ." (Acts 17:24, 26). There is also the intersecting of a troubling Christian idea: All men are persons of worth to God and must be regarded as such by Christians. These collide with my own long-standing ideas and practices. At last, I see that I must rearrange the furniture of my mind and my conscience: Indians in my community are objects of God's affection. I must show the love of Christ in my relationships with them and invest my energy in ministering to their needs.

When I pass the point of "insight," I am then confronted with further implications of my understanding. I infer these from what I have tested and found to be reality in developing my insight. I have never cultivated the friendship of an Indian; that must change. I have never tried to see things from an Indian's point of view—history, values, culture, for example; my task is clearly growing.

At each stage of the learning experience I must decide whether I will move into the next. But no decision is more crucial than the final one. Will I *act* on the understanding with all of its implications for me as I understand them at the present time? Implementation is the test of effective learning; it also is the lifelong task of the learner who must live out his understandings on many hundreds of concepts.

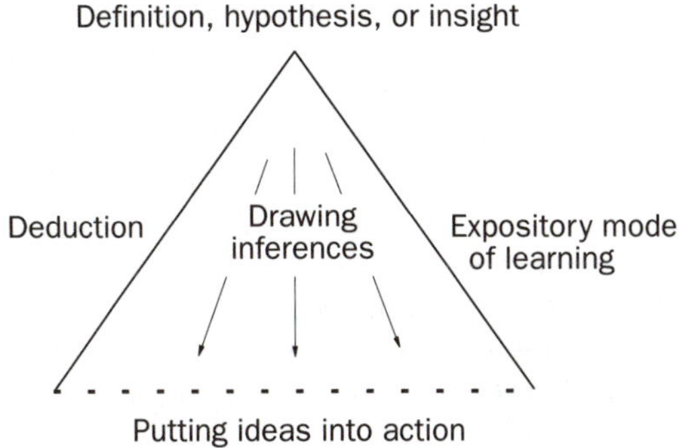

I have suggested in the model that the top portion of the diagram represents inductive reasoning. With induction, we begin with the understandings, feelings, actions, and issues as they really are with a person. But we add ingredients which will bring his attention to focus on a certain kind of problem. He will then find himself having to cope with the problem or idea by using his previously acquired equipment—his ideas, emotions, and habits. As he stirs in the new information and responds to new curiosities, he is trapped into making some kind of judgments or ground rules to cope with the new mixture he is

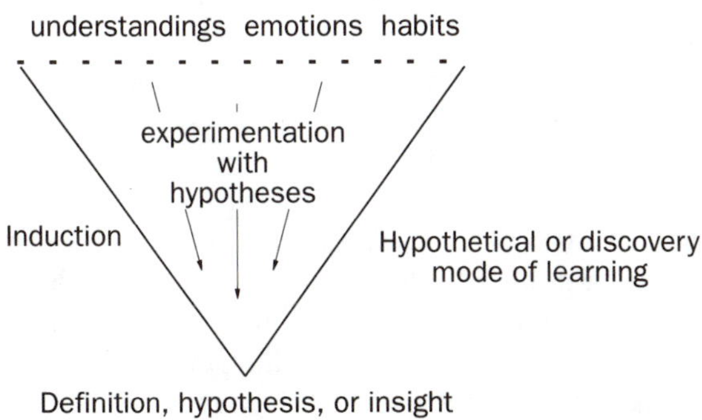

now dealing with. He narrows his hypotheses until the best one emerges: the definition or insight.

The lower portion of the "Life-Changing Learning" model represents deductive processes. With deduction we take an idea or hypothesis and work it over to get its message for us—we deduce its applications. Our entire attention is caught by the idea. We push it down in all directions to apply it to various aspects of life. If teaching begins here it makes one of two assumptions: (1) The learners are all wide awake to the profound importance and relevance of the definition about to be expounded for their benefit. (2) The definition, in itself, commands universal attention and banishes all other competing needs of the listeners. Either of the assumptions leaves us open to the comic tragedy of the Greek philosopher who loved to close his eyes while addressing his students—the more to follow his interesting train of thought. But alas, when he opened his eyes, he often found that he was left alone.

I have proposed the inductive-deductive model to represent life-changing learning in an effort to help us avoid the perils surrounding both modes of inquiry. The peril of induction or the hypothetical mode of inquiry *when used alone* is that it may lead nowhere in particular. It assumes that man by himself can find his way, and that man by himself can discover all that he needs to know. The peril of deduction or the expository mode of teaching is that *when used alone* it tends to disregard the real needs of learners, seems to ignore the fundamental nature of man and of the processes of learning, and, in short, may be answering questions which are not being asked by the learners.

In the educational work of the church we are committed to the view that if man is to find his way, it will be by the grace and wisdom of God. This means that the hypothetical mode of inquiry is always carried out in such a way as to unmask ultimate evidences. The learner is accepted where he is, with the needs he possesses, but evidences from the revelation of God in Jesus Christ and Holy Scripture are injected into his experience as he begins to formulate a meaningful pattern for himself. For example, we use the ultimate truth, not to bludgeon our "woman of Samaria" to death, but to dissolve the shackles of her ignorance, superstition, and sin so as to open to her the vision of what she was meant to be. What is more, finding her where she is with the real needs she possesses, we furnish the percepts only as she can take them in. The concept is what she builds from them. She did it, but not by herself. We entered her perceptual field—her real life as she saw it—and expanded her vision by injecting evidences leading to ultimate truth. The Spirit of God and of truth thus grants both the "message" and the "insight" in the mystery of learning in the church.

The point at which the two triangles meet in the "Life-Changing Learning" model represents discovery that is more than human discovery. It represents the insight that comes when a person has wrestled to reconcile what he already knows with what he has found to be ultimate reality—God's revelation of himself in Jesus Christ and in Holy Scripture. The "intersection" is always a confrontation of life as it is with clues about life as it may become. Thus "insight" always gives us a hypothesis which has both the dimensions of man's experience and of God's grace.

From this point on, we are ready for exploration in the expository mode. What are the implications of this insight for me? What can I infer from what I have understood and experienced? We met our candidate where she was (life=Samaria); she then formulated a hypothesis about what she might become. It now becomes important for her to know the implications of all of this for now (life=Samaria). Definitions become important to her when she has advanced to the level of asking for meanings; they might have had no interest to her before she felt the restlessness awakened by the claims of Christ upon her. By the grace and power of God she can then put into action the new understandings she has about herself.

Thus, the "Life-Changing Learning" model combines the hypothetical and the expository modes of inquiry for the special purposes of Christian education. Such education respects both the dilemma of man as he is and the authority and vitality of the Christian revelation as the vision which transforms man. We are able, in this way, to imitate our Lord who always began with life as it is in order to help a man discover what it ought to be. Our traditional limited "expository mode" has probably been the product of laziness; we were not so attentive to Jesus' method with men as we were to grasp and proclaim the essence of what he taught.

In this model we may have achieved the best of two possible worlds. We have found the learner where he is and have planted seeds of discontent and renewal that will help him begin his discovery of his real needs and appropriate solutions. When he has discovered those solutions, has felt the vibration of their ring of truth, we can then help him to find the definitions and the implications for turning his knowledge into action in his world. Perhaps there is no more concise description of meaningful learning in the church.

For Reflection

1. Why does Joy suggest that a "master list of concepts for Christian education" would be useful for the church?
2. What strategy does the author identify for the "recurring exploration and development" of concepts?
3. What influences are suggested to be brought to bear on "home curriculum"? Why?
4. State four key words in a formula for meaningful teaching. Give a brief example of such a formula in action.

References

Bruner, J. 1960. *The process of education*. New York: Random House.

———. 1965. *On knowing*. New York: Atheneum.

21

Lois E. LeBar

The Teaching-Learning Process

(1958)

Lois LeBar earned an M.A. degree from Wheaton College, where she studied, along with her sister, Mary, under Rebecca Price. Both went on to earn a Ph.D. in religious education from New York University; both returned to Wheaton College, where they taught for over thirty years. After retiring they journeyed to Africa for a brief but fruitful teaching ministry.

Education That Is Christian, published in 1958, is still in print and has enormous value even today. Its most recent publication includes commentary by one of Dr. LeBar's former students. Harold W. Burgess (1975) places LeBar in the traditional theology category, in which emphasis is placed on transmission of religious content. Even so, LeBar stresses the activity of the learner and life connection to the centrality of Christ and the Word of God.

Professor LeBar shows teachers how to begin with those learner needs most evident to the learners and move toward the most important needs in the learner's life. Scripture is widely used in the book as a basis for its philosophy and for examples of the author's perspective on Christian education. Professor LeBar considers the use of the Bible in teaching and the general method of Jesus the Teacher. Teachers must, according to LeBar, join partnership with the Holy Spirit

From *Education That Is Christian* (Old Tappan, N.J.: Revell, 1958), 142–73.
Unless otherwise indicated, Scripture references are from the King James Version of the Bible.

if they are to be truly "Christian" educators. The life and spiritual example of the teacher and a sense of "ministry" as a teacher are also key components of the author's approach to Christian education.

This chapter, "The Teaching-Learning Process," stresses the life-involvement of the student in learning: "A pupil's growth is determined not by what he hears, but by what he does about what he hears" (143). Spiritual maturity, rather than outward conformity, is the teacher's goal. Discovering the Bible, linking to life, group activities, and biblical psychology are all components of teaching-learning.

References

Burgess, H. W. 1975. *An invitation to religious education*. Birmingham: Religious Education Press.

After discovering the scriptural foundations for Christian teaching, we come to the practical question of "How." How can we help pupils to get through the written Word to the Living Word? How can we help them translate Scripture into life? How can we help them take the next step toward maturity in Christ? Even in asking these questions, we see that the pupils must have a large place in the process, for it is they who must have dealings with the Lord; they must change their daily conduct, they must grow in grace. Our problem is to bring them to Christ, help them grow in Christ, and send them out for Christ. We can't receive Christ for them. We can't learn for them. According to the old adage, "You can lead a horse to water, but you can't make him drink." What is teaching but helping people to learn? Therefore the basic problem is not teaching, but learning. Unless we discover how people learn, we won't be able to teach as we ought.

Transferring the Learning Process from Teacher to Pupil

It is true that pupils are always learning something, but often what they learn is not what the teacher intended to teach. While a lackluster teacher talks on and on, they may be deciding that they'll leave Sunday school just as soon as their parents stop forcing them to come. While a scholarly teacher strings generalization after generalization, they may be learning that the Bible is a very dull book. While an unprepared teacher rambles on in prayer, they may be learning that prayer time is the moment for carrying out their own ingenious devices.

A pupil's growth is determined not by what he hears, but by what he does about what he hears. The important thing is what is happening inside the pupil. He may accept or he may reject whatever is going on outside. Learning is what the pupil does and what outer forces do to him. We teachers can influence these inner factors only by manipulating the outer. If we work with the Spirit of God, he can use us to effect inner changes.

Modern man cannot hope to improve upon the concept of teaching that the Lord God himself has given in John 16:13. Because the Holy Spirit is the only teacher who is able to work both inside and outside the pupil, Christ told his disciples that the Spirit would guide them into all the truth and declare to them the things that are to come. Teaching then is guiding and declaring, guiding pupils and declaring truth. A real teacher does not hesitate to declare truth in a context of guidance. But if he only declares, he becomes a preacher. A teacher must be skilled in guiding, directing, helping pupils in their learning.

Teaching may be compared to conducting a guided tour. The tourists have decided whether they wish to see Europe, South America, or the Holy Land. The competent guide is one who has previously taken the trip, usually many times, and who is familiar with all the points of interest, so that he can help the group map out their itinerary and answer their questions. He facilitates the trip by making necessary arrangements and leads them to the main attractions so that every hour brings new experiences. The satisfaction of the tourists comes from their firsthand experiences with new people and places. Can you imagine the manager of a tour saying to a group who wanted to sightsee, "Since I've already made this trip, you won't need to go. I'll tell you all about it"?

Yet that's what many of us teachers are doing. We have learned a great deal because we have enjoyed rich, new experiences with the Lord. In teaching we always learn more than our pupils because we get more involved in the process than they do. But instead of guiding them through the type of experiences that we have had, we try to shortcut the process by giving them only the end result of our experience. They don't want to know merely what happened to other people, not even to the people of the Bible; they want exciting new experiences to happen to them—firsthand, personally.

Of course the easiest way to teach is merely to tell. We can tell what we have to say without any regard for the pupils. It matters not if Jerry feels homesick with an aching void inside, if Alice is feeling spiteful because of what happened last Sunday, if Nancy is full of questions about what we're saying, if Alden has heard it many times before. But guide pupils? Guide them into firsthand experiences? Jerry and Alice and Nancy and Alden? How can we do that? That will take some doing. Yes, it will. But nothing else will suffice for the Christian teacher. Christ wants to teach in his own way through us today. . . . Every area of life that God's revelation enters is changed, teaching being no exception.

Our big job as teachers is to set up a situation that is propitious for learning, in which Jerry and Alice and Nancy and Alden will want to find God's higher ways. We can make everything in the classroom situation favorable to learning rather than militating against it, as is often the case.

In the first place we'll project ourselves into the place of our pupils, and try to feel as they feel, think as they think, walk in their shoes. We'll put aside the fact that we know the lesson of the day, but remember only that they don't. We won't stay in our own world and try to call across a great gulf into theirs. We'll try to tap their world. We'll transfer the learning process from the teacher to the pupil. Then teaching becomes a great adventure with the Master Teacher himself.

The Nature of Growth

Scripture often speaks of spiritual growth in terms of physical growth: "Thy wife shall be as a fruitful vine by the sides of thine house: thy children like olive plants round about thy table" (Ps. 128:3); "Every plant, which my heavenly Father hath not planted, shall be rooted up" (Matt. 15:13).

. . . While there are many instructive similarities between natural and supernatural growth, there is one great difference. The lower order of plant life has no will of its own; it merely follows the sequence marked out for it by its Maker according to its kind. The action of the human will is necessary in regeneration to receive God's gift of his Son. This decisive action has no parallel in nature. No matter what a person's training or mental understanding may be, we won't assume that he is a Christian until we observe unmistakable evidence of his being born from above. However, just as there is a period of prenatal development before physical birth, there is a period of prenatal development before spiritual birth, sometimes longer, sometimes shorter. Before regeneration, the young child's parents try to help him to say no to his own selfish ways and yes to the Lord's higher ways; yet strictly speaking, only after spiritual birth can the new creation in Christ be said to grow. Our concern is to see the individual making steady spiritual progress from physical birth to death.

Scripture's Analogy with Physical Growth

Although the human sapling may suddenly spurt ahead in his development when he makes right decisions, spiritual growth as well as natural growth is usually a gradual ongoing process. Just as in a cornfield we see "first the blade, then the ear, after that the full corn in the ear" (Mark 4:28), so we are to grow up into Christ in all things, for he is the head of the body the church (Eph. 4:15). Under healthy conditions growth is steady and consistent. Though startling changes may not be seen day by day, progress should be evident. If reliance is placed on periodic revivals or contests, the result is likely to be a spurt followed by a decline, then another effort to rally, followed by relapse.

Growth takes place from within outward. "The righteous flourish like the palm tree, and grow like a cedar in Lebanon . . . They still bring forth fruit in old age, they are ever full of sap and green" (Ps. 92:12, 14 RSV) The roots of the tree take nourishment from the soil up through the trunk, out through the branches to every last leaf and bud. Bud, blossom, and fruit are all an integral part of the very life of the tree.

How different the Christmas tree, that has been severed from its source. For a few weeks we doll it up with lights and bright balls and tinsel. For a short time it is truly a spectacle, but soon it is thrown away. It was only meant to be decoration. But don't we teachers sometimes work for "Christmas tree" effects? We train our pupils to repeat verses that are only words to them or to say pretty little poems in special-day programs. These words may perhaps entertain adults, but what is happening inside the pupils as a result? Is the Word of God merely "hung on" the pupil for decoration, or is it being assimilated into his inner being? The Book of Proverbs admonishes us to keep our heart with all diligence, for out of it are the issues of life (4:23).

The issues of life for "every blooming thing" depend upon the nature of the soil, whether or not it has been prepared. "Behold, a sower went forth to sow," said Jesus, "and some seed fell by the wayside, some fell on stony ground, some fell among thorns, and other seed fell on good ground" (Matt. 13:3–8 [author's paraphrase]). In most of our Bible classes we have several kinds of soil represented. How can we expect to teach without knowing what kind of seed which pupil is ready to receive? When eternal destiny of souls is at stake, how can we be content to take whatever seed is nearest at hand and scatter it broadside regardless of the soil? Some type of seed will grow in even the poorest soil if we care enough to find out what type that is.

Even the sturdiest of plants continually need sunshine, rain, and pruning. "The Lord God is a sun and shield" (Ps. 84:11); "He shall come down like rain upon the mown grass: as showers that water the earth" (Ps. 72:6). Christ said, "Every branch in me that beareth not fruit he taketh away: and every branch that beareth fruit, he purgeth it, that it may bring forth more fruit" (John 15:2). Nourishment and exercise are needed every day of one's life, from birth to death. Some teachers relax their efforts after a soul has been born from above. What, leave a newborn spiritual babe to fend for himself when he needs constant care and feeding?

The Test of Real Learning

"By their fruits ye shall know them" (Matt. 7:20). The righteous man "shall be like a tree planted by the rivers of water, that bringeth forth his fruit in his season; his leaf also shall not wither; and whatsoever he doeth shall prosper" (Ps. 1:3).

What kind of fruit has been the result of our teaching? Have we been satisfied when our pupils have been able to recite Bible verses, repeat Bible facts, earn awards for perfect attendance? What aspects of our teaching have we been particularly concerned about? How smoothly we could tell a Bible story or give a lecture? How quiet our classroom is? What is the real test of our teaching, the test of real learning on the part of the pupils?

During the week when our pupils mingle with non-Christians, is it evident that the Word of God is operating in their lives? On the playground could a stranger pick them out as most unselfish, loyal, truthful, cooperative? In school or in the office are they most dependable? At home are they obedient, courteous, lovable? Do their families ask, "What have you been doing to my boy?" because his conduct is changing? When you aren't with them, do they manifest the fruit of the Spirit (Gal. 5:22–23)?

In our own spiritual experience we find that when God gives us new truth he soon puts us to the test over it. The minute we refuse to act on his truth, that minute we begin to backslide. The minute we act on it we begin to pulsate with new life and to go on to spiritual victory.

One of the most haunting phrases in Scripture is "nothing but leaves" (Mark 11:12–14). When Jesus saw in the distance a fig tree in leaf, he went to see if he could find anything on it to assuage his hunger. He found nothing but leaves. May this phrase characterize the efforts of none of us! It is possible to go through all the motions of Bible teaching, to speak Bible words, sing hymns, pray, mark attendance books and prepare object lessons, without spiritual fruit. But if we do the Lord's work in the Lord's way, "in due season we shall reap, if we faint not" (Gal. 6:9).

Today when the Lord seeks in our churches for "the fruit of the travail of his soul" (Isa. 53:11 RSV), is he satisfied with what he finds? Or does he find "nothing but leaves"? The fruit that he seeks is disciples, for he has commanded us to go and teach all nations, make learners of all nations, make disciples of all nations (Matt. 28:19). Disciples are Christians who can stand alone in Christ, who are multiplying themselves, who are dying to their old self-life, falling like a grain of wheat into the ground in order that they may reproduce themselves (John 12:24). Disciples are following Jesus, are daily walking with him rather than continuing their old selfish ways.

But alongside disciples in our churches today are many converts. Yes, they've been saved, they once met Christ, they have eternal life. But like the fig tree that Jesus cursed, they are bearing no fruit. They are producing "nothing but leaves." They go to church, they sing gospel songs, they know the cardinal doctrines. But they are not multiplying themselves. They have turned around from dependence upon themselves to dependence upon the Lord for salvation, but they are not walking in the faith that saved them. The Lord never asked us to make converts.

Our methods of teaching are largely responsible for the number of converts who should be disciples. When our boys and girls have repeated Bible words, we have said that they have "learned" them, and perhaps have given them a star for it. That, to the children, was the end of the process. Therefore to say Bible words like "love one another" was to learn the verse. Is "love one another" an easy memory verse? When has a person learned to love others? Have *you* learned to love others? What is the real test of love for others? How *easy* to say three little words! How *hard* to show love to people who are unlovely, in circumstances that impel self-preservation!

How can we help converts to become disciples by practicing love? We can provide opportunities for practice as part of our program. Right in our classrooms we can set up situations for the practice of sharing, working together, being courteous, thinking of others, taking turns, denying self. Projects and parties planned during the Bible school hour but carried out during the week call for other kinds of Christian conduct. But the real test comes when the pupils leave the realm of our supervision and are on their own. If they actually show love in new situations at home, on the playground, in school, or in the office, they have truly learned to love one another. If not, they have failed to learn those Bible words.

Individuality in Growth

If each leaf on a tree differs from any other, how much more the complex human personality, each with its unique combination of traits. Each of us has been fashioned by the great Designer to bear a special manifestation of his own Son. He needs every one of us in our own place to show forth his whole character. It may be natural for us to feel that some defect mars the symmetry of our makeup or the usefulness of our service, but we are exactly as he planned in his perfect knowledge and power.

Just as some seeds do best in light, sandy, well-drained soil, while others prefer rich heavy ground, human personality is even more sensitive to environing conditions. Some seeds need full sunshine, while others will grow in shade. Some will grow year after year in the same location, while others should be removed to another place. Some of our pupils need very tender, delicate treatment for they are sensitive and easily bruised. Some respond best to harsh shock treatment. Some are so eager that they grasp even the incidentals that are tossed in as extras. Some are so dull to spiritual things that the core of the truth must be approached from many angles before they catch a glimmer of its meaning. Each has his own rate of development, his own special needs.

How can we expect to make one lesson fit all the different individuals in our class? At every contact our aim is nothing less than to help each one take a step toward maturity in Christ. The first thing we'll do is to pray definitely for each one each day. What changes do we want to see in Jerry? Why does Jerry feel and think as he does? Can we visualize the world as it looks from his back porch? If not, we'll find out these things. We'll visit his home, his schoolroom or his office, his gang, his recreation center. Then we'll be able intelligently to pray for him. Moreover, as we get the Lord's viewpoint on Jerry, we'll be ready to work with the Spirit in his own way to help Jerry.

Learning as an Inner Process

Of course true learning has outward manifestations, yet they will not represent real and permanent changes unless something has first happened inside. The truth of God must progressively control the inner life.

If we are going to work with the Lord to change pupils inwardly, we must begin where the change is needed, with what already controls their behavior. What is it that prompts our actions? It is our needs, our strong innate drives, which the Almighty himself has put within us. The concept of need is one of the key concepts of education. All mankind have physical needs, for the satisfaction of which we expend prodigious efforts, lie, steal, or go to war. We have emotional needs of security, affection, recognition, freedom from guilt, and new experiences. In advanced cultures where standards of living are high, these psychological needs motivate most of our actions. Mentally we all need activity along the lines of present interests, challenges to our current abilities, and broadening new intellectual experiences. Spiritually we need to be reconciled with our Creator-Redeemer, to mature in the privileges and responsibilities of life in Christ, to work creatively with him in order to apprehend that for which we were apprehended of Christ.

Although many of these needs are concurrently present, whichever need is most basic and most pressing will claim our attention, our interest, our effort. Our whole being is consciously and unconsciously searching for the means of meeting these needs. If we see no relation between an event and our own needs, we pay no attention to it.

Why did the Creator constitute us with these needs? So that he could satisfy them with himself. He is waiting to supply all our needs according to his riches in glory by Christ Jesus (Phil. 4:19). He wants to speak to us daily in the language that we know best, the circumstances of our everyday lives. Every problem in life ought to drive us to him for its solution. Most of the lessons Christ taught in the Gospels started with these personal needs. We as teachers help our pupils to see and appropriate the Lord as the answer to the personal needs that he has ordained.

When we bow before Christ as King of kings and Lord of lords, we find all our needs met in this one glorious Savior! As Christ delivers us from the power of sin in the form of the world, the flesh, and the devil, we become increasingly free to devote ourselves to him. As we delight ourselves in him and become identified with him in his death and resurrection, he can take us up into his divine purposes and give us a spiritual burden that he will accomplish in us. As the self-life is denied, he becomes the center of all of life. Then our entire concentration is that we may know him, and the power of his resurrection and the fellowship of his sufferings. We are no longer concerned about our own needs but about his great plan of redemption for the world.

Sometimes the needs that are felt most urgently by our pupils are inconsequential in the light of eternity. Yet we may be obliged to start with these "felt needs" in order to make a point of contact. Our purpose then will be to lead from these "felt needs" to real spiritual needs, just as Christ did when he led the Samaritan woman from physical water to spiritual water. He might never have had a hearing with her if he had started with living water and true worship. Starting with "felt needs" doesn't mean that we're stopping there.

Is starting a lesson with the pupils' interests the same as starting with a need? What is the distinction between an interest and a need? If we are teaching children the story of David and Goliath, we might begin with their interest in slingshots, which would probably enlist immediate attention. They would be glad to share their experiences with slings, they'd be able to project themselves into the story of David, and would listen especially for the part about the sling. After the story, what would most likely be their comments? "Wish I had a sling. How could I get one? I wouldn't need a giant to hit. I'd settle for a bird, or a man's hat. I want a sling." Is that the response we're seeking as the result of the story?

Contrast the approach to that lesson in terms of a personal need. Discuss with the children the things they know they ought to do but they find hard to do. "These are our giants, the things that may slay us if we aren't careful. David had his giant too, and he overcame his. How did he do it? Can we too be strong in the Lord and in the power of his might? How? This week?" Yes, a need pierces deep into the inner life while an interest is often superficial.

Our Bible lessons may relate pupils more or less personally to the Word of God, the degrees of which may be expressed as follows:

being exposed to the truth
being interested in the truth
doing something about the truth
being controlled by the truth

If our pupils see no connection between their own needs and the Word, it may be spoken into the air in their vicinity, but will yield little fruit because it doesn't get inside. If it is associated with an interest, they will listen with attention which may lead to something deeper. If they see how the Bible meets a need, they will make some effort to find God's answer. And if they find by experience that the Living God meets other needs, they will continue to appropriate him inwardly.

But though we have probed to the heart of the problem when we begin with pupils' needs, the process of change is far from automatic. We naturally resist change because it means a new organization of the personality structure that we have been building. It's much easier to continue the line of least resistance than to disrupt old patterns of thinking and acting. If an individual is asked to make too many adjustment at once, he is overwhelmed. We teachers ought to appreciate what is required of a young person who goes back into a godless home and school to live Christ. He needs a great deal of reinforcement from the Lord and the Lord's representatives on earth.

When a man feels the pull of the spiritual world, he will submit to any amount of external routine rather than take himself apart within. It is much easier to fall into the habit of quoting words and assuming that they are meeting God's requirements. If we teachers demand nothing more than words, the pupils will try to quiet their consciences with them. They may be very quick to defend the truth against all comers. But the Lord comes looking for the fruit of the Spirit in life situations. The strength of the heathen religions is that they are intimately bound up with daily life.

Our task as teachers is not so much to motivate as to use the pupils' current motives and values and purposes. They come to us with many needs. As far as possible we should already have discovered these needs, and planned our lesson on the basis of them. If we converse informally with them during presession, we can learn what is uppermost in their thoughts at the moment, and often begin there. On a chalkboard we can write personal questions that point to the Bible content. We can pick up the comments that indicate inner problems. Often personal needs will come out casually in the midst of a lesson and provide rich leading-on values for the next lesson.

Experienced teachers who observe young teachers are often dismayed at the number of excellent leads given by the pupils that go unheeded by the teacher. Questions and comments and suggestions that would lead to thrilling discussions and projects are not even heard. The teacher is so absorbed by the content, he's so uncertain of the sequence of points in his outline, that he isn't teaching content to people, he's just teaching content. He expects the pupils to hear what he says, but he doesn't hear what they say. Is that fair? If pupils' inner needs and ideas and suggestions are woven into the lesson, it will penetrate to the mainsprings of action.

Either we'll seek to meet our pupils' needs by means of the lesson, or they themselves will meet them in a way that will disrupt or negate the lesson. What the pupils want to learn is as important as what the teachers want to teach.

Learning as an Active Process

Overheard in a first-grade class:

Teacher: Dickie, what am I going to do with you? The closing bell has rung, and your picture isn't colored, and you don't know your memory verse. I don't suppose you have learned a thing today. Now why is that, Dickie?

Dickie: Well, you made me sit down and be still, and you told me to be quiet and listen, and you *teached* me and *teached* me and *teached* me until I couldn't *learn* anything! (Peck 1953, 11)

'Lizbeth was just seven and she loved school. Her dolls sat in chairs and read and counted and did all the happy things that 'Lizbeth did in school.

Aunt Edith, who lives at 'Lizbeth's house, was a teacher, who often got tired of the reading and counting and other lessons that had to be taught, so one day she offered a suggestion for a new play for dollies. "Why not play Sunday school, 'Lizbeth? I should think your dollies would like the change."

"No," said the little lady, "my dollies are going to be educated. All we do in our Sunday school is sit and listen, and they'd never learn anything just doing that."

That gave Aunt Edith, who taught Sunday school as well as day school, a lot to think about. (Etecht 1929, 80)

Letting Pupils in on the Activity

Through sermon after sermon, Bible lecture after Bible lecture, are the churches training "professional listeners" who become expert at tuning out what isn't vital to them personally? It is estimated that only about one-fourth of a congregation is really listening to the preacher at any one time. When people are also "talked at" in the so-called teaching sessions, it is no wonder that spiritual results are not more in evidence. Pupils are actually being trained not to listen.

The peculiar genius of teaching is the small intimate group in which overt interaction is possible. Our pupils are often divided into small classes. Why? If we teachers only talked to them, we might as well talk to large groups. The preacher in his sermon should stimulate thinking, but people in the congregation cannot answer him back. Teaching should provide interchange. In teaching, the whole personality should be involved. True is the old saying that we get out of an experience just about what we put into it. There is no such thing as receiving an education. Said Elbert Hubbard, "Education is a conquest, not a bequest; it cannot be given, it must be achieved."

"I will conquer that boy no matter what it may cost him," boasts the misguided teacher; "I will help that boy conquer himself no matter what it may cost me," says the wise teacher. Through the years teachers have been frustrated trying to get pupils to sit still, with pupils frustrated because it is against their nature to sit still. "When teachers do most of the learning, pupils get only the 'dehydrated' product, which is tasteless and dull" (Ruth Bailey). With or without a teacher and a classroom a boy in action is learning.

In transferring the learning process from teacher to pupil, the pupil ought to get half the activity so that he can cash in on the profits. This doesn't imply that the pupil does anything he wants to do or that he goes undisciplined, but he shares with the teacher the responsibility and the activity and the results.

He can help devise plans, make his own discoveries in Scripture, evaluate his own efforts. The teacher should do nothing that the pupils can *more profitably* do. We should seek a maximum of self-propulsion, a minimum of absorption of the teacher's words.

What a challenging adventure to help pupils find out for themselves the thrilling possibilities of life in Christ, to guide eager workers rather than to talk to people who are indifferent or actually bored! If people discover the truth for themselves, they are much more ready to obey it.

> Teaching by the printed or spoken word is made really effective when indoctrination becomes inspiration, when precept becomes practice, when illustration becomes experience. We learn best by doing the right things, and we can only hope that our information and exhortation will suffice to keep our boys and girls from the wrong kind of experience. (Edman 1953, 10)

Experience is the best teacher in the sense that her lessons are always learned. Whether or not they are the right lessons is something else again. Experience is a hard teacher, for she gives the test first, the lesson afterward.

The writer of the Book of Hebrews chides his hearers for being dull of hearing and for failing to progress to spiritual maturity (5:11–14). They have had sufficient opportunities to be ready to teach the Word, yet they are still subsisting on the milk of the first principles of eternal truth when they should be ready for strong meat. By reason of use (experience) the mature have their senses exercised (by new understanding and insight) to discern both good and evil (evaluated on the basis of scriptural norms). Likewise in our churches we should be guiding our young people into experiences that will give them practice in discernment so that they will be maturing as the competent leaders of tomorrow.

Compare the training an athlete gets with that of a spectator at a game. The latter may note the sequence of plays, may shout and cheer at crucial points, may even learn to appreciate some technical skills. But he is not changed by the process. He couldn't duplicate what he saw if he were to get out on the floor or the field. The player on the other hand must plan each strategic move, be very sensitive to the movements of the other players, exercise judgment, take advantage of openings, practice and practice techniques. He comes out of the game a different person because every power has been brought into play. Too long have teachers been the active participants in the game of learning, with the pupils merely spectators. It's time the pupils got into the game.

> Somehow, in the process of the development of traditional education, the roles of the student and the teacher have become the reverse of what they should be in participative education. The student should be the primary participant. In traditional education the teachers do what the students should do and the students act as disinterested observers of the process. The college frequently becomes

> an institution where the students pay tuition to subsidize the teachers, who do the learning. This topsy-turvy condition is well evidenced by a kind of job analysis of the teacher activities. The teacher robs the student of each of these vital experiences: he sets the goals for the students, formulates the questions and problems, evaluates progress, organizes the experience of the student, "integrates" the curriculum, plans the course and the lectures, thinks about the course problems outside of class hours, and does most of the talking. In short, the teachers are the students, the learners, the *participants* in the educative process. It is commonplace to hear teachers say: "I never learned so much as in my first year of teaching." It is questionable how long our society can support institutions where "students" sit and watch teachers learn. (Gibbs, Platt, and Miller 1951, 65)

Making Discoveries in the Bible

On Sunday morning junior high young people sauntered into their Sunday school room buzzing in groups about their new clothes, the fun they'd had the previous evening, the new boy at school, the girl with the new haircut. The room was filled with the cheerful hum of their comments and exclamations until the quiet music began to call them to the worship service. Reluctantly most of the buzz then gave way to passive lethargy while the superintendent and later the teachers talked to them about events that happened long ago and far away, that had little connection with their lives. The leaders made no connections, the pupils saw none. With the exception of some lively choruses that the group sang for fun—they got nothing spiritual out of them—they merely tolerated the proceedings either because it was their habit to come to Sunday school, or they had been trained to be courteous, or on the whole they enjoyed the social situation. The cleverest of them could occasionally get in a sly remark that provoked clandestine merriment from their friends but which the teacher did not notice because he was wholly absorbed with his content. The sound of the closing bell again released the merry chatter right in the middle of the teacher's sentence.

Every week pupils in Sunday school classes ought to be making discoveries in the Bible that are more thrilling than the discoveries in science that are being made in our day. The secrets of the Christ-life that the Lord God is eager to disclose to seeking hearts are more personal and potent than the secrets of the world of nature. If we teachers start right where the pupils are, with their needs, they'll be ready to seek God's answers. Our responsibility then is to guide them in making the discoveries that they need at the moment or that we know they will soon need.

Until a child is able to read, he is unable to search the Scriptures for himself. In the early years the best way of conveying scriptural truth is the well-told Bible story, in which the teacher himself relives the event so realistically that the boys and girls go through the experience vicariously. No, the children in this case don't actively use their own Bibles, but they can be active in the use of the Bible.

Though the teacher tells the story, the children may listen actively in order to find out something. They should think of it as more than an interesting tale such as they sometimes hear on Saturday at a library story hour. If they have discussed a personal problem that is real to them as the approach to the lesson, they will be discovering how the Bible story meets that need. They will be listening to the story in terms of the need. After the story, the teacher won't have to moralize while they fidget; they will be able to draw their own conclusions and make their own applications. After the story of David and Goliath, the teacher may say, "We don't need a sling and pebbles for our giants (that we discussed as the approach to the lesson). How can we today 'be strong in the Lord and in the power of his might'?"

Because children must listen quietly to the Bible story, the rest of the Bible school hour should contain much activity for them. If there is not enough, we can't expect them to sit still to listen to the story. In presession they may examine objects related to the Bible lesson; in worship they actively sing and pray and use familiar Scripture; in expressional work after the story, they do something that helps to bridge the gap between knowing and doing God's will.

By the time children become juniors, they can read well enough to do a lot of experimenting with their own Bibles. Since Bible vocabulary is not the same as that which they read in school, they cannot be depended upon to read well or to get the meaning. They should never be allowed to read before a group if they stumble through a portion haltingly. They should practice whatever they are going to read so that the group hears the Bible read expressively whenever it is read aloud. But if the teacher gives them the setting and problem of a biblical narrative, they will like to read for themselves the exciting climax to discover the wonderful way in which the Lord worked.

Juniors need plenty of drill in locating the books of the Bible, but they shouldn't get in the habit of using God's written Word mechanically. They derive little benefit from scrambling to see who can first find hit-and-miss verses, rattling off the words with no thought of their meaning. In Bible drills the same mature children usually find the verses first, while the others don't bother to try. Juniors should often look up verses in various parts of Scripture that are related to the problem at hand, and should discuss how these ideas would work out in their own lives during the week.

Junior high [students] through adults should regularly experience the thrill of making their own discoveries in Scripture. The teacher's part is to steer them from their personal needs to the passages that meet those needs. When a group begins this type of direct, inductive, laboratory Bible study, the teacher will probably supply sufficient leading questions to bring out all the major answers. As the group gains experience in comparing Scripture with Scripture, it will soon be able to furnish many of the questions also.

The first step in active Bible study is to ask the Author of the Book for his illumination of the page, for his divine enabling in order that we may know, love, and obey the truth. The passage which answers the need is then placed in its historical setting and read as a whole to get the main thrust. As the student rereads and rereads the whole, he makes concrete factual observations, first about the outstanding characteristics of the passage, then the details. He tries to put himself in tune with the Author of the material, to see as he sees, to feel as he feels. He notes words and phrases that are repeated for emphasis, that are compared, that are contrasted. He asks the questions: What? Why? When? Where? How? He sees interesting relationships take form, and finds out why each section, verse, phrase, and word is where it is, is expressed in a certain way. As he continues to observe, the structure of the literature takes shape. As he makes these factual observations, his perception becomes keener, his discernment sharper.

Not until we have seen what a passage actually says are we ready to interpret its meaning. Marshaling the facts first enables us to get God's message rather than to "prove" our own prejudices.

After students have learned this type of study under the supervision of a teacher, they will be able to prepare their lessons in this way at home during the week. The assignment should be given out in relation to a need that the group currently feels. If students have studied the Bible passage at home, they come to class with the discoveries that they have made, ready to share them with the others. In class the teacher uses their contributions to solve the assigned problem and perhaps others related to it. If no questions remain regarding the initial problem, others involving the same Scripture may be discussed. In class pupils want a new spiritual experience, not the repetition of an old one. This is not difficult since we all have so many needs, with new ones constantly arising.

In answer to questions given out by the teacher or raised by the pupils, the group continues to search the passage to find facts and relationships that they have missed, to ascertain whether or not observations that they contribute are factually valid, to answer objections to viewpoints that are expressed, to see what light other passages shed on this one, to discuss the practical implications of the truths discovered. One of the first things a group learns is that in an hour or two no one of us begins to get from a Bible passage all its rich meaning. Thus the class members are alert and active intellectually, emotionally, and volitionally as they participate in lively group interaction.

Making Pupils Work—and Like It!

"Hi, Miss Reid! You're just the person I'm looking for. Are you free?" The speaker was tall Don Rose, insurance salesman and teacher of the junior class of boys in Forward Baptist Church.

"Come in, Don," answered Miss Reid.

Don closed the door behind him and pointed his thumb over his shoulder in the direction of the bulletin board in the foyer of the church. “I’ve just read your new poster,” he said, “and decided it was time to talk with you.” He was referring to the attractive placard which boldly proclaimed some of the most glaring flaws that were to be found in the Sunday school. In a few words Miss Reid had skillfully painted the characteristics of both a good and a poor teaching situation. Don’s inquiry was just what she had been hoping and praying for.

“I’ve read and reread those words, Miss Reid,” he said. “In some spots it describes my class perfectly. I’d like to reach my fellows in the way that that poster says they can be reached.”

“What do you like, what don’t you like about your lesson period?” encouraged Miss Reid.

“Well, I feel that there was a oneness in the class that you described—the boys and the teacher seemed to be working together, almost unconsciously pulling for the same thing. I’d like an atmosphere like that in my class. The Word of God is so wonderful. The truths there mean so much to me; I want my boys to feel the same way about it. But I feel that I’m just preaching at them. They listen politely for a while, but then I lose them and discipline gets to be a problem. They are so active. It has left me feeling discouraged time and again.”

“Look,” said Miss Reid, “here’s the essence of what you have said. Your aim is to teach the Word; the fellows won’t take it when you ‘preach’ at them. They’re full of life and vigor. They want to be active, to be doing things all the time. Can you see any significant relationship in these facts?”

“The Word and their energy,” Don thought aloud. “I suppose my problem would be solved if I could harness that energy and get them to expand it in studying the Word.”

“Exactly,” returned Mess Reid. “That’s not easy and yet it can be done.”

“I wish you’d show me how,” said Don.

“What’s your next lesson, Don?”

“We’ve been working in Mark.” Don began thumbing through his Bible. “The next incident coming up is the story of the rich young ruler in chapter 10.”

“That’s a good one to discuss,” said Miss Reid as she reached for her Bible. “The ruler came looking for eternal life. That’s what your boys need. Why don’t you read through the passage as if you were a junior. Forget that you’re teacher and put yourself in the place of one of the boys.”

Don began to read. Almost immediately he looked up. “I don’t want to read this,” he said. “It doesn’t make sense.” Don grinned. “That’s the way my boys would react. Some of them would stare a little longer at the book, but there would be no interest.”

"You're honest enough to see that very real difficulty," encouraged Miss Reid. "How can you make them *want* to read that Bible story, to help them answer some problem of their own, something that's bothering them today?"

Don leaned forward. "Let's see. My boys have it good too, and they aren't bad boys. I could start by describing the rich young man with his houses and lands and servants to wait on him. What could prompt him to kneel in the dust of the road before Jesus, in his fancy clothes? What more could this man want who seemed to have everything? I think the boys could read what he wanted in verse 17. But what would eternal life mean to them?"

"Could one of the sharper boys who is a Christian tell what it means to him?"

"I think Roger could."

"Then you could add the rest, in junior terms. Maybe, eternal life is the fullest kind of life, the kind that makes you feel good deep down inside, like the life of the mighty Creator who made this tremendous universe with all its galaxies, and its individual people."

"Should the boys read Jesus' answer? Maybe I better express that."

"Yes, for the commandments, you could say don't steal, don't lie, don't cheat, obey your parents."

"Then the class could give the man's answer in verse 20, and find how Jesus felt about the man in 21."

"You're getting the hang of it. It's a real skill to word questions that are not too hard or too easy for a group. Now your boys are ready for the key question that will carry the rest of the lesson, that will direct all we do. How can we express the focal question in the boys' words?"

Don was thinking fast. "Who wouldn't want this full life? The problem is how to get it. So for the boys—if we don't steal or lie or cheat or disobey our parents, is God satisfied with us? How can we have this best kind of life? Hooray! I think that will challenge them!"

"Great! Now they have something to look for, to find out."

"I'll write these important questions so I won't lose them. But the next thing Jesus said made this man hang his head—this rich man who is also called a ruler. What did Jesus say in verse 21? Jesus may not say to us today all that he said to the rich man, but two of those words he is saying to us today. Will we go away sad because we want what we want, or will we pick up Jesus' challenge?"

"Don't feel that the boys need to read everything themselves. You might read 23 and ask how the disciples felt about that in 24. And again you read Jesus' answer in 24–25 and the boys find the disciples' response in 26."

"I could ask why that would be so hard for a rich man. And would anything be too hard for the boys to give up if they love Jesus."

"Then Peter was delighted to discover that the disciples had done something that the rich man couldn't do."

"And Jesus told how he rewards people who follow him. As the class members read 29–30, they can look for a few words they don't expect. A hundredfold reward *with persecutions!* Who opposes and fights the followers of Jesus? Juniors appreciate the need to be strong to overcome the Enemy."

A big smile came over Don's face as he read verse 31. "Verse 31 is a riddle; juniors like riddles. How can the first be last, and the last first? How was the rich man first? Last? How are we today?"

Miss Reid was so pleased with the insights that had been discussed. "There's your Bible content outlined," she said.

"At the end I won't have to preach at the boys, the way I usually do. I'll ask personal questions about us. Think what happened to you last week. Did you follow Jesus in any way? Did you do some things your own way instead of his best way? Let's make a list of things that boys and girls love more than Jesus. We should get down to nitty-gritty specifics in order to be practical."

"We can't expect them to reform their living overnight, but we can ask them to think of one thing they could do this week to put Jesus first."

"We may not feel like doing these things; they may not be easy. But the Lord will be glad to help us if we ask him. Let's think what the hard thing might be, and ask him right now."

"When in the Sunday school hour have you been having your worship service?"

"At the beginning."

"Why not switch it to the end, when the boys are psychologically ready to meet the Lord on the basis of their Bible study? They could sing "Hear the Savior Call, Follow Me" and "I Will Follow Jesus" IF they mean to follow him. They could study a picture of the rich young ruler, read Mark 10:29–31 in two or three Bible versions, and have a modern illustration of the truth."

"Thanks so much, Miss Reid," Don concluded. "It's going to be fun to give my fellows a workout! Make them work and like it."

Guiding Group Discussion

Recent experience in the field of group dynamics has demonstrated how much can be learned and how much interest generated when young people and adults discuss common problems with open, face-to-face interaction. Basic personality needs are met when we have the opportunity to add our own outlook to a discussion, to voice our questions and doubts without fear of rejection, to hear more than one side of a controversial issue, to find out what problems we share and what others are thinking.

But group discussion requires wise leadership if it is not to waste precious time and degenerate into the pooling of ignorance. The leader establishes a warm spiritual atmosphere by coming well-informed on biblical and current issues, by insisting that the group be small enough so that the members feel free with each other, by clearly focusing the problem in the direction of scriptural answers, and by helping each member regardless of his background to make his own contribution. He makes it clear that no person has a monopoly on the Holy Spirit, that spiritual illumination comes primarily from obedience to the Word rather than from intellectual acumen. Every believer has an important place in God's program.

The leader respects every personality, every contribution, every honest question, and helps the group to do so. Every contribution cannot be accepted, but it can be respected. If a group member is assured that the group and the leader accept his whole being as a person, he does not feel crushed or dismayed if one comment or opinion is rejected, for that represents only a small part of him. But if a comment is rejected when he isn't sure of his acceptance as a person, he may not broach an idea again, and the group won't be able to help him because it won't know what he is thinking. If a person is allowed to voice an opinion, even if it is rejected, he usually feels satisfied with the discussion. If not, he has at least looked at the scriptural basis of the question.

In Christian work a large measure of unity may be expected since all are dependent upon one Holy Spirit, all are studying the relevant Scriptures, and all are learning to appreciate each other. Basic doctrinal issues in Scripture are so clear that all seekers of the truth agree on them. Even on minor questions there is much less difference of interpretation when students approach the Bible factually and objectively. Yet some conflict is to be expected because God's ways are so much higher than man's ways, and traditional ways of thinking and acting have to be disrupted to make room for new ways that are discovered. Group members can make it easy and not hard for others to change by understanding why they have felt as they did and by helping them to ease into the new patterns. Experiments have shown that it is usually easier to change individuals formed into a group than to change any one of them separately.

Learning as a Continuous Process

As we noted earlier in this chapter, spiritual growth resembles physical growth in that it is usually steady, ongoing, continuous. In the home the young child lives in the midst of daily activities of people who are much older than he is. Without the direct intention of anyone to teach him, he is continually learning. What is he learning? The next steps for his own stage of development. Though he is ever imitating, he is not able or interested in imitating everything he sees. Some of the activities of his home hold no meaning for him because they have no connection with his own current stage of growth. He doesn't skip any of the major stages, but takes one after another in a distinct pattern of growth. "First the blade, then the ear, after that the full corn in the ear" (Mark 4:28). Never the ripe fruit before the earlier stages, nor the ear before the blade. These stages of development are part of the orderliness of God's universe that he has ordained in infinite wisdom.

Unlike the plant, the human creature, made in the image of God with self-consciousness and self-determination, may spurt ahead spiritually when he makes significant decisions in the direction of maturity in Christ. He may take several steps at the same time, which is often God's best way, yet even these follow the divine order. At each age level a child should be a healthy mature specimen for that stage. At five he should not regress to the self-centeredness of three; neither should he be expected to act like a ten-year-old.

At each stage of growth the child is ripe for certain kinds of truth, principles that he can comprehend and act upon. At that time he sees the need for them; they make sense to him; he can weave them into his life. To try to teach them earlier is to waste our time and discourage our pupils. Timing is important.

For example let's take the question of the proper age to teach the books of the Bible. An alert three-year-old who was the darling of her family was taught to spiel off the names of all the Bible books. She could hardly get her tongue around those awkward sounds that were simply gobbledygook to the small child. But she continued to repeat them for the praise she received. She could show off better with those long names than with anything else she had discovered, so she didn't mind saying them. But when are children ready to learn the books of the Bible with meaning and usefulness? When they are juniors, when they can read, when they have Bibles of their own, when they've had enough Bible stories so that some of the names are familiar, when they're mature enough to understand the organization of the various sections, when they are gaining some acquaintance with history and geography. It is wise for primaries to learn to find their way around in the first five books of the New Testament. There is plenty of material here for them to explore; they know many of these stories, can understand what the names of the books mean, and can mark and memorize many of the verses.

But the question may be asked, Don't we need to prepare our pupils for the future? Surely we do, but how? What happens when we try to store their minds with information that they will need at a later date? Unless content can be integrated into one's present thinking and living, it is merely words. What would happen if we removed from a boy's pocket his magnet, flashlight, screwdriver, nail, compass, and substituted things that he'll need when he grows up—driver's license, car insurance, voter's identification, social security card?

How can we best prepare the boy to take his place as a dependable citizen of both his earthly and heavenly country? Can we help him meet tomorrow's needs today? How? By helping him solve today's problems. If he is a spiritually healthy boy of ten today, that's his best guarantee for the future. If he forms habits of relying upon the Lord and obeying him today, he is headed in the right direction. The best way to insure his being a genuine prayer warrior at fifty is to see to it that he takes to the Lord all the juvenile affairs of life today.

It is foolhardy to concentrate on vague future needs at the expense of pressing current needs.

Yet there are some aspects of the future that we all can and should appreciate ahead of time. We can be warned away from disastrous experiences. We can be prepared—to some extent at least—to meet the normal shocks of life. When our friends are going through crises, we may be close enough to them to learn from them. When a loved one or acquaintance dies, we're ready to think seriously about heaven. When an accident happens to someone in our circumstances, we can imagine that it might have happened to us, and we'll heed the warning. When we can visualize a personal experience like taking a job or a trip or adjusting to new family arrangements, the experience is close enough to stir us to get ready for it. If we teachers take advantage of vicarious opportunities like this that have roots in present experience, our pupils will be able to project themselves to some extent into the future.

Learning as a Disciplined Process

When we begin with pupils' needs and proceed according to their developmental level, are we pampering our pupils, are we guilty of "soft pedagogy," will we cover as much content as if we concentrated on subject matter? Yes, we'll be able to teach—actually teach rather than cover—more subject matter, we'll be developing inner control rather than enforcing outer conformity, and we'll be engaging all our pupils' powers.

In their attempts to meet needs, teachers have sometimes erred in lowering the standards of the group to fit the abilities of the least gifted, of the slowest. Then the needs of the average and the superior are not met. Is it possible to challenge everyone to give everything he's got to the lesson at hand? It is if we teach individuals rather than classes. We can make our plans for the average—still the average varies so much! Special attention is then given to those above and below the middle. We must keep before each one a high vision of his untold possibilities in Christ, of the next step toward that vision, not so far ahead that he'll grow discouraged in trying to reach it, but just far enough so that he'll strain every nerve to reach attainable goals.

Formerly many pupils spent their energies trying to get out of work or to get around the teacher or to frustrate his efforts. When pupils accept a goal as worthwhile, as their own, they concentrate their energies on reaching it, they make suggestions as to the best methods of attaining it, they scurry around for the materials they need, they enlist others in the enterprise, they keep evaluating their progress. In other words, the goal is theirs, the Bible class is theirs, not just the teacher's.

Contrast the prodigious labor that a boy puts into the tree house he has decided to make with a routine job that he considers a boring chore, such as mowing a lawn. The latter is easier, yet he creates much more fuss about it.

When pupils come to church because it is their duty or habit to come, because they are prodded by parents or teachers or friends, or because it affords a pleasant social situation, motivation is weak. It takes strong personality drive to discipline oneself, to hold in check strong natural tendencies. Some other dynamic must take precedence over desire for self-will and self-indulgence. The only motive strong enough to control the old self-life is love for the Lord. Unless divine love is drawing a soul and that soul is responding, self-control cannot be expected.

A new teacher must start out firmly because control is necessary in any group situation and he cannot depend upon a new group to exercise any control of its own. But the aim of Christian teaching is not mechanical regimentation, rather the development of inner control on the part of all believers. A strong teacher may force outward control; a winning teacher may charm a group into doing as he wishes; a clever teacher may beguile a group. The Christian teacher trains his class to assume more and more responsibility in directing their own affairs under God's authority. A sudden transfer of control would be fatal. At each stage of development the group should be given as much responsibility as it can manage. A good test of a teacher's strength is to watch what happens when he steps out of his room for a minute. Do the "mice" immediately stop their work and begin to play because the "cat" is away, or do they continue their work because it is theirs and they are used to directing their own activities?

Is the Christian curriculum light and thin in content? Students cover more ground faster when they see the need of it. Then they're eager to learn all they can about their Beloved, they get excited about the insights they discover, they themselves connect ideas in doctrinal systems, with the result that every minute is made to count for eternity. Sometimes a group takes longer to explore for itself a passage than would be required for a teacher to lecture on it, but when they dig into it, it becomes their own, whereas the teacher's words often go in one ear and out the other.

"Teach your disciples to observe all things that I have commanded you," directed our Lord (Matt. 28:18–20). Every believer is entitled to know the whole counsel of God. If we obey the great commission, we'll have to do more than learn to speak the words of truth—we'll also have to acquire the art and science of guiding pupils into the truth.

In summary, effective learning may be defined as an inner, active, continuous, disciplined process under the authority of the Word of God and the control of the Holy Spirit in the direction of maturity in Christ.

Christian teaching is guiding experience and declaring truth. God says, "I will instruct thee and teach thee in the way which thou shalt go: I will guide thee with mine eye" (Ps. 32:8).

Why It Is Hard to Practice the Truth

We all agree that it is much easier to gain a new truth than to practice that truth. Sometimes teachers comment that young children could have longer memory verses than the educators suggest, longer than verses like "obey your parents." What are the implications of these comments? That the children are able to repeat more words? That they are just saying words? How easy is it for them to practice these few words?

Not much research has been done in biblical psychology. Yet the nature of man is of crucial importance in Christianity. One reason is that the Bible is not a textbook in science; it does not use its terms precisely. But it does yield valuable insights in working with people.

The most common biblical word in referring to our human makeup is the word *heart,* which is usually used to designate the self, the ego, the essential person. Scripture reflects a healthy respect for the *body* that acts, that relates us to our material world. Our *spirit,* the inner breath that survives death, that relates us to God, is dead until the Holy Spirit quickens it in regeneration.

The term *soul* has no clear-cut designation for us today. Many exegetes hold that it refers to the mind, emotions, and will that relate us to our social world. The problem is which of these three aspects of human nature will have control over the others. Which of the three should have the upper hand, and which actually does in individuals?

Our *emotions* clamor to be in control so that life can be as easy and pleasant as possible. We can neither deny nor rely on feelings. They energize, are the natural mainsprings of action. They add color, heights, and depths to life. Their pressures give power to the whole being. They can even compel the mind to supply rationalizations for what they want to do. They can also be fickle, can distort reality, can carry away the other aspects of life. They must be disciplined. They cannot be intellectualized away.

For most people *mind* is not as directive as they like to think. It is seldom adequate to move to action. Knowledge may puff up. We cannot find God by reasoning, though, most amazingly, he has enabled us to think his thoughts after him. God usually gains access to man's inner being through his mind by means of written revelation.

God has given man a *will* that should be strong enough to integrate the whole being by making decisions in the light of the whole for the good of the whole being. This human nature finds very hard to do. For spirit, body, mind, and emotions often disagree on what is good. They all have their own outlooks and interests. *Will* must get it all together, must try to unify the pulling and hauling of the other parts. It must keep a balance between being independent and being programed, must be free within legitimate authority. Will must keep priorities and principles clear, attitudes and habits disciplined. This isn't easy.

Unregenerate man often lives in conflict because when he is out of tune with his Maker, he is usually out of sorts with himself and his world. How does he get back into right relationships? Probably through his mind as some witness communicates the truth of written revelation. The Holy Spirit without and his conscience within testify that Scripture is true. When he makes the slightest overture to the living God, the loving Father answers and keeps seeking the lost. If the Spirit reveals the Savior, the mind avers that this is sensible, and the will can decide to commit its being to its Creator. If the emotions are exuberant over becoming a child of the Most High, the feeling is tremendous! But it may be that the emotions are not excited about a life with a cross in it. . . . The body too may be opposed; it may be tired or sick or sleepy.

Can the will be strong enough to hold its being together with emotions pouting or indifferent? Yes, for God himself works in us to will and do his good pleasure (Phil. 2:13). If we put our weak will on his strong will, he is strong enough to hold it there. If we ask him to will and do in us, he takes control of the unconscious depths beyond our control. If we are tied only to the Lord, and are one with the Spirit, he will overpower our lower nature. We can be inwardly renewed each day (2 Cor. 4:16) to experience the good, acceptable, and perfect will of God (Rom. 12:2). As we move in his direction, our emotions gradually come to enjoy the process too, until they rejoice in fulness of life. When one's whole being is enthusiastically moving toward the Lord, that is life indeed. Nothing is so attractive or fruitful as wholeheartedness.

Still one of the greatest mysteries of the universe is how the material and the immaterial parts of us can interact with each other when they have no elements in common.

Now we see why it is so difficult to practice the truth that we easily understand. The will must be able to get the mind, emotions, and body to move as the Spirit directs. Unless we teachers involve the whole persons in our classes, they may give assent to our teaching but remain unchanged in conduct. The will of a child must be gradually bent but not broken; he will need all the strength of will he can muster to stand for God in this wicked world.

For Reflection

1. What does "transferring the learning process from teacher to pupil" mean?
2. What methodological implications do you see for the concept of inner process?
3. Relate LeBar's idea of the teaching-learning process to the metaphor of pilgrimage.
4. Give an example of how this (#3) might work in a Christian education setting.

References

Edmon, V. R. 1953. *Storms and starlight.* Wheaton: Van Kampen.

Etecht, M. F. 1929. *Moody Monthly.* October.

Gibb, J. R., G. N. Platt, and L. F. Miller. 1951. *Dynamics of participative groups.* St. Louis: John S. Swift.

Peck, K. B. 1953. "Jottings." In *Church School Builder*, March.

22

Thomas H. Groome

Shared Praxis in Praxis: The Five Movements

(1980)

Thomas Groome is a Catholic religious educator, originally from Ireland. His education in America includes a master of arts degree in religious education from Fordham University and a doctorate in religion and education from the joint program of Union Theological Seminary and Teachers College, Columbia University. He has taught religious education and theology for several years as a member of the faculty of the Institute of Religious Education and Pastoral Ministry, Boston College.

Professor Groome's book, *Christian Religious Education,* is considered one of the most important books in religious education of the past fifty years. It treats the nature, purpose, context, approach, and stages of Christian education and the role of teachers. In addition, he critically analyzes such theorists as Dewey, Piaget, Habermas, Fowler, and Freire. The very heart of the book, however, is the *shared praxis approach* to Christian education. For Groome the critical component of Christian education is the sharing of life as it is being lived in the light of the Christian tradition, by a small group of believers committed to each other and to God. His approach is flexible in that its content is drawn from the individuals and what they consider important in their own Christian tradition. The flexibility of this approach allows its methodology to be used by people of any denomina-

From *Christian Religious Education* (San Francisco: Harper and Row, 1980), 207–23.

tion without violating their various theological/biblical positions. Above all the method calls for honest *koinonia*, life-sharing.

In the reading below, part of chapter 10 of the book, Groome describes and discusses the implications of each of the five movements of shared Christian praxis. He tries to show how a dialectic process is used to hold theory and praxis in tension. In the presentation of each movement are examples of its use, including children's groups, adult programs, and graduate classes.

Although not as evident in this reading as in other parts of the book, Groome uses Scripture widely and appropriately. His use of the word *tradition* may cause some Protestants discomfort, but one should consider his or her own tradition even when it might not be so named. While Groome himself tries to be inclusive in terms of theological background, he seems to be representative of Union Seminary from a Catholic perspective.

In a context of Christian religious education using shared praxis, one should expect to find an opportunity for the participants to name some dimension of their present Christian action, to reflect critically to whatever extent they are capable on what they have named, and to share their reflections in dialogue. Since the critical reflection on present action is to be informed by the Christian faith tradition, then the Story and its Vision as they pertain to the issue or topic being dealt with must be made accessible to the group. Finally, in keeping with "present dialectical hermeneutics" and the dialectical unity between *theoria* and praxis, there should be an opportunity for participants to personally appropriate the Story and its Vision to their own lives and choose what may be a fitting lived response.

Over the past years I have used a shared praxis approach with adults and high school and grade school students (in both school and parish contexts), in weekend retreats, seminars, symposia, conventions, community renewal, and teacher training programs, and so on. Gradually, from both apparent successes and failures, five recognizable pedagogical movements[1] have emerged. These are the five movements I generally follow now (possible variations will be dealt with later). I will outline them briefly before moving into a more detailed description of each one.

Each praxis exercise has a particular focus of attention.

1. The fact that I now call the five activities *movements* is a development beyond my earlier published articles, where I called them *steps*. *Steps* can be a misleading term and may give rise to an inflexible mentality where the activities are seen to be rigidly separate and necessarily sequential. *Movement,* on the other hand, is intended with something of its musical overtones. The movements flow together, overlap, are repeated, and blend into an orchestrated activity with its own wholeness and aesthetic.

1. The participants are invited to name their own activity concerning the topic for attention (present action).
2. They are invited to reflect on why they do what they do, and what the likely or intended consequences of their actions are (critical reflection).
3. The educator makes present to the group the Christian community Story concerning the topic at hand and the faith response it invites (Story and its Vision).
4. The participants are invited to appropriate the Story to their lives in a dialectic with their own stories (dialectic between Story and stories).
5. There is an opportunity to choose a personal faith response for the future (dialectic between Vision and visions).

There is nothing sacred about the number five, and other educators may find it helpful to adjust, combine, or increase the movements. I hope that we can improve upon them as our praxis continues. The movements can be put into operation by a variety of teaching methods, and many different pedagogical techniques can be used within each movement.

In the following accounts I first describe each movement, then give some samples[2] from my own praxis, and finally make some general reflections upon the process. For the sake of clarity I draw generally from the same instances throughout the five movements.

Each shared praxis unit must have a particular focus, that is, some dimension or experience of Christian faith to which the group will attend. The educator is usually the one who establishes the focus of attention in the group. This can be done in a myriad of ways. In one sense, the focusing exercise becomes a common experience for the participants. Sometimes this may require an overt activity by the group. However, I have also begun with a Scripture reading, a film, a photograph or painting, a poem, a story, an example of the issue, a case study, a role-playing exercise, a simple statement of the focus, and so on.

First Movement: Naming Present Action

The first movement is an invitation to the participants to name their present action in response to the particular focus of the unit. I described *present action* as "every doing that has any intentionality or deliberateness to it . . . whatever way we give expression to ourselves. It includes what we are doing physically,

2. I purposely use the word *sample* here in preference to *example,* lest the impression be given that I am posing what I have done as model examples. Indeed, there is ample room for critique of my handling of any other movements. Creative educators will hopefully devise much more imaginative ways of putting the five movements into operation.

emotionally, intellectually, and spiritually as we live on personal, interpersonal, and social levels." Thus, depending on the focus of attention, the opening movement could invite an expression of the participant's reactions, feelings, sentiments, overt activity, valuing, meaning making, understanding, beliefs, relationships, and the like. The important task is to elicit a personal statement on present action rather than a statement of *theoria* based on what "they say." For example, in units on the Eucharist I have formed the opening question as "What do you do with the Eucharist in your life?" or "What does the Eucharist mean in your life?" "What is your own basic reaction to Eucharist?" or some other variation of such questions, instead of asking "What is the Eucharist?" (the latter question being more likely to elicit a *theoria* response). In other words, the goal is to elicit an expression (it could be in words, art, mime, etc.) of one's own "knowing" (doing) as that arises from the person's own engagement in the world. With some issues this will also require a naming of the present action that the participants experience in their social context and community, but it must be their own perspective on that particular social praxis.

In forming the opening question, I often find the old distinction between systematic and moral theology to be helpful. When the group is attending to a particular belief, I usually begin with a question like "What is your own understanding of [the belief]?" If an ethical issue or some Christian practice is being dealt with, I begin by inquiring how they presently respond to that issue in their lives. The actual forming of the opening question will depend greatly on the characteristics of the particular group, but the form is crucial if a statement of praxis rather than *theoria* is to be elicited. Some samples from my own praxis may clarify what I intend here.

In a weekend seminar for eighteen faculty members and administrators from a university concerned about its role in educating for social justice, the opening question was: "What can you name at your university that promotes or prevents education for social justice?" In a graduate course for religious educators when the topic was the purpose of Christian religious education, I opened by asking, "As you look at your own work in parishes, schools, or wherever, what for you is the purpose of Christian religious education?" In a group of church education leaders who were focusing on the Emmaus story of Luke 24, having read the passage slowly, my opening question was, "What is the primary message *you* hear from this passage?" In a workshop preparing people to be evaluators of a Catholic school network and intended to focus especially on the Christian environment of the schools, the opening question was, "How do you feel about being evaluated?" With a group of eleventh-grade students dealing with loneliness, I focused the topic by showing a short movie on loneliness and then invited them to reflect on and share the feelings the movie stirred in them (thus causing them to name their "present action" in regard to loneliness). In a unit on Eucharist with ninth-grade students the opening question was "What do you do with the Eucharist in your life?"

Some examples from a fourth-grade class indicate what the first movement might look like for students at that age level. In a unit on a prayer (other than prayers in church, which we had covered in previous units) I began by asking a series of questions such as, "What prayers do you say? How do you say them? What do you say when you talk to God? When do you pray? Tell me about the time that you prayed really hard." In another fourth-grade unit on Reconciliation, focusing in particular on the Penitential Rite at the beginning of the Roman Mass, I began by asking the students to draw a picture of a fight they had had recently. Then I had each of them tell the group about the fight. I asked what caused the fight, whether they were "really mad with the other person," and how they felt. In another unit on the Offertory of the Mass, I began by asking the fourth-graders about gift giving and receiving. I asked questions such as, "Do you ever give a gift to anyone? Do you ever receive a gift? Can you tell me about a time that you gave a gift to someone? Tell me about a time that you received a gift from someone."[3]

This movement is where the shift from a *theoria* to a praxis way of knowing begins. After the focusing activity the opening question must be put in such a way as to elicit a naming of the participants' praxis rather than their *theoria*. This can be especially difficult with topics of a systematic theological and more abstract nature, for instance, the Blessed Trinity. But even there the opening question can inquire about the participants' understanding of it and way of making meaning out of it, and the implications this belief has for their living of the Christian faith. When I prepare for a shared praxis unit, a great deal of my time is spent in formulating the opening question.

It is important to pose the opening question in a gentle, nonthreatening manner. I have learned the hard way that if a praxis-type question is asked without prior explanation, adults can hear it as a challenge to justify their existence, especially if they are unaccustomed to the process. With all age levels I attempt to eliminate the feeling of being investigated by explaining that they are not being cross-examined in an evaluative manner, but rather are invited to come to self-awareness of their own knowing and name it for themselves. It has also helped, especially with participants who are strangers to each other, to begin with some "ice-breaking" and community-building exercises to establish at least a minimal level of trust in the group. After a

3. With my fourth-grade C.C.D. class I use the Benziger "The Word Is Life" series. I have found it to have much in common with a shared praxis approach. In fact, many of the standard grade school Christian education series are easily adaptable to shared praxis. I especially recommend the "Shared Approaches" developed by Joint Education Development and published by United Church Press, Philadelphia.

group has been through the process a number of times, the opening question is rarely heard as a challenge.

Before the participants share their statements, it is important to make clear that each one should feel free to remain silent. I often invite a large group of adults to move into smaller groups of four but to feel free not to join a group or to join a group and not speak. When the group is small enough to be kept together for the sharing (the setting and time frame will often decide this), I have learned by mistake not to "go around the circle." This can force people to speak when they do not wish or are not ready to do so. It is the educator's role in this first movement to facilitate participants in articulating as clear a statement as possible. This sometimes means inviting a person to say more or explain further. It is also the educator's task to keep the group focused on the question posed. The opening movement is not the time for "explaining why," telling anecdotes, and so on, and the educator should gently bring the group back to the question at hand as necessary.

The different ways that people can be brought to express their naming of present action are myriad, and many are more imaginative than the ones I have described here. I often find it helpful to have groups of adults write a brief statement in response to the topic. A more imaginative example is one from a weekend retreat with college-age people focusing on the church, where the leaders opened by giving the participants playdough and having them fashion their "impression" of the church and then explain their representations.[4]

Second Movement: The Participants' Stories and Visions

The second movement is the beginning of critical reflection proper. It takes different forms for different age levels, but for all participants it is a reflection on "why we do what we do and what our hopes are in doing it" as related to the topic for attention. In this sense the movement is the participants' becoming aware of their own stories and visions as they are expressed in present action. This second movement is first looking discerningly at present action to see the "obvious" about it, but it is also an attempt to go below the obvious, to become aware of its source, the genesis of present action. In this the movement attempts to help participants come to a consciousness of the social conditioning, norms, assumptions, and the like that are embodied in their present action. This can be achieved by using critical memory to probe into the biography of the self and by trying to uncover the social influences that bring us to do what we do—in other words, one's own story. As critical reflection the movement also entails the use of imagination, a "looking forward"

4. For a description of this retreat see Kennedy, "Young Adults Confront a Bishop."

that attempts to ascertain the likely consequences of one's action and to determine what one would want the consequences to be (i.e., one's own vision). A discrepancy between the likely and the desired consequences often arises; however, in the dissonance lies the possibility for change, development, and growth. The movement often releases dialogue that was previously repressed, which is part of its purpose.

I usually introduce this movement by posing some questions that invite the participants to explain to themselves what brought them to give the expression they gave in the first movement. I then follow with questions about the likely consequences and the desired consequences of their present action. Here again, the questions are not meant to challenge the participants to defend what they do. Instead, they are an invitation to reflect upon one's reflection (children, of course, are capable of no more than a very rudimentary form of such reflection)[5] and to articulate for oneself and the group why one takes that present action and what the intended consequences of that action are. Some examples from my own praxis may clarify the activity of the second movement.

In the weekend with the university group I introduced the second movement by posing three questions, which we addressed separately: "Why is what we do or fail to do to promote social justice at the university happening? How likely is it that our students will graduate with a commitment to social justice? What would we want to do to promote education for social justice at the university?" The third part I introduced as "blue-sky time" and encouraged some dreaming. The second movement questions are not always set out as separately as this, and responses often overlap. Some people concentrate on their stories and others on their visions.

With graduate students reflecting on the purpose of Christian religious education (a unit I have done many times) I have asked questions like, "What brought you to have that purpose?" (their story) and then, "How does that purpose shape your religious educating?" (their vision). In the group of church educators reflecting on the Emmaus story I asked two questions, and we dealt with them separately: "What memories does this passage raise up for you?" and then, "What hope does it give you?" With the people preparing to be evaluators I asked, "What has brought you to feel that way about being evaluated?" and then, "How could those memories influence you when you become an evaluator?"

In the unit on the Eucharist with ninth-graders I began by having them remember their first communions and then invited them to describe how

5. I am well aware that critical reflection in anything like its fullness is not possible for children. But they are capable of concrete reflection, of asking Why? at least from the stage of what Piaget calls concrete operations. In chapter 11 I claim that unless some rudimentary form of reflection is encouraged from the beginning, anything like the fullness of critical reflection will be unlikely in adulthood.

the role of the Eucharist in their life had changed since then. I finished the second movement by asking, "What do you want the Eucharist to become in your life?"

With the fourth-graders I have attempted to encourage reflection according to their capacity, promoting Why? questions in the hope that when they are developmentally capable, they will be more likely to do what could properly be called critical reflection. In the unit on prayer I set the scene by asking them to imagine that I was a little man from outer space. (Most of them had recently seen the movie *Star Wars.*) "I land in my space ship beside you on the way home from school and say, 'Please do not run away. I have a question. I was on this planet one night last week, and I looked through a bedroom window and saw a little boy kneeling beside his bed. He was talking to someone, but there was nobody in the room with him. What was he doing?'" The fourth-graders entered into the spirit of the scene and explained elaborately that the little boy was praying. "Praying," I asked, "what is that?" Now they had to explain to me what praying was, and it was fascinating to hear their explanations. I pushed them further by asking, "Why do you pray?" Invariably the answers were along the lines of "to get things from God." I did not settle for this answer because to do so would have been to affirm them in what Fowler would call the "reciprocity" of stage-two faith. I affirmed for them that prayers of petition are important, but asked if there were any other kinds of prayer we could say or any other reasons for praying. In this I was inviting them to undertake critical reflection of a sort, affirming but pushing beyond present attitudes. After further dialogue they agreed that we could also pray simply to tell God that we love God, without asking for anything. In fact, they concluded, the only reason we pray is that God loves us. One girl said reflectively, "Praying wouldn't make any sense if God didn't love us." I then asked them what happens when they pray, how it makes them feel, and how they think God feels about it (their visions). At the end of this dialogue one of them gave the perfect transition to the third movement (community Story and Vision) when she said, "Okay, let's pretend that we are people from outer space and we meet you on the way home from school and ask you the same question. What would you say?" The transitions do not always come so easily.

In the unit on Reconciliation (and specifically on the Penitential Rite of the Catholic Mass) movement two focused on the questions "Why do we fight?" and "What are the consequences of fighting?" A general answer seemed to be that we fight because we want "to get our own way." I asked, "Why do we want things our own way?" and "Is it possible to always get what we want?" I inquired into the feelings they have when they are angry, how it affects them and others when they fight, and if it is possible to "make up" after a fight. I also asked how they think God feels about fighting and if God would want us to make up. They agreed that God does not like us to fight. I inquired if God forgives us when we do, and not all of them were sure about that. One girl said that God would forgive us only if we promised "not to be mad" at the person with whom we had had a fight.

In the unit on the Offertory of the Mass I asked such questions as, "Why do we give gifts? How do you feel when you get a gift? How do you feel when you give a gift? How do you think it makes the other person feel? To whom can you give gifts? What gifts has God given us? Is there any gift we can give back to God? Is God pleased when we offer gifts?"

This second movement can also take many forms and be effected in many ways. The movement looks and sounds quite different with participants of different age levels and in various contexts, but there is a basic similarity no matter who participates or what the focus may be. The primary task is always to enable participants (the educator included) to reflect critically on their present action, their reasons for it, and the consequences of it. Any pedagogical strategy or teaching model which can promote such reflection and dialogue is appropriate for this second movement.

Children take to this movement quite readily, and they often appear to enjoy it. For adults, on the other hand, it seems to be the most difficult and painful movement of the whole process. I am often reminded of Dewey's warning that education grounded in experience "involves reconstruction which may be painful."[6] For this reason, again, it is important not to put pressure on people to speak. We should not assume, however, that the silent ones are not participating in the dialogue. My own experience has been that when I am truly listening, I find myself entering into dialogue within myself with each person who speaks.

Although I described critical reflection as a combination of reason, memory, and imagination, the examples above make clear that not all three dimensions are equally attended to in every unit. The emphasis varies from one topic to another and with different groups. When I work consistently with the same group over a number of units, I often attend to different dimensions for variety, one time concentrating on reason, at another on memory, or again on imagination.

Third Movement: The Christian Community Story and Vision

The third movement is an opportunity for the group to encounter the Christian community Story concerning the topic of attention and the Vision or response that the Story invites in light of the kingdom of God. As indicated before, I use Story and Vision as metaphors to represent the faith tradition of the Christian community and the lived response toward which this tradition invites us.

6. Dewey, *Art as Experience*, 41.

Normally the Story and its Vision are made available to the group by the educator, though I have frequently been with groups of adults where this was done by a well-prepared group member or by an outside resource person. It is crucial that the Story and Vision made accessible to the group be an accurate representation of the faith understanding of the broader Christian community in whose name the education is being carried on. This requires that the presenter be well informed (as should be true with any approach) by contemporary scholarship and church teaching. This does not mean that every Christian religious educator should be a professional theologian or Scripture scholar, but he or she must have reliable resource material from which to draw. The Story/Vision presented at even the earliest grade levels must be a version that will not have to be contradicted later, but rather can be added to. Bad theology is harmful to the faith life of people at any age.

This is the most obviously catechetical movement in the process. It is the "echoing," the handing down, of what has come to us over our past pilgrimage. Presenting the Story and proposing its Vision can be done in many different ways using a variety of teaching techniques;[7] I have personally used a number of different styles of lecturing, audio-visuals, and research assignments. It is vitally important that the Story be made available in a dialogical rather than in a monological manner. This does not mean that the presenter and the group constantly talk back and forth to each other. Rather, it requires that the Story/Vision be made present in a disclosure rather than a closure way, that is, a way that invites people, bringing their own stories and visions, to reflect upon, to grapple with, question, and personally encounter what is being presented. One key condition is that the presenter must never make his or her version of the community Story/Vision sound like the fullness and final statement of the "truth." If the presentation is absolutized and made to sound as if "this is exactly what you must believe or do . . . and as I say so," then a personal appropriation by the participants, in dialogue with their own lived experience, is unlikely. The tradition can give life, but dogmatism is barren and arrests the journey toward maturity of faith.

One wonders if the fact that the great majority of people remain at stage three of faith development is not due, at least in part, to a religious education that taught too much, too soon, too finally, and from outside lived experience. If our expression of the Story/Vision is to be part of an "education toward adulthood"[8] and toward maturity in Christian faith, then they must be

7. Many of the models of teaching that Marsha Weil and Bruce Joyce have worked out can be used at different movements. However, the advance organizer model and the concept attainment model are particularly suited to this third movement (see Weil and Joyce, *Information Processing Models of Teaching*).

8. I take this phrase for the title of Gabriel Moran's most recent book, *Education Toward Adulthood*. Moran has done more than any religious educator to promote the idea that all religious

presented in a disclosure rather than a closure manner. They must be made accessible in a way that invites people to reflect, to personally appropriate, to see the why and the wherefore of the tradition—in a sense, to rediscover it for themselves. This is also essential to prepare for the fourth movement, where the present dialectical hermeneutics . . . begins. A rule of thumb I have found useful in my own presentations and that helps to promote a dialogical disclosure-type presentation is to end with a statement such as, "And that is my understanding of the tradition on this topic. What do you think?" Such an admission gains respect for my position while inviting the participants to appropriate it to themselves and to their own knowing, out of their own Christian praxis.

When I describe this third movement as a making present of the Christian community Story and its Vision, this should not be understood as two separate presentations, the first of the Story and the second of the Vision. Two foci are sometimes called for within the same presentation, but most often I find that as I present the Story I also present its Vision, the response it invites and promise it offers. A more detailed account of samples from my own praxis may make the workings of this movement clearer.

During the weekend with the university people considering their university's role in educating for social justice, the third movement was handled by three resource people. The first person gave a summary, as she had heard it, of the corporate Story and Vision of the group as it had emerged from the previous two movements. The second two "input" people, who were from outside the group, worked full time in social justice ministry. Drawing heavily from Scripture, current theological writings, and papal documents, they gave presentations on their understanding and rationale for social justice and outlined what they envisioned as the possible contribution of the university in meeting that challenge.

With religious educators attending to the purpose of Christian religious education, I gave a summary of the purpose. . . . In the unit on the Emmaus story the third movement was an exegesis of the passage which drew from a number of Scripture commentaries and proposed it as a model of Christian education. . . .

In another adult group dealing with the role of women in the church I talked about the low status of women in the pre-Christian world, the oppressive attitude of the Fathers toward women (looking especially at Tertullian, Jerome, and Augustine), and the poor treatment of women in church legislation and practice down to our own day. Then, bringing some present consciousness to the reading of Scripture, I contrasted this story with the open and liberating attitude of Jesus toward women. Many of his words and actions directly contravened the

---

education should be adult centered, in the sense not of excluding children, but of promoting life-long learning toward adulthood.

laws and sexist mores of his cultural context. I shared some insights from current feminist theology and spoke about the Vision of the kingdom in which there is no longer to be discrimination of any kind, where Jew and Greek, slave and free person, male and female will all be one in Christ Jesus our Lord (Gal. 3:28).

With the ninth-graders on the Eucharist I emphasized the responsibility which Eucharist places on us (receiving requires giving) and then screened a film titled *Eucharist*, which very powerfully develops this theme.

In the unit on prayer with the fourth-graders I used a narrative format. I explained how Jesus had told us to pray and pray often. Using Scripture stories, I explained how Jesus had given us an example of saying to God what was most on our mind, be it joy and praise or pain and petition; how he had prayed at different times and in various places and had even taught us a special prayer to say. We said the Lord's Prayer together. I told them about prayers that are not just prayers of petition and about prayers of petition that are not just for members of our own family or group. I concluded by explaining that Christians are called to be praying people and that God will always hear our prayers, though not always as we think they should be heard.

In the unit on Reconciliation I used a short film, *The Dropout*, a children's version of the parable of the prodigal son. I explained how God is always willing to forgive us when we say we are sorry for what we have done wrong. Then, using the Scripture passage about leaving our gift at the altar and being reconciled with our brothers and sisters before offering it (Matt. 5:23–24), I explained the meaning, purpose, and structure of the Penitential Rite at the beginning of Mass and how this prepares us as a community to celebrate the Eucharist in a spirit of love and forgiveness. I explained further that we could always be confident of God's mercy if we say that we are sorry, but we must also be willing to forgive those who hurt us.

Again, in this third movement a great variety of teaching modes and methods of presentation can be used. It may be done in a ten-minute presentation or take a number of weeks or even months. The primary purpose is to enable the group to encounter the broader community Story and Vision that arises from the Christian faith tradition. Fourth-graders, for example, should not have to invent the idea of a loving and forgiving God who offers us mercy and wants us to forgive each other. That is part of the revelational heritage of our faith community which they deserve to inherit. However, if they are to personally appropriate this idea for their lives, then they need, first, to have it made present in the context of their lived experience and, second, to be enabled to take it to themselves and accept responsibility for their response to it. The second point is the agenda for the next two movements.

The fourth and fifth movements combined are a bringing together of what was done in the first two movements with what was made accessible in the third movement. They place *theoria* and praxis in a dialectical unity with each other. The stories and visions are placed in dialogue and dialectic with the

Story/Vision to invite appropriation of the tradition to lived experience and decision making for further praxis. In my own praxis, especially with younger children, the two movements often overlap. However, with adults especially it is often important to keep them separate in the praxis, and I will present them separately here.

Fourth Movement: Dialectical Hermeneutic between the Story and Participants' Stories

The fourth movement is a critique of the Story in light of the stories and a critique of the participants' present stories in light of the past Story. Though I would rarely pose the question in such metaphorical language, the fourth movement asks, in essence, What does the community's Story mean for (affirm, call in question, invite beyond) our stories, and how do our stories respond to (affirm, recognize limits of, push beyond) the community Story?

Let me repeat again here that I am speaking of critique in the dialectical sense, and not of criticism in the narrowly negative sense. Thus there will be affirmation as well as negation, and very often there will be much more of the former than of the latter. There are times when the Story comes to us as a source of affirmation, encouragement, healing, and hallowing. But knowing that we—in our personal, interpersonal, and social/political lives—are never completely faithful to our faith commitments, there are also times when the Story confronts us, calls us in question, and calls us forward. God's self-revealing and reaching out into the world should always be recognized as both consolation and confrontation, encouragement and correction, affirmation and invitation. Conversely, as our stories respond to the community Story, there are whole dimensions of the larger Story with which our own lived experience resonates (since it arises from the lived experience of the Christians who went before us). Thus we can readily affirm it. On the other hand, there may be dimensions of the larger Story or at least the presentation of it as encountered in movement three in which we recognize limitations.

That there are limitations in our understanding of the Story seems inevitable since we can never exhaust its meaning and truth for our lives. The ground of our Story is a God of ultimate mystery and thus no version or understanding we have of God's activity among our people (our Story) can ever be the last word. Rather than passively accepting or simply repeating the version made accessible, we need to recognize the limitations in our present understanding and attempt to move beyond them.[9] This is far from being an exercise in

9. What I intend here is very close to what I understand David Tracy to mean by "critical correlation." Tracy sees that there are "two main 'sources' of fundamental theological reflection" (*Blessed Rage for Order*, 64), namely, "the Christian fact" and common human experience and language. Both sources must be themselves critiqued and then critically correlated with each other.

negative criticism. On the contrary, the dialectic is a liberating and creative process that uses the tradition itself to empower us to move forward. Some examples of how I have done the fourth movement, and then a more precise description of the fifth movement, may clarify what I am saying here.

In the weekend on social justice with the university people, I opened the fourth movement by asking for general reactions to the input of the morning (third movement). How had the input shed light on their situation at the university, what did they see as feasible or not feasible, and what would they add to what was said that morning? In the unit with people preparing to be evaluators of Christian schools the third movement (presented by a well-prepared member of the group) was a very moving presentation on stewardship, well grounded in Scripture and rich in imagery. For the fourth movement I invited the participants to choose and share the image that had spoken most powerfully to them and to explain why. (This puts the two stories in dialogue with each other.) With the group focused on the Emmaus story after my presentation I asked the participants, "What insights did my presentation renew for you, and what would you add to or clarify in my statement?" In units with graduate students on the purpose of Christian religious education I typically ask them to write down three points they particularly agree with in my presentation, and three points they want to question, add to, or rephrase. I then have them share their notes with the whole group, or in groups of four if the whole group is too large.

In a unit on "freedom of conscience in a teaching church," one woman made a very moving statement that is a good example of what can happen at this fourth movement. She said, "In my own life the church as teacher lost a lot of its credibility after the encyclical on birth control. For some time I just turned it off when it tried to offer me moral directives. Yet I have realized from this evening that I need the consensus and support of a Christian faith community in my ethical decision making. I do not want to decide everything for myself as a private, isolated Christian." Here, I felt, neither the individual story nor the community Story was having the only word, but the two were in a creative dialogue with each other.

After screening the film with the ninth-graders on Eucharist I asked, "If you lie in bed tonight and think about that film, what image or scene will jump out at you first and why?"

In the unit on Reconciliation and the Penitential Rite of the Mass with the fourth-graders, I asked what they thought of the Rite and if it was a good idea to have it at the beginning of Mass (the Story and their lived experience in dialogue). Most of them seemed to think that it was a good idea. We spent some time talking about how it could help us prepare to celebrate Mass with feelings of peace and love. In that class there was also an interesting example of a small story talking back to the big Story. One boy had difficulty pronouncing the words *Penitential Rite*. Then it occurred to me that, for fourth-graders, I had used very poor language. What does that big word *penitential* mean to children? And is it *write* or *right* or *rite*? They did not know. So I asked them to think of a better name for it. After some discussion, one girl volunteered, "It's the time for forgiveness." We settled for that name, the time for forgiveness, and that was how it was referred to for the remainder of the semester. They had come to name it for themselves far better that I had named it for them.

I draw attention also to the difference between asking them what *they* think and feel about the time for forgiveness during Mass and playing the traditional role of teacher by asking them to tell me what the Penitential Rite is. The latter procedure, though typically followed by teachers after their presentation to a class, is not likely to achieve the purpose of the fourth movement. The expectation that usually underlies such a question is that the students will feed back to the teacher the "right answers," that is, the answers the teacher has given them. This is not to imply that the fourth movement is reduced to an exercise in personal opinions or feelings. On the contrary, the participants are indeed expected to know their community Story. In this case I wanted the fourth-graders to know clearly what the Penitential Rite was, and when it is obvious that that was not clear, I repeated my explanation of it. But even more important, I wanted them to come to see what the Penitential Rite might mean for their lives.

At the fourth movement in the unit on prayer I asked the participants what they now thought about prayer and about how Jesus had prayed. They seemed to agree that we should talk to God not only to ask for things, but also to express love and gratitude. This led to a discussion about whether or not we really can talk to God in our own words, at any time or place, or about anything. This seemed strange to them, and many were reluctant to accept the idea. Two people said that prayers we make up ourselves are not "real prayers." Real prayers, they insisted, are the Our Father, Hail Mary, and other set prayer formulas that they had learned. In response I pointed out that Jesus did not often use a set formula and that I very often talk to God in my own words. Here is an example of the discussion that followed: When I asked one little boy, "Billy, what is the most important thing in your life right now?" he said, "My dog." I did not expect that answer, but this was a dog he had received just a few days previously. I inquired if he could talk to God about his dog. He laughed ("What a stupid question") and said, "No." "Why not?" I asked. He said, "Cause he's not sick." We talked about that with the group, and they agreed that Billy could talk to God about his dog even though the dog was not sick. I asked Billy if he could thank God for his dog and do it in his own words. After a good deal of thought, Billy agreed that he could. I then asked, "Will you?" (fifth movement overlapping), and with some enthusiasm he said that he would.

The vital task to be promoted by the educator in the fourth movement is twofold: that lived faith experience be informed by the Christian faith tradition and that the appropriating of the tradition be informed by, and be in the context of, lived faith experience. Only thus can a praxis way of knowing be promoted. There is also a sense in which the fourth movement is an opportunity for the participants to see the "why" of the Christian Story or, as Piaget would say, "to reinvent it." As the second movement is an opportunity to reflect on their individual knowing, the fourth movement is an opportunity to reflect on the community knowing, to appropriate it, to name it their "new" knowing of it with a sense of discovery. It attempts to promote a moment of "aha" when the participants come to know the Story as their own, in the context of their lives.

At first, people who are new to the process, be they young or old, tend to feed back the answers they presume the teacher expects. This tendency decreases as they continue to use the process. The way in which the fourth movement questions are posed is crucial for moving beyond such a "right-answers" mentality (e.g., not saying, "Now tell me what the prayer is," but rather, "How do you understand prayer? What could it mean for your life?" etc.).

Fifth Movement: Dialectical Hermeneutic between the Vision and Participants' Visions

The intention for the fifth movement is to critique the visions embodied in our present action in the light of the Vision of God's kingdom and to decide on future action that will be an appropriate response to that Vision. Stated in its technical language, the fifth movement is asking, "How is our present action creative or noncreative of the Vision, and how will we (I) act in the future?" Stated more simply, the movement is an opportunity for the individual and the group to choose a faith response, a Christian praxis, in light of all that has gone before.

In the dialectic that is intended here there is a recognition of the signs of the kingdom already among us, but there is also a perception of its not-yetness and a decision of how to respond to both in our lives. To people who are new to the process especially (and given our penchant for abstractions), it is difficult at first to make praxis decisions about our future action. This became obvious in my first experience using shared praxis with adults. All of us tended to make statements like, "People need to realize that . . ." or, "The church should. . . ." But such are likely to be *theoria* statements, at best, and decisions for other people rather than for ourselves. To help us come to our own new knowing, we found it helpful to preface our remarks with statements like "I will do . . ." or "For me this means. . . ."

Remembering again our comprehensive description of action, the decision for future action here can be a decision for overt activity, or it can be an articulation of a new awareness, understanding, sentiment, feeling, hope, and so on. It could also be a decision for further reflection and attempts at clarification. Many times during this movement participants have said something like, "I have never thought of it this way before, and I need to think a lot more about it." Such a statement is actually a decision for future action.

The examples of what has happened during this fifth movement are almost as varied as the number of people who have participated multiplied by the number of times I have used a shared praxis approach. In the unit on social justice this final movement was spent in outlining concrete strategy for the next step. Many ideas were shared about what might be done, the suggestions were noted, and a committee was formed to write a proposal. The proposal was later circulated to the other members of the group for comments, and then a final statement was prepared for submission to the university administration.

In the Emmaus story unit we began the fifth movement by asking ourselves, "How will these reflections influence how we educate in the future?" In units on the purpose of Christian religious education, my graduate students are invited to write a reflection paper on "What for me is the purpose of Christian religious education?" The fifth movement with the evaluators began with a half hour of silence during which the participants were invited to reflect upon and write down five sensitivities or awarenesses they would want to bring to their task as evaluators. These were later shared with the whole group.

With the ninth-graders on Eucharist we ended by responding to the question, "How will I give 'Eucharist' to people?" Some offered concrete suggestions, while one said, "I will have to think a lot more about that." In other units on Eucharist we have ended by celebrating a liturgy together, and on one occasion a group of high-school boys decided to organize a fast for world hunger.

With the fourth-graders in the unit on prayer I simply asked questions like, "Will you pray? What will you say? When will you pray?" They talked about praying in the morning and at bedtime, before and after meals, saying prayers of petition and also prayers of praise and thanksgiving. One little girl was missing from class that day because she was in the hospital. The class decided that they would pray for her. I suggested that we each write out a prayer and I would take them to her in the hospital. I had the children read their prayers aloud before I collected then, and one boy said that he would say his again that night.

In the unit on Reconciliation we talked about how we might enter into the "time of forgiveness" at Mass the next Sunday. I asked if there was anyone whom they could forgive or "make up" with. Everyone had someone to whom they needed to say "sorry," and I invited them to do that when they had an opportunity. It so happened that two of the boys had had a fight before class that day, and this was reported to the group. The class suggested that they shake hands with each other, and they did. In the unit on the Offertory we spent some time talking about what we might try to remember at the Offertory of the Mass next time we participated. It was just before Christmas time, so there were many decision concerning Christmas gifts.

The fifth movement is essential if our religious education is to lead to further Christian praxis. . . . Christian faith is a whole way of being in the world, a lived response rather than a theory about, and our religious education should invite people to decision. Many contemporary curriculum materials, especially at the grade-school level, cover the first four movements of shared praxis in one way or another (though the dialectical element is often absent). But unfortunately the fifth movement is frequently left out. An opportunity for choosing needs to be built in as a consistent part of the process, rather than simply being taken for granted.

Even as I pose the fifth movement as an opportunity for choosing a faith response it is important to remember that . . . this movement is certainly not a free-for-all in which people are invited to choose arbitrarily as they please. On the contrary, the guidelines of continuity, consequences, and community/church must guide the decision-making, It is also relevant to recall the description of the kingdom as both invitation and mandate, and the description of Christian freedom as very different from rugged individualism and the antithesis of license. An example may clarify what I mean here: in a unit on justice, the educator could never pose the fourth and fifth movement questions in the forms of "Will you or won't you be just?" as if the Christian Story and Vision offer an option on the question. Justice is a mandate of the kingdom. The participants may indeed choose to overlook injustice in their lives, but the educator can never pretend that it is a valid response to the kingdom. The educator can, however, invite students to discern what justice means, why they are called to it, and how they will live justly in their own lives.

But even when the guidelines for decision-making and the mandate of the kingdom are kept in mind, there still remains an obvious risk in inviting our students to such decision-making and personal appropriation. All of us have hopes for what our students will choose, and we should never be without purpose and intentionality. We have the right to give witness to what our hopes are, and our students have a need to hear them. But I am often asked, "What if the participants make choices contrary to what we hope they will choose?" This is a risk we must take. Indeed, we have a responsibility to provide an environment of openness in which they will have that option. Otherwise, we are likely to fall back into domination, rather that education. The model here is Jesus himself. When the rich young man came to him inquiring, "What must I do to share in everlasting life?" he received the invitation to "sell all you have and give to the poor. . . . Then come and follow me." The rich young man refused the invitation. Jesus, while saddened by that refusal, respected the young man's choice (Luke 18:18–25). In John 6, after the discourse on the bread of life, "many of his disciples broke away and would remain in his company no longer" (John 6:66). Far from refusing their choice and trying to cajole or threaten them into accepting his position, Jesus turned to the Twelve and asked, "Do you want to leave me too?" (John 6:67). Throughout the Bible the call of Yahweh and the call to discipleship always carry with them the right of refusal. That is the risk God takes in giving us free will. Our risk as Christian religious educators can be no less.

We must never presume that because our students do not choose the response we had envisioned for them that they are inevitably being unfaithful to the Story and Vision. *Our* intentions for them are not necessarily God's intentions. In fact, our students may choose other than as we had hoped, but in that go beyond our limited vision as teacher to a more faithful Christian response. One mark of a great educator is the ability to lead students out, not just to his or her own position but beyond that to new places where even the educator has never been. On many occasions in shared praxis groups I have been brought to decisions I never set out to make. Such moments remind us again that the educators should be the "leading learner" and that, especially in the journey of faith, we are all brother and sister pilgrims together.

For Reflection

1. From your experience, how does Groome's approach to Christian education differ from "business as usual"?
2. How does the author deal with the interaction between theory and practice?
3. What do you understand *praxis* to mean?
4. The fifth movement focuses on action in light of the four previous movements. Is there an appropriate limit to action generated in this way? Is there a range of acceptable action? What might that be?

23

James W. Fowler

Stages of Faith

(1981)

Currently the director of the Center for Faith Development at Emory University, Professor James W. Fowler is a doctoral graduate of Harvard and previously taught at Boston College. Fowler's book, *Stages of Faith,* begins with a distinction between religion and faith. Following the work of the comparative religionist Wilfred Cantwell Smith, Fowler says that religion is a "cumulative tradition," like a dynamic gallery of art: "Faith, at once deeper and more personal than religion, is the person's or group's way of responding to transcendent value and power as perceived and grasped through the forms of the cumulative tradition. Faith and religion, in this view, are reciprocal" (9). Each is dynamic and nurtures the other. However, faith and belief are not to be taken as synonymous. Belief is the holding of ideas while faith is the relation of trust in and loyalty to the transcendent about which beliefs are fashioned. ". . . faith involves an alignment of the heart or will. . . ."

How the heart is aligned might be said to be the key to visioning faith development. It is a structural approach attempting to locate the frame upon which to hang the full clothing of belief. Professor Fowler and his associates, building upon the work of Piaget, Erikson, and Kohlberg, interviewed 359 persons ranging in age from four to eighty-four. These were of all religious backgrounds, including atheist, though more than 80 percent were Protestant or Catholic. Over 97 percent were

From *Stages of Faith: The Psychology of Human Development and the Quest for Meaning* (San Francisco: Harper and Row, 1981), 119–213.

white; male and female were about equally represented. Where old enough, they were asked questions that helped them review their lives, life-shaping experiences and relationships, present values and commitments, and their religion. Probes were used to move toward deeper and deeper considerations of these issues. Each interview took from two to two-and-one-half hours to complete. The results were analyzed, and out of this work came six stages describing what the interviewees held in common and where they differed.

This selection from the book, subtitled *The Psychology of Human Development and the Quest for Meaning,* covers several chapters that describe the stages of faith developed by Fowler.

Infancy and Undifferentiated Faith

It is morning. A very young baby awakens. Feeling the discomfort of hunger, a wet diaper, and a vague anxiety, she cries out. Nearby, a mother wakes up, attending to the cry. Soon she is in motion. Approaching the baby, she calls out a name. She follows this with verbal greetings and phrases of tenderness. The baby's head turns; its eyes grow animated. Their eyes meet. Face to face now, the greetings are repeated. Then with her face expressive of interest and concern, the mother picks up the child, nuzzling and embracing her, while sniffing and feeling in order to determine the extent of her need. Continuing the verbal caresses all the while, the mother carries out the necessary operations of cleansing and replacing soiled clothes. The baby watches the mother's face as she works; their eyes meet frequently. Picking the baby up again, the mother produces a warm bottle or a breast. As she holds the infant in her arms, perhaps rocking her gently, the baby begins to suck vigorously. As her lips, tongue, and palate draw warm milk into her mouth and stomach, her eyes play on the face of the mother. The mother's eyes are bright and attentive, her features mobile. Frequently she speaks, producing familiar, soothing, or playful sounds. As the sharp edge of her hunger eases, the baby pauses. Lifting her to her shoulder the mother pats her on the back while continuing words of encouragement. After a burp or two the feeding continues, only now it is a little more relaxed.[1]

We all begin the pilgrimage of faith as infants. Formed in the profound symbiosis of prenatal life in our mother's womb, at birth we are thrust into a new environment for which we have potential but not yet fully viable abilities. For another nine months after birth we are more dependent on the care

1. Paraphrased and shortened from Erik H. Erikson, *Toys and Reasons* (New York: Norton, 1977), 85–90.

of those who welcome us than are all but a few of our mammalian companions. We are wonderfully endowed with innate potential for adapting to this new world, but the activation and elaboration of our adaptive capacities depends both on the progress of our overall maturation and on the way the persons and conditions of our environment greet us and beckon us into interaction. If there is not enough holding, rocking, or stimulation from communication, our adaptive capacities for relationship and loving attachments can be severely retarded or non-activated. If our environment presents us with no change, with no novelty or physical objects to call forth and challenge us, our movement and our coordination, our curiosity and operations of knowing may be severely limited. If the quality and consistency of our feeding and cleansing are inadequate and if there is no person (or persons) with whom we can achieve a dependable complementary relationship of mutuality, our trust of the world and in ourselves can be outweighed by distrust and infantile despair.[2]

Only gradually do we begin to know objects in our environment as separate from us and as continuing in existence when out of our sight or attention. Initially it is as though the breast or bottle, the maternal face, and the objects we grasp and taste are extensions of us, there at hand miraculously when need or curiosity direct us to them. A kind of primal "fall" into consciousness occurs as our interaction with persons and objects enables us cognitively to construct what Piaget calls the "schema of object permanence." By seven or eight months we form and retain mental images of missing objects—people and things—and we are on the way toward knowing that we are separate from those we love and toward needing to experience ourselves as central in a world of "others." This fall is traumatic. Some think that our primal innocence gives way to the first split of conscious and unconscious as we experience the new anxiety, emerging on the average around eight months, of remembering our mothers when they are absent from us and the panic about whether our mothers when they are absent from us and the panic about whether they will return. This panic is so severe, these observers tell us, that it is repressed by our first psychic defenses and "forgotten" (Lowe 1980). This healthy forgetting is made possible by the timely returns of the mother or other primary giver of care. As she returns, calling the baby's name and blessing it with the gift of her eyes and face, the baby is reconfirmed in being and well-being and restored to a sense of centrality in its world of objects growing increasingly separate. In such a way does trust take form—trust in the caregivers and the environment they provide; trust in the self, its worthiness and its being at home; trust in the larger world of meaning inchoately surrounding the infant and the caretakers, mediated through their bodies and voices and the patterns of their ways of

2. For a fine survey of recent literature on these topics see Selma Fraiberg, *Every Child's Birthright: In Defense of Mothering* (New York: Basic, 1977).

parenting the child, even as a baby, toward their (and their culture's) images of worthy womanhood or manhood (Erikson 1963, 249).

Those observers are correct, I believe, who tell us that our first *pre-images* of God have their origins here. Particularly they are composed from our first experiences of mutuality, in which we form the rudimentary awareness of self as separate from and dependent upon the immensely powerful others, who were present at our first consciousness and who "knew us"—with recognizing eyes and reconfirming smiles—at our first self-knowing (Rizzuto 1979). I call these *pre-images* because they are largely formed prior to language, prior to concepts and coincident with the emergence of consciousness.

Summary of Undifferentiated faith. In the pre-stage called Undifferentiated faith the seeds of trust, courage, hope, and love are fused in an undifferentiated way and contend with sensed threats of abandonment, inconsistencies, and deprivations in an infant's environment. Though really a pre-stage and largely inaccessible to empirical research of the kind we pursue, the quality of mutuality and the strength of trust, autonomy, hope, and courage (or their opposites) developed in this phase underlie (or threaten to undermine) all that comes later in faith development.

The emergent strength of faith in this stage is the fund of basic trust and the relational experience of mutuality with the one(s) providing primary love and care.

The danger of deficiency in the stage is a failure of mutuality in either of two directions. Either there may emerge an excessive narcissism in which the experience of being "central" continues to dominate and distort mutuality, or experiences of neglect or inconsistencies may lock the infant in patterns of isolation and failed mutuality.

Transition to Stage 1 begins with the convergence of thought and language, opening up the use of symbols in speech and ritual play.

Stage 1: Intuitive-Projective Faith

For several weeks between her fifteenth and eighteenth months my older daughter conducted daily a curious ritual. In our four-room graduate student's apartment she had a small bedroom adjoining that of her parents. In what had been an old New England farmhouse there were long windows, almost from floor to ceiling. As early morning sunlight bathed the room, Joan would awaken, stand up in her crib and through the open door demand her parents' sleepy attention. When she was sure that we were both in attendance she began, in her tentative English, to name the various pictures and objects of furniture in her little room. After she had named each of the eleven or twelve items she knew, waiting after each one to get our confirmation and praise, she then turned to other play and the day could begin.

What was the meaning of this ritual? At the time I had done very little study in developmental psychology and simply assumed that it was a playful step in language acquisition. Certainly it was this, but now I know that it was more. The operations of our thought and the beginnings of language have different roots in infancy. Our first "reasoning" involves sensorimotor knowing—the coordination of movements and the construction of practical schemata of space, object permanence, and causal action. The production and repetition of vocal sounds, which elicit response and mutual imitation between parents and child, do not effectively come into the service of thought until the beginnings of the second year of life. At that point, when the convergence of thought and language begins to occur, the child takes hold of a qualitatively new and powerful kind of leverage on the world of experience (Vygotsky 1962, 33–49). I think our daughter's morning ritual had to do with this revolutionary convergence of thought and language. Minimally, I believe, it represented a daily celebration (and reconfirmation) that the external world was made up of dependably permanent objects, that they had names, and that she, in mastering their names, could daily reconstitute a repertoire of shared meanings with her parents.

The Intuitive-Projective child, whose age ranges from two to six or seven, uses the new tools of speech and symbolic representation to organize her or his sensory experience into meaning units. With words and names the child explores and sorts out a world of novelty, daily encountering new elements for which he or she has no previously developed categories or structures. In this era the two- and three-year-old's endless questions of "what" and "why" may drive responsive parents, on some days, to wit's end. Close observation of the parent-child interchange helps one realize that often the logic that formulates the questions works in quite different ways than does the logic that produces the answers. Hence, the questions frequently are not satisfactorily answered. The child's thinking is not yet reversible. Cause-effect relations are poorly understood. The child's understanding of how things work and what they mean is dominated by relatively inexperienced perceptions and by the feelings these perceptions arouse.

Intuitive-Projective children exhibit cognitive egocentrism. . . . Being as yet unable to coordinate and compare two different perspectives on the same object, they simply assume without question that the experiences and perceptions they have of a phenomenon represent the only available perspective. This means that many conversations between Intuitive-Projective children have the character of dual monologues, each speaking in a way that assumes identity of interest, experience, and perception, while neither coordinates his or her perspective with that of the other, testing for fit or aptness. Seen from the cognitive developmental perspective the child's thinking is fluid and magical. It lacks deductive and inductive logic; it has an episodic flavor in which associations follow one another according to imaginative processes not yet constrained by stable logical operations.

Our interviews begin with children at age four. What they articulate in these talks appears to bear out the descriptions of cognitive process just presented. We will not make the mistake of assuming that what children are able to bring to word in these talks with strangers exhausts their faith constructions, but it does provide a beginning point. I want to let you overhear parts of an interview with Freddy, an alert six-year-old from a Catholic family. He had been told the outlines of a simple story about a brother and sister (the boy his age, the girl somewhat younger) who go on a family picnic in a large park. In the course of the afternoon the brother and sister wander off from the family and become lost in the deep woods that border the park. He is invited to tell some of the things they might see and experience in the woods.

Freddy: They see—you can see deers, you can get sunshine. You see beautiful trees. You see lakes and you see clear streams.
Interviewer: Well tell me, how did all of these trees and animals and lakes and things get there?
Freddy: By rain. . . . Mothers get the babies. The sunshine shines through the clouds and that's a lot of fun. Yeah, the stream and the water lakes. The lakes—the lakes get um, more—the forest—you have a deep hole and then it rains and then when it gets full enough they—it's a—it's a lake. But when it gets stinky you can't swim.
Interviewer: Oh, I see. Well why do you think we have trees and animals?
Freddy: 'Cause God made them.
Interviewer: I see. Why do you think he made them?
Freddy: 'Cause. 'Cause there's two reasons why. Number one is 'cause trees give off oxygen and number two is animals protect other animals.
Interviewer: I see. I see. Well why are there people?
Freddy: Uh—I don't know.
Interviewer: Can you think what it would be like if there weren't any people?
Freddy: The beautiful world would become ugly.
Interviewer: How come?
Freddy: 'Cause, nobody would be down and the world would be ugly.
Interviewer: Yeah?
Freddy: I think it would be like in the old days and things.
Interviewer: Um-hum. And what was it like in the old days?
Freddy: Like there was big holdups. There was wagons going fast.
Interviewer: But what—but what about even before that? What if there weren't any people at all anywhere?
Freddy: Just animals? I think it would be like—be like an animal world.
Interviewer: Would that be good?
Freddy: No, if there weren't any people, who would be the animals?
Interviewer: Well, how did people get here?
Freddy: They—they got here from God? That's all I know about the old days.

In Freddy's responses to a classic Piagetian moral dilemma we learn something about both his form of moral reasoning and his location of authority. The interviewer told him about a dinner table incident involving the same two children who had been lost in the woods. The sister, reaching for the margarine across the table, accidentally spills her glass of milk, ruining the front of her dress. Later the brother gets mad because he is not allowed to have a second piece of cake. In his anger he pushes his glass of milk over, but he gets only a small spot on his shirt.

Interviewer: Now which one of those people do you think did the worse thing?
Freddy: The sister.
Interviewer: Why?
Freddy: 'Cause—'cause she got a lot of milk all over her dress.
Interviewer: Yeah, and that's worse?
Freddy: Yeah.
Interviewer: I see. Do you know when you've done something bad?
Freddy: When I break a cup.
Interviewer: How do you know that's bad?
Freddy: 'Cause my mother gets upset and then she starts spanking and she starts screaming. When she sees the rug she screams real loud.
Interviewer: Well, how does your mother know that that's bad? Who told her?
Freddy: Her mother when she—when my—her mother—her mother got mad.
Interviewer: How did her mother find out?
Freddy: From her mother.
Interviewer: Well how did the first mother find out?
Freddy: From her mother.
Interviewer: How about the very first mother?
Freddy: Uh, I bet she was real smart.

At a later point in the conversation the interviewer introduces a series of questions about sickness and death. Freddy tells us that if a person is not getting well ". . . you just go to the hospital." Then he adds, "But the hospital can't fix you up sometimes."

Interviewer: What happens when they can't fix you up?
Freddy: You die.
Interviewer: You just die?
Freddy: Yeah.
Interviewer: What happens to you when you die?
Freddy: I don't know. Never been up in heaven before, only when I was a baby.
Interviewer: When you were a baby you were in heaven?

Freddy: Yeah.
Interviewer: How do you know that?
Freddy: Well, 'cause I felt the cold.
Interviewer: It's cold in heaven?
Freddy: Yeah, no, I think it's warm, real warm.
Interviewer: Where is heaven?
Freddy: Uh, high, high, high up in the sky.
Interviewer: What's it look like?
Freddy: Uh, high mountains, so I know about heaven.
Interviewer: Who is in heaven?
Freddy: God.
Interviewer: Just God? Is he by himself?
Freddy: No.
Interviewer: Who else is there?
Freddy: There's, there's the shepherds—the shepherd man—I mean the wise men that are dead.
Interviewer: Is there anyone else in heaven?
Freddy: Baby—no, not baby Jesus.
Interviewer: No?
Freddy: 'Ca—yeah, baby Jesus is God.
Interviewer: He is?
Freddy: Yeah.
Interviewer: Okay. Is anybody else in heaven?
Freddy: There's Mary. Saint Joe—that's all I know.
Interviewer: So heaven is where people go when they die?
Freddy: Your spirit goes up.
Interviewer: Oh, your spirit. What is your spirit?
Freddy: It's something that helps you—helps you—helps you do everything.
Interviewer: Yeah, where is it?
Freddy: In your body.
Interviewer: Inside you?
Freddy: Yeah.
Interviewer: And what does it help you do?
Freddy: Helps you do lots of things.
Interviewer: Like what?
Freddy: I don't know. Maybe—maybe walking. Maybe seeing around and stuff. That's all I know.

Freddy's account of spirit reminds me of a scene in a frieze on the front of the twelfth-century cathedral in Arles, France. Portraying the death by stoning of the first Christian martyr, Saint Stephen, the artist depicted Stephen's spirit in the form of a child-sized body being drawn gently upward by angels from the dying witness's mouth.

I conclude our quotes from Freddy's interview by combining several brief passages were he speaks about God. In one section he is shown a picture of a church. The interviewer asks him how the people in the picture feel about going to church.

Freddy: They feel sad.
Interviewer: How come?
Freddy: 'Cause all the things about God.
Interviewer: What kind of things about God make them feel sad?
Freddy: Well, God dies. God dies and then he comes back to life. That—coming back to life is good but—
Interviewer: But the other part is sad?
Freddy: Yeah, 'cause when you stay dead. That's all I know about that.
Interviewer: All right. Can you tell me what God looks like?
Freddy: He has a light shirt on, he has brown hair, he had brown eyelashes . . .

At this point Freddy brought in two small statues of Christ which he showed to the interviewer. After remarking about the statues she asked him, "Does everybody think that God looks like that?" Freddy's answer, suggesting a typical inability to construct other perspectives, is arresting: "Mmm—not when he gets a haircut." The interviewer follows these questions with one that asks how we can find out about God. The answers, probably a mixture of spontaneous construction and Freddy's efforts to make sense of some things he has heard, are interesting:

Freddy: When you go up—when your spirit goes up to heaven.
Interviewer: Is there any way we can find out before that?
Freddy: I don't know, really . . . when you take off in space.
Interviewer: Well how do *you* know about God?
Freddy: My teacher tells me about him sometimes. Sometimes I see him on cards and I see, uh—all those people up in heaven.
Interviewer: Do people ever talk to God?
Freddy: Yeah.
Interviewer: How?
Freddy: Well, well God can hear them, but he's in signs. He doesn't talk.
Interviewer: [Mis-hearing him]: He doesn't? What kind of songs does he sing?
Freddy: He sings songs about—I don't know, really. But he's in *signs.* Signs like stop signs.
Interviewer: Stop signs? Can you guess what kind of signs he might send?
Freddy: Like peace signs.
Interviewer: Peace signs?
Freddy: Yeah. That's all I know about that.

For a final sample of Freddy's theology we hear him talk about God in a quite different way than the anthropomorphic images of the Christ.

Interviewer: When you do something bad, does God know?
Freddy: Yes. He spreads all around the world in one day.
Interviewer: He does? How does he do that?
Freddy: He does 'cause he's smart.
Interviewer: He's smart? How does he get all around the world in one day?
Freddy: Uh—he can split or he can be like a God.
Interviewer: He can split into lots of things?
Freddy: Yeah.
Interviewer: There's not anything he can't do?
Freddy: He can do things, things that are good, not bad. God never tells a lie in his life.
Interviewer: Never?
Freddy: Nope.

Freddy has been exposed to a relatively rich range of symbols for composing his images of the character of an ultimate environment. His eclectic appropriation and extension of some of these help to make clear that children in Stage 1 combine fragments of stories and images given by their cultures into their own clusters of significant associations dealing with God and the sacred. Children from non- or anti-religious homes show similar tendencies, though their sources of images and symbols may be more limited. In an interview with Sally, four and a half, whose parents have made intentional efforts to avoid exposing her to religious symbols, we talked about belief in God.

Sally: Sometimes I believed in God, but my mother and father never believed in God.
Interviewer: Why do you believe in God?
Sally: Because on those shows they believe in God, like on "Leave It to Beaver" and Davey [the Lutheran Church in America's animated cartoon series, "Davey and Goliath"] you know that? Especially on Davey; there's a lot of that. Saturday morning we wake up kind of early and we watch Davey. And like today I watched Beaver and "Father Knows Best," but they don't have much about God.
Interviewer: Is God real to you?
Sally: Ummm—yeah . . . sometimes I think it's real.
Interviewer: What does God look like?
Sally: He doesn't look like anything. He's all around you.

Other sources of knowledge about God to which Sally referred included wedding and funeral scenes which occasionally occur in TV westerns. Sally's comments underscore the point of Dr. Ana-Maria Rizzuto (1979) in her rich psychoanalytic study of the origins of God images. Dr. Rizzuto finds that despite our secularization and religious fragmentation, religious symbols and language are so widely present in this society that virtually no child reaches school age without having constructed—with or without religious instruction—an image or images of God.

Preschool children typically do not yet generate (or faithfully retell) narratives that could give order and a kind of causal connectedness to their image clusters. They appreciate long stories and follow their details, but have limited abilities to retell them. And while the precursors of conceptual abstractions are present (Freddy's statement that God "spreads all around the world in one day"), only concrete symbols and images really address the child's ways of knowing.

One of the questions in our interviews with young children asks them to share what kinds of things make them feel fearful or afraid. Almost invariably, from boys and girls alike, the answer is some variant of "Lions, tigers, bears, and monsters!" When I first began to administer the interviews I would frequently respond to this by saying, "But you don't *really* have any of these things around your neighborhood, do you?" And they would say no. Then I would ask again, "What makes you feel afraid or fearful?" The answer would return: "Lions, tigers, bears, and monsters!" Puzzling over this with some of my research assistants, I was helped when one of the women pointed out to me that these fearsome, archetypal creatures are what the children dream and daydream about, and that "reality" and fantasy interpenetrate for them. Since then I have been helped tremendously by Bruno Bettelheim's book *The Uses of Enchantment: The Meaning and Importance of Fairy Tales* (1977). Drawing on his work as a child therapist, Bettelheim shows how fairy tales provide powerful symbolizations for children's inner terrors and for the hidden fantasies of violence or sex that bring them secret feelings of guilt. They also provide the child with tangible models of courage and virtue and with conviction-awakening stories showing that goodness and resourcefulness triumph over evil and sloth. Bettelheim's position makes a strong case against the effort, in children's literature or early childhood religious education, to present children only with the sunny or cheerful sides of life. By the third or fourth year children have developed an often preoccupying fear of death, particularly fear of the death of a parent or parents. Similarly, they have begun to internalize—often with a harshness far greater than parental adults ever intend—the taboos and prohibitions that surround and make mysteriously attractive things sexual and religious. The useful realism of fairy tales—and of many biblical narratives—provides indirect yet effective ways for children to externalize their inner anxieties and to find ordering images and stories by which to begin to shape their lives. One of Bettelheim's examples can be shared:

> Encouraged by discussion about the importance fairy tales have for children a mother overcame her hesitation about telling such "gory and threatening" sto-

> ries to her son. From her conversations with him, she knew that her son already had fantasies about eating people, or people getting eaten. So she told him the tale of "Jack the Giant Killer." His response at the end of the story was: "There aren't any such things as giants, are there?" Before the mother could give her son the reassuring reply which was on her tongue—and which would have destroyed the value of the story for him—he continued, "But there are such things as grownups, and they're like giants." At the ripe old age of five, he understood the encouraging message of the story: although adults can be experienced as frightening giants, a little boy with cunning can get the better of them. (1979, 27)

Testimony of another kind helps us appreciate more fully the immense responsiveness of children in this stage to symbols and images that awaken and shape conviction. One of our adult respondents, a male in his thirties, recalls that as a four-year-old he was required to take an afternoon nap. At the beginning of these naps his mother would sometimes read a story from the Bible. After reading the stories and responding to some of his curious questions, she would leave him "to go to sleep." Sleep came, he says, less frequently than rich fantasies and daydreams, often stimulated by the stories. He shared two of these with us. The first was the Daniel sequence, which tells of the heroic purity, faithfulness and defiance of Daniel and his three Hebrew friends in face of the king of Babylon. The story culminates, of course, with Daniel and his friends being subjected to a fiery furnace and to dangerous lions and being protected against all harm by God in both instances. Our respondent was particularly fascinated with the trial in the lions' den. He asked his mother many questions about how God "shut-mouthed" those lions. His own image of how it happened, he recalls, had to do with the instantaneous appearance in the lions' mouths of something like dental braces, locking their teeth together. After his mother left the room that day, and for some days to come, he relived that dramatic situation. He remembers that on at least one occasion he thought to himself, as though saying it out loud, "God, I'm brave like Daniel. Put some lions here in this room and I will show you that I am not afraid." Then, he said, he began to feel real fright at the possibility that God might really do what he asked.

The other story this man shared centered on his hearing the account of Samuel's call in the temple (1 Sam. 1–3). As his mother told him the story of the dedication by Hannah of her son Samuel to the work of God, it made a strong impression on him. It seems likely that just as he identified with Daniel in his fantasies, he also saw parallels with Samuel and felt identification with the latter's relation to a religiously serious mother. He felt, he said, a special closeness to the boy Samuel as he served in the temple. As the story continues, Samuel, on two different occasions, hears a call in the night. Two times he goes to Eli, the high priest, responding to what he took to be Eli's call. After the second call, Eli, perceiving that God was addressing the boy, instructed him when the call came again to respond: "Speak, Lord, for thy servant hears" (1 Sam. 3:9). Later in his childhood and adolescence, this man says, he would frequently awaken in the middle of the night and in the pregnant darkness would find himself feeling, "Speak, Lord, for Thy servant hears." It comes as no surprise to learn that today he is a minister and theologian.

In the following passage from Bettelheim I would prefer to substitute for his somewhat pejorative word *fantasy*—which suggests "make-believe" and "unreality"—the stouter word *imagination.* Imagination can indeed be fanciful, but it arises in this stage, for reasons Bettelheim helpfully sets forth, as a powerful and permanent force by which we compose an ultimate environment and orient ourselves toward the being or beings that constitute its character (Lynch 1973).

> A young child's mind contains a rapidly expanding collection of often ill-assorted and only partially integrated impressions: some correctly seen aspects of reality, but many more elements completely dominated by fantasy. [Here the phrases "correctly seen aspects of reality" and "completely dominated by fantasy" point to the limits of Bettelheim's appropriation of his own thesis.] Fantasy fills the huge gaps in a child's understanding which are due to the immaturity of his thinking and his lack of pertinent information. Other distortions are the consequences of inner pressures which lead to misinterpretations of the child's perceptions. (Bettelheim 1979, 61)[3]

While we reject Bettelheim's bias in this passage that imagination merely fills temporary "gaps" in knowledge and that it "distorts" reality, his statement helps us recognize both the robustness of imaginative processes at this stage and their inevitability. This and our previous examples also help us to see how the imagination and fantasy life of the child can be exploited by witting or unwitting adults. For every child whose significant others have shared religious stories, images, and symbols in ways that prove life-opening and sustaining of love, faith, and courage, there must be at least one other for whom the introduction to religion, while equally powerful, gave rise to fear, rigidity, and the brutalization of souls—both one's own and those of others. There are religious groups who subject Intuitive-Projective children to the kind of preaching and teaching that vividly emphasize the pervasiveness and power of the devil, the sinfulness of all people without Christ, and the hell of fiery torments that await the unrepentant. This kind of faith formation—and its equivalent in other religious traditions—can ensure a dramatic "conversion experience" by the time the child is seven or eight. It runs the grave risk, however, of leading to what Philip Helfaer calls "precocious identity formation" in which the child, at conversion, takes on the adult faith identity called for by the

3. Remarks in brackets are mine.

religious group (1972). This often results when the child is an adult in the emergence of a very rigid, brittle, and authoritarian personality.

Our research convinces me that education at this age—in the home, in synagogues and churches, in nursery schools and kindergartens—has a tremendous responsibility for the quality of images and stories we provide as gifts and guides for our children's fertile imaginations. Because the child's appropriations of and personal constructions of meaning with these symbolic elements is unpredictable and because insisting on conceptual orthodoxy at this age is both premature and dangerous, parents and teachers should create an atmosphere in which the child can freely express, verbally and non-verbally, the images she or he is forming. Where this expression is allowed and encouraged, the child is taken seriously and adults can provide appropriate help in dealing with crippling, distorted, or destructive images the child has formed. Dr. Jerome Berryman's approach to the use of parables with children ("being in parables with children" he calls it) provides an extremely helpful model for the approach I am advocating (1979, 271–85). Berryman's method builds on developmental theory, Montessori principles, and current research on the narrative functions of parables (Crossan 1973).

Finally, we must warn against a possible misunderstanding of the position taken here. The desirability of children's exposure to death, poverty, treachery, and maliciousness in the context of fairy tales and Bible stories, when told to them by trusted adults with whom their feelings can be tested and shared is one thing. It does not, however, translate into approval of hours spent passively before a television, absorbing the mixed bag and unending commercials of the Saturday morning cartoons. Nor does it sanction children's exposure to the super-realistic violence, materialism, and sexploitation of prime-time television programming (Sullivan 1980, 549–73).

Summary of Intuitive-Projective faith. Stage 1 Intuitive-Projective faith is the fantasy-filled, imitative phase in which the child can be powerfully and permanently influenced by examples, moods, actions, and stories of the visible faith of primally related adults.

The stage most typical of the child of three to seven, it is marked by a relative fluidity of thought patterns. The child is continually encountering novelties for which no stable operations of knowing have been formed. The imaginative processes underlying fantasy are unrestrained and uninhibited by logical thought. In league with forms of knowing dominated by perception, imagination in this stage is extremely productive of longlasting images and feelings (positive and negative) that later, more stable and self-reflective valuing and thinking will have to order and sort out. This is the stage of first self-awareness. The "self-aware" child is egocentric as regards the perspectives of others. Here we find first awarenesses of death and sex and of the strong taboos by which cultures and families insulate those powerful areas.

The gift or emergent strength of this stage is the birth of imagination, the ability to unify and grasp the experience-world in powerful images and as presented in stories that register the child's intuitive understandings and feelings toward the ultimate conditions of existence.

The dangers in this stage arise from the possible "possession" of the child's imagination by unrestrained images of terror and destructiveness, or from the witting or unwitting exploitation of her or his imagination in the reinforcement of taboos and moral or doctrinal expectations.

The main factor precipitating transition to the next stage is the emergence of concrete operational thinking. Affectively, the resolution of Oedipal issues or their submersion in latency are important accompanying factors. At the heart of the transition is the child's growing concern to know how things are and to clarify for him- or herself the bases of distinctions between what is real and what only seems to be.

Stage 2: Mythic-Literal Faith

The mind of the ten-year-old is an amazing instrument. It can virtually memorize the *Guinness Book of World Records.* It can guide a pair of hands to victory in a game of chess, sometimes over more experienced adult competitors. It can take an hour and a half to tell, in vastly inclusive detail, what the movie *Star Wars* is about. It can write and tell good stories, perform arithmetical operations, create and use systems of classification and consistently and accurately take the perspective of another on some object or interest in common. The ten-year-old mind can reverse its operations; it therefore understands constancy of volume and weight when objects or liquids are changed from one form to another. It can think in terms of processes—particularly if the processes in question are ones for which it has experienced concrete analogies. It can make inferences regarding the cause and effect relationships linking two "states of affairs" and it can reconstruct plausible intermediate steps in the process to test and refine its inferences.

In contrast with the preschooler, the ten-year-old constructs a more orderly, temporally linear and dependable world. Capable of inductive and deductive reasoning, the ten-year-old has become a young empiricist. Where the Intuitive-Projective child fuses fantasy, fact, and feeling, the Mythic-Literal girl or boy works hard and effectively at sorting out the real from the make-believe. Within the range of his or her ability to investigate and test, this youngster will insist on demonstration or proof for claims of fact. The concrete operational boy or girl does not cease to be imaginative or capable of a highly developed fantasy life, but the products of imagination are confined more to the world of play and will be submitted to more logical forms of scrutiny before being admitted as part of what the child "knows." Gone or vastly diminished are the epistemological egocentrism and the "blooming, buzzing confusion" of Stage 1. Replacing them are the ability to coordinate one's own perspective with that of another and the experience of a more predictable and patterned—if more prosaic—world.

The great gift to consciousness that emerges in this stage is the ability to narratize one's experience. As regards our primary interest in faith we can say that the development of the Mythic-Literal stage brings with it the ability to bind our experiences into meaning through the medium of stories. Younger children, as we have seen, depend upon rich stories to provide images, symbols, and examples for the vague but powerful impulses, feelings, and aspirations forming within them. Stories for the Stage 1 child provide symbolic representations that both express and provide models for their constructions of self and others in relation to an ultimate environment, but the preoperational child does not yet generate stories. He or she does not yet narratize experience. Concrete operational thinking brings new capacities. The convergence of the reversibility of thought with taking the perspective of another, combined with an improved grasp of cause-effect relations, means that the elements are in place for appropriating and re-telling the rich stories one is told. More than this, the elements are in place for youngsters to begin to tell self-generated stories that make it possible to conserve, communicate, and compare their experiences and meanings.

This capacity for and interest in narrative makes the school-age child particularly attentive to the stories that conserve the origins and formative experience of the familial and communal groups to which he or she belongs. Stories of lives and of great adventures—true or realistically fictional—appeal because of their inherent interest, but they also appeal because they become media for the extension of the child's experience and understanding of life. Of course, we never lose this fascination with stories, just as we never lose Stage 1's capacity for composing and responding to the symbolic and fantastic. Any speaker recognizes the relaxation of facial expressions and the grateful shifts in body posture that occur when the talk calls for a change from conceptual prose to the telling of a story. But with further development we will later construct the ability to step back from our stories, reflect upon them, and to communicate their meanings by way of more abstract and general statements. Stage 2 does not yet do this. If we picture the flow of our lives as being like a river, Stage 2 tells stories that describe the flow from the midst of the stream. The Stage 2 person—child or adult—does not yet step out on the bank beside the river and reflect on the stories of the flow and their composite meanings. For Stage 2 meanings are conserved and expressed in stories. There is also a sense in which the meanings are *trapped* in the narrative, there not being yet the readiness to draw from them conclusions about a general order of meaning in life.

Let's listen to some sections of a lively interview with a *real* ten-year-old. Millie, a fourth grader from a Protestant family, plays the viola and loves singing and acting. Math, she says, is her hardest school subject: "It's so hard and so confusing—put this over there and everything!" (She's just been introduced to large multiplication problems and to long division.) A short way into the talk Millie is asked the question about why there are people in the world.

Millie: People in the world? Let's see. If there weren't any people, there wouldn't really be a world. And if there wasn't a world then the world would be blank. I mean everything—that's a tough question. Let's see. Why would there be people?

The concreteness of Millie's thinking and the unreadiness yet to formulate conceptual meanings of more general order mark her responses to this and the next several questions. A short time later she is asked if she can imagine a world without her and what it would be like.

Millie: It would be the same only there'd be a different person without me in it. . . . Well there wouldn't be a Millie T. Well, there might be somewhere. And Sue T. [her sister] wouldn't have a person to share a room with. And there wouldn't be a little girl in the Willingham School who plays the viola. And there wouldn't be Millie T., Jacqueline M.'s best friend. There wouldn't be Millie T., who plays viola in the all-city orchestra. And it would be different, I think, it probably would be.

To her, Millie's identity is the story of Millie's relationships and roles. The concreteness of her thought leads her to depict a world without her in terms of the gaps in relationships and roles her absence would mean. Interestingly, her depiction of a world without people conceives it in terms of the gaps in roles and relationships *God* would experience:

Interviewer: Okay, now let's go back to the first question and see if you can tell me now why you think there are people here in the world. Are they here for any purpose?

Millie: There—well, if there wasn't any people in the world, who would keep God company?

Interviewer: Is that why people are here?

Millie: I don't know, but that question just popped into my mind. How—how would God keep busy?

Interviewer: And what does God do with people?

Millie: He—he makes the people. He tries to give them good families. And he, he, um, made the world. He made trees and everything. If you didn't have trees you wouldn't have books. And if you didn't—like he made the whole world, which has a lot of beauty and that makes up things. Like rocks make metals and some kinds of rocks make metal.

Interviewer: Well, since God made all of these things for us, does he expect anything from us?
Millie: He just expects us, probably, to believe in him. To love each other and forgive and try to follow the Ten Commandments.
Interviewer: Is that all?
Millie: I—let's see, to love and to forgive and to try—to try to be happy in the world.
Interviewer: And how can you be happy?
Millie: To not—to not do things that you don't want to and to try to keep ourselves, you know, used. Not just sit around and mope.

In the next several passages Millie shares some of her images and thoughts of God. Here we see the concrete operational mind working creatively, within its limits, to grasp and express paradoxical insights. We see a typical example of the literal quality of Stage 2's use of symbols. The interviewer has just asked her what God looks like.

Millie: Well, I don't know. But do you want me to tell you what I imagine that he looks like? I imagine that he's an old man with a white beard and white hair wearing a long robe and that the clouds are his floor and he has a throne. And he has all these people and there's angels around him. And there's all the good people, angels and—and um, cupids and that he has like—I guess I—he has a nice face, nice blue eyes. He can't be all white, you know, he has to—he has blue eyes and he's forgiving. And I guess that's the way I think he is.
Interviewer: How do you get to be a good person?
Millie: To believe in God and try your hardest to do what is good.
Interviewer: When we do something wrong, does God know?
Millie: Yeah. God's with you all the time.
Interviewer: He is? How is that?
Millie: Well, God's inside of you in a way. In a way God's inside of you but in a way God isn't. He's inside of you because you believe—if you believe in him then he's inside of you, but he's also all around.
Interviewer: How can he be all around?
Millie: Well, that's a good question. Um, well he's—he lives on top of the world, so in a way he's all around.

The anthropomorphic elements in Millie's image of God (the old man with the white beard who lives on top of the world), as in many of our Stage 2 interviews, are far more developed than the nascent anthropomorphic images in Freddy's depiction of God quoted in our discussion of Stage 1. And as the next passage will show, Millie's God has the capacity to take her perspective and the perspectives of his other people. He takes account of intentions and the struggles of people; he is inclined to be compassionate. Before we began this research I had assumed that full-fledged anthropomorphic images of God like Millie's would primarily be found among preschool children. What we have found, in fact, is that Stage 1 youngsters are far more likely to answer questions about God in terms of his being "like the air—everywhere," or as Freddy put it, "He spreads all around the world in one day," or "He can split or he can be like a God." As I suggested in a previous writing (Fowler and Keen 1978, 46), this unexpected delay in the emergence of fully anthropomorphic God-images until Stage 2, where it is very common, makes sense if we take account of the revolution in perspective-taking that concrete operational thinking makes possible. The egocentrism of Stage 1 limits the child's ability to differentiate God's perspective from his or her own, just as it limits the ability to take the perspective of other persons. Stage 2's capacity to construct the perspectives of others ("Sue T. wouldn't have a person to share a room with. . . . And there wouldn't be Millie T., Jacqueline M.'s best friend.") means that the youngster now can also construct God's perspective, giving it as much richness—and some of the same limits—as the perspectives now consistently attributed to friends and family members. Let's listen to Millie again:

Interviewer: Does God care when you do something wrong?

Millie: Sure he—he cares. And he knows that you're—he knows that you are sorry about it. And he always tries—he always forgives you usually.

Interviewer: What if you're not sorry about it?

Millie: Then he knows, probably. He probably will still forgive you probably because he knows that you're probably going through a rough time. And I think that probably like some people who don't even believe in God, God still probably believes—uh, forgives them, because he knows that, you know, people have their own ideas and beliefs.

The concreteness and literalism that keep Stage 2 grounded come through plainly in this next passage, which sets forth the outlines of Millie's cosmology:

Interviewer: Well, what if somebody just came up to you and said, I've heard lots about this God. Can you tell me what God is? What would you say to them?

Millie: God is like a saint. He's good and he like—he like rules the world, but in a good way. And—

Interviewer: How does he rule the world?

Millie: Well, he—not really rule the world, but um—let's see, he like—he lives on top of the world and he's always watching over everybody. At least he tries to. And he does what he thinks is right. He does what he thinks is right and tries to do the best and—he lives up in heaven and—

Interviewer: Well can anyone go to heaven?

Millie: If people want to and believe in God then they can go to heaven.

Interviewer: What if people don't want to or don't believe in God? Then what happens to them?

Millie: They go just the opposite way.

Interviewer: And where's that?

Millie: Down under the ground where the devil lives.

Interviewer: Oh, I see, okay. Can you tell what the devil is?

Millie: Devil is a saint too, but he believes in evil and doing things wrong. Just the opposite of God. And he's always doing things that God doesn't want people to be doing.

Interviewer: Does he have power over the world?

Millie: The devil? Well like, no. God—no. I don't think. . . . That's a hard question. God doesn't really have power over the world. He just kind of watches it. And the devil's just like a little mouse trying to get cheese. Like he's trying to get into it, but I guess he just doesn't.

In the next several passages we see Millie bringing to word some of what she feels and knows about death and the justice of God. It seems likely that here we are getting thoughts that grasp and repeat some things her parent or parents have recently offered her. Yet one judges that Millie is not merely parroting, but that she has passed the meanings they shared with her through the filters of her own structures of knowing and valuing and that we are getting her first formulations on these matters. The interviewer has just asked why people die.

Millie: Well, if everybody stayed alive then, I mean, the world would just be so overcrowded. And, and things—it would make it harder for a family like to lead, to get money, to work, to find jobs and to find food and it would just be hard for the world. So God has to let some people die.

Interviewer: Is it up to God?

Millie: Well, well yeah. But like you know, he has to—let's see. Well, in a way, yes. Because he kind of controls. And I think that probably that—well actually he can't help it if somebody's going to die. Like he can't say that person's good, he can't die. He'd just say well I'm sorry but he's going to have to die. I mean like he can't really help. Like my friend, she had a puppy and he got ran [sic] over. And she was so mad. And she says, "I hate God, I hate God!" And I go, you know, that you shouldn't say that, 'cause God does work in mysterious ways. And you know you never know what's going to happen next. And neither does he.

Interviewer: But is it always the best thing?

Millie: It's always the best thing. Because if that puppy didn't die, then you know, you never know what would have happened next. And usually what God does is the best thing.

Interviewer: Usually?

Millie: Most of the time. All the time.

Interviewer: Which one?

Millie: All the time he does the best thing and the thing he thinks is best for us.

Interviewer: How does he know what's best?

Millie: Well, it's like your parents. They think they know what's best for you and so they try to do what they think is right. So that's what God does. And usually it turns out that he—what he does is the right thing.

With Millie's mentioning that God's doing what he thinks best is like parents doing what they think best for their children we are in position to grasp a useful insight. Millie's God-image takes forms offered by her culture, both the larger Western culture and the more particular Protestant culture of her family. But the forms are filled with the contents of Millie's perspective taking with her parents as decision makers. A little further in the interview, after she has likened God's actions to those of parents (God, too, is doing what he thinks is best for his people), she is asked if parents always do the right thing.

Millie: No, they don't always do the right thing, but they think what they do is best. Sometimes they make mistakes and I guess God probably makes mistakes too. See I keep changing my mind. You know, after I think, parents make mistakes because they think what they think is try to do the best. Sometimes it doesn't turn out to be the best and—well, God still I guess probably does what he thinks is right and it usually turns out—it turns out to be the right thing. But parents I guess don't always do the right thing.

Interviewer: How do parents find out what's right?

Interviewer: They have to think it over. Get all the things that happened and put them together and decide which would be the best thing to them.

This perspective taking with her parents and their apparent willingness to make their own processes of decision making accessible to their children enable her to construct an understanding of God that allows for divine mistakes and limitations of power. These factors help account for the fact that, in contrast to that of many of our Stage 2 respondents, Millie's God is not seen in excessively simple terms of strict reciprocity, invariably sending bad fortune to bad people and sending good fortune to the virtuous. Though still confined to the concreteness of the Mythic-Literal stage in this area of theodicy (explaining God's ways with humanity), Millie shows evidences of an emerging structuring in which seeming inequalities and differences in human fortune actually work for good. She is asked why some people seem to be luckier than other people.

Millie: Um, if God—if God evened up the whole world exactly even, then there wouldn't be good because there wouldn't be people who you could buy things from because I guess—to own like a company, you have to be very wealthy. You couldn't buy things from those people because there wouldn't be any companies and also you couldn't have jobs from other people because they wouldn't have enough money to give you because they have to use it, and things wouldn't work out . . . and usually—and usually it's the person who's wealthy is the lucky—I mean, it's he—you can't really call him lucky because he worked really hard for that money and so like you can call him lucky for the money, but he still has to work very hard to get the money.

At the end of this passage, an eloquent ten-year-old formulation of a rationale for capitalism, we see Millie drawn back toward Stage 2's typical commitments to reciprocity and fairness in God's dealing with humans, but in a more subtle and sophisticated form than it is usually stated. ("You can't really call him lucky because he worked really hard for that money.")

Eleven-year-old Alan, for example, was also asked why some persons seem to be luckier than others.

Alan: I can't really say that there's any such thing as luck because, um, this, it's just that it's like coincidences most of the time.

He goes on to give a somewhat unclear explanation that suggests that what people get has to do with their intentions. His meaning comes clearer when the interviewer asks him whether God has anything to do with whether people get what they want or not.

Alan: No, because, um, after the first sin, then the Lord, he punishes the people who do wrong, but he can't make them do wrong.

Interviewer: Can't make them do wrong?

Alan: So, it's like he's seeing what they're going to do. . . . So, um, he really has no, no charge of whether they're lucky or unlucky.

Interviewer: Are you saying that people who do wrong things get punished and are therefore unlucky?

Alan: No, they aren't unlucky. It's, um, it's punishment if you, if you did something wrong then you would deserve it.

Interviewer: So, that people who don't get the things they want or who get disappointed in life are somehow being punished?

Alan: Yeah, yes. Not if they don't get things that they want, but if they do something wrong and then they don't get the things that they want, then they're sort of being punished. . . . Oh, could I say that answer over again? See, it's like, not if they're doing wrong. Some, like in the first story you told me [the "Heinz dilemma"], he did wrong for good, so they don't always punish wrong, but if you do wrong deliberately for yourself, then you would most likely get punished.
Interviewer: I see. And God does that?
Alan: Mm-hm.

Alan's construction, while less sophisticated than Millie's, implies a similar understanding of reciprocal justice as an immanent structure in our lives. Presumably God created this ordering of things and even God is bound to the lawfulness he has created. This comes out even more plainly in our last excerpts from Millie's interview. Toward the end of the interview Millie too, was given the "Heinz dilemma" developed by Kohlberg for his research. A sparse story, it tells of a man in Europe whose wife is dying of cancer. He learns about a druggist nearby who has developed a new drug, derived from radium, which may help his wife get better. The druggist pays $200 for the radium, and charges $2000 for the finished drug. Heinz does all that he can to raise the needed money, but is only able to get $1000. The druggist refuses to sell the drug for that price. Heinz grows desperate and he breaks in and steals the drug.

Interviewer: Should Heinz have stolen the drug?
Millie: Um—that's—I knew you were going to ask that, and that's a hard question. Well in a way yes, but in a way no. Because—his, because his wife really needed it and if God forgave him, then probably everybody says, oh, that's okay, and everybody would steal. And the world wouldn't be right.
Interviewer: The world wouldn't be right?
Millie: No, because it wouldn't be the way that God would want it to be, if everybody stole and did what was wrong.

This is fascinating. Here we see Millie, like Alan, working with the same structuring of fairness that typifies Kohlberg's stage two. This is the fairness of instrumental exchange, where whatever one person is entitled to each other person is also entitled to. But she has extended that to the construction of a kind of rudimentary social system in which ("even if God forgave him" and "probably everybody else says, oh, that's okay") it would still be wrong for Heinz to steal. Why? Because, in fairness, everyone else would also be entitled to steal. And more, the structure of rightness in the world would be violated: "And the world wouldn't be right . . . because it wouldn't be the way that God would want it." I think that here we see justice as fairness, based on a prelegal understanding, extended into what amounts, for Millie, to an ontological structure of rightness—a functional, preconceptual system of natural law. Even God, who might personally make allowances for Heinz, cannot change the fact that stealing, which could become generalized if Heinz "gets by" with it, goes against "the way that God would want it to be." So powerful is this sense that stealing is wrong in some ontological sense that Millie shows very limited readiness to take the perspective of Heinz's wife. She is asked, "Is it worse to steal than to save someone's life?

Millie: Um, I guess, but—I guess in a way it's better to save somebody's life.
Interviewer: In what way?
Millie: In a way that the person's dying. But in a way no, because in a while that person's going to die anyways.
Interviewer: So you're just kind of putting it off.
Millie: Yeah, Yeah.
Interviewer: So what do you think Heinz should do?
Millie: Heinz should have gone to try his best. He should have like tried to make a lot of money, like work really fast. He could have gone to some place like a high authority like the mayor.
Interviewer: And why would he go to the mayor?
Millie: To ask them if, um, if that there was anything that he could do to get the money for the medicine. And if anybody could help him with his wife, help take care of the wife if she was sick right now.
Interviewer: So he shouldn't have stolen the drug?
Millie: He should have tried his hardest. 'Cause when he—when his wife died he would have known—Say his wife died anyways. He would have known that he did something wrong and he was going to have to pay for it. He would have known he did something wrong.
Interviewer: How would he know?
Millie: He, he would know, 'cause he a feel—he would have a feeling inside him, now I did all this wrong just to save my wife's life.

The connection between God and the necessity of accepting punishment, even for well-intentioned infractions against the "natural law" comes clear in the next eloquently concrete passage. Millie has just said, "He would have a feeling inside him, now I did all this wrong just to save my wife's life."

Interviewer: And where would that feeling come from?
Millie: From his conscience—conscience.
Interviewer: And what is your conscience?
Millie: It's like a person in you who always like talks inside of you, it talks like in your brain.
Interviewer: Um-hum. And where does it come from?
Millie: What?

Interviewer: Your conscience.
Millie: God. God gives everybody a conscience.

As the next passages indicate everyone's conscience is not the same (indicating again that Millie recognizes differences of perspective and judgment). Yet, still it is clear that, at least regarding stealing, everyone's conscience is likely to oppose it:

Interviewer: And everybody has the same conscience?
Millie: Uh-uh [no]. It depends on who you are. Like if you're an adult you have an adult conscience inside of you.
Interviewer: Um-hum. Well how is my conscience different from yours?
Millie: Because you—if you're older and you have different personalities than I do. And you probably have different thoughts than I do.
Interviewer: So—what kind—so Heinz had a different conscience than you?
Millie: Yeah. He probably thought what he was doing was right.
Interviewer: Why would he think that?
Millie: Because he was saving his wife's life. But then when his wife died, he would have said, why did I steal that?
Interviewer: What if his wife didn't die? What if she got well?
Millie: Then he would still know that he did something wrong, and he'd probably, probably, probably, he'd probably have to be put in jail and probably pay—have to work very hard to pay for the money for the thing.

In both Millie's and Alan's responses we see a structuring of the ultimate environment based on the strong intuition of a built-in, divinely constituted, natural lawfulness. Though there is some allowance for motives and intentions and the experiences that affect them in Millie's answers, she, like Alan, believes that even God is bound by the structures of reciprocity built into the order of things.

Though Stage 2 typically takes form in the elementary school years, some of the adolescents and a few of the adults we have interviewed exhibit the structural characteristics of Stage 2 as they speak of their faith. A few passages from one such respondent, a woman in her fifties, will provide an example. Please recognize that I could have chosen a man for this and that other examples one might have used could have included atheists or persons of religious orientations other than Catholicism.

Mrs. W., a mother of several grown or near-grown children, is in her fifties. Before her children began to leave home she devoted her full time to being a mother and to directing the affairs of their home. As the children have gone off to college or other pursuits she has returned to teaching school and seems to be kept very busy with her work. This seems to have cut her off from frequent conversations with friends. There is an undercurrent of loneliness and depression in her interview. As we look in on her conversation with our interviewer Mrs. W. is describing a talk given by one of the parish priests, a man whom she admires and whose approach to religion she appreciates.

Mrs. W.: Well I tell you now, last week he was saying that it was Advent and that, you know, just do one good thing, he said, for someone—just one this week. Some kind of thing—hold a door for someone that doesn't expect it. Just one little thing, and offer it up. [Pause] Y'know, 'n this is what, this is what I find I need, you know. Sometimes you keep doing big things; you think, oh I have to say a whole rosary or any—to say a whole thing. Now I have a little picture of the Pope—oh, I have great faith in him, that Pope—Pope John—and over my sink I have a picture of him, and everyday I say an Our Father, a Hail Mary, and a Glory Be to God. And then when I need it, it's in the bank. And now I have my children doing it, when they're walking to class and all, I say, "Build up your bank account." And when you sit in that dentist's chair, and it goes, Oooh! You just say, "open the bank" and out it pours, and it works. . . . Well, it, you just know that if you get in a mess, you have that bank and it will open up and it will help you through the mess.

At another point in the interview Mrs. W. is asked about her faith.

Interviewer: Let me ask you in general to describe what your faith is. What sort of descriptions would you use to, to try to tell somebody what your faith means to you?

Mrs. W.: Well, I don't know if other people feel this way, but I sort of sometimes feel you're plodding along, you know, all by yourself. But . . . because I have this great . . . because I have faith and believe in God, it seems to make the bumps a little easier, or the good times, you know, you have someone to share it with, really. Now I don't know why I say—I say this, because I was brought up with a sister. And we chatted and chatted, and chatted. And that's all we had, you know, each other. Then I married, and Ben is not a gossipy type person. So that, I mean, you know, if . . . well, I can just sort of share my feelings with God more easily than I can with a person, I guess.

Interviewer: Do you find yourself during the day just kind of casually . . . chatting . . . chatting with God?

Mrs. W.: Yeah. Yeah, and I'd say, you know, "I don't mean to complain—I know I have my health, and I know I have feet, and I know I have food, but what do you say, you know, uh, let's have . . ." And I think we've tried to bring the children up this way to make it more human, so you don't feel that. . . . Now I thought that one of the greatest things was Tom [one of her sons]. He decided, you know, that this going to mass was too much and all. And then, oh the draft came along for Mack [another of her sons], and then it came along for himself. And he said, "You know, Mother, I go to church every Sunday now because I felt I can't be asking for a big favor and then not be showing up. And then when something else happens," he said, "so it's easier for me to make a little effort each week." So . . . , so I just feel that . . ., uh . . . Well, it, it just, I mean I can only talk about my children and myself's feeling because . . . other people just don't discuss it. But everyone seems to enjoy having this thing to share.

From these few passages the concreteness and narrative character of Mrs. W.'s outlook become evident. Her meanings are contained in her stories. And like Millie and Allan, our ten- and eleven-year-old respondents, Mrs W. constructs her understanding of God and the world in terms of reciprocity. Daily, or even hourly prayers and acts of praise enable her to "put money in the bank"—to store up God's good favor against times when special help or forgiveness may be needed. She has tried to teach this way of structuring the world to her children and is pleased when she sees evidence that they understand that if they want God's help and protection they have to do their part.

Later in the interview we get indications that Mrs. W.'s God is somewhat remote and impersonal. She says that her husband, in praying, "goes straight to the top," meaning that he prays directly to the God-head. She, however, finds a meaningful and personal mediation in her relation to God through a group of saints, who are for her also protectors and companions:

Mrs. W.: Oh, down in that church I have it all there. I have both—Tom was born the day after Christmas, and there's a painting of the Blessed Virgin holding the Christ Child. Well, I pray to the Christ Child—the Christ Child takes care of Tom, and the Blessed Virgin Mary. And there's a lady with Christ, and she's Saint Anne—she takes care of Joan [a daughter]. And then there's a Saint Anthony over in the corner that takes care of Mack. So every time I walk into church I thank all of them for what they've done for them. [Pause] But it's these pictures, I think . . . that . . . that's who they all pray to . . . And Mim [another daughter] has a little Indian girl—Tekawitha, is that her name? . . . [Pause] I love that little chapel . . . But I, now, as I say, I, now when I pray to Saint Anne—I used to pray to Saint Anne for myself—and I'd think of her there in a rocker rocking there praying for me to God, you know . . . to help me along. But maybe I'm too friendly with them, you know?

Interviewer: With the saints?

Mrs. W.: Yeah, I mean, you know, . . . Saint Anne sitting there and she's telling her beads, and she'll say, "Throw one in for S. W.," you know. And that Christ Child; I mean, I say to him, you know, Tom's really working awful hard, and, and he'll, I mean he certainly—has come through, and I'll say Saint Anthony worked for Mack like there's no tomorrow. . . . We're doing pretty well, and I say to him, "I don't mean to keep asking, but. . . ." As I say, I'm kind of friendly with them. But this gives me a feeling of satisfaction. I mean I don't feel so alone. . . . They're like friends.

Mrs. W.'s account of her faith shows some elements of Stage 1's magical thinking. It also has hints of the interpersonal constructions that we will encounter as a key structuring characteristic of Stage 3. On the whole, however, the modes of her faith are best described as Stage 2, given the almost exclusive reliance on narrative as the means of organizing her meanings, and the central importance of reciprocity as the principle governing divine-human relations. Other Stage 2 qualities include the overall anthropological character of her meaningful symbols and the literalism involved in her reliance upon those symbols. Had we looked further at the interview you might have begun to see more clearly that Mrs. W.'s forms of faith and her isolation from actual friends and family are probably interrelated. At one point she begins to characterize herself as a child. The interviewer failed to pick up on this self-description, but it appears that Mrs. W. is pretty painfully aware that her form of faith does not serve her very well as an orientation in a complex and dangerous world. One wonders if her college-age children really find her faith formulas helpful or viable or whether they collude with her childishness by telling her only what she seems to want to hear.

Summary of Mythical-Literal faith. Stage 2 Mythic-Literal faith is the stage in which the person begins to take on for him- or herself the stories, beliefs, and observances that symbolize belonging to his or her community. Beliefs are appropriated with literal interpretations, as are moral rules and attitudes. Symbols are taken as one-dimensional and literal in meaning. In this stage the rise of concrete operations leads to the curbing and ordering of the previous stage's imaginative composing of the world. The episodic quality of Intuitive-Projective faith gives way to a more linear, narrative construction of coherence and meaning. Story becomes the major way of giving unity and value to experience. This is the faith stage of the school child (though we sometimes find the structures dominant in adolescents and in adults). Marked by increased accuracy in taking the perspective of other persons, those in Stage 2 compose a world based on reciprocity. The actors in their cosmic stories are anthropomorphic. They can be affected deeply and powerfully by symbolic and dramatic materials and can describe in endlessly detailed narrative what has occurred. They do not, however, step back from the flow of stories to formulate reflective, conceptual meanings. For this stage the meaning is both carried and "trapped" in the narrative.

The new capacity or strength in this stage is the rise of narrative and the emergence of story, drama, and myth as ways of finding and giving coherence to experience.

The limitations of literalness and an excessive reliance upon reciprocity as a principle for constructing an ultimate environment can result either in an overcontrolling, stilted perfectionism, or "works righteousness," or in their opposite, an abasing sense of badness embraced because of mistreatment, neglect, or the apparent disfavor of significant others.

A factor initiating transition to Stage 3 is the implicit clash or contradiction in stories that leads to reflection on meanings. The transition to formal operational thought makes such reflection possible and necessary. Previous literalism breaks down; new "cognitive conceit" (Elkind) leads to disillusionment with previous teachers and teachings. Conflicts between authoritative stories (Genesis on creation versus evolutionary theory) must be faced. The emergence of mutual interpersonal perspective-taking ("I see you seeing me; I see me as you see me; I see you seeing me seeing you.") creates the need for a more personal relationship with the unifying power of the ultimate environment.

Stage 3: Synthetic-Conventional Faith

Puberty brings with it a revolution in physical and emotional life. The adolescent needs mirrors—mirrors to keep tabs on this week's growth, to become accustomed to the new angularity of a face and to the new curves or reach of a body. But in a qualitatively new way the young person also looks for mirrors of another sort. He or she needs the eyes and ears of a few trusted others in which to see the image of *person*-ality emerging and to get a hearing for the new feelings, insights, anxieties, and commitments that are forming and seeking expression. Harry Stack Sullivan speaks of the "chum" relationship—a first experience of adolescent intimacy outside the family. In the chum—of either the same or opposite sex—a youth finds another person with time and with parallel gifts and needs. In their endless talking, scheming, fantasizing, and worrying, each gives the other the gift of being known and accepted. And more, each gives the other a mirror with which to help focus the new explosiveness and many-ness of his or her inner life. Puppy love, as Erik Erikson tells us, is by no means merely a matter of glandular changes and sexual interests. In the assured regard and idealizing affections of the new love, one fathers and falls in love with a forming personal myth of the self (1963, 262).

Formal operation thinking may first make its appearance in an algebra class or in an advanced biology lab. As it emerges it brings with it the ability to reflect upon one's thinking. It appraises a situation or a problem and forms a variety of hypothetical solutions or explanations. It generates methods of testing and verifying the hypotheses. In problem solving formal operational thinking can work with propositions and symbols, manipulating them to find solutions prior to any contact with the actual physical objects or contexts they represent. And just as it can generate hypothetical propositions of explanation, so it can envision a universe of possible realities and futures. Formal operational thought can conceive ideal features of persons, communities, or other states of affairs. It can be idealistically or harshly judgmental of actual people or institutions in light of these ideal conceptions.

In social and interpersonal life the advent of formal operations has several significant consequences. In Stage 2, you remember, persons' meanings tend to find expression in their stories, the network of narratives that recall and represent their significant experiences. At Stage 2 the story teller speaks from within the flow of experience and does not typically reflect upon it in such ways as to formulate more general, propositional insights that could convey a synthesis of meanings. Formal operational thinking, with its new capacity for reflection on one's own thought and ways of experiencing, invites one mentally to step outside the flow of life's stream. From a vantage point on the river bank, as it were, one can take a look at the flow of the stream as a whole. One can see and name certain patterns of meaning arising out of her or his collection of stories. A myth or myths of the personal past can be composed; this represents a new level of story, a level we might call the *story of our stories.* And with this comes the possibility and burden of composing myths of possible futures. The youth begins to project the forming myth of self into future roles and relationships. On the one hand this projection represents faith in the self one is becoming and trust that that self will be received and ratified by the future. On the other it brings dread that the self may fail to focus, may find no place with others and may be ignored, undiscovered, or shunted off into insignificance by the future.

A key to both the forming of a personal myth and to the dynamics of chumship or first love is the emergence of interpersonal perspective taking. With the formal operational ability to construct the hypothetical, there can emerge the complex ability to compose hypothetical images of myself as other see me. This, of course, is the mechanism by which the friend or first love becomes a mirror for us. . . .

> I see you seeing me:
> I see the me I think you see.

The new burden of "self-consciousness" that the realization of this capacity brings is part of an adolescent version of egocentrism. The youth believes everyone is looking at him or her and may feel either a narcissistic inflation or a self-questioning deflation regarding "the me I think you see." Part of what helps to moderate this self-consciousness—and to overcome the usually temporary excesses of egocentrism—is the functional realization of the reciprocal of our earlier couplet. For soon one begins to recognize that,

> You see you according to me:
> You see the you you think I see.

The relational situation described by these two couplets is what we call mutual interpersonal perspective-taking.

Stage 2 constructs a world in which the perspectives of others on the self are relatively impersonal. Lawfulness and reciprocity, as we have seen, are the principal characteristics of such a world. In its constructions of God or an ultimate environment, Stage 2 typically employs anthropomorphic images. These anthropomorphisms, however, are largely prepersonal, lacking the kind of nuanced personality in relation to which one could know oneself as being known deeply. With the emergence of mutual interpersonal perspective-taking God undergoes a recomposition. Both the self and the chum or young love come to be experienced as having a rich, mysterious, and finally inaccessible depth of personality. God—when God remains or becomes salient in a person's faith at this stage—must also be re-imaged as having inexhaustible depths and as being capable of knowing personally those mysterious depths of self and others we know that we ourselves will never know. Much of the extensive literature about adolescent conversion can be illumined, I believe, by the recognition that the adolescent's religious hunger is for a God who knows, accepts, and confirms the self deeply, and who serves as an infinite guarantor of the self with its forming myth of personal identity and faith. It is not surprising that so many of the images for transcendence that appeal to persons in Stage 3 have the characteristics of a divinely personal significant other.

By the time of the teen years a young person has begun to relate to a widened set of environments. In addition to the sphere of the family now there are spheres of influence represented by peers, by school or work, by media and popular culture, and perhaps by a religious community. In each of these spheres of influence there are peers and adults who are potentially significant others. With this term I refer to those persons whose "mirroring" of the young person has the power to contribute positively or negatively to the set of images of self and of accompanying meanings that must be drawn together in a forming identity and faith.[4] The "identity crisis" of adolescence, as Erikson has taught us to call it, derives in signal ways from the discrepancies

4. In the past I have, mistakenly, attributed this phrase to George Herbert Mead. See *Mind, Self and Society* (Chicago: University of Chicago Press, 1934). His phrase is the "generalized other," a kind of composite representation of the recognition, expectations and evaluation of the self accorded by one's experience of social relations. I am unable to trace the origin of the phrase "significant other," though it clearly resembles the I-Thou relation described by Martin Buber.

and dissonances between the images of self and value reflected by our significant others. Who of us can fail to remember the tightness we felt as adolescents when the significant others from our various spheres of influence were occasionally assembled in one place, focusing on us all at once the vectors of our sense of their different expectations?

Their expectations: in the interpersonal world of Stage 3 faith *their* expectations help us focus ourselves and assemble our commitments to values, but there is always the danger of becoming permanently dependent upon and subject to what Sharon Parks calls the "tyranny of the they" (1980). For Stage 3, with its beginnings in adolescence, authority is located externally to the self. It resides in the interpersonally available "they" or in the certified incumbents of leadership roles in institutions. This is not to deny that adolescents make choices or that they develop strong feelings and commitments regarding their values and behavioral norms. It is to say, however, that despite their genuine feelings of having made choices and commitments, a truer reading is that their values and self-images, mediated by the significant others in their lives, have largely chosen them. And in *their* (the youths') choosing they have, in the main, clarified and ratified those images and values which have chosen them.

When God is a significant other in this mix—and the divine is always potentially what James Cone has called the "Decisive Other" (1975)—the commitment to God and the correlated self-image can exert a powerful ordering on a youth's identity and values outlook.

Let us consider now some passages from interviews with two of our adolescent respondents which will give flesh to our discussion so far of the dynamics of the forming of Stage 3 faith and identity.

Linda is a petite and startlingly blonde fifteen-year-old of Finnish descent. Though born in this country, her first language was Finnish. The family continues to speak only Finnish at home. Her father works in construction. In his ongoing search for work the family has moved fourteen times in the last fifteen years. Her mother, a blonde woman even tinier than her daughter, works as a housecleaner and her services are in great demand in the area of the Florida city where they now live. The family, including Linda's baby brother Matt, live in a newly built tract house decorated elegantly, if sparsely, with modern Finnish furniture. Her family's move to Florida has been a happy one for Linda. She is popular and a good student. Very much in tune with her age group, she thinks a lot about fashion, boy friends, and popularity. She sees herself as standing somewhat apart from her peers, however, because of her strong religious and moral beliefs. Linda is a Lutheran, active in teaching church school and playing the organ on occasions at church.

Earlier in their talk, Linda told our interviewer a lot about the experiences of her life. In that part of their conversation she spontaneously talked about the importance of her religion to her. Acknowledging that Linda seems to know how she feels about things, the interviewer asks her to talk about those feelings:

Linda: Well, I feel like I'm not afraid of anything now because I know what I believe in and I know what I want to do in life, and nothing could really set me off course. We're not going to move any place now. Before, if we moved (like I told you we did) I got into people, different people, and I sort of changed as the people went. But I have learned that just the best thing is to be yourself.

Interviewer: Linda, when you say you *know* what you believe in . . . can you try to trace *how* you came to know what you believe in?

Linda: I guess religion. I've always gone to church and everything. And my parents, they always guided me. . . . They've always taught me that God's always there and, you know, he's the only way that you can really make it. . . . You depend upon him and I really believe in him and, you know how they say God talks in many mysterious ways? Well, in a sense he's told me lots of times . . . I really think that he's led me to where I am today. 'Cause lots of times I've just thought the world is just, you know, I just don't feel anything. But then that morning I'll just have a feeling that . . . I guess there is Somebody, you know?

Interviewer: What do you think God is?

Linda: God is different to a lot of people. . . . I don't go exactly by the Bible. I think you should try to make the world . . . you should try to make people happy and at the same time enjoy yourself, you know? In a good kind way . . .

Asked further about her conception of God, Linda answers, "I just feel, I just feel he's there. There might not be any material proof but I *know*. I can bet my life on it. Really. I know because he *has* talked to me." Linda explains that God's talking to her comes in the form of feelings she gets when she has really struggled with a problem, feeling that God cares and that there is something she can do. Once when one of her friends had turned against her she went into her bedroom, thought about her situation, and cried. She said, "Then I remembered that, you know, there was *God* and I just asked him to tell me something, tell me what I could do, because why do I have to be glued to one person? Why can't I be good friends with everybody? Go places with her one time and then with her and him, and you know, with everybody? And that's really true."

Notice the concerns with identity and interpersonal relations in Linda's conversation about her religion and God. Note also her reflection on her past and her future and on the effort to pull the diffusion of her life of fourteen moves into a dependable and stable unity. God for her is personal. Although some concrete imagery from a previous Stage 2 lingers in the next passages, Linda's dominant images of God have the Stage 3 qualities of companionship, guidance, support, and of knowing and loving her. Her warranty for her beliefs comes from what she has been taught and what she *feels.*

In her talks with friends Linda often speaks about religion. She recognizes that frequently they are turned off by her talk. Our interviewer asked why that was so.

Linda: They get *scared* or something. . . . I guess they are just afraid of dying. . . . But I'm not afraid to die at all.

Interviewer: What do you think happens to you when you die?

Linda: Well, I *know*. I have this feeling, like, when *I* die I'm going to go to heaven because I've tried on earth to be good to people and I believe in God and I'm a *follower*.

Linda shows us further characteristics of Stage 3 when she speaks of the limits of knowing and acknowledges the penumbra of mystery she chooses to live with around her central convictions and beliefs.

Interviewer: What does it mean when you say you are going to go to heaven?

Linda: Well, nobody really knows. It's supposed to be paradise. And, I guess I'll find out sometime. But, see, I don't want to ask too many question like that. I always want to . . . well, lots of people have really done research on religion and they've gone insane, you know? I've never wanted to go *that much* into it. I just want to do what the Bible says. Lots of people think how the earth started and everything. I, only, . . . there's a limit to me. I know that it started from God. God made it and I don't ask any more questions, you know? I'll find out later on.

Linda was asked if she ever had doubts about God.

Linda: Yeah. I have felt times when I have doubted God. But then I realize that it's just *me*. I'm walking *away* from God. I should have, like, at times like this people need to be so close to someone like God. You need to be so close and you need to have something to wake up to every morning. I mean, . . . and have a feeling inside you that, that it's worth living. I think people who live, go to work, come home, go to sleep, go to work, you know, I mean it's a regular *routine*, so that I think people should just believe in God and just follow him.

Authority for Linda's beliefs, religious and moral, resides principally with her parents. She has strongly identified with their teachings and standards and feels that they are her own. An instance is her firmly held belief that sexual intercourse prior to marriage is wrong. Our interviewer asked her where she thought she got that feeling.

Linda: I don't know. It's just . . . my mom. She's against it, but I haven't gotten it from her. I've thought about it lots of times, believe me, there *have* been chances and everything. But I've never done anything.
Interviewer: How important do you think your parents' influence has been?
Linda: My parents have guided me in the right direction. . . . I'm glad that they've done what they've done. They've taught me to do the right from wrong and everything, and I've taken it from there. From what I know. . . . They brought me to church and taught me about God and love and everything, and now I know what it is and . . . and I'll be telling *my* daughter or my son, or whatever, the same thing.

Linda's fervent religiousness gives us one example of the forming of a Synthetic-Conventional faith in adolescence. Brian, whose interview we next listen in on, provides an instance of a similar Stage 3 *structuring* of faith. The *contents* of Brian's faith, however, are quite different from Linda's. Where her faith community has encouraged a limit to questions about belief, Brian's has encouraged just the opposite.

Tall for his sixteen years, Brian has lived in his upper middle-class New England suburb since he was six. His father, an engineer, grew up in this town. The family continues their involvement in the local Unitarian church. Brian loves hiking and canoeing. He has traveled some and spends a part of each summer in rural Maine. He is bright; his marks are above average. He confesses, however, that he daydreams a good bit in class. He reads a lot on his own and seems more interested in learning than he feels free to admit among the friends with whom he hangs around. He sees his parents as strict and seems to feel considerable tension between their expectations of him and those of his peers.

Initially Brian's conversation strikes one as indicating that he is far more individuated than Linda. His outlook involves more questioning, less reverence, more cynicism than hers. Further reflection on his interview, however, helps us see how "conventional" the perspective Brian offers is in the context of the community and Unitarian church that have formed him. While it is likely that this rich, stimulating, and critical environment will ensure that Brian constructs a Stage 4 perspective much sooner than Linda, it is important to see how conformist, how concerned with the "tyranny of the they" Brian still is and to recognize the degree to which the positions he takes are really his own versions of what his community stands for rather than being self-composed perspectives.

Brian was asked what his own approach to life involves, what rules or guidelines he finds important.

Brian: Just, not to pick on other guys. I don't think you ought to interfere with a person's way of life. For example, a lot of kids now who are going out with someone, they try to change to become more suitable for the kid they're going out with, and I don't think you ought to change. I think a person is going to grow up and should grow up the way his life is going to lead him and anyone who tries to change that person's character . . . is really . . . infringing on his rights."

Brian's way of continuing this thought indicates his concern with identity and continuity in his life.

Brian: And, you know, it is hard to change, it really is. . . . I couldn't just all of a sudden become a really goody-goody and really study in school and love mother and American flag and apple pie and be Jack Armstrong or whatever.

A bit later the interviewer asked Brian if he has a group of people or a community of peers who share his basic outlook on values.

Brian: Well, people who I'm really close to . . . like a few of my friends who are really good friends of mine and who I really talk to a lot about this sort of stuff. We just sit around and talk about girls or whatever, past experiences and stuff like that. My really close friends that I really talk to, most of them are girls, because they talk about this stuff a lot, and I feel that I can talk about it more freely with a girl than with a boy, because the boys try to impress each other and impress the girls. But you can have a lot better talk with a girl on stuff like this than you could with a boy.

With girls Brian finds he can talk about "screwed up relations with your parents and stuff," and with a few "about deeper things like what we appreciate and what we don't." The interviewer then asked him what types of things *he* appreciated.

Brian: Just life. It fascinates me. I don't know what goes on before or after birth and death. And some things scare me. The unknown is really a factor in my life because I like to think about it a lot and the reason why everything got here. It really bothers me a lot because I don't know the answers, and no one knows the answers, and I can't turn to anyone to get the answers—except to God, if there is a God. Maybe someday I'll get a vision from the Almighty!

Brian had recently been looking for "answers" by reading some philosophical or religious books. He had just finished *The Prophet* by Kahlil Gibran. He was asked to characterize what it and some Buddhist thought he had heard about meant to him.

Brian: What they are trying to do, I think, is understand each other. They appreciate that everyone has faults and things of that nature, and they try to accept that and accept the world in general, which I think should be done. Certain people go around knocking the world, like I have been, but it's all we got, so why not make the best of it? . . . I'm sort of mixed up on what I'm trying to prove by anything that I do. It is sort of hard to explain what the meaning is to life and what the meaning is to your conscience; but it's just something . . . I guess the reason everyone knocks [the world] is because someone started knocking it, and other people started knocking it, and more people started knocking it, and pretty soon everyone was doing it. . . . But if everyone would stop procrastinating, then we wouldn't have the problems that everyone knocks.

Brian returns to one of his key themes as he explains why people don't overcome their negativity and apathy and really work together to transform the world. He also exposes where the authorities he appeals to clash in his life.

Brian: I would like to see them get involved; but then again there is the peer pressure where, you know, a person should like to get involved, but if his friends found out he was doing something like that they'd call, stand around, and laugh at him, and he'd be sort of an outcast. So everyone doesn't want to get involved for the sake of keeping their friends or saving face—which I have done many times.

Interviewer: So there is a cost to being committed, if you really were, to changing things in the world in that your peers would look down on you?

Brian: Right. Like everyone is always trying to impress everyone in this world; it's a matter of social status and all this trying to be better than the Joneses or whatever. And if we stop doing that—which is impossible, but—well, just to say if we could stop that, the world would be a lot better because people wouldn't mind getting involved. They'd just go out and get involved for the sake of what they wanted to do.

Toward the end of Brian's interview the questioner seeks to get him to return to some earlier reflections about his questions regarding life's meaning.

Interviewer: Are there any specific things about meaning or value in life that you are uncertain about. Earlier you said you were concerned about the unknown. Right?

Brian: All right, well, I think actually that it bothers everyone, because if you have doubts about what is going to go on afterwards . . . like the idea—everyone talks about reincarnation and stuff like that and if it really is real—but I can't think of myself as being anything else. I do experience things like *déjà vu*, which is the feeling that you've seen something that you've just seen before; I think that's the right definition for it. I get quite a few *déjà vu's* a day. And just not knowing what's going to happen after you're gone. Let's just say life is: you're born, you gain knowledge, you die, and that's the end of your life, and there is nothing else, and you'll know nothing else of what happened after you die. That really bothers me because like gaining knowledge I like, and I'd like to know what's going to happen after I'm gone, whether someone appreciates what I've done or tried to do—if I've done anything, if I'm not apathetic about life after I grow up and I'm an old man. I'd like to leave at least some kind of mark in this world, and I'd like to see what my mark has proven or what it's done. And if you die and that's just the end of everything—which I cannot see—I don't know what the feeling would be. It's just a weird feeling.

Interviewer: It bothers you, this sense of the unknown about what happens at death?

Brian: Right, because it's unexplainable. We only make up what we feel is the answer. Just take that. Maybe the answer is something that no one can grasp because no one is really smart enough or it's something completely beyond our conceptions of being able to grasp what life is about and something like that. It makes me think quite a bit; I don't know about anyone else, but not being able to grasp an idea—it's physically impossible to grasp that idea—really bothers me and makes me think about it.

In these last passages we get some clear indications that Brian is thinking for himself and will soon be ready to challenge the conventions of his peers and of his liberal church. Though this observation is too simple, I think it is helpful to point out that Linda's Synthetic-Coventional faith has been formed in what seems to be a dominantly Stage 3 faith community. Brian's Synthetic-Conventional faith, on the other hand, is taking form in a faith community that is more likely to be modally Stage 4. That is to say, the *average expectable stage-of-faith development* for adults in the families and churches of Linda and Brian are probably Stage 3 and Stage 4, respectively. This will have a bearing on the rapidity and difficulty of their respective experiences of transition to Stage 4.

We have now to come to terms with the fact that a considerable number of the adults we have interviewed—both men and women—can be best described by the patterns of Stage 3 Synthetic-Conventional faith. For some adolescents, such as Brian, the forming of identity and faith in Stage 3 is open-ended and clearly anticipates a transition, in the late teens or early twenties, to Stage 4. But for others (and Linda may be one of these) it becomes a long-lasting or permanently equilibrated style of identity and faith. To see how this can happen we need to look at several other structural characteristics of Stage 3.

For both adolescents in the forming phases and adults who find equilibrium in Stage 3 the system of informing images and values through which they are committed remains principally a *tacit* system. Tacit means unexamined; my tacit knowing, as Michael Polanyi calls it (1966), is that part of my knowing that plays a role in guiding and shaping my choices, but of which I can give no account. I cannot tell you *how* I know with my tacit knowing. To say that Stage 3's system of images and values is tacitly held reminds me of a statement attributed to the philosopher George Santayana. "We cannot know," he said, "who first discovered water. But we can be sure," he continued, "that it was not the fish." To live with a tacit system of meaning and value is analogous to the situation of the fish. Supported and sustained by the water, it has no means of leaping out of the aquarium so as to reflect on the tank and its contents. A person in Stage 3 is aware of having values and normative images. He or she articulates them, defends them, and feels deep emotional investments in them, but typically has not made the value system, *as a system*, the object of reflection.

It is significant when persons at Stage 3 encounter and respond to situations or contexts that lead to critical reflection on their tacit value systems. Under such circumstances they begin the transition to Stage 4's *explicit* system. A new quality of choice and personal responsibility for their values and for their membership in the communities that bear them becomes possible. For many reasons, however, people resist or avoid these invitations to awareness of and a more conscious responsibility for their beliefs and values. They reaffirm their reliance on external authority and their commitments to their particular values and images of which they are aware.

The awareness or unawareness of *system* is a factor in another aspect of Stage 3's structuring of the world. Caught up in its sensitive orientation to the interpersonal, Stage 3 typically orients to other groups or classes than its own as though they were merely aggregates of individuals. It constructs social relations as extensions of interpersonal relationships. It does not think of society in terms of a network of laws, rules, roles, and systemically determined patterns. This means that other persons are known and evaluated in terms of their supposed personal qualities and interpersonal ways of relating. In a real sense, in this way of knowing, persons are separated from the social system factors shaping and limiting their lives. When anyone says "Some of my best friends are *X*," and *X* refers to some racial, ethnic, religious, or national "out-group," this kind of structuring toward the interpersonal is likely going on.

What happens is that the speaker assimilates her or his friends from the outgroup into her or his notions of personal worthiness, while effectively excising them from the social contexts and political realities—and the group histories—which actually determine their lives in powerful ways.

Finally, our account of the structural characteristics of Stage 3 needs to indicate how persons best described by this stage employ symbols and relate to the transcendent through them. Previously we have seen that faith forms powerful and longlasting images of an order of meaning and value—an ultimate environment. For persons in Stage 3, with its largely tacit system of meaning and value, the symbols and ritual representations expressive of their faith are organically and irreplaceably tied to the full realities of their meaning systems. Said another way, the symbols expressive of their deepest meanings and loyalties are not separable from the what they symbolize.

At Stage 4, as we will see, as part of the reflection on one's system of meanings taken as a system, a kind of demythologization can occur. Meanings can be separated from the symbols that bear them. This gives the symbols a status as media for meanings that can be expressed in other ways. For Stage 3, however, demythologization feels like a fundamental threat to meaning, because meaning and symbol are bound up together. Consider an example. In the 1960s confrontations over the American flag occurred between construction workers and harsh young critics of the Vietnam war. For both groups, I suspect, the flag and its meaning were inextricably and non-negotiably intertwined. For the construction workers it represented a concatenation of dreams and loyalties that participated in their deepest levels of meaning and identity. Any attack on the flag—and protesters carrying it constituted an attack for them—amounted to an attack on a sacred set of images and myths that grounded identity and worth: "My country, right or wrong." For the protesters the flag similarly stood for a powerful coagulation of images of and feelings toward "America." But for the latter group it symbolized a history and present reality that had to be changed, purged, or cleansed. These sometimes bloody struggles, often representing conflicts between two generations of Americans whose experiences of the nation seemed deeply different, cannot be explained without recognizing how the flag, for both groups, was inseparable from their powerfully felt meanings.

Religiously, at Stage 3, meaning and symbol impinge on each other in similar ways. It is not so much that persons at Stage 3 are locked into their particular symbols in a kind of fundamentalism of symbolic forms. Rather, symbols of the sacred—their own and others—are related to in ways which honor them as inseparably connected to the sacred. Therefore, worthy symbols are themselves sacred. They *are* depths of meaning. Any strategy of demythologization, therefore, threatens the participation of symbol and symbolized and is taken, consequently, as an assault on the sacred itself.

The other side of this coin, as regards Stage 3's way of relating through symbols, is that when persons' symbols have undergone trivialization, or when a person has absented him- or herself from the ritual celebrations of shared central symbols, the sacred itself is emptied. When this kind of emptying of the sacred is widespread in a society—as it is in ours today—the vacuum of meaning and of meaningful symbolic representations results in rampant anxiety and neuroses and in a resurgence of interest in all kinds of occult and spiritualistic phenomena.

Now let's review for a moment. We have pointed to the *tacit* character of Stage 3's system of values and meanings. We noted the way interpersonal relationships provide the paradigm for constructing social and political relations. Finally, we described Stage 3's way of relating to the transcendent through symbol and ritual, seeing these as inseparable, related to the realities they symbolize. Perhaps this discussion helps make more clear why persons and groups can and do find equilibrium in Stage 3. In many ways religious institutions "work best" if they are peopled with a majority of committed folk best described by Stage 3.

Many critics of religion and religious institutions assume, mistakenly, that to be religious in an institution necessarily means to be Synthetic-Conventional. This mistake by critics is understandable. Much of church and synagogue life in this country can be accurately described as dominantly Synthetic-Conventional. Moreover, television evangelists and the highly profitable media religious clubs have mastered the art of addressing and secularizing religious hungers of Synthetic-Conventional folk. They constitute a new set of charismatic external authorities, appealing to the residual resonance of central Christian symbols and offering a tacit version of Christian theology that centers in vicarious interpersonal warmth and meaning. In the so-called electronic churches all of this is ambiguously joined under the sacred mana of powerful electronic media, attractive personalities, and sentimental "God talk." They constitute a parody of authentic Christianity and an abomination against biblical faith.

Let me introduce several adults we have interviewed. These persons, best described by Stage 3, will help illustrate the characteristics we have described and some of the variety of contents of Synthetic-Conventional faith.

Our first respondent is Mr. J. D.[5] He was sixty-three at the time of his interview (1976). He described himself as a retired teamster who had driven a truck for a living for almost twenty-five years. He grew up in a poor white section of Gary, Indiana, where he attended Catholic and public schools. He

5. This interview was conducted and written up in the summary form presented here by Dr. Richard Shulik. It will appear in Lawrence Kohlberg's *Collected Works*, vol. 2, in an article by Kohlberg and Shulik entitled, "The Aging Person as Philosopher; Moral Development in the Adult Years." I have altered Dr. Shulik's writing style at certain points to make the narrative more consistent with my own writing. The quotes from Mr. J. D., of course, have been left untouched.

dropped out of high school in his sophomore year to enlist in the United States Army. He served through the last two years of the World War II and spent some time in Japan after the war. A serious health problem forced him to give up driving at the age of fifty-eight. He regarded himself as a man who had worked very hard in life. He seemed to feel that his life had been rewarding and intrinsically satisfying. He was asked about his work:

Mr. D.: I am familiar with the Detroit-to-New England route, and I often drove Chicago to Detroit. When I was working for another firm for a short time, I also had a Minneapolis-Seattle run, and on another occasion a Maine-to-Florida run. I know of nothing more satisfying than getting together with some of the other drivers at a truck stop or a tavern after a long day's haul.

Despite his illness and semi-retirement, Mr. D. still viewed himself as a teamster. When the interviewer asked him to describe his basic values and beliefs he tended to doubt that his views could really be of very much importance.

Mr. D.: There is really very little that I could tell you. I am really not much of a thinker; my views are quite the same as those of any teamster, or any working man.

This was his way of saying that his philosophical system held nothing remarkable or very interesting. To him it was like that of "many other people."

When the interviewer pressed him to talk further, Mr. D.'s responses showed the global and non-analytical features of many adults best described as at the Synthetic-Conventional level. He acknowledged, for example, that present-day society faces a great many problems. But he persisted in the belief that society generally has not changed.

Mr. D.: Hell, there are problems today, and there were the same problems when I was a boy. And I expect that there will be the same problems forty years from now, long after we are gone.

He believed that there is the *appearance* of social change, but that underneath this appearance everything really remains quite the same. In discussing specific social issues Mr. D. tended to attribute controversies and concerns to corrupt politicians:

Mr. D.: Since moving here from the greater Chicago area to New England I have learned that absolutely all politicians are corrupt. And so they create these issues for themselves and for their own benefit. . . . All of this hubbub about President Nixon, hell! Nixon was no different from Kennedy or Johnson or Eisenhower or any of the rest. And the fellas over here in our city all are all the same ilk. And you watch and see that Jimmy Carter will show himself in the end to be exactly like all the rest of them, or I'll be very much surprised.

He was asked if there truly is an energy crisis going on.

Mr. D.: Of course there isn't! It's just that some politician somewhere is making a great deal of money convincing everyone that there is!

Recently Mr. D. suffered a serious illness that threatened and altered his life. He had an extremely rare malignant tumor, described by his physician as a "floating tumor"—not fixed in its position—and therefore difficult to remove. In all previous cases of this condition surgery had been unsuccessful, leading to the death of the patient. Mr. D., so weakened by the tumor that he had to give up working, agreed to surgery despite its risks. Having survived the operation his case became well known in medical journals.

Mr. D.: I am somewhat famous in the medical journals, you know, and I'm still living on borrowed time, thanks to the very intelligent doctors at my hospital.

The discussion of these issues led to a consideration of life's basic meaning and to his thoughts about death and dying.

Mr. D.: . . . I'm not now a religious man, never was, and never will be. Religion is just a lot of nonsense as I see it. As I see it, we are born, we live here, we die, and that's it. Religion gives people something to believe in, that there's something more, because they want there to be something more, but there isn't. So . . . you see, I'd rather put some money down on the bar and buy myself a drink, rather than put that same money into a collection plate! Wish others would do the same, too. They'd spare themselves a lot of needless bother.

Mr. D. indicated that these had always been his basic convictions, and that even his close brush with death, due to his unusual illness, had not changed anything.

Mr. D.: No reason to see why an experience like that *should* change what I believe. That's just the way the cards fall. But I am grateful that this old body still has some life in it, if that's what you mean.

Mr. D. tended to dismiss the interviewer's question about the basic purpose or meaning behind human life as being an essentially meaningless or incomprehensible question. It was, in his opinion, a question that really could not be comprehended well, let alone answered, and so it wasn't worthy of much serious reflection. Hence he answered with some humor.

Mr. D.: You go and ask a seventeen-year-old boy this question, and he may give you an answer or he may not, but the real answer to this question for him is some pretty young woman that he wants to take into his arms. And the pretty young woman, her answer to this question is that handsome young man. And that is how nature has made us, and that is it. . . . And [moreover], I am proud to be able to tell you that, even at the age of sixty-three, I still have an eye for pretty young women! And so! What do you think of that! I think it's great.

In brief, Mr. D. can present the interviewer with the outlines of a faith system, but it is, in reality, a loosely aggregated collection of opinions or convictions that he identifies as being essentially "just the views of one common man." And, in a sense, he is right: he is not particularly reflective, but he makes no pretense of reflection. Some of his views appear to be almost platitudes (e.g., all politicians are corrupt, without exception; all political crises are merely the fabricated contrivances of corrupt politicians). As his statement of a personal philosophy his view is not genuinely the result of an introspective process. Rather, it makes him one with the community—or his perceived community of hard-working men. This is the central meaning behind the terms *synthetic* and *conventional.* The Stage 3 individual's faith system is conventional, in that it is seen as being everybody's faith system or the faith system of the entire community. And it is synthetic in that it is non-analytical; it comes as a sort of unified, global wholeness. In truth, for Mr. D., the discussion of values and convictions is a means of asserting his solidarity with the community he calls his own. He does not discuss values to distinguish himself, or to examine the values, or to be sure that his views are correct. Rather, in such discussion he seeks to establish a sense of commonality or relatedness with the other person present.

Now let's consider another example. At forty Anthony R. owns his own modest home in a predominantly Italian section of a New England city. Describing himself as a "working man," he takes pride in being the provider for his wife and two children. Anthony feels that his values and outlook are different from those of his immigrant parents and his brothers and sisters. This sense of being different from his family of origin is more a feeling he has than something he can put into words. Anthony speaks rapidly and talks a lot. Yet, as he himself says, he has a hard time really communicating what he feels and knows. Anthony believes, deep down, that the world is going to be much tougher for his two children than it has been for him. He is at a loss for anything he can do, either to help alter the world or to better prepare his children to cope with it. He trusts that values are transmitted in the family by parental example and that his children can pick up on those that he and his wife hold. She may be primarily responsible for the fact that they send the children to parochial school. Anthony shows no interest in religion and is not a practicing Catholic. He says he worries a good bit about the possibility of losing his job. His worst fear, in that connection, is that he might even lose his "manliness"—understood, I believe, both in the sense of being a good economic provider and of being a sexually potent male. His major center of value seems to be his family. He uses the image of a car with four wheels to symbolize the family. As head of the household he is driver and chief mechanic. He has responsibility to see that the wheels are going in more or less the same direction and that the engine is running efficiently and harmoniously. He knows, also, that family members—including the father—are mutually accountable.

Anthony: There's like four wheels turning here, right? And we've got to keep them all in the same line. And no matter which one gets out of line, you bring it back in. So, hopefully, no matter who the individual is, even though the—say the man, the big wheel—he's moving along on the straight path, you know, and he's supposed to keep order. Well, he can run off too and so, you know, it's a family relationship where somebody's got to take over and say, "Hey, wait a minute . . . you're running out of line and you better get back in." So you've got to be open too for suggestions and what-not and criticism.

At the midpoint of his life, Anthony R. shares his evaluation of how his life is going. It is just as much oriented to the judgment and the level of success of his peers as anything our two teenagers, earlier considered, would have said.

Anthony: My personal life? Well, I'm happy. . . . I'm adjusted. . . . The only thing I believe in is that, you know, just playing the game right, going by the rules, and life is going to continue, and then, you know, poof! all at once, you know, it's just like a guillotine falling down. It comes to a complete halt. Now, my personal life, I feel is going along the normal . . . you know . . . an even keel with the normal working man. I'm, you know, no different. I don't feel I'm any better off or any worse off. I get up and go to work, you know. It's the routine, it's the general routine. I think it's a rat-race, but like I say, I'm adjusted to accept it. See, if I didn't think it was right, I wouldn't be here. Or if . . . I didn't think working was right, I wouldn't work. But I feel these are all the right things to do. Now whether it was the way I was brought up or what, I don't know. I mean, you know, it's me. I feel that, you know, everything's all right. It must be all right if I get, you know, I've got my wife that seems to think it's all right, or we wouldn't be here together, you know? . . .

In the world of Anthony R. it appears that coherence comes from fitting into a network of expectations and duties that spread out from his central commitment to the maintenance and welfare of his family. We have already heard him speak about "going along on an even keel with the norm for a working man." We have seen his image of the family as an auto, each member being a potentially unruly wheel. At one point he speaks about his sense of what gives order or rightness to his life.

Anthony: When everything you're doing—let's face it—when you're abiding the laws that were made—uh, not only the laws—it depends on your—uh, we won't get into the religious thing—say, laws. If you're going by—uh, what can I say? If you have, you know, a set of rules to live by—whether they write them down openly, you know—and let everybody know what they are actually—are—the rules and laws are or what they think their rights and wrongs are—if you're going by that, then what you're doing is right. . . .

Interviewer: Well, what are some—what are some of the rules you really think—you've got inside your head in terms of your family?

Anthony: Being truthful with my family. Not trying to cheat them out of anything—not breaking promises. . . . I feel like all of them are the right things to do. I'm not saying that God or anybody set my rules. I really don't know. It's what I feel is right. . . . I still feel like what I've been doing is right.

With both Mr. J. D. and Anthony R. we recognize several related factors that may help account for their having remained in the Synthetic-Conventional stage. Both come from backgrounds of limited education. Both exhibit difficulty in using language to communicate inner states or their attitudes, values, and feelings for others. Both show a need to feel that their life stances are right. They are limited in their self-reflection, however, to either comparisons with or the approval of others perceived to be like them. Both men, for reasons that may have to do with traditions of male withdrawal from religious involvement in working-class urban Catholicism, have had no sustained and meaningful relationship with the church.

Now for a final instance of adult Synthetic-Conventional faith we turn to Mrs. H. M., a Southern woman who grew up on tenant farms in poverty, and who, at age 61, recently "rededicated her life to Christ" and is back in the Southern Baptist Church.

Mrs. M. grew up in various parts of the South on farms where her father shared one-fourth of what he produced with the landowners as rent for the land he used. She was the third child in a large family. Her father she characterized as a very stern man who would allow his children to do little for fun besides go to school, attend Sunday school, or visit their grandparents. Their mother, a woman with some education and from a more privileged background than their father, never seemed able to stand up to him or to protect the children from his anger and excessive restrictions. At seventeen H. ran away from home to get married. She married a man a lot like her father. She had three children with him. He worked in construction and they moved frequently. He eventually began to run around with other women and became a borderline alcoholic. When he drank, he was abusive. When H. was thirty years old, her father and mother talked her into getting a job and divorcing her husband. Her mother kept the children while she worked. She enjoyed her work. Soon she began to form a relationship with a man at work. When they decided to get married, both families objected so strongly (because he was much younger than she) that they gave up their jobs and went to another state to the home of a relative of hers. They took her three children with them. In a few days were married and found a place of their own. They both got jobs with the same company.

H. and her second husband had two children together. Socially, she says, their friends tended to be his friends. Their leisure activities focused principally on his interests in auto and motorcycle racing, and on football. Eventually she tired of going with him to these events. They did not find new ways to celebrate and enjoy their relationship. After a serious illness in his late forties he divorced her in order to marry his secretary. They had been married twenty-four years. Five years after her divorce at age fifty-seven, Mrs. H. M. tells us of the central theme in her life review and self-assessment.

Mrs. M.: I have never done with my life what I could have done after I was old enough to realize that you have to do something to get anything out of life. . . . I could have taken courses at [name] College, . . . but I didn't do anything but work. And I've always been unhappy. I think it was because I didn't do what other people did. Although I was saved during World War II, I did not go to church very long, because I was always moving. Then when I married the last time we tried to go, but the difference in our ages always separated us in Sunday school so we quit. All we ever did was go to the drive-in, out to nice restaurants for dinner, and to drag races and baseball games. He played golf and went to the Masters at Augusta several years. He used not to want to go anywhere without me and I'd finally just say, "I want to stay with the kids, find somebody else to go with you." . . . But I've always been frustrated. I've always wanted to write, and I've always

> wanted to paint. And I've never tried either one. I have never made any effort to really do anything that I wanted to do. I think the reason that I've felt unhappy so much of my life is because I don't like *me*. I don't like what I've done to other people. I hurt my parents and took my three older children away from family and friends because of what I wanted. My last husband is a good person and was very good to me and my children—all of them. As I look back I see that so much was my fault. But now that I have rededicated my life to the Lord, and am back in church, I feel much better.

Mrs. H. M.'s despair comes from the sense that she has not done what everyone else has done. This deep-going sense of failure is the other side of Mr. J. D.'s and Anthony R.'s sense that their lives are "normal" or going along all right. The norm lies in the conventional pattern of life of those who constitute "everybody." Part of this social conscience tells her that she did well, waiting on and spoiling her children. But in a time when assertiveness and liberation in women have become a new consensual set of norms, Mrs. H. M. looks at her life choices with sadness.

Living now with a married daughter, Mrs. H. M. has to travel nearly fifty miles round trip to attend her church. She drives this sometimes twice on Sundays as well as on other evenings in the week. She is finding challenges there to be part of the church's outreach to new people.

We close our look into the world of Mrs. H. M. with her sharing some of her religious outlook. Here the Synthetic-Conventional reliance on external authority and its construction of meaning in interpersonal images and terms can be seen.

Interviewer: Do you think that life on this earth will continue for some time in the future, or do you think we're coming near the end of the world?

Mrs. M.: The Scripture tells of many things that will happen in the last days and these very things are happening now. I think that we are very near the end of time. A very learned Bible teacher that I hear each week tells us that according to Scripture, the end will come before the year 2000.

Interviewer: Would you agree with her?

Mrs. M.: The more I listen to her, the more convinced I am that she is right.

Interviewer: You mentioned God. When you hear that word what do you feel?

Mrs. M.: I feel very sad and ashamed for the way I have wasted my life. I do know that God has forgiven me for every wrong that I've done, and that he loves me. I feel very close to God most of the time, now that I am active in the work of the church again. Of course there are times that I don't feel as close to him as I'd like to, but I know that I am the

> one who moves away, not he. I've learned that we all have so much to be thankful for, if we only stop and count our blessings.*

Now a review and summary of the features of the Synthetic-Conventional stage of faith.

Summary of Synthetic-Conventional faith. In Stage 3 Synthetic-Conventional faith, a person's experience of the world now extends beyond the family. A number of spheres demand attention: family, school or work, peers, street society and media, and perhaps religion. Faith must provide a coherent orientation in the midst of that more complex and diverse range of involvements. Faith must synthesize values and information; it must provide a basis for identity and outlook.

Stage 3 typically has its rise and ascendancy in adolescence, but for many adults it becomes a permanent place of equilibrium. It structures the ultimate environment in interpersonal terms. Its images of unifying value and power derive from the extension of qualities experienced in personal relationships. It is a "conformist" stage in the sense that it is acutely tuned to the expectations and judgments of significant others and as yet does not have a sure enough grasp on its own identity and autonomous judgment to construct and maintain an independent perspective. While beliefs and values are deeply felt, they typically are tacitly held—the person "dwells" in them and in the meaning world they mediate. But there has not been occasion to step outside them to reflect on or examine them explicitly or systematically. At Stage 3 a person has an "ideology," a more or less consistent clustering of values and beliefs, but he or she has not objectified it for examination and in a sense is unaware of having it. Differences of outlook with others are experienced as differences in "kind" of person. Authority is located in the incumbents of traditional authority roles (if perceived as personally worthy) or in the consensus of a valued, face-to-face group.

The emergent capacity of this stage is the forming of a personal myth—the myth of one's own becoming in identity and faith, incorporating one's past and anticipated future in an image of the ultimate environment unified by characteristics of personality.

The dangers or deficiencies in this stage are twofold. The expectations and evaluations of others can be so compellingly internalized (and sacralized) that later autonomy of judgment and action can be jeopardized; or interpersonal

*In reviewing this synopsis of her interview Mrs. M. asked me to insert the following description she wrote of herself; I agreed to do so (JWF). "More than a year has passed since this interview with Mrs. M. She now has her own apartment (she lived with a daughter at the time of the interview) and is feeling much better about her life. She still has many regrets, but leads a very active life and tries to help others when the opportunity arises. She is active in her church and has many Christian friends with whom she enjoys life."

betrayals can give rise either to nihilistic despair about a personal principle of ultimate being or to a compensatory intimacy with God unrelated to mundane relations.

Factors contributing to the breakdown of Stage 3 and to readiness for transition may include: serious clashes or contradictions between valued authority sources; marked changes, by officially sanctioned leaders, of policies or practices previously deemed sacred and unbreachable (for example, in the Catholic church changing the mass from Latin to the vernacular, or no longer requiring abstinence from meat on Friday); the encounter with experiences or perspectives that lead to critical reflection on how one's beliefs and values have formed and changed, and on how "relative" they are to one's particular group or background. Frequently the experience of "leaving home"—emotionally or physically, or both—precipitates the kind of examination of self, background, and life-guiding values that gives rise to stage transition at this point.

Stage 4: Individuative-Reflective Faith

At the time we interviewed him Jack was twenty-eight. He grew up in a large family in a lower-class ethnic enclave of a northeastern city. His Irish father and Italian mother had a stormy marriage. Jack, the fourth of their ten children, seems to have been particularly sensitive to their marital fights. He felt anger and sadness for his alcoholic father and genuine fear for his mother. People in his neighborhood, he said, never troubled to learn his and his brothers' first names. They just called them all "Donovan" (not their real name). Jack says that sometimes when he heard one of his brothers speak it was as though he himself was speaking, they sounded so much alike.

For the first six years of his education Jack went to public school. In the seventh grade he transferred to a Catholic parochial school, at considerable cost to the family. Parochial school was harder. He had been on the honor roll in public school. He suspected that he attained that status simply because he attended regularly, came clean, and seemed interested. Then—and now—Jack has never allowed himself to think of himself as particularly bright or gifted.

In the parochial school, he said, teaching about religion pervaded everything. In his seventh-grade year Jack experienced a kind of religious conversion. In the spring, building up to Easter, he went to mass every day. He made two special observances called Novenas. He said, "I began to think of myself as one of Jesus' special children. I kind of made a bargain with him," he continued. "I promised that I would be his special boy if he would help my father sober up a bit."

Toward the end of that seventh-grade year his teacher, a nun, made a fateful error. She called Jack up before the class and said, "Jack is the only member of the class I have seen attending mass faithfully every day this spring. I'm really proud of him." "That did it," Jack said. "They got me then. The bullies."

For the next two years his peers made him pay painfully for that moment of religious recognition. "I quit going to church," he said. "It was just as well, I guess, because my old man didn't quit drinking. In fact he began going out on Thursday nights to drink, in addition to Friday, Saturday, and Sunday."

At age nineteen Jack joined the army. His travel to Maryland for basic training and his first base assignment marked the first time he had ever been out of his city. "It opened me up a bit," he said. "I seemed to get along well with people from other parts of the country, especially those from cities like me." He learned a lot in the service, he said, because, "just like in jail, there's nothing much else to do but talk. You talk a lot in the army."

Jack came to spend a lot of time in several bars that specialized in playing music by black artists. He came to love that music and his conversations with black soldiers opened up a whole new world to him. In those years *Ramparts* magazine ran a series of articles on the Black Panthers. This series included writings by Huey Newton, Eldridge Cleaver and, posthumously, Malcolm X. As he talked about these articles and about black power, Jack discovered a whole new world of politics.

"When I grew up," he said, "politics meant speeches, hoopla, voting, and payoffs. I thought I knew about politics, but now I began to see politics differently. I began to see that the prejudice against blacks that I had been taught and that everybody in the projects where I grew up believed in was wrong. I began to see that us poor whites being pitted against poor blacks worked only to the advantage of the wealthy and powerful. For the first time I began to think politically. I began to have a kind of philosophy."

During this period Jack had a brother who had also been drawn into radical political thinking. When Jack got "busted" and put in the stockade for fighting, this brother sent him some money and wrote him about the political ideas that excited him. This encouraged Jack in his new perspectives.

When he came home from the service his old neighborhood bristled with tension over the threat of court-ordered busing to achieve racial desegregation in education. Jack tried out some of his new political philosophy on his old friends and acquaintances. "When anyone began making prejudiced statements about blacks," he said, "I found myself starting to preach. I explained how blacks had done nothing to make our neighborhood like it was. It was always bad. I told them that the rich people benefited from our being set against the blacks."

Jack soon found himself an alien in his old neighborhood. He began to seek the company of other groups in the city who shared something of his new political outlook. He felt marginal. His new political acquaintances were mostly college educated. They made him feel quaint and their articulate use of words made him feel uncomfortable. He missed the rhythms and style of his neighborhood. Yet, he didn't fit in there any more either. His new awareness seemed strange and threatening to his old friends. They had little capacity for or interest in the kind of political analysis in which he engaged. *His* new ways of using language intimidated them.

During this period Jack married a bright young woman from a middle-class family. She shared his new interests and commitments. He soon took a low-level bureaucratic job in state government. As their two children came along she eventually gave up her medical technician's job. At the time of our interview she worked in the evenings as a waitress to supplement his $12,000 a year income. Jack and his wife, when we talked with them, had emerged as leaders of a tenants' rights movement in their part of the city. Due to their success as organizers, they were each involved in lawsuits totaling a million dollars brought by landlord associations. Jack, explaining their commitments, said, "I don't know too much philosophy; I don't know Hegel and Marx too good. But I do know my class. I know we're getting stepped on. And I know that there are others worse off than us, who are fighting for their chance at life, too. If we're fighting in the alleys, then they're fighting in the cellars, you might say. We have to be careful not to step on those fighting below us. As long as there are people like these suffering and struggling for their rights, I'll still be in the fight."

Among other things, Jack's story shows us rather vividly one of the crucial steps in the transfer from a Synthetic-Conventional position to a Stage 4 Individuative-Reflective faith stance. In going to the army Jack left home, both emotionally and geographically. As he encountered the ideologically potent and threatening teachings of the Panthers, it drove him, for the first time, to look with critical awareness at the assumptive system of values he and his family had shared with most of their neighbors as he grew up. Here we see Santayana's fish leaping outside the fish tank and finding a place to stand in order to look at his own value ethos seriously. The analysis of "the system" provided by the Panthers awakened him to the insight that ideologies have particular histories and that persons and groups have world views that grow out of their particular experiences and the conditions with which they have had to deal. He began to see other people not just as individual persons with their particular quirks and qualities of temperament. Now he recognized that people get shaped by their social class, by the group histories they inherit, and by the economic conditions and opportunities with which they and their groups struggle. Jack, we may say, became disembedded from his Synthetic-Conventional, assumptive world view. His first move beyond it, in a kind of counter-dependent step of opposition to it, was to embrace the explicit ideology of the Panthers, with its combination of black empowerment strategies and Marxist economic and semipolitical analysis. The tacit values and meaning system of his Stage 3 began to be replaced by the explicit system of Stage 4.

Some other factors in Jack's experience of stage transition help to illumine the character of the Stage 4 faith position. Previously, Jack's identity had derived from his belonging to a family, to a peer, and to a neighborhood world. The religious world, so important to him for a brief time in his early teens, seems to have diminished markedly in what may be seen as a Stage 2 to Stage 3 transition. Although Jack kept his promise faithfully at thirteen, God did not make his father cut back on his drinking. This collided with the structure of reciprocity in Jack's Stage 2 faith. Then the bullies and his peers hammered him into conformity with their conventional male aloofness from religion.

In the "hanging out" period of his mid- to late teens, Jack said, he had no special badge of distinction to make him stand out from—or in—the crowd he ran with. "I was not the lover, or the fighter, the leader, or anything special," he said. His identity derived from his memberships; he was who he was able to be in those face-to-face groups in which fate placed him—family, school, peer group, and neighborhood.

This is not to say that Jack's personhood was either exhausted or fully expressed in his derivative teen years' identity. He tells us that as a teen he spent long hours alone listening to his older brother's record player. He tells us how uncomfortable it made him feel when his gang would single out a guy in a bar, provoke a fight with him, and then beat him up. He tells us how especially uncomfortable it made him when his gang baited black people and blamed all problems in the projects on "the niggers." But these aspects of his personhood could find little expression in the identity his groups were willing to allow him. And with no good clothes and little money, Jack said, the thought of trying to get a girl's attention seemed hopeless as well.

For Jack, going into the service meant being extracted from the interpersonal groups that had largely formed, maintained, and limited his identity. For many other youths going to college represents a similar extraction. In addition to encountering an ideology that enabled (and forced) him to examine his own conventional values, Jack now had the freedom (and burden) to explore who he could be away from home.

This represents a moment of crucial importance in the transition from Stage 3 to Stage 4. It can be a frightening and somewhat disorienting time of being apart from one's conventional moorings. Whether a person will *really* make the move to an Individuative-Reflective stance depends to a critical degree on the character and quality of the ideologically composed groups bidding for one's joining. Social fraternities or sororities in colleges often represent conventional ideological communities that in effect substitute one family group for another, making any genuinely individuative move as regards identity and outlook difficult. Many religious groups similarly reinforce a conventionally held and maintained faith system, sanctifying one's remaining in the dependence on external authority and derivative group identity of Stage 3. Marriage, for many young men and women, can serve to create a new Synthetic-Conventional ethos, and because the couple are playing adult roles they are able, at least for a time, to evade the challenges of the individuative transition.

But when Jack identified himself with that group of black soldiers, held together by their commitment to soul music and the Panther ideology, he burned his bridges. Without full assurance of where it would lead, he began to shape a new identity and faith. His identity had previously derived from and been a function of the groups he grew up with in fated membership. Now, as is the case in any genuine Stage 4, his choice of groups, with the ideological perspectives they bear, became a function of the identity he was forming. He shaped his new identity in relation to the groups and outlooks whose invitation to life-redefining membership he accepted.

For a genuine move to Stage 4 to occur there must be an interruption of reliance on external sources of authority. The "tyranny of the they"—or the potential for it—must be undermined. In addition to the kind of critical reflection on one's previous assumptive or tacit system of values we saw Jack undertake, there must be, for Stage 4, a relocation af authority within the self. While others and their judgments will remain important to the Individuative-Reflective person, their expectations, advice, and counsel will be submitted to an internal panel of experts who reserve the right to choose and who are prepared to take responsibility for their choices. I sometimes call this the emergence of an *executive ego.*

The two essential features of the emergence of Stage 4, then, are the critical distancing from one's previous assumptive value system and the emergence of an executive ego. When, and as these occur, a person is forming a new identity, which he or she expresses and actualizes by the choice of personal and group affiliations and the shaping of a "lifestyle."

We find that sometimes many persons complete half of this double movement, but do not complete the other. By virtue of college experience, travel, or of being moved from one community to another, many persons undergo the relativization of their inherited worldviews and value systems. They come face to face with the relativity of their perspectives and those of others to their life experience. But they fail to interrupt their reliance on external sources of authority—and may even strengthen their reliance upon them—in order to cope with this relativity. On the other hand there is a significant group who shape their own variant way of living from a shared value ethos, break their reliance on consensual or conventional authorities, and show the emergence of a strong executive ego. Yet they have not carried through a critical distancing from their shared assumptive values system. In either of these two cases we see an interesting and potentially longlasting equilibrium in a transitional position between Stages 3 and 4.

To complete our discussion of this stage let us look at several other correlated structural features of Individuative-Reflective faith. In social perspective-taking, for example, Stage 4 constructs a perspective genuinely aware of social systems and institutions. It retains Stage 3's orientation to persons and its richness of mutual interpersonal perspective-taking, but it adds to it two related features. First, Stage 4, aware that the self has an ideology that it has formed and re-formed over time, works at apprehending other persons in terms of their personal qualities as well as taking into account the determinative shape of their ideologies and the group experiences that fund them. Second, it achieves an understanding of social relations in systems terms. No longer constructing social relations as merely the extension of interpersonal relations, Stage 4 thinks in terms of the impersonal imperatives of law, rules, and the standards that govern social roles.

In keeping with Stage 4's critical reflection upon its system of meanings, its relation to and use of symbols differs qualitatively from that of Stage 3. Symbols and rituals, previously taken as mediating the sacred in direct ways and therefore as sacred themselves, are interrogated by Stage 4's critical questioning. In its critical reflection Stage 4 regards meanings as separable from the symbolic media that express them. In the face of a liturgical ritual or a religious symbol the Individuative-Reflective person asks, "But what does it *mean*?" If the symbol or symbolic act is truly meaningful, Stage 4 believes, its meanings can be translated into propositions, definitions, and/or conceptual foundations.

This demythologizing strategy, which seems natural to Stage 4, brings both gains and losses. Paul Tillich, writing about religious symbols and their powers, says that when a symbol is recognized to be a symbol by those who relate to the transcendent through it, it becomes a "broken symbol" (1957, chap. 2). A certain naive reliance upon and trust in the sacred power, efficacy, and inherent truth of the symbol as representation is interrupted. Instead of the symbol or symbolic act having the initiative and exerting its power on the participant, now the participant-questioner has the initiative over against the symbol. For those who have previously enjoyed an unquestioning relation to the transcendent and to their fellow worshipers through a set of religious symbols, Stage 4's translations of their meanings into conceptual prose can bring a sense of loss, dislocation, grief, and even guilt.

I once heard theologian and cultural analyst Harvey Cox share with a class a memory of his experience of the loss of the primal naïveté regarding a central symbolic act for Christians. Though himself a Baptist, Cox said that as a high-school lad he often attended services with his friends at the Catholic church next to his home. In one period he had been dating a Catholic girl a year or so older than he. She went off to college while he stayed at home to finish high school. When she came back for Christmas vacation Harvey went with her to a beautiful midnight Christmas Eve mass. As the mass climaxed and the people were receiving the Eucharist, Harvey said his college-aged girl friend, who had just completed Anthropology 101, turned to him and whispered, "That's just a primitive totemic ritual, you know." Harvey said, "A what?" She replied with great self-assurance, "A primitive totemic ritual. Almost all premodern religious and tribal groups have them. They are ceremonies where worshipers bind themselves together and to the power of the sacred by a cannibalistic act of ingesting the mana of a dead god." Communion, Cox said, was never the same again. A symbol recognized as a symbol is a broken symbol.

But there are gains as well. Meanings previously tacitly held become explicit. Dimensions of depth in symbolic or ritual expression previously felt and responded to without reflection can now be identified and clarified. The "mystification" of symbols, the tendency to experience them as organically linked with the realities they represent, is broken open. Their meanings, now detachable from the symbolic media, can be communicated in concepts or propositions that may have little direct resonance with the symbolic form or action. Comparisons of meanings become more easily possible, though a certain tendency to reductionism and the "flattening" of meanings is difficult to avoid.

Jack's time of transition from Stage 3 to Stage 4 occurred at the most ideal time for this movement—his early to mid-twenties. Levinson calls this "novice adulthood" and sees it as the time when persons form their first adult life structures. Erikson identifies the crisis of Intimacy vs. Isolation with this period. Intimacy requires the ability to stand alone as well as to risk one's forming self and sense of identity in close engagement with other persons and with ideological commitments that channel one's actions and shape one's vision of life goals (Levinson's "dream").

For some adults, however, the transition to Stage 4, if it comes at all, occurs in the thirties or forties. It can be precipitated by changes in primary relationships, such as a divorce, the death of a parent or parents, or children growing up and leaving home. Or it can result from challenges of moving, changing jobs, or the experience of the breakdown or inadequacy of one's Synthetic-Conventional faith.

This transition represents an upheaval in one's life at any point and can be protracted in its process for five to seven years or longer. It typically is less severe for young adults, however, coming in that era as a natural accompaniment of leaving home and of the construction of a first, provisional adult life structure. When the transition occurs in the late thirties or early forties it often brings greater struggles. This is because of its impact upon the more established and elaborated system of relationships and roles that constitute an adult life structure.

Summary of Individuative-Reflective faith. The movement form Stage 3 to Stage 4 Individuative-Reflective faith is particularly critical for it is in this transition that the late adolescent or adult must begin to take seriously the burden of responsibility for his or her own commitments, lifestyle, beliefs, and attitudes. Where genuine movement toward Stage 4 is underway the person must face certain unavoidable tensions: individuality versus being defined by a group or group membership; subjectivity and the power of one's strongly felt but unexamined feelings versus objectivity and the requirement of critical reflection; self-fulfillment or self-actualization as a primary concern versus service to and being for others; the question of being committed to the relative versus struggle with the possibility of an absolute.

Stage 4 most appropriately takes form in young adulthood (but let us remember that many adults do not construct it and that for a significant group it emerges only in the mid-thirties or forties). This stage is marked by a double development. The self, previously sustained in its identity and faith compositions by an interpersonal circle of significant others, now claims an identity no longer defined by the composite of one's roles or meanings to others. To sustain that new identity it composes a meaning frame conscious of its own boundaries and inner connections and aware of itself as a "worldview." Self (identity) and outlook (worldview) are differentiated from those of others and become acknowledged factors in the reactions, interpretations, and judgments one makes on the actions of the self and others. It expresses its intuitions of coherence in an ultimate environment in terms of an explicit system of meanings. Stage 4 typically translates symbols into conceptual meanings. This is a "demythologizing" stage. It is likely to attend minimally to unconscious factors influencing its judgments and behavior.

Stage 4's ascendant strength has to do with its capacity for critical reflection on identity (self) and outlook (ideology). Its dangers inhere in its strengths: an excessive confidence in the conscious mind and in critical thought and a kind of second narcissism in which the now clearly bounded, reflective self overassimilates "reality" and the perspectives of others into its own worldview.

Restless with the self-images and outlook maintained by Stage 4, the person ready for transition finds him- or herself attending to what may feel like anarchic and disturbing inner voices. Elements from a childish past, images and energies from a deeper self, a gnawing sense of the sterility and flatness of the meanings one serves—any or all of these may signal readiness for something new. Stories, symbols, myths, and paradoxes from one's own or other traditions may insist on breaking in upon the neatness of the previous faith. Disillusionment with one's compromises and recognition that life is more complex than Stage 4's logic of clear distinctions and abstract concepts can comprehend, press one toward a more dialectical and multileveled approach to life truth.

Stage 5: Conjunctive Faith

I have not found or fabricated a simple way to describe Conjunctive faith. This frustrates me. I somehow feel that if I cannot communicate the features of this stage clearly, it means that I don't understand them. Or worse, I fear that what I call "Stage 5" really does not exist. I cannot accept either of these explanations. The truth, I believe, is that Stage 5, as a style of faith-knowing, *does* exist and it *is* complex. Moreover, while it has been—and is—exemplified in the lives of persons, in their writing and in writings about them, its structural features have not been adequately described, either in my own previous writings or in the writings of others.

As a way of opening our consideration of Conjunctive faith let me offer a few analogies, which may tease out an image of the character of the transition from Stage 4 to Stage 5. The emergence of Stage 5 is something like:

> Realizing that the behavior of light requires that it be understood both as a wave phenomenon *and* as particles of energy.
>
> Discovering that the rational solution or "explanation" of a problem that seemed so elegant is but a painted canvas covering an intricate, endlessly intriguing cavern of surprising depth.
>
> Looking at a field of flowers simultaneously through a microscope and a wide-angle lens.
>
> Discovering that a guest, if invited to do so, will generously reveal the treasured wisdom of a lifetime of experience.
>
> Discovering that someone who shares your identity also writes checks, makes deposits, and stops payments on your checking account.
>
> Discovering that one's parents are remarkable people not just because they are one's parents.

Stage 5, as a way of seeing, of knowing, of committing, moves beyond the dichotomizing logic of Stage 4's "either/or." It sees both (or the many) sides of an issue simultaneously. Conjunctive faith suspects that things are organically related to each other; it attends to the pattern of interrelatedness in things, trying to avoid force-fitting to its own prior mind set.

The phrase *dialectical knowing* comes close to describing Stage 5's style, yet the term is too methodologically controlling. Better, I think, to speak of *dialogical* knowing. In dialogical knowing the known is invited to speak its own word in its own language. In dialogical knowing the multiplex structure of the world is invited to disclose itself. In a mutual "speaking" and "hearing," knower and known converse in an I-Thou relationship. The knower seeks to accommodate her or his knowing to the structure of that which is being known before imposing her or his own categories upon it.

Stage 5's dialogical knowing requires a knower capable of dialogue. Epistemologically, there must be sufficient self-certainty to grant the known the initiative. What the mystics call "detachment" characterizes Stage 5's willingness to let reality speak its word, regardless of the impact of that word on the security or self-esteem of the knower. I speak here of an intimacy in knowing that celebrates, reverences, and attends to the "wisdom" evolved in things as they are, before seeking to modify, control, or order them to fit prior categories.

Stage 5's willingness to give reality the initiative in the act of knowing, however, is not merely a function of the knower's self-certainty. It also has to do with the trustworthiness of the known. In this sense Stage 5 represents a kind of complementarity or mutuality in relation.

In theological seminary I learned methods of studying Scripture that employed language study, source criticism, form criticism, and text criticism. All of these methods involved things I could learn to do to texts in order, as Martin Luther once said, to "crack them open like a nut." Not until I was in my thirties, undergoing my first experience of spiritual direction in the tradition of Saint Ignatius's *Spiritual Exercises,* did I begin to learn a method of working with Scripture that breathed more of the spirit of Stage 5. The Ignatian approach did not require me to give up or negate my critical skills, but it did teach me to supplement them with a method in which I learned to relinquish initiative to the text. Instead of *my reading,* analyzing, and extracting the meaning of a Biblical text, in Ignatian contemplative prayer I began to learn how to let the text *read me* and to let it bring my needs and the Spirit's movements within me to consciousness.

Put straightforwardly, Stage 5 Conjunctive faith involves going beyond the explicit ideological system and clear boundaries of identity that Stage 4 worked so hard to construct and to adhere to. Whereas Stage 4 could afford to equate self pretty much with its own conscious awareness of self, Stage 5 must come to terms with its own unconscious—the unconscious personal, social, and species or archetypal elements that are partly determinative of our actions and responses. Stage 5 comes to terms with the fact that the conscious ego is not master in its own house. As in the analogy of the mysterious *Doppelgänger* who also funds and draws on our bank account, Stage 5 recognizes the task of integrating or reconciling conscious and unconscious.

Stage 5 accepts as axiomatic that truth is more multidimensional and organically interdependent than most theories or accounts of truth can grasp. Religiously, it knows that the symbols, stories, doctrines, and liturgies offered by its own or other traditions are inevitably partial, limited to a particular people's experience of God and incomplete. Stage 5 also sees, however, that the relativity of religious traditions that matters is not their relativity to each other, but their relativity—their *relate*-ivity—to the reality to which they mediate relation. Conjunctive faith, therefore, is ready for significant encounters with other traditions than its own, expecting that truth has disclosed and will disclose itself in those traditions in ways that may complement or correct its own. Krister Stendahl is fond of saying that no interfaith conversation is genuinely ecumenical unless the quality of mutual sharing and receptivity is such that each party makes him- or herself vulnerable to conversion to the other's truth. This would be Stage 5 ecumenism.

This position implies no lack of commitment to one's own truth tradition. Nor does it mean a wishy-washy neutrality or mere fascination with the exotic features of alien cultures. Rather, Conjunctive faith's radical openness to the truth of the other stems precisely from its confidence in the reality mediated by its own tradition and in the awareness that that reality overspills its mediation. The person of Stage 5 makes her or his own experience of truth the principle by which other claims to truth are tested. But he or she assumes that each genuine perspective will augment and correct aspects of the other, in a mutual movement toward the real and the true.

Conjunctive faith cannot live with the demythologizing strategy of Stage 4 as regards the interpretation of story or myth or the understanding of symbol and liturgy. Stage 4 is concerned to question symbolic representations and enactments and to force them to yield their meanings for translation into conceptual or propositional statements. As such, Individuative-Reflective faith wants to bring the symbolic representation into its (Stage 4's) circle of light and to operate on it, extracting its meanings. This leaves the person or group in Stage 4 clearly in control. The meaning so grasped may be illuminating, confronting, harshly judgmental, or gently reassuring. But whatever its potential impact, its authentication and weight will be assigned in accordance with the assumptions and commitments that already shape the circle of light in which it is being questioned. It will not be granted the initiative. Nor will its self-authenticating character be fully translated into the conceptual or propositional communication.

Conjunctive faith, on the other hand, is not innocent of the critical impulse or critical capability. In Paul Ricoeur's powerful language, Conjunctive faith is not to be equated with a "first naïveté," a precritical relationship of unbroken participation in symbolically mediated reality (1967, 351–52). That style more aptly describes Stage 3 Synthetic-Conventional faith. Conjunctive faith has experienced the breaking of its symbols and the "vertigo of reality." It is a veteran of critical reflection and of the effort to "reduce" the symbolic, the liturgical, and the mythical to conceptual meanings. But it cannot rest content with that strategy. It acknowledges the powerlessness of anything *it* can control to transform and redeem its myopia. It discerns the powerful residues of meaning that escape our strategies of reductive interpretation. With its attention to the organic and interconnected character of things Stage 5 distrusts the separation of symbol and symbolized, sensing that when we neutralize the initiative of the symbolic, we make a pale idol of any meaning we honor.

Ricoeur's term "second naïveté" or "willed naïveté" begins to describe Conjunctive faith's postcritical desire to resubmit to the initiative of the symbolic (1978, 36–58). It decides to do this, but it has to relearn how to do this. It carries forward the critical capacities and methods of the previous stage, but it no longer trusts them except as tools to avoid self-deception and to order truths encountered in other ways.

Now, lest my descriptions make you believe that only professors, theologians, or adepts in hermeneutics become Stage 5, let me tell you about J. T. (not her real initials). At the time we interviewed her Miss T. was seventy-eight years old. She lived in a university city where she rented rooms to four graduate students, something she has done for the past twenty years. She has arthritic hips, walks with great difficulty, and is expecting soon a third operation to improve her mobility and reduce her pain. She spends her time reading, conversing with "her students" and with other friends by phone. She currently devotes time most days to revising for publication a small book on life truths which she wrote during a period of recovery from a nervous breakdown in her early fifties. She has already published another, more popular book, about how to approach life problems. Reading the interview with Miss T. (I did not do the interview) one forms the image of an exceedingly lively, highly intelligent woman who looks squarely into life. She preserves few illusions and is not easy on those of others. But she seems to have found a ground of hope, of courage, and of love for her life that is beyond illusion.

Across the years of her life Miss T. has done many things. She founded and operated a puppet theater on the West Coast. She taught art, having begun her own small art school in New York. She studied acting and worked for a number of years in the theater and movie industry in varying capacities from actress to make-up artist to script writer. She had an unusually productive voluntary career in mental health work. Except for the sudden onset of arthritis in her late fifties one suspects this would have become a late professional career of great significance. Miss T. devoted twenty years of voluntary work effectively aimed at the racial integration of summer camps for children and of the recruitment of black children to attend them. She traveled a good bit, lived on both coasts of the United States, and has apparently been a seeker after moral and religious truth for most of her life.

Miss T. was born in New England in 1898. The daughter of a lawyer with inherited wealth and literary aspirations and a mother whom she characterized as "really wanting to have been a minister herself," she grew up privileged in many ways. About 1910, the quarreling between a headstrong father and an outspoken mother led to the latter's taking her two young daughters to Europe for the winter. Miss T., the older, was then twelve. She had just been confirmed in the Unitarian church, an event that she would always remember.

Miss T.: I joined the Unitarian church and my uncle, who was a darling, saintly person . . . was minister of that little church. I remember that service. I had a little white dress and my pink hair ribbons, I remember, all fresh and new and lovely. And the service that he gave at that time I think was a religious experience for me. It went very deep; I felt as if I were going to be pure and holy for the rest of my life.

Years later at a time when she sought psychiatric help for recurring illnesses she suspected were psychosomatic, she recalled the pain of her parents' deep conflict over their children. She describes her first sessions with the psychiatrist.

Miss T.: And it came, it came piling out in that first session, first few sessions, of what it had meant to me as a child to have our parents pulling in opposite directions over us. There was the scene in the railroad station when mother brought us home from camp and my father wanted to take us and my mother wouldn't let us go. People gathering around believe it or not. See parents fighting over their children. Well, these stories all came piling out and I was so tired when I got out of that office that I had to hold onto the railings to get down to the subway.

In her early teens the parents divorced. Her father remarried and had two sons with his new wife. The younger of those sons, who developed a lifelong mental illness in his teens, was to play an important role in Miss T.'s life. She was asked about her father.

Miss T.: We adored him when we were little children and he adored his two little girls that came first, and I think I developed a father complex. I, when it came to picking a mate for myself, I wanted somebody as gifted as my father but who didn't have all his hazards, which was a very difficult proposition. This I never found. So I really lost those first dear fellows that loved me. And, well, I feel that my father gave me by inheritance a great deal that was splendid, and I've gotten way past the place where I hold him any grudges.

Miss T. recalls her mother as a "devout Unitarian, almost Episcopalian in her feelings." She had attended some of the first courses in religious education at Radcliffe College in her student years. Miss T. remembers her as a woman who always continued to study and grow.

Miss T.: I think that mother, mother's integrity was superb. And I saw her grow, I saw her right under my eyes as a growing up young woman, developing from a spoiled child, which she certainly had been, although she wasn't an only child. She worked away every morning. I would find her with the little books that she was studying, and I think before she died she was a very simple, wonderful person. I saw her develop; it was an inspiration for me to see it.

Miss T. also attended Radcliffe. While she was a student there the United States entered World War I. She read a book by a famous Unitarian minister of that era, John Haynes Holmes. It made her a lifelong pacifist. She left the church at about age twenty when, at someone's urging, the local Unitarian minister came to see her and to try to "correct" her pacifism. She speaks about the minister.

Miss T.: I really felt sorry for him because he was a marvelous man. And he knew I was right; he knew that what I said about love and peace and understanding were true, and he was in a false position for him to try to tell me what attitude to take toward World War I. Any rate, I got in that war disillusioned in the church.

Disappointed that the church failed to take a stance critical of U.S. entry into the war, Miss T. turned in other directions.

Miss T.: That's when I came to know the Quakers, God love 'em. I would say that I went with my whole heart instead into the labor movement which was then gathering strength. And A.J. Muste was leaving his parish and going in as a labor leader, and Roger Barwin was organizing the American Civil Liberties Union.

Her religion, she said, became a search for beauty.

Miss T.: I think I've always been a religious person, but I had to stop calling myself a church-goer. I didn't go to church for years and years and years, except to please my mother at Christmas and Easter.

Details of Miss. T.'s life from her early twenties to her mother's death about 1940 are sketchy in the interview. In its main lines it looks like this. Immediately upon graduating from college she travelled to the West Coast. There, with another young woman she met, she started a puppet theater and they began to tour in California. They planned to do a tour to the Far East, but ran out of money. She then returned to New York where she began a small art school for children. After a time she moved, apparently to her mother's home in upstate New York, where she taught art history and studio art in a girls' boarding school. After a few years she left home again, going to New York to work in theater. For what must have been ten to twelve years she worked as an actress and as a professional make-up artist for stage and screen. It was during those years that she sought a psychiatrist's help for her psychosomatic illnesses. It seems likely, also, that in these years she had some of the "unfortunate relationships" she mentions in talking about why she never married. She said, "I had unfortunate relationships, several important relationships. In lonely periods I made some mistakes."

Apparently in these years her mother wanted to bind Miss T. closer to herself than Miss T. could stand. She speaks of when she was working in theater and films.

Miss T.: I used to go home for weekends to be with mother. . . . She was wrapped up in humane education for children—that was her old-age career when she found that I wouldn't let her make me into an old-age career for her. I had to be independent and she learned that the hard way, I think. But she did learn it and she went ahead with her own career.

The period from Miss T.'s early twenties to her early forties seems to have been a time when she dealt with issues of separation from her mother, with finding a career, and with unresolved emotional binds with her father. We have seen how she earlier set herself critically over against her Unitarian background and left organized religion. She made her faith a search for beauty. Taken together, all this suggests that by around age thirty Miss T. had developed a pretty well equilibrated Stage 4 Individuative-Reflective faith stance.

The death of her mother in 1940 represented for Miss T. the end of an era. She was in her early forties. It appears that she had remained in the East, at some detriment to her career chances, in order to fulfill what she took to be her responsibilities to an aging mother. About a year after her mother's death Miss T. left for California. She took with her a book manuscript she had begun after her mother's death, one apparently dealing with a person's responsibility for how one meets, deals with, and transcends adversities. For four or five years she worked in and around Hollywood. She used her make-up artist's skills to make a living while taking screen tests to see if she could get going a career as a character actor. She also did some screen writing. Her breakthrough never came.

At about age forty-eight Miss T. had what she called "an acute nervous breakdown" in Hollywood. I suspect that today's name for what she suffered would be an acute, delayed mid-life crisis. In the midst of that crisis she was helped by a doctor who was a student and adherent of Rudolph Steiner. She also discovered the writings of Carl Jung and of other depth psychologists. Through friends she found a small cottage where she could live apart until she got herself together. In a kind of religious and artistic community near a river she began to write again and to find a new basis for her life. Through the friends who helped her find this place to live and write she had earlier come into contact with the Vedanta society of Hollywood and, through it, with the Indian sage Krishnamurti. His teachings, available to her for two weeks in each of the three or four preceding summers, had given her powerful religious images with which to work.

Miss T.: He [Krishnamurti] gave me so much of wisdom, I think, deeper than any other help I have ever received. He gave me a foundation for Christianity. I think Christians can get into trouble.

Interviewer: What kind of trouble?

Miss T.: The Christians who believe in hell and damnation for instance. That's a wicked philosophy and it's Christians who put it forth. And many people have been injured, have been damaged psychologically with that fearful philosophy.

Interviewer: And what kind of foundation did Krishnamurti give you?

Miss T.: That it doesn't matter what you call it. Whether you call it God or Jesus or Cosmic Flow or Reality or Love, it doesn't matter what you call it. It is there. And what you learn directly from that source will not tie you up in creeds . . . that separate you from your fellow man.

If Krishnamurti gave her the kind of help that brought her into a new and more inclusive religious community, it was a man from a group called the Camp Farthest Out who precipitated her return to Christianity. Hearing her speak of her religion as a quest for beauty, he responded, "But J., beauty can be pagan. . . . Where in that way of life is righteousness?" Miss T. remembers that question.

Miss T.: That word righteousness sent shivers right down my back. It gave me the whole thing in one word. . . . I got the perspective on all that was lacking in my life. It was that one word, righteousness, opened up the whole thing of what's lacking without a religious foundation. A wonderful swami in California, in Hollywood, Swami Prabhabananda said religion meant: *re* "back, again," *ligio* "to bind,"—"to bind again." The word religion means to bind again. And I felt that that one word *righteousness* bound me back again to those things I had been brought up to understand.

Shortly after that experience Miss T. returned to her native New England. Her half brother—her father's second son from his second marriage—had been rehospitalized with severe mental illness. She does not speculate on why she went back to try to care for him and help him recover, but she did. Her involvement with him led to a remarkable period in which she pioneered in teaching art, dance, and folk music to patients in mental hospitals. Her stories of carrying a hand-crank Victrola into the wards and leading patients in singing and dancing are fascinating. She would take them out on the lawns for dancing and gymnastics. Nurses and psychiatrists apparently were impressed with the effectiveness of what she did. After several years it appeared that there might be state funding to support and broaden her program. At that time, however, late in her fifties, Miss T. began to develop serious arthritis and had to decline this opportunity.

In what she calls her "old-age career" Miss T. devoted a lot of time and energy with the Quakers, whom she joined in 1952, to integrating their summer camps for children. This meant establishing contacts in the black communities of her city and spending considerable time there each year recruiting children and their families for the camps. This she did with characteristic energy, verve, and effectiveness for nearly twenty years.

As Miss T. talks today about her life and her outlook, her words and phrases disclose an almost textbook Stage 5 structuring underlying her faith. Before turning to some quotes that show this, perhaps it is worthwhile to reflect on the transition from the Individuative-Reflective stage of her thirties and forties to the Conjunctive stage that emerged after her breakdown. The factors leading to her mid-life breakdown—or at least some of them—seem to be obvious. With the death of her mother a few years before, she was now alone in the world. She suffered several years of career disappointment and probably began to face the conclusion that she would never be a success as an actress. Though we have few details, she had watched chances at marriage pass her by. Near fifty and childless, the state she vowed she would never accept—that of being an "old maid"—loomed more certainly as her future. For all these reasons, and more perhaps that we do not know, her faith, centering in the search for beauty, wore thin. The meanings sustaining her life collapsed.

As she had done after the death of her mother, she wrote herself back toward wholeness. The teachings of Krishnamurti, the psychology of Jung, and the witness of her friends from the Camp Farthest Out sponsored her toward a new beginning in faith. As is characteristic of Stage 5, it was a new beginning that had to reclaim and reintegrate elements of strength from her childhood faith. It is revealing that in the interview her telling about the powerful impact of the question about righteousness upon her is followed immediately by the account of *religio* as a "binding back." Then she tells of her confirmation at twelve in the Unitarian church and of the power of that religious experience. With her return to New England, her joining the Quakers, and her continuing and deepening relation with the Camp Farthest Out, she began to build a new faith stance, one that could sustain her in the second half of *her* life and ground her in finding fulfillment in service to others. What is the shape of that faith? What are its animating themes and anchoring convictions?

Miss T. was asked if there are beliefs and values everyone should hold.

Miss T.: If somebody asked me that and gave me just two minutes to answer it, I know what I'd say. It's a line from George Fox, the founder of Quakerism. It's old-fashioned English and it seems to me to have the entire program of anybody's life. It's a revolution, it's an enormous comfort, it's a peace maker. The line is: "There is that of God in every man." Now, you can start thinking about it. You can see that if you really did believe that, how it would change your relationships with people. . . . It's far-reaching. It applies nationally and individually and class-wise; it reaches the whole. To anyone that I loved dearly I would say, "Put that in your little invisible locket and keep it forever."

Mindful of her own suffering and of her devotion to other sufferers, our interviewer asked Miss T. how, if at all, she makes sense of the inequality and maldistribution of suffering in the world. Her answer began with her sharing her feelings about her younger half-brother, with whom she has worked for nearly thirty years in the state hospital.

Miss T.: Well, I can go back to my own experience with the problem of suffering. Take my brother R. If there ever was a pure, sinless, human soul, it's my brother R. Why did he have to have a life like this? I said to myself, I've got to solve it if I am going to believe in a good God, a kind God. And I came out of it more or less this way: human life is a moment in eternity. I think there were two courses at college that meant more to me, philosophically, than any other two. One was astronomy. . . . You get a vista if you study astronomy. Your perspective opens out to an absolutely incredible degree. The other course was anthropology, where you get some idea of the development of the human being on this planet earth. They were both exercises in perspective. So I decided that a human being's life was his moment in eternity. It may be that R.'s—to use a figure of speech about the caterpillar—in the cocoon stage and the butterfly stage—it's a very telling figure because if you put that together with man as but a moment in eternity, maybe this is R.'s moment in the cocoon. I have had a sense that I should somewhere someday, along the pathways of God, meet R. when he is come into his own, and he comes with rushing wings. . . . I can't help but feel that all the suffering of all these people, all the people that are starving to death, that their time will come.

Miss T. continues with references to the vastness of eternity and the limited capacities for understanding of even the most enlightened human beings. She talks about suffering with finality:

Miss T.: I know it has nothing whatsoever to do with guilt or sin or purity. That the pure in heart, Christ's line was, that they shall see God. And I believe that. At the same time there are a lot of human beings who have not had a chance to see God. So, as Christ told us, if we can believe without seeing, those are the real faithful. And I guess the trick is to be able to give your all to the people that are suffering, without losing your faith that there is some meaning to it.

When asked how she would speak about God to someone who knew nothing of what the term referred to, Miss T. took on the challenge. She began with an appeal that we acknowledge that there is a power beyond ourselves. Then she speaks of her convictions regarding the power beyond us.

Miss T.: The Quakers call it The Light Within. I don't think it matters a bit what you call it. I think some people are so fed up with the word God that you can't talk to them about God. Call it Reality—all these would be spelled with a capital—let us say Reality, or Cosmic Flow or Love. And nobody can tell another about it. It has to come from within the individual, because, of course, everyone has the same inheritance. Religious structures in the mind. That interested me very much: that Carl Jung says if the analyst explores deeply enough he comes across the religious symbols that are in every human mind. It doesn't matter whether they call themselves agnostics or atheists.

Toward the end of her long interview Miss T. is asked about her understanding of sin.

Miss T.: Sin!? I don't use the word sin, *ever.*
Interviewer: Why?
Miss T.: I think, on the whole, people are doing the best they can with what light they have. And I think more in terms of mistakes than I do of deliberate sin. Everybody's made plenty of mistakes. In my own life I would perhaps describe it more as blundering because I didn't have the experience to handle things right. You blunder your way along. And you keep open to getting more light and to . . . well, sin surely. A good definition of sin would be thoughts and actions that bear no relation to the light within, call it what you will. They're severed, like a branch, severed. As Jesus said, the branches that are not functioning should be cut off and burned up. But I am absolutely convinced that there will have to be sin, have to be. Gigantic blunderings and mistakes and stupidities. It's past belief the stupidity of the world today. The American people that are shipping arms to the whole world because their industry has to make money. I think that's such a colossal stupidity. I call it stupidity rather than sin. . . . You go through life thinking that humanity . . . or you start as a young one thinking that people in general have sense. How is it that a concept of that sort can be a fact of today's experience? . . . You really have to have a deep faith in Almighty God and the power of good not to just go down under that gigantic stupidity and say it's hopeless. So I think sin, in one sentence, is the result of being cut off from God.

A few paragraphs later Miss T. speaks about how she struggles with that powerful temptation "to just go down under that gigantic stupidity and say it's hopeless." In the sense that Erikson means it, I think this statement breathes the integrity, hard won, that Miss T.'s struggle has yielded and the power on which her faith has depended.

Interviewer: When do you feel you are changing or growing now in your life as a religious person?

Miss T.: Have to give me a moment to think about that one! {Pause.} I wrote this little second book of mine in California before 1950. Basically I had a hideout in the woods; I lived in a canyon as a little community there. And I found this place in the woods that was ideal for working out of doors and the people who owned the place let me take out an old kitchen table and a chair and we hid the typewriter in an abandoned beehive in the brush. And this was written under the most ideal circumstances. Complete peace, complete sharing of nature, fragrance of the flowers from those slopes above, the Santa Barbara mountain range there. And the animals in the woods that visited me and the horses in the meadow out there that I made friends with. So I wrote something that I probably couldn't have written anywhere else. This place where I live now, that I love very dearly, is just full of interruptions. But I have succeeded; what I have been doing here in this last few years as my hobby is editing this material. And I find that this material helps me enormously. My own high moments help me. I would say that one of the things that has come to me in the immediate last few days is that this Cosmic Flow, which is God, call it what you will, is the life back of every cell in the body. It's a nice metaphor, the river is the flow, because it has come to me more deeply that I am just sort of porous. That this refreshing, healing love of God is flowing through me, and that's a very marvelous thing to believe if you are seventy-eight and you've got arthritis, and you're burdened with the racial concept of old age that everybody gets sick and peters out and gets carried away. But it doesn't matter where you are physically, if you're sick or if you're well. That this Reality, of this actual life, all spelled with capital letters, Life flows through you at every moment of your waking-sleeping experience. Consequently you can be creative to your last breath.

There's even an illustration that was made by a man who produced the illustrations for the brochure of the place I was living. He made a drawing of the river flowing along over the rocks. There are some people who will think perhaps this is superstitious, but I think it's all right to use your imagination. I could almost feel that if I touch that illustration that it strengthens me to know that that river's flowing. You see an advantage to putting down your thoughts when you're a little bit depressed physically, or if someone you do not vibrate too well has jarred on your nerves. Just let this thing flow through and know it flows through the other person. And peace comes.

Summary of Conjunctive faith. Stage 5 Conjunctive faith involves the integration into self and outlook of much that was suppressed or unrecognized in the interest of Stage 4's self-certainty and conscious cognitive and affective adaptation to reality. This stage develops a "second naïveté" (Ricoeur) in which symbolic power is reunited with conceptual meanings. Here there must also be a new reclaiming and reworking of one's past. There must be an opening to the voices of one's "deeper self." Importantly, this involves a critical recognition of one's social unconscious—the myths, ideal images, and prejudices built deeply into the self-system by virtue of one's nurture within a particular social class, religious tradition, ethnic group, or the like.

Unusual before mid-life, Stage 5 knows the sacrament of defeat and the reality of irrevocable commitments and acts. What the previous stage struggled to clarify, in terms of the boundaries of self and outlook, this stage now makes porous and permeable. Alive to paradox and the truth in apparent contradictions, this stage strives to unify opposites in mind and experience. It generates and maintains vulnerability to the strange truths of those who are "other." Ready for closeness to that which is different and threatening to self and outlook (including new depths of experience in spirituality and religious revelation), this stage's commitment to justice is freed from the confines of tribe, class, religious community, or nation. And with the seriousness that can arise when life is more than half over, this stage is ready to spend and be spent for the cause of conserving and cultivating the possibility of others' generating identity and meaning.

The new strength of this stage comes in the rise of the ironic imagination (Lynch 1973)—a capacity to see and be in one's or one's group's most powerful meanings, while simultaneously recognizing that they are relative, partial, and inevitably distorting apprehensions of transcendent reality. Its danger lies in the direction of a paralyzing passivity or inaction, giving rise to complacency or cynical withdrawal, due to its paradoxical understanding of truth.

Stage 5 can appreciate symbols, myths, and rituals (its own and others') because it has been grasped, in some measure, by the depth of reality to which they refer. It also sees the divisions of the human family vividly because it has been apprehended by the possibility (and imperative) of an inclusive community of being. But this stage remains divided. It lives and acts between an untransformed world and a transforming vision and loyalties. In some few cases this division yields to the call of the radical actualization that we call Stage 6.

Stage 6: Universalizing Faith

As our structural-developmental theory of faith stages has emerged and undergone refinements, it has become clear that we are trying to do both descriptive and normative work. Our empirical studies have aimed at testing whether there is a predictable sequence of formally describable stages in the life of faith. The hypothesized stages with which we began, however, and the versions of them that have withstood empirical scrutiny exhibit an indisputably normative tendency. From the beginning of our work there has been a complex image of mature faith in relation to which we have sought for developmentally related prior or preparatory stages. It is this normative endpoint, the culminating image of mature faith in this theory, with which I want to work now. What *is* the normative shape of Stage 6 Universalizing Faith?

In the little book *Life-Maps* I described Stage 6 in the following way:

> In order to characterize Stage 6 we need to focus more sharply on the dialectical or paradoxical features of Stage 5 faith. Stage 5 can see injustice in sharply etched terms because it has been apprehended by an enlarged awareness of the demands of justice and their implications. It can recognize partial truths and their limitations because it has been apprehended by a more comprehensive vision of truth. It can appreciate and cherish symbols, myths, and rituals in new depth because it has been apprehended in some measure by the depth of reality to which the symbols refer and which they mediate. It sees the fractures and divisions of the human family with vivid pain because it has been apprehended by the possibility of an inclusive commonwealth of being. Stage 5 remains paradoxical or divided, however, because the self is caught between these universalizing apprehensions and the need to preserve its own being and well-being. Or because it is deeply invested in maintaining the ambiguous order of a socioeconomic system, the alternatives to which seem more unjust or destructive than it is. In this situation of paradox Stage 5 must act and not be paralyzed. But Stage 5 acts out of conflicting loyalties. Its readiness to spend and be spent finds limits in its loyalty to the present order, to its institutions, groups, and compromise procedures. Stage 5's perceptions of justice outreach its readiness to sacrifice the self and to risk the partial justice of the present order for the sake of a more inclusive justice and the realization of love.
>
> The transition to Stage 6 involves an overcoming of this paradox through a moral and ascetic actualization of the universalizing apprehensions. Heedless of the threats to self, to primary groups, and to the institutional arrangements of the present order that are involved, Stage 6 becomes a disciplined, activist *incarnation*—a making real and tangible—of the imperatives of absolute love and justice of which Stage 5 has partial apprehensions. The self at Stage 6 engages in spending and being spent for the transformation of present reality in the direction of a transcendent actuality.
>
> Persons best described by Stage 6 typically exhibit qualities that shake our usual criteria of normalcy. Their heedlessness to self-preservation and the vividness of their taste and feel for transcendent moral and religious actuality give their actions and words an extraordinary and often unpredictable quality. In their devotion to universalizing compassion they may offend our parochial perceptions of justice. In their penetration through the obsession with survival, security, and significance they threaten our measured standards of righteousness and goodness and prudence. Their enlarged visions of universal community disclose the partialness of our tribes and pseudo-species. And their leadership initiatives, often involving strategies of nonviolent suffering and ultimate respect for being, constitute affronts to our usual notions of relevance. It is little wonder

> that persons best described by Stage 6 so frequently become martyrs for the visions they incarnate. (1978, 87–89)

Before commenting on the passages I have just offered from *Life-Maps* let me share another effort to describe the shape of Stage 6, this time from a more recent writing. This will serve as our summary in advance:

> Stage 6 is exceedingly rare. The persons best described by it have generated faith compositions in which their felt sense of an ultimate environment is inclusive of all being. They have become incarnators and actualizers of the spirit of an inclusive and fulfilled human community.
>
> They are "contagious" in the sense that they create zones of liberation from the social, political, economic, and ideological shackles we place and endure on human futurity. Living with felt participation in a power that unifies and transforms the world, Universalizers are often experienced as subversive of the structures (including religious structures) by which we sustain our individual and corporate survival, security, and significance. Many persons in this stage die at the hands of those whom they hope to change. Universalizers are often more honored and revered after death than during their lives. The rare persons who may be described by this stage have a special grace that makes them seem more lucid, more simple, and yet somehow more fully human than the rest of us. Their community is universal in extent. Particularities are cherished because they are vessels of the universal, and thereby valuable apart from any utilitarian considerations. Life is both loved and held to loosely. Such persons are ready for fellowship with persons at any of the other stages and from any other faith tradition. (Fowler 1979, 13–14)

Even as I read these descriptions I am haunted—as I am sure you are—by memories of Jonestown, Guyana, and the Reverend Jim Jones. Also in my mind, images of the deeply angry, mystical eyes of the aged Ayatollah Khomeini look out across the frenzied, impassioned mobs he inspires with his mixture of chauvinistic nationalism and religious absolutism. The followers of both these men—and those of many other persons like them—would likely hear my descriptions of Stage 6 as depictions of their revered, and feared, leaders. To hear the qualities of Stage 6 in these ways, however, is to miss some extremely important qualifications and dimensions of Stage 6 faith. Fascinated with the charisma, the authority, and frequently the ruthlessness of such leaders, we must not fail to attend in the descriptions of Stage 6 to the criteria of inclusiveness of community, of radical commitment to justice and love, and of selfless passion for a transformed world, a world made over not in *their* images, but in accordance with an intentionality both divine and transcendent.

When asked whom I consider to be representatives of this Stage 6 outlook I refer to Gandhi, to Martin Luther King, Jr., in the last years of his life, and to Mother Teresa of Calcutta. I am also inclined to point to Dag Hammarskjöld,

Dietrich Bonhoeffer, Abraham Heschel, and Thomas Merton. There must be many others, not so well known to us, whose lives exhibit these qualities of Stage 6. To say that a person embodies the qualities of Stage 6 is not to say that he or she is perfect. Nor is it to imply that he or she is a "self-actualized person" or a "fully functioning human being"—though it seems that most of them are or were, if in somewhat different senses than Abraham Maslow or Carl Rogers intended their terms. Greatness of commitment and vision often coexists with great blind spots and limitations. Erik Erikson, writing his book on Gandhi, set out to illumine the religious and ethical power of Gandhi's doctrine of *satyagraha*, the reliance on non-violent strategies in the aggressive pursuit of the social truth that is justice. In the middle of the book Erikson had to stop. He found it necessary to write a stern and sad letter of reprimand to the Mahatma—dead those twenty-five years—pointing out the unfairness and the muted violence of Gandhi's treatment of his wife, Kasturba, and of his sons (1969, 229–54). (Gandhi, in forming his ashram, had insisted on bringing Untouchables into the household. Kasturba had accepted this without complaint. She found it too much, however, when Gandhi insisted that she take on the job of removing their toilet wastes from the house—something he himself was patently unwilling to do.) To be Stage 6 does not mean to be perfect, whether perfection be understood in a moral, psychological, or a leadership sense.

I do not believe that people set out to be Stage 6. That is not to say that some, who later come to fit that description, did not set out to be "saints." Thomas Merton, while still a student at Columbia University, came to be clear in his own mind that he wanted to become a saint. Students of his career, however, recognize that his growth toward what we are here calling Stage 6, took paths and required difficulties that were unforeseen in Merton's early visions of sainthood (1948, 233–34). It is my conviction that persons who come to embody Universalizing faith are drawn into those patterns of commitment and leadership by the providence of God and the exigencies of history. It is as though they are selected by the great Blacksmith of history, heated in the fires of turmoil and trouble, and then hammered into usable shape on the hard anvil of conflict and struggle.

The descriptions I have read to you of Stage 6 suggest another note of realism in our efforts to understand the normative endpoint of faith development in the Universalizing stage. Here I refer to what has been called the "subversive" impact of their visions and leadership. Even as they oppose the more blatantly unjust or unredeemed structures of the social, political, or religious world, these figures also call into question the compromise arrangements in our common life that have acquired the sanction of conventionalized understandings of justice. King's "Letter from Birmingham Jail" was written not to "Bull" Connor or the Ku Klux Klan, but to a group of moderate and liberal religious leaders who had pled with King to meliorate the pressure his followers were exerting through non-violent demonstrations on the city. King's assault on the more blatant features of a segregated city proved subversive to the genteel compromises by which persons of good will of both races had accommodated themselves in a racist society.

This subversive character of the impact of Stage 6 leadership often strikes us as arising from a kind of relevant irrelevance. Mother Teresa of Calcutta's ministry illustrates this powerfully (Muggeridge 1971). Mother Teresa, a foreign-born nun in her late thirties, head of a girls' boarding school, was going on retreat. As she traveled through the city she became overwhelmed by the sight of abandoned persons, lying in the streets, left to die. Some of these forgotten people were already having their not yet lifeless limbs gnawed by rodents. Under the impact of those grim sights she felt a call to a new form of vocation—a ministry of presence, service, and care to the abandoned, the forgotten, the hopeless. In a nation and a world where scarcity is a fact of life, where writers and policy makers urge strategies of "triage" to ensure that resources are not "wasted" on those who have no chance of recovery and useful contribution, what could be less relevant than carrying these dying persons into places of care, washing them, caring for their needs, feeding them when they are able to take nourishment, and affirming by word and deed that they are loved and valued people of God? But in a world that says people only have worth if they pull their own weight and contribute something of value, what could be *more* relevant?

In these persons of Universalizing faith these qualities of redemptive subversiveness and relevant irrelevance derive from visions they see and to which they have committed their total beings. These are not abstract visions, generated like utopias out of some capacity for transcendent imagination. Rather, they are visions born out of radical acts of identification with persons and circumstances where the futurity of being is being crushed, blocked, or exploited. A Martin Luther King, Jr., prepared by familial and church nurture, by college, seminary, and doctoral studies, influenced theologically and philosophically by Gandhi's teachings on non-violent resistance, gets drawn into acts of radical identification with the oppressed when Rosa Parks refuses any longer to let her personhood be ground underfoot. Gandhi, steeped by a Jain mother with the doctrine of *ahimsa* (the doctrine of non-injury to being), influenced by a tradition of public service in his father's family, prepared by legal study in Britain, is physically abused and removed from the first-class section of a South African train. Through this shock of recognition of his identification with the oppressed and despised minority of a colonized people he is drawn eventually into the leadership of a non-violent struggle for Indian independence. We have already spoken of the identification with the hopeless and abandoned dying street people that launched Mother Teresa's vision of a ministry where one meets Christ in the person of the forgotten ones.

In such situations of concrete oppression, difficulty, or evil, persons see clearly the forces that destroy life as it should be. In the direct experience of the negation of one's personhood or in one's identification with the negations experienced by others' visions are born of what life is *meant* to be. In such circumstances the promise of fulfillment, which is the birthright of each mother's child and the hope of each human community, cries out in affront at the persons and conditions that negate it. The visions that form and inform Universalizing faith arise out of and speak to such situations as these.

Stage 6 and the Jewish-Christian Image of the Kingdom of God

Since I began systematically to work on a theory of faith development it has been clear to me that my normative images of Stage 6 have been strongly influenced by H. Richard Niebuhr's descriptions of radical monotheistic faith (1960). As we saw in Part I of this book, in speaking of "radical monotheism" Niebuhr chose a category from anthropology and comparative religion. Originally it was intended to characterize the religions of the West—Judaism, Christianity and Islam—which lay stress on the oneness and the sovereignty of God. Niebuhr's use of the term in no way compromises the conviction of God's oneness or sovereignty. He does not, however, want to identify the term simply as a generic category by which to designate traditionally monotheistic religious groupings. Radical monotheism, for Niebuhr, means a faith relationship characterized by total trust in and loyalty to the principle of being. Radical monotheism, in Niebuhr's usage, describes a form of faith in which the reality of God—transcendent and ever exceeding our grasp—exerts transforming and redeeming tension on the structures of our common life and faith. In radical monotheistic faith the particular forms of religious and ethical life to which a people hold are seen as partial apprehensions of and responses to the true state of affairs, namely God-ruling, or the kingdom of God. In radical monotheistic faith all our beliefs, practices, and images of the divine-human relationship are seen as relative to the reality they try to apprehend. This is not to fall into an assertion of relativ*ism*—the assertion that all religious outlooks are relative to each other and to the circumstances, experiences, and interests of the communities who form around them. Rather, it is to call for a theory of relativ*ity* in faith in which forms of religious life are considered as relative representations or modes of response to that determinative center of power and value that is the sovereign reality with which we humans have to deal in life, whether we know it or acknowledge it or not.[6]

Radical monotheistic faith has powerful ethical correlates. With roots deep in the Jewish tradition, yet in a manner resonant with Eastern ideals of non-attachment, radical monotheism interrupts all attachments to centers of value and power that might be prized for ego or group-ego reasons. The sovereign God of radical monotheistic faith is an enemy to all idolatrous gods. This includes the gods of nation, self, tribe, family, institutions, success, money, sexuality, and so on. These partial gods are not *negated* in the judgment of a sovereign God, but they are relativized to the status of proximal goods. Any claims of ultimacy for them or by them must be avoided or relinquished. In radical monotheistic faith the commonwealth of being, unified in the reign of God as creator, ruler, and redeemer, is universal. This means that principles by which human beings divide themselves from each other—and from other species in the orders of creation—are not divisions that finally determine their relative worth and value. The sovereign God of radical monotheistic faith intends the fulfillment of creation and the unity of being. This is not a homogenous unity in which differences and particularities are molded into a monolithic oneness. Rather, the unity envisioned in the kingdom of God, as expected in radical monotheistic faith, is richly plural and highly variegated, a celebration of the diversity and complexity of creation. The hallmark of the kingdom of God is a quality of righteousness in which being is properly related to being, a righteousness in which each person or being is augmented by the realization of the futurity of all the others.

In developing the concept of radical monotheistic faith, Niebuhr understood himself to be bringing to expression the dominant thrust of biblical faith. He understood it as the central element in the covenant relationship between a liberated Israel and the God of the Exodus. He understood that the Torah was given and elaborated in order to give form to a righteous community, a community fit to be priests to other nations. He saw Jesus as steeped in the Jewish vision of a covenant relationship with God and in the Jewish hope of a coming reign of God that will redeem, restore, and fulfill God's creation in a kingdom of right-relatedness between God and humanity, between peoples, and between people and nature. Niebuhr saw Jesus as the pioneering embodiment of radical monotheistic faith, the "pioneer and perfector" of the faith to which we are called. He saw the resurrection of Jesus, in power and glory, as God's ratification of the truth for all people, of the proclaimed coming kingdom of God.

I suspect that by now many of you find yourselves forming objecting questions to what I have said. I suspect you are asking yourselves, "Does he think he can take a Jewish-Christian image of faith in the kingdom of God and generalize it to serve as the normative and descriptive endpoint of a supposedly formal and inclusive theory of faith development?" For some of you—Jews and Christians alike—there is undoubtedly some offense in my designating "radical monotheism," as developed here, as "Jewish-Christian." I am sure that the position, as I offer it here sounds more Christian than Jewish. I hear you asking, "What kind of religious and cultural imperialism are we being asked to buy?"

6. For a similar call for a theory of relativity in faith see Wilfred Cantwell Smith, *Faith and Belief* (Princeton, N.J.: Princeton University Press, 1979), 155–56, and esp. 208 n. 41.

These are legitimate objections. They point to serious issues we must face and deal with. In my previous published works on the faith development theory I have chosen to avoid them. In writing the present book, however, a book I hope will give adequate expression to the full range of findings and insights that this work has yielded, I find I cannot and do not wish to avoid the issues raised in this instance of trying to move from the particular to the universal.

The case I am trying to make is this: the fact that the image of the most developed faith that informs the normative and descriptive endpoint of the faith development theory derived initially from a theological formulation of the central thrust of *biblical* faith need not disqualify it as more generally or universally valid. Put another way, the fact that descriptions of Stage 6 seek to express in a formal and inclusive way the contours of radical monotheistic faith does not negate the possibility of its universal truth and usefulness.

To keep this from becoming something other than a solipsistic confession of my convictions or the arrogant assertion of a biblical apologist, I need to deal with three critically important kinds of claims. First, in a way that I believe potentially applies to the central thrusts of *any* of the lasting great religious traditions, I think we must learn again to take seriously what I will call the "absoluteness of the particular." Second, with regard to Jewish and Christian understandings of the kingdom of God, I will want to explore with you the significance of the claim that the kingdom of God is an *eschatological reality*—a reality that is coming to us from the future and that comes to us as the unifying power of the future (Pannenberg 1969, 72ff.). And third, I want to test with you how seriously we are prepared to take the category *revelation*—revelation when it is connected with the truth claims of our own religious traditions and revelation when it is claimed for truths of others' traditions.

The Absoluteness of the Particular

We all know something about "the scandal of the particular." The particular is the time-bound, the concrete, the local. The particular means *this* relatively undistinguished group, and not another. The particular has warts, and dust from the road; it has body odors and holes in its sandals. The scandal of particularity arises from the fact that over and over again disclosures of ultimate moment find expression to and among very finite, undistinguished, local, and particular peoples. Cryptic phrases and questions express our sense of the scandal of the particular: "How odd of God to choose the Jews." "Can any good thing come out of Nazareth?" Or more straight forwardly we ask, "Why Abraham, why Moses? Why Mary and Jesus? Why Gautama, why Confucius, why Muhammad?" These particulars are scandalous precisely because something of transcendent and universal moment comes to expression in them or through them.

Concern about particularity arises out of the collision of communities of faith, each of which—directly or indirectly—makes claims of universal truth and validity for their faith. With these implicit or explicit claims of universality there are usually clear assertions that the alleged universal truth is an exclusive possession of the community that has been formed around it. Religious wars, inquisitions, heresy trials, persecutions, pogroms, holocausts, and histories of prejudice and suspicion have been the results. Out of the blood and ashes of such struggles have come efforts by philosophers of religion to generate criteria, independent of any one tradition, by which the truth claims of each and all can be tested, evaluated, and generalized in relation to presumably more universal standards. The responses of many others go in the direction of the adoption—often in considerable disillusionment—of forms of secularist relativism, marked by varying degrees of tolerance, indifference, and cynicism toward religious faith. From this latter perspective the truth claims of religions are evaluated, if at all, on the basis of utilitarian criteria. Whatever truth a faith may have is seen, from this angle, as a matter of its pragmatic usefulness for particular individuals or groups.

Sometime ago Orbis Press published a fine collection of papers called *Christian Faith in a Religiously Plural World* (1978), edited by Donald G. Dawe and John B. Carman. In it the topic indicated by the title was addressed by Christians, a Buddhist, a Hindu, a Jew, and a Muslim. Dawe, in the keynote address, pointed out, with proper irony, that secularist solutions to the clash of religious truths neither overcome the divisions in the human family that prove so destructive, nor do they address the pervasive hunger for truth that characterizes our age. Let me quote Dawe:

> Modern secularity has offered another way of dealing with religious pluralism. As religious traditions lose their importance as means of self-understanding and community identification, their differences and mutual exclusiveness diminish in importance. Alienation from any particular religious faith tends to move the question of religious particularity into the realm of indifference, as life is determined by non-religious values and institutions. Yet secularity has been no more successful in establishing human community than has the religious vision. The competing claims of nationalism, economic imperialism, and ideological triumphalism are also demonic forms of particularity that have not been able to establish a new universality in human community. . . . So the fact remains that the religious question has to be dealt with in the religious perspective. The problem of Christian faith in a religiously plural world cannot be solved by ex-Christians learning to relate to ex-Jews, ex-Buddhists, ex-Muslims, or ex-anything else, in the name of conceptions that do not take these traditions seriously. (1978, 16–17)

For persons committed to and through religious faith to work together on questions of religious truth means to take with radical seriousness *the absoluteness of the particular*. Now let me say what I mean when I use this intentionally provocative term. Absoluteness means here "bearing the quality of ultimacy." Absoluteness in a tradition of religious faith is constituted by those moments in it in which the structure and character of the ultimate conditions of existence are disclosed. Absoluteness in a tradition of religious faith is a function of the faithful shape it gives to human life as a correlate of the revelation of divine character and intention that it has been given. Absoluteness is that quality of a tradition of a religious faith given to it by the instances in which the unconditioned has come to expression in it.[7]

Now let me make some crucial clarifications. The absoluteness that comes to expression in some moments of a religious tradition is not to be identified with the absolutes that adherents of that tradition may fashion about it. Put another way, absoluteness is a quality of the transcendent that comes to expression in revelation, but not necessarily of the symbols, myths, propositions, or doctrines formulated to represent or communicate it. Further—and this is the most important point—absoluteness, as a quality of the transcendent that comes to expression, is not *exclusivistic.*[8] Presumably, the absoluteness of the divine character can come to expression in different forms and in different contexts, with each of these instances bearing the full weight of ultimacy. All of this means—if it is correct—that the most precious thing we have to offer each other in interfaith encounters is our honest, unexaggerated, and nonpossessive sharing of what we take to be the moments of absoluteness in the particular faith traditions in which we live as committed participants.

The descriptions of Stage 6 Universalizing faith are offered for that kind of testing and refinement. I take those descriptions to be formal and generalized expressions of that radical monotheistic faith with which Jews and Christians respond, in trust and loyalty, to the present and coming reign of a God of sovereign universality. This I take to be a worthy offering in the faithful effort to which we all are called, to discern and respond to the absoluteness in the particular.

The Eschatological Character of the Kingdom of God

Radical monotheistic faith is faith oriented toward the coming kingdom of God. One of the reasons why the reality referred to by Christians and Jews with the political metaphor "kingdom of God" may claim absoluteness has to do with its being an *eschatological* reality. To take eschatology seriously is to see that present and past come to us out of the future. Out of the freedom of God came creation and possibility. Freedom and responsibility in our present

7. This language is indebted, of course, to Paul Tillich. See especially *The Protestant Era*, 2d ed. (abr.), trans. James Luther Adams (Chicago: University of Chicago Press, 1957), 32 n. 1, and 78.

8. In this crucial respect my position differs markedly from that of Ernst Troeltsch in *The Absoluteness of Christianity and the History of Religions*, trans. David Reid (Richmond: John Knox, 1971). See especially his chapter 4, "Christianity: Focal Point and Culmination of All Religious Developments." It is precisely the claim embodied in this title (which Troeltsch subsequently gave up) that I, in principle, do not want to make.

come to us out of the freedom of God's future for us and for all being. Receiving the present from God's future, we are freed over against the past. As the power of the future, God is the promise of a unified and unifying future for all being (Pannenberg 1969). In ways that surely transcend the specificity of Jewish and Christian images of the coming kingdom, God has disclosed the divine intention to redeem, restore, and fulfill all being.

Seen in the light of this vision the human vocation—and it must be understood as a universal human vocation—is to live in anticipation of the coming reign of God. The human vocation is to lean into God's promised future for us and for all being. It is to be part of the reconciling, redeeming, and restoring work that goes on wherever the kingdom of God is breaking in. It is to be part of the suffering rule of God, to oppose those structures of life that block and deny the future of persons and being in God. The human vocation in response to the coming kingdom of God is to live so as to honor—in others and in oneself—the futurity grounded in the promises of the faithful, sovereign God.

In light of their particular vision of the reality they call the coming kingdom of God and of the understanding of the human vocation that flows from it Christians and Jews have a witness to offer. First, we are called to live as pioneers of the coming kingdom of God, to give flesh and communal form to the anticipatory righteousness that is an advance colony of the kingdom. Second, without expecting or requiring that others become Christians or Jews, we are called to point to the futurity of God and to the coming kingdom as the universal, shared future of all being. Intrinsic to that witness is the assurance that the reality and character of the coming reign of God exceeds and spills over all our images, symbols, and beliefs about it. Equally intrinsic to that witness, however, is the conviction that through the symbols, metaphors, and beliefs with which we have tried to apprehend the disclosure of God's promised and powerful future, there comes to expression a calling to divine-human partnership that bears the weight of ultimate truth. Third, we bear *special* responsibility for testifying to the depths of the human capacity for distorting our apprehensions of and our efforts to respond to the coming kingdom. The reality of *sin* as personal, corporate, and cosmic in character comes clear to us from moments of disclosure in our histories of revelation. The reality of sin comes clear to us as well, when we reflect upon the intractability of our own and of our companions' capacities for self-righteousness and destructive hatred in dealing with each other.

The bearers of Stage 6 faith, whether they stand in the Jewish, Christian, or other traditions, embody in radical ways this leaning into the future of God for all being. I have noticed that whenever I speak on stages of faith and try to describe the structural features and style of each stage, it is always Stage 6 that people are most interested in. The more "secular" the audience, the greater the interest. I ask myself, "What is it about those people best described by

Stage 6 that enlivens our excitement and draws us out of our embeddedness in the present and the past? What is it about these persons that both condemns our obsessions with our own security and awakens our taste and sense for the promise of human futurity?" I believe that these persons kindle our imaginations in these ways because, in their generosity and authority, in their freedom and their costly love, they embody the promise and lure of our shared futurity. These persons embody costly openness to the power of the future. They actualize its promise, creating zones of liberation and sending shock waves to rattle the cages that we allow to constrict human futurity. Their trust in the power of that future and their trans-narcissistic love of human futurity account for their readiness to spend and be spent in making the kingdom actual.

For Reflection

1. How might the structure of the stages of faith be useful for a Christian educator within a congregational context?
2. What could be done to support and encourage movement from one stage to another?
3. Could two persons of different belief, say Christian and Muslim, be at the same faith stage? Explain.
4. Having studied the stages, where would you like to be yourself? Why?

References

Berryman, J. 1979. Being in parables with children. *Religious Education* 74, 3 (May–June): 271–85.

Bettelheim, B. 1977. *The uses of enchantment: The meaning and importance of fairy tales.* New York: Random House.

Cone, J. M. 1975. *The God of the oppressed.* New York: Seabury.

Crossan, J. D. 1973. *In parables: The challenge of the historical Jesus.* New York: Harper and Row.

Dawe, D. G., and J. B. Carman, eds. 1978. *Christian faith in a religiously plural world.* Maryknoll, N.Y.: Orbis.

Erikson, E. H. 1963. *Childhood and society.* New York: Norton.

Erikson, E. H. 1969. *Gandhi's truth.* New York: Norton.

Fowler, J. 1979. Perspectives on the family from the standpoint of faith development theory. *The Perkins Journal* 33, 1 (Fall): 13–14.

Fowler, J., and S. Keen. 1978. *Life-maps: Conversations on the journey of faith.* Waco: Word.

Helfaer, P. M. 1972. *The psychology of religious doubt.* Boston: Beacon.

Lowe, W. J. 1980. Evil and the unconscious. *Soundings* 63, 1 (Spring).

Lynch, W. F. 1973. *Images of faith.* Notre Dame, Ind.: Univ. of Notre Dame Press.

Merton, T. 1948. *The seven storey mountain*. New York: Harcourt, Brace.

Muggeridge, M. 1971. *Something beautiful for God*. New York: Ballantine.

Niebuhr, H. R. 1960. *Radical monotheism and Western culture*. New York: Harper and Row.

Pannenberg, W. 1969. *Theology and the kingdom of God*. Philadelphia: Westminster.

Parks, S. 1980. Faith development and imagination in the context of higher education. Th.D. diss, Harvard Divinity School.

Polanyi, M. 1966. *The tacit dimension*. Garden City, N.Y.: Doubleday.

Ricoeur, P. 1967. *The symbolism of evil*. Trans. E. Buchanan. Boston: Beacon.

———. 1978. The hermeneutics of symbols and philosophical reflection. In *The philosophy of Paul Ricoeur*, ed. C. E. Reagan and D. Stewart. Boston: Beacon.

Rizzuto, A. M. 1979. *The birth of the living God*. Chicago: Univ. of Chicago Press.

Sullivan, E. V. 1980. The scandalized child: Children, media, and community culture. In *Toward moral and religious maturity*. Morristown, N.J.: Silver Burdett.

Tillich, P. 1957. *The dynamics of faith*. New York: Harper and Row.

Vygotsky, L. S. 1962. *Thought and language*. Ed. and trans. E. Haufmann and G. Vahar. Cambridge, Mass.: M.I.T. Press.

24

Sharon Parks

Imagination: The Power of Adult Faith

(1986)

The work of Sharon Parks is an example of the conjunction of theory from developmental psychology, education, religion, and Christian education. The subtitle of her book, *The Critical Years,* is *The Young Adult Search for a Faith to Live By.* This has become a popular approach to thinking about faith development. The selection by James Fowler represents the current state of the art structurally; alongside of it this excerpt by Parks should be considered. While Donald Joy speaks of working "with the grain" or working with men and women as created by God and as fallen, Parks has presented a well thought-out conceptualization for this purpose, which she, then, applies to young adults in higher education.

Parks brought wide experience in ministry and education to the writing of this book. She was at Whitworth College for some time and, over an eighteen-year period, served as residence director, director of student activities, instructor, chaplain, teaching fellow, and professor. Afterward, when Parks attended Harvard for doctoral studies, her experience, as a "freshman" provided her with a renewed point of reflection on what she and others were going through in a university setting. At the time of the writing of *The Critical Years,* Parks was associate professor of developmental psychology and faith education at the Harvard Uni-

From *The Critical Years: The Young Adult Search for a Faith to Live By* (San Francisco: Harper and Row, 1986), 107–32.

versity Divinity School and a fellow of the Clinical Developmental Institute in Massachusetts.

Parks, like Fowler, approaches *faith* and *belief* in the manner of the study of these words by Wilfred Cantwell Smith. Faith is the noun and belief its verb form. Smith points out that the contemporary usage of these words neglects the Latin (lit., being, "I set my heart") Today belief means to give cognitive assent to propositions. To recover a more generic meaning of faith as "that upon which one sets his or her heart" is possible, primarily in the activity of making meaning of life through a dialogue with theories of imagination. Parks sees this as one of the major tasks of young adulthood.

This approach to faith means that whatever we depend on for the meaning of our existence functions as "God" for us. Obviously this includes the God known through the various expressions of Christianity. Professor Parks brings together the faith definition of Smith, the structural-developmental concept of faith, à la Fowler, and the content of faith-images, symbols, concepts, stories. Later in the book, she identifies Groome's *praxis* approach to Christian education as a primary "way to go." By her endorsement of Groome and her high view of community, Parks demonstrates her openness to conservative church and college approaches to faith nurture and to maturity enhancement. However, Parks warns authority-bound institutions that a faith divorced from life may well be rejected by young adults, especially in its "religious" form.

Some years ago, I began in the course of my studies to notice that various authors boldly declared what they perceived to be *the* unique characteristic of human beings. I began to record these declarations at random and, among them, accumulated the following:[1]

> The human is first of all a promise-making, promise-keeping, promise-breaking creature.
>
> —Martin Buber

> There is a primary need in people which other creatures probably do not have . . . This basic need is the *need of symbolization.*
>
> —Suzanne Langer

> The gorilla, the chimpanzee, the orang-outang, and their kind, must look upon humans as feeble and infirm animals, whose strange custom it is to store up their dead.
>
> —Miguel de Unamuno

1. As quoted by H. R. Niebuhr (1943, 41); Langer (1942, 40–41); Unamuno (1921/1954, 20); James (1958, 397).

> No fact in human nature is more characteristic than its willingness to live on a chance.
>
> —William James

On first reading, each of these statements appears distinctly different from the others; a closer reading suggests, however, that this is not the case. Rather, each one reflects what Philip Wheelwright describes as the experience of "threshold existence." Human beings live "always on the verge, always on the borderland of something more." Human beings bear a consciousness of something beyond the immediate. Human life finds itself forever on the thresholds of time, of space, and of the unseen—"reaching up to the gates of Heaven while one foot is slipping off the edge of the Abyss" (Wheelwright 1954, 8–16). In spite of the massive evidence of the mundane and the ugly in our experience, we human beings tenaciously harbor the conviction that we were "made for more." Something more was promised. There is more for us to live into, to embrace, or to be embraced by. We have a sense that we participate in something wider and deeper than we have yet realized—a more inclusive patterning of relation, a more profound ordering of justice, a richer loving of life in its manifold forms. We intuit a unity of the whole. Time, the world-as-it-is, the world of space and sense—all may be lived into and transcended. We human beings harbor a conviction of a "Beyond filled with Holiness" (Langer 1942, 40). Having the capacity to intuit the whole, we have the capacity for faith.

Young adulthood is, as we are beginning to see, the critical period for forming a conviction of threshold existence and a passion for the "ideal." But the strength of the formation of vision and commitment in young adulthood is contingent upon two factors. The first is the evolution of its undergirding structure: for example, the development of critical thought. The second, equally indispensable, is an ability to adequately recognize and name the ideal, the worthy, the good.

This second, crucial factor, the apprehension of the unseen potential of life, occurs only by means of metaphor. We can name the unseen and intuit the character of ultimate reality only by indirection. We can only say, "It is like . . ." The seen provides a vehicle for the unseen.

We know this on many levels of experience. For example, if we want to name tears (as in weeping) we need only point to them and agree upon a single sound that serves as a sign. If, however, we want to express sadness, we must point to a tear, meaning "sadness is like tears," or we may speak of a "heavy heart." Likewise, whatever we know of transcendent truth, we know by means of an image—an object or act of the sensible world—that gives form to our intuition of the character of ultimate reality. And so we speak of ultimate reality as like No Exit, or a father, or a mother, or Nothingness, or the Way, or a unified field, or the Holy One.

If, therefore, we recognize that the quality of faith utterly depends upon the adequacy of the images it employs and how those images are held, then we will see that the composing of faith is, in essence, an act of imagination conditioned, in part, by structural development.

Young adults share a similar way of composing meaning—a particular structure for seeking and holding images of faith—but this structure may hold various contents. Those who become young adults in faith have the capacity to think critically, to passionately search for the ideal, to be appropriately dependent upon a self-chosen authority outside the self, to fiercely affirm what is ambivalently held, and to pledge fidelity to a community that will hold and confirm the promise of the merging self and its vision of the world and ultimate reality. This structure, however, may hold the faith of a peace activist whose life is ordered by a commitment to the preservation of the planet, a marine whose life is ordered by allegiance to a nation, a newlywed homemaker whose life is ordered by the values of marriage and family, a medical student whose life is ordered by the desire to heal and by the priorities of the medical institution, a drug pusher whose life is ordered by financial survival, a junior executive in an advertising firm whose life is ordered by material success, or a computer entrepreneur whose life is ordered by the delight of intellectual and business puzzles and the desire to belong to the crowd in the fast lane of the career track. Each of these may represent the same structure of meaning, but each meaning structure holds a different content. Therefore, their forms of faith are similar in significant ways, yet distinctly different.

Constructive-developmental theory has tended to separate the issues of structure and content and to focus almost exclusively on the development of structures. Yet we can neither adequately understand the dynamics of young adult faith nor assess the relative worthiness of various faith choices if we do not attend to the matter of content as well. We must recognize that the function of structures is to hold life in meaningful patterns and that, as this chapter will attempt to make clear, life's patterns are given form, not only by the structures already described, but also by the images the structures hold.

The character of the structure and the quality of the content it holds are mutually interdependent in the activity of meaning-making. Piaget described the dynamic interdependence of structure and content as the process of assimilation and accommodation. Content—images, symbols, concepts, stories—gives form to our intuitions of life; but the power of the content is conditioned by the capacity of the structures that hold it (much the way a computer program conditions what the images of letters or numerals can or cannot do). Images (the content), in turn, have the power to modify structures, because, as Piaget described it, it is only when one encounters images that cannot be assimilated into the present structures that the structures must be transformed so as to more adequately accommodate the image or pattern of images. The character and quality of one's faith, therefore, are dependent upon both structure and content.

Recognition of the mutual interdependence of structure and content draws us inexorably beyond the fact of the formal structure of meaning-making (a fascination with stages per se) and more deeply into the process of meaning-making itself and the question of its correspondence to truth. It compels us to attend to both of the questions of epistemology: How do we know? and What can we know?

Therefore, once we recognize that everything of importance to us is inevitably and unavoidably shaped and determined by the meaning-making activity of faith, we are overwhelmed both by our need to know the character of ultimate reality and by our awareness of the finite nature of all knowledge. In other words, we must find meaning in order to act; we must orient our action to a center or centers of power, confidence, loyalty, and affection—to a fabric of trustworthy pattern. We must compose a "God." And yet we recognize simultaneously that even the most worthy composition of faith is, finally, partial and inadequate—that is, an idol—insofar as metaphor is a vehicle that can convey no more than a limited aspect of the real, and the structures, which determine how profoundly metaphors are held, also cannot match the complexity of reality.

Hence, we must realistically appraise the strength and the limits of the human activity of meaning-making; as we shall see, this is to say that we must understand and test the power of imagination.

Piaget and the Neglect of Imagination

Piaget was primarily interested in the formal properties of knowing. But, as we are beginning to see, if we are concerned with faith and therefore with image as well as with structure, an exclusively structural appropriation of Piaget's thought is inadequate. The concerns of faith development require attention to an element of Piaget's insight that Piagetians have "forgotten," and about which psychologists, educators, theologians, and others may be usefully reminded.

Earlier, in chapter 3, we noted that the Piagetian paradigm has manifested a number of "neglects"—namely affect, being, continuity, process, and the social dimension of experience. Kegan has addressed these by arguing that Piaget's insight into cognition partakes of a larger conception—meaning-making activity—and that this larger activity embraces all of these "neglects." However, there is another "neglect" that Kegan has not addressed. Piagetians and other developmentalists have attended to structure to the neglect of content.

Piagetians have forgotten that the power of developing structures, or "operations," of the mind is the power of their enhanced capacity to handle images—what Piaget termed representations.[2] This power of symbolization is the power of imagination. Piagetians have participated in the Enlightenment myth that one can shear structure (or method) from content, separate the subject who knows from the object that is known. Consequently, developmental theorists have separated development from imagination, neglecting to recognize the power of the latter. They have focused on seeking to understand the method or conditions of seeking truth. In so doing, they have neglected to give comparable attention to the adequacy of the "truth" itself. The power of process and method has been divorced from the power of content and name. Yet Piaget himself recognized that the significance of each new developing structure is precisely its greater capacity to hold and handle representations. Thus when we appropriate this paradigm to make linkages between the structure and the content of faith, we are again in continuity with Piaget's essential genius. His thought is, however, rooted in the thought of the Enlightenment and, as already suggested, reflects both the strengths and limits of that intellectual tradition. It is useful, therefore, to examine earlier understandings of imagination if we are to renew our understanding of the relationship of structure and content in the composing of faith.

Kant, Coleridge, and Imagination

We have already remarked that, at least since Kant, we have been aware that all of our knowing is a composing activity. The human mind does not receive the world as it is in itself; rather, we act upon it to compose it (or better, we interact with it in a mutual composing). In the era of the Enlightenment (1675–1830), it was almost as though Western philosophical-theological thought came to the same point in the epistemological pilgrimage as does the emerging young adult described earlier. Philosophical reflection articulated a renewed awareness of the powers and limits of its own knowing. Philosophers began anew to critique, to purify, and to restore their understanding of the power and processes of the knowing mind.

In Germany, Immanuel Kant (1724–1804) made distinctions between theoretical, speculative, and practical reason, thereby distinguishing the knowing of the sensible from the supersensible.[3] Only that which could be apprehended through the immediate senses could be "known." The apprehension of moral and religious claims was perceived as inaccessible to "knowing," but he perceived the postulation of religious categories as necessary to practical

2. Piaget (1968, 88–92); see also Loder (1981, 40–41, 128–29). Loder perceives his "transformational logic" as the pattern that governs the stage transition process, but does not seem to extend it to the activity between stages, or "the motion of life itself."

3. Kant (1788/1956, 3–19, 92–93). Pure reason, reason in its theoretical and speculative employment, cannot know matters of "eternal truth"—God, immortality, etc. Practical reason, reason in its practical employment, may only postulate (rather than know) freedom, immortality, self, world, and God, but must do so because one must determine the legitimacy of one's acts in the context of the phenomenal world in which actions have consequences.

or moral life. Philosophical and theological reflection became aware of and responsible for its own composing activity—particularly in the realm of the supersensible or the spiritual.

As a part of his critique of the powers of the mind, and central to our concerns here, Kant identified imagination as the active, creative, constructive power of the knowing mind. He recognized imagination as the power that acts upon the *sense* in a way that organizes perception, unifies, and creates the categories of interpretation, or "understanding"—at the same time that it is free from the laws of "understanding." Imagination for Kant, then, is the free composing activity of the mind, essential to all perception and to the power of the mind to hypothesize.[4] But as critical a role as Kant gave to imagination in the knowing of the sensible world, he did not allow imagination a central role in practical reason, the deducing of the supersensible world necessary to moral choice and action.

In England, Samuel Taylor Coleridge (1772–1834), influenced by the Enlightenment and specifically by Kant, also identified imagination as the composing activity of the mind. Coleridge was intrigued with Kant's word for imagination, *Einbildungskraft: Kraft* denoting power; *Bildung,* shaping; and *ein,* one. Imagination—the power of shaping into one.[5] However, Coleridge not only noted this meaning but, as we shall see, brought it to a level of significance that went beyond Kant. In so doing, he made visible the indivisible bond between imagination and faith—understanding both as shaping and unifying activities integral to being human and to discerning the character of "eternal truth" (or ultimate reality, as we have termed it).[6] Therefore, in order to understand the relationship of imagination and faith, we first direct our attention to the thought of Coleridge. (As William F. Lynch has noted in his own reflections on imagination, "new theorists are modest because they acknowledge that poets like Coleridge and Wordsworth anticipated them by far." [1973, 119])

Before proceeding further it is essential to distinguish imagination from mere fancy, fantasy, or the fanciful. *Fanciful* in its common usage connotes "the unreal." And, indeed, Coleridge identified fancy as having a function quite other than the act of composing reality. In his perception, fancy sim-

4. Lindsay (1934, 95, 275). Kant perceived that imagination can contemplate but cannot know the sublime. However, as the imagination strains to its utmost to know the sublime, the imagination has a sense of being unbounded. It thereby activates practical reason, which then deduces the nature of the sublime (247–51). Lindsay suggests that Kant did not extend the role of imagination because he never saw that freedom and necessity somehow had to be reconciled within reason itself (288).

5. Coleridge remarked in a notebook entry: "How excellently the German Einbildungskraft expresses this prime and loftiest faculty, the power of coadunation, the faculty that forms the many into one—in-eins-bildung!" Quoted in Hart (1968, 338).

6. For this particular interpretation of Coleridge's thought I am indebted to Linda L. Barnes.

ply takes the images already in the memory and arranges and rearranges them in an associative or aggregative manner.[7] Fancy, for example, can associate talking and mice and can compose a Mickey Mouse to reign over Fantasyland. This is not to say that fancy is necessarily trivial. The free association of fancy can play a role in the composing of more adequate truth, as demonstrated in psychoanalytic method. Fancy alone, however, cannot finally compose truth. By contrast, the task of the imagination, and particularly of the religious imagination, is to compose the real (Lynch 1973, 63).

Coleridge describes imagination itself as the highest power of Reason, which includes all of the powers of the mind. Coleridge's sense of Reason is like Kant's "practical reason" in that Reason can apprehend transcendent, moral truth. But, unlike Kant, Coleridge is persuaded that Reason "knows" eternal truth and does so by means of the imagination. "Reason is the power by which we become possessed of principle (eternal verities) and of ideas (N. B. not images) as the ideas of a point, circle, Justice, Holiness, Free Will in Morals" (Coleridge 1969, 1:177).

> Reason is the knowledge of the laws of the whole considered as one; and as such it is contradistinguished from the understanding, which concerns itself exclusively with the quantities, qualities, and relations of particulars in time and space . . . The reason . . . is the science of the universal, having the ideas of oneness and allness as its two elements or primary factors. (Coleridge 1972, 69)

Above all, writes Coleridge, Reason is the integral *spirit* of the regenerated person, reason substantiated and vital, "one only, yet manifold, overseeing all, and going through all understanding; the breath of the power of God."[8]

7. "FANCY on the contrary, has no other counters to play but with fixities and definites. The fancy is indeed no other than a mode of Memory emancipated from the order of time and space; while it is blended with, and modified by that empirical phenomenon of the will, which we express by the word CHOICE. But equally with the ordinary memory the Fancy must receive all its material ready made from the law of association." Coleridge (1907, 1:202).

8. Coleridge continues, "'and a pure influence from the glory of the Almighty; which remaining in itself regenerateth all other powers, and in all ages entering into Holy Souls maketh them friends of God and prophets' (Wisdom of Solomon, c. vii)." By "Sense" Coleridge denoted the imitative power, which is both voluntary and automatic. Coleridge (1907, 1:193). Sense is "Whatever is passive in our being, . . . all that the person is in common with animals, in kind at least . . . sensations, and impressions . . . recipient property of the soul, from the original constitution of which we perceive and imagine all things under the forms of space and time." (Language modified to be inclusive. The reader will find quotations from Coleridge to follow customs of his day in style of writing, to be preserved as far as present printing practices will allow.) Coleridge (1969, 1:177). "Understanding" he perceived (with Kant) as the "regulative, substantiating and realizing power" (Coleridge 1907, 1:193). Understanding is "the faculty of thinking and forming judgments on the notices furnished by the sense according to rules existing in itself which constitutes its true nature." (Coleridge 1969, 1:177).

The power within Reason by which the contradictions of understanding are transcended and the oneness of reason is accomplished is the imagination—"the completing power."

Thus, for Coleridge, Reason, which "dwells in us only as far as we dwell in it," and which constitutes the human relationship to the divine, is the highest and most complete power of any human mind; it is, if you will, the "animating essence" of the mind. And its completing, unifying, transcending activity is wrought by means of the imagination. Reason grasps the infinite, unseen ideal, and does so by means of the power of imagination. Since Reason is the regenerate Spirit in the human, imagination is also the activity of Spirit—"the breath of the power of God." For Coleridge, imagination—the power of shaping into one—is the power by which faith is composed.

A central insight of Enlightenment thought was the insistence that if human beings were to awake to the fulfillment of their own humanity, they must become aware of and responsible for their own humanity, they must become aware of and responsible for the power of imagination. Mature faith was perceived to depend upon an awakening to the nature, power, and limits of imagination. The human being is thus most true to his or her own nature when the powers of imagination are fully awake—alive to the presence of Spirit and to the power of the human person and community to compose (and to distort) self and world.[9]

We turn, therefore, to examine the process of imagination and its relationship to human development. After we have explored these dynamics we will consider the adequacy of the imagination to determine truth. Finally, we will consider the role of human community—specifically the academy—in shaping the imagination, and therefore the truth, of the young adult. To explore these dynamics is to examine further the "how" of human development and the underlying grammar of the formation of adult faith.

Imagination: Essentially Vital

Coleridge's most focused statement describing imagination is a brief, "packed" definition in his *Biographia Literaria:*

9. Northrop Frye (1947, 389–90) describes the maturing of the imagination when he writes: "To the individual visionary the upper limit of Beulah is the limit of orthodox vision, and as far as a church of any kind will take him [or her]. It is a state in which nature is seen as beatified, God as a father, man as a creature, and the essence of mental life as the subjection of reason to mystery. It is, or may be a state of genuine imagination, but, because still involved with nature and reason, with a Father God, and perhaps a Mother Church, it is imaginative infancy, the child's protected world. Many visionaries remain in this state indefinitely, but those who reach imaginative puberty become aware of an opposition of forces, and of the necessity of choosing between them. Ahead of them is the narrow gap into eternity, and to get through it they must run away from their protecting parents, like Jesus at twelve, and become adult creators themselves. They must drop the ideas of a divine sanction attached to nature, of an ultimate mystery in the Godhead, of an ultimate

> The IMAGINATION then, I consider either as primary, or secondary. The primary IMAGINATION I hold to be the living Power and prime Agent of all human Perception, and as a repetition in the finite mind of the eternal act of creation in the infinite I AM. The secondary Imagination I consider as an echo of the former, coexisting with the conscious will, yet still as identical with the primary in the *kind* of its agency, and differing only in *degree,* and in the *mode* of its operation. It dissolves, diffuses, dissipates, in order to re-create; or where this process is rendered impossible, yet still at all events it struggles to idealize and to unify. It is essentially *vital,* even as all objects (*as* objects) are essentially fixed and dead. (Coleridge 1907, 1:202)

For our purposes, there are five concepts in this definition that are important. First, imagination participates in all human perception as its "living Power and prime Agent." This is to say that all people imagine their world into being. It is not to say that the world somehow does not really exist and that the imagination conjures it up. Rather, we compose what we find.[10] The imagination orients one to choose and notice certain details over countless others. The imagination then informs the way in which one makes sense of the details, forming pattern out of disparate elements. In other words, it acts first as a kind of filter and then as a kind of lens. Consequently, the mind is never a mere onlooker—it composes its world. Everything that we sense or perceive is "created" by the power of the imagination. "To know is in its very essence a verb active" (Winnicott 1965, 246). Second, some of the activity of imagination is conscious (and this dimension we will discuss at some length). Third, the imagination is a power that "dissolves . . . to re-create" and "struggles to unify." Fourth, it is essentially vital; the imagination, as we shall see, is the motion of life itself, enlivening existence. And, therefore, fifth, as Coleridge saw, it participates "in the eternal act of creation." (It is one with the Spirit that in the biblical story of creation "hovered over the face of the waters" at the dawn of Creation—imagination is the activity of Spirit.)

Coleridge was a powerful thinker, but not a systematic one. Nowhere did he lay out a comprehensive statement of his reflection on imagination. Instead, he tucked his thoughts here and there into notebooks, elaborated upon them in poetry, and wove them into other writings as fleeting flashes of insight. In our own consideration of the imagination, therefore, we are assisted by others who reflections on imagination serve to order the thought of Coleridge.

I find particularly helpful the work of James Loder, an educator, clinical psychologist, and theologian. Loder describes a grammar of transformation

---

division between a human creature and a divine creator, and of recurrent imaginative habits as forming the structure, instead of the foundation, of the imaginative life. . . . Imaginative puberty may occur at any time, or never, in a person's life." (Language modified to be inclusive.)

10. Winnicott (1965, 181) has addressed this paradox by observing that the child composes that which the child finds. See also Rizzuto (1979).

or a paradigm of the process of creativity that identifies the critical elements of the process of imagination as these bear on human development. He has described what I term five "moments" within the act of imagination: (1) conscious conflict (held in rapport), (2) pause (or interlude for scanning), (3) image (or insight), (4) repatterning and release of energy, and (5) interpretation (Loder 1981, 31–35).

1. *Conscious conflict:* Whether or not we hold a theory of change and growth, we know from our own experience that new life, insight, and transformation often arise out of circumstances that are initially at least somewhat uncomfortable. The moment of "conscious conflict" occurs when one becomes aware that "something is not fitting." Conflict may be present in an unconscious or preconscious sense, but it does not become available for the recomposing of meaning and for the transformation of faith until it is brought to the conscious level. This may emerge as an increasing curiosity, a devastating shattering of assumptions, a vague restlessness, an intense weariness with things as they are, a body of broken expectations, an interpersonal conflict, or a discovery of intellectual dissonance. In this moment, equilibrium is thrown off balance. Individuals (and sometimes whole communities) from time to time experience some degree of such disequilibrium. Within the moment of disequilibrium lies a threefold task: the conflict must be felt, allowed, made conscious; the conflict must be clarified; the conflict must be suffered with the expectation of a solution.

The conflict is initially experienced as a "baffling struggle with irreconcilable factors" (Loder 1981, 32). Whatever the factors, they generally represent a tension between established meaning that is deeply rooted in both mind and heart—and new experience, which now stands in strong opposition over against established meaning. In this tension are embedded echoes of the yearnings described earlier, the simultaneous longings for preservation and transformation, for continuity and for new life, for communion and for distinctness: "the tendency at once to individuate and to connect, to detach, but so as to either retain or reproduce attachment" (Barfield 1971, 155). (Therefore, this is typically the moment of trying to figure out and to name "what's wrong," while at the same time feeling some resistance to "finding out.")

It is Coleridge's great conviction that this moment of opposition must serve to distinguish, but not to divide (Coleridge 1969, 1:cii). To distinguish is to clarify; to divide is to destroy the underlying and ultimate unity, which would preclude the activity of recomposing the whole that is the activity of imagination when vitalized by Spirit. Thus, for Coleridge, thought distinguishes but is essentially connective.

Philip Wheelwright sharpens the description of this moment with his discussion of the *"confrontive imagination"* (Wheelwright 1954, 79). The confrontive imagination particularizes; it makes things specific. The moment of conflict has not exercised its potential power as long as there is only a contradiction of vague generalities. One must enter into the particularity of the puzzlement, tugging unruly thoughts and feelings into view. In so doing, one faces an enlarged complexity and sometimes a deepened terror. This not only demands rigorous and disciplined care for thought, but may sometimes also require a measure of courage.

This is to say that, in the activity of faith, "the bombardment of forces" experienced in the disparate character of existence must be transformed from a welter of overwhelming blur into a perception of the particular nature of each element of power in the force field of life. This particularizing function, integral to the search for truth, accounts, in part, for the vitalizing, intensifying nature of imagination; for in the moment of conscious conflict "everything comes alive when contradictions accumulate" (Bachelard 1969, 39).[11]

This particularizing requires also the imaginative distancing of the *"stylistic imagination."* Wheelwright uses this term to identify the imaginative achievement of "right distance." Right distance is "not mere distance in space and time," but a "putting of the phenomenon, so to speak, out of gear with our practical, actual self" and thereby looking at it with a freshness of attention. This distance is "the primary factor of style, both in life and in art" (Wheelwright 1954, 82).

The perils of this moment of conscious conflict are two: overdistancing and overwhelming anxiety. Overdistancing, or a reified objectifying, breaks the connection with one's own field of receptivity, with affective grounding, and with Spirit. Overdistancing breaks the felt tension of conscious conflict by dividing the conflicted self from the rest of self at the cost of a broken spirit and the emptying out of all that is vital. Overdistancing has occurred when intellectual engagement with significant issues becomes mere academic swordplay, alienating the student from learning; overdistancing is manifested when domestic conflict shifts to domestic violence; and this same dynamic marks the erosion of political passion into a mere exercise of power.

The moment of conscious conflict that serves to recompose meaning and fulfill the promise of life is not one of brokenness in this sense; it is, rather, a distinguishing that fosters an enlivening restlessness (or even torment) suggesting new possibility—be it intriguing, irritating, painful, or awesome. The moment of conscious conflict is the location of much of the suffering dimension of faith, and the temptation to avoid this moment is understandable.

If either overdistancing within the conflict or an avoidance of the conflict altogether are to be averted, the conflict must be held in a "context of rapport" (Loder 1981, 53) lest the maintaining of the tension create an overwhelming anxiety. We must particularly note that when faith itself is being reordered, when meaning at the level of ultimacy is disordered and under review, a com-

11. See also R. R. Niebuhr (1972, xi–xiv).

munity of rapport is especially crucial. This notion is similar to Winnicott's concept of a "holding environment."[12] If disequilibrium is to be tolerated, there must be a sustaining "holding environment." Moreover, it must continue to hold over time, for once the conflict is conscious there is an inner momentum that drives toward resolution, seeking and waiting for its fulfillment. Momentum of this kind can only be ignored, thwarted, or submerged at the great cost of the betrayal and diminishment of the potential self and the consequent impoverishment of the human community. Yet here, once again we see that transformation is dependent upon the strength of the community itself, in this case, the capacity of the community to tolerate, sustain, and even nurture conscious conflict.

2. *Pause:* Once the nature of the conflict has been clarified, it is no longer fruitful to continue to focus intensely upon it. This is the time for the second moment in the composing process, the moment of *pause,* or incubation, an "interlude for scanning." One puts the conflict out of consciousness, but not out of mind. This moment is one, not of escape, but of relaxed concentration. In the moment of pause the conscious mind remains passive, or better, "permissive." Here, the mind is asleep, but "the soul keeps watch with no tension, calmed and active" (Bachelard 1969, xviii).[13] The activity beneath the surface may be likened to "an interlude for scanning" (Loder 1981, 32)[14] for integrative patterns—some of which may already be present, others of which may have yet to appear in experience. Coleridge described consciousness as "connected with master-currents below the surface" (Coleridge 1907, 1:167). In the moment of pause, the master-currents are at work.

Humankind has formalized modes of giving itself over to the deep master-currents of the soul, and a recognition of the essential and powerful nature of pause is embodied in all contemplative traditions. One finds it in Quaker silence and in yoga meditative practice, as well as in such contemporary for-

12. Winnicott (1965, 43–46) has used the term *holding environment* in his discussion of the mother and the infant. Kegan (1982, 115–16) has appropriated this concept to describe the necessary conditions of relation upon which human development depends in every developmental era.

13. Coleridge (1907, 1:85–86) described this moment of intellection by using the images of the waterbug and the snake—images incorporating pause as a factor of locomotion.

14. Here Loder draws on Harold Rugg, who described this moment as allowing the "transliminal mind to be at work. The true locus of the creative imagination is the border state that marks off the conscious from the nonconscious. This is the stage between conscious alert awareness, about which Dewey wrote for fifty years, and the deep nonconscious in which Freud was intensely absorbed. James was aware of it, calling it 'the fringe,' 'the waking trance.' Others spotted it long ago. Galton names it 'antechamber'; Varendonck, 'foreconscious'; Schelling, 'preconscious'; Freud, 'subconscious'; more recently Kubie, 'pre-conscious'; and Tauber and Green, 'pre-logical.' This is the Taoists' state of 'letting things happen,' where daydreaming and reveries go on, where Whitehead's prehension and Wild's intuition, as primal awareness, function; where we know before we know we know . . . the true creative center. . . .

"I think of it as 'off-conscious,' not unconscious, for the organism is awake, alert, and in control" (Rugg 1963, 39–40).

mulations as Transcendental Meditation. But "pause" also occurs in more mundane forms, which is to say that something really does happen to us while the bathtub is filling. An intuitive sense of this moment is reflected in such phrases as "Let me put it on the back burner for a while," or "I'll sleep on it."

The experience of "pause" is illustrated in a passage in which Virginia Woolf begins to account for how it was that when she was asked to speak about women and fiction, she came to speak about "a room of one's own:"

> Here then was I . . . sitting on the banks of a river a week or two ago in fine October weather, lost in thought . . . . Women and fiction, the need of coming to some conclusion on a subject that raises all sorts of prejudices and passions, bowed my head to the ground. . . . The river reflected whatever it chose of sky and bridge and burning tree, and when the undergraduate had oared his boat through the reflections they closed again, completely, as if he had never been. There one might have sat the clock round lost in thought. Thought—to call it by a prouder name than it deserved—had let its line down into the stream. It swayed, minute after minute, hither and thither among the reflections and the weeds, letting the water lift it and sink it, until—you know the little tug—the sudden conglomeration of an idea at the end of one's line: and then the cautious hauling of it in, and the careful laying of it out? Alas, laid on the grass how small, how insignificant this thought of mine looked; the sort of fish that a good fisherman puts back into the water so that it may grow fatter and be one day worth cooking and eating. I will not trouble you with that thought now, though if you look carefully you may find it for yourself in the course of what I am going to say.
>
> But however small it was, it had, nevertheless, the mysterious property of its kind—put back into the mind, it became at once very exciting, and important; and as it darted and sank, and flashed hither and thither, set up such a wash and tumult of ideas that it was impossible to sit still. (Woolf 1929, 5–6)

This "pause" after the recognition of the conflict may require only a few seconds, or many years. Its gift is a unifying image or insight—a gift that, no matter how intense the struggle that precedes it, always "takes awareness by surprise" (Loder 1981, 36).

3. *Image (or Insight):* The period of pause has completed its work when it gives rise to an image or insight capable of simplifying and unifying all that had seemed so unreconcilably disparate and complex. The image incorporates the conflict into a single unified whole, thereby repatterning it. This is the moment of insight, the moment of "ah-ha!" Hitherto unrelated frames of reference converge to create a wholly new outlook.

The image that works creatively simplifies and unifies the disarray of the conflict, "shaping it into one." The image is in itself merely an object or act of the sensible world; it becomes an "outward form that carries an inward sense" (Bushnell 1976, 20–21). When wishing to express a thought, emotion, or intuition that cannot be pointed at because it lies beyond the senses, we must use objects and acts of the sensible world as mediators. To convey our meaning, we point to an object or act of the sensible world, not as a one-to-one correspondence, but as metaphor. The image then loses its own "gross material quality," so to speak, and lends its form as a vehicle to convey inner life or spirit. For example, "the word *sincerity* is supposed to be the same as *sine,* without, and *cera,* wax; the practice of the Roman potters being to rub wax into the flaws of their unsound vessels when they sent them to market. A sincere (without-wax) vessel was the same as a sound vessel, one that had no distinguished flaw." To take another example, the word *spirit* originally meant "breath" or "air in motion," suggesting a power that moves unseen (Bushnell 1976, 24–25).[15]

Thus, as Bushnell saw, "the soul that is struggling to utter itself, flies to whatever signs and instruments it can find in the visible world, calling them in to act as interpreters, naming them at the same time, to stand, ever after, as interpreters in sound, when they are themselves out of sight" (Bushnell 1976, 23).[16] Objects and acts of the sensible world serve as forms for thought. "Thinking . . . is the handling of thoughts by their forms" (Bushnell 1976, 52).[17]

This awareness of image used as metaphor leads us to the important insight that every image that functions as a bearer of inner life is at once both "true" and "untrue." Since the image only gives *form* to the truth it attempts to convey, it can only represent that truth; it cannot fully reproduce or embody it. Consequently, the image is simultaneously both like and unlike the intuition or feeling it mediates. This occurs of necessity, if only in that the image gives form to what is without form. Thus, there is inevitably some distortion in every image, and, therefore, in every apprehension of truth. All images, as well as the words, concepts, and rituals that derive from them, are merely forms we employ for the handling of reality. Insofar as they convey some essential aspect of truth, they are faithful to that truth. Their deception—their untruth—lies, in part, in their tendency, as earthen vessels in which truth is borne, to offer "their mere pottery as being truth itself." When the earthen vessel is regarded as truth itself (rather than a participant in truth), we lapse into idolatry.

15. Bushnell extends this premise even to conjunctions: "So the conjunction *if,* is known to be the imperative mood of the verb *to give*, and is written in the Old English, *gif,* with the particle *that* after it. 'I will do this *gif that* (if) you will do the other'" (p. 27).

16. "The Latin word *gressus,* for example, is one that originally describes the measured tread of dignity, in distinction from the trudge of the clown, or footpad. Hence the word *congress* can never after, even at the distance of thousands of years, be applied to the meeting or coming together of outlaws, jockeys, or low persons of any description. It can only be used to denote assemblages of grave and elevated personages, such as councillors, ... ambassadors, potentates" (p. 51).

17. Note that *conception (con-capio)*, meaning "to take up with" or "to hold together," may be thought of as "form only." Concepts are "formal" modes of thought refined and abstracted from the "gross material" of image.

Such idolatry is further conditioned by the fact that when any image is appropriated to grasp, name, and give form to unseen reality, the image is always peculiar to the individual or group who selects it. The image carries particular associations—social, political, and psychological. The same image, therefore, may bear quite another meaning (or no meaning) for another person, or for a different group.

This awareness of the strengths and limits of images, and of the words that derive from them, enables Bushnell (perhaps overstating the point) to assert that there are few creeds one could not affirm if one were to return to the standpoint of those who made the creed and were to receive it in its "most interior and real meaning." Conversely, he also notes that, given the fluctuations of language and its ongoing "peculiar" appropriation of images, over time "we cannot see the same truths in the same forms. It may even become necessary to change the forms to hold us in the same truths" (Bushnell 1976, 81–82, 80).

Whether as mathematicians, physicists, sociologists, philosophers, theologians, or historians, human beings give form to their meaning with images. When the image becomes so complex as to serve as a key to a whole pattern of relationships, the image becomes a symbol. Meaning is constituted by a pattern of connections, unified and expressed by symbols. Because the task of faith is to shape into one the whole force field of life, when an image functions to give form to meaning at the level of faith, it necessarily engages a degree of complexity only held by symbol. Its form may be that of concept (i.e., God), event (i.e., Passover), person (i.e., Muhammad), or thing (i.e., bread and wine); its function is to grasp and to shape into one a conviction of fitting reality.[18]

As noted earlier, Langer asserts that the distinctive activity of the human being is this act of symbolization. She writes:

> I believe there is a primary need in human beings which other creatures probably do not have, and which accentuates all . . . apparently unzoological aims, . . . wistful fancies, . . . consciousness of value, . . . utterly impractical enthusiasms, and . . . awareness of a "Beyond" filled with holiness . . .
>
> This basic need, which certainly is obvious in any person is the need of *symbolization*. (1942, 40–41)[19]

18. See Kaufman (1981), esp. chaps. 1, 10; and McFague (1982).

19. Langer uses *symbolization* to connote all the activity of the imagination, at the level of sense and understanding. "Symbolization is pre-rationative, but not pre-rational. It is the starting point of all intellection in the human sense, and is more general than thinking, fancying, or taking action. For the brain is not merely a great transmitter, a super switchboard; it is better likened to a great transformer. The current of experience that passes through it undergoes a change of character, not through the agency of sense by which the perception entered, but by virtue of a primary use which is made of it immediately: it is sucked into the stream of symbols which con-

For example, every nonutilitarian act of humankind—including the "chattering" speech-play of small children that occurs apart from the need for communication, as well as ritual, art, laughter, weeping, love, talk, superstition, dreaming, and scientific genius—is the transformation of experiential data into symbolic forms. Such symbolic transformation has no purpose in the sensible world apart from the human need for "meaning," which transcends, permeates, and shapes into one the whole of being (Langer 1942, chap. 2).

Thus, we may now be prepared to recognize that religion, at its best, is a distillation of images (symbols) powerful enough to shape into one the chaos of existence—powerful enough to name a community's conviction of the character of ultimate reality. "Religion . . . is a metaphysical poem tied to faith."[20] The great religions of the world have survived only because countless people have been able to confirm that, "Yes, life is like that."

The moment of image/insight in the process of imagination is, in religious experience, the moment of revelation. Revelation is that part of the inner experience of a people that "illuminates the rest of it" (Niebuhr 1952, 93). Revelation is the event that provides an integrative, unifying image of meaning. H. Richard Niebuhr writes:

> By revelation in our history . . . we mean that special occasion which provides us with an image by means of which all the occasions of personal and common life become intelligible. What concerns us at this point is not the fact that the revelatory moment shines by its own light and is intelligible in itself but rather that it illuminates other events and enables us to understand them. Whatever else revelation means it does mean an event in our history which brings rationality and wholeness into the confused joys and sorrows of personal existence and allows us to discern order in the brawl of communal histories.

Niebuhr likens such revelatory images to a luminous sentence in a difficult book, "from which we can go forward and backward and so attain some understanding of the whole." This is to suggest that the new image or insight enables us to do and to see the whole of life in ways that previously eluded us. Occasions of just such revelatory insight are the motivating purpose of all truly liberal education, and it is this moment in which the purposes of education and the journey of faith are most inextricably linked. As Niebuhr expressed

---

stitutes a human mind" (42). It is Coleridge who reserves symbols for the grasping of complex pattern, as when he writes that imagination is "that reconciling and mediatory power, which incorporating the reason in images of the sense and organizing (as it were) the flux of the sense by the permanence and self-circling energies of reason, gives birth to a system of symbols" (Coleridge 1972, 26). It is this sense that Langer echoes when she identifies symbols as having to do with a relationship. "Meaning is not quality, but a *function* of a term. A function is a *pattern* viewed with reference to one special term around which it centers; this pattern emerges when we look at the given term *in its total relation to the other terms about it*. The total may be quite complicated" (55).

20. Quoted in Chadwick (1975, 209). See also Cox (1984), chap 17.

it, "When we speak of revelation we mean that moment when we are given a new faith." This is what Whitehead understood when he wrote that finally the essence of education is religious (Whitehead 1929, 25).[21]

That one is now able to engage the whole of reality in a new way points us toward the next moment in the process of imagination: the repatterning and the release of energy made possible by the new image.

4. *Repatterning and Release of Energy: Repatterning* is the term I use to name the moment that Loder refers to as release of energy or release of tension and reconstruction of phenomena. "This is a felt decathexis of the conflict that makes new energy available for reorganization of the personality and its 'world' relative to the insight gained. New energy is available because the mind has found an easier way to assemble all the aspects of the conflict" (Loder 1981, 55). At the level of faith, the recomposing of the whole, this moment must include what in educational contexts is described as teaching for transference. This is to say that, in light of the new insight, the whole of one's knowing and being is reordered. There is a re-visioning of the connections between things—from the point of insight there is a "going back and forth" so as to order a new pattern, a new seeing of the whole; whether the transformations be dramatic or subtle, the reordering of the particular is, in actuality, a repatterning of the whole.

Such repatterning may be recognized in everyday experience. It happens, for example, when one notices that something one has known for a long time in one arena of life also pertains to another aspect of one's world. This is the continual making of connections, the recognition and deepening of associations. One of the consequences of the release of tension and energy is a feeling of enlargement, a new quality of openness to self and world. Releasing one from the tension of the conflict, it also frees one for a measure of fresh awareness and engagement. "We might say consciousness is expanded by, and to the measure of, the resolution" (Loder 1981, 33). The surest sign of healing insight is this release of tension and new openness. Repatterning makes possible a "freshness of sensation" that is a "seeing with new eyes as on the morning of the first day of creation."[22]

Obviously, therefore, this moment also contributes to the vitalizing power of imagination. New vision combines with new energy; together they compose and exhilarate the soul so as to affectively ground a sense of confidence, assurance, and new power. There is a sense of more adequate access to reality. Imagination is, therefore, the power of realization: to image is to realize. And as imagination is the activity of faith, the task of faith is to imagine the real

21. He continues, "A religious education is an education which inculcates duty and reverence" (26).

22. This phrase is from a lecture by R. R. Niebuhr and is, I think, perhaps a paraphrase from Coleridge (to whom it was attributed): "with feelings as fresh as if all had then sprang forth at the first creative fiat" (1907, 1:59).

(Lynch 1973, 63; Unamuno 1921/1954, 192–93). Faith is, indeed, something quite other than wishful thinking or mere assent to irrelevant dogma. But if the image which gives form to faith is to serve its vocation to truth, the image, no matter how compelling it may appear, must be tested before the act of imagination is complete. The testing of this new reality and the power of its energy is the next moment, and the completion, of the act of imagination.

5. *Interpretation:* The transformation of knowing and trusting is not complete until it has found public form. This moment brings "insight" to a public test of its validity (Loder 1981, 56).[23] This effort to interpret the revelatory insight to an interested public functions in two ways: First, we do not seem to grasp the new insight fully, and we are not at ease with it, until it has been confirmed by others. In other words, we are dependent upon a community of confirmation for the completion and anchoring of our knowing. We feel this to be necessary because we feel a need for assurance of correspondence, coherence, and connection between the original conflict, the new image, and a concerned or interested public. Hence, we test our knowledge with the knowledge of others. This test is crucial in a second respect as well.

Having examined this process of imagination as the process by which we formulate our knowledge and our trust, we cannot help but recognize both how strong and powerful a process it is and how seemingly precarious. That so much depends on the search for fitting and right images, and that images are so conditioned by context, should give us pause. Northrop Frye has said that the use of metaphor can seem "like crossing a deep gorge on a rope bridge: we may put all our trust in its ability to get us across, but there will be moments when we wish we hadn't" (Frye, 591).

We most wish we did not have to when haunted by the question, How is the knower to be saved from the distortions of subjectivity in his or her quest for a truthful faith? Sometimes even the most compelling images are, nevertheless, seriously distorting, unfitting images that lead away from truth. Images may be held with deep feeling, but "depth" is no guarantor of truth.[24] If we compose our knowing by means of the imagination, how do we account for, and how are we saved from, what H. Richard Niebuhr calls the "evil imaginations of the heart" (Nicbuhr 1952, 95–109)? Is it not the case that though we have been following Coleridge's perception of imagination as the act of Reason—the divine in the human—imagination, nevertheless, persists in com-

23. Note that the sequence of moments as presented here does not presume that the process always begins with conscious conflict. It may begin, for example, with an "image" or an "interpretation," but once the process is entered it drives toward completion.

24. Loder also alerts us to the "seduction of the depths," indicating that "depths" are as "capable of error and distortion, seduction, and corruption as are the routinized patterns of behavior that others use to keep them from ever exploring matters of depth. The creative process surely *has* a depth dimension but is is not validated thereby." (Unpublished draft ms).

mon usage as a "slippery term designating a power that penetrates the inner meaning of reality but also a power that creates substitutes for reality" (Sparks 1976, 4)?

Indeed, Coleridge also recognized the possibility of an evil imagination. He understood the evil imagination to be the isolated imagination, divided from the unity of the "One Life" and therefore cut off from its Source (Barfield 1971, 155).[25] This is to suggest that when the imagination of an individual, a community, or a nation becomes isolated, whether as a result of arrogance or oppression, such isolated imagination becomes vulnerable to the distorting features of its own metaphors.

All images must be brought to the test of "repeated, critical, and common experience" (Niebuhr 1952, 96). The interpretive moment is essential, not only as the completion of an inner process, but as a participation in the forum of common experience that alone can confirm or refute the capacity of the image to grasp the real. For which "gods [images of defining and unifying power] are dependable, which of them can be counted on day after day and which are idols—products of erroneous imagination—cannot be known save through the experiences of . . . history" (Niebuhr 1952, 80). This is to say that the human community must serve not only as a community of confirmation but also as a community of contradiction. Emancipation from "narrow faith" and from distorting subjectivity may occur only in a community that distinguishes between evil images—those that separate and diminish selves and communities—and life-giving, truthful, vital images.

However, we must not give a too-facile endorsement of the power of finite communities to serve the search for truth. It must be acknowledged that even a rudimentary acquaintance with the history of faith communities abounds with examples of the abuse of the process in which "spirits" and "images" are discerned. Too often, inadequate images are greeted with acclaim, whereas the true prophet is rarely popular. Therefore, the community of confirmation must be defined finally in terms of the historical experience (past and future) of the whole human community.

Having recognized that all images are finite and now acknowledging that the process of imagination itself is fragile and vulnerable to distortion, one may ask if one can have confidence at all in any meaning, truth, or faith so composed. An awareness of the imagination process could lead us into the

25. Barfield suggests that this detachment, when it occurs in a self-conscious will, is the nature of "apostasy" or "original sin." In the following passage, Coleridge elaborates the same: "The ground work, therefore, of all true philosophy is the full apprehension of the difference between the comtemplation of reason, namely that intuition of things which arises when we possess ourselves, as one with the whole, which is substantial knowledge, and that which presents itself when transferring reality to the negations of reality, to the ever-varying framework of the uniform life, we think of ourselves as separated beings, and place nature in antithesis to mind, as object to subject, thing to thought, death to life." Coleridge (1969, 1:520).

cul-de-sac of unqualified relativism. Yet as Niebuhr states so clearly, "the heart must reason," and "the participating self cannot escape the necessity of looking for pattern and meaning in its life and relations. It cannot make a choice between reason and imagination but only between reasoning on the basis of adequate images and thinking with the aid of evil imaginations." Thus "anyone who affirms the irrationality of the moral and religious life simply abandons the effort to discipline this life, to find right images by means of which to understand oneself, one's sorrows and joys" (Niebuhr 1952, 107).[26]

Mary Moschella, while a graduate student in religion, gave a baccalaureate address, the following excerpts from which illustrate something of the dynamics of imagination as the power of shaping into one—the power of adult faith:

> Many of us might admit that we . . . were drawn to this place by the modest desire to learn to see everything clearly. Though it sounds presumptuous, we who have spent two or more years here, dissecting holy Scriptures, comparing world religions, constructing and deconstructing the concept of God, cannot pretend any lack of ambition. We did not come here to satisfy cool academic curiosities, but rather to learn how to see everything—the whole picture of life—clearly. We came to explore the very mysteries of God, to expand our view of the world, and to discern what it is that the universe demands of us.
>
> After being here for a while, we have discovered that the process of learning to see religiously is a difficult, if not overwhelming, endeavor. For in delving into questions of ultimate meaning, we have learned how blurred is our vision, how tentative and partial our . . . insight. In this, we are like the blind man from Bethsaida, who even with a miracle, could only slowly and gradually learn how to see . . . .
>
> Our studies and our common life have bombarded us with more . . . than we know how to manage. For our study . . . has caused us to examine our own faith and values: To decide what it is that we treasure . . . and what is essential to human be-ing.
>
> Thus we have been involved in the process of naming our Gods. This process has demanded not only that we clarify issues of personal faith and belief, but also that we regard anew some of the global issues of human struggle. It is not that horrors such as world hunger have just recently come into being. But somehow before we hadn't quite seen (or faced) the magnitude of suffering involved, or the ethical challenges that such suffering presents.
>
> So in the process of naming the Gods, we have been naming some demons too. We have seen and named the terrifying demons of militarism, racism, and sexism in our world. These appear to us as horrifying patches of darkness, frightening shadows that make us want to shut our eyes tightly and return to the comforts of our former blindness . . .

26. (Language modified to be inclusive.) For further discussion of the dynamics of revelation and the quest for the moral life see Dykstra (1981), esp. chap. 3.

Last summer I was in Israel, working on an archaeological dig. At the site of the ancient city of Dor, each day as I swung my pick into the age-old soil, I was inwardly chipping away at just these sorts of issues. I expended a good deal of energy cursing the facts of human suffering in the world, and trying to imagine some kind of hope of restoration.

Excavating at the level of the Iron Age can be rather tedious; only rarely did we turn up any precious small finds. Most of the time was spent staring at dirt walls and broken pottery shards. In my square, not even one whole vessel was uncovered all season—just so many broken pieces, scraps of ancient civilization. All of the brokenness appeared to me as an accurate metaphor for understanding the world. Broken and crushed, every piece of it; broken with small personal pains, as well as with overwhelmingly large human struggles. Yet as the summer went on, and I kept staring at the pottery, I slowly started to notice something more than just the brokenness. Some of the pieces of clay, however broken, were really quite beautiful.

Later in the summer, I found out about the business of pottery mending. This tedious work goes on year-round in a cathedral-like building not far from the tel. Here ancient vessels have been slowly and carefully reconstructed. I remember being completely amazed at seeing those huge restored jugs for the first time. How could anyone have possibly managed to piece together so many small nondescript chips of clay?

Seeing those restored vessels encouraged me to imagine perhaps that at least some of the world's brokenness could be overcome. I began to picture myself in a kind of vocation of mending, of repairing some of the world's brokenness.

To mend the world. To proclaim a radical vision of social transformation that would prevent future brokenness from occurring. These are the tasks that I perceived the world to be demanding of me. (1983)

Robert Lifton has written that "human existence itself can be understood as a quest for vitalizing images" (1979, 39). Not only to the study of religion, but to every discipline, academic department, and professional school, the young adult comes seeking vitalizing, fitting, and "right images" by which to name self, world, and "God." The young adult has a unique capacity to receive images that can form the vision and fire the passion of a generation to heal and transform a world. It is the vocation of higher education to inform and nurture the young adult imagination—the power of adult faith.

For Reflection

1. How can imagination lead to "truth" in any substantial way?
2. Where might "conversion" and "the Bible" fit in Parks's notion?
3. Do you envision higher education being the only place young adults might grow spiritually? If not, what other?
4. Give an example for Parks of avoiding unqualified relativism.

References

Bachelard, G. 1969. *The poetics of space*. Trans. M. Jolas. Boston: Beacon.

Barfield, O. 1971. *What Coleridge thought*. Middleton, Conn.: Wesleyan Univ. Press.

Bushnell, H. 1976. "Dissertation on language." In *God in Christ*. Hartford, Conn.: Brown and Parsons.

Chadwick, O. 1975. *The secularization of the European mind in the nineteenth century*. New York: Cambridge Univ. Press.

Coleridge, S. T. 1907. *Biographia Literaria*. Ed. J. Shawcross. Oxford: Oxford Univ. Press.

———. 1969. *The friend*. Ed. B. Rooke. 2 vols. Princeton, N.J.: Princeton Univ. Press.

———. 1972. "The statesman's manual." In *Lay Sermons,* ed. R. White, vol. 6 of *The collected works*. Ed. K. Coburn. Princeton, N. J.: Princeton Univ. Press.

Cox, H. 1984. *Religion in the secular city: Toward a postmodern theology*. New York: Simon and Schuster.

Dykstra, C. 1981. *Vision and character: A Christian educator's alternative to Kohlberg*. New York: Paulist.

Frye, N. 1947. *Fearful symmetry: A study of William Blake*. Princeton, N.J.: Princeton Univ. Press.

———. "The expanding world of metaphor." *Journal of the American Academy of Religion* 53, 4.

Hart, R. L. 1968. *Unfinished man and the imagination: Toward an ontology of rules and rhetoric*. New York: Herder and Herder.

James, W. 1958. *The varieties of religious experience: A study in human nature*. New York: New American Library, Mentor.

Kant, I. 1788/1956. *Critique of practical reason*. Trans. L. Beck. Indianapolis: Bobbs-Merrill.

Kaufman, G. 1981. *The theological imagination: Constructing the concept of God*. Philadelphia: Westminster.

Kegan, R. 1982. *The evolving self: Problem and process in human development*. Cambridge: Harvard Univ. Press.

Langer, S. K. 1942. *Philosophy in a new key: A study in the symbolism of reason, rite, and art*. Cambridge: Harvard Univ. Press.

Lifton, R. J. 1979. *The broken connection: On death and the continuity of life*. New York: Simon and Schuster.

Lindsay, A. D. 1934. *Kant*. London: Ernest Benn.

Loder, J. E. 1981. *The transforming moment: Understanding convictional experiences*. San Francisco: Harper and Row.

Lynch, W. F. 1973. *Images of faith: An exploration of the ironic imagination*. Notre Dame, Ind.: Univ. of Notre Dame Press.

McFague, S. 1982. *Metaphorical theology: Models of God in religious language.* Philadelphia: Fortress.

Moschella, M. 1983. Baccalaureate address. Howard Divinity School. June 8.

Niebuhr, H. R. 1943. *Radical monotheism and western culture.* London: Faber and Faber.

———. 1952. *The meaning of revelation.* New York: Macmillan.

Niebuhr, R. R. 1972. *Experiential religion.* New York: Harper and Row.

Piaget, J. 1968. *Six psychological studies.* Ed. D. Elkind. New York: Vintage.

Rizzuto, A-M. 1979. *The birth of the living God: A psychoanalytic study.* Chicago: Univ. of Chicago Press.

Rugg, H. 1963. *Imagination.* New York: Harper and Row.

Sparks, P. M. 1976. *The female imagination.* New York: Avon.

Unamuno, M. de. 1921/1954. *Tragic sense of life.* Trans. J. E. Crawford Flitch. New York: Dover.

Wheelwright, P. 1954. *The burning fountain.* Bloomington, Ind.: Indiana Univ. Press.

Whitehead, A. N. 1929. *The aims of education and other essays.* New York: Free Press.

Winnecott, D. W. 1965. *The maturational processes and the facilitating environment.* New York: International Univ. Press.

Woolf, V. 1929. *A room of one's own.* New York: Harcourt Brace.

Bibliography

Bruner, J. 1968. *Process of cognitive growth: Infancy*. Worcester, Mass.: Clark Univ. Press.

———. 1973. *Beyond the information given: Studies in the psychology of knowing*. New York: Norton.

———. 1985. *Child's talk: Learning to use language*. New York: Norton.

———. 1987. *Actual minds, possible words*. Cambridge: Harvard Univ. Press.

———. and Haste, H., eds. 1988. *Making sense*. New York: Routledge Chapman and Hall.

Coe, G. A. *The psychology of religion*. 1916. Reprint. New York: AMS Press.

———. *The motives of men*. 1928. Reprint. New York: AMS Press.

———. 1969. *Social theory of religious education*. Salem, N.H.: Ayers. (Original work published 1917.)

Dewey, J. 1933. *How we think: A restatement of the relation of reflective thinking to the educative process*. Lexington, Mass.: Heath.

———. 1956. *Child and the curriculum and the school and society*. Chicago: Univ. of Chicago Press.

———. 1963. *Experience and education*. New York: Macmillan.

———. 1966. *Democracy and education: An introduction to the philosophy of education*. New York: Free Press.

———. 1980. *The school and society*. Carbondale, Ill.: Southern Illinois Univ. Press.

Dobbins, G. S. 1960. *Ministering church*. Nashville: Broadman.

———. 1968. *Learning to lead*. Nashville: Broadman.

Edge, F. B. 1956. *Teaching for results*. Nashville: Broadman.

———. 1959. *Helping the teacher*. Nashville: Broadman.

Erikson, E. H. 1963. *Childhood and society*. 2d ed. New York: Norton.

———. 1968. *Identity: Youth and crisis*. New York: Norton.

———. 1979. *Dimensions of a new identity*. New York: Norton.

———. 1980. *Identity and the life cycle*. New York: Norton.

Freire, P. 1970. *Cultural action for freedom*. Cambridge, Mass.: Harvard Educational Review.

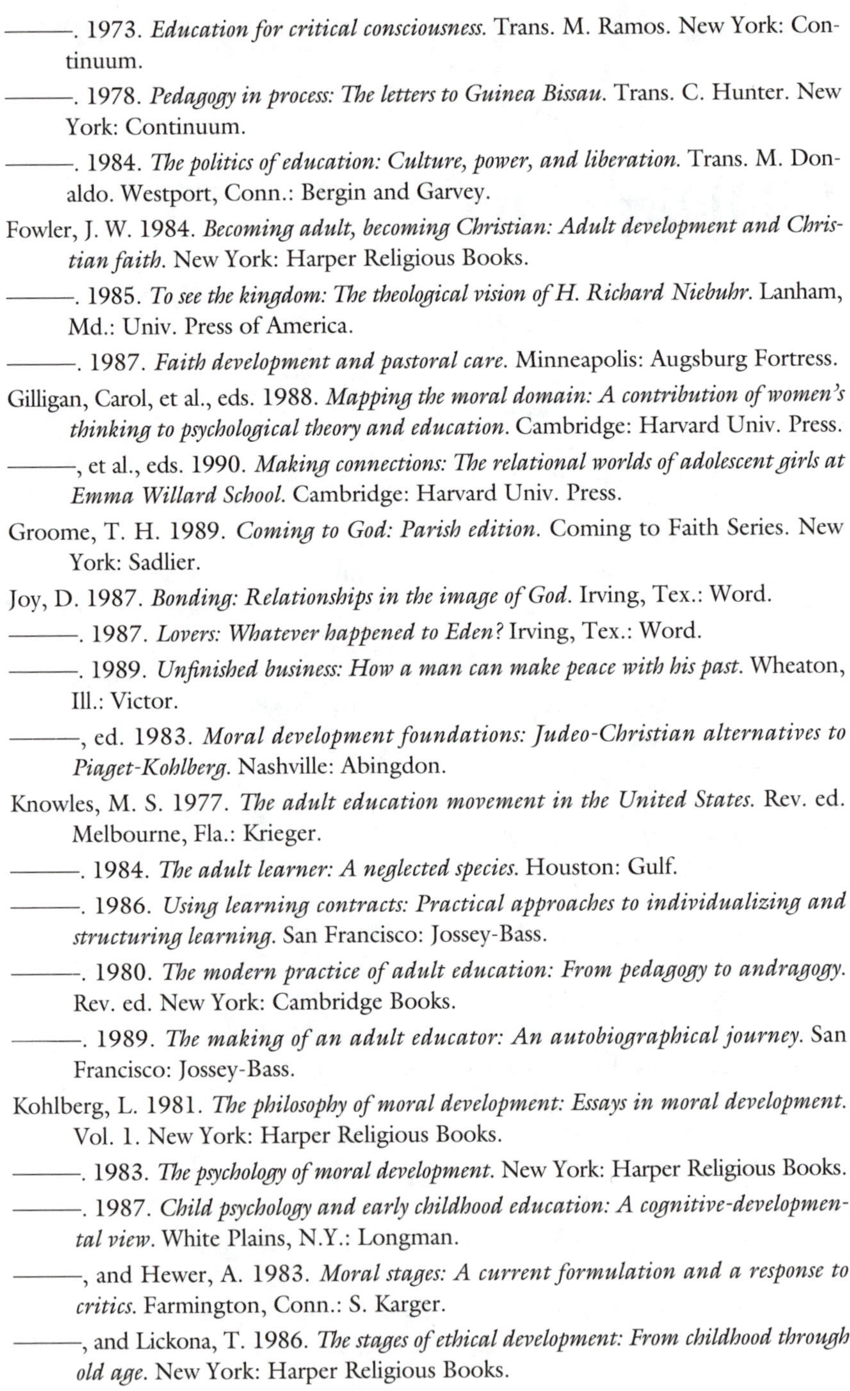

———. 1973. *Education for critical consciousness.* Trans. M. Ramos. New York: Continuum.

———. 1978. *Pedagogy in process: The letters to Guinea Bissau.* Trans. C. Hunter. New York: Continuum.

———. 1984. *The politics of education: Culture, power, and liberation.* Trans. M. Donaldo. Westport, Conn.: Bergin and Garvey.

Fowler, J. W. 1984. *Becoming adult, becoming Christian: Adult development and Christian faith.* New York: Harper Religious Books.

———. 1985. *To see the kingdom: The theological vision of H. Richard Niebuhr.* Lanham, Md.: Univ. Press of America.

———. 1987. *Faith development and pastoral care.* Minneapolis: Augsburg Fortress.

Gilligan, Carol, et al., eds. 1988. *Mapping the moral domain: A contribution of women's thinking to psychological theory and education.* Cambridge: Harvard Univ. Press.

———, et al., eds. 1990. *Making connections: The relational worlds of adolescent girls at Emma Willard School.* Cambridge: Harvard Univ. Press.

Groome, T. H. 1989. *Coming to God: Parish edition.* Coming to Faith Series. New York: Sadlier.

Joy, D. 1987. *Bonding: Relationships in the image of God.* Irving, Tex.: Word.

———. 1987. *Lovers: Whatever happened to Eden?* Irving, Tex.: Word.

———. 1989. *Unfinished business: How a man can make peace with his past.* Wheaton, Ill.: Victor.

———, ed. 1983. *Moral development foundations: Judeo-Christian alternatives to Piaget-Kohlberg.* Nashville: Abingdon.

Knowles, M. S. 1977. *The adult education movement in the United States.* Rev. ed. Melbourne, Fla.: Krieger.

———. 1984. *The adult learner: A neglected species.* Houston: Gulf.

———. 1986. *Using learning contracts: Practical approaches to individualizing and structuring learning.* San Francisco: Jossey-Bass.

———. 1980. *The modern practice of adult education: From pedagogy to andragogy.* Rev. ed. New York: Cambridge Books.

———. 1989. *The making of an adult educator: An autobiographical journey.* San Francisco: Jossey-Bass.

Kohlberg, L. 1981. *The philosophy of moral development: Essays in moral development.* Vol. 1. New York: Harper Religious Books.

———. 1983. *The psychology of moral development.* New York: Harper Religious Books.

———. 1987. *Child psychology and early childhood education: A cognitive-developmental view.* White Plains, N.Y.: Longman.

———, and Hewer, A. 1983. *Moral stages: A current formulation and a response to critics.* Farmington, Conn.: S. Karger.

———, and Lickona, T. 1986. *The stages of ethical development: From childhood through old age.* New York: Harper Religious Books.

———, et al. 1988. *Moral education, justice and community: A study of three democratic high schools.* New York: Columbia Univ. Press.

LeBar, L. E. 1989. *Education that is Christian.* Wheaton, Ill.: Victor.

Lee, J. M. 1971. *The shape of religious instruction: A social-science approach.* Birmingham, Ala.: Religious Education Press.

———. 1985. *The content of religious instruction: A social science approach.* Birmingham, Ala.: Religious Education Press.

———, ed. 1985. *The spirituality of the religious educator.* Birmingham, Ala.: Religious Education Press.

———, ed. 1990. *Handbook of faith.* Birmingham, Ala.: Religious Education Press.

Miller, R. C. 1973. *Live until you die.* New York: Pilgrim.

———, ed. 1946. *Church and organized movements.* Salem, N.H.: Ayer.

Parks, S., and Dykstra, C., eds. 1986. *Faith development and Fowler.* Birmingham, Ala.: Religious Education Press.

Piaget, J. 1965. *The moral judgment of the child.* Trans. M. Gabain. New York: Free Press.

———. 1970. *Genetic epistemology.* Trans. E. Duckworth. New York: Columbia Univ. Press.

———. 1976. *Psychology of intelligence.* Lanham, Md.: Littlefield Adams.

———, ed. 1981. *Intelligence and affectivity: Their relationship during child development.* Trans. C. E. Kaegi. Pal Alto, Calif.: Annual Reviews.

Richards, L. O. 1970. *Creative Bible Teaching.* Chicago: Moody.

———. 1987. *A practical theology of spirituality.* Grand Rapids: Zondervan.

———. 1988. *Children's ministry: Nursing faith within the family of God.* Grand Rapids: Zondervan.

———. 1988. *Christian education: Modeling the gift of new life.* Grand Rapids: Zondervan.

Selman, R. L. 1980. *The growth of interpersonal understanding: Developmental and clinical analysis.* San Diego: Academic.

———, and Schultz, L. H. 1990. *Making a friend in youth: Developmental theory and pair therapy.* Chicago: Univ. of Chicago Press.

Skinner, B. F. 1976. *Walden two.* New York: Macmillan.

———. 1976. *About behaviorism.* New York: Random House.

———. 1978. *Reflections on behaviorism and society.* Englewood Cliffs, N.J.: Prentice-Hall.

———. 1989. *Recent issues in the analysis of behavior.* Columbus, Ohio: Merrill.

Ward, T. W. 1984. *Living overseas: A book of preparations.* New York: Free Press.

———. 1989. *Values begin at home.* Rev. ed. Wheaton, Ill.: Scripture.

Westerhoff, J. H. 1979. *Inner growth-outer change: An educational guide to church renewal.* New York: Harper Religious Books.

———. 1980. *Bringing up children in the Christian faith.* New York: Harper Religious Books.

———. 1983. *Building God's people in a materialistic society.* New York: Harper Religious Books.

———. 1984. *A pilgrim people: Learning through the church year.* New York: Harper Religious Books.

———. 1985. *Living the faith community: The church that makes a difference.* New York: Harper Religious Books.

Wyckhoff, D. C., ed. 1986. *Renewing the Sunday school and the CCD.* Birmingham, Ala.: Religious Education Press.

———. and Richter, D., eds. 1982. *Religious education ministry with youth.* Birmingham, Ala.: Religious Education Press.

Index

Absoluteness of the particular, 489, 491
Absolutism, 484
Abstract learning, 333
Accepting, 336
Accomodation, 110, 126
Achievements, 35n
Acquisitions, 118, 120, 122
Action, 126
Activity, 259, 380
Actualization, 482–84
Adolescents, 26–27, 45, 46, 93, 97, 279, 299, 301, 324–25, 437, 441, 443–44, 447, 450–51, 461, 468
Adult education, 181, 403n. *See also* Andragogy
Adult faith, 425–26, 504, 515, 517
Adults and Synthetic-Conventional faith, 450–51
Affective deprivation, 101
Affective education, 82, 96, 98
Affective nature, 120
Age levels, 291, 322, 323, 352, 353, 354, 356, 386
Aiken, W., 311
Ajuriaguerra, J., 118n, 124
Allport, Gordon, 298
Altruism, 82, 91, 220
American religion, 206, 209, 213
Amos (prophet), 213
Andragogy, 181, 184, 186, 189
Angelism, 319
Anglican church, 299
Anthropology, 338, 352
Anthropomorphism, 440, 443
Anxiety, 506, 507
Apostles' Creed, 260, 261
Application, 293, 380
Approval, 63
Apraxia, 117, 122–25, 128, 130–31
Aristocracy, 27
Aristotle, 135, 137, 138, 297
Arnold, Franz, 319n
Aronfreed, Justin, 301n
Arrogance, 514
Articulated representative regulations, 115
Assimilation, 110, 114, 120–21, 126
Association, 121, 345
Associationist model of learning, 119–20
Athlete, 378
Atonement, 18, 274, 277
Attachment, 37, 43, 54
"Attention-getting devices," 359
Attitudes, 155–56, 186, 195, 358
  religious, 304–5
Augustine, 315, 320, 403
Ausubel, D. P., 84
Authoritarian personality, 426
Authoritarian teaching, 360
Authority, 63, 64, 220, 290, 346, 419, 444, 446, 449, 461, 462, 484
  external, 451, 460, 465–66
  within self, 466
Autonomous man, 140–41, 143, 144, 145, 147
Autonomy, 19, 21, 22, 33–35, 36n, 46, 50, 53, 54, 71, 302, 416, 461
Autonomy of congregation, 221

Bachelard, G., 506, 507
Bacon, Francis, 144

Bailey, Ruth, 377
Banking concept of education, 160, 161–71
Baptism, 219, 220
Barbara, Anna, 301
Barfield, O., 505, 514
Behavior, 19, 61, 96, 97, 98, 100, 105, 135, 136–38, 139–47, 242, 262, 298, 299, 301, 302, 304, 306, 328, 337, 374
Behavior modification, 297–98, 313, 318, 319–20, 322–24, 327, 328, 362
Behavioral objectives, 133, 243
Behavioral sciences, 243
Behaviorism, 109, 110, 133–34, 138, 333, 335–36, 338–40
Being, 297, 487, 488
Belief, 496
  and moral practice, 303, 305
Belonging, 208–9, 464
Benedek, Therese, 16
Berelson, B., 310
Bergson, Henri, 169
Berkowitz, Leonard, 301n
Berryman, Jerome, 426
Bettelheim, Bruno, 46–47, 423, 425
Bible, 272, 276, 283, 284–86, 290, 292, 393, 302–3, 308, 360, 364
  and Christian education, 336, 376
  content, 376
  criticism, 471
  as developmental book, 339–40
  discoveries in, 379–81
  drills, 380
  examples of behavior modification, 322
  history, 357
  meets needs, 375
  orthodox view of, 292
  study of, 380, 381, 384
Bible reading, 380
  in public schools, 239
Bible stories, 379–80, 386, 424–26
Biblical psychology, 389
Biblical-historical approach, 320–21
Biology, 135, 136, 137, 138, 141, 145, 146
Biophily, 164
Biosocial development, 342
Biting stage, 16–17
Blank slate, 339
Blatt, M., 96, 97
Bloom, B. S., 193n, 320
Body, 389, 390
Bonhoeffer, Dietrich, 485
Boredom, 175
Botanical model for leadership, 340–42
Bower, W. C., 213
Bowlby, John, 301n
Broken symbol, 467–68
Bronfenbrenner, Urie, 342
Broverman, I., 50
Brown, Daniel, 313
Bruner, Jerome, 237, 353
Buber, Martin, 443n, 496
Bultmann, Rudolf, 286
Burgess, Harold W., 271, 367
Burrows, Millar, 275
Bushnell, H., 508–10
Bussmann, Esther, 125
Butterfield, H., 137

Care, 16, 36n, 38, 49–51
Carman, John B., 490
Caster, Marcel van, 323
Castration anxiety, 22, 42
Catechism, 260, 299–300, 357
Cause, 136–37, 142
Cause-effect relations, 417, 428
Chadwick, O., 511n
Chandler, M. J., 84
Change, 159, 169, 213, 215, 218, 229, 291, 374, 376
Character education, 263
Charisma, 484
Charity, 16
Cheating, 60–62, 67, 68
Chekhov, Anton, 40
Chenu, M. D., 303, 315
Child psychologists, 301
Child-control, 243
Childhood, 43–45, 46, 279
Children, 354–56
Children's games, 43–45
Chodorow, Nancy, 42–43, 45
Choice, 502
Christian eucation, 234–35, 237, 242, 245, 248, 254–55, 333
  and behaviorism, 339

education and the ministry of the church, 231, 234, 336
future focus, 248
guiding principle of, 272, 273, 281
laboratories in, 357–58
as nurture, 337
problems in, 232, 332, 333
purpose of, 259, 261, 263
and theology, 204, 214, 333
theory of, 272–74
Christian education specialists, 359
Christian growth, 260, 262
Christian life, 224
Christian teacher's dilemma, 248, 251–52
Christianity, 487, 489, 491, 492, 493
Chum relationship, 441, 442, 443
Church, 218–21, 240, 272, 274, 275, 277, 302, 318
as Christian school, 225
and classroom, 298
and culture, 278, 278
and gospel, 281
as institution, 210–11
and the kingdom of God, 228
Church attendance, 205, 305
Church educators, 237–38
Church growth, 334, 338
Church membership, 204, 208, 211
Church polity, 221
Church schools, 238, 239, 240
Church, Joseph, 301n
Church-related colleges, 325, 352–53
Circular reactions, 119
Clarkson, F., 50
Class differences and moral development, 70–71
Classroom as laboratory for Christian living, 325–27
Clergy-laity distinction, 337
Cliques, 27
Closed retreat, 305n
Closure, 353, 402, 403
Coeducation, 324–25
Cognition, 120, 166–67, 169
Cognitive conceit, 441
Cognitive development, 82, 83, 84, 99, 100, 101, 105, 109, 113, 342, 343
Cognitive psychology, 149
Colby, A., 94, 96
Coleman, J. S., 310
Coleridge, Samuel Taylor, 501–5, 507n, 508, 511n, 513n, 514
Combinative operations, 115
Commitment, 208
Communication, 82, 85, 161, 164, 166, 328
Communications technology, 359
Communion. *See* Eucharist
Communist education, 357
Community, 239, 242, 243, 348, 456, 496
of confirmation, 514, 515
of contradiction, 514
of faith, 244–45, 246
hetereogeneous, 240
inclusiveness of, 485
Compensation, 121
Competence, 46
Competition, 44–45, 47–49
Completion, 112
Compulsion neurosis, 20
Concept curriculum, 351–52, 356
Concepts, 352, 353, 355, 357, 359–62, 509n, 510
Concrete operations, 114, 115, 124–25, 128, 339n, 427–31
Concrete reflection, 399n
Conditionality, 309
Conditions of learning, 309–12, 322–23
Conduct, 292, 372, 390. *See also* Behavior
Cone, James, 444
Confession, 224
Confidence, 16
Configurations, 114
Conflict, 390, 441, 506, 508, 509
Conformist stage, 461
Conformity, 292, 368, 387, 388, 465
Confraternity of Christian Doctrine, 240
Confrontive imagination, 505
Congratulating, 335–36
Conjunctive faith, 469–72, 478, 482
Connectedness, 38
Conscience, 42, 63, 351, 390, 436–37
Conscious conflict, 505–7
Consciousness, 163, 165, 166, 167, 168, 169, 170, 415, 471, 507–8
Conservation, 115
Consistency, 66

Constructive-developmental theory, 498
Content, 262, 306, 376, 386, 387, 498, 500
  and method, 261, 262, 263, 327–28
Content-centered teaching, 181, 258, 259, 261. *See also* Traditional education
Continuous creation, 252
Contract, 68
Contractual legalistic orientation, 63
Conventional role conformity level, 63, 68
Convents, 324
Conversations, 354, 355–56
Converts, 372–73, 425
Convictions, 304–5, 318
Coordination, 113, 116, 117, 118, 121
Core curriculum, 311–12
Corporal knowledge, 129
Council of Trent, 307
Counseling and instruction, 318–19
Courage, 416
Covenant, 274, 488
Cox, Harvey, 467–68, 511n
Cox, Claire, 205
Creation, 254, 324, 504
Creational developmentalism, 340
Creativity, 251, 252, 254, 293, 294, 356, 359, 361
Creeds, 510
Crisis, 21, 45–46
Criteria and means of validating evidence, 187, 188, 191
Critical correlation, 405n
Critical memory, 398
Critical reflection, 395, 398, 399n, 400, 401, 469
Critique, 405
Crossan, J. D., 426
Cultural milieu, 323
Curiosity, 185, 505
Curran, C. A., 319
Current issues curriculum, 358–59
Curriculum, 261, 283, 290–92, 299, 302, 326, 351–53, 359, 388, 410
  and the gospel, 280
  design, 151–52, 157, 323
  evaluation, 292–93
Curriculum publishers, 290–93, 352, 358, 360
Custom, 250
Darlington, C. D., 134
Dawe, Donald G., 490
de Beauvoir, S., 162
De-schooling society, 236
Dean, T. W., 304
Death, 31, 32, 419–20
Decision-making, 405, 410
Decisive other, 444
Deductive reasoning, 315, 361, 363–64, 417, 427
Deficiency, 416
Definitions, 363, 365
Deharbe, Joseph, 299–300
Delinquent behavior, 62
Demeter, 54
Democracy, 220
Democratic view of man, 354
Demythologization, 169, 452, 467, 469, 472
Denial, 23
Denominational history, 357
Denominational magazines, 359
Denominations, 218, 229, 318
Dependency, 43
Descartes, René, 142–43
Despair, 31, 34, 36n
Detachment, 470
Determinism, 336, 339
Developmental education, 333
Developmental leadership, 340
Developmental level, 387
Developmental psychology, 495
Developmentalism, 338, 339, 340, 342–43, 426
  male bias, 41
Deviance, 68
Deviation, 61n
Devotion, 36n
DeVries, R., 84
Dewey, John, 57, 58, 59, 82, 236, 247, 326, 393, 401, 507n
Dialectic, 395, 404, 405–6, 408, 410, 470
Dialectical hermeneutics, 394, 403, 405, 408
Dialogue, 160, 166, 167, 169, 171, 357, 394, 399, 400, 401, 402, 404, 406, 470
Dictatorship, 220
Digestive education, 164n

Dignity, 133, 145, 147
Dilthey, Wilhelm, 126
Diplomas, 185
Discernment, 378, 381
Disciples, 345, 347, 372–73
Discipleship, 372, 411
Discipline, 382, 387–88, 389
Disclosure, 402–3
Discovery, 113, 152, 153, 359, 360, 363, 364, 365, 378, 408
Discussion guides, 358, 359
Disequilibrium, 505, 507
Disillusionment, 469
Dislocation, 467
Dissonance, 444, 505
Distantiation, 28, 466
Distrust, 61, 415
Divorce, 468
Dobbins, Gaines, 203
Doctrine, 272, 385
  and experience, 261
Dodds, E. R., 138
Dogmatism, 402
Doing and understanding, 156–57
Domination v. education, 410
Doubt, 19, 20–21, 33, 34, 36n, 46
Dread, 442
Driver education, 236
Durkheim, Emile, 58
Dyad, 91, 92, 93
Dykstra, C., 515n

Eckardt, R., 206, 209
Ecology, 232, 239, 240
Economic ethos, 24
Ecumenism, 471, 491
Edman, V. R., 378
Education
  as domination, 165–66, 167, 243, 410
  and experience, 174, 175, 176–78, 401
  as practice of freedom, 167
  purpose, 183
  as response to the present, 252
  as transmission, 183, 251, 252
Educational ecology, 240
Educational ministry and pastoral ministry, 337–38
Educational psychology, 173, 333
Educational research, 353
Educational technology, 234, 242
Edwards, C. P., 51
Edwards, Jonathan, 271
Effectiveness, 311
Ego, 43, 137, 389
Ego development, 53, 83, 84, 99, 102, 105, 466
Ego identity, 26, 31
Ego integrity, 34, 36n
Ego strength, 62, 342
Egocentric role taking, 87–89, 95
Egocentrism, 417, 426, 427, 431, 442–43
Einbildungskraft, 501
Election, 226
Elitism, 336
Elkind, David, 321n
Emotional integration, 32
Emotions, 363, 389, 390
Empathy, 42, 45, 85
Empirical research, 300–303, 306, 307, 308, 310–15, 322–25
Encouragement, 344
Enlightenment, 500, 501, 503
Ennui, 175
Environment, 15–16, 133, 134, 141, 142–43, 145, 146, 147, 339, 373, 415, 416, 422, 441, 443, 461
Epigenesis, 15, 32–33, 35
Epistemology, 499
Equality, 68
Equilibrium, 110, 112, 115–17, 121, 126, 453, 461, 466
Erikson, Erik, 26, 36n, 38, 45–46, 47, 48–49, 342, 413, 414n, 416, 441, 443, 468, 481, 485
Eschatological reality, 489, 492
Etecht, M. F., 377
Eternity, 479
Ethnic churches, 238
Eucharist, 396–97, 399, 404, 406, 409, 467, 468
Evangelicalism, 284, 285, 287, 290
Evangelism, 223, 225, 228, 263. *See also* Persuasion
Evidence, 362
Evidence of accomplishment, 187, 191
Evolution, 35n, 36n, 139, 142, 147
Ewert, D. M., 159
Examinations, 157, 186, 312

Example, 347
Exclusivism, 491
Expectations, 444
Experience, 19, 174–79, 185, 259, 272, 378, 379, 387, 405, 514, 515
Experience-centered curriculum, 261, 333
Experiential religion, 214–15
Explicit system, 451, 464, 468
Expository mode of learning, 363–65
External coordinations, 117, 119, 121
External degree programs, 182
Extrinsic motivation, 344

Facilitation, 319–22, 323, 326, 328, 333, 341, 345
Fairness, 82, 85, 435
Fairy tales, 423–24, 426
Faith, 16, 35, 219, 223, 224, 226, 246, 274, 302–3, 318, 437–38, 440, 442, 443, 451, 452, 478, 510, 513
- capacity for, 497
- content of, 499
- definition, 496
- and education, 232, 243
- and knowledge, 225
- as purpose of Christian education, 244–46
- quality of, 498–99
- and revelation, 512

Faith commitments, 405
Faith development, 416, 425, 499–500
Faith response, 395
Faith tradition, 401, 402, 404, 406, 408
Faithful leadership, 341
Fall, 337
Family, 239, 240, 354, 457, 458, 461, 465
Family development, 342
Family devotions, 356
Fancy, 502
Fantasy, 83, 423–24, 425, 427, 501
Fear, 61
"Fear failure," 48
"Fear success," 48–49
Feeling, 113, 140, 141, 142
Feffer, M. H., 84
Felt needs, 375
Female development, 37, 38, 40–48, 50, 51, 54, 55
Femininity and success, 48–49
Feminist theology, 404
Fidelity, 16, 36n
Figurative aspect, 123–24, 126, 127, 129
Filthaut, Theodor, 314
Fink, C. F., 310
First naivete, 472
Fixation, 65
Flaherty, Mary Rita, 325
Flavell, J. H., 84, 342
Flexibility in teaching, 294
Folk religion, 206
Forgiveness, 275
Form, 510
Formal operations, 115, 441–42
Fowler, J. W., 393, 400, 431, 496
Fox, George, 478
Fraiberg, Selma, 415
Free will, 370, 411
Freedom, 133, 144–45, 147, 492, 493
Freire, Paulo, 393
Freud, Sigmund, 25, 28, 30, 32, 41–43, 45, 46, 50, 51, 61, 109, 139, 141, 144, 507n
Friedenberg, Edgar, 70
Friendship, 92
Fritz, B., 96
Fromm, E., 61, 164–65
Fry, Margery, 301n
Frye, Northrop, 513
Function, 156
Functional assimilation, 120
Fundamentalism, 315
Fundamentals of technology, 24–25
Future action, 408–9
Futurity, 492, 493

Gandhi, 485, 486
Gardner, H., 85
Gender identity, 42–43
General science, 155–56
Generalized other, 93, 95, 443n
Generalized perspective, 91
Generalizing assimilation, 120
Generation gap, 354
Generativity, 30, 34, 36n, 46
Genetic endowment, 139, 141
Genetic epistemology, 110
Genitality, 28, 29, 46
Gestalts, 121
Gesture, 122, 127, 128, 130, 131
Gibb, J. R., 379

Gibran, Kahlil, 449
Giraldo, M., 94
Goal setting, 347
Goals, 387
God, 421, 422–23, 429–30, 432–35, 439, 479, 480
  adolescent images, 443–46, 448
  anthropomorphisms, 430–31, 443
  as cosmic flow, 481–82
  grace, 364, 365
  remote and impersonal, 439
  sovereignty, 487, 488, 491
  transcendence, 304
  wsdom, 385
God-centered curriculum, 261
Godin, Andre, 326
Goethe, J. W. von, 131
Goldbeck, Angela Dolores, 309–10
Goldbrunner, Josef, 300, 304, 318
Golden rule, 91, 95
Goldman, Ronald, 321n
Good works, 226, 336, 346
Good-boy orientation, 63
Goodman, Paul, 70
Gospel, 274, 277–81
  and Christian education, 273, 278–79, 280
Gourevitch, V., 84
Grace, 351
Grades, 185, 292
Graham, Billy, 313
Grande, Peter, 299
Greeks, 136, 138, 140, 144, 333, 345
Groome, T. H., 496
Groping, 113
Group, 58, 93, 394, 397–98, 402
Group discussion, 381, 384–85
Group of displacements, 112, 121
Groupments, 115
Growing, 336
Growth, 368–69, 370–71, 373
Grünbaum, A. A., 126
Guided self-application, 288–90
Guillaume, P., 129
Guilt, 22, 33, 34, 36n, 46, 61

Habits, 363
Hammarskjöld, Dag, 485
Hartshorne, Hugh, 59, 60, 62, 66, 67, 68, 301n
Harvey, Marie Edmund, 325
Hassenger, Robert, 325
Hate, 61
Havighurst, Robert, 61, 62n, 234
Heart, 389
Hécaen, H., 124
Helfaer, Philip, 425
Hendrick, Ives, 24
Hendrilite, Rachael, 234
Hennessey, Thomas, 305
Herberg, Will, 206
Heschel, Abraham, 485
Heterogeneous ecology, 232
Heuristic approach, 156
Hickey, J., 94, 96–97
Hidden curriculum, 241, 242
Higher education, 517
Hirst, P., 98
History, 276, 277, 280, 281
Hofinger, Johannes, 317, 320, 321
Holding environment, 507
Holding on, 19
Holstein, C., 51
Holt, E. B., 143
Holy Spirit, 293, 308, 319, 364, 367, 369, 388, 389, 390
  fruit of, 372, 375, 376
Home curriculum, 354, 355, 356
Home, formation of values, 67n, 69, 354, 356
Homer, 54
Honesty, 59–62, 66–69, 70, 71
Hope, 16, 36n, 245, 416
"Hope success," 48
Horizontal lags, 112
Horner, Matina, 47–48, 49
Horney, K., 61
Hubbard, Elbert, 377
Human development, 333, 342, 347, 348
Human nature, 350, 496, 497
Human potential, 350
Humanism, 340
Humanization, 166, 170
Humankind, 337, 339, 340, 364, 389
Hunkins, Francis P., 193n
Hurlock, Elizabeth B., 301n
Husserl, E., 168
Hutchinson, P., 208
Huxley, Julian, 35n

Hypotheses, 360, 362, 363, 364, 442
Hypothetical mode of learning, 363–65
Hypothetico-deductive operations, 125

I.Q., 69, 70, 71, 105
I-Thou relationship, 443n, 470
Id, 137
Ideal, 497
Identity, 15, 25, 34, 36n, 45–46, 445, 448, 451, 465–66, 468, 469, 482
  and intimacy, 46, 47
Identity confusion, 27
Identity crisis, 443
Identity formation, 425, 443
Ideology, 27, 461, 464, 467, 469
Idolatry, 488, 510
Ignatius, 471
Illumination, 385
Illustration, 378
Image, images, 126–28, 428, 482, 492, 497–500, 508–14, 515, 516
  in worship, 222
  of faith, 498
Image of God, 386
Imagination, 114, 361, 398, 401, 425, 426, 427, 498, 499–506, 511–15, 517
Imitation, 126, 129, 130, 252, 385
  interiorized, 122, 127, 128, 129
Implementation, 359, 361–62
Inadequacy, 61
Incarnation, 274, 277, 483, 484
Incest taboo, 22
Independent learning. *See* Self-directed learning
Individual study, 357
Individualism, 170
Individuality, 373, 468
Individuation, 37, 43, 45, 46, 50, 51, 54
Individuative-Reflective faith, 462, 464–68, 472, 476, 478
Indoctrination, 261, 262, 263, 357, 378
Inductive reasoning, 115, 315, 335–36, 361, 363–64, 417, 427
Inductive-deductive model, 364
Indulgences, 317
Industry, 24, 25, 34, 46
Infants, 16–19, 45, 414–15, 417
Infantile sexuality, 22, 31
Inference, 359, 360–64
Inferiority, 25, 34, 46
Inhelder, B., 104
Initiative, 21, 22, 23, 24, 25, 33, 34, 36n, 46
Inner control, 387–88
Inner hindrances, 25
Inquiry plan, 185, 192–94
Insight, 361–62, 363, 364, 513
Inspiration, 378
Institutionalism, 203, 209–12, 214, 215
Institutions, 210, 212, 243, 453, 466
Instruction and counseling, 318–19
Instructional religion, 297–98
Instrumental orientation, 91, 95, 104, 435
Integration, 263, 386
Integrative characteristic, 111
Integrity, 31–32, 35
Intellectual operations, 116
Intelligence, 126, 140
Intentionality, 90, 102, 166, 169
Interaction, 358, 377, 384
Interchange, 377
Interiorization, 113–14, 119, 122
Internal coordinations, 117, 120
Interpersonal perspective taking, 440–41, 442–43, 460, 461
Interpretation, 381, 505, 513
Intersection, 359–62, 364
Intervention, 97
Intimacy, 27–28, 29, 34, 36n, 43, 46, 47, 50
  v. isolation, 468
Intrinsic motivation, 344
Introjection, 17
Intuitive-Projective faith, 416–17, 425, 426–27
Inversion, 116
Investigation, 359–62
Invisible church, 228
Ironic imagination, 482
Islam, 487
Isolation, 28, 29, 34, 36n
Israelites, religion, 213

James, William, 140, 497
Jerome, 403
Jersild, Arthur T., 301n

Jesus Christ, 225–26, 227, 276, 277, 280, 353, 407
attitude toward women, 403
fulfillment of history, 275
lordship, 348
resurrection, 488
teaching method, 367, 410–11, 345–47
use of empirical verifiers, 303–4
Jones, Jim, 484
Josselyn, I. M., 61
Joy, Donald, 495
Joyce, Bruce, 402n
Judaism, 239, 487, 488, 489, 491, 492, 493
Judeo-Christian view of man, 354
Jung, Carl, 476, 478, 480
Jungmann, Josef, 300, 309
Justice, 38, 42, 50, 51, 82, 435, 483–85, 486
Justification, 275

Kagan, Jerome, 342
Kant, Immanuel, 500–501
Kaufman, G., 510n
Keen, S., 431
Kegan, R., 499, 507n
Kennedy, Patricia, 300
Kenoyer, Marie Francis, 324
Khomeini, Ayatollah, 484
King, Martin Luther, Jr., 485, 486
Kingdom of God, 227–28, 488–89, 492
Kingston, Maxine Hong, 47
Knowing and doing, 347
Knowing as composing activity, 500–501
Knowledge, 155, 161, 162, 164, 194, 195
Knowles, Malcolm S., 195
Kohlberg, Lawrence, 37, 38, 44, 50–53, 61, 62, 68, 69, 70, 71, 85–86, 94, 96, 97, 100, 103, 342, 413, 435, 453n
Kohn, M., 70
Koinonia, 394
Kounin, Jacob, 69
Kraemer, Hendrik, 210
Krebs, R., 67, 69
Krishnamurti, 476–77, 478
Krutch, Joseph Wood, 144
Kuhn, D., 94

Lag, 112
Langer, Suzanne, 496, 497, 510–11
Language, 113, 114, 118, 417
Latency stage, 25
Law, 21, 70, 70n–71n
Lawfulness, 443
Laws of learning, 306
Lay leadership, 350
Leaders, 378
Leadership, 332, 334–36, 337, 339, 340–43, 345, 346, 347, 348, 384–85
Learner, 248–51, 280, 292, 377, 379
and God, 261–62, 263–64
as dependent personality, 185
needs, 360, 367
Learner-centered education, 174
Learning, 182, 183, 237, 243, 296, 337, 351, 360, 368, 369, 371, 379, 388
by doing, 174, 326
environment, 308, 323–25, 326, 327, 370
and living, 183
process, 183, 364, 374–75, 376–77, 306, 385
resources and strategies, 187, 188, 191
Learning contract, 186–88, 191
Learning objectives, 187, 188, 191
Learning outcomes, 311–13, 324, 326
Leaving home, 462, 464
Lee, James Michael, 299, 308n, 310, 311, 318n, 325n
Legalism, 292
Lenski, Gerhard, 301, 312
Letting go, 19
Lever, Janet, 43, 44, 45, 49
Levi-Strauss, Claude, 342
Liberal approach to religious education, 247
Liberal education, 279
Liberal theology, 234
Liberalism, 287, 307, 315
Liberation, 161, 163, 165–66, 170, 484, 493
Lieberman, M., 97
Life cycle, 15–16, 18, 32, 40, 46, 47, 50, 54, 55

Life-centered teaching, 258–59. *See also* Progressive education
Life-changing learning, 361, 363–65
Life-involvement of student, 368
Lifestyle, 466
Lifton, Robert, 516
Ligon, Ernst, 203
Lindsay, A. D., 501n
Lippett, Ron, 342
Listening, 377
Literacy education, 159
Literalism, 431, 440–41
Little, Sara, 234
Liturgy and education, 338
Live curriculum, 358–59
Loder, James, 500n, 504, 507–8, 512, 513, 514n
Loevinger, Jane, 53, 105, 342
Logic of propositions, 114, 116
Logical domain, 99
Lord's Prayer, 404
Love, 28, 36n, 61, 485
Love and hate, 21
Lowe, W. J., 415
Luther, Martin, 471
Lutheran church, 299
Lynch, William F., 425, 482, 501–2, 513
Lynn, Robert W., 232

Mabry, J., 143
Magisterium, 302–3, 315, 318
Male moral development, 41–47, 49, 54–55
Management, 334
Manipulation, 22, 345, 357, 369
Marquand, John P., 208
Marriage, 465
Martin, Alex, 276, 276
Marty, Martin, 205, 206, 208
Martyrs, 484
Marx, Karl, 30
Maslow, Abraham, 485
Mass, 249, 317, 397, 400, 401, 404, 406, 407, 409, 410
Materialistic conception, 104
Maternal care, 16–17
Maturation, 185, 186, 322
Mature faith, 483, 502, 503
Maturity, 51, 54, 279, 279, 279, 378
May, M. A., 59–60, 62, 66–68
May, Rollo, 298
Mayer, R., 100
Mayr, M., 257, 295
McClelland, D. C., 48, 54
McFague, S., 510n
McGuffey Readers, 239
McLuhan, Marshall, 326
Mead, George Herbert, 43, 45, 99, 443n
Meaning, 468, 482, 499
Meaning and symbols, 452–53, 467
Meaningful learning, 359, 365
Media, 453
Meister, J., 211
Memorization, 260, 372, 373, 380, 386
Memory, 154, 401
Mental health, 58–59
Mental pictures, 118, 122
Mercy killing, 64–65
Merton, Thomas, 485
Metaphor, 497, 499, 509
Methodology, 242, 259, 291, 294, 302, 318, 328, 356, 373, 402
Metz, Johann, 298
Mid-life crisis, 476, 478
Middle-class values, 70
Miller, L. F., 379
Miller, Randolph Crump, 203, 234, 302, 313–14
Mind, 138–39, 141, 146, 389, 390, 503
Mirroring, 443
Mistrust, 33, 34, 36n, 46
Moir, D. J., 94
Monologue, 402
Montaigne, 144
Montessori principles, 426
Moore, O. K., 84
Moral behavior, 59, 67n, 69, 343
Moral character, 61, 68
Moral development, 38–39, 43, 44, 50–52, 57–58, 65, 69–72, 84, 342
  male bias in, 44, 47
Moral dilemmas, 40, 57, 62, 84, 85–87, 97, 103, 419, 435
Moral education, 58–61, 69, 71–72, 279
Moral judgment, 62, 67, 70, 94, 96, 97, 100, 104, 343
Moral knowledge, 66, 67
Moral reasoning, 85, 87, 419

Moral responsibility, 22–23
Morality, 52–53
Moralizing, 380
Moran, Gabriel, 308, 319n, 327–28, 402n
Moratorium, 27
Morocco, Robert, 316
Moschella, Mary, 515
Mother Teresa, 485, 486, 487
Motivation, 149, 335, 336, 343–45, 348, 351, 376, 388
Movement, 394–95
Muggeridge, M., 486
Munich method, 304
Murray, John, 307–8
Mutual role taking, 91–92, 95
Mutuality, 92, 415, 416, 470
Mystery, 446
Mystification of symbols, 468
Mythic-Literal faith, 427, 428, 433, 440
Myths, 442, 443, 452, 461, 469, 482, 483, 491

Naively egoistic orientation, 63
Narcissism, 54, 416, 442
Narrative, 428, 440–41, 442
Narrative education, 160, 167
Natural law, 436–37
Natural reason, 302
Neale, J. M., 84
Necrophily, 164–65
Needs, 343, 364, 365, 374, 375, 376, 379, 381, 387
Negative reinforcement, 321
Neglect, 416, 441
Nelson, C. Ellis, 234
Neo-orthodoxy, 234, 271, 286–87, 292
Neugarten, Bernice, 342
New curriculum, 182, 235
New Testament, 275
  faith, 209, 214
  principles, 218–19, 220–29
  religion, 210, 213, 215
Niebuhr, H. Richard, 487–88, 511–12, 514–15
Niebuhr, R. R., 506n, 513n
Niebuhr, Reinhold, 165
Nihilism, 462
Nonanalytic faith, 454, 456
Nonconscious, 507n
Nonjudgmental leadership, 341
Nontraditional study programs, 182
Nourishment, 371
Novice adulthood, 468
Novitiates, 324
Nurture, 224-25, 337, 354

Obedience, 62, 63, 69, 224, 301–2, 318
Object permanence, 415
Objective verification of learning outcomes, 312–14
Objectivity, 468
  of social sciences, 315
Observations, 362, 381
Obsessiveness, 19, 29
Oedipal stage, 24–25, 41–42, 46, 427
Offertory, 397, 401, 409–10
Old Testament, 275, 313, 314
Ontologism, 319
Open classrooms, 182
Open retreat, 305n
Operations, 117, 123–24, 125, 128, 129, 131,
Oppression, 161–65, 170–71, 486–87, 514
Order of succession, 111, 122
Organismic model of education, 181
Organization, 177–78, 211. *See also* Institutions
Organized religion, 18
Orthodoxy, 426
Outer hindrances, 25
Overcompensation, 23, 29
Overdistancing, 506–7
Overobedience, 23

Pallone, Nathaniel J., 318n, 325n
Pannenberg, W., 489, 492
Parables, 426
Parents, 322, 353, 354–56, 358, 416
  of adolescents, 446–47, 448
Parks, Sharon, 444
Participation, 293
Participative education, 378–79
Particularity, 489, 490
Pastor and Christian education, 356
Patient leadership, 341
Paul (apostle), 320
Pause, 505, 507–8

Pavlov, Ivan, 142, 357
Peck, K. B., 377
Peck, R. F., 61, 62n
Pedagogy, 181, 184, 186, 189, 233, 237, 244, 245, 292, 299
Peers, peer groups, 43, 102, 103, 104, 306, 322, 354, 443, 448, 449, 450, 457, 463
Penitential rite, 397, 400, 406–7
Perfection, 351–52, 353, 485
Perfectionism, 441
Permanence, 169
Perry, E., 207
Persephone, 54
Personality, 66, 249–51, 262, 299, 307, 308, 377
Perspective, 87–91, 93, 101, 104, 428, 430, 437
Perspective-taking, 431, 433, 436, 440, 441, 442–43, 466
Persuasion, 222–23
Peters, R., 98
Phenix, Philip, 298
Philosophy, 245
Philosophy of education, 176
Philosophy of experience, 176–77, 179
Philosophy of teaching, 293, 294
Physical causality, 83
Physical domain, 99
Physical growth, 370–71
Physical needs, 374
Physics, 135, 136, 137, 138, 141, 145, 146
Physiology, 139
Piaget, Jean, 37, 43, 44, 49, 50–51, 57, 62, 85, 104, 342, 393, 399n, 408, 413, 415, 498–500
Piagetian developmental theory, 69, 84, 94, 96, 102
Pictures, 126, 128–29, 131
Pietism, 319
Pius XI, 324
Planning, 291
Plato, 128, 135, 236
Platt, G. N., 379
Play, 43–45
Pluralism, 240, 490
Poincaré, H., 112
Polanyi, Michael, 451
Political science, 338
Popper, Karl, 138
Popular culture, 443
Positive reinforcement, 306, 321
Possession, 427
Postponed imitation, 122
Powers, Edward A., 234
Practical reason, 500–502
Practical theology, 326
Practice, 373
Praxis, 116–17, 119, 121, 122, 124–25, 130, 160, 161, 166, 169, 394, 395, 396, 397, 399, 403, 404–5, 408, 496
Prayer, 373–74, 397, 400, 404, 407, 439
Prayer in public schools, 239
Pre-images, 416
Preaching, 222, 223, 224, 337–38
Preadolescents, 97
Precepts, 353, 378
Precision teaching, 133
Precocious identity formation, 425
Predestination, 144
Predicting behavior, 306–9, 328
Prejudice, 28, 381
Premoral level of moral judgment, 62, 68, 95
Preoperatory representations, 114, 124
Preparation, 112
Present action, 395–96, 398, 399, 401
Prestige, 346, 348
Presuppositions, 337
Price, Rebecca, 367
Priesthood of believers, 220
Principle, 63
Privileges, 346, 348
Problem-centered learning, 166–71, 181, 185
Problem solving, 82, 272
Process of formation, 112
Process theology, 258
Process, reality as, 168
Production and care, 36n
Programmed instruction, 339, 356–58
Progressive education, 173, 175, 176, 177, 179, 258, 262
Projection, 17
Propositional revelation, 292
Propositions, 442

Protestants, 248, 249, 250, 251, 315
Pseudo-intimacy, 30
Psychoanalysis, 17, 28–29, 30, 61, 137, 338
  male bias, 42
Psychological assessment, 324
Psychological causality, 83
Psychological needs, 374
Psychology, 237, 242, 243, 245, 338, 352
Psychopathic personality, 61n
Psychophysiological functioning of learner, 295, 323
Psychosocial approach, 16, 18n
Psychotherapy, 139, 140
Puberty. *See* Adolescents
Public schools, 233, 236–37, 239, 240, 291, 311
Pulz, Louis J., 308n
Punishment, 62, 63, 64, 67, 69, 95, 306–7, 339, 357, 436
Pupil. *See* Learner
Puppy love, 441
Pure reason, 501n

Quakers, 475, 477, 478, 480, 508
Quantification, 316–17

Radical monotheism, 487–89, 491, 492
Rahner, K., 314
Ranwez, Pierre, 301
Rapport, 506
Rating scales, 196–98
Reality, 163, 423, 425, 469
Realization, 513
Reason, 401, 417, 502–3, 513
Reciprocal assimilation, 121
Reciprocity, 101, 102, 104, 116, 400, 433, 435, 437, 439, 440, 441, 443, 465
Recognitive assimilation, 120
Reconciliation, 161, 397, 400, 404, 406, 409
Reconstruction, 248, 254, 401
Redemption, 273, 275–78, 375
Redemptive history, 351
Reflection, 160, 399, 442, 451, 456, 461, 462, 466, 468
Reflex, 113, 117, 118, 142
Reformation, 214
Regeneration, 219, 220, 224–25, 370, 389
Reinforcement, 150, 357
Relationships, 37, 38, 43, 46, 49, 51, 52, 263, 283, 336, 347, 348, 353, 390, 451, 453
Relativism, 90, 487, 490, 515
Relativity, 471, 487, 488n
  of perspectives, 462, 466
Release of energy, 505, 512
Relevance, 287, 288, 292, 293, 360
"Relevant irrelevance," 486
Religio, 477–78
Religion, 19, 21
  and faith, 232, 244–45
Religion-controlled development, 251
Religious education, 233–34, 238, 239, 241, 245, 246
Religious Education Association, 233, 247, 257
Religious instruction, 59, 297, 299, 301
  conditionality, 309, 311
  empirical nature, 298–300, 302
  facilitation process, 319–21
  not mystical experience, 319
  as social science, 296–98, 304, 308, 326
  verification in, 302–4
Religious periodicals, 240
Religious variation, 250–51
Renunciation and wisdom, 36n
Repatterning, 505, 512
Repentance, 219, 223, 224
Replication, 312, 337
Representations, 500
Representative intelligence, 118, 127
Repression, 45
Resources, 360
Response, 142, 143, 292–94, 401, 403, 404, 408, 410, 411
Responsibilities, 38, 49, 50, 51–54, 68, 69, 388, 492
Retreats, 305
Revelation, 273–74, 389, 489, 512
Reversibility, 116, 428
Revival of religion, 204–5, 207, 370
Revolution, 165, 169, 171
Rewards, 59, 62, 63, 69, 185, 339, 356–58

Rey, A., 125
Richards, Lawrence O., 292n
Richardson, Alan, 275
Ricoeur, Paul, 472, 482
Righteousness, 477
Rights, 38, 51, 52, 54
Rituals, 222, 482, 483, 510
Rizzuto, Ana-Maria, 416, 422–23, 504n
Rogers, Carl, 342, 485
Rokeach, Milton, 303
Role confusion, 26, 34, 36n
Role taking, 81–82, 84–90, 93–94, 96–99, 101, 104, 342
Roman Catholic church, 210, 239, 240, 248, 249, 250, 251, 299, 301–2, 305, 307, 317, 319, 462
Roman Catholic schools, 315, 317, 324–25
Rosenkrantz, P., 50
Rugg, Harold, 507n
Rules, 49, 51
Russian psychology, 357

Sacraments, 219, 222
Sacrifice, 220
Sadistic personality, 61n
Sainthood, 485
Salvation and education, 224–25, 226
Santayana, George, 451, 464
Sartre, Jean-Paul, 164n, 168
Satyagraha, 485
Sassen, Georgia, 48
Scharf, P., 97
Schemes, 118–21
Schizophrenia, 17
School, 24–25
Schooling-instructional paradigm, 232–37, 238, 239, 241–45
Schools and education, 236, 337, 241
Science, 134, 136, 137–38, 141, 145, 247, 326, 335, 337, 348
  neutrality of, 41
Sears, R., 307
Second naivete, 472, 482
Secular education, 245, 279–80, 345
  and religion, 243
Secularism, 346–47, 490, 493
Secularization, 423
Segal, S. J., 319
Self, 99, 389
Self-absorption, 28
Self-actualization, 319, 342, 468, 485
Self-awareness, 426
Self-consciousness, 442–43
Self-control, 21, 36n, 243, 388
Self-directed learning, 181, 182–87, 189, 190, 192
Self-discovery, 293
Self-esteem, 21, 46, 61, 104, 185
Self-fulfillment, 468
Self-propulsion, 378
Self-reflective role taking, 90, 95
Self-righteousness, 23
Selman, R. L., 84, 94, 97, 99
Seminary training, 307–8, 345, 352
Senses, 501
Sensitivity, 45
Sensorikinetic apraxia, 130
Sensorimotor intelligence, 113, 117, 119, 120, 121, 123, 126, 127, 130
Separation, 37, 38, 43, 52, 54
Sequence, 150
Sermon, 377
Servanthood, 346–47
Service, 59, 225–27
Sex, 27–29, 314
Sex differences, 41–47, 50, 54, 55
Sex education, 236
Sex-role stereotypes, 50
Shame, 19–21, 33, 34, 36n, 46
Shared praxis, 393–95, 397n, 408, 409, 410, 411
Sharing, 336, 344
Shaw, George Bernard, 48–49
Sheen, Fulton, 317
Shinn, Roger, 234
Shulik, Richard, 453n
Sidgwick, H., 74
Significant other, 443n 444
Simpson, R. M., 51
Sin, 274, 277, 374, 480, 492
Situation, 59, 60, 61, 67, 68
Skills, 183, 195, 361
Skinner, B. F., 136n
Sleeping Beauty, 47
Smart, J. D., 213
Smith, Wilfred Cantwell, 413, 488n, 496
Snow White, 47

Snyder, Ross, 234
Social adjustment, 59
Social agreement, 68
Social and conventional system role taking, 93, 95
Social-cognitive development, 97, 98, 102, 104, 105–6
Social development, 82, 96, 252, 337, 398
Social gospel, 227
Social-informational role taking, 89, 95
Social isolation, 104
Social justice, 396, 399, 403, 406, 409, 410
Social order, 70–71, 93, 95, 99, 467
Social-order maintaining orientation, 63
Social pressure, 354
Social problem solving ability, 85
Social psychology, 149
Social science, 245, 296, 299–305, 327, 332, 333, 338, 340, 343
  and prediction, 306–9
  and objectivity, 312–15
  and quantification, 316–17
  and behavior modification, 319–23
  and learning environment, 324–26
Social scientists, 310, 311, 335, 336
Social structure, 342, 451
Socialism, 354
Socialization, 43, 232, 241–42, 283
  adult, 342
Socioeconomic background, 323
Sociology, 338
"Soft pedagogy," 387
Solidarity, 164, 170
Soloman, L., 84
Somato-spatial apractognosis, 130
Soul, 389
Sparks, P. M., 514
Specificity, 297
Spectator, 378
Spiral curriculum, 353–56
Spirit, 389
Spiritual growth, 287
  and physical growth, 370, 385
Spiritual maturity, 368, 373, 386, 388
Spiritual needs, 375
Spontaneity in teaching, 294
Sprinthall, N. A., 109
Sprinthall, R. C., 109
Stachnik, T., 143
Stage analysis, 83–85, 87–90, 101, 102, 104, 106, 112
Stages of development, 98, 110–11, 124, 291, 344, 385, 386, 388
Stages of faith. *See* Faith development
Stages of life, 342
Stages of moral judgment, 62–66, 82, 87, 94, 343,
Stagnation, 30, 34, 36n
Stealing, 435–36
Steiner, G. A., 310
Steiner, Rudolph, 476
Stendahl, Krister, 471
Stimulation, 345
Stimulus, 142–43
Stoller, Robert, 42
Stone, Lawrence J., 301n
Stories, 398, 426, 428, 429, 440, 442, 469
Story, 394–95, 400, 401–3, 404, 405, 406, 407, 408, 410, 411
Strand theory of ego development, 105
Structural aspect of role taking, 84, 87, 89, 90, 93
Structural-developmental analysis, 103, 496, 498
Structure, 111, 150, 155
  and content, 498–99, 500
Strunk, William, 41
Student. *See* Learner
Stylistic imagination, 506
Subject-centered orientation, 185, 311
Subjectivity, 89, 468, 513–14
Subversiveness, 486
Success, 35n, 44, 48–49, 61
Suffering, 479, 492
Sullivan, E. V., 426
Sullivan, Harry Stack, 441
Sunday school, 211, 233–34, 236, 238, 240, 290, 316, 345, 351, 353, 377, 379, 382, 384
  enrollment, 211
Superego, 22, 23, 42, 137
Supernatural, 302
Symbol, 510
Symbolical function, 114, 117, 118, 119, 122, 124, 130, 131
Symbolism, 127

Symbolization, 500, 510–11
Symbols, 422, 423, 424, 425, 428, 430, 440, 452, 453, 467–68, 469, 482, 483, 491, 492, 511
Sympathy, 82, 85
Synthetic-Conventional faith, 447, 450, 453–54, 456, 458, 460–61, 464, 465, 468, 472
Systematic instruction, 24
Systematic theology and moral theology, 396
Systems logic, 334

Tacit system, 451, 453, 461, 464, 466, 468
Taft, R., 84
Taoism, 507n
Teacher, 185, 248–51, 280, 283, 287, 291, 292, 293, 294, 306, 308, 374, 379, 380
  distinct from clergy, 298
  as facilitator, 182
  as social scientist, 310–12
  training, 234
Teacher-directed learning, 174, 184–86, 189
Teacher-pupil relationship, 248–51
Teaching, 224
  as guided tour, 369
  and learning environment, 370
  results, 372
Teaching machine, 356–57
Teaching plan, 293–94
Teaching standards, 387
"Teaching-learning process," 327, 368
Technical education, 279
Techniques. *See* Methodology
Technological ethos, 25
Technology of behavior, 134–35, 138, 143, 145, 146–47
Television, 240, 320, 359, 426
Television evangelists, 453
Ten Commandments, 305
Tertullian, 403
Thematic Apperception Test (TAT), 47
Theological Education by Extension (TEE), 331
Theological science, 296–98, 302–6, 308–10, 312, 314, 317–20, 322, 325, 326
Theology, 258, 274, 292, 306, 308, 315, 317, 352
  and Christian education, 261–63
Theoria, 394, 396, 397, 404, 408
Theory and practice, 272
Thinking, 130, 351
Thomas, E. J., 310,
Thomism, 315
"Three languages," 46
Thrower, J. S., 94, 96
Tillich, Paul, 286, 315, 467, 491n
Time management, 334
Toffler, Alvin, 183
Tracy, David, 405n
Tradition, 218, 229, 302, 303, 346, 347, 402, 403, 405, 406, 471, 489, 490, 491
Traditional curriculum, 311
Traditional education, 174–76, 179, 258, 262, 378
Traditional theology, 367
Transcendence, 443
Transcendental Meditation, 508
Transfer of principles, 150, 154, 155
Transformation, 123, 131, 160, 168, 170, 285, 287, 500n, 505, 506, 507, 511, 512, 513
Trivialization, 453
Troeltsch, Ernst, 491n
Trueblood, Elton, 214–15
Trust, 16–19, 21, 32, 33, 34, 35, 36n, 45, 61, 67, 68, 397, 415, 416, 442
Truth, 259, 261, 364, 372, 375, 376, 385, 386, 389, 390, 472, 490, 491, 502, 504, 509
  as multidimensional, 471
Turiel, E., 76
"Tyranny of the they," 444, 447, 466

Ulrich, R. T., 143
Unamuno, Miguel de, 497, 513
Unconscious, 19, 83, 471, 482
Understanding, 153–54, 195, 304–5, 501, 503n, 511n
Understandings, 358, 363
Undifferentiated faith, 414, 416
Unitarian church, 473, 474, 476, 478
Universalizing faith, 483–87, 489, 490, 491

Urbanization, 236
Utilitarianism, 490

Value-freedom, 317–18
Values, 59, 145, 147, 195, 303, 318–19, 348, 351, 358, 361, 456–57, 458, 466
  sex differences, 49
Van Bunnen, Christian, 321n
Varied applications, 288, 289
Vatican II, 307
Vaughan, Richard, 307–8
Vernon, G. M., 313
Verplanck, William, 321
Vertical lags, 112, 113
Vertigo of reality, 472
Violence, 426
Virtues, 36n
Vision, 394–95, 400, 401–5, 408, 410, 411
Visions, 398–99, 408
Vocation, 492
Vogel, S., 50
Vorgrimler, H., 314
Vygotsky, L. S., 417

Wallon, H., 127
Weil, Marsha, 402n
Wertheimer, Max, 157
Wessell, Alice, 325
West, Morris L., 296
Wheelwright, P., 497, 505
White, E. B., 41
Whitehead, A. N., 507n, 512
Whitman, A., 207
Whole persons, 283, 390
Whyte, W. H., Jr., 207
Will, 389, 390
Willed naivete, 472
Willpower, 36n
Winnicott, D. W., 504, 507
Winter, G., 210
Witness, 223
Women in the church, 403
Woolf, Virginia 49, 508
Word and deed, 346
Word of God, 273–74, 280
Wordsworth, William, 502
Work, 28
Works-righteousness, 441
World-view, 464, 469
Worship, 212, 221–22, 260, 260, 298, 379, 380, 384
Wrightstone, Wayne, 311
Wyckoff, D. Campbell, 234, 297

Yoga, 508
Young adults, 358, 468–69, 497–98, 504, 516, 517
Youth. *See* Adolescents

DATE DUE